BY THE RIVERS OF WATER

BY THE RIVERS OF WATER

A Nineteenth-Century Atlantic Odyssey

ERSKINE CLARKE

BASIC BOOKS

A Member of the Perseus Books Group
New York

Books published by Basic Books are available at special discounts for bulk purchases in the United States by corporations, institutions, and other organizations. For more information, please contact the Special Markets Department at the Perseus Books Group, 2300 Chestnut Street, Suite 200, Philadelphia, PA 19103, or call (800) 810–4145, ext. 5000, or e-mail special.markets@perseusbooks.com.

TEXT DESIGN BY JEFF WILLIAMS

Library of Congress Cataloging-in-Publication Data
Clarke, Erskine, 1941-author.
    By the rivers of water : a nineteenth-century Atlantic odyssey / Erskine Clarke.
        pages cm
    Includes bibliographical references and index.
ISBN 978-0-465-00272-6 (hardcover)—ISBN 978-0-465-03769-8 (e-book)—
ISBN 0-465-00272-2 (hardcover)—ISBN 0-465-03769-0 (e-book)
1. Wilson, J. Leighton (John Leighton), 1809–1886. 2. Wilson, Jane Bayard, 1809–
1885. 3. Missionaries—Liberia—Biography. 4. Missionaries—Gabon—Biography.
5. Missionaries—United States—Biography. 6. Presbyterian Church in the U.S.—
Missions—Liberia. 7. Presbyterian Church in the U.S.—Missions—Gabon. 8. Grebo
(African people)—Missions. 9. Mpongwe (African people)—Missions. I. Title.

BV3625.L6W554 2013
266.51092—dc23

                                                                    2013021385

10 9 8 7 6 5 4 3 2 1

To Judy and Will

And he shall be like
a tree planted by the
rivers of water, that
bringeth forth fruit
in his season.

—PSALM 1:3, KJV

CONTENTS

Part III: Life Among the Mpongwe

Part IV: Homeward Journey

1. Bird's Eye View. In this view of antebellum Savannah, Hutchinson Island can be seen in the distance. The Bayard slave settlement was toward the left end of the island.

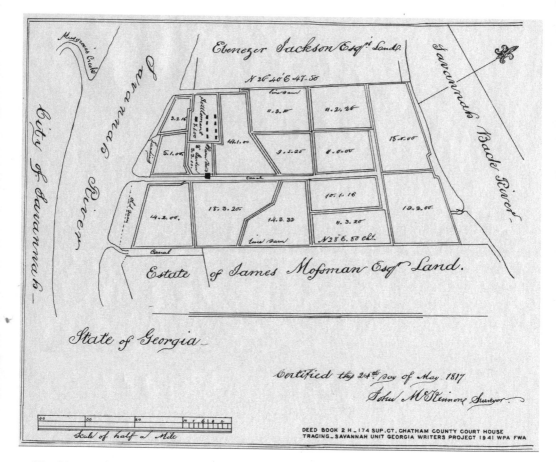

2. Hutchinson Island. This map shows the layout of the Bayard property on Hutchinson Island. Note the slave settlement, the landing, and the old rice fields with their canals and dams. Courtesy of the Georgia Historical Society.

3. Georgia Coast *(facing page)*. A network of tidal rivers and creeks marks coastal Georgia. Both Bayard slaves going to General's Island and Jane Bayard going to Fair Hope Plantation frequently travelled the inland waters between Savannah and Darien.

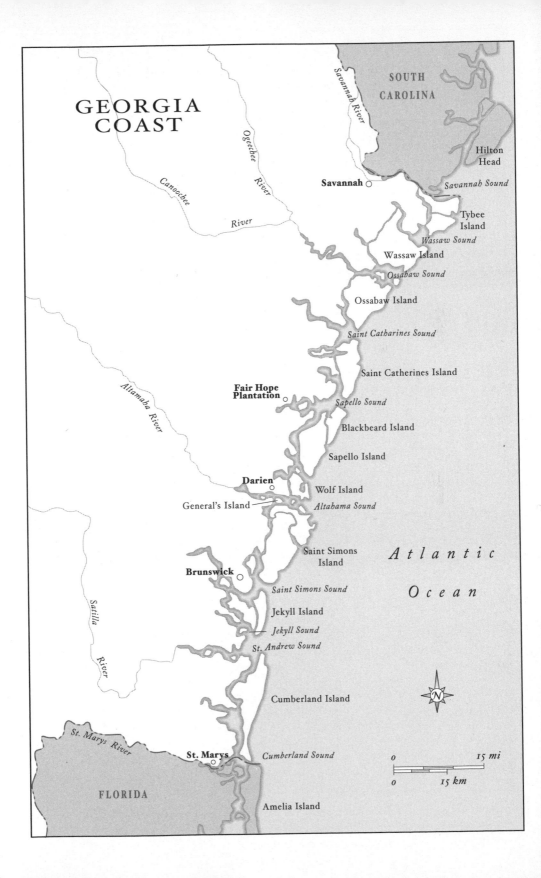

GEORGIA
COAST

SOUTH
CAROLINA

Savannah River

Ogeechee River

Canoochee River

River

Savannah ○

Hilton
Head

Savannah Sound

Tybee
Island

Wassaw Sound

Wassaw Island

Ossabaw Sound

Ossabaw Island

Saint Catharines Sound

Saint Catherines Island

**Fair Hope
Plantation** ○

Sapello Sound

Blackbeard Island

Sapello Island

Altamaha River

Darien ○

Wolf Island

General's Island

Altahama Sound

Saint Simons
Island

Brunswick ○

Saint Simons Sound

Atlantic

Ocean

Jekyll Island

Jekyll Sound

St. Andrew Sound

Satilla River

Cumberland Island

St. Marys River

St. Marys ○

Cumberland Sound

0   15 *mi*

0   15 *km*

FLORIDA

Amelia Island

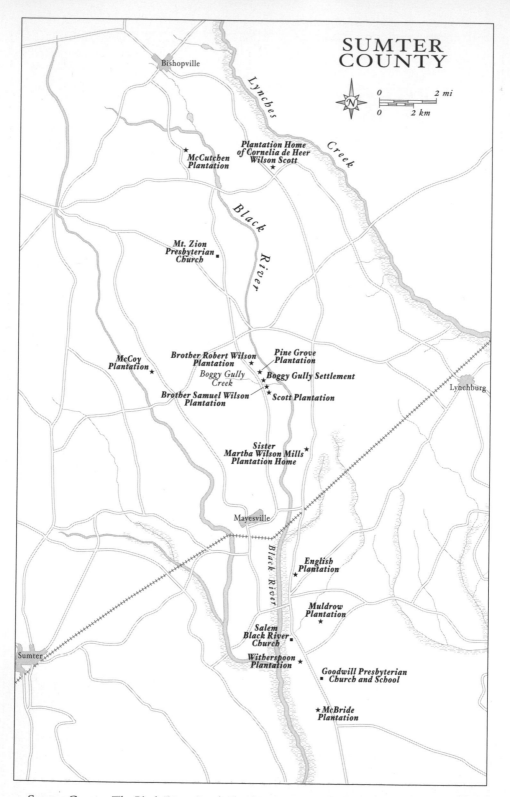

4. Sumter County. The Black River, South Carolina, served as a highway for Scotch-Irish settlers in the eighteenth century. By the 1850s, the plantations and churches of their descendants reflected the wealth created by a rapidly growing slave population.

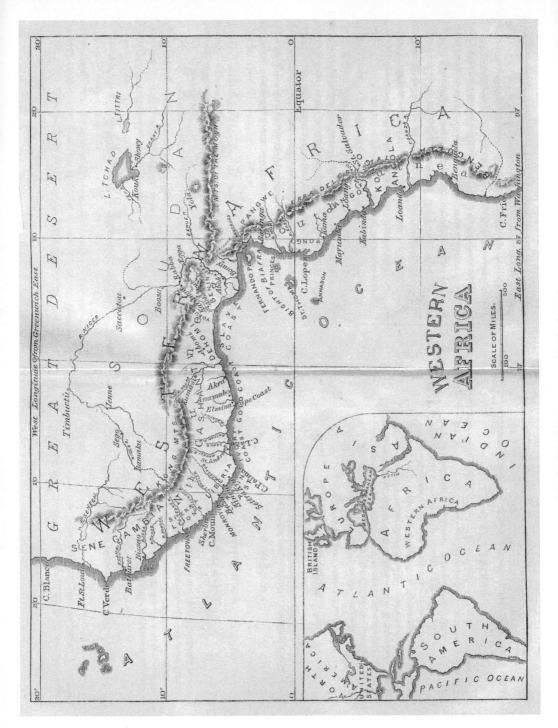

5. Western Africa. This map, from Leighton Wilson's *Western Africa*, provides an overview of the coast and shows the geographic relationship of Cape Palmas to Gabon and the major places the Wilsons visited on their travels in West Africa.

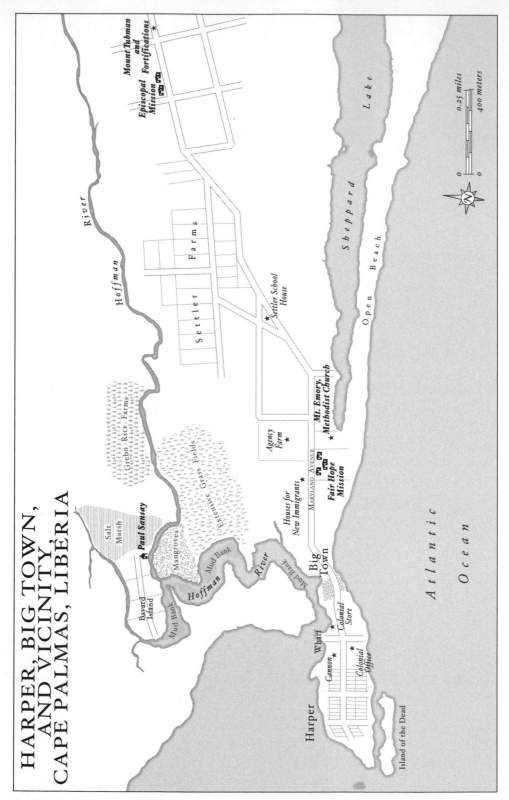

6. Harper, Big Town, and Vicinity. This map shows the relationship of the Fair Hope mission to its setting at Cape Palmas. Note Bayard Island.

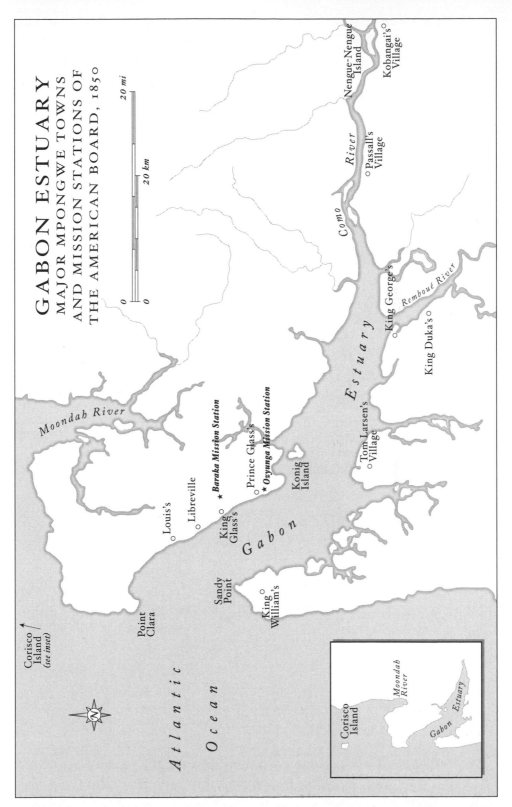

7. Gabon Estuary. Gabon rivers and their estuary provided easy access in the nineteenth century to Mpongwe towns and villages.

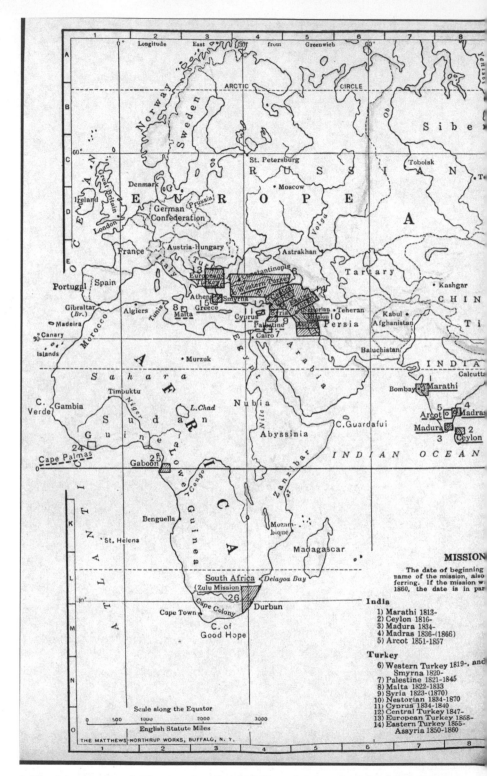

The date of beginning and the
name of the mission, also that referring. If the mission w
1860, the date is in par

MISSION

India

1) Marathi 1813–
2) Ceylon 1816–
3) Madura 1834–
4) Madras 1836–(1866)
5) Arcot 1851–1857

Turkey

6) Western Turkey 1819–, and
     Smyrna 1820–
7) Palestine 1821–1845
8) Malta 1822–1833
9) Syria 1823–(1870)
10) Nestorian 1834–1870
11) Cyprus 1834–1840
12) Central Turkey 1847–
13) European Turkey 1858–
14) Eastern Turkey 1855–
     Assyria 1850–1860

8. The American Board. The American Board of Commissioners for Foreign Missions was one of many Protestant mission agencies rapidly expanding its work around the world during the nineteenth century. Note that "Indian Nations" were regarded as "foreign missions."

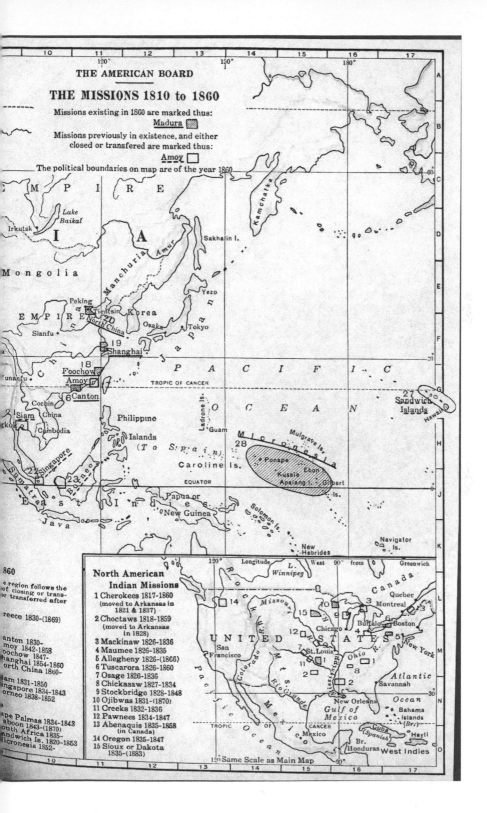

THE AMERICAN BOARD

THE MISSIONS 1810 to 1860

Missions existing in 1860 are marked thus:
Madura ▨

Missions previously in existence, and either
closed or transferred are marked thus:
Amoy □

The political boundaries on map are of the year 1860

E M P I R E
Lake Baikal
Irkutsk
I A
Sakhalin I.
Kamchatka
Mongolia
Manchuria
Amur
Yezo
Peking
Tientsin Korea
North China
Osaka Tokyo
EMPIRE
Sianfu
Shanghai 19
18 Foochow
Amoy □
unanfu
6 Canton
Cochin China
Siam
China
Cambodia
Philippine
Ladrone Is.
Guam
Islands
(To Spain)
Micronesia
Caroline Is.
Ponape
Mulgrave Is.
Ebon
Kussie
Apaiang I. Gilbert Is.
EQUATOR
Singapore
Borneo
Sumatra
East Indies
Java
Papua or
New Guinea
Solomon Is.
New Hebrides
Navigator Is.
P A C I F I C   O C E A N
TROPIC OF CANCER
Sandwich Islands
Hawaii

North American Indian Missions

1 Cherokees 1817-1860 (moved to Arkansas in 1821 & 1837)
2 Choctaws 1818-1859 (moved to Arkansas in 1828)
3 Mackinaw 1826-1836
4 Maumee 1826-1835
5 Allegheny 1826-(1866)
6 Tuscarora 1826-1860
7 Osage 1826-1836
8 Chickasaw 1827-1834
9 Stockbridge 1828-1848
10 Ojibwas 1831-(1870)
11 Creeks 1832-1836
12 Pawnees 1834-1847
13 Abenaquis 1835-1858 (in Canada)
14 Oregon 1835-1847
15 Sioux or Dakota 1835-(1883)

Longitude West from Greenwich
L. Winnipeg
Canada
Quebec
Montreal
Buffalo Boston
Chicago
New York
UNITED STATES
San Francisco
St. Louis
Ohio R.
Atlantic
Savannah
Mississippi
Colorado R.
Rio Grande
Mexico
New Orleans
Gulf of Mexico
TROPIC OF CANCER
Mexico
Br. Honduras
Cuba (Spanish)
Hayti
Bahama Islands (Br.)
West Indies
Pacific Ocean
Same Scale as Main Map

860
region follows the
of closing or trans-
or transferred after

reece 1830-(1869)

anton 1830-
moy 1842-1858
oochow 1847-
hanghai 1854-1860
orth China 1860-
am 1831-1850
ngapore 1834-1843
orneo 1838-1852

pe Palmas 1834-1843
aboon 1843-(1870)
outh Africa 1835-
andwich Is. 1820-1853
icronesia 1852-

PREFACE

By the Rivers of Water is a history set in the midst of a nineteenth-century Atlantic world. It is a story of a strange odyssey by a young white couple from the Georgia and South Carolina Lowcountry who left plantation homes and the elegant little city of Savannah and sailed ocean highways to West Africa. There they lived for seventeen years, first in a cottage above the pounding surf at Cape Palmas and later in a cottage by the broad waters of the Gabon estuary. Odysseus-like, they sailed along what was for them an exotic coastline and sometimes ventured up great rivers and followed ancient paths. They encountered different peoples, found cultures that evoked both admiration and horror, and visited landscapes of great beauty and waiting dangers. But unlike Odysseus, they did not undergo in their travels a journey from a great estrangement to a spiritual restoration; this was no odyssey from a war-torn city to a longed-for home. Rather, their odyssey was a journey into a wider world and into an expansion of the human spirit. And their return to home was a return that followed the call of familiar voices, places, and scenes—a seductive call that emerged from deep within their memories and that echoed in their hearts. They returned because they were unable to resist the voice of a beckoning Southern homeland, unable to ignore the call of those who had loved them since their childhood, unable to abandon those who were waiting at home for them.

By the Rivers of Water is the story of John Leighton Wilson and his wife, Jane Bayard Wilson, the best-known and most influential American missionaries in West Africa during the first half of the nineteenth century. Around their story—with all of its startling contradictions and deep ambiguities—are gathered the stories of other men and women whom they encountered on their odyssey: Gullah slaves from Georgia and Philadelphia bankers; Grebo kings and a brilliant young woman at Cape Palmas; Portuguese slavers and African slave traders; African American colonists in Liberia; white missionaries, black missionaries, Mpongwe kings, and merchants in Gabon; French imperialists; and South Carolina secessionists. Here in this Atlantic world—in the midst of this cacophony of disparate voices, cultures, and societies—the Wilsons made their way, guided, they believed, by a divine providence. On their journey, they found their lives entangled not only with the lives of diverse peoples, but also with the landscapes through which they traveled, which reached out to embrace and engulf them in the sights and sounds and tastes of particular places.

The Wilsons were members of affluent—and in the case of Jane, aristocratic—families in Georgia and South Carolina. Their grandfathers had been officers in the American Revolution—Major General Lachlan McIntosh, Colonel Bubenheim Bayard, and Captain John James, son of Major John James. Through the Bayards they were closely connected to the families of prominent bankers and physicians in Philadelphia, to US senators in Delaware, lawyers in New York, and professors in New Jersey. Through the Wilsons they were part of a dense network of increasingly prosperous planting families who, through the labor of their slaves, were turning Sumter County in South Carolina into one of the wealthiest regions in the nation.

When Leighton and Jane Wilson decided to become missionaries in West Africa, many of their family members and friends were deeply alarmed. The Protestant missionary movement was young, and to many of the Wilsons' contemporaries, their decision to become missionaries appeared quixotic, if not fanatical. And to go to Africa with its raging fevers seemed nothing less than suicidal. Although there was a growing enthusiasm for Christian missions as the nineteenth century proceeded, many whites regarded the missionary effort as ridiculous, as an act of religious hubris. And in regard to Africa, many thought mission efforts doomed to failure. They asserted—especially as a new scientific racism began to develop in the nineteenth century—that Africans were unable to comprehend the Christian gospel or to adopt the "civilized" ways of Christian people.

Such nineteenth-century ideas, when added to the widespread distrust and often disdain of missionaries in our day, make it difficult to enter the Wilsons' world and travel with them on their odyssey. The perceived presumption, and, all too often, the obvious arrogance of missionaries—and indeed, of the mission movement itself—make the world of Leighton and Jane Wilson seem distant and uninviting. Yet, to begin to understand the stunning religious transformations of the twentieth and early twenty-first centuries, in particular the development of a truly global Christianity, requires that we try to cross the distances that separate us from these early Protestant missionaries. We must try to peer as deeply as we can into their world with its commitments and sorrows, its adventures and failures, its travels and homecomings, and to listen as carefully as we can to their often surprising voices.

If the odyssey of Leighton and Jane Wilson seems strange and distant, the worlds and voices of those whom they encountered along the way seem equally strange and distant. The distinctive accents of Gullah slaves in the Lowcountry of Georgia and South Carolina sound peculiar to most twenty-first-century ears. The Gullah left few written records, and for generations their voices have been largely ignored or regarded as merely quaint and entertaining. Yet today their story and stories are beginning to be heard more clearly as archaeologists dig into old slave settlements, as anthropologists investigate Gullah storytelling, and as historians gather records of Gullah life from courthouses and plantation records and from the letters of whites and from even a few precious letters Gullah slaves themselves wrote or received. Their history is a part of the history of the American South, and their lives were entangled with and interpreted and challenged the lives of Lowcountry whites—including Jane and Leighton Wilson.

The free African Americans whom the Wilsons encountered in Liberia were on their own odyssey—from the land of slavery to a homeland in West Africa. Their voices sound at first clear and familiar to contemporary ears. Their records are abundant and their efforts to escape US slavery and racism resonate with the deep sensibilities of many twenty-first-century people. Yet the peculiar ambiguities of their colonialism and of their relationship with the indigenous people of Liberia make their world and their perspectives also seem strange and often surprising and difficult to understand. These ambiguities are perhaps best seen in the life of a remarkable governor of the colony at Cape Palmas, and in the life of a former Charleston barber who died as a patriot of his new homeland, fighting the Africans who had long lived there.

During their odyssey, the Wilsons met many different African peoples—from the Mandingo and Vai in the north, to Fanti on the Gold Coast, to the Fang in tropical rainforests. But most of all, they encountered and lived among the Grebo at Cape Palmas and the Mpongwe on the Gabon estuary. Modern Western people must strain—and strain hard—to hear the voices and catch intimations about the nineteenth-century world of the Grebo and of the Mpongwe. Most daunting is trying to hear individual voices—attempting to recognize the sound of a king's voice at Cape Palmas or the voice of his precocious niece; or trying to hear the voice of a wise Mpongwe merchant or of an old Mpongwe king struggling to maintain the traditions and independence of his people. Yet their voices—hard to hear as they are—rise up in documents and what anthropologists call "hidden transcripts," and they demand that we try to hear them, too, and that we look, that we squint hard, and peer across the great distances that separate us from them, and try to get glimpses into their world. They call us to acknowledge that they, too, had lives and were part of cultures worthy of acknowledgment and understanding. They speak and insist that they, too, were travelers, and that they were on their own and sometimes surprising odysseys. They were not silent and passive participants in a larger Atlantic world, but were vocal and active players in that world. And they point us to their own stories as revealing interpreters of modern Western assumptions and power.

TO LISTEN TO these disparate voices, to attempt to explore at least the most important aspects of these diverse cultures and societies, and to hear a coherent story emerging from many individual stories, requires a disciplined imagination. The discipline demands a careful reading and rereading of texts; one must listen to many witnesses, and pay special attention to what is odd and local. Such discipline requires one not only to listen to many nineteenth-century voices, but also to engage the voices of many twentieth- and twenty-first-century specialists—especially anthropologists and archaeologists and historians of the American South, of an Atlantic world, and of the diverse societies of West Africa. The research for this intense listening leads to wondering, and the listening and the wondering together prepare the way for the historian's imaginative reconstruction of a coherent distant story.

To be sure, any persuasive reconstruction of the past must demonstrate careful research and faithful attention to details. But the historian's task is not primarily to present a catalog of discovered "facts." Rather, the historian attempts to enter as deeply as possible into past lives and into the social and cultural contexts of those lives in order to interpret and re-create for the present a past world. The study of history is, finally, an exploration of mysteries, the continuing exploration of—and arguments about—the lives of particular people, and about the dynamics and forces that influence the course of human life. The writing of history is plunging into other times and other places and into the story and stories of other people and then emerging with the historian's account of what has been seen and heard even in the empty places and silences of the past. Among the many things encountered, as one follows the strange odyssey of the Wilsons, is the mystery of good intentions and cruel consequences, and the enigma of human freedom in the midst of slavery and the contingencies of human life.

PART I

Starting Places

Chapter One

A Slave's World

From the slave settlement on Hutchinson Island, Paul could look across the river to Savannah with its waterfront of toiling men: sweating stevedores loading and unloading sailing ships from exotic, unknown places; slave porters pushing and pulling heavy carts up steep cobblestone dray-ways to city markets; sailors dropping rusty anchors, swabbing decks, and hoisting sails. In the midst of all this activity, Paul could see and hear, as an almost unnoticed part of the landscape, white-bodied seagulls and terns calling wildly to one another as they flew back and forth above the dark river waters.[1]

Since the founding of Savannah in 1733, the Savannah River had shaped much of the life of the little city. Its waters connected Savannah to London and Liverpool, to Cuba and Jamaica, to Boston and Charleston, and to the cities, villages, and rivers of West Africa. From its port flowed the produce of a Georgia hinterland, and to its port came riches from a wider world. Savannah's tree-lined parks and slave markets, its soaring church steeples and sturdy warehouses packed with lumber, cotton, and rice—all in one way or another depended upon the river waters.[2]

By early December 1832, the river had also played its part in shaping Paul's life and the lives of those who lived with him in the slave settlement. Most mornings he crossed the river in a little bateau to work in the city as a carpenter. And most evenings he returned to the settlement across waters stirred by tide and river flow and sometimes by night winds that made the paddling hard and the crossing dangerous. Over the years he had learned well the moods of the river, and he knew the coming in and going out of its waters. When the moon was full and the time right, he had to paddle against the tide as it surged strongly up the river pushing back its waters and bringing past the slave cabins on Hutchinson Island hints of the Atlantic and its wider world. But when the moon was new, and especially when there had been heavy rains inland, and swamps had emptied dark, cypress-stained waters into the Savannah, he had to direct his bateau against the river's flow as it pushed hard against the tide and brought downstream reminders of a Southern landscape.[3]

Paul, now thirty-one, was too young to remember slave ships unloading their frightened cargoes of men, women, and children, but his father, Charles, remembered. Charles had worked the waterfront as a porter and had witnessed the foul-smelling ships as they sailed slowly past Tybee Island at the mouth of the Savannah and unloaded their slave cargoes at the waiting wharfs—the *Mars* and the *Betsy*, the *Aurora* and the *Franklin*, the *Polly* and the *Mary*, and many others.[4]

Each ship had arrived carrying its own bitter history. The *Mary*, constructed in Philadelphia, had left Liverpool, England, in 1802 and had cruised the coast of West Central Africa flying the flag of Great Britain and buying slaves before setting her sails for Georgia. Her captain had taken on board and stored beneath the *Mary*'s deck 310 men, women, and children drawn from the kingdoms and tribes of a great interior region of West Africa. In late 1803, after months on the open Atlantic, he had sailed up the Savannah and unloaded 279 slaves for the city's slave market. In this manner, for almost half a century, the ships had been arriving one by one at the Savannah wharfs to disgorge from wretched holds those who—in their work and in their bodies—were to create in the coming years much of the wealth of the land.[5]

The last international slaver to sail boldly up the river had been the *Flora*—a sleek sailing ship that had arrived at a Savannah wharf in October 1807, flying the US flag. Its captain had purchased 267 slaves from the Vili kingdom of Loango, north of the Congo River, and had disembarked 201 of them in Savannah. Some of the missing 66 may have been sold in a Caribbean market, but some no doubt had succumbed to dysentery or dehydration, to the trauma and brutality of the Middle Passage. The dead, and perhaps even the dying, would have simply been tossed overboard.[6]

The importation of slaves into Savannah had come to an end two months after the arrival of the *Flora*. The US Constitution had declared that the importation of slaves "shall not be prohibited by the Congress prior to the Year 1808"; and in 1807, Congress had passed the Act Prohibiting Importation of Slaves, to go into effect on January 1, 1808. The federal legislation was largely effective in stopping an open trade in Savannah, and while slavers occasionally glided cautiously into some isolated tidal river along the Georgia coast to unload their illegal cargoes, none would be so reckless as to sail directly to a Savannah wharf. Whatever the motives behind the congressional action in 1807, and the motives were no doubt many, the law was a boon to those who already owned slaves and who watched both the number of their slaves and the value of their slaves grow in the years that followed.[7]

Paul had been only six when the *Flora* sailed into Savannah Harbor. But although new slaves were no longer arriving on the banks of the river, slaves were still pushing and pulling carts up the steep dray-ways to the city, still working the rice and cotton fields, still being sold in slave markets, and still having their lives pushed, pulled, and managed to suit the needs and whims of whites. Now, in December 1832, Paul had learned alarming news, most likely from his sister, Charlotte, who lived in Savannah and worked as a domestic servant for the Bayard family—their owners, Jane and Margaret Bayard, had both become engaged. A handsome young South Carolinian, John Leighton Wilson, had shown up in Savannah and suddenly proposed to Jane, and she had accepted. And James Eckard, a Philadelphia lawyer and seminary student at Princeton, had arrived in Savannah at about the same time and had quickly proposed to Margaret, and she, too, had accepted. Such news must have been deeply troubling for those who lived on Hutchinson Island, because the marriage of an owner—especially a woman owner, and most particularly two women owners—meant, all too often, the breakup of a slave settlement and slave families. For even a marriage, even a happy event in the lives of white slave owners, could have devastating effects on the lives of black slaves.[8]

Paul's family, like the other families living on Hutchinson Island, had been shaped and reshaped for generations by the choices and vagaries of their owners' lives. Paul's parents, Charles and Mary, had been owned by Major General Lachlan McIntosh. McIntosh, as the commander of the Western Department of the Continental Army, had endured the bitter winter at Valley Forge with George Washington and his troops. McIntosh's family had originally come to Georgia with other Scottish Highlanders, settling south of Savannah at the mouth of the rich and muddy Altamaha River. In 1739, the Scots had signed an antislavery petition seeking to keep the young colony of Georgia free of the slaves who were increasing so rapidly in neighboring South Carolina. Again in 1775, on the eve of the American Revolution, McIntosh had led his fellow Scots in declaring their "disapprobation and abhorrence of the unnatural practice of Slavery in America." But when the allure of wealth created by slaves, especially from the burgeoning trade in rice—Carolina Gold, it was called—when that allure overcame the antislavery sentiments in Georgia, the Scots had laid aside their reservations and had soon become wealthy planters and slave owners.[9]

The old General died in 1806, and in the division of his estate, his daughter Esther McIntosh received some of his slaves, together with lands scattered along the Georgia coast. These selected slaves, willed to her and her heirs forever, became upon Esther's death in 1822 the property of her young daughters, Jane and Margaret. With them came the children of the slave women and any future issue and increase of the females. In this way, the sisters had become the owners of thirty-nine slaves who lived in the Bayard settlement on Hutchinson Island as well as the owners of much rich and productive land scattered along the coast of Georgia, from Savannah to Cumberland Island far to the south.[10]

With such a history, Paul surely pondered and perhaps stayed awake at night wondering about and worrying about the engagements of these two young white women. What would the engagements mean for those who lived in the island settlement? Families would almost certainly be divided. Which sister would get which slaves and what land would go to which sister? Where would Paul and the others live? Would they be scattered, friend from friend, husband from wife, children from parents, and carried to distant places? Such were the harsh questions faced by all who lived in the Bayard settlement, and Paul knew that the answers would largely be determined by two unknown white men. These men, as the sisters' new husbands, would soon assume responsibility for their wives' property, and for the lives and destinies of those who were called Bayard slaves.[11]

Nicholas Bayard, Jane and Margaret's older half-brother, had become the trustee of the property in 1822, after their mother's death. The girls' father had died a short time before their mother, and Nicholas had already taken responsibility for managing the estate, of which he also owned a share. When their father had died, Margaret had only been eleven years old, and Jane had been fourteen.[12]

One of the first things Nicholas did was to make Paul an apprentice to the carpenter Jack. Slave carpenters—especially good ones—were valuable, not only for what they would bring on the slave market but also because they were in much demand in a young city. Young Paul had to carry much lumber and make many cypress shingles and saw many pine and oak boards, always watching Jack at his work and listening to his instructions, before he finally received his own carpenter's tools in 1830. There were hammers and saws, augers, gimlets, and chisels. And there were planes for different work—a jackplane, a fore plane, and a joiner plane—and he had to know which one to use when. Jack taught him how to use each tool, and he taught him that much of the work of a carpenter was solving problems—you had to be able to look at a task and figure out how to do it and do it right. What was to be the pitch of a roof, or how was a joist to be connected to a beam, or how were window frames to be measured and built, or floorboards tightly laid? It took time to learn such a trade, and it took a good teacher to teach it, and Paul spent the time, and he was fortunate to have in Jack a good teacher.[13]

Paul's work meant that he had to move around Savannah and learn its streets and handsome squares, its rhythms of work, and its rules and secrets. In spite of restrictive legislation, blacks moved freely through the city, running errands for owners, driving wagons and pushing carts, selling fruit and vegetables brought in from the countryside, or hawking fish or shrimp or crabs caught in a creek, or oysters gathered on a muddy bank. Some slaves were allowed by their owners to hire themselves out for work—to clean privies or work in a garden or wash and iron—paying their owners most of the wages for their labors. Most slaves lived in quarters behind their owners' houses, in a kind of compound that it was hoped would restrict their movements. But the boundaries of the compounds were generally porous, and little alleys ran off the straight streets and connected the quarters to city life. With care and knowledge of the ways of whites, and especially of the police who walked the streets, a slave could sneak out at night and visit other quarters or go to a waterfront tavern to mingle with white sailors from distant places, and drink a little rum, and do a little carousing. In all of this, Paul learned that slaves had to be careful. They had to anticipate white anger and white discipline and learn strategies for avoiding and resisting white power. The slave markets of the city were constant reminders that whites could sell any slaves they considered unruly or troublesome—and sell them to some slave trader on his way out of the city, perhaps heading to the new cotton country being opened up in Alabama or Mississippi. And the jail and the workhouse and the whipping post—they, too, had their lessons to teach about caution and dangers. Some of the Bayard slaves had spent time in the jail, and no doubt Paul had heard from them that it was a wretched place and that he should use every available strategy to stay out of it.[14]

As Paul moved around the city, going from one job to the next, he could see that along parts of the waterfront, and in certain other, largely rundown neighborhoods, free blacks lived. They were only a small part of the black population of Savannah—and an even smaller part when the population of the surrounding county was included—but they played an important role in the city's life. Among them were carpenters and butchers, seamstresses and washerwomen, and a few shopkeepers, fishermen, nurses, and cooks. They lived in a kind of twilight zone between freedom and slavery, with many restrictions on their lives. Their status provided some freedom, but because they were people of color, whites regarded them as almost slaves. Unlike Paul and those who lived in the Bayard settlement, they could have legal marriages, but only if they married another freed person. If a woman was free, her children were born free; but if a free father had a child by a slave woman, the child was born into slavery. Free people could own property and keep for themselves what they earned by the sweat of their own brows, but they were subject to many of the same harsh punishments as slaves.[15]

Mixed up among the slave and the free were runaways, slaves who had made their own break for freedom and were living by their wits, hiding out in the shantytown below the bluff that ran along the river, or in some back street, pretending to be employed by their owners. When one young woman from the settlement on Hutchinson Island disappeared for a time in 1823, Nicholas hired a slave catcher, and she was quickly captured. She had been attempting to hide in the city, but hiding was not easy and the risks were high in a city full of spies who made their living catching slaves on the run for freedom.[16]

During the years of Paul's apprenticeship, the religious life of Savannah's black community was increasingly dominated by First African Baptist Church and Second African Baptist. Andrew Marshall, the pastor of First African, was the preeminent leader of the city's slave and free black community. For Paul, as for other blacks in Savannah, Marshall was a source of encouragement and hope. During his long ministry (1826–1856), Marshall baptized some 3,800 blacks, welcomed into First African's membership more than 4,000, and married some 2,000 black men and women. He and Henry Cunningham at Second African taught and preached a Protestant Christianity that had emerged from a radical wing of the Reformation. It had been deeply shaped by the revival fires that first swept across colonial America in the Great Awakening of the mid-eighteenth century, and that had burst out again in a Second Great Awakening at the beginning of the nineteenth century. This Protestant Christianity, with its roots in a European Baptist tradition, had been adopted and transformed by African and African American converts into good news for slaves.

Paul and other blacks in the city no doubt began going to the churches for many reasons, but certainly among these reasons was that they heard in the churches an offer of hope in what appeared a hopeless situation. In sermons and Sunday schools, in river baptisms and communion services, the present order of masters and slaves did not appear eternal but passing and contingent. In the churches—circumspect as the pastors had to be—singing, praying, worshiping congregations were able to imagine an alternative to the present system of slavery. "There Is a Fountain Filled with Blood," so popular among singing Baptists, white and black, would have brought hope. But so, too, would the spiritual "There is a balm in Gilead, to make the wounded whole." And, when the time was right: "Go down Moses, way down in Egypt's land; tell old Pharaoh, to let my people go!" "God," proclaimed Andrew Marshall in a sermon, "would deal impartially with 'the poor and the rich, the black man and the white.'" Years later, as an old man not far from death, he reflected on the glory of his redemption in Christ and declared to his congregation: "Our skins are dark, but our souls are washed white in the blood of the Lamb. . . . How many of those to whom we are subject in the flesh have recognized our common Master in heaven, and *they are our masters no longer?* They are fellow-heirs with us of the grace of life."[17]

This city—Savannah with all of its distinctiveness—had become home for Paul. Savannah, a particular place with its flowing river and social arrangements, was the primary environment in which he had grown up, and it continued to provide the conditions for his development as an African American man. Here, and at the settlement across the river, he was learning his way in the world—how to think about himself, how to carry himself, how to act with other blacks, and how to act before whites. And here he was also learning how to see Savannah and understand it in ways that were fundamentally different from the ways in which Nicholas and his young sisters and other whites saw the city. He knew that this city was a place of deep oppression, and consequently, he had begun to discover, as the years passed, that Savannah was not home for him. In spite of deep memories of the city and its shaping influence on his life, he was beginning to long for another home and another homeland where he could be a free man.[18]

IN JANUARY 1825, early in Paul's apprenticeship, Nicholas decided to move most of those who worked the Bayard land on Hutchinson Island to a rice-growing plantation that had been part of General McIntosh's estate. General's Island, some sixty-five miles south of Savannah, lay near the mouth of the great Altamaha River close to the little village of Darien. The island and the county in which it was located—McIntosh—were named for the old General, but the McIntosh plantation on the river island, in spite of its rich alluvial land and abundant water, had never been fully developed. Nicholas was a banker and not a planter by practice or inclination. He had, however, a keen eye for profits, and he knew that a rice plantation, properly managed, could yield rich rewards for its owner.[19]

After making careful arrangements, Nicholas had all who were being sent south gather with their possessions at the Savannah customhouse. Among them were Jack and Paul—the carpenter and his young apprentice—who were to repair and enlarge the old slave settlement and work on the trunks and gates that regulated the flow of water into the rice fields. Nicholas paid for their clearance at the customhouse and no doubt gave them words of instruction and encouragement. Then he saw them settled on board a little coastal schooner that sailed the inland waters between the mainland and the sea islands that lined the Georgia coast.[20]

For young Paul, it must have begun at least as a great adventure—they cleared the customhouse, moved slowly down the river toward Tybee Island, and then, before reaching the open Atlantic, they turned south onto broad inland waters. The schooner sailed close to Ossabaw Island, home to several plantations and many slaves. St. Catherine's Island came slowly into view with its slave settlement of white tabby houses. Massive sea-island oaks, gnarled and twisted, soared over dense thickets of myrtle, saw palmetto, and razor-sharp yucca. To a traveler on a passing boat, such island scenes presented contrasting images that seemed to overwhelm the senses—a landscape enchanting yet threatening, inviting yet seemingly impenetrable. Off to the right on the mainland, Paul could make out in the distance the little village of Sunbury where the Medway River's dark waters emptied into St. Catherine's Sound.

The schooner was entering a region of great isolated plantations. Ospreys and eagles cruised the waters. Marshes stretched out to the horizon while creeks and small rivers wound their way reluctantly toward the Atlantic. The travelers sailed past Blackbeard and Sapelo Islands where palmettos ran to the water's edge and brightly colored crabs and innumerable seabirds fed along rich mudbanks. The air became heavy with the fragrance of the marsh and an occasional porpoise moved gracefully through the water hunting shrimp and mullet. They entered Doboy Sound and ran up the Rockdedundy River, an arm of the Altamaha, gliding silently past Catfish Creek until the village of Darien appeared, and finally General's Island.[21]

It was a miserable place—flat, hot, and buggy: just the kind of place where rice could thrive in tepid waters. Here the Altamaha River had formed islands of river swamps by dividing into several channels. Through years of slave labor, the islands had been banked and the swamps drained and plantations created. Fanny Kemble Butler, the English actress and a reluctant plantation mistress, described neighboring Butler's Island as "quite the most amphibious piece of creation that I have yet had the happiness of beholding. It would be difficult to define it truly by either the name of land or water, for 'tis neither liquid nor solid but a kind of mud floating on the bosom of the Altamaha." The product, she wrote, of "this delectable spot is rice—oranges, negroes, fleas, mosquitoes, various beautiful ever-greens, sundry sort of snakes, alligators and bull rushes enough to have made cradles not for Moses alone but the whole Israelitish host besides." Such was the landscape of General's Island, not so different in fact from Hutchinson Island, but Darien was no Savannah, and the isolation of the island was palpable. Yet such isolation, together with similar isolated places up and down the Georgia and South Carolina coast, had provided the land-scape for the development of a distinctive culture and speech among the slaves of this Lowcountry region.[22]

Paul, by moving to General's Island, was entering the land of the Gullah—a people who had forged, while drawing from their varied West African lin-guistic and cultural traditions, a distinctive African American culture and pattern of speech. Paul was himself, of course, already a part of this Gullah community, but he had been living on its margins. Savannah moderated and inevitably diluted the strength of Gullah culture for the black men and women who lived within its urban environment. The city had too many whites and the power of European culture was all too clear, even as one looked across the river from the slave settlement on Hutchinson Island. City blacks, espe-cially those born and raised in the city, were famously different from country blacks—they were wiser in the ways of whites and more acculturated into white patterns of thought and behavior. But McIntosh County was another matter. The white population was barely a fourth the size of the black com-munity, and many of the whites were clustered in the little village of Darien, and others spent the summer and fall months of the sickly season away from their plantation homes. Such isolation from whites and their European Amer-ican culture provided the geographical and social space for the blacks of the Lowcountry to shape their own folkways and cultural traditions.[23]

For Paul, General's Island was consequently an immersion into one of the strongest centers of Gullah culture. The name "Gullah" most likely came from a corruption of the word "Angola," but it had come to refer to all of the Africans and their descendants who lived in the Lowcountry, the coastal region of South Carolina and Georgia. Their Gullah language had slowly evolved out of several sources: the diverse languages of West Africa, an English pidgin that had long been used on the coast of West Africa for trading, and the English of Lowcountry whites. Through a complicated process of language formation, the isolated slaves of the Lowcountry had grafted, generation by generation, the vocabulary of whites onto the shared grammatical structures of West African languages. The result was a distinct Gullah language. To be sure, some African words survived—*da* or *na* for "mother," *tata* for "father," *li* for a "child." And there were translations into African-style equivalents, so that "to speak" was to "*crack one's breath*," "to envy" was to "*long eye*," and "to cry" was to "*eye water*." But it was the deep grammar of Gullah, more than anything else, that linked it to the diverse languages and cultures of African homelands. The language consequently reflected both the isolation of the Gullah and their connections to swirling currents linking Europe and Africa with the Americas. The ways in which the Gullah people saw and interpreted the world around them, the ways in which they endured their suffering and responded to their oppression, and the ways in which they met the contradictions and mysteries of human life were all carried and expressed by their language.[24]

Most whites not raised in the Lowcountry had difficulty understanding Gullah and thought it was simply "bad English." And even among the Gullah themselves, young people, more acculturated to white ways, sometimes had to struggle to understand the language of older generations. Years after Paul traveled to General's Island, a former slave who had lived on neighboring Butler's Island remembered that "Sebral uh dem hans wuz bery old people. Dey speak a funny language an none uh duh res of us couldn hahdly ununstan a wud dey say." As one who lived and worked in Savannah, Paul may have had some difficulty himself in understanding the country blacks. Ironically enough, however, the Gullah he heard on General's Island and in isolated McIntosh County was not some lone phenomenon without a language family. He would discover, after a much longer journey to unexpected places, an Atlantic Creole that echoed the vocabulary, intonations, and grammar of the Gullah people of the Lowcountry.[25]

Paul could see and hear all around him the evidences of a Gullah culture that was both distinct and related to this wider Atlantic world. On some days when he and Jack needed lumber and supplies, Gullah boatmen carried them into Darien in a long canoe. Six or eight men, paddling in rhythm, pushed the canoe through river currents and sang in rich Gullah tones their boatmen songs—songs that echoed a West African world transplanted and adapted to life along the Altamaha and its hinterlands. And on some nights, when the work of the day was done, Paul and the others from Hutchinson Island gathered around bright-burning fires to hear stories with deep West African connections. All around them in other settlements such stories were being told, and they no doubt made their way into the evening hours on General's Island as well—stories of the spider Anansi, the trickster who won by guile, not strength, or of the trickster Buh Rabbit, who used his wits to get the best of powerful figures like Buh Wolf, Buh Alligator and Buh Bear. And arriving with these stories were their traveling companions, Gullah proverbs, which also moved from settlement to settlement. Polished by their telling and retelling, the proverbs carried Paul and his companions into the inner world of ances-tors. They revealed in a few memorable lines the accumulated wisdom and warnings of those who had gone before in Africa, and of those who had de-veloped strategies for surviving in the Georgia Lowcountry. You should keep your promises, for "anybody wuh gwine back on eh prommus, an try fuh harm de pusson wuh done um a faber, sho ter meet up wid big trouble." And you should always be a faithful friend, because "en yet [it doesn't do], in dis wul, fuh man fuh ceive [to deceive] he fren." Some stories and proverbs warned blacks to always be careful around whites, while others taught them how to trick a master or mistress. And some stories rose up out of the toil and pain of bondage and told of the deep longing of a people for freedom and a re-membered homeland. A former slave who lived near General's Island remem-bered popular stories of slaves flying back to Africa. "Duh slaves wuz out in duh fiel wukin. All ub a sudden dey git tuhgeddu and staht tuh moob roun in a ring. Roun dey go fastuhnfastuh. Den one by one dey riz up and take wing an fly lik a bud . . . back tuh Africa."[26]

Sometimes when the sun had set and the moon was high and the people had a little time for themselves, the Gullah danced. Gathering in the open space of a settlement, illumined by their evening fires, they danced the snake hip and buzzard lope, the camel walk and fish tail. Young Paul—he was twenty-four when he arrived on the island—no doubt knew the popular dances and songs of Savannah blacks, but these dances in the isolated settle-ments around Darien reflected more clearly and vigorously the rhythms and cultural style of West Africa. Still, however exotic they may have seemed to Paul with his city ways, the Gullah dances had English names, and those names—no less than the styles and rhythms of the dances—shaped their character and meaning. Paul was living, after all, on General's Island, and the dances of the Gullah settlements were being danced on the sandy soil of Georgia plantations, not in a distant home across the Atlantic. In Georgia, the dances could be subversive of white authority, and they often aroused anxiety and sometimes disdain among white planters. Whites worried that dancing could stir strong and dangerous emotions among their slaves, for dances had stories to tell and were an alternative to the disciplined and or-derly world that owners tried to create in order to keep slaves submissive. Their dances, one nearby planter complained, "are not only protracted to unseasonable hours, but too frequently become the resort of the most dissolute and abandoned, and for the vilest purposes."[27]

To be sure, some owners and plantation managers, seeking to be wise as serpents, encouraged dancing in the settlements. Twenty years before Paul moved into the settlement at General's Island, Roswell King, the overseer of the neighboring Butler's Island plantation, had ordered a dozen fiddles. They were to be a diversion for the people and to keep them from thinking about and acting on more serious matters. "I must" he wrote the owner, "try to break up so much preaching as there is on your Estate. Some of your Negroes die for the Love of God and others through feir of Him. Something must be done. I think Dancing will give the Negroes a better appetite for sleep than preaching."[28]

But Paul would have heard not only the music of fiddles coming across river waters and marshes. On clear nights when the moon was bright and the wind was still, the often haunting sound of banjoes would have come from the settlements around Darien, and perhaps would have risen irrepressibly within the settlement on General's Island. Drawing from a variety of West African and Caribbean traditions, Gullah craftsmen had created their own Lowcountry banjoes. They dried a gourd, cut an opening in it, stretched a cat hide across the opening, added a wooden stick neck, and attached horsehairs for strings. And then they played their music and the people danced their dances. And their rising music and their ecstatic dances poured from their hearts and memories and told, often in powerful and mystical ways, of their world by the dark waters of the Altamaha.[29]

Above all, however, Paul would have heard drums. They were like nothing he had ever heard in Savannah with its rush of many people and rumbling wagons and creaking carts. But here in the great loneliness of McIntosh, the drums sounded and their messages flowed not only across river currents and marshes to General's Island but also through inland swamps and forests, isolated settlement to isolated settlement, and even from mainland settlements out to the sea islands. And in reply came sea-island messages surging back above the murmur of the tide and swelling surf to tell their stories and make known well-disguised intentions. Whites were often alarmed by these slave drums, for they talked across plantation boundaries, and their messages rolled over white efforts to control slave talk—Who knew, whites wondered, what secret and threatening plans might be announced by these talking drums?[30]

Still, in spite of white opposition, the drums were built and kept in the settlements, often concealed. In the area around General's Island, a man would kill a raccoon for the supper pot, then dry its hide and stretch it across a hollow cypress log to create a drum with its own distinct sound. Sometimes a drummer beat a call to a dance and sometimes to a funeral. When dancing was the intent, the beat was fast. When a death was announced, the beat came long and slow. One former slave remembered: "Right attuh duh pusson die, dey beat um tuh tell duh udduhs bout duh fewnul. Dey beat a long beat. Den dey stop. Den dey beat anudduh long beat. Ebrybody know dat dis mean somebody die. Dey beat duh drum in duh nex settlement tuh let duh folks in duh nex place heah." No wonder whites feared what secret things the drums might say or what plans they might make known.[31]

Paul would not have been surprised to hear the drums announce a night-time slave funeral—such funerals were also the general practice in Savannah. Daytime, after all, was a time to work for the master or mistress or overseer; nighttime was the time when slaves could bury their dead. Slave carpenters made simple pine coffins, and Paul, no doubt, had been learning from Jack how to construct these final beds.

Among the Gullah, the body of the dead was placed in the coffin as soon as the box was built. Then when the evening sun had set over the marsh and rice fields, the mourners took up the filled coffin and, under starlight and moonlight and by the light of fatwood torches, they made their way to the slave burying ground. There they opened a grave in the sandy soil, and there they gazed for the last time upon their friend or loved one whose face was forever fixed in death. They nailed the lid on the coffin and lowered the body into the ground and into the deep anonymity of a slave cemetery. Then singing and praying, the mourners began to march around the grave, tossing sandy soil over the coffin and into the wide-gaping earth. Once the grave was covered, the people brought some possessions of the deceased, a few things from among the few things a slave may have claimed to own—perhaps a pail and dish, maybe a piggin, bottle, and spoon, or even a little mirror or an old cup. They placed them on the grave and warned one another that these fragile reminders of a slave's life were not to be disturbed: "The spirit need these," a former slave declared years later, "jis lak wen they's live." The living and the dead were close to one another, and Gullah graves, though real and deep, did not hold the spirits of their dead. "Duh spirit," another explained, "nebuh go in duh groun wid duh body. It jis wanduh roun. Dey come out wen duh moon is noo."[32]

Paul most likely heard on the island stories of ghosts wandering the countryside. He would have been no stranger to such stories, for ghosts were said to move quietly along the backstreets and alleys of Savannah, frightening whites as well as blacks. On General's Island and the surrounding plantations, ghosts sometimes appeared when a person walked at night along a lonely stretch of road. The white sand of the road provided a dim path leading into the darkness. Cypress and black gums, oaks, and Spanish moss loomed over-head and cast their shadows—shadows that conjured in their shape and movement the appearance of a spirit traveling the same road. "They peah jis as nachral as anybody," said one Lowcountry resident. "Most of them ain got no heads. Jis go right along down the path."[33]

More threatening than the wandering spirits were witches—a neighbor or friend might be one; it was not easy to tell. Witches, like ghosts, were no strangers to Savannah, and Paul may even have encountered one before his move to General's Island. Certainly some whites in the city seemed no more immune to them than blacks. But witches seemed to prefer life in the isolated settlements of the countryside to the orderly grid of streets and squares in Savannah. A witch or hag could, after slipping quietly into a cabin at night, change identity by hanging up her—or his—human skin behind a door. Then, with a new, terrifying appearance, the witch would pounce upon a vic-tim's chest and ride it hard until the victim awoke terrified, fighting for breath as if being suffocated. Sometimes a witch would become an animal in order to do its victim harm—a buzzard or a cat, or perhaps an alligator hiding on the bank of a swampy creek, waiting to grab the leg of its prey at some un-expected moment—not unlike a leopard man of a remembered African homeland. When the identity of a witch was discovered, the accused was feared and sometimes punished by the Gullah community.[34]

Because wandering spirits and witches roved the woods and muddy marshes around General's Island, the Gullah hung charms over their doors, buried them in front of their cabin steps, hid them where paths crossed, and wore them to keep sinister forces at bay. White travelers frequently reported seeing charms throughout the Lowcountry, and former slaves later reported on their wide-spread use in the area around Darien. Paul and the other Bayard slaves would have seen charms in Savannah, too, but charms were more visible, perhaps more necessary, in the scattered settlements of McIntosh, where spirits and witches seemed more likely to roam. A former slave who lived near Darien described the charms used in the area: "They's made of haiah, an nails, an graveyahd dut, sometimes from pieces of cloth an string. They tie em all up in a lill bag. Some of em weahs it round wrist, some of em weahs it roun the neck, and some weahs a dime on the ankle." Although some charms were used to guard against a witch or threatening spirit, others might be used to cure an illness, or to make a person brave or invincible in the face of danger, or to cause an enemy harm.[35]

Conjurers were the specialists with charms—they knew what was needed for certain purposes and what incantations were necessary. Some conjurers were also root doctors with an intimate knowledge of Lowcountry herbs, roots, and barks. In Savannah when Paul or others on Hutchinson Island had become sick, Nicholas Bayard had sent Dr. Joseph Habersham to treat them, and he had paid him handsomely for his trips across the river to the settlement. But on General's Island, apparently no white physician was available, and whenever Bayard slaves became sick or suffered wounds, they undoubtedly turned to root doctors for help. Though these doctors drew on West African traditions of healing, they had of necessity become familiar with the flora of the Lowcountry. They had discovered from long trial and error that chewing sweet-gum leaves or drinking a tea of marsh rosemary could cure diarrhea; that an infusion of dogwood bark helped cool a fever; that the juice of Jerusalem oak could clean hookworms and tapeworms out of a child; and that boiling the roots of Devil's Walking Stick and drinking its tea could give a man courage and sexual prowess. Learning such secrets took time, generations, and the result was an evolving Gullah tradition of healing. Old West African assumptions about healing, about what caused illness or misfortune, remained; but root doctors, no less than conjurers with their rusty nails and dimes, were Gullah practitioners and not West African ones.[36]

Charms and conjuring could also be used against whites as a means of resistance when black rage boiled and the desire for revenge or justice could no longer be suppressed but came rushing to the surface. For a people with no military or legal power, the powers of a secret world could be invoked to hide an illicit barbeque in the woods or to defend a family from separation or to strike back at a cruel master. An experienced conjurer could create a charm intended to make a master ill or to blight a crop, or to bring misery and death into a white family. What slave owners most feared, however, were the poisonous roots and concoctions that could be slipped into foods, stirred into drinks, or dropped into a well. Stories of such poisonings were whispered by whites in plantation parlors and behind closed doors in city mansions; and over the years, more than a few slaves in the Lowcountry had been charged and executed for poisoning or attempting to poison white owners or overseers.[37]

SUCH WAS THE world that Paul entered when he and the other Bayard slaves sailed the inland waters to General's Island in 1825. He found much that was familiar, but he no doubt discovered much that was new. He was, after all, a city person and not a country fellow. He knew the sounds of Savannah—wagon wheels on cobblestone dray-ways and sandy streets, church bells and sailors' voices, country women hawking vegetables and fishermen selling shrimp. Paul spoke in city accents, understood city manners, and practiced city ways of resisting white control. He had listened to Andrew Marshall preach, had heard the congregation of First African Baptist lift its voice and sing, and had learned where runaways hid and free blacks worked. This world of Savannah was the world that had most fundamentally shaped him. Here he had learned to think of himself as a carpenter, to carry himself upright, and to walk without the shuffle that slavery tried to teach.

But his time among the country Gullah also helped to shape his understanding of who he was as an African American man, and it helped to prepare him for a surprising West African home that would be both familiar and strange. When he arrived on General's Island, he entered a largely secret world that whites saw only in glimpses and from a great distance. The music and the dancing, the stories and the proverbs, the charms and root doctors populated a sacred cosmos, an interior landscape of the mind and imagination. On General's Island, the details of this landscape became more familiar to Paul. And because he internalized parts of this Gullah world, his deepest assumptions, his dispositions, and his inclinations were all unavoidably informed—in part at least—by what he had experienced during his years in McIntosh County. Stories and proverbs once learned by a young Paul would not easily fade into forgetfulness but must have rumbled far down in his heart and mind. Nighttime scenes of dances and funeral rituals surely lingered in his memory, ready to emerge when called forth by some new scene at some new place. And roaming spirits and chest-riding witches—they, too, must have loitered about in his imagination, waiting for their chance to appear in a troubled dream.

Yet, in a few years, Paul would vigorously reject this internal world of the mind and imagination and seek to disassociate himself from it. He was, he would insist, a "civilized American" from Savannah who stood in great contrast to the "savage" Africans around him. And yet his rejection would be the rejection of an insider, of one who had lived within the world of the Gullah, who knew not only star rise and moon rise on General's Island and the sound of talking drums flowing across the Altamaha, but also the fear of roaming spirits and threatening witches. And so, like many others around the world struggling to be "civilized," to be modern and escape the traditions of ancestors, his rejection would carry an intensity and passion that could easily lead to violence.

NICHOLAS BAYARD LEARNED the hard way that it was no easy thing to operate a rice plantation from a banker's office in Savannah—nor was his experiment as profitable as he had hoped. And so after a few years of buying supplies and sending clothes and food to the island and gaining little in return, he abandoned his plans, rented the land to a neighboring planter, and brought the Bayard slaves back to Savannah. Most likely they were all glad to leave the plantation and its fetid rice fields to return to Hutchinson Island, even if going back to the old life had its own burdens.[38]

On Hutchinson Island they at least did not have to plunge into miry rice fields. The Bayards had entered an agreement with the city in 1818 to practice only "dry culture" on Hutchinson. It was thought that *miasmas*, the noxious and deadly vapors of summer swamps and rice fields, were somehow the cause of what was called "the bilious remitting fever," or "country fever," or "marsh fever"—or sometimes simply "malaria." The miasmas were also associated with the devastating epidemics of yellow fever that periodically swept the city. These miasmas had apparently claimed the lives of the Bayard parents in the early 1820s. Both Jane and Margaret Bayard had most likely had the fever as well—it was not so devastating for children. Their immunity to the scourge would stand them well in the future.[39]

With his full labor force of slaves back in the city, Nicholas now handed out work assignments to each. As a banker, he wanted to utilize them in the most rational and profitable manner possible. Most of those who were newly returned from General's Island he put to work raising cotton and oats on Hutchinson Island. Two old men he hired out in the city as house servants, while a few others he hired out as common laborers. Charles, Paul's father, had never left Savannah, and Nicholas had him continue his work as a porter, pushing large carts loaded with cotton, rice, and other goods along Bay Street and Factor's Row. Nicholas gave Mary, Paul's mother, and a few other older women space on the island to tend a large garden for the Savannah market. He rented a stall at the market on Ellis Square where the women sold potatoes and okra, beans and benne seeds, tomatoes, field peas, and arrowroot cakes. He had them bring him regularly the proceeds of their labors—although there was obviously room for the women to fudge when the time came to settle accounts.[40]

Nicholas was pleased with Paul's progress in carpentry. He rented him out for various jobs around the city, and the wages Paul earned for the Bayard estate grew steadily as he became increasingly skilled. He had learned his numbers—how to add and subtract, how to multiply and divide—as a necessary part of his carpentry. He needed to be able to measure the length of a board and determine how much of it to cut off to make it fit; how many feet of lumber he needed for a job; how to figure a quarter of an inch or three-eighths of an inch; and how to cut a board at just the right angle. And as a part of his training, Paul also learned to read and write, even though it was illegal for a slave to do so. Nicholas apparently turned his head and ignored this illegality, knowing that a slave carpenter's ability to read and write made him more profitable. Now Paul could receive written instructions about how a window was to be framed or a roof laid, or send written questions about where a door was to go, or where he was to secure lumber or nails. But literacy was not only a valuable skill—it was also an opening for Paul to a wider world. He could now read newspapers and pamphlets, the Bible and city signs. To be sure, he had to read and write with great caution and circumspection in order not to alarm whites. But literacy provided a new freedom within the constricted world of a slave. And that freedom also offered, perhaps ironically, a path that led not only away from white control, but also away from the world of the Gullah. Literacy was a pathway for Paul to a modern world, to his identifying himself as a "civilized" American from Savannah. At any rate, Nicholas bought more tools for his bright carpenter, and Paul began to receive special treatment when clothes and shoes were distributed to the Bayard slaves.[41]

So Paul prospered—as such things are measured for a slave—and he entered ever more deeply into the life of the black community of Savannah. As he moved around the city, he met a young woman who was a "domestic servant" of an affluent white family. Perhaps he met her in the market on Ellis Square, where his mother sold produce. Or perhaps they met at First African Baptist—the church was one of the few places where blacks, slave and free, could gather in large numbers. Wherever they met, they fell in love and were able to convince Nicholas and her owner to give them permission to marry. The service would have been simple—even though the bride was a domestic and the groom a skilled carpenter—but not so simple as a country wedding, in which slaves sometimes simply jumped across a broomstick together to become married. Because their marriage was widely recognized by whites, a minister most likely conducted it—perhaps Paul and his bride were one of the thousands of black couples married by Andrew Marshall of First African. But slave marriages were not announced in the newspaper or recorded in court documents, and so the details of their wedding—even the bride's name—entered a silence as deep as a slave's grave.[42]

After the marriage, Paul had a "wife house"—his wife's room where she lived in slave quarters behind a Savannah house. Paul could visit her on weekends, so they could have a little time together before he had to return to his own home on Hutchinson Island. Whites often allowed such divided housing arrangements for slave couples with different owners—and with such arrangements, Paul and his wife struggled to create a family and life together.[43]

SO PAUL WAS a married man, a slave husband on his way to becoming a slave father, when he learned the deeply troubling news in 1832 that the Bayard sisters had become engaged. Now the danger of a separation from his wife loomed as an alarming possibility. How would the slave property—the men, women, and children in the Hutchinson Island settlement—be divided between the sisters, and where might they be scattered? When Paul and his wife fell in love and decided to marry, they knew that a slave marriage ran the risk of separation. Such knowledge had not deterred them from taking such a risk and claiming some freedom in the midst of their bondage. In the years ahead, however, this risk, and its fragile freedom, would extract a bitter cost, demanding of Paul a decision that could not staunch a terrible pain.

Chapter Two

Many Mansions

While Paul was becoming a skilled carpenter and immersing himself in the life of Savannah and General's Island, his two young owners, Jane and Margaret Bayard, were growing up and being shaped by very different circumstances. They were, after all, white children of great privilege. Their father, Dr. Nicholas Serle Bayard, had made a name for himself as a respected and well-connected Savannah physician. Much to the gratitude of city authorities, he had stayed at his post during deadly outbreaks of malaria and yellow fever during the first two decades of the century. Rather than flee to the countryside, as did many physicians, he had visited the sick and dying and had done what he could to ease their suffering. And as one of the incorporators of the Georgia Medical Society, he had worked hard to make the practice of medicine the work of scientific men—of professionals, not roaming quacks promising wonderful remedies for all the ailments of man and beast.

Moreover, when he was so inclined, Dr. Bayard was ready to remind his proud Savannah neighbors of his Huguenot ancestry and to point to a family tree loaded with colonial leaders. By the time Jane and Margaret were old enough to understand family connections, one of Dr. Bayard's brothers was clerk of the US Supreme Court, another was a wealthy Philadelphia banker, one sister was married to the chief justice of the New Jersey Supreme Court, and a cousin was a US senator from Delaware.[1]

The immediate patriarch of this Bayard clan—the paternal grandfather of the two young sisters—was Colonel Bubenheim Bayard. He had been an honored patriot during the Revolution and had spent the difficult winter of 1777–1778 at Valley Forge with Jane and Margaret's maternal grandfather, Lachlan McIntosh. So the sisters grew up knowing that they were descendants of distinguished Revolutionary War officers and hearing stories of their grandfathers' bravery and patriotism.

Dr. Bayard had married his cousin Ann Livingston Bayard of Philadelphia in 1798. Nicholas, their only child, had been born in New York in 1799 and was three when his mother died in Savannah in 1802. Three years later, Dr. Bayard had married Esther McIntosh in Savannah, Jane and Margaret's mother. Jane had been born in 1807 on her grandfather McIntosh's Cumberland Island plantation some forty miles south of Darien and General's Island. There, amid the luxurious growth of the island and with the sound of the surf flowing across the land, she had had her earliest sensory impressions. Margaret had been born in 1810 in Savannah, where carriages and wagons rattled on cobblestones and black men and women walked down sandy streets hawking shrimp and crabs.[2]

The sisters and their half-brother, Nicholas, grew up in Savannah in a handsome house in Franklin Ward—a house filled with black servants and frequent guests. From their earliest days, the white sisters heard whites telling blacks to come here and to go there and to do this and to do that. When they went with their parents to visit friends, or to go to church, or to take an outing for their health, they inescapably saw—although they may not have consciously noticed—blacks building, cleaning, and feeding Savannah. For privileged white children growing up in the city, such arrangements must have seemed natural, like the rising of the sun in the east and the setting of the sun in the west and the movement of the moon and stars at night. Whites had their place and blacks had theirs, and each moved in their own place, in their own orbit, as a part of daily life. These distinctive social arrangements were quiet guides for the sisters as they were learning what it meant to be white girls and young Bayards in Savannah.

With their distinguished ancestry, and Dr. Bayard's lucrative medical practice, the Bayard family moved easily in the city's highest social circles. They were members of Savannah's Independent Presbyterian Church, where Dr. Bayard rented a pew and brought his family to listen to the long, logical but passionate sermons of their greatly loved pastor, Henry Kollock. The sermons and the arrangements of the congregation reinforced the sisters' understanding of the world's ordinary ways—blacks had their place in the balcony, whites had their place in rented pews. When the congregation's new sanctuary was completed in 1819, the local papers declared it one of the most beautiful church buildings in the country. Its steeple soared high above any other structure in the city, announcing its prominence, and its great domed ceiling declared the blessings of heaven on what was below. When the new sanctuary was dedicated, the young Bayards watched President James Monroe and his entire cabinet arrive and take their seats in the front of the church to join the celebration, while blacks looked on from above.[3]

Dr. Bayard died in 1821 when Jane was fourteen and Margaret eleven. He was, declared the *Savannah Republican*, a man who did "ample justice to his talents, the excellence of his character, and the urbanity of his manners." The paper described him as public spirited and hospitable—a man endowed with an independent mind who had honor and honesty as his only guides. He was said to be "religious, moral and candid." He lived life, said the paper, "without fear and so ended his days without reproach."[4]

A few months later, Esther McIntosh Bayard was dead, apparently a victim of yellow fever. She possessed, the *Georgian* noted, "all the qualities that ought to render a lady dear to her relatives, and estimable in the view of the public. She was friendly, hospitable, affectionate, and in all respects filled her station in society, as an honorable, useful and good member of it. She was the eldest surviving daughter of Major General Lachlan McIntosh, a patriot of the revolution, and inherited his patriotic feelings, and firmness of character."[5]

Much of the character of the parents had already been inherited by Jane and Margaret—a spirit of generous hospitality and hearts that were affectionate, independent, and surprisingly fearless. But the home in Franklin Ward had now become a painful reminder to them of happier times. They began to withdraw to themselves and turned to one another for comfort in their grief. Nicholas, a twenty-two-year-old bachelor, did his best to look after his young half-sisters, but he quickly realized they needed more than he could provide. They needed a full and happy home life, and they needed to continue what they had already begun in Savannah—an education to prepare them for their place in society as Bayard women.

EARLY ON THE morning of July 4, 1822, Nicholas and his sisters arrived at a wharf across from the Hutchinson Island settlement. Black porters loaded their extensive luggage on the packet ship *Garonne*. A number of other prominent whites in the city joined them on board. Then, when the wind and tide were right, sailors hauled anchor, and the captain steered the ship out into the river to follow its flow.[6]

Two weeks later, Nicholas and the sisters were in New York visiting Bayard relatives. After a short stay, they boarded a coach loaded high with their luggage and set off across the countryside for Philadelphia. They stopped in Princeton to visit their Hodge cousins—their grandmother Bayard had been a Hodge. During his early teens, Nicholas had spent several years living with the Hodge household and going to school in Princeton, and he was eager to revisit the little village and the family that had welcomed him so warmly. Nicholas had become particularly close to his cousin Charles Hodge—they were the same age—and when the travelers arrived at the Hodge home they discovered that Charles had been elected, only a few weeks earlier, professor of biblical and Oriental literature at Princeton Theological Seminary. Young Charles was on his way to becoming one of the country's most influential theologians, and in the years ahead he would have a close and affectionate relationship with his cousin Jane and her distinguished husband.[7]

When the travelers arrived in Philadelphia, they went straight to the home of their uncle Andrew Bayard, their father's oldest brother. A wealthy merchant and president of the Commercial Bank of Philadelphia, he lived in one of the city's most elegant homes, where white servants did the polishing of silver, the cleaning of dishes, the washing of clothes, and the cooking of meals. Nicholas brought his young sisters and their luggage to the Bayard house on Washington Square, and there Andrew and his wife, Sarah, welcomed them as their own daughters and brought them into their large, affectionate, and pious family. For the next five years, Jane and Margaret called their uncle's home their home, and they began to think of their Bayard cousins as their brothers and sisters.[8]

Jane and Margaret quickly became especially close to their cousins Theodosia and James. For the rest of their lives, even during long and sometimes terrible separations, they would all regard one another with genuine affection. Theodosia Bayard later visited Jane and Margaret in Savannah and traveled with them in New England, and James Bayard—who was close to Jane in age—made his home in years to come a second home for them and a refuge in times of illness or distress.[9]

After their arrival in Philadelphia, Nicholas met quietly with his uncle Andrew and negotiated the financial support his sisters would require. He left funds for their immediate needs and made arrangements to send his uncle regular payments to cover the girls' expenses. Drawn from the proceeds of their father's estate, the payments came largely from the profits that flowed from the labors of Paul and the other Bayard slaves. So even in Philadelphia, Jane and Margaret were attached by the webs of slavery to those who lived in the settlement on Hutchinson Island and by the rice fields of General's Island. Uncle Andrew, careful banker that he was, used the funds prudently for the girls' education, for their clothing, and for visits to various family members in New Jersey, New York, and Delaware. They frequently went with Theodosia to visit her sister Elizabeth Bayard Henry in Germantown, and in this way the young Savannah girls became a part of the Henry family as well.[10]

The Bayards, Hodges, and Henrys were all Presbyterians, and many of the men—including Uncle Andrew—were Presbyterian elders. A few, like Charles Hodge, were Presbyterian ministers. They believed that their religious life had at its heart a deep personal devotion to Christ and to his continuing ministry in the world through the church. Their Calvinist piety was both warm and disciplined. During the week, each family had morning and evening prayers as well as daily devotionals and Bible reading at their breakfast tables. These disciplined practices were part of the rhythm of life in their households, nurturing the hearts and minds of family members. They were all strict Sabbatarians. Sunday was the Lord's Day when they refrained from all work—not as a burdensome law but as a gift in the midst of the continuing work and rush of the world around them. The Sabbath, they thought, served as a reminder that in all of life they were utterly dependent upon God's grace and love and not on their own labors or willpower. They believed that Sabbath rest, when they joined with others in worshiping God as their Creator and Redeemer, was a foretaste of heaven. On the Sabbath, they heard God's Word read and interpreted in long, carefully prepared sermons intended to inform the mind and touch the heart. They sang praises to God with hymns—both old and new—whose words and music penetrated to the deepest parts of their self-understanding. And at the communion table they felt themselves united in the Body of Christ with believers around the world and across the ages. These daily and Sabbath practices of their Calvinist faith nurtured in Margaret and Jane—together with their cousins—a deep sense of privilege and of the responsibilities that flow from a gratitude rooted in God's grace. Disciplined work and a life spent seeking to do God's will was, they believed, a faithful response to God's love and the sacrifices of Jesus, whom they called their precious Redeemer.[11]

For the Bayard men, the spirituality nurtured by such practices of their faith meant a commitment to philanthropy and a concern for the public good. They became directors of the House of Refuge for juvenile delinquents, of the Magdalene Society for the "fallen women of the Philadelphia," of the Sunday School Union, and of the College of New Jersey (Princeton). They contributed liberally to their churches and to education societies. And they sought, perhaps above all, to be responsible in their vocations—in their callings—as bankers, merchants, and physicians, as professors and politicians, and in the ordinary comings and goings of their lives. They believed that the ordinary, everyday work of their lives—and not some sheltered holy place—was the great arena for the practice of their Christian faith. Much to the frequent irritation or amusement of their neighbors, they thought of themselves as the chosen means of bringing learning, culture, and sophisticated religion to a waiting world.[12]

If, however, they thought that their Christian faith and Presbyterian practices informed and fueled their everyday work and commitments, they were less well aware of the ways their religious life and philanthropic activities were shaped by their work as bankers, merchants, and physicians, as professors and politicians. Their orderly worship, their disciplined devotional life, their interpretation of the Bible and of their responsibilities as Christians were all, in one way or another, deeply influenced by the character of their work and by the comfortable and affluent homes in which they lived. To be sure, they believed that they made decisions—decisions that mattered. Not all bankers, after all, knelt and prayed morning and evening, or read the Bible daily with their families, or supported philanthropic causes. And certainly many around them—"worldly people," they called them—did not keep the Sabbath as they kept the Sabbath. These Bayards, Hodges, and Henrys believed that they had, within the circumstances and contingencies of their lives, the freedom to make real choices. But they also believed at some deep level of their self-understanding—or at least it was what they confessed—that their freedom was not unlimited, and that the mysterious providence of God directed their lives and the course of human history. In the coming years, these complex and even contradictory ideas about human freedom would shape their thinking about the black slaves who, like Paul and his family, labored in the cities and fields of the American South.[13]

For the Bayard, Hodge, and Henry women, the practices of the faith also had to do with their ordinary everyday lives. But their daily lives, their vocations, were focused on the home and family and led to no public engagements in philanthropy or vocations outside the home. The world of these women—even these affluent white women—offered them no directorships of benevolent societies, much less jobs in banking or politics. What the world of these women offered were busy homes where dinners were ordered, guests welcomed, and children loved and disciplined. To be sure, the women could reach out from this place, from within this restricted arena, to the world around them in Christian discipleship—they could be faithful members of congregations and could support philanthropic societies with their prayers and contributions. But their vocation was above all the creation of a Christian environment in their homes where the language that was used, the manners that were practiced, and the order that was maintained contributed to a deepening love for Christ.[14]

Margaret and Jane internalized this world of affluent Philadelphia Presbyterians. It helped to shape the way they saw themselves and carried themselves as privileged young white women. It influenced their temperaments, dispositions, and postures. It provided many of the deep assumptions that they carried for the rest of their lives. Yet their Philadelphia home also began to nurture within them, even in their youth, a restlessness to break out and go beyond the boundaries assigned to women. Precisely because they felt deep religious stirrings as young women, they wanted to respond with their whole lives and not some restricted, assigned roles. They began to consider themselves—no less than their uncles and male cousins—among those chosen to go beyond the home and to help bring Christian love, learning, and salvation to a waiting world.[15]

AFTER FIVE YEARS in Philadelphia, Margaret and Jane returned to Savannah in 1827 and to the home of their brother, Nicholas. Jane was now twenty and ready to move into the social world of Savannah. Margaret, at seventeen, was not far behind. All around them were reminders of the life they had known before their parents' deaths—the elegant home where they had lived with their mother and father and the sights and sounds of the city with its parks and gardens and busy markets. And everywhere, from the moment they stepped once again onto a Savannah wharf, they were surrounded by black men and women who were moving about—hauling and cleaning; butchering, selling, and building; sweating in the hot sun and always keeping an eye on whites.[16]

The sisters arrived in Savannah about the same time that Paul and the other Bayard slaves were returning to the city from their sojourn on General's Island. Jane and Margaret most likely did not know most of those who were returning—before their parents died, the sisters would have had few opportunities or little reason to know field hands and laborers on Hutchinson Island. But the domestics who worked in the Bayard home were another story. The sisters found Jack the butler at his post still carrying himself erect, still practicing his old-fashioned good manners—they called him House Jack to distinguish him from Jack the Carpenter, Paul's mentor. Paul's sister, Charlotte, who had been Jane's personal servant for years when they were both little girls, was waiting to take up her responsibilities with her returning mistress. And Suzanne, who had looked after Margaret as a little girl, now had a seventeen-year-old mistress.[17]

Jane and Margaret, as young women who had been living in Philadelphia, were now able to look around them and see Savannah with new eyes. There was, of course, still much that they could not see and much that they could not understand. But they inescapably knew that Savannah was different from Philadelphia. For one thing, blacks were everywhere, and their presence made Savannah look different, sound different, and move in different rhythms from what they had known in the North. After five years away, the world of Savannah was more visible in all its distinctiveness, and they now began to notice and to pay attention to what had before seemed only ordinary. This meant that Jane and Margaret began to look at, to actually see, the black slaves who were all around them—including those who lived on Hutchinson Island and whose labors provided most of the comforts the sisters enjoyed. And with their looking and their noticing, they began to have questions about slavery and about their ownership of slaves.[18]

They met John, the new driver—the "boss man" who was in charge of directing the work on the island and distributing rations to the people in the settlement. A religious man held in great confidence by whites, he crossed the river weekly and came to the Bayard home to confer with Nicholas. And Paul came as well to bring his wages, and Jane and Margaret had opportunities to meet the young carpenter so recently returned from General's Island. They met Paul's father, Charles, who brought his porter's wages, and Paul's mother, Mary, who came to the house to report what vegetables and how many eggs had been brought from the island and sold in the Ellis Street market. They watched Nicholas talk with them, and saw him collect wages from those hired out, as well as the money from the market, and they knew he wrote it all down carefully, banker like, in the estate account book.[19]

Jane and Margaret returned to Savannah not only with new eyes but also with hearts that had been nurtured and awakened to deep religious feelings, and those feelings also added to their growing misgivings about slavery. They returned to their family's pew at the Independent Presbyterian Church, where they had sat as children with their parents. Now they heard the eloquent preaching of Daniel Baker, one of the great preachers of his generation. His preaching was said by a Southern editor to move "thronged assemblies as the trees of the forest are moved before the wind," and his impassioned appeals were said to touch "the learned and unlearned, cultivated and uncultivated." Standing in a great mahogany pulpit placed high above white worshipers, Baker preached to a congregation that included some of the most influential and affluent members of the community—Barnards, Bryans, and Cummings; Gordons, Habershams, Stoddards, and Telfairs. And above them all, gathered in the balconies, blacks sat and watched and worshiped.[20]

This congregation of blacks and whites not only listened to Baker preach, they also sang hymns together and listened to the soaring music of the church's great organ being played by Lowell Mason. Mason was a prolific writer of hymn tunes, and his music would become deeply identified with the piety of evangelical Protestantism not only in the United States but also abroad. In the coming years he would compose "Bethany" ("Nearer, My God, to Thee"), "Olivet" ("My Faith Looks Up to Thee"), "Dennis" ("Blest Be the Tie That Binds"), and "Hamburg" ("When I Survey the Wondrous Cross").[21] But it was Mason's music for a stirring missionary hymn—"From Greenland's Icy Mountains"—that most deeply touched Jane and Margaret and ignited their imaginations about the future direction of their lives. Composed by Mason in Savannah, the hymn rang out:

> From Greenland's icy mountains,
> From India's coral strand;
> Where Afric's sunny fountains
> Roll down their golden sand:
> From many an ancient river,
> From many a palmy plain,
> They call us to deliver
> Their land from error's chain.[22]

ON THEIR RETURN to Savannah, Jane and Margaret found Nicholas an attentive and affectionate older brother. He looked out for the best interests of his young half-sisters and sought to provide them with a home where they could continue to have nurtured both a high-toned sense of Christian morality and a propriety that reflected their station in life. But his relationship to them, while good, was never particularly close. Affection was there, but it always seemed to be rooted more deeply in duty and responsibility than in the feelings of the heart. The sisters consequently grew closer to one another, drawing on their shared memories of Philadelphia and their continued grief over the death of their parents.

But the sisters also made new friends. They became especially close to Eliza Clay, who was three years older than Jane. Eliza's father, a distinguished Savannah judge, had become, after a powerful conversion experience, a Baptist minister and had served as pastor of the First Baptist Church of Boston, Massachusetts. Eliza had spent years in the North and had returned to Georgia only the year before Margaret and Jane returned. An independent spirit—she would remain single all her life—she did not hesitate to break out of roles assigned to affluent white women; nor was she afraid to do work ordinarily reserved for affluent white men. She learned how to manage a large rice plantation, and in the years ahead she gave advice to neighboring planters about the best time to plant, about the sprout flow of waters into rice fields, and about when to have black men and women go down into the miry earth to hoe between long rows of rice. In her willingness to break social expectations, she modeled for the Bayard sisters a certain freedom of spirit and helped to give them courage to explore little-known paths.[23]

Particularly important for Jane and Margaret were Eliza Clay's efforts on behalf of the religious instruction of slaves. The Clay plantation, Richmond-on-Ogeechee, a short distance from Savannah, was one of the most beautiful in the South. There Eliza and her brother, Thomas Savage Clay, were establishing schools where they were teaching their many slaves biblical stories and Protestant hymns. And there, in the evenings after their students had come in from their heavy labor in rice fields, the Clays began to instruct Gullah men and women about family life and about avoiding the enchantments of charms and witches and late night dances. Such instructions soon came under fierce attack from conservative whites, who thought it encouraged insubordination and said that religious instruction of blacks was little more than "casting pearls before swine." The future governor of South Carolina, Whitemarsh Seabrook—a kind of lingering rationalist of the Jeffersonian sort—would be particularly venomous in his attack on the Clays. But Eliza, like Jane and Margaret, felt her religious convictions drawing her toward some special effort of Christian benevolence, and the schools seemed a kind of home mission work that needed to proceed in spite of the arrogance and impiety of a South Carolina radical.[24]

WHILE SAVANNAH THUS became a home for the Bayard sisters, they began to spend time with relatives near Darien in McIntosh County. Their cousin William McIntosh was a contemporary of their mother's and became "Uncle William" to them. His plantation, Fair Hope, became, especially for Jane, a place of special memories, a home that evoked for her joy, gratitude, and a deep peace of heart.

During the six years following her return to Savannah (1827–1833), Jane traveled regularly to Fair Hope, a little north of Darien and General's Island, for leisurely visits, especially during the balmy months of winter and spring. Margaret went with her sometimes, but Charlotte was Jane's constant companion as her personal servant. The young mistress and her maid always sailed, like Paul on his journey to General's Island, on one of the little schooners that ploughed the inland waters, where the sea wind mingled the fragrance of salt and marsh, and an occasional fisherman could be seen in the distance. Each trip made the landscape more familiar—they had time to learn the contours of the sea islands: Ossabaw and St. Catherine's, Blackbeard and Sapelo. And each trip slowly invited Jane and Charlotte to enter through all of their senses a world of isolated plantations, of rice fields that yielded their crops in season and slave settlements that stretched out in long rows.[25]

Each time their schooner arrived in Darien, Jane and Charlotte were only a short distance from General's Island, where Paul had had his immersion in Gullah life. But the island plantation was rented during these years, and Jane and Charlotte apparently never visited its flat, hot, and buggy settlement on any of their trips. Rather, they met in Darien a McIntosh coachman—he was always waiting for them with a carriage. After he loaded their luggage with care, he would drive them along sandy roads past rice and cotton fields where Gullah men and women were hoeing and plowing, reaping and picking. The carriage rolled through great stretches of barren pine forests and around cypress swamps before finally turning down the long plantation avenue, where oaks heavy with age and moss reached out to enclose all who traveled this way to Fair Hope house. There, William and Maria McIntosh, together with their children, welcomed Jane into their loving family and Charlotte to the servant quarters.[26]

Even more than in Savannah, Jane learned at Fair Hope what it was like to be surrounded by black men, women, and children. Over seventy slaves lived in the McIntosh settlements, and many more populated the surrounding plantations. Daily she would have heard them speaking in their Gullah accents, and daily she would have seen them going about their work in the house or going to and from the rice and cotton fields. In the evenings she would have seen their settlement fires and heard the distant sound of their voices and their preparations for slave suppers. Such scenes would not have seemed alien to her, although she saw them only from the distance of her race and class. Unlike many whites who felt awkward and often threatened or repulsed when in the midst of blacks, Jane felt at ease among the Gullah people, even as they knew they had to keep their eye on her and other whites—and perhaps especially on her, with her growing benevolent sensibilities toward them.[27]

As in Savannah, Jane no doubt noticed particular slaves that surrounded her and wondered about them. Perhaps her years in Philadelphia—where she had been largely surrounded by whites—made her attentive to, and curious about, life in the settlements. Or perhaps what she had seen in Savannah led her to look more carefully at those who lived and worked at Fair Hope. Or maybe her growing religious sensibilities led her, on occasion, to walk through the settlement and talk to the women who were fixing supper, or to the men returning from feeding a horse or a mule. Whatever the cause, Jane was beginning to think of slaves as individuals with distinct personalities, with their own sorrows and hopes, anxieties and concerns. And so at Fair Hope she continued to wonder—and to wonder more intensely—about her Christian duty in regard to them and to those she would come to regard as their injured and neglected relatives in their African homeland.[28]

At the same time that Jane was paying careful attention to the blacks of Fair Hope, she was also growing to love the quiet of the plantation—especially compared to Philadelphia and Savannah, where wagons and carriages constantly banged and clanked down the streets. She was becoming a quiet and reserved young woman, possessed of much self-confidence, to be sure, but preferring the pleasures and pieties of a quiet life to the social swirl that preoccupied many young women of her class. And the beauty of Fair Hope, in all its isolation, had great appeal for her. The plantation house was located on a little bluff above the Sapelo River, and it provided Jane on each of her visits a grand scene of the marshes and tidal rivers that lay between Fair Hope and Sapelo Sound. In the early mornings, she watched the marshes begin to glow as sunlight spread across them. And in the evenings, she watched the marshes slowly dim in the lengthening shadows of twilight—egrets flew in long white lines to roost and the night wind stirred the marsh grass and surrounding oaks. Wildlife roamed the Fair Hope woods, and on occasion she saw animals along the edges of the marsh—deer and raccoons, possums, rabbits, otters, and cooters. The birds were a wonder for Jane, especially in the winter when migrants found their way south. Buntings, warblers, and vireos joined the homebound who stayed year round—the red-winged blackbirds that sang while clinging to a marsh reed, and the wood storks and great blue herons that hunted shallow waters for frogs and fish. And the ducks! Mallards and pintails, teal and widgeons—they arrived in the fall by the thousands to feed in rice fields and under oaks that dropped their acorns into tepid waters.[29]

Both the social landscape of Fair Hope—with its black population and Gullah culture—and the physical landscape of Fair Hope—with its lonely marshes, rivers, and swamps—played a part in shaping how Jane saw the world and how she felt about the world and how she saw herself as a young white woman in the world. Like Philadelphia with her Presbyterian relatives, and Savannah with its memories and associations, Fair Hope provided a home—a home that encouraged her quiet temperament and that nurtured her love for flowing rivers and the beauties of a lonely countryside. Even the rhythms of her Southern speech, the way she walked, and the way she held herself with confidence showed the influence of her time beside the marshes of Sapelo Sound. Yet Fair Hope's social and physical landscape did something more—it helped to prepare Jane for what would be the great adventure of her life and the consuming passion of her religious commitments.

In early 1832, Jane and Margaret announced that they wanted to become missionaries. Their friends were stunned. The Protestant mission movement was young, only a few decades old in 1832, and the movement still seemed to many—including many church folk—to be a largely questionable activity.[30]

For Margaret and Jane to say they wanted to be missionaries seemed, if not insane, at least naive, quixotic, and fanatical, especially given their comfortable social status. Why would they go, many wondered, to some distant and dangerous land and live among a barbarous people? But the sisters were determined. They wrote the American Board of Commissioners for Foreign Missions in Boston and offered their services. Back came the reply: the board did not accept single women as missionaries. If they wanted to be missionaries, each of them needed to marry a man headed for the mission field.[31]

And so word went out that two young women, attractive and well-placed, were waiting in Savannah for husbands who would take them to a distant mission field. The arrival of two such men—John Leighton Wilson from South Carolina and James Eckard from Philadelphia—and the quick engagements of the sisters was the troubling news that Paul heard in early December 1832. What he did not know was what this news would mean for him and for the other slaves on Hutchinson Island in the years ahead. There was no way for him to know that it was the beginning of a chain of events that would eventually lead them on a journey as remarkable in its own way as the journey of the Gullah who were said to "riz up and take wing an fly lik a bud . . . back tuh Africa."[32]

Chapter Three

A Black River Home

John Leighton Wilson, the youngest of the suitors to arrive in Savannah in 1832, had been born near the cypress-stained waters of the Black River in South Carolina. His great grandfather, Major John James, and his grandfather, Captain John James, had fought with the "Swamp Fox"—the wily Francis Marion—against the British and their Tory allies during the American Revolution. Striking quickly from their camp in dense swamps, Marion and his partisans had hit British outposts and lines of communication time and again only to disappear into the cypress bogs and muddy flats that surrounded their hidden camp. Young Leighton had grown up hearing the embellished stories of their exploits and learning that free men and women were called to resist the arrogance and rule of imperial powers—a sentiment he would carry with him to far places.[1]

The Wilsons and the Jameses had come to South Carolina in the 1730s with other Scottish and Scotch-Irish immigrants. Settling in what seemed to them a savage wilderness along the Black River northwest of Charleston, they had slowly cleared the land, built modest homes, and farmed the rich soil that lay between the river, creeks, and swamps of the region. Gradually the children and grandchildren of the early settlers moved further up the river. They established new homes and farms, using the river as their primary highway to carry deer and cow hides, corn, and indigo downstream and to bring back goods purchased on the coast. Before too many years passed, they began to return upriver with a few slaves whom they had bought in the booming slave markets of Charleston.[2]

As soon as they had secured a shelter for their own households, the first settlers organized the Williamsburg Presbyterian Church, after the pattern of the Church of Scotland, and called a Scotsman to live and minister among them. In this way the Williamsburg congregation became the mother church to an expanding line of Presbyterian churches that followed the flow of set-tlers up the Black River—Indiantown, Black Mingo, Salem Black River, Mt. Zion, and Bishopville. Each congregation was at the center of a little community, and in time, Mt. Zion became the home congregation of the Wilson family and at the heart of much of Leighton's world.[3]

William Wilson and Jane James Wilson, Leighton's parents, had married in 1801 and had established a farm about forty miles up the river from the original settlement. The home they built was a plain clapboard farm house, two stories high, with a chimney on each end of a gabled roof. A wide porch—a *piazza* they called it in their Lowcountry way—provided a place for relaxing at the end of the day and for visiting when neighbors or relatives came calling. As children were born and the farm began its evolution into a plantation, more rooms were added—not with any particular aesthetic sen-sibility, other than a concern for what was practical, so that the house grew room by room in a rather gangly, awkward fashion.[4]

Leighton was born in 1809, the fifth of eight children. He became par-ticularly close to his two older brothers, William and Samuel, and to his two younger sisters, Sarah and Mary Martha. It was a loving family marked by deep commitments to one another and to the community in which they lived. All around them—and up and down the river—were families that were con-nected in bewildering webs of relationships: Witherspoons and Scotts, Muldrows and Chandlers, McCutcheons, McBrides, McCoys, and McLeods, and a host of other entangled families. Young Leighton grew up calling many of the white adults around him "aunt" or "uncle," and most of his contem-poraries he called "cousin."[5]

As rooms were being added to the Wilson home, acres were being added to the Wilson farm. The original tract ran from the little road that paralleled the river to the river itself. Along the eastern boundary was Boggy Gully, a stream that meandered north until it was lost in swamps and a narrow section of the river. To this original tract of some 500 acres were added lands—some across the road, some down the road, and some on the far side of Boggy Gully. Cotton, after the invention of the modern gin in 1794, was becoming a highly profitable crop and had begun to make the settlers along the Black River prosperous—including William Wilson as he added acre upon acre to his holdings.[6]

Raising cotton, however, was no easy task, and the Black River farmers believed that they needed slaves to chop the cotton, pick the cotton, and press the cotton into bales for the waiting gins. Like rice planters before them, they began to invest—with loans from Charleston merchants—in black men, women, and children, becoming ever more deeply entwined in a rapidly expanding slave economy. In this way the few slave cabins that had been built on the edge of Boggy Gully in 1801 had become by the 1830s a substantial slave settlement, and what had been called the Wilson farm began to be called the Wilson plantation.[7]

Among those who lived in the slave settlement were some who had been given by Captain John James to his daughter Jane when she was a child. They and their descendants—that is, the descendants of the women—were entailed to Jane and her children. Leighton had thus become the owner of some young slaves who, as he said years later, became entailed "to me twenty years before they or I had an existence." In time, these and the other black men and women who lived in the settlement would have their own memories of this land, their own stories to tell around communal fires, and their own interpretations of life as lived close by the Black River. These memories, stories, and interpretations would challenge what whites remembered, the stories whites told, and the interpretations whites gave to how things had been at the Wilson place and on the other plantations of the area.[8]

LEIGHTON GREW UP on the Wilson farm before it became a plantation. From an early age he had his chores—he helped in the kitchen garden, he learned how to plow a straight furrow, and he worked side by side with the black slaves who were carrying the burden of the day. He learned the way they spoke and how to talk with them in their dialect. And no doubt he heard their stories—at least the ones they wanted him to hear. He listened to their proverbs about how a person should live wisely, and in the evenings he heard the sound of their voices, and sometimes their singing, in the settlement. On occasion he watched root doctors make a poultice to heal an ache or pain and caught glimpses of charms used to keep evil at bay, and he learned of a secret world inhabited by ghosts and haunts and how hags could come at night and take your breath away by riding on your chest. All of this he remembered later, as these early experiences made deep impressions upon his mind and imagination and helped to shape the way he saw a broader world.[9]

But Leighton also remembered black men and women in church with him and his family. Sharper and Ben, Nelly and Sabrina, Abraham and Matilda were among those from the Boggy Gully settlement who made their public confession of faith and were baptized and numbered among the members of the Mt. Zion congregation. They, along with slaves from neighboring settlements, traveled weekly down sandy roads to the Mt. Zion meetinghouse, where they heard the scriptures read and long sermons preached. Together with the Wilsons and other whites they sang the hymns that did so much to shape a Protestant piety among them. And twice a year these black men and women came and sat at a long table that stretched across the front of the church while white elders served them the bread and wine of the communion service. And like the whites who had been served before them, these black slaves took from the elders the plate with bread and the cup with wine and passed them around the table to one another. These scenes made their own impressions upon young Leighton. They, too, helped to shape the way he saw a broader world and stirred feelings that in the years to come marked the deepest commitments and clearest contours of his life.[10]

The people of the settlement consequently did not seem strange or threatening to Leighton. They were people with names and familiar personalities. Jacob was the patriarch, and as he grew older he was moved from working the fields to working around the farmhouse. There he began to help in the kitchen, a little house located behind the Wilsons' home. Kitchen work was unusual for a black man, but Jacob learned to cook the peas, collards, and sweet potatoes from the garden; how to make rice dishes with chicken and its broth, mixed together with okra and tomatoes; and how to prepare the hams from the smokehouse and the sausages stored in crocks packed with lard. He became a favorite with Leighton and was respected by all in the white family.[11]

Leighton knew, of course, that Jacob and the other blacks on the place lived in the little cabins down by Boggy Gully, and not in his parents' expanding farmhouse. And he came to understand as a young white boy that beyond the distance between house and cabin was the greater distance between owner and owned, between white and black. Each day taught him who was boss and who was bossed, who ate the food prepared in the kitchen and who ate from the cook pots of the settlement, who cleaned the stable and who rode the horses, who made the beds in the house and who slept in the beds. And Sundays had their lessons as well—he saw where whites sat and where blacks sat, and he heard sermons preached by whites, and he sang hymns chosen by whites. It all came to seem natural to him, the way the world was ordered, a part of a coherent moral universe.[12]

In the midst of these daily routines, Leighton began to become aware that although Jacob and the others in the settlement were a part of his world, there was much of their world that he did not know or understand. Still, his experience taught him that these two worlds—and their histories—while separate, overlapped and were entwined. When the Wilsons gathered on the piazza in the evenings with visiting aunts and uncles, cousins, or friends to talk about what was going in the county or to remember earlier times, Jacob and other slaves came creeping into their stories from the margins—sometimes as central players in a scene, sometimes as incidental actors, but always as a seemingly natural part of the landscape and of the imagination of a white world.[13]

For their part, Jacob and those who lived by Boggy Gully knew only too well that the Wilsons' world was a powerful and bitter reality in their own lives. A white world not only overlapped their black world, it also lay heavy on it; it was a great pressing, breathtaking burden that intruded into every aspect of their lives. Where they slept, what they ate, the clothes they wore, and the work they did, from the rising of the sun to the last dishes were cleared away and the horses fed at night—in it all, whites tried to govern what blacks did and what they thought, to control the imagination of the settlement and to limit the horizon that lay beyond Boggy Gully. And standing behind these white attempts at control, waiting and watching, was white military power and its readiness to use bloody, terrifying violence.[14]

Because Jacob and the others in the settlement knew all of this only too well, they tried to use strategies to frustrate white control without provoking white wrath. They could shuffle along during the day when told what to do, and in the evening when they were alone together before the settlement fires, they could tell their own stories and laugh at jokes about whites. And when rage boiled and someone could take no more white bossing, the swamps offered a temporary refuge even with the threat of a whipping. In these ways the Wilson place became contested ground, and young Leighton grew up hearing, in the daily coming and going of his Black River home, the often muffled sounds of conflict.[15]

THE WILSONS CALLED their home "Pine Grove"—not "Fair Hope" or "Richmond-on-Ogeechee" or "Strathy Hall" or some other such name used on one of the great rice plantations of the Lowcountry—but rather a modest name to fit the home's modest character and the character of those who lived in its spreading, gangly farmhouse. Longleaf pines, *Pinus palustris*, surrounded their home and—together with cypress swamps and growing cotton fields—dominated the landscape where the whites of Pine Grove and the blacks of Boggy Gully lived separate but tangled lives. The pines, soaring high above scattered oaks and sweet gums, were largely impervious to the fires that burned the undergrowth, and they created open, park-like stands with a ground cover of grasses where deer could graze and quail flourish.[16]

Leighton became a fine horseman in these open forests, and in the Black

River swamps he learned to hunt and became aware of the physical world around him. He knew the explosive flight of quail rising before a pointing dog, and the quail's evening whistle calling together a scattered covey. He could distinguish a buck's track from a doe's and could read the bloodstained story of rabbit fur and bobcat track. He became skilled at quietly paddling a little boat through swampy waters—a skill that later served him well—to hunt the wood ducks and mallards that fed in the dark waters of a cypress swamp. And in the evenings after a hunt as he walked home along the hedgerows that lined the cotton fields, he could hear the lonely song of the cardinal settling over the land, and the twilight hoot of an owl could sometimes be heard coming up from the swamp and in the distance the mordant bark of a fox.[17]

In all of this Leighton was not only learning how to look and to listen and to interpret the natural world around him—he was also becoming deeply rooted in the landscape as place and personality mingled. No less than the social world of family and church, of slave and owner, this physical world was becoming an intimate part of Leighton's world. At some deep level of affection and self-understanding, he began to identify with this spot of ground, this particular place along the Black River. No matter how far he traveled from these pine forests, cypress swamps, and cotton fields, no matter how long he stayed away from these home grounds, they lingered in his heart and in the places of his imagination. Leighton's memory and therefore his sense of self became intertwined with this specific place as the place insinuated itself into his most elemental senses: the sound of the night wind in the pines outside his bedroom window, the fragrance of new-plowed ground in the spring, the feel of matted pine straw beneath his feet, the taste of food prepared in a plantation kitchen, the sight of winter smoke rising from home fires, and the light of a winter sun on a forest floor. Leighton's experience of distant places would always be filtered through these early memories, and his voice, however tempered by other places, always carried the sounds and intonations of a Black River home.[18]

What surprised Leighton was how those who lived by Boggy Gully also began to claim in the years ahead this same landscape as theirs. They had, after all, worked the land in the heat of the day, plowing straight furrows and picking bale after bale of cotton. They had gathered at night before leaping flames to eat their suppers, do their flirting, and warn their children. Here, on this particular spot of earth, they had been living their lives, and over the years they had watched the rich soil of the land receive their dead, and they had sensed the land beneath them shifting and becoming the sacred home of their ancestors. So in later years they, too, claimed this landscape as theirs, and their voices, however suppressed and muted by slavery and racism, also began to carry the sounds and intonations of a Black River home.[19]

AT SOME POINT in his early years Leighton's parents realized that he was a bright, eager student. They had themselves received modest educations, as might be expected among a people settling new land. Most likely, they had gone for only a few years to a little school taught by a Presbyterian clergyman living nearby. But they valued education, and they gathered in their home a small library and made sure that their children had ample opportunities for an education suitable for rising young gentlemen and ladies. While his brothers and sisters did well enough with their studies, Leighton showed himself to be the promising scholar of the family. He loved to read, and there were enough books in the family library to keep him busy—six volumes of *Ancient History* by the French historian Charles Rollin, with their stories of Greeks and Persians, and Romans and Carthaginians; John Bigland's two-volume *History of England* and a *Life of Napoleon*, and Matthew Henry's *Complete Commentary of the Whole Bible*. And of course there was the Bible itself to be read daily, and the Westminster Shorter Catechism to be memorized, and John Fox's *Book of the Martyrs* to be scrutinized, with its pictures of tortured Protestants that so deeply influenced Leighton's view of Catholics and what he and his Protestant ancestors regarded as Rome's tyranny over Christian people. From an early age he plunged into Latin, memorizing vocabulary, mastering declensions, and learning to conjugate verbs. When he was sixteen, he was sent to the little Mt. Zion academy in Winnsboro in the South Carolina upcountry, where many of the state's prominent families were sending their sons for the foundations of a classical education. When he was eighteen, his father sent him to Union College in Schenectady, New York, then under the presidency of the highly regarded and deeply pious Eliphalet Nott. With his background at the Mt. Zion academy, Leighton was able to enter the college as a junior, to take up the more difficult Latin writers, to study natural sciences, mathematics, and moral philosophy, and to begin his study of the Greek language, and then, in his last term, Hebrew.[20]

Schenectady was a long way from the Black River—its winters were cold and its students, mostly from New York and New England, seemed at first to be equally cold, lacking the warmth and easy manners of the Lowcountry. "There are too many Yankees for my pleasure," he wrote his sisters. He found that "they possess no confidence in each other, nor for anyone else. They destroy all confidence that one student has for another. I am sorry to say it, but instead of having my Southern prejudices against the Yankees removed I have had mine confirmed." He was clearly a homesick Southern boy, and he confessed to his sisters that he spent much time thinking about home. He remembered with longing "our dwelling with everything that pertains to it. The little shade trees in the yard, the little water oak in front of the milk house, the one behind it, the many pines in front of the piazza. The large pines on every side of the house." And he thought about "going into the house and taking my seat by the fireside with you all; taking a part in the chit chat; but above all, the privilege of kneeling together around the family altar. This is the place to enjoy a foretaste of heaven!"[21]

But this homesickness did not last long, and Leighton soon turned his attention to the adventure of being in a new place with new people. He found he had a Witherspoon cousin from Alabama at the college, and to his delight he found a new friend from Charleston, John Adger, who became a lifelong friend. And he began to discover as well that he actually liked Yankees, and that they actually liked him. And he began to make friends with them.[22]

As for the landscape, he was stunned by the beauty of upstate New York with its lakes and mountains and rich fertile fields. During his first summer break he began to take long hikes with his new friends. He wrote home that with "knapsacks on our backs and muskets on our shoulders," they walked from Schenectady to Albany, a distance of some twenty miles. They took a steamer the next day down the Hudson River to the village of Catskill, then hiked twelve miles to a house in the mountains where they spent the night. Early the next morning, they climbed a high peak of the Catskills, where they had splendid views of the surrounding countryside dotted with cities and towns. They hiked on toward the falls of the Catskill River. As they drew near, they heard the roar of the falls and saw mists rising from the river. Then came the falls themselves with their thundering power—light and shadows flashed on their waters and a sudden coolness flowed through the air. All seemed to draw Leighton into the grandeur of the place, creating within him a feeling of awe in the presence of a sacred mystery.[23]

There were other hikes to be made—one to the junction of the Mohawk and Hudson Rivers, then down to Troy, then back to Schenectady, a distance of forty miles in one day. Leighton loved the countryside and the mountains, and whenever in the future he climbed other mountains in distant places and saw magnificent views, he compared them to the magnificence of the Catskills.[24]

Leighton returned to South Carolina in the fall of 1829. After a few months at Pine Grove enjoying the company of family and friends, he went to study in the home of his uncle, the Reverend Robert James, pastor of the Salem Black River congregation. James was a highly regarded and greatly loved pastor, and he reminded Leighton of his mother, who had died a few years earlier. Leighton, who had been very close to his mother, rarely mentioned her in the years to come when he wrote home or when he wrote of home. Rather, like Jane Bayard in Savannah, he seemed to carry painful memories in the silences of his correspondence and in the quiet places of the heart. William Wilson had remarried, and his second wife was a kind, affectionate woman fourteen years his junior. Leighton was always respectful toward her, but their relationship was distant; when he wrote home, his greetings to her always seemed an afterthought.[25]

Robert James directed his nephew's studies—they read the New Testament together in Greek, and the Old Testament in Hebrew, and took up the study of theology. James had a special passion for ministry among the growing slave population along the Black River, and Leighton had opportunities to see his uncle teaching, preaching, and visiting among the black slaves in the neighborhood. Under James's leadership, the Salem congregation began to develop a sense of responsibility for the religious life of the slaves, and by the time Sherman's army shook the land, Salem had 100 white members worshiping with 610 slave members. Leighton looked to his uncle as a mentor and guide and admired his piety, his pastoral ways with people white and black, and his disciplined intellect. His uncle was said by others to "have much of the milk of human kindness," and his relationship to those around him was said to be "marked by gentleness and urbanity." Leighton sought to develop these characteristics in his own life, becoming much like his mother's brother. And he began to have questions about slavery as he went with his uncle from slave settlement to slave settlement, visiting with the people, hearing them talk about their sorrows and anxieties, and getting glimpses of the ways in which slavery not only oppressed them, but also hung like a building cloud over the whole land.[26]

Leighton, however, was not yet sure what he wanted to do with his own life or what vocation to pursue. Law was a possibility, and so was the ministry, but he was unsettled. And so, like many recent college graduates in his situation, he decided to teach for a while. He accepted a position in Mt. Pleasant across the Cooper River from Charleston. It was a good choice. He enjoyed his teaching, had time in the afternoons to study, and took time to walk and ride horseback in the surrounding countryside and to ponder the questions that troubled his sleep. On the weekends he went into Charleston and stayed with the parents of his college friend John Adger, who was in seminary at Princeton. He found their home to be remarkable, and their family life filled him with admiration. "There is," Leighton wrote his sister, "more domestic happiness and harmony in this family than I have ever seen in any other. Love appears to be the ruling principle, and peace the consequence." The Adger home was also large and wealthy far beyond anything Leighton had known. James Adger, the father, was a merchant and cotton factor who sold crops for planters and supplied them with seeds and fertilizers, with harnesses and slave clothing, with barrels of molasses and bacon and all the supplies needed to run a plantation. He was hugely successful and had extensive business connections in the North and in England. He also had his own shipping line, which included his pride, the *James Adger*. Although he was a prudent man when sharing his opinions, Adger apparently had little sympathy for the parochialism of many of the planters who came into the city from Charleston's hinterland. They often needed to borrow money from him on next year's crop, and they often seemed to have little awareness of the larger world that lay beyond South Carolina, or even beyond their home county or their plantation. The Adgers, in contrast, summered at the Virginia Springs, at Newport and Saratoga. They went shopping in New York and Philadelphia, visited friends in New Jersey and Boston, and made extended trips to Britain and the continent. They were also members of the Second Presbyterian Church, and on Sunday mornings Leighton went with the family to worship at the large and imposing sanctuary at the end of a small park. He soon began to teach Sunday school and to become acquainted with some of the ministers of the city.[27]

A few months after Leighton began going into the city for the weekends, a series of revival services began to be held in a number of the churches. He began going on weekday evenings and quickly was attracted to Dr. Benjamin Morgan Palmer of the Circular Congregational Church. Palmer was the most progressive church leader in the city and the leading advocate for a number of benevolent causes. His congregation was politically powerful, numbering among its members US Senator Robert Young Hayne; former governor Thomas Bennett; and Hugh Swinton Legare, a leading intellectual in the city who would later become US attorney general and then US secretary of state. Along with Hayne, Bennett, and Legare, many of Charleston's oldest and most respectable families were members of Circular, including DeSaussures and Porchers, Aikens and Vanderhorsts, Hutsons and Perroneaus and a host of other Lowcountry grandees. Leighton, while still staying with the Adgers, began attending Circular regularly.[28]

A religious awakening was beginning to move among both whites and blacks in the city. This local awakening was part of a Great Awakening—a religious revival that had been for several decades sweeping back and forth across the country from colleges in the East to frontier camp meetings in the West. Indeed, it was a part of a larger evangelical awakening that included Great Britain and the Protestant churches of continental Europe. In Charleston, such diverse figures as Henry Laurens Pinckney, editor of the *Charleston Mercury* and soon to be a US congressman, and Charles Snetter, a black barber on Market Street, were touched by the deep soul-searching flowing from the religious services in the city. They, together with a number of others, joined Circular and became a part of Palmer's large and growing congregation. Palmer was inviting his hearers to move beyond orthodoxy, a belief in the truth of Christian faith. For Palmer, knowing the catechism was important, but more important was knowing Jesus. Living an upright, moral life was also important, but more important was a grateful heart—the very foundation for a faithful Christian life. Palmer was inviting his hearers, in powerful and winsome ways, to open their hearts to God's love and to claim Jesus as their personal redeemer. Listening to Palmer and to other preachers in the city, Leighton experienced his religious faith being challenged and the foundations of his life trembling.[29]

Not long after Leighton began to attend the evening services, he began to feel the absence of God in his life in spite of his churchgoing and his daily Bible reading and prayer. "God," he wrote his sister, "has hidden his face from me and if I really ever had a hope, for the present it is absent." The absence of God and a sense of absolute loneliness and abandonment left him deeply shaken. After one service, he suddenly had a vision of hell and eternity—not a hell of fire and brimstone, but a hell where he was utterly alone and abandoned, cut off from those whom he loved and from those who loved him, cut off in profound isolation from love itself. He saw himself standing before the judgment seat of God before whom all pretenses were swept away and all was made clear. In that moment, he saw "the deceitfulness and obstinacy of my heart of which I had no previous conception and the depth and nature of that deceitfulness!!" And he found himself without hope for a Redeemer. In his imagination, he wrote, he saw himself "surrounded by a beloved father, Mothers, sisters and brothers and innumerable host of friends, all dressed in white robes and glittering crowns, to bid me an eternal adieu. And I could almost feel the last pressure of the cold grasp." "Think of my feelings!" he exclaimed. Then he saw eternity. "In vain I tried to fathom its depth. I rolled years upon years and centuries upon centuries, until my imagination was exhausted and I could not see that I had begun to measure the duration of this torment. My feelings were so much tortured that I could no longer bear even to imagine myself the subject of it. I placed another in it and could hear him century after century as he sank deeper and deeper exclaim 'is there no end?' and the reply was as often 'Eternity.'"[30]

His conversion followed several weeks later. With overwhelming emotion he experienced the "perfect love of God which casts out all fear." Christ, the love of God incarnate, had not abandoned him, Leighton confessed, but had come after him and was his Redeemer and Friend, the Lamb of God who takes away the sin of the world, who, in the final day, would stand in Leighton's place before the judgment seat of God. This conversion experience was the turning point of Leighton's life. From then on he measured his journey from this place, a journey that would not end with a final "eternal adieu" but with a joyful reunion in an eternal home where, with believers of all generations, he would feast at the banquet table of the Lord.[31]

Leighton's conversion experience and the convictions that flowed from it meant that in the coming years he was not afraid of death. To be sure, he saw death as an enemy that stalked him and those whom he loved. He would struggle and fight with death, and as colleagues and friends fell under its power, he would learn over and over again how cruel and ruthless death could be. But Leighton was convinced that death did not have the final word on those who had "a precious Redeemer in Jesus Christ." Death for them, in spite of its enmity and all of its terrors, was transformed into a friend in God's gracious providence and an entry into an eternal home. To tell this good news, to point people to this amazing grace, became the consuming passion of his life—he now sang "'Twas grace that taught my heart to fear, And grace my fears relieved," with the conviction of his own experience.[32]

To have Jesus as his Friend and Redeemer, however, meant for Leighton that he must discipline himself as he sought to follow his Lord. And critical for this discipline were self-reflection and a daily examination of his heart and life through prayer and Bible reading. He came to love and to pray the Psalms—Psalm 51: "Behold, thou desirest truth in the inward being; therefore teach me wisdom in my secret heart. . . . Create in me a clean heart, O God, and put a new and right spirit within me." And Psalm 139: "Search me, O God, and know my heart! Try me and know my thoughts! And see if there be any wicked way in me, and lead me in the way everlasting!" He must, he was convinced, struggle to avoid the illusions, the self-deceptions, and the deceitfulness that had marked his life before his conversion. He must seek to see himself as he was and not as he pretended to be. This struggle, this warfare of the heart, made others—friends and foes alike—see in him a man of great integrity. Yet he himself confessed that despite his disciplined efforts there was much about himself that he did not see, or perhaps could not see, or maybe refused to see. And what was most difficult for him to see were the waters in which he always swam, the waters of his Black River home, and how the fear of being cut off from that home continued to linger in the deep places of his heart in spite of his conversion. A great struggle lay ahead of him between the freedom that he claimed in his conversion and the confining power of love for a particular people and a particular place.[33]

LEIGHTON AND OTHER whites, however, were not the only ones being touched by the Charleston revival services. Some African Americans in the city also felt a new stirring as they peered into the light of the revival fires and saw new hope rising. Many began to seek membership in Charleston churches.

Those African Americans who wished to join the Circular Congregational Church had to spend time in a class under the supervision of one of the black leaders of the congregation. The purpose of the class was for Bible study and for an introduction to great themes of the Christian faith. All were expected to learn the questions and answers of a catechism that the congregation's pastor had written specifically for slaves and free persons of color. Charles Snetter, the black barber, was assigned to the class of Charles Henry. Both men were literate free blacks, and both had influential whites as friends and supporters. Henry was particularly close to the pastor, Benjamin Palmer, who held him in high regard for his piety and leadership. Snetter had as a patron Thomas Grimké, one of the most respected men in the city. Grimké was from an aristocratic Huguenot family and was deeply involved in benevolent causes and national benevolent organizations. Two of his sisters, Sara and Angelina, had moved north and were soon to become deeply involved in the growing antislavery movement and the struggle for women's rights.[34]

Among the causes that both Palmer and Grimké supported was the colonization of African Americans in what was being called Liberia in West Africa—a cause closely linked to the evangelical enthusiasm stirred by the Great Awakening. Those who felt themselves transformed by God's grace and benevolence—by God's goodwill toward humanity—felt themselves called to follow the admonition of the Epistle of James to be not only "hearers of the Word," but also "doers of the Word." They were to act with benevolence toward all. And so they had begun to organize a new kind of religious institution—voluntary societies of private individuals for reform and for missionary or charitable purposes. During the early decades of the nineteenth century, the converted had been organizing societies for prison reform, for education, for temperance, for orphans, for aid to seamen, and for missions at home and abroad. Sometimes these voluntary societies not only came into competition with one another but also clashed directly with one another. Antislavery societies challenged vehemently the assumptions of colonization societies, and missionary societies were to challenge and be challenged by both colonization and antislavery societies. The zeal to do good had already led by the 1830s to divisiveness and bitter accusations among the converted.[35]

In Charleston, colonization was a cause that was bitterly opposed by many—both whites and blacks. For many whites, colonization seemed like a threat to slavery, and for many blacks it appeared to be a kind of deportation of free persons of color. But colonization had great appeal to both Charles Henry and Charles Snetter, and they were apparently encouraged by Palmer and Grimké. Since an attempted slave revolt in 1822, said to be led by the free black Denmark Vesey, white authorities had made life increasingly difficult for free blacks in the city. The limited privileges they enjoyed had been further restricted—free black males who had recently entered the state were heavily taxed; any free blacks who left the state were prohibited from returning; free black sailors arriving in Charleston were to be imprisoned until the time for their ship's departure; and all free blacks had to secure white guardians or face expulsion from the state. In addition, the state legislature made the emancipation of a slave by a white owner even more difficult than it had been before 1822.[36]

Given these new restrictions, Henry and Snetter had paid attention when a colony of freed African Americans had been established at Cape Mesurado, West Africa, in the 1820s. Already the colonists had established a little town they called Monrovia after President James Monroe, one of the supporters of the movement. The American Colonization Society, which was promoting the effort, was urging free blacks throughout the country to return to their "motherland," join the settlers in Monrovia, and become a powerful force for bringing Christian faith and civilization to "benighted Africa."[37]

A few months after Snetter joined Henry's class at Circular, the two men gathered with other free blacks at the home of Titus Gregorie, an old friend of Henry's, in order to discussion emigration. Henry was elected secretary of the meeting and took careful minutes, which were later polished in the rhetoric of colonization and published. After much discussion, Henry rose to speak. "Africa," he said, "the land of our fathers, although surrounded with clouds of darkness, seems to me to be extending her arms towards us as her only hope of relief, and calling on us loudly for help—saying, 'I struggle for light and for liberty, and call upon you by the names of your ancestors to come to My help and Your rightful possession.'" He then moved that they answer the call and "that we take the Bible for our chart, with a full Supply of love, hope, and faith, and leave the land that gave us birth, and emigrate to Liberia, in Africa, the land of our ancestors, there to spend the remnant of our days, in peace and harmony." They were, said Henry, to "go to Africa as harbingers of peace, in the fullness of the blessing of the Gospel of Christ, and determined by every virtuous deed, to set such examples as shall be worthy of the Christian name." Snetter then rose and declared that he approved the motion and that "he and his family would leave the shores of Carolina for those of Africa, as soon as an opportunity was afforded them."[38]

In the spring of 1832, both Henry and Snetter, along with their families and a number of other free blacks from Charleston, left the land of slavery to sail to the land of their ancestors. Henry and most of his family lived only a few months before succumbing to African fever. But Snetter and his family survived the fever, and in a few years they found their lives entangled on those distant shores with the lives of Leighton, Jane Bayard, and those who had lived in the slave settlement on Hutchinson Island.[39]

WHILE HENRY AND Snetter were making plans to take their families to Liberia, Leighton was making arrangements to enter the newly established theological seminary in Columbia, South Carolina. Charleston Union Presbytery had examined him to see if he was prepared to study for the ministry. The presbytery asked him about "his experimental acquaintance with religion and his views in desiring to enter the gospel ministry," and then, a few days later, it had rigorously examined him on his knowledge of Latin and Greek; on geography and astronomy; on moral philosophy, mathematics, and botany; and finally, on rhetoric and logic. The presbytery sustained his exam and approved him as a candidate for the ministry. The ministers and lay elders of the presbytery wanted to be sure not only about his piety and moral rectitude but also about his education. Did he possess a broadly based classical education? Was he able to be a bearer of civility and tradition, a representative of an established order? Was he ready to plunge deeply into the history and theology of the Christian faith and to utilize classical languages in his work as a minister of the gospel?[40]

The presbytery was clearly guarding the entrance into its clergy membership—an elite and disciplined clergy, together with supportive lay elders, was asserting its legitimacy and authority. The exam, along with the even more rigorous exam that followed Leighton's theological education in Columbia, was intended, among other things, to distance him from the farmer preachers of the backwoods who plowed their fields during the week and sowed the Word on Sunday as the Spirit moved them and from the Methodist circuit riders, who, with little formal education, were sweeping west with amazing success. These popular preachers were speaking the language of the people, challenging old authorities, and ushering in a leveling and democratic spirit that was beginning to reshape much of the nation's religious life. In the years ahead, Leighton learned to admire—and even have deep affection for—many of these "brothers" and to think of them as colleagues. But he never gave up the idea of a learned ministry, and he was hard pressed not to be dismissive of preachers who shouted in what he regarded as an unseemly fashion and who did not engage as he thought they should in a learned and careful study of a biblical text.[41]

Leighton was in the first class of students at Columbia Theological Seminary. The seminary, located in a handsome mansion, had been organized by affluent whites—primarily from the Lowcountry—who wanted a Southern seminary to throw the light of the gospel into such howling wildernesses as Alabama and Mississippi and the frontier regions of Georgia, to "shine," as its founding document declared, "upon the pathway of the benighted, and those who have long groped in the dim twilight of unenlightened reason." Palmer was on the seminary's board of directors, as was Leighton's uncle Robert James; James Adger was soon also on the board, adding his business acumen to the management of the seminary's growing endowment. George Howe, a New Englander, left Dartmouth College to accept a position at the seminary and quickly established himself as the leading member of the faculty. Leighton felt an immediate admiration for Howe and looked to him as a mentor whose judgment he could trust.[42]

The little band of students—only seven that first year—soon became close friends. Moultrie Reid was a Charlestonian and a member of Circular church. Francis Goulding was a son of one of the professors and came from a family with deep roots in the Georgia Lowcountry. James Merrick, a graduate of Amherst, was from Massachusetts and was soon encouraging in Leighton a vision of an expanding mission movement. There was more than enough room in the mansion for everyone in this first class, but there was no easy way for them to get their meals—the idea of their doing their own cooking seemed beyond them. They struggled through their early months eating here and there, but when more students joined them they decided to band together and form an eating club. Leighton wrote his father and asked if they could hire old Jacob for their cook, and he added, in a note to his sister Martha, "and we need some other servants immediately." William Wilson was apparently unwilling to hire out his old cook, so Jacob stayed at Boggy

Gully, and the seminarians found help in Columbia to do their cooking and washing and cleaning.[43]

In his senior year at the seminary, Leighton decided to offer himself as a missionary under the American Board of Commissioners for Foreign Missions in Boston. The board—one of the most influential of the voluntary societies—had had its origin among college students. In 1806, some students from Williams College had been caught in a summer rain and had taken shelter in a haystack. There they had talked and prayed and had committed themselves to missionary work abroad. In 1810 at Andover Theological Seminary, they had organized, in the spirit of the time, the American Board of Commissioners for Foreign Missions. The board, along with other mission societies that were beginning to be organized, marked a shift in Protestant life in the United States, in Britain, and in the continental churches. Since the Reformation, Protestants had been largely uninterested in foreign missions—leaving the "heathen" to the providence of God. But with their new evangelical enthusiasm aroused by the revivals of the awakening, they were on their way to making foreign missions one of their great efforts in the nineteenth century. The American Board quickly made itself a leading agency for missions. While it drew support from several denominations, it was largely run by New England Congregationalists with significant help from Presbyterians in the Middle Atlantic and Southern states.[44]

Early in 1832 Leighton wrote his sister in the language and piety of the new mission movement: "I suppose you were all surprised at the subject of my last letter to Pa, but I hope you would all cheerfully consent and be even proud to see me so much honoured as to be a Foreign Missionary. If a man of the world were appointed to negotiate for our government with other nations of the earth, he would feel honoured and everybody else would look upon him as an honoured and a distinguished man." Ought then, he asked, "that man to feel honoured who is commissioned by Jesus Christ, King of Kings, to carry and proclaim the glad news of salvation to those who 'sit in the dark places of the earth'?" He soon found that not everyone—even among church people—shared his views.[45]

Leighton turned his eyes toward Africa. There were American pastors among the settlers in Liberia, but their attention was focused on the African American settlers, not the Africans. The British had missionaries in a few scattered parts of West Africa, as did some of the continental mission societies, but there were no focused missionary efforts by Americans in West Africa. As Leighton continued to think carefully about the black men and women whom he knew in the Black River settlements, and about the bitter history of slavery in the South, he began to feel, as a white Southerner, a particular responsibility for Africa. Like "benighted" white settlers on the Southern frontier who "groped in the dim twilight of unenlightened reason," Africans were regarded by most whites as "benighted," as people who walked in deep darkness and not in the light. Leighton talked to Howe, who said that he would prefer that Leighton stay in the South, where there was such a great need for civilized Christianity, but he would not try to influence him one way or another.[46]

Leighton wrote to the American Board of Commissioners for Foreign Missions in Boston and immediately received an enthusiastic reply. They had been waiting, they said, for a Southern man to offer himself for the West African field. A Southerner, it was supposed, could better survive the climate and the deadly African fevers than a Northerner, and there was a great need to start a mission in this large and populous region of the earth. So Leighton made his decision and began to make ready his application to the board. Several others in his small class were also thinking about foreign missions—they had organized their own Society for Inquiry on Missions, and one classmate, James Merrick, was soon to leave for Persia. But most in Leighton's class and in the classes that immediately followed found strong opposition from their families, or had health problems preventing them from embarking on such a vocation, or simply felt called to a nearby church. Still, there were young graduates from other seminaries who were going abroad. Among them was Leighton's friend John Adger, who was already on his way to Turkey to work as a translator of the Bible and religious tracts. Leighton was committed to mission work; he faced, however, his own pressing difficulty. He did not want to go alone, but with a wife.[47]

He had in fact been looking for a wife for some months, ever since he had started thinking about being a missionary. But where was he to find one? He wrote his sister that he would like to find a companion near home, "but where is she?" And if he found one, "a mountain of parental objection is to be climbed and a thousand painful circumstances met before there is any prospect of success. My heart faints at such an undertaking. I believe I can contemplate the *stake* with more composure than I can the act of taking away a girl from the bosom of unwilling parents." Leighton did make a try at romance with Margaret Adger, John's sister. She wanted to go to the mission field, and her parents would not stand in the way, having already agreed to support John in his mission work. But Leighton's overtures seemed more pragmatic than romantic, and Margaret saw the difference and responded in kind. John wrote her that when she knew him better she may "find him an object to love." But she was adamant. "Affection," she wrote John, "is not to be forced, and it is a fearful risk to run, the *usefulness*, as well as the *happiness* of *his* future life and *my own*, may depend, indeed I may say *does* depend upon it. . . . Ought I to consent to marry a man, whom I do not love?—would it not be doing *him* injustice—would you not consider it a poor compliment from any woman?" So Leighton consoled himself with the idea that he was called to go alone to Africa.[48]

Then his classmate Francis Goulding told him about the Bayard sisters in Savannah.

Chapter Four

A Place Seen from Afar

L eighton made immediate plans to go to Savannah to see for himself if the Bayard sisters were, as reported, "very intelligent and amiable"— and, not least, if he had any chance of persuading one of them to become his wife. Leighton was particularly intrigued by what Francis Goulding had told him about Jane—she seemed, from what his friend said, to be attractive beyond his wildest hopes. So he wrote his father for money to make the trip. He wrote his sister Sarah that Goulding "has made me believe that Miss B is the next to the best Girl in Savannah—Mary Howard his own being not only the best in Savannah but in the world." Leighton was nervous as a cat about what he called his "projected scheme," remembering, no doubt, how he had botched his attempt at romance with Margaret Adger. He confessed to Sarah: "If Miss B is the next to the best in the world, she must be a great many times too good for me." He insisted that Sarah not say a word about the trip, and he worried that his other classmates would learn why he was suddenly going to Savannah—"I am trembling for fear I shall be suspected," he said. Still, he was determined to go, although he seemed to go back and forth between thinking about both Jane and Margaret Bayard and thinking only about Jane. "The young ladies," he wrote, "have already made up their minds to the world of missions and they have no parents to say they shan't go." But then, gathering his courage, he added: "It is a long way from here, but if she is a worthy girl, she is worth going for." His plan was to stay in Savannah for two weeks or more and "to have effected something definite one way or the other before I leave." He sounded like a businessman exploring the possibilities of a good deal, but he was much more the novice at romance. He simply trusted, perhaps wisely, in the providence of the Lord, rather than his own charm.[1]

Leighton arrived in Savannah in mid-November 1832 and went to the home of Joseph Cumming, an elder in the city's First Presbyterian Church and one of the leading citizens of the city. There he learned that Jane Bayard would be teaching a Sunday school class for African American children at the First African Baptist Church. He made his plans accordingly. When he arrived at the church, he found Jane surrounded by children and deeply engaged in her teaching. He was stunned. Before him was a young woman— tall and slender, with blond hair, blue eyes, and a very pretty face. She was moving among the children with ease, had the confidence of a well-connected Bayard, and projected modesty and earnest piety. He was not only stunned, he was smitten. On her part, Jane looked up in the midst of her teaching and saw a young man enter her class. He was tall—six feet two inches—with a handsome face and broad shoulders, and he possessed what friends would later describe in fine Victorian fashion as a "manly physique" and "splendid chest." With his transparent character, Jane may very well have sensed his startled, smitten heart.[2]

Mary Howard, Goulding's fiancé, made arrangements for them to meet at the Howard home, one of the city's fashionable mansions with its formal parlor one level above the street. There, with Mary Howard and Francis Goulding coming and going, Jane and Leighton sat and talked together for hours about their shared commitments to missions and their dreams of being a part of a great movement of the church across the earth. They took long walks through Savannah's streets and parks in the balmy days of late November as all about them black men and women went about their work of hauling, cleaning, and building. Leighton called at the Bayard home and met Margaret as well as a young man from Princeton seminary, James Eckard, who had arrived in the city hoping to propose to Margaret. Eckard already knew Nicholas Bayard—the families had connections in Pennsylvania. Leighton also met Nicholas, and he liked the young banker and the kind way in which he treated his sisters. And, very quickly, Leighton and Jane fell deeply in love. After one of their evenings together, Leighton returned to his room at Joseph Cumming's home and wrote, "to her, who tho' a stranger two weeks ago, now is the *nearest* and *dearest* object to my heart on the face of the earth." He confessed that he had feelings "which I never before dreamed of. Again and again have I asked myself is this not a pleasing dream. No, no, I am awake—I have my pen in hand and my paper is before me. It is no dream. Jane is *mine* and my heart exults with joy." He later wrote that they had been together long enough "for you to master the best feelings of my heart." Their "long and sweet walks" were, he said, "forever engraved on my memory. I delight in the reflection that you *love me, trust me, and pray for me*."[3]

In early December, Jane left for a planned trip to Fair Hope to visit with her McIntosh relatives. Leighton gave Nicholas a letter of intent announcing their engagement. Nicholas had been cordial to the young seminarian, and Leighton hoped he would have no serious objection to their plans. Nicholas did say that he thought they were acting in a precipitous manner, but Jane, he said, was an adult and was to make her own decisions.[4]

James Eckard and Margaret also had a whirlwind courtship. A graduate of the University of Pennsylvania, James had practiced law for several years before entering Princeton Theological Seminary. He was a serious young man—studious, but not brilliant—with a mother who had long hovered over him in a protective manner. James nevertheless possessed a bright and friendly outlook on life, and he was committed to foreign missions in spite of his mother's alarm and opposition. Within a few weeks, he and Margaret announced both their engagement and their intention to become missionaries. He and Margaret also received Nicholas's blessing, although Nicholas must have had similar misgivings about the precipitous way in which they had become engaged. The young couple was soon accepted by the American Board of Commissioners for Foreign Missions, and by the spring of 1833, plans were under way for them to go to Ceylon to work in the expanding mission among the Tamil people there and in southern India.[5]

The news of these two engagements could not have been kept a secret from those in the settlement on Hutchinson Island. No one—including Jane, Margaret, and Nicholas—knew what the engagements would mean for Paul and his family, or for the others who lived in the settlement. But they all knew that Leighton Wilson and James Eckard would now be playing key roles in shaping the future of the black men, women, and children who were called Bayard slaves.

LEIGHTON HAD RETURNED to Columbia in mid-December 1832. Shortly after his arrival back at the seminary, he received a letter from Jane. Now, she wrote, I will "leave kindred, friends and happy country and uniting my destiny with yours, seek and find a home in some savage wild." She confessed that she "looked for one to whom in every emergency I could look for support, comfort and advice. Such I *think*, I fondly think, I have found in you— time alone must undeceive me." And Leighton wrote back: "The longest time that we may be companions, I hope will only prove that it is my delight and study to make you happy. But Jane, do not overrate me—do not expect too much. The fact that you repose such implicit confidence in me has drawn forth *feelings* from my heart towards you which I could scarcely believe existed there." However precipitous their engagement, they were clearly in love with a love that would only deepen and grow over the coming years.[6]

So Leighton and Jane continued their courtship and their correspondence. They wrote of their dreams and plans. They worried about the nullification controversy swirling in South Carolina. Following the lead of John C. Calhoun, Lowcountry planters were insisting that the state had the right to nullify tariffs passed by the US Congress that the nullifiers regarded as antislavery acts. Unionists in the state, primarily from the nonplantation Upcountry, were horrified and condemned the nullifiers as unpatriotic. Leighton and Jane feared the state was in danger of plunging into a civil war between the two parties, a war that would swallow up family and friends in a bitter conflict. The two parties finally compromised, and the crisis passed, but Leighton saw nullification as a clear signal of dangers to come. South Carolina radicals had shown themselves willing to act in reckless ways to split the nation and protect slavery.[7]

The young couple were also deeply troubled about what was happening to the missionaries who were working among the Cherokees in Georgia. The state, in its bloody aggression against the tribe, had arrested and imprisoned several missionaries who stood with the native people. Leighton wondered if Andrew Jackson would send federal troops into the state to liberate the missionaries and to protect the Cherokees from white aggression. Much to his disgust, during the coming years he watched the federal government's treachery toward the native people unfold as the Jackson administration aided in the usurpation of Cherokee lands by whites. In a few years, Leighton would see parallels between this treachery, the aggression of white Georgians, and the treatment of Africans by African American colonists.[8]

Leighton plunged back into his studies in Columbia, but he took time in the spring to visit Jane at Fair Hope. He was now the one to sail down the inland waters to Darien and to ride out to Fair Hope past rice and cotton fields and through pine barrens and under the long avenue of oaks. William and Maria McIntosh welcomed him like a son and were delighted that their Jane had found such a man as Leighton. For his part, he loved Fair Hope, took an interest in the Gullah people around him, and found the McIntosh family to be welcoming and loving. Back in Columbia, he wrote Jane: "I have a peculiar out goings of affection towards your Uncle and family, and sometimes wish I was there to tell them how much I love them. I love them because they are so kind to you. No one can find a more direct access to my heart than by showing the least kindness to my Jane. . . . You must tell my Fair Hope friends how much I love them."[9]

By the late winter of 1833, Leighton had begun serious negotiations with the American Board. They agreed that he would spend part of the coming spring and the first part of the summer at Andover Theological Seminary in Massachusetts studying Arabic in preparation for his time in Africa. So in early March he made his way north. The plan made sense—given how little they all knew about West Africa—but it would have been better for him to study Portuguese, Spanish, or even French. Still, the time was not wasted. He was once again thrown into language study, a task that was going to demand disciplined, strenuous work from him for the next two decades. While he was near Boston, he would be able to make frequent visits to see Rufus Anderson and Benjamin Wisner, secretaries of the board, and discuss his plans with them.[10]

During his time in New England, both Jane and Leighton felt pressure from friends and acquaintances who were stunned by their decision to go to Africa. They insisted that it was dangerous, even suicidal. Even James Eckard's mother—never hesitant to make her opinions known—entered the fray. Writing to Leighton and Jane from Pennsylvania, she urged them not to go. Her objections, Leighton wrote Jane, "I could regard . . . in no other light than fanciful and framed with too much indifference to poor benighted Africans, to deserve a very serious consideration." But Leighton acknowledged that "many hard things have been said about us—such as 'going to Martyrdom,' 'pursuing shadows' etc." The objections were not simply that Africa was deadly with its fevers and dangerous with its "savage people." More formidable and fundamental were objections rooted in the deepest racism, objections that rested on the claim that Africans were not capable of understanding and receiving the Christian gospel. Leighton's memory of the piety and Christian faith of African Americans at Mt. Zion and at Circular made him dismiss such claims as ridiculous and dangerous, but he was to spend years challenging such claims in his reports and in his descriptions of Africans and of the rich and varied cultures of Africa. Such objections, he wrote Jane, "affect me in no other way than to grieve my heart for the narrow and contracted feelings of those with them, and as long as you are firm and unmoved in our present plans, I shall move right forward in prosecuting them and be one of the happiest men in the world."[11]

After conversations with Anderson and Wisner in Boston, they all agreed that he should make an exploratory trip to West Africa to determine the best place to establish the mission. Leighton hoped for a while that one of his seminary classmates would join him, but one by one they dropped out of the plan, some because of parental objections or the objections of a fiancé, others because they feared their health was not adequate for the challenge. So it was agreed that he should try to find an African American who would accompany him and help with the necessary arrangements for the establishment of the new mission.[12]

Upon completion of his studies in July 1833, Leighton headed south. He stopped in New Haven to visit with the faculty and students at Yale, and then again at Princeton to talk about missions and the new mission to Africa. In Philadelphia, he met Jane's relatives, who, he wrote Jane, "gave me a very warm grasp and treated me as kindly as if I had been their real cousin." Margaret and James Eckard were there, having already married, and were making their final arrangements before they sailed for Ceylon. "They are both cheerful," he reported to Jane, "Margaret as much so as I ever saw her. She has told me a great deal about you."[13]

Leighton arrived in Savannah in the middle of August. He was eager to get to Fair Hope and see Jane, but first he had to find an African American who was free and willing to accompany him on his exploratory trip. After several false starts, he was put in touch with Joe Clay, a literate free black with close connections to Thomas and Eliza Clay of Richmond-on-Ogeechee. A leader among blacks in the city, he was a deacon and one of two clerks of the First African Baptist congregation. As clerk he had recorded much of the early history of the congregation—it was later said by a church leader that he was consequently clothed by the people with great dignity and made by them "an [object] of emulation." Leighton was genuinely impressed by Clay, and Clay agreed to accompany him. The African American deacon was apparently deeply interested in a mission to Africans. He wanted to see for himself the homeland of his ancestors and evaluate the progress of the new colony of Liberia. Leighton and Clay agreed to meet in Philadelphia in October, and Leighton made arrangements for the deacon's travel.[14]

At the same time, Leighton met Margaret Strobel, a free woman of color, a prominent seamstress in the city, and the mother of a young daughter, Catherine. She was eager to go to Liberia and be a teacher, and Leighton told Jane that he very much approved of her. Leighton consulted with Mary Howard—who had been teaching Margaret Strobel—and some other white women who were to be her sponsors, and then a plan was proposed. "Mrs. Strobel," as Leighton came to call her, could go to Richmond-on-Ogeechee to study under Eliza Clay and learn from Eliza's teaching experiments with the plantation slaves. When Jane returned to Savannah, she could take responsibility for the oversight of the young seamstress's education. Margaret Strobel agreed to the plan, and so did Jane. But, Leighton warned Jane, she must be careful "not to pursue any course with her instruction that would be exceptionable in the eye of the law." Teaching even a respected free woman of color more than basic reading and writing required great prudence in Savannah if serious problems with the white authorities were to be avoided. Whites feared not only the content of what might be taught but also the disturbing image of an educated black person.[15]

Leighton left Savannah in late August 1833 to visit his family at Pine Grove and to be ordained at Mt. Zion before his departure for Africa. He expected to meet in Columbia the Reverend John Brooke Pinney, a New Englander and a graduate of Franklin College (the University of Georgia) and Princeton Theological Seminary. Pinney was headed to Liberia to work among the settlers and had already spent much of 1833 traveling for the American Colonization Society to promote colonization. When Wilson arrived in Columbia, he found to his dismay that Pinney's life had been threatened by an angry mob while he spoke at the First Presbyterian Church. A rowdy crowd of whites had gathered at the church and had become indignant when they found blacks in the audience listening to Pinney talk about freed men and women going to Liberia. There, he said, they could enjoy all the benefits of freedom in their own country. Leighton wrote Jane that Pinney "had been *driven* off the day before by a mob! And for what? For the great and unpardonable crime of speaking about the Colonization society in a public address where there were Negroes!!" An excited "*rabble*" had endangered Pinney's life, and his friends had been forced to smuggle him quickly out of the city. Wilson felt that "such an outrage has seldom ever occurred before and the excitement in Columbia seldom ever equaled. The whole transaction will be published and I trust the indignation of the religious community will be aroused against such an affair." And then he confessed to Jane: "To tell you the truth Jane, I must acknowledge that there is in my native Carolina *much of the spirit of revolutionary France.*" What was foreboding for Wilson about the incident was not only the chaos and excitement of the "rabble," but an eighteenth-century rationalism that still lingered in the state among those hostile to religion. The most virulent racism and radical proslavery ideology would flow, he feared, from this "spirit of revolutionary France," and these forces would attack not only the work that Thomas and Eliza Clay were doing among their slaves in Georgia, but also any claim to the full humanity of Africans or African Americans.[16]

Leighton left Columbia in disgust and hurried to Pine Grove. There he found his extended family and many friends waiting to attend his ordination and to say their tearful goodbyes. The Saturday night before the ordination,

Pine Grove was crowded with guests—including eight ministers and four Presbyterian elders, who must have slept several to the bed in the sprawling plantation house. The next morning, Leighton's uncle Robert James preached the ordination sermon at Mt. Zion and struggled to contain his emotions when he spoke of his nephew's impending departure for an unknown land. Leighton's father began to weep freely, and the staid congregation heaved with waves of emotion that could not be suppressed as they thought of young Leighton, one who had grown up among them by the waters of the Black River, leaving for Africa. In what appeared to many of them to be the mysterious providence of God, he was embarking on a journey toward certain death on behalf of Africans from whose villages and cities their own slaves had been drawn.[17]

That afternoon, Leighton preached before a huge congregation of slaves who came from the surrounding plantations to stand in the park-like area that surrounded the church. Leighton spoke of missions and of sailing to the land of their ancestors with the message of Jesus Christ. They, too, were overcome with emotion as he spoke of Africa and of his hopes for its people. They swayed and moaned and wept, like an ocean that cannot be at rest, and they pressed around him as he spoke. Afterward, they came one by one in a long line to shake his hand. One old man, an "Elder in Israel," a leader in the black community, came forward and declared his own responsibility for Leighton's going to Africa. Leighton's going, he told Leighton, was in answer to his prayers. Perhaps the old man was remembering the land of his birth, for he held out his hand to Leighton and said "he would add to his prayers one dollar for the spread of the Gospel in that country." The old man was, Leighton wrote Jane, a poor slave who in the midst of his poverty gave for Africa. Others came forward, but their weeping became so intense that Leighton had to tear himself away before he had told the tenth part goodbye. So he left them there at Mt. Zion, near the waters of the Black River, and they swayed and moaned and wept when they remembered Africa, when they remembered the land of their ancestors.[18]

TWO WEEKS LATER, Leighton was in Philadelphia making plans for his exploratory trip. He had stopped in Baltimore and had visited the offices of the Maryland Colonization Society. The society, originally a part of the American Colonization Society, having established its independence, had received generous financial support from the Maryland legislature. The hope was that a new colony, Maryland in Liberia, could be established, and that it would avoid some of the difficulties faced by the Liberian colony at

Monrovia and its surrounding settlements. The Liberian colonists were reporting frequent shortages of food. In letters to friends and family that often ended up in newspapers, they told of being ravaged by disease, and they seemed to be in constant conflict with the indigenous people of the area. The American Colonization Society, many were complaining, had largely abandoned them once they had arrived in Liberia, and some were saying they wanted to return to their true home, the United States.[19]

John H. B. Latrobe, the principal organizer and corresponding secretary of the Maryland society, believed that with the financial support of the Maryland legislature a new and more successful colony could be established on the West Coast of Africa. As an enterprising manager, however, he was looking for other support wherever he could find it. Consequently, when Leighton showed up as a representative of the growing American mission movement, Latrobe gave him an enthusiastic welcome. He strongly encouraged him to establish a mission at the society's proposed new settlement at Cape Palmas, 250 miles south of Monrovia. But Latrobe also learned that Leighton had very influential personal connections—especially with the Bayard family. Jane's cousin James Bayard was the secretary of the Philadelphia branch of the American Colonization Society, and Latrobe wrote him shortly after Leighton's visit asking if a public meeting could be organized in Philadelphia for the purposes of supporting the Maryland colonization efforts. Bayard had replied that it was not possible, since the Philadelphia branch was committed to the parent society. Latrobe was, of course, disappointed, but he was apparently pleased that Leighton and Jane had personal connections with influential members of philanthropic movements—not an indifferent matter for the promoter of a new American colony. He hoped the young couple's involvement would bring positive attention to the Maryland experiment. But in the future, when disagreements began to emerge between the young missionaries and colonization officials, Latrobe would discover the downside to their influence. He would have to take into account not only Leighton's and Jane's growing reputation as missionaries, but also their deep connections with social and religious elites.[20]

Latrobe was himself an exceedingly complex man. He shared the widespread belief among Maryland whites that the state's growing population of free blacks constituted a serious threat to Maryland's peace, stability, and prosperity. Like other supporters of colonization in Maryland, he envisioned removing free blacks and recently emancipated slaves to West Africa as a way of whitening the state, and he hoped that national colonization efforts would give America what he called "a homogenous white population." Convinced that blacks could not survive in freedom in America, Latrobe thought that colonization afforded a "refuge for the weaker" African race. It was not that he feared a race war, as many did, but he believed that the natural superiority of whites would mean a "dwindling away" of free blacks "under the force of circumstances" that neither blacks nor whites were able to control. Yet Latrobe also believed—unlike most whites—that blacks were fully capable of governing themselves, and in the coming years he worked tirelessly to promote black leadership in the Cape Palmas colony. He also welcomed blacks into his home as his guests, and on occasion he challenged conventional lines of separation between blacks and whites in Baltimore. But many blacks in Baltimore were quick to point out that even his benevolence and good intentions were undergirded by the deepest racism.[21]

William Watkins, a free black teacher, led the opposition in the city to colonization. "Why," he asked, "should we abandon our firesides and everything associated with the dear name of *home?*" Two years before Leighton's visit to Baltimore, Watkins had written in William Lloyd Garrison's *Liberator* that he and other blacks in the city would "rather die in Maryland under the pressure of unrighteous and cruel laws than be driven, like cattle, to the pestilential clime of Liberia, where grievous privation, inevitable disease, and premature death, await us in all their horrors." Colonization, Watkins argued, was simply deportation—a way to strengthen slavery by insisting that "our natural color" is an "obstacle to our moral and political improvement in these United States."[22]

But a minority of strong voices in Baltimore's black community supported colonization. They believed that the racism of white America was so deep, so entrenched in every aspect of American society, that blacks—whether free or slave—had no true home in the United States. They were convinced that to escape from daily insults and harsh physical subjugation, and to be free from the assaults upon their sense of self-worth and dignity, they had to leave the land of oppression and return to Africa, their Motherland. Already a small number of blacks had left the city for Liberia. Most prominent among them was George R. McGill, a teacher and Methodist minister. He had quickly established himself as a leading merchant in Monrovia and had been back in Baltimore promoting colonization a short time before Leighton began his conversations with Latrobe. In contrast, he said, to being demeaned in America for their skin color, "colored men [in Liberia] from the United States, being thought by the natives to be men of information, are received and treated as white men, and denominated by the same epithet."[23]

Leighton was consequently entering deeply disputed territory when he began his conversation with Latrobe. Some whites, like the rabble in Columbia and radical proslavery elites, thought colonization was an attack on slavery. Others, like Latrobe, thought colonization was an answer to what they regarded as the problem of free blacks in American society and a way to whiten the nation. And the blacks were themselves divided between those who believed that colonization was nothing more than deportation—one more indication of the racism of whites—and those who thought colonization was the only means of escaping white oppression and racism. Wilson was clearly aware of these competing claims, their emotional power, and how they could be a distraction from his intended missionary efforts—especially if his mission station was to be located in the midst of the new Maryland colony. But, much to his later regret, he felt that Latrobe's offer provided an opportunity for establishing a base in a land that was to him unknown. At least he could go on the ship that was to carry the first colonists to Cape Palmas. Once there, he could see for himself if the new colony of Maryland in Liberia was the place to establish an American missionary presence in West Africa.

Latrobe's offer held particular appeal for Leighton because he was deeply impressed by the appointed governor of the new colony—Dr. James Hall, a white physician who already had extensive experience in West Africa. "He is," Leighton wrote Jane, "a small man, lame and uses a crutch—appears to be good natured and has a good deal of philanthropy, but not pious." Leighton thought his chief characteristic was his "*good common sense*." He knew the Africa fever and how to treat it—indeed, he had suffered recurrent bouts of it himself. The opportunity to accompany such an accomplished physician helped Leighton decide to sail with the colonists.[24]

The board in Boston agreed with Leighton's decision, and he began to make immediate preparations for his departure. He contracted with a builder in Baltimore to construct a house to carry out in parts. He began to purchase necessary supplies for himself and for Joe Clay, who had arrived after a detour through New York. And he greeted with delight the decision of an old Union college classmate, Stephen Wynkoop, to join him on the exploratory trip.[25]

While making his preparations for the trip, Leighton preached to large congregations in Philadelphia, Washington, and Baltimore. His mission to West Africa had caught the imagination of many and evoked growing support for the cause of mission. "What an interest is now felt in the welfare of Africa," he wrote Jane. "No part of the world is attracting half the same interest. God grant that it may increase, not exclusively, until all the injuries inflicted for ages shall be repaired and the light of the gospel pervade the whole continent."[26]

ONE PRESSING QUESTION remained before Leighton left for West Africa—What were he and Jane to do about the African American slaves they had inherited? They had apparently been discussing this question since they first met in Savannah. Perhaps Jane's maid, Charlotte, had entered the room as the young couple talked together about the "poor benighted Africans," and they had suddenly realized that their commitment to foreign missions had deep implications for this young black woman who stood before them. Or maybe they had seen Paul bring his carpenter's wages to Nicholas while they were discussing the practical matters of marriage. Or perhaps, when they talked about leaving behind family and friends to go to some unknown place on the coast of Africa, they had realized that they would also be leaving behind black men, women, and children who were legally their property—human beings for whom they felt a burden of responsibility. Whatever the particular occasion that first raised the issue for them, Leighton and Jane knew they had to make some decisions about their slaves. Most immediately pressing was the question of what to do about those who lived in the settlement on Hutchinson Island and in the quarters behind the Bayard home in Savannah. This question was pressing not only because Leighton and Jane were making plans to go to West Africa, but also because Margaret and James were preparing to leave shortly for Ceylon. As co-owners of the slaves they had inherited through their mother, Jane and Margaret—together with their husbands—needed to reach some agreement about the life and destiny of those who were theirs.[27]

Leighton went to Philadelphia to say his goodbyes to Margaret and James and to discuss this daunting question with them. Both of the couples knew that, even if they wanted to, they could not manage slaves from some distant place. Selling them was out of the question. The couples felt that such an act would be morally abhorrent. Furthermore, if they sold their slaves, their own character would be deeply tarnished in the eyes of many—perhaps especially in Boston and among supporters of the American Board. None of the four wanted to undermine their future work as missionaries. But freeing slaves was no easy thing—Georgia had passed laws that required any freed slave to leave the state, and many free states had made it very difficult for freed persons to enter. And what about the slaves themselves? Were they willing to leave Savannah, if given the choice, and say goodbye forever to family and friends left behind?[28]

Margaret had already been seeking Leighton's advice—as a Southerner from Pine Grove he knew better than James both the possibilities and the difficulties owners faced when thinking about the future of their slaves. Jane also wrote to Leighton wondering if anything should be done about the slaves before he sailed for Africa. Already their friend Thomas Clay, who was traveling in the North, had advised Margaret to free her slaves and have them join the new colony at Cape Palmas. Leighton agreed tentatively—he would have no legal say until after his marriage to Jane—but he was clear about several things. "Every human being," he wrote Jane, "who is capable of self-government and would be happier in a state of freedom than in bondage *ought to be free*." He was, however, not "a friend to immediate and universal emancipation and for the simple reason that all Negroes are not ready for freedom and would be worse in that than in their present conditions."[29]

Leighton did believe that Jane and Margaret's slaves should be freed and helped to settle in Africa. But, he said, the decision must depend on three things. First was their willingness to go. "No Negro," he wrote, "ought to be forced to go to Africa." Since it was now almost impossible to free slaves and let them remain in Georgia, he advised that if they could not be persuaded to emigrate, she should "let them be continued in the hands of some kind master." Second, the freed slaves would need to be fit for the demands of colonizing under very difficult conditions. Thinking of the deep privation that many settlers were reporting from Liberia, he wrote that "I do not conceive that all Negroes are fit to colonize—not having been accustomed to provide for themselves, they may suffer, as many have in Liberia." Like most other whites, he thought of the houses the slaves lived in, the food they ate, and the clothing they wore as things that slave owners provided for their slaves. He seemed strangely unaware that the houses were built by the slaves themselves, the food largely raised by slaves, and most of the clothing sewn by slaves. He shared the widespread belief that blacks needed whites to look after them. Third was the issue of where they would settle in Africa, which had not yet been determined and might influence the decision. He had heard such discouraging reports about turmoil in Monrovia and the Liberian settlements around it that he was unwilling to recommend Liberia proper. The new settlement at Cape Palmas was a possibility, but if the Bayard slaves went there, Jane and Margaret would have to bear the cost of transportation and of providing the necessary supplies for an extended period. "You know the character of your Negroes," he concluded, "and can judge best whether they are fit subjects for colonization. Upon the whole I think you had better let things remain just as they are and say nothing about the subject until I return to this country or until you hear from me after I have returned to this country or until you hear from me after I have reached Africa. And after all, I want you to act entirely according to your own feelings and judgement. Do what is right and I promise to be satisfied."[30]

In this way Margaret, James, Leighton, and Jane discussed and began to make decisions about the life and destiny of those who lived in the Hutchinson Island settlement and in the quarters behind the Bayard home. So Paul continued his carpentry in Savannah; his sister, Charlotte, continued to see after Jane's needs; and his mother, Mary, continued to bring vegetables to the market while they and all those known as Bayard slaves waited and no doubt wondered.

PART II

Journey to a West African Cape

Chapter Five

Testing the Waters

On a cold, rainy morning in late November 1832, the pioneer settlers of Maryland in Liberia struggled up the gangplank of the brig *Ann*. William Cassell, a freeborn barber and saddler, came on board with his wife, Frances, and their two-year-old son, Charles. Jacob Gross, a farmer, along with his wife, Rosanna, and their five children, had been freed by a Maryland planter in order to emigrate. They, too, came on board as part of the little band of emigrants, only eleven adults in all, who carried with them bundles of their carefully gathered possessions together with ducks and cackling chickens, stubborn goats, and squealing pigs. After securing all amidships, the emigrants assembled on the deck with their children. They were, no doubt, both excited and anxious, for they were leaving all that was familiar, all those places and memories they had known as home, for a distant homeland, for what they believed was a better country. As sons and daughters of Africa, they believed they were on their way to a promised land to receive and possess an inheritance, a freedom and dignity they had only seen from afar.[1]

Leighton, Joe Clay, Stephen Wynkoop, and Dr. James Hall, all filled with their own emotions and hopes, joined them on deck. The new flag of the colony, heavy with rain, hung above them all. A crowd gathered on the wharf. Speeches were made. Prayers were said. And a hymn, composed by Latrobe, was sung: "For Africa, For Africa, our way lies o'er the deep / For Africa, For Africa!—oh who would stay behind?" Musically it was an inauspicious beginning, and the hymn apparently faded quietly into oblivion. But the embarkation marked a new moment in the colonization movement and the beginning of Leighton's journey to Africa.[2]

The *Ann* was a wretched little ship, hard to handle even as it left port. "The *Ann* fairly *rolled* down river," wrote Dr. Hall. "It could scarcely be called *sailing*." It took two weeks to get out of the Chesapeake. From the outset, the vessel seemed designed for seasickness. Leighton shared a little cabin—seven feet by ten—with five others, including Stephen Wynkoop, James Hall, and the ship's crusty, cursing captain. The settlers were lodged in even more crowded quarters amidships, where families had to share the little space that was theirs. Joe Clay found a place among them and must have heard during the coming weeks not only the crying of the children and the sounds of sea-sickness, but also their stories about life in Maryland and their hopes for life in Africa.[3]

In this way they tossed and rolled out into the Atlantic following winds and currents that for three centuries had provided highways for sailing ships. The *Ann* and its passengers were riding a world in motion, an Atlantic world that moved clockwise with winds, with currents sweeping eastward in the north and westward in the south linking four continents in great, complex networks of human activity. As the *Ann* rolled through the waters of the open ocean, it was riding a world with a past, a world with a human history. Along these Atlantic highways had come traders and settlers, priests and preachers, soldiers and government officials. And with them had come plants and animals, diseases and medicines, religious beliefs and social systems, gold and guns, and the products of human ingenuity. But, above all, what had ridden these highways in the holds of ships had been African slaves and the sugar, tobacco, rice, and cotton that had been drawn from their labors and sorrows. The passengers on the *Ann* knew that they were traveling a highway of bitter memories, and that they were, in some small way, trying to reverse the flow and direction of a brutal history.[4]

After eight weeks at sea and what seemed an interminable time of tossing and seasickness, the ship became becalmed off the coast of Sierra Leone. Now her only movement was a dead, heavy roll in the swells of the sea. The heat seemed unbearable. "No awning or deck-house," wrote Hall. "The sun pouring down upon the deck, the pitch frying out of the seams, all felt that the voyage must end there, and we suffer the fate of sundry cockroaches, brought occasionally on deck with fire wood and ship stores, who failing to reach shadow or shelter, would keel over and die."[5]

With the mainland not yet in sight, Hall and Leighton could not bear the waiting any longer, and so they determined to take the little sailboat Hall had brought along and launch out on their own for Monrovia. The decision was uncharacteristically impetuous for men who were ordinarily prudent, but the captain provided a seaman to help with the sail and four equally impatient settlers volunteered to go and help row if the wind failed.

The group set out on Wednesday evening, January 22, 1833, with a light breeze and beautiful moonlight and soon went out of sight of the ship. They sailed all day Thursday without seeing land, but they did obtain soundings in the evening. On Friday they passed in the distance Sherbro Island, where there had been a disastrous attempt to establish an American colony in 1818, but they saw no sign of habitation. Early on Saturday morning, they discovered two ships bearing down on them. They feared they might be "Guineamen," ships of the infamous slave trader Pedro Blanco, for their little sailboat was passing almost within sight of Gallinas, where Blanco had a thriving slave depot. The Cuban and Brazilian slave markets were booming, and the Guineamen must have seemed sinister reminders of the fate of those who fell into Blanco's hands. So the travelers from the *Ann* set their sails directly before the wind and soon were out of sight of the pursuing ships. That afternoon, they hauled in near to the land, where they could see numerous towns and villages along the beach. Leighton noted their diversity—some were laid out with much uniformity, others consisted of nothing but clusters of thatched houses.[6]

A land breeze carried them briskly through the long, rolling swells of the Atlantic and eased the heat as Leighton gazed at the passing coast. Here at last was Africa, a land that he had seen only in his mind's eye as he had read books and pored over maps. Now the mainland stretched out before him, a place vast and to him unknown, a place said to be dangerous, but to Leighton a place calling out to his deepest commitments. A great continent, diverse and complex, was introducing itself to a young man who had grown up by the Black River not far from Boggy Gully. And the four settlers, they too gazed at the passing shoreline, and they no doubt wondered about this land that had previously existed for them only in remembered stories and their deepest hopes.

Early Monday morning, they came in sight of Cape Mesurado. In the distance they could see Monrovia tucked on the Cape's landward side. They were, wrote Leighton, "not a little revived at the prospect of finding a resting place after so long and tedious a voyage." A canoe came out with a pilot to guide them into the harbor. The pilot, they discovered, was a native of Cape Palmas, with the English name of Joe Wilson. He spoke the Pidgin English of the West African coast, and when he and Leighton found they shared a name, they gave each other, wrote Leighton, a hearty shake of the hand and soon became "decided friends."[7]

The travelers crossed the harbor bar and landed, and for the first time in eight weeks they put their feet on solid ground. Leighton went immediately to visit the American missionaries and found them all sick with the

African fever—including John Pinney, the colonization advocate who had been chased out of Columbia the previous summer. He was serving as both acting governor of the colony and as a Presbyterian missionary, but the fever had given him a terrific battering, and he had been able to do little in either capacity.

Leighton looked for Charles Henry, the former black leader at Circular Congregational Church in Charleston, and found that he had died from the fever shortly after his arrival in Monrovia. But Henry's colleague Charles Snetter, the black barber from Charleston, had survived and was there with his family. He and Leighton soon became reacquainted far from their South Carolina homes and laid the foundation for future work together. That evening, Leighton had dinner with a settler family he had first met in Savannah and learned about the troubles they had seen in the struggling young colony—especially the food shortages and the difficulties of making a living. Later Leighton returned to the sailboat and spent the night on board rather than expose himself to the deadly nighttime miasmas that were believed to be the cause of the fevers.[8]

The next day the *Ann* arrived—she had caught a breeze shortly after the departure of the little sailboat. While Hall began to recruit settlers to join the new colony at Cape Palmas, Leighton and Wynkoop, together with Joe Clay, began to explore the town. Clay was quite pleased with Monrovia, and he began to evaluate the colonization experiment carefully so he could give a full report on his return to Savannah and First African Baptist. They visited several schools established by missionaries and learned that the children of the settlers were doing remarkably well. Wynkoop observed that "there was as much vivacity and intelligence expressed on their countenances as among children of a different complexion." Teachers told Leighton that some children had learned in the course of two or three years no less than six different native languages. Even if such reports were exaggerated, Leighton and Wynkoop were clearly impressed, and they would soon use such reports to counter dismissive white claims about blacks.[9]

As they visited various parts of the town during the next several days, they saw a number of Africans who were working as servants for the settlers—hauling, cleaning, cooking, and clearing land. Wynkoop thought that the Africans were "regarded by the colonists much in the same light as the coloured population in America are by the whites. They are employed as servants in their houses and for all the hard drudgery of business." Hall later wrote that the settlers modeled their relationship to African servants after white masters and black slaves in the United States, resulting in "an imperious deportment on the part of the master or mistress and an obsequious sub-servancy on the part of the servant." Hall saw African American settlers cuff and kick African servants, and some critics of colonization seized on such reports to claim that the settlers were treating the indigenous people no better than slaves. Not all Africans in Monrovia, however, were servants. Some were coming into town in long lines, carrying great bundles of camwood to trade to the settlers. The settlers, in turn, exported the wood to Europe and the United States for its rich red dye and for cabinet making, building links be-tween the colony and distant markets.[10]

Leighton wrote Jane that many Africans lived in the vicinity of Monrovia and that most of them spoke some English. He thought that he had an easier time understanding them than many of the missionaries and other whites because he had grown up hearing the language of Southern slaves—their vo-cabulary, intonations, and grammar. What he was discovering was an Atlantic Creole that linked West Africa to the voices he had known since his youth by the Black River and Boggy Gully, and that he had heard echoing through the streets of Charleston and Savannah and in the Gullah settlement at Fair Hope.[11]

One day, Leighton had an interview with a Mandingo man who said he had been at the Cape for several weeks to learn about Christianity. Leighton later reported that he was a handsome and impressive person—six feet four, slender, with a light copper complexion. He wore a *tobe*—a long, straight piece of blue cotton cloth draped around his body and tied at the left shoul-der. A Muslim, he could read and write Arabic with ease. He carried an Ara-bic Bible with him, often referring to it as he made inquiries about Christianity. But he also wore around his neck two *greegrees*, African fetishes or charms, most likely intended to protect him from harm. For Leighton, this mixing of different religious practices and beliefs was perplexing. He thought of religion as a coherent and systematic set of beliefs and the prac-tices they enjoined—like the catechism he had been taught as a child. Now, however, during his first week on the African coast, he was encountering a different understanding of religion. It wasn't just that the Africans had a dif-ferent system of belief, but that the nature of religion itself seemed different. Indeed, the whole idea of religion, as Leighton understood it, seemed alien to the languages of the surrounding peoples that he was beginning to explore. "It will be extremely difficult to communicate any ideas on the subject of religion through any of them," he noted.[12]

In the years ahead, Leighton would have to contend with an understand-ing of religion that was fluid and rooted in individual practices, and that allowed Africans to add new beliefs and practices onto old ones. The Mandingo Muslim reading from the Bible and wearing African greegrees provided a hint of the challenge that lay before him. The young missionary had, he believed, a call—a vocation—to proclaim the Christian gospel that he had learned and internalized in a home across the Atlantic at Pine Grove, in the meetinghouse at Mt. Zion, and in the classroom in Columbia. As he was now beginning to realize, this meant trying to persuade Africans not only that the gospel was true, but also that it was exclusive, that it demanded the abandonment of many of the deeply held beliefs and practices of their people.[13]

Yet, as Leighton became more familiar with the land and its people, he would learn that Africans who became Christians did not give up being Africans but brought with them into their new faith a deep continuity with their religious past. Perhaps ironically, years later Leighton discovered within himself the difficulty of abandoning the deeply held beliefs and practices of his own people—the whites who lived near the Black River or who moved with grace and pride among the elegant homes and churches of Charleston and Savannah.[14]

On his last day in Monrovia, Leighton saw a man coming in from the bush whom he quickly identified as a *"fetish priest."* An animal skin, Leighton wrote, "decorated with sea shells sat upon his head and tumbled over his forehead and down onto his shoulders." Around his neck were long strings of beads and around his wrists and ankles were rings of iron and ivory. A long tail reached toward the ground with a bell on its end that made a loud dinging sound at each step, and around his waist he wore only a narrow strip of cloth. He had a war horn under one arm and carried a long iron spear in his hand, which he struck forcefully upon the ground as he walked into town. While Leighton found his dress "singular and ludicrous," he immediately perceived that the man carried himself erect with great dignity and with a sense of self-confidence. In a remarkable encounter, Leighton approached the man and began to examine minutely what Leighton called "his articles of ornament." This examination gave the man great offense. "He resented my curiosity," Leighton confessed, "by taking hold of the sleeve of my coat and twisting it with an air of contempt." In this way the missionary and the "Fetish Priest" examined and confronted one another across the great cultural divide that separated their worlds. Leighton, far from Charleston or Savannah or his Black River home, had to learn quickly to be more circumspect and prudent as he sought to engage proud and independent Africans and to learn something of their world. He was beginning to discover that it is not easy to comprehend the interior life of other peoples, and that Africans "naturally shun the scrutiny of white men."[15]

THE *ANN* PREPARED to leave for Cape Palmas a week after it had arrived in Monrovia. Dr. Hall had persuaded thirty settlers in Monrovia to join the little Cape Palmas colony, and they came crowding onto the already crowded ship. With them came George McGill, the merchant and Methodist minister recently returned from his recruiting visit to Baltimore. As an experienced African trader, he was going along to help Hall negotiate with the Grebo, who had a large town at the Cape. McGill brought his assistant, the Grebo Joe Wilson, the same who had acted as the pilot for Hall and Leighton. As a Grebo who spoke a little English, he was to serve as a translator.[16]

They weighed anchor and sailed south along the coast. On the first day, they passed a Spanish slaver headed for Cuba with its frightened cargo. Soon they would pass others. Wynkoop noted that Africans sold slaves to the Spanish. Some slavers, he found, left goods with an African trader on the promise of being supplied with slaves on a return trip. Others opened a store at a carefully selected location in order to buy slaves as soon as they were brought by African traders from the interior. So as the colonists, free African Americans, sailed south toward a new home, they watched slave ships sail toward a Middle Passage with men, women, and children destined for a Cuban slave market and the brutal labor of sugar plantations.[17]

Several Kru, natives of this part of the coast and intrepid sailors, were on board the *Ann*. A broad, bluish-green mark extended from the peaks of their foreheads down to the tips of their noses. Around their waists they wore cloth that reached to their knees, and around their necks they hung greegrees. They used a variety of materials and shapes for their greegrees— antelope horns filled with secret ingredients; handsomely prepared cloths covered with beads and cowry shells and tied so as to hold powerful contents; and small leather bags containing hair and fingernail clippings or some other mixture prepared by a greegree man. The Kru told Leighton and Wynkoop that the greegrees were worn to prevent illness and to protect the wearer from danger. One Kru explained: "Me wear him, me no get sick; me no fall overboard, no slave man snatch me."[18]

Leighton talked with the Kru about the greegrees and tried to persuade them that the charms provided no protection, but they were unimpressed. Leighton, however, was impressed by the men—"Every visitor to this coast must be struck with their appearance and their character," he wrote. "They are of ordinary size—stand very erect—quick and graceful in their movements and exhibit a most extraordinary development of muscles." He thought they had "fine faces—their foreheads are high and large—their countenances are always animated and very intelligent for uncultivated men." He was amazed by their skill as watermen and noted that they had an intimate knowledge of all the bars and harbors along the coast. Leighton was to see much of the Kru during the coming years. They were present along the coast all the way to Angola, and they were eagerly sought by European and American captains for their seamanship.[19]

The *Ann* passed numerous towns and villages as they sailed close to the coast. The travelers had a good view of Bassa Cove and could see a small struggling American colony not far from a slave factory. At Garroway, they saw a beautiful native town surrounded by a substantial barricade. And at Fishtown, another handsome native town, they sailed slowly past a broad tranquil bay, where they saw, spreading inland, beautiful fields of grass covered with flocks of sheep and herds of cattle, with rows of majestic palms standing in strong relief against the eastern sky.[20]

Finally, nine days out from Monrovia, they anchored about twelve miles from Cape Palmas. Hall sent Joe Wilson ashore that evening to inform the king of the local Grebo of the impending arrival of the *Ann* and of the proposed purchase of land for a colony. When Wilson arrived late in the night, the town was "all dark," he later told Hall and Leighton, "all still—no man go about." He went to the house of Pah Nemah—or King Freeman, as he was called by English speakers—and woke him. "What news?" Freeman asked. "Me come in Merica ship—me bring Merica man to look Cape Palmas—spose he like, and King say yes. Merican man den set down." "You speak true?" the king asked. "Yes true," Wilson replied.[21]

Already, no doubt, some news had reached Freeman of the approach of the *Ann*. The ship had been besieged for miles along the coast with eager Grebo traders who had come out in their canoes to offer rice and palm oil, chickens, and fish for some European or American goods. Freeman was certainly familiar with European and American traders, who often plied the coast with their ships filled with the products of distant lands—cloth, rum, guns, iron bars, and various tools and household items. The Grebo were themselves skilled traders; they bought goods from the visiting ships not only for their own use but also for trade with interior tribes. Moreover, the Grebo were—like their Kru relatives—noted seamen, who had been traveling great distances along the coast in Western ships. They had had opportunities to learn something of the ways of white men, with their seemingly inexhaustible wealth and their ability to build and navigate large ships and produce great quantities of tobacco and rum and guns and iron pots and kettles and fishhooks and spoons and cloth of various kinds and colors. But Freeman must have also known that the American settlements around Monrovia had brought trouble and disputes and even warfare.[22]

Whatever he thought of Joe Wilson's report, Freeman was not the one to make a decision about a proposed colony, even if he carried the title "king" among English speakers. Grebo society was more of a democracy than a monarchy, and any important decision had to be approved by a *palaver*, a deliberative assembly of the Grebo men. So Freeman thought about the impending negotiations and sent Wilson back to the *Ann* to invite the newcomers ashore.[23]

Early the next morning, Joe Wilson returned to the ship and its anxiously waiting passengers. Hall took him down into the cabin, where he took his seat without saying a word, and, as Leighton noted, "it was impossible to judge from his countenance whether he had favorable or unfavorable news to communicate." Hall asked him, "What news?" Wilson replied, "Very good news," and told how he had gone in the night to the Grebo town and how he told the king about how the Americans were looking for a place to settle. "What did the king say?" asked Hall. "He very glad," said Wilson. He "say you must come look at the place you self, if you like um, you can sit down dere." So the *Ann* weighed anchor and was soon under way. That evening, they anchored quite near the Cape and fired four guns as a signal that they had come to live among them. Leighton found the harbor to be beautiful, with its long Cape extending almost a mile into the Atlantic. He could see a large Grebo town, Gbenelu or Big Town, at the juncture of the Cape with the mainland.[24]

The next morning, Hall, McGill, Wynkoop, and Leighton went ashore in the ship's boat, escorted by a canoe to pilot them over the bar. As they approached the shore, they were astonished by the number of people who could be seen crowding every vantage point. Naked boys lined the beach for a considerable distance. Men, women, and children covered the brow of a hill, and a great crowd was assembled at the place of landing. The boat stranded not far from shore, and immediately men plunged into the surf and carried the travelers ashore on their backs. They formed a little procession and a man with a staff went before each newcomer to clear the way. The great crowd swayed with what seemed to Leighton the most "heartfelt joy," and the noise of their welcome, together with the clanging of the bells and the iron rings worn around Grebo wrists and ankles, was almost deafening to the little company from the *Ann*.[25]

The procession entered Big Town and wound its way through narrow streets before spilling out into a kind of town square. Freeman, sitting on a stool with a small striped umbrella held over his head, was waiting for them. The crowd pressed around the travelers, cutting off almost any flow of air, making it difficult to breathe and almost intolerably hot. *Dashes*—gifts—were exchanged, and the visitors took their seats on sturdy Grebo stools.[26]

Leighton was immediately impressed by the king. He was, Leighton wrote, "a fine looking man—very stout and fleshy—dignified, modest and sensible in his appearance." He wore a common black hat with a red cap underneath. A striped cloth fastened around his waist extended down to his knees. A string of beads hung around his neck, and he had iron rings around his wrists and ankles. His wives stood behind him, and to his left sat Simleh Ballah, the king's interpreter, and Joe Wilson, the interpreter for the newcomers.[27]

Hall explained that he wished to buy land for a colony. Freeman expressed a willingness to sell, but said he needed to bring the kings and people from two neighboring towns into the negotiations. So they quickly agreed to meet the next day, and Freeman sent word to the nearby kings to come to Big Town for a grand palaver.[28]

The next morning, Joe Clay and the whole company from the *Ann* came ashore through the surf and were met by a great, thronging crowd of Grebo. For Clay it must have been a remarkable experience as he looked around and felt the pressure of African bodies—black men, women, and children—welcoming them and escorting them through Big Town to the place of the palaver. Leighton had been talking with Clay about bringing his family to Cape Palmas and serving as a kind of business manager, handling the secular affairs of the mission. So Clay must have looked around and wondered what it would be like to leave Savannah and First African Baptist behind and move to this place on the West Coast of Africa as a part of the Christian mission-ary movement. Here was a handsome landscape and a handsome people, a place far removed from Savannah's slave markets and arrogant whites. Yet it was also a place where greegrees hung before every door, and the people, though clean and neat, must have seemed desperately poor to a free black who was a deacon and clerk at First African Baptist.[29]

Once again, Freeman was waiting on his stool as the newcomers were ush-ered into the shade of a tall tree. Shortly after they were seated, a drum began to beat to announce the arrival of the other kings. The crowd parted as Baphro, king of Grand Cavally, came striding forward and in a commanding style took his place in the circle. Leighton was not impressed with this new king; he found him a "coarse, stout man with a countenance rather morose and forbidding." The young missionary, however, thought the king's wife "a most beautiful woman." She wore a piece of striped cloth that reached from her waist to her knees, and she had not less than a dozen brass rings around each ankle and an equal number of steel and ivory rings around each wrist.[30]

Whatever his first impressions, Leighton would learn to respect Baphro with his commanding ways and beautiful wife. The king, who was over six feet tall, spoke a Creole English with ease and was a savvy leader who knew how to deal with the European and American ship captains who sailed along the coast buying and selling. Baphro's town was at the mouth of the Cavally River, about twenty miles east of Big Town, and it was large and prosperous, as it controlled much of the trade, especially the huge volume of locally grown rice coming down the river.[31]

Weah Bolio, or King Yellow Will, of Graway, whose town lay immediately east of the territory of Big Town, arrived next and entered the circle straining to match the dignity of Freeman and Baphro. Dressed in a blue broadcloth coat with metal buttons and white trousers that reached halfway down his jet black legs, he took his seat not far from the other kings. With the two kings came the headmen of various families and other Grebo dignitaries. They sat nearby, constituting what Leighton took to be something of a senate. The grand palaver was ready to begin.[32]

Simleh Ballah, Freeman's interpreter, stood in the middle of the gathered circle. A stoutly built and robust man, Ballah knew as well as anyone in Big Town what was at stake in the palaver. He was a leader among his people and wore his Grebo identity on his face—the inner corners of his two upper teeth were filed away, and a blue line was tattooed from the root of his hairline along his nose down to his chin. His skin was very black and possessed the luster of one who washed and oiled his body daily. He was heart and body a Grebo, but he was also a Grebo who spoke English, a Grebo who lived in a Creole world connected by the highways of the Atlantic. As such, he was a man in the middle of two worlds, a man being asked to translate and to interpret each world to the other.[33]

Ballah cried three times "*Bateo*" (Listen) and three times the people said "*Bate*" (We listen). As silence descended on the gathering, Ballah spoke quietly with Freeman. He then turn to Hall: "King say, what you come for? King want your full, true word." Hall answered that they wished to purchase land and settle a colony in their territory. He then enumerated the advantages the colony would bring the Grebo—trade, education, and defense. Freeman, in response, insisted that the Grebo would not sell their independence or their town or their right to their farms or their right to go to sea. Hall responded slowly, trying to use the Pidgin English that many understood—"We no want your town, you shall keep all, nor the land you cut for farm," he said. "You keep your canoes, fish, trade with vessels as before." But, he added, "when a ship comes, it comes to the governor and no captain must land goods except to the port officer." Then came the question from Freeman: "What you pay for it?"[34]

The bargaining commenced in West African style with derisive laughter by both Freeman and Hall as amounts were proposed and dismissed. Finally, as the sun began to set, an agreement was reached. The Colonization Society would provide a wide variety of goods—from guns and tobacco to fishhooks and iron pots—that were valued at about $1,200. For the cost of two strong field hands in the Baltimore slave market, the society received approximately twenty square miles of West African territory.[35]

During the palaver Leighton had opportunities to talk with the kings about the proposed mission and the promise of establishing schools for the Grebo. He emphasized that the mission was not a part of the settlement, but would be for the benefit of the Grebo people. The kings were much pleased. The people, Leighton noted in his journal, had had enough contact with whites to appreciate the value of a Western education. The day after the palaver, Leighton picked out a beautiful spot for the mission some distance from the new settlement and not far from Big Town. Hall designated seven acres for the mission property, and the two men made arrangements to have the mission house erected that had been brought out from Baltimore, so that it would be ready when Leighton returned with Jane.[36]

In this way the palaver was settled and plans made for a mission station. A new colony—Maryland in Liberia—was ready to be established at Cape Palmas. Dr. Hall and his little band of settlers immediately began to unload the provisions that had been shipped from Baltimore. Coming ashore with their trunks and barrels and lumber and livestock were their visions of a new homeland—a place free from the burdens of a bitter past, a place in Mother Africa, a promised land flowing with milk and honey.[37]

Two days after the palaver, Leighton, Clay, and Wynkoop sailed for Monrovia on board the *Edgar*, a schooner out of New York that was trading along the coast. The ship's captain, Richard Lawlin, was very kind to them, and the voyage marked the beginning of a mutually respectful relationship between Lawlin and Leighton. The *Edgar*, however, had a tedious voyage up the coast—the winds were against them and frequently the currents were, too—but the delays provided opportunities for the travelers to observe the coast, to visit some of the towns, and to begin making careful notes about the environment and the cultures and activities of the costal peoples.

When they arrived in Monrovia they found that two of the missionaries had died of the fever—both had been in the country less than a year. Leighton and his two companions dined with the little cluster of missionaries who remained, some of whom had come in from outlying settlements. Trying to be upbeat, Leighton remarked that "the company was remarkably cheerful not withstanding sickness and death had invaded their ranks. I do not know any set of people more happy than a group of missionaries assembled together in a foreign land."[38]

Leighton hoped to book passage quickly with Wynkoop and Clay on a ship returning to the United States, but they were frustrated and delayed for days by the absence of any returning vessel. They spent their time exploring the town and the nearby countryside and talking to as many settlers as they could in order to reach their own conclusions about the colonization project. Finally, after two weeks of waiting, they learned that a ship called the *Jupiter*, at Cape Mount north of Monrovia, would be leaving for the United States. Leighton chartered a little schooner, and they sailed north through a harrowing thunderstorm before they became becalmed close, they thought, to Cape Mount. Taking a canoe that was on board the schooner and two Kru men to paddle, the five men set off for the port. It turned out they were twelve miles from their destination, and it took all the skill of the Kru to get them through the crashing West African surf into the safety of the port.[39]

They had some time at the Cape before the *Jupiter* was to leave for New York—the captain was busy trading with the local Vai people. Leighton visited the native leader of the town, a man named Gomas. His father, a rich merchant, had sent him at an early age to England, where he had spent eight years in school. He had returned to his home country about twenty years before Leighton's visit and, noted Leighton, had immediately "conformed to the habits of his countrymen," entered the slave trade, and developed a lucrative business with Spanish and Portuguese slavers. Gomas told Leighton that he had recently abandoned the trade from principle. Leighton thought his change of heart was more likely a reflection of his own self-interest or of some necessity—Gomas was, Leighton noted, a great advocate of domestic slavery among the Vai and owned almost a hundred slaves himself.[40]

Leighton found Gomas to be a "*tall, stout, fine* looking man, not ostentatious, but graceful and dignified in his common deportment." He had received a good education in England and spoke and wrote English with ease and grace. A number of his wives and children were sitting near him, and

Leighton asked him how many wives he had. The question embarrassed Gomas—perhaps he wanted to present himself as a proper Englishman, or maybe such a question seemed intrusive and a reflection of poor manners among the Vai. At any rate, he avoided giving an answer. Then his chief wife came forward, and Leighton was stunned by her beauty. She was, he wrote in his journal, dressed more like Americans than any native woman he had yet seen on the coast. She seemed to "possess much of the 'milk of human kindness.'" She had a fine meal prepared for Leighton and served it upon a beautiful china plate with a silver spoon.[41]

In this way Leighton ended his first experience of West Africa. Whatever else he had learned, he had learned that West Africans were not simply Africans after the manner of Western stereotypes, but many peoples with diverse cultures. Within those cultures were individuals with different histories and different personalities and different ways of responding to great changes—changes that had been sweeping over their lands for generations as ships traveling over ocean highways had arrived from far-off places.

DURING THE RETURN trip, Leighton and Wynkoop worked hard on a report they were writing for the American Board. They had both kept journals that they intended to submit to the board, but they also wanted to present a joint, confidential report on their findings in regard to the American settlements in Liberia. In particular, they want to give their evaluation of the colonization project and the possibilities of a mission adjacent to a colonial settlement. After long conversations together, Leighton wrote the report for the two of them.

They began by asking why there were such conflicting and contradictory accounts of the settlements. The primary cause, they wrote, was that different expectations shaped what people saw. Some visitors came with great expectations and found much to encourage them. Others came with lower expectations and found much to confirm their biases. With the colonists, however, it was a different manner. Leighton and Wynkoop had found, as they had talked with the residents of Monrovia, that those who came with exaggerated expectations had been greatly disappointed and often dissatisfied, while others, expecting much less, had often been energized and had soon prospered.

The real issue, however, for Leighton and Wynkoop was not with the settlers but with the colonization societies themselves. The deep hopes of the societies for the success of colonization had led their supporters to an unfair representation of things—they were concealing discouraging circumstances, magnifying small things into matters of great importance, and representing Liberia as if it had already reached what they hoped it would be in the future. Leighton and Wynkoop found the official reports of the American Colonization Society to be particularly misleading. They consequently "severely deprecated" the reports and speeches and regarded them as "*unwarranted fraud*" and the source "of more *misery and heartburning disappointment* in Liberia than can well be imagined." What was needed was a more honest course so that potential emigrants might know what to expect—both the great challenges of colonization and the demanding opportunities that the settlements offered.[42]

For their part, Leighton and Wynkoop said that their own expectations had—not surprisingly—been largely confirmed by their first impressions and subsequent conversations with the colonists. Liberia's prosperity was what they thought could be expected from a young colony. "It was certainly highly gratifying to our feelings on our arrival there to see men who a few years ago were wearing the galling yoke of servitude in a foreign land now the masters of *respectable fortunes* and enjoying *freedom and comfort and every blessing* that could be desired." The founders of this colony, they said, "were men who were freed from the *tyranny of slavery*." The very existence of the colony "at the present moment on the coast of Africa," they said, was "an honorable tribute to the humanity of the age and its future prosperity." But the colony had a double testimony—it was both a witness to "the philanthropy which gave it birth" and "a lasting monument of the atrocities and injustice which were once practiced on the benighted shores of Africa." Leighton, as he wrote out the report, seemed clear about the atrocities of the international slave trade, the "galling yoke" of slavery, and "the tyranny of slavery" in the United States.[43]

The colony itself, however, faced many difficulties. Leighton and Wynkoop thought that while many of the settlers were industrious, active, and enterprising, many others were poor and destitute—their poverty the result of indolence, sometimes protracted sickness, and frequently both. But their poverty also came, Leighton and Wynkoop insisted, from "some kind of indefinable expectation of subsisting upon *freedom*, expecting all the provisions and luxuries of life without suitable exertions to procure them, and it is not till the pressing hand of poverty grinds them that they find out their mistake. Then their eyes are turned back to the fleshpots of America." What Leighton and Wynkoop were wondering was how the recently freed slaves could be expected to suddenly internalize the disciplines needed for freedom and prosperity when the primary discipline they had experienced had been brutally imposed. The transition, they thought, from slavery to freedom was difficult, and it was difficult precisely because of the way slavery insinuated itself into the deep habits and dispositions of the enslaved. Some leaders of the colonists were soon to come to the same conclusion.[44]

Those who supported colonization had, from the first, said that it would be a powerful means for the evangelization of Africa, a beachhead for the spread of the Christian gospel into the interior of the continent. Leighton and Wynkoop now believed such expectations to be false and fanciful. The colonists were too preoccupied with their own struggles and affairs to give attention to the evangelization of the surrounding African peoples. Moreover, explorers and missionaries had been calling attention to the conflicts between colonists and indigenous peoples around the world. Using the white Dutch settlers in southern Africa as an example, Leighton and Wynkoop saw colonization as a worldwide threat to indigenous peoples and an impediment to the mission movement, regardless of the race of the settlers. They saw no reason not to expect conflicts to arise between the black settlers in Liberia and the Kru, Grebo, and other peoples of the area. There was, they thought, nothing so distinctive about the colonization of African Americans in Liberia that it would prevent black settlers from becoming powerful enemies of the Africans who lived around them.

Although Leighton and Wynkoop still supported the establishment of the mission at Cape Palmas, they did so with reservations and with the understanding that the Cape would be only a launching point for missionary efforts. "The more remote missionary operations are from settlements," they concluded, "the better." Leighton later lamented that he had not taken his own advice.[45]

Chapter Six

Fair Hope Among the Grebo

In April 1834, as the *Jupiter* moved to anchor in New York harbor, Leighton wrote eagerly to "My dearly beloved Jane." With you, he confessed, "all my hopes of earthly happiness are associated." You are "dear to me as ever," he said: "Neither *time, distance* nor a multitude of cares have ever crowded thoughts of my dear Jane from my mind." Leighton wrote Jane that he longed to be in Savannah to see her, but first he and Wynkoop had to go to Boston to deliver their reports to the officers of the American Board and give them their recommendations about the mission.[1]

Shortly after the three travelers came ashore, Leighton and Wynkoop said their goodbyes to Joe Clay, who was returning directly to Savannah. Clay took with him the only souvenir they had brought back—a small box of seashells gathered along the beaches of Cape Palmas. They all agreed there was nothing exceptional about the shells except their origin, but Clay's family and friends in Savannah could hold the shells in their hands, feel the molding of their surfaces, and imagine the sounds of a faraway surf and a Grebo welcome as Clay told of his adventures in Africa. Leighton worried that Clay, by returning first to Savannah, would tell everyone about their experiences, leaving no new stories for Leighton to tell when he finally arrived in Savannah. But he was grateful that Clay had accompanied them and he had found him to be a good traveling companion and a good man. Leighton wrote the treasurer of the American Board and asked that Clay be paid the agreed $120 beyond his expenses.[2]

So Clay returned to Savannah and to his family, and word no doubt went out to many in the city's African American community about what he had seen and heard in Africa. Clay had decided that Savannah was his home, and that he would not go out with his family as a settler or accept Leighton's offer to join the mission and run its secular affairs. Rather, he would return to First African Baptist and to the familiar sights and sounds of Savannah with its tree-lined parks and rumbling wagons, its sweating stevedores and Gullah voices and the bitter cry of its slave markets. His visit to Liberia had apparently made clear to him that he was an American, an African American, and that he would cast his lot with the life and struggles of his people in Savannah.[3]

Leighton and Wynkoop hurried to Boston and met with the Prudential Committee of the American Board. They gave their journals to Rufus Anderson, who quickly published extracts of them in the board's *Missionary Herald*. The travelers turned over their report on the colonies and talked with the committee about why they thought Cape Palmas was the place to begin the West African mission. But they noted their reservations—colonial efforts at Cape Palmas could lead to conflict between the Maryland settlers and the Grebo and disrupt the work of the mission. Both Leighton and the committee would later regret that they had not taken these reservations more seriously.[4]

Their reports to the board complete, Leighton and Wynkoop parted after having spent six months in each other's constant company. Wynkoop never returned to West Africa, but years later he and his wife traveled to Japan, China, India, and throughout the Middle East, taking two years to visit the stations of a rapidly expanding American Protestant mission movement.[5]

IN EARLY MAY 1834, Leighton headed for Savannah. On arrival he found Jane eagerly awaiting him. "Miss Bayard," he wrote Anderson, is "well, cheerful, glad to see me, and more a missionary than ever." They took long walks through the city's streets and parks as Leighton told her about what he had seen and heard and how plans were proceeding for the mission. They were impatient to marry as quickly as possible, but first they wanted to visit Fair Hope together and see Jane's McIntosh family. So once again they took a schooner south through the inland waters. This time Leighton saw the sea islands—Ossabaw and St. Catherine's, Blackbeard and Sapelo—through eyes that had seen the African mainland and the swelling surf that pounded its coastline. Here was a landscape as impenetrable as an African mangrove swamp, and here were signs of land cleared and crops raised. But no great towns came into sight as they sailed the inland waters, and no canoes came clustering about their schooner to bargain and trade.[6]

From Darien they hurried together along sandy roads to the plantation's long avenue with its arching oaks before finally being enveloped by Fair Hope and the waiting family. Leighton had written that he wished never to be parted from Jane again until death did its parting, and they were now beginning years of almost constant companionship. They made their plans for a simple wedding in Savannah—Jane, true to character, wanted only family and a few friends to attend the service. And they enjoyed their springtime together at Fair Hope. The plantation gardens were luxurious, and the fragrances of the Lowcountry—tea olives and wisteria, marshes and sea breezes—filled the air.[7]

In the settlement and the plantation house Gullah men and women went about their work of laboring for and serving the white family as it celebrated the reunion of a young white man and young white woman in love. Perhaps when Leighton looked into the faces of these African Americans he remembered the Mandingo man with his Arabic Bible, and the fetish priest twisting Leighton's sleeve, and the Kru guiding ships, and Joe Wilson translating, and Freeman negotiating the palaver. And perhaps Leighton told the Gullah some of his stories—how he had sailed to Africa, and what he had seen and heard in that distant, remembered land. But if he did any of this, he didn't write it down, because he was finally with his Jane.[8]

They were married in the Bayard home in Savannah on May 22, 1834, by the pastor of the Independent Presbyterian Church. Nicholas was there with his new wife, Sarah, but Margaret and James Eckard were not. After three and a half months at sea, they had arrived the previous February in Ceylon and were now settled at the mission station at Batticotta. Charlotte, Jane's personal servant, was no doubt at the wedding—in the background—along with other domestic slaves. They would have been busy dusting, polishing, cleaning, and baking—doing all that they were told to do so that the wedding could be a simple and happy affair for Jane and Leighton.[9]

After a few days in Savannah, the young couple headed for South Carolina and Pine Grove to spend June and July with Leighton's family before saying their goodbyes. Arrangements had already been made to have Margaret Strobel and her daughter Catherine join the Wilsons in Philadelphia in September. Once there, they would all sail on the first suitable passage that could be secured. Eliza Clay, Jane, and Mary Howard had been working with Mrs. Strobel, helping to prepare her to teach when she arrived at Cape Palmas. A number of prominent white women in the city from several Protestant denominations had organized a mission society, and they had pledged to provide for Mrs. Strobel's salary and expenses. They gathered clothes for her and for Catherine, making sure they had what they needed for such a place as Leighton and Joe Clay had described, and when the time came, they helped mother and daughter pack their trunks before seeing them off to Philadelphia.[10]

Leighton and Jane spent eight weeks at Pine Grove—it was a kind of honeymoon for them, although they were surrounded by family and friends in the big sprawling house. Still, there was space for them to be alone, and time for them to take long walks down sandy roads through a landscape embedded in Leighton's heart and imagination. Now Leighton heard with Jane the song of the cardinal settling over the land at twilight and together they felt the wind moving through the pines and saw smoke rising from evening fires in the settlement by Boggy Gully. They visited in the settlement and Leighton told about what he had seen of the African coast, what he had learned of the African people, and what he and Jane hoped to do at Cape Palmas.[11]

Two children in the settlement were of particular interest to Leighton— they were his slaves, John and Jessie, entailed to him through Leighton's mother. John was eleven and Jessie was five. Leighton hardly knew them— he had been away from home so long and had seen them so seldom that, years later, he would have difficulty remembering if Jessie was a boy or a girl. He hoped that John would join them at Cape Palmas when he was a little older, but seemed perplexed about what he should do with the children. The South Carolina legislature had passed draconian measures that made it illegal for newly freed slaves to remain in the state, and Leighton did not want to take the children from their mother, who belonged to William Wilson and was a part of her own dense network of family and friends. John in fact said emphatically that he did not want to leave and go anywhere. So Leighton left the children at Boggy Gully, and he and Jane hurried to Philadelphia at the beginning of August.[12]

While Jane visited family in the city and at Princeton, Leighton was busy making preparations for their departure. Trade goods had to be purchased in order to transact business with the Grebo, so Leighton bought knives and beads, cloth and scissors, pots, pans, and kettles. Jane's cousins organized interested supporters in Philadelphia who purchased bedsteads and mattresses, dressers, chairs, and tables for the mission. Leighton ordered books to take out—medical books and travel books, books on the history of Africa and books on natural philosophy and even a complete set of the American Encyclopedia—all to be added to his own personal library. He bought supplies for the proposed schools—slates and pencils, quills, ink, and writing books. All had to be carefully packed in barrels and boxes along with clothes and food supplies—sugar and tea, flour, salt fish, and corned beef—provided by friends in the city.[13]

Leighton and Jane were frustrated, however, in their efforts to find transport to Africa. They considered going with a group of colonists who were leaving Norfolk, but the ship was already crowded. There was a possibility of a ship going from Baltimore to Cape Palmas, but it was uncertain. For a while, they thought they would go with a fast schooner from Philadelphia, but it didn't work out. Finally Leighton heard that his friend Richard Lawlin of the *Edgar* was in New York and was planning to leave for West Africa in early November. Leighton made immediate arrangements for them to join Lawlin and to go out with "the good captain" on the *Edgar*.[14]

In late October a service was held in the Central Presbyterian Church of Philadelphia to commission Leighton as a missionary to West Africa. Jane, of course, was also going, and was expected to play a critical role in the work of the mission, but she was to go as a missionary wife. Margaret Strobel was also going, in order to teach in the mission, but she was going as a "coloured assistant" to the missionary. Jane and Margaret, and Catherine, too, were not invisible to those doing the commissioning—their presence was noted—but they were simply secondary in a world of white men.

Rufus Anderson came from Boston to lead the service, which was attended by representatives of several Protestant denominations. He began by insisting that Leighton be careful about the health of those going out. News had recently arrived that three of the missionaries whom Leighton and Wynkoop had visited in Monrovia had died of malaria, and many Christians had become discouraged about the prospects of a West African mission. The preservation of life, said Anderson, was consequently especially important at the Cape Palmas mission in order to avoid deeper discouragement among mission supporters. Anderson expressed great confidence in the progress of science as it sought to ease the terrors of malaria. He insisted that science, together with experience and intelligent piety, was opening a way for a West African mission. Soon, he said, malaria would "cease to be regarded as the mere agent of blind fate, or chance. The connections between causes and their effects are fast being developed in these latter days." He confidently predicted that science would soon provide a life preserver for missionaries as they entered the miasmas of tropical climates.[15]

Anderson then turned to the mission strategy that was to guide the work at Cape Palmas—and in important ways the American Protestant missionary movement for years to come. First, in regard to Cape Palmas, Leighton needed to understand clearly that he was laying a foundation for the future. What was needed in West Africa was a starting point and base of operation. From such a base, other missions could later be established. Leighton, said Anderson, needed to be content with such work and build up as firm a foundation as possible. Second, Leighton needed to remember that the preeminent objective of the American Board was to raise up Christian leaders from among the native people. To do this, Leighton was to start schools in the native towns around Cape Palmas—schools for both males and females. The American Board, said Anderson, intended to recruit "coloured teachers" from the United States to work with Leighton. They had, it was thought, a better chance of withstanding the immediate dangers of an African climate. As for the children of the schools, they were to live with their parents. Then, from among the promising boys, a boarding school was to be established after the successful model of boarding schools in the Ceylon mission. With proper nurture and education, native leaders would begin to emerge from the boarding school. But native leaders would need books—and above all the Bible—in their own language. So Leighton was to learn the Grebo language and reduce it to writing. A printing press was to be established so that books could be prepared and printed in Grebo. From such a start, and in cooperation with other mission agencies in the United States and abroad, Anderson envisioned the spread of Christianity across the continent. Indigenous leaders would carry the gospel throughout Africa not only from the west coast of the continent but also from the south and east.[16]

While Africans were to be the primary evangelists for Africa, Anderson insisted that European and American whites were not relieved of their responsibility for missionary efforts on behalf of the African. "Shall the white man," he asked, "after having trampled upon Africa for two centuries, after having drawn myriads of slaves from its unhappy shores, and made his influence felt, like that of a demon, in every valley, plain and mountain of its fertile regions, and on every oasis of its mighty deserts—shall the white man now turn his back from that unhappy continent? Shall the *Church* do this? Shall *we* risk nothing to heal the wounds of Africa which our fathers inflicted?" Then, turning to Leighton, he said: "Long since, dear brother, you have answered these inquiries, and answered them like a disciple of the blessed Jesus."[17]

THE NEXT MORNING, Leighton and Jane met with a lawyer to draw up their wills and other documents in preparation for their departure. They appointed Nicholas Bayard to be their attorney and gave him power to manage their affairs while they were outside of the United States. After enumerating how he was to handle various properties, they instructed Nicholas to manage and take care of the slaves belonging to Jane—and then they added that when they notified him, he was "to send them to Africa if they shall be willing to go." Thomas and Eliza Clay, having come to Philadelphia for the commissioning service, were witnesses, and Thomas took a copy of the document with him and had it recorded in Savannah.[18]

So Leighton and Jane joined Margaret and James Eckard in making the decision to free those who lived in the Hutchinson Island settlement and to send them to one of the new American colonies in West Africa. What remained for Leighton and Jane was a decision about timing: When should the emancipation take place? When should those who lived in the Bayard settlement sail for Africa? But Paul and Charlotte, Charles and Mary, and all the others in the settlement—they, too, had a decision to make: Did they want to go? Did they want to leave the land of their birth for a distant unknown land? Was the burden of slavery so great, was the weight of it so oppressive, that they would be willing to leave behind family and friends for the free air of Africa?

THE *EDGAR* DEPARTED New York Harbor on November 7, 1834. Jane became violently seasick as they headed out into the North Atlantic and needed Leighton's constant care. Once they reached calmer waters, however, she enjoyed being on deck, where she felt the warmth of the sun and the pleasure of a steady breeze. Jane was entering the great adventure of her life. Behind her lay the comforts and privileges of Philadelphia and Savannah and the deep peace she had felt at Fair Hope plantation. Before her lay what she could only know in her imagination—a mission station on an African coast above a pounding Atlantic surf. She was embarking with her handsome young husband into a new world that beckoned her and that seemed to be drawing her into a life of noble purpose and Christian discipleship. She knew that the way ahead would be filled with dangers—especially the waiting African fevers. But the approaching hardships only added to her sense of being a part of a great nineteenth-century movement of Christianity around the globe. Her sister was already in Ceylon. And now she—Jane Bayard Wilson, granddaughter of Major General Lachlan McIntosh—was to be a missionary pioneer for the conversion of West Africa.[19]

On December 7, 1834, the *Edgar* anchored off Goree Island, a short distance from the mainland. The crew needed to repair a damaged yard. Leighton went ashore and found it a melancholy place, for, as he wrote Anderson, it had been the site of one of the most extensive slave markets on the northern coast of Africa. Although the trade had been suppressed for a number of years, Leighton imagined he could see traces of human guilt and cruelty upon the island. The whole place seemed like an immense prison that had been built to confine slaves before they were shipped across the Atlantic.

He was told that the 7,000 slaves still held by the wealthier citizens of Goree constituted three-fourths of the population.[20]

After a short stop in Monrovia, the *Edgar* arrived at Cape Palmas on Christmas Eve. Once again, the Grebo gave a tumultuous welcome. Fifteen men paddled out in the largest canoe at the Cape to take them ashore. The four newcomers made their way carefully down the side of the ship as the *Edgar* rocked in the swells of the Atlantic. Stepping into the long, narrow dugout, they struggled to seat themselves, and then the Grebo suddenly sent the canoe springing forward, the men singing and paddling with great spirit as they plunged through the surf to the beach and a waiting crowd.

King Freeman was the first to welcome them, and a multitude escorted them to the newly erected mission house. Walking up the hill from the beach, the three women from Savannah—Jane, Margaret, and young Catherine—looked around for the first time at the leaping, shouting, welcoming Grebo with their iron anklets and bracelets ringing from largely naked bodies.[21]

When they reached the top of the hill and the mission station, they found the house—brought out the year before from Baltimore—largely complete and surrounded by stunning views. "The situation of our house," Leighton wrote, "is remarkably pleasant. I do not know that I have ever seen any place where the beauty and grandeur of nature are more harmoniously united." Standing in front of the house, on the ocean side, they saw the Atlantic reaching out to the horizon, and almost immediately below them, they saw a surf heaving and crashing onto a long white beach. To their left a salt lake stretched out finger-like for eight or ten miles. To their right the pointed roofs of Big Town marked the home of King Freeman and the Grebo, while close by, the little colonial settlement clustered on the Cape's peninsular. When they walked to the other side of the house, they saw before them, extending inland, a rich and green plain, with a beautiful freshwater stream winding its way toward the Atlantic. In a letter to a Bayard cousin in Philadelphia, Jane noted: "We are elevated fifty feet above the water, and between us and it, a distance of one of your Philadelphia squares, we have a very pretty but irregular descent." Indeed, they were close enough to the beach for their house to be constantly jarred by the pounding of the waves.[22]

They found the house itself an attractive cottage, a story and a half high, thirty-four feet long, and nineteen feet wide. A hall, eight feet wide, ran through the center of the house on the first floor, as in many a Lowcountry home. When the doors were opened, a strong, steady breeze flowed through the hall from the sea toward the land, or from the land toward the sea, depending on the time of day. On one side of the hall was a single room, wrote

Leighton, for "sitting, eating, school and a 'palaver' room." On the other side, two rooms had been built—a bedroom and a study. Upstairs were two bedrooms, to be occupied for the time being by Margaret and Catherine, until their own home could be constructed. Two piazzas stretched across the house—one facing inland, and one facing the Atlantic. They were intended to protect the walls during the rainy season, but they were also to serve, as in the Lowcountry, as a place for visiting and relaxing and as a location for evening prayers together.[23]

Leighton and Jane were encouraged by the welcome they received and were clearly enchanted by their new home and its setting. They had already decided to name their new home Fair Hope. It seemed such a good name, an expression of their deep if modest hopes for the work they were about to begin. They apparently did not see any irony in the fact that they were naming this place on the African coast after a plantation on the Georgia coast where Gullah men and women lived and labored as chattel slaves. Leighton and Jane, after all, loved Fair Hope plantation, with its white family and seductive landscape and its happy memories of their springtime together. Such a love, such affection for a Southern home, blinded them to much that was peculiar and bitter.[24]

As soon as they had their goods unloaded, Leighton presented Freeman with a *dash*—presents from the trade goods brought out—and Freeman presented Leighton with a young bullock. Leighton thought the Grebo felt "interested in our object and claim me as *their man* in distinction from the colony," and for the next few days, crowds pressed around the mission house to see the white couple who were taking up residence there with Margaret and Catherine. Jane was apparently the first white woman many of them had ever seen, and she must have appeared very odd to them, with her blue eyes and pale white skin—largely covered by her long dress—and with her blond hair carefully tucked under her bonnet.[25]

As the Grebo, curious and eager to learn about the newcomers, continued to crowd around the mission house, they ignored what Leighton and Jane—and no doubt Margaret and Catherine—regarded as private space. With their compact towns and villages, the Grebo saw space and how people occupied it differently from the North Americans, so Leighton found he had to have a fence erected around the mission yard. The fence, he thought, was very serviceable, as it allowed him to regulate the visits of the people. Still, he and Jane welcomed the visits and the interest the visits seemed to indicate.[26]

Freeman came regularly and enjoyed sitting on one of the piazzas and talking with the young white couple, and with Margaret and Catherine as well. He ate frequently with the newcomers, and he was quick to learn that if he wanted to eat inside, and not on the piazza, he had to wear more than a cloth around his waist reaching down to his knees. Jane explained to him that in her home he must clothe himself more fully, a requirement he apparently accepted without complaint as one of the peculiarities of the newcomers. With him came his translator, Simleh Ballah, and Freeman's brother William Davis, who was eager to have his daughter enrolled in the proposed school. Baphro, king of Grand Cavally, also came on occasion. He wanted to know when a school would be established in his town.[27]

In this way, the Grebo began to observe the mission and to form some ideas about its purposes, about the character of those who had arrived on the *Edgar*, and about the customs and ways of the newcomers—how they held themselves and related to one another; how and what they ate; how their house was built and how the different rooms were used; how they thought of time, how they prayed, and how they had so many marvelous things brought from some distant place. Jane wrote relatives in Philadelphia that the Grebo had begun to call Leighton "true man" because "he never changes his word." And an officer from a visiting American ship wrote home that the Reverend Mr. Wilson together with his lady appeared "to be admirably well adapted by their conciliating manners to win the affections of the natives."[28]

Leighton and Jane called the king and his brother by their English names rather than their Grebo names. The colonists did the same. But in Big Town, the King was Pah Nemah, not Freeman, and his brother was Mworeh Mah, not William Davis. To the newcomers the brothers were men adapting to the new world that had come ashore and established itself at Cape Palmas. To the Grebo the brothers were Grebo, leaders among their own people. Both brothers, each in his own way, struggled in the coming years to live in both worlds and sought to help the Grebo find their way as they were attracted by the power of this new world. Freeman would be the wise political leader, negotiating with the colonial authorities, recognizing the economic benefits the colony brought to Big Town and the military power supporting the colony, but always remembering that as Pah Nemah he was a Grebo and had to do his best to protect the interests of the Grebo. William Davis would be a leader in engaging the culture and religion of the newcomers. A man whose brilliance startled whites, Davis understood that beneath the power and wealth of the newcomers was a new way of seeing and being in the world, a way that seemed to offer not only more cargo, but also some freedom from many of the fears that marked life in Big Town. Davis was to probe and wonder about—and finally to enter deeply into—that new world, but he would do so as Mworeh Mah, a Grebo man.[29]

Simleh Ballah and Baphro also had English names—Bill Williams (Ballah) and Joe Holland, (Baphro)—but the settlers and the missionaries seldom used them. Both men spoke the Pidgin English of the West African coast. Ballah would soon visit Baltimore, where he could communicate with Latrobe and other leaders of the Maryland Colonization Society without difficulty. Baphro already had a son studying in the United States, and in 1837 he sent a young wife to the mission school at Fair Hope. But both Ballah and Baphro lived more fully in one world, the world of the Grebo, even as they saw another world approaching. To be sure, both, like Freeman, sought to negotiate with that other world, but neither had Freeman's insight about what the Grebo were facing. And both were thought to be open to the changes arriving at their shores, but neither followed Davis by entering deeply into the assumptions and commitments of that new world. Leighton and Jane seemed to know this intuitively, calling them Simleh Ballah and Baphro even as they also called them friends.[30]

The settlers also began to visit Fair Hope. Dr. Hall came and welcomed the young missionaries to "Maryland in Liberia" and talked with Leighton about developments in the colony. He had named their little town Harper after the Revolutionary War hero General Robert Goodloe Harper, a former fiery congressman from South Carolina who had moved to Maryland. Harper had been one of the founders of the American Colonization Society and a mentor of Latrobe's. In a letter widely circulated in Maryland, Harper had argued that free blacks were largely paupers who lived at the expense of the community, that they had the potential of stirring up slaves against their masters, and that colonization would remove "a population for the most part idle and useless, and too often vicious and mischievous." Hall had also named the nearby salt lake "Lake Sheppard" after Moses Sheppard, a Quaker and wealthy flour merchant in Baltimore. Sheppard, a leading member of the Maryland Colonization Society, largely shared Harper's views on the need for colonizing free blacks. So the settler town and its nearby lake, like Fair Hope, bore odd names deeply rooted in the landscape of American slavery and racism.[31]

DECEMBER BROUGHT THE end of the rainy season at Cape Palmas, but before it expired, great thunderstorms rolled over the Cape. The thunder and lightning were more violent than anything the newcomers had yet experienced, and they were awed by the power of the storms that sailors called "tornados." They were not the funnel clouds called "tornadoes" in the United States, but sharp, tumultuous line squalls that could sink a ship or bring terror to a village. Once the rainy season had ended, however, and the storms had passed, a regular weather pattern settled over the land. Leighton found the climate pleasant—perhaps as agreeable, he thought, as in any part of the United States. In the morning, from eight until eleven o'clock, the air was rather still and sultry. Then a sea breeze began to build, and from eleven until twelve at night the air was cool and damp. It was most likely at night after the sea breezes had subsided that the bearers of malaria arrived at Fair Hope.[32]

Among the many species of mosquitoes that filled the air at Cape Palmas was *Anopheles*. From deep in time it had brought much suffering and death to the coast of West Africa, and its body appeared to be designed for the task. From its compact head emerged thick spikes of hair, two antennae, and powerful mandibles. Its six legs were bristled and jointed, its wings light and strong, and its back arched for attack. Most formidable was the female. Hunting at night, from dusk to dawn, she punctured the skin of victims with her long proboscis and sucked blood until her body turned red and was full. When she bit a person infected with the protozoan *Plasmodium*, the *Anopheles* became infected herself with a malaria parasite. When she bit another person, that person became infected. The parasite entered the person's liver, grew, spread into the blood, and invaded the red blood cells.[33]

Of course, in 1835 no one knew the role of a little mosquito in spreading malaria. The whites and the African Americans thought that the miasmas, the noxious vapors of swamps and decaying matter, were somehow the cause of the fevers, which were sometimes "intermittent" and sometimes "remittent." When they were "intermittent," the sufferer had periods of normal temperature followed by a high fever. When they were "remittent," there were fluctuations of higher and lower temperatures, but no intervals of normal temperature. The two patterns, however, often seemed to overlap, and there was often uncertainty about the nature of the fever and how best to treat it.[34]

Whether intermittent or remittent, the fevers were devastating. The person struck felt first a sledgehammer attack of fever. Soon afterward, the whites of the eyes became tinged with yellow, and the tongue became covered with what nineteenth-century physicians called a "brownish fur." The sufferer became sick to the stomach and would now and then vomit bile as the fever began to climb. And so the disease progressed, day by day, with rising and cooling, until it came to a crisis. Then the lips became purple and swollen, the tongue dark brown or black, clammy and offensive to the smell. The eyes became either dry or red and watery, and the urine was either much reduced in quantity or nonexistent; what urine remained was of a dark brown color and had a bad smell. The evacuations of the bowels were either black, bloody, and in quantity, or reddish and watery. The stomach became soft, as if filled with air. And sometimes, just before the sufferer died, blood was discharged from the bowels, nose, or mouth.[35]

Over long generations of suffering, West Africans had developed certain immunities to various kinds of malaria, and while they—and especially their children—continued to suffer its assaults, they did not have the extreme vulnerability to the disease that Europeans and European Americans had, who died like flies when they ventured onto the West African coast. Indeed, malaria had long acted as a kind of African shield against an invasion of whites and as a vengeful fury that pursued any slaver who dared to linger too long on the African coast.[36]

Sometime in early January 1835, *Anopheles* mosquitoes began entering Fair Hope, seeking a human blood meal. Leighton was struck first—then Margaret and Catherine, and finally Jane. Leighton wrote his family that they were all recovering, "yet we all expect occasional relapses. The fever is severe, and we all suffered much for a week or ten days, especially myself." The headaches were excruciating, but Margaret and Catherine had relatively mild cases and quickly recovered. Jane, however, had a violent relapse: "My dear wife has been the greatest sufferer," wrote her distraught husband. She was confined to her bed almost steadily for four weeks, and during this time she had a miscarriage. They did not know it then, but Leighton and Jane were to be childless—apparently the result of the repeated assaults of the fevers—a fate of most of the early missionaries to West Africa. Leighton later wrote Anderson about the dangers malaria posed for pregnant women: "A woman hazards her life by coming here in a state of advanced pregnancy. Very few indeed, thus situated, survive the ravages of the fever." Jane's miscarriage and their inability to have children was a deep sorrow for the young couple, especially for Jane, who took great delight in children. As the months and years passed and she began to realize she was not going to have children, she began to turn with even greater intensity and more tender care to the children who came to the mission schools.[37]

Leighton thought that he had passed through the worst of the fever, but in the middle of March he was suddenly struck with great violence. For weeks he appeared near death. Jane, weak and still recovering, struggled to nurse him back to health. She bathed and cleaned his fevered body, changed his bedding, prayed and prayed again and again, and watched Leighton fighting for his life. A growing apprehension and sense of isolation came over her, this young white woman from Savannah, as she struggled to ease Leighton's suffering. The vastness of a great continent seemed to be engulfing her as she listened to the pounding surf and looked out across a lush, and to her unknown, African landscape and prayed beside the bed of her fevered husband. Dr. Hall, who was himself fighting the fever, sent instructions about what to do, so Jane gave Leighton powerful purges, including calomel, and then regular doses of opium intended to quiet him. But Leighton sank deeper into his suffering and became severely anemic, pale as death, and deranged.[38]

Freeman and other Grebo leaders were alarmed, for if Leighton died, so, too, did the promised schools. Because they believed the fever came not from some noxious miasmas or pestiferous vapors but from a malignant spirit lurking under the mission house, the Grebo gathered at Fair Hope to fight with their own medicine. First one and then another and then altogether they began to howl and shout as they hurled threatening and deprecatory language at the lurking spirit in a ritual intended to frighten it and chase it away. But their threats did not intimidate the spirit; the fever remained, and Leighton drew near to the grave. Hall struggled out of his own sickbed, came out to Fair Hope, and now began giving Leighton some quinine. Hall stayed beside Leighton for days and nights, not sure how much quinine to give, when to give it, or what else to give with it, but Leighton began to improve, although the recovery was slow.[39]

On June 15, Jane wrote Rufus Anderson that Leighton had been suffering from "brain fever." "You would scarcely recognize," she wrote, "the robust and cheerful young man in the now feeble and fevered frame of Mr. Wilson. Should he continue in this state of health would it not be duty dear Sir to return to our fathers' land?" But she was not ready to give up. "The cause of God in Africa will ever be dear to our hearts and we both hope to spend and be spent for the good of her sons and daughters."[40]

BY THE MIDDLE of July, Leighton was much better, and he and Jane, at Dr. Hall's recommendation, took a short trip for their health on one of the trading ships going up and down the coast. They found being at sea refreshing, loved the feel of the wind and sun, and returned much restored in health and strength. But they were distressed by the slave ships they passed off the Liberian coast. "They hover along this coast," wrote Leighton, "like so many birds of prey, and seize their victims under the eyes of Americans, but nobody is found for their relief." They did not realize it at the time, but many of the slave ships they saw were American built and sold in Cuba or on the

African coast for a handsome profit—especially the fast clippers built in Baltimore, the home of the Maryland Colonization Society. Leighton hoped that the introduction of Christianity among the coastal peoples would lead them to stop selling slaves to the Portuguese and Spanish for the Cuban and Brazilian markets, but he apparently did not have much hope for the Portuguese and Spanish who sailed the ships.[41]

In early August, the Wilsons finally plunged into their work. Leighton focused on learning Grebo—Simleh Ballah was his teacher, and they met every day of the week in the study at Fair Hope. Leighton quickly learned that the language presented more difficulties than he had anticipated. He would learn one pronunciation of a word or the structure of a sentence from Ballah, and then hear another pronunciation of the same word, or a different sentence construction, from someone else. He concluded that the language was more fluid than English because it was unwritten, which, he thought, must be the case, more or less, with every unwritten language. If there were a written standard, he wrote Anderson, "there would be of course fewer innovations and variations." He thought "euphony in words and sentences seems to be the governing principle," a principle that appeared to rule out any "uniformity whatever that I have been able to discover." What was most strange to Leighton, however, was the way the Grebo frequently separated the syllables of a verb and inserted between them the noun which was governed by the verb. He gave Anderson an example: "The verb *occausea* signifies to build and the noun *ki* is a house. Then the natural construction to us would seem to be *occausea ki* 'to build a house.' But they speak it *occau-ki-sea*." So Leighton and Ballah met daily as Ballah sought to respond to Leighton's questions and to teach him something about the language, and Leighton went into Big Town and tried out what he was learning. The Grebo laughed at his awkward use of the language—and he laughed with them—but Ballah encouraged him, saying that one day, he would speak it better than any of them. Leighton kept careful notes and began a vocabulary list, which in time he would have printed as the first Grebo dictionary. He also continued to struggle with the language's grammar, seeking to systematize that which was so fluid, and from his notes he composed the first Grebo grammar, which he also had printed. He knew it was incomplete and most likely contained serious errors, but it was a beginning.[42]

This demanding language study by Leighton ultimately would have a profound impact on Grebo culture and society, imposing Western ideas of order and system onto the language. As he worked on his Grebo dictionary and grammar, Leighton was creating a standard Grebo dialect, used first in the mission schools and later in government schools. And he was also preparing the way for a shift in Grebo authority from oral storytellers to those who could read and write.[43]

But more immediately, working with the language opened for Leighton a window into Grebo life. As he met daily with Ballah and as he tried to talk with the residents of Big Town, he was visiting another world of thought and encountering a web of cultural practices that were a part of that world. Not incidentally, the Grebo—and especially Ballah and later William Davis—were his guides into that world. They were not passive as Leighton made his inquiries and drew his conclusions; rather, they actively made decisions about what to tell him and what not to tell him, interpreting for him the meaning of words and the significance of what Leighton was observing as he visited among the Grebo of Big Town and the neighboring villages. In this way, Leighton himself was being changed by the Grebo as they by him. The world he had brought with him to Cape Palmas—the world of Pine Grove and Union College and Charleston and Columbia—that world continued to rumble deep in his mind and imagination and to dominate his feelings, thoughts, and basic assumptions. But the world he brought with him was being enlarged by what Ballah was teaching him and by what he was learning as he walked through Big Town or sat on the piazza with Freeman.[44]

A primary reason for the study of the language was to prepare books in Grebo for Jane's school. While Leighton had been working on the language, Jane had been organizing her school with Margaret as her helper. At first they included both settler and Grebo children in the same class, but they found that it was difficult to teach the Grebo using English books. So Leighton hurried to prepare a primer to teach the Grebo children to read, even though he knew it would contain inaccuracies. Other difficulties, however, caused them to move ahead and separate the Grebo and American children.

Tensions had been building with Mrs. Strobel since the outset of their journey. On the voyage out, when Jane had been seasick and needing constant attention, Margaret had not offered to help but had left Jane's care to Leighton. The Wilsons had thought at the time that her behavior was because of her "elation at her promotion and the attention that was paid her" before she left Savannah, and that she might fear being regarded as a "menial" if she helped. Moreover, they had found her generally to be a cheerful person possessed of "a good Christian spirit." They had consequently decided to overlook what they regarded as a lack of Christian sympathy and help, hoping that once they arrived at Cape Palmas she would act differently. "But," wrote

Leighton in a confidential note to Anderson, "in this we were also disappointed." When the fever had struck Jane and Leighton, she offered no help, although she and Catherine were living with them in the mission house. Rather, after she had recovered from her slight bout with the fever, she went off daily to visit settler friends in Harper. When Leighton finally recovered from his fever in July, she let it be known that she hoped to go to Monrovia to live with a man coming out from Savannah. But then a few weeks later, she received a letter informing her that he was a "fallen character," and she had come to her meals with Leighton and Jane depressed and unhappy.[45]

For the Wilsons, Margaret was becoming a distraction. They became increasingly irritated and thought of her as irresponsible and unworthy of the trust and help that had been given her in Savannah. Leighton had a long, frank conversation with her and, he wrote Anderson, "she acknowledged her faults and promised to do better." But nothing seemed to change. So Leighton told Margaret that she had become an encumbrance for the mission and gave her three choices. She could return to her friends in Savannah. She could go to her friends in Monrovia. Or she could stay at Cape Palmas in the employment of the mission, stay in a house in Harper rented for her by the mission, and have a small school under her own control for the settler children.[46]

Margaret decided to take the last proposal, and Leighton wrote Anderson "that we are doing all we can to make her contented and useful." The whole business, however, was perplexing for Leighton and Jane, for they liked Margaret, felt close to Catherine, and thought they had been trying to do their Christian duty in regard to them. For Margaret's part, she appeared to be glad to get away from the Wilsons and from their "Christian duty," their assumptions of authority, and their constant supervision. She had come to Africa to breathe its air freely, not to be bossed about by white people.[47]

Margaret and Catherine moved into Harper. There, Margaret could—among other things—use her snuff and smoke her pipe away from the disapproving eyes of Leighton and Jane. She began to teach the settler children, and she and Catherine began to be more a part of the little colony. Jane then turned her attention to the fifteen Grebo boys who gathered every morning in a little school located at the edge of the Fair Hope garden. The Wilsons and the Strobels thus parted and divided their work, but they continued to be drawn toward each other in a kind of mutual affection tempered by deep memories, old habits, and long-established systems of power and authority. For the next twenty-five years, they would find their lives overlapping and intertwining, long after Cape Palmas had become for them all a receding memory.[48]

By late 1835, the mission appeared to be well established. Two schools had been started, Leighton was busy studying the Grebo language, and the mission's relationship to the Grebo people appeared promising. Jane and Leighton, as well as Margaret and Catherine, had passed through the acclimating time with the fever, so deadly among whites, and while they all continued to have regular attacks, the fevers were not so severe or debilitating after that first year, for the Americans had acquired immunities that greatly reduced their suffering. Leighton wrote home that he and Jane were as cheerful and as happy in Africa as they had ever been in America. And, he noted, "we enjoy the cheering conviction that we are laying the foundation of a super-structure, which, under the hands of others, and with the blessing of Almighty God, will prove the glory of West Africa."[49]

Chapter Seven

Beneath an African Sky

Early on a bright and sultry November morning, 1835, Leighton and Jane walked to the north side of the Cape as the pounding whitecaps of the surf reflected the dawn of a West African day. The young couple climbed carefully into a narrow canoe that had been dug out from a single tree trunk and sharpened and peaked at both ends. They were eager to learn more about the Grebo—the details of their daily lives, their beliefs and rituals, and the ways in which they saw the world—and they also wanted to find a promising location for a new school. Rock Town, about six miles north of the Cape, was known as an important Grebo center and seemed by its prominence to invite an exploratory visit.[1]

Leighton and Jane settled in the canoe. Seven Grebo men, laughing and talking, grabbed the sides of the canoe and pushed it from shore as they splashed through the water. When the canoe was fully afloat, the men threw their bodies across it, pulled themselves up, and scrambled artfully aboard. They edged the canoe toward the heaving surf while carefully watching the rise and fall of successive waves. Then suddenly with a cry, they leaned forward in unison, dug their paddles deep into the water, and shot the canoe out between the rising swells.[2]

The Grebo, like their Kru relatives, were accomplished swimmers, using a freestyle that combined alternate overarm strokes with fast scissor kicks. If the canoe had capsized, they could easily have swum ashore, especially since they wore only cotton cloths lightly wrapped around their waists. But Leighton, like most Westerners, knew little about swimming, except for perhaps a dogpaddle, and Jane was most certainly not a swimmer. Dressed as they were in Western-style clothes and with boots on their feet, they would be in serious danger if a wave caught the canoe sideways and flipped it over.

The Grebo, however, knew what they were doing and quickly took the couple through the surf to the smoother waters beyond the breakers.[3]

Turning the canoe north and apparently enjoying the morning, the men were soon singing and reciting poetry—not unlike the Gullah boatmen Leighton and Jane had seen in Georgia. "Had we been better acquainted with their language," wrote Leighton, "we would have enjoyed these poetical effusions much more than we did."[4] But it was a grand adventure for the young couple, especially for Jane. How far away Savannah and Fair Hope plantation must have seemed to her—and especially Philadelphia! Holding onto her bonnet as the ocean breeze flowed over them, General McIntosh's granddaughter gazed on a passing African landscape illumined by the morning sun.

When the travelers arrived at Rock Town, they were given a tumultuous Grebo welcome. Leighton and Jane climbed a high bank, helped along by many Grebo hands, and walked into the town as the growing crowd pressed around them. They passed a post with greegrees hanging from it warning all who came that way that the entrance to the town was protected by powerful fetishes. Years later, Leighton wrote, perhaps remembering this visit to Rock Town, that when a stranger first plants his feet upon the shores of Africa, his eyes immediately encounter greegrees or fetishes. The traveler, wrote Leighton, finds fetishes "suspended along every path he walks; at every junction of two or more roads; at the crossing-place of every stream; at the base of every large rock or overgrown forest tree; at the gate of every village; over the door of every house, and around the neck of every human being whom he meets."[5]

Now, as Leighton and Jane entered Rock Town, they no doubt remembered that the Gullah—and other African American slaves—also used charms—what Leighton called "real fetishes, though not known by this name." These remembered charms that they had seen here and there throughout the Lowcountry seemed deeply connected to what they were now seeing at Rock Town. But in a telling comment, Leighton wrote that Lowcountry charms were used "in a less open form" than what they were seeing in Rock Town. Lowcountry conjurers used their charms—made of material available to them from their own landscape—in the midst of the social, cultural, and religious power of a US slave society. American slaves had to be discreet, "less open," with their charms, just as they had to hide many areas of slave life from the eyes of whites.[6]

In contrast, as Leighton and Jane walked into Rock Town they were surrounded by fetishes that were displayed for all to see. What they now saw were fetishes that reflected in their composition a Grebo landscape—here was a piece of camwood, there the hoof of an antelope; here the yellowing horn of a goat, over there the long white tooth of a leopard. With so many of them openly displayed around them, the young missionaries were beginning to understand that these fetishes were not only rooted in this particular spot of earth, they were also an embodiment of a Grebo world, of a Grebo way of understanding human life. The missionaries could sense as they looked around them that these Rock Town fetishes moving slowly in the morning breeze had beneath them and in them the authority of Grebo society. So what Leighton and Jane saw, when they climbed the hill and entered Rock Town, seemed both familiar and unfamiliar to this young white couple who had lived close to Boggy Gully and the settlement at Fair Hope plantation. What was familiar was the presence of the fetishes or charms. What was unfamiliar was their omnipresence, their composition, and their relationship to the dominant Grebo culture and society. And what Leighton and Jane were just beginning to realize was that beneath the familiar and the unfamiliar were deep assumptions that linked the Gullah to the Grebo and other West Africans—assumptions about what causes people to get sick or hurt, or what causes the fishing to be good or bad, or what causes a woman to run away from her husband, or a man to die suddenly.[7]

The people led the young missionaries to the center of the town, to the palaver house, where they were seated on little stools while a great crowd pressed close around them. Finally a little man came out. He seemed to Leighton silly and stupid looking—a startling contrast to Freeman or William Davis or Simleh Ballah—but he represented the king, who was away. He and Leighton exchanged dashes, and Leighton told him he was considering establishing a school for the children of Rock Town. Everyone seemed very pleased by this announcement, but before the discussion could go further, the little man insisted that Jane take off her bonnet. The people of Rock Town had never before seen a white woman, and as they crowded around Jane they were particularly curious about her hair, which they saw peeking out from beneath her bonnet. So Jane untied the bonnet and took it off. She ran her hand through her hair and shook her head so that her long blond hair fell around her shoulders to what Leighton called "the profound gratification and admiration of the surrounding multitude."[8]

If the Rock Town people were surprised by Jane's blond hair, Leighton and Jane had their own surprise. They were invited to the home of a leading trader, where they discovered, to their amazement, that he had spent five years in Newport, Rhode Island. He spoke English well and had much of the manners and ways of an American. So Leighton and Jane were learning day by day that the Grebo did not fit easily into a stereotype. Grebo culture was not static but already in flux as part of a wider world connected by great ocean highways. And the Grebo, for their part, were also beginning to learn more about whites, and most particularly about this young white couple that had come among them.[9]

Leighton and Jane were pleased with what they saw at Rock Town—the size and character of the population and the location of the town on a massive rock high above the surrounding country. Before they left in the afternoon for their return to Fair Hope, they decided that Rock Town would be an excellent location for another school.[10]

NOT LONG AFTER their return, the young missionaries heard gunfire in Big Town. Leighton went into the town to see what was happening, and he learned that an important man had died and that his funeral rites had begun. He found the body laid out in a small canoe in front of the man's house. Already the people had brought and placed in the canoe gifts of cloth, beads, china, and rice, so that the canoe was overflowing, and the dead man was well prepared for his last journey. His chief wife sat beside his head and brushed flies away with a handkerchief while pouring out her lamentations.

When all was ready, two men lifted the canoe over their heads and began hurrying with the body down one of the narrow streets of Big Town toward the little island a few hundred yards off the shore—the place of the dead. The wail of the women grew more intense, but the Grebo men showed no emotion except through the sound of their beating drums and the noise of their guns, which they fired continuously as the procession flowed quickly toward the edge of the town. Suddenly the pallbearers began to stagger and then they turned around and rushed back along the route that they had come. Leighton asked what was happening and was told "the dead man was not willing to go." Finally, after some entreaties and assurances by Freeman that he would not be forgotten by the living, the dead man consented and was carried to the island, where he and his accompanying provisions were placed on the ground. The men tipped the canoe over to protect him as best as they could from exposure to the wind and torrid sun.[11]

Leighton and Jane could see the island from Fair Hope, and during the days that followed they watched as the man became a ripening feast for gulls and scurrying crabs. And in Harper windows had to be closed for several days when the wind blew in from the sea.[12]

Who was responsible for the death of the man lying on the little island beneath the canoe, sun, and swirling gulls? The death of anyone—but especially the death of an important man—led the Grebo to search for the person who caused the death. The Grebo knew, of course, that the man might have died because he had a fever, or because he slipped and hit his head on a rock, but the question was, why did he have the fever, or slip and hit his head? And while they might acknowledge multiple causes for a misfortune, they looked beneath any empirical reason for some sinister intention and act—the grudge of a neighbor, perhaps, or the jealousy of a husband who utilized witchcraft or sorcery to inflict harm. In order to discover the specific cause of a misfortune and to identify the person who had inflicted the harm, they relied on divination.[13]

In contrast, when Leighton had been commissioned in Philadelphia, Rufus Anderson had spoken of a modern understanding of cause and effect. The connections, he had said, "between causes and their effects are fast being developed in these latter days." Anderson and those gathered in Philadelphia may have known nothing about the role of mosquitoes in causing malaria, but as children of the Enlightenment they believed that science would soon provide an answer—an answer that would furnish what Anderson called "a life preserver for every man." They believed that natural causes were behind sickness and death and misfortunes.[14]

But Leighton and his people, like the Grebo, also looked beneath empirical causes to a deeper question of "why?" And what they found when they asked why was not sorcery or witchcraft or the breaking of some taboo, but the providence of God's will and purposes. They believed that human history had a purpose and a direction guided by the Holy One of Israel, the God of the Bible, who used natural causes for God's own good, loving, and just purposes. This tension between natural causes and God's providence marked Leighton's and Jane's world—indeed, it marked with growing intensity the world of much of nineteenth-century Protestant life, even as it encountered an increasingly secular understanding of human life and human history.[15]

For Leighton and Jane, the tension between these two understandings of history—of whether it was driven by natural causes or guided by God's providence—was ultimately resolved by the deep and unfathomable mystery of God's being, the God of the Bible, who had declared in Isaiah: "For as the heavens are higher than the earth, so are my ways higher than your ways and my thoughts than your thoughts." This high and holy One, they believed, had revealed Himself most completely and clearly in Jesus, "the Word made flesh." And what they believed Jesus revealed was God's love and gracious purposes, which sustained and guided human history, even the seemingly inexplicable suffering and sorrows of human life.[16]

As missionaries, it was Leighton's and Jane's task to invite the Grebo into their world—a world with a modern understanding of cause and effect where at the same time the providence and will of God governed and directed human life. What was clear and unambiguous to Leighton and Jane was that this world, their world, was not the world of the Grebo, and that the world of the Grebo was not only wrong but also barbaric. Such claims were rejected by many of their contemporaries in the United States and Europe and would come in time to be viewed with disdain as "missionary hubris" and expressions of cultural imperialism. Others, however, scorned such missionary efforts as "casting pearls before swine," as attempting to convert Africans who by their very nature were unable to be anything more than "primitive," people who could not give up their attachments to their world of fetishes—or who, for the entertainment of whites charmed by the exotic, were to be kept primitive, undisturbed by either Christianity or modernity.[17]

Jane and Leighton, however, saw their work as an invitation to the Grebo—an attempt to persuade them to change their beliefs about the causes of sickness and death, suffering and sorrows. And they thought their work was also an invitation to the Grebo to experience and practice a new freedom. They believed that the Christian gospel freed people from the constant fears that the missionaries saw lurking everywhere—behind greegree posts at the entrances to towns, hanging with greegrees over doorways, and suspended like heavy weights around the necks of the people. Leighton wondered if the fetishes, rather than making the people feel more secure, did not make them feel a deeper insecurity. "A man," he said, "must be careful whose company he keeps, what path he walks, whose house he enters, on what stool he seats himself, where he sleeps. He knows not what moment he may place his foot or lay his hand upon some invisible engine of mischief, or by what means the seeds of death may be implanted in his constitution." He and Jane believed that Christian faith could free the Grebo—as they believed and hoped it had freed them—from the fears that surrounded death and the reluctant trip to the island of the dead.[18]

Moreover, for this young couple from South Carolina and Georgia, Africans, for all their differences and distinctive ways, were not, finally, a wholly other people, different from other humans, especially those of European ancestry. They were, rather, as fully human and as fully capable as any other people; they held within them the potential to reject their fetishes as unreal, and to acknowledge their own agency in what was happening to them and around them. This belief in the full humanity of the Africans, this belief which had led Leighton and Jane to Cape Palmas, deepened as they sat on the piazza and talked with Freeman and Simleh Ballah and taught Grebo children and walked into Big Town and visited in Grebo homes and observed Grebo life. They believed that these men, women, and children were fully able to claim what Leighton and Jane believed to be "the glorious liberty of the children of God." And so the young couple went about their missionary labors at Fair Hope, studying the Grebo language and teaching the Grebo children and preaching the Christian gospel, while the surf rolled and thundered nearby and while, in Big Town, the people went about their traditional ways.[19]

THE WORLD OF THE Grebo and the world of the missionaries collided at many places, but they collided most dramatically when a Grebo died an unexpected death or when there seemed to the Grebo to be sinister forces at work in some area of their common life. Not long after Leighton and Jane returned from their visit to Rock Town, several men were accused of crimes, had to undergo the "sassy wood ordeal" to determine if they were guilty or innocent, and had died from its consequences. Each had been forced to drink great quantities of "red water," a decoction from the sassy wood bark. If the accused vomited freely and suffered no serious injury, he was pronounced innocent. Each of the three men, however, had suffered vertigo, fallen down in great pain, and lost control of his bowls. His guilt thus proven, a general howl of indignation had sounded. The assembled crowd had mocked him, pelted him with stones, spit upon him, and then pulled him about by his heels until he died in great humiliation and anguish.[20]

Shortly after these men had been executed, Leighton and Jane learned that another man had been accused of poisoning a neighbor—an act the Grebo regarded as a form of witchcraft—and was being required to undergo the same ordeal to determine if he was guilty or innocent. Friends of the man came to Leighton and pleaded with him to intervene, for they apparently were learning that both the missionaries and the colonial authorities regarded the ordeal with abhorrence. Leighton went to a road leading out of Big Town, where the ordeal was to take place, and found the scene appalling. People were lined up on both sides of the road, and the sassy wood was piled in the middle, beside the mortar in which it was to be pounded. The accused sat alone and had grown almost white with fear. His anguish grew more intense moment by moment as the people began to laugh at him and to show their indifference at what was about to happen to him. Leighton began to entreat and remonstrate with the people, trying to make them acknowledge that such a trial was arbitrary and cruel. But they resisted his appeals and felt he was intruding into their affairs. A fetish priest then came toward Leighton with angry looks and menacing gestures and told him to go away. But Leighton was not intimidated and looked him steadily in the face, and after a short time, the priest turned around and walked back into the crowd. Leighton continued to remonstrate, and then he bent down and gave the accused man his hand to show his support. Suddenly, the mood of the people changed, and they gave what Leighton called "a hearty assent" to his "taking the man." Leighton evidently thought that by bringing the authority and self-confidence of a white missionary to the encounter he had been able to stare down the priest and change the mood of the crowd. But what he apparently did not realize at the time was that when he had taken the hand of the accused, he was enacting a part of the Grebo ritual that allowed the man to go free. For the Grebo, Leighton was assuming responsibility for the man and could be required to pay heavy damages.[21]

So Leighton took the man to Fair Hope and made a place for him there, and from then on, Leighton said, the man regarded him "as the best friend he has in the world." And Leighton wrote up the whole episode and sent it to Rufus Anderson, who published the story in the *Missionary Herald*. In this way the rescued man became part of a missionary narrative about life in distant lands where missionaries were portrayed as taking brave stands against the barbaric practices of those called "benighted natives."[22]

WHILE LEIGHTON AND Jane were learning about the world of the Grebo and going about their missionary labors, Dr. Hall was preparing to return to Baltimore. He had suffered regular attacks of fever during his first months at the Cape and had written Latrobe that he needed to return home at an earlier date than originally anticipated. Latrobe had to scramble to find someone quickly. He was relieved when a young white Baltimore dentist, Oliver Holmes, agreed to go out as an agent of the Maryland Colonization Society and temporary governor of the colony.

Holmes proved to be a terrible choice and just the opposite of Hall in background and character. He had no experience in West Africa, was impetuous and immature, lacked the skills needed for negotiating with ship captains and African kings, and was generally disdainful of both the settlers and the Grebo. He was also very fond of rum, an item the Baltimore board had banned from the colony.[23]

At the same time came news that the colony's secretary and storekeeper,

James M. Thomson, had received an appointment from the Domestic and Foreign Missionary Society of the Episcopal Church to establish a mission station with a school at the Cape. Thomson, who had originally gone out as a settler to Monrovia, had been Hall's most capable assistant, but he eagerly accepted the new appointment and began an Episcopal mission several miles from Fair Hope. In this way the leadership of the colony was suddenly removed, leaving the colonists alarmed and the Grebo perplexed.[24]

To make matters worse, Hall did not leave immediately, but, after turning over the affairs of the colony to Holmes, continued to make important decisions. On a quick trip to Monrovia, Hall secured the Charleston barber Charles Snetter to replace Thomson, promising Snetter a fine salary. He said Snetter could stay in a room in the agent's house with Holmes until he was able to secure his own housing. Hall wrote Latrobe that Snetter was "possessed of sterling honesty, cool and undaunted courage, profound sagacity, and the warmest Patriotism." Leighton was delighted with his old friend's appointment, but he was troubled by what he saw as a growing disorder within the colony.[25]

Hall finally left for Baltimore in the early spring of 1836, taking Simleh Ballah with him. Ballah was to negotiate with the Maryland board a code of laws for the Grebo. From the first the board had insisted that their colony would be a means of civilizing the Africans—and preparing a Western code of law for the Grebo seemed a reasonable way to encourage the process. Wanting to do what they could to get the Grebo to accept the code, and thinking it wise to have some immediate Grebo response to what they were proposing, the board invited Ballah to join them in Baltimore. He went as "the king's mouth"—he would speak on behalf of Freeman and help the board understand the ways of the Grebo—but his going meant that Freeman lost his translator for a while. Not only that, but Leighton lost his teacher of Grebo, and the settlers and the Grebo lost a person skilled in negotiating their differences. Leighton sent a note to Anderson saying that Ballah was "the most favorable specimen of the native character that could be selected from this place both for appearance and sagacity," and asking that if he visited Boston, for Anderson to treat him with special kindness.[26]

THE DEPARTURE OF Hall and Ballah for Baltimore led to the immediate escalation of tension between the colonists and the Grebo. Hall, with his long experience in West Africa, understood the Grebo better than anyone who was left in Harper. Ballah, for his part, was not only Freeman's translator, but also his counselor, helping him understand the ways of the settlers. Their absence from the Cape meant that both the colonists and the Grebo had lost skilled diplomats. What made matters even more difficult was the new governor—Holmes had no knowledge of Grebo ways, and his contempt for the settlers was apparent to all.

Two weeks after Hall's departure, Holmes cut off trade with the Grebo in retaliation for their constant pilfering—digging up cassava in settler gardens, taking any tool left unguarded for a few minutes, stealing plates and supplies out of settler houses. Holmes's action was rash—Hall had been having a series of negotiations with Freeman about the matter—but the problem was real. Even Fair Hope had become a target. Leighton had thought that the enthusiasm of the people for the school would protect the mission from petty theft, but he was mistaken. "They hold," he wrote Anderson, "our effects to be as good game as anybody else's." It was difficult, he thought, for anyone not familiar with the Grebo to form any idea of their expertness in pilfering. No matter how vigilant a person might be, no matter what precautions a settler or missionary might take, Leighton found that where a Grebo was, there your property was in jeopardy. Leighton quoted what Dr. Hall had told Freeman: "If Merica man no look sharp, country man steal he chair from under him."[27]

Still, Holmes's decision to break off of trade was rash, and he found it necessary to prepare for war. He had the colony's cannons moved and trained on Big Town. The settlers supported his action—even though they knew that Holmes had only contempt for them—for here at last it seemed something was to be done about the Grebo and their constant pilfering. Moreover, the settlers were increasingly repulsed by what they regarded as the savage ways of the Grebo—they were beginning to think of the Grebo as people beneath the civilized colonists from the United States. They would soon be sending a message to the Maryland board insisting that the Grebo were "Savages"; the Grebo, they said, "thirsts for our blood."[28]

Freeman was eager to negotiate and called for a palaver to settle the colonists' complaints. He had been the primary advocate for selling land to the colonists, understood the trade advantages that the colony brought to the Grebo, and believed that the mission school and Grebo contacts with the settlers held the promise of bringing some of the power and wealth to his people that he had seen in the ships that sailed to the Cape. But Freeman insisted that the Grebo also had their complaints. The colonists were intruding on Grebo lands and were violating the original agreement that had been reached with Dr. Hall. The settlers were not to invade Grebo farmland, and they were doing just that.[29]

The Grebo complaints about the settlers' appropriation of their land emerged, in part at least, from the very different techniques they and the settlers used for cultivating the land. After farming some cleared land, the Grebo would leave it fallow for several years before returning to farm the land again. For the Grebo, this fallow land was farmland, but for the settlers it was empty land. The settlers were not naive—they knew the land was being left fallow—but because the land was empty, it was, they insisted, fair game for them to take.

Adding to the tension were different understandings of land ownership. Leighton later explained what he learned from the Grebo about their understanding of land. For the Grebo, he wrote, an individual could appropriate land only for temporary purposes. Land was common property, and any man could use as much of it as he needed, but he could not sell any land. It was true, Leighton noted, that the whole community, by the common consent of the men, could sell any portion of its common property to a stranger for the purpose of erecting a trading post, or a garden, or a farm. But even then, even when the transaction was subjected to a written contract, the transaction was simply an agreement that allowed a stranger to live among the Grebo and to enjoy the rights of Grebo society. The Grebo assumed that the land would revert to them, as a matter of course, should the stranger die or leave their country.[30]

Such different interpretations of the original treaty and of the meaning of landownership meant years of conflict between the American settlers and the Grebo. In this first conflict, Holmes was adamant and uncompromising in the palaver, and Freeman knew the cannons were aimed at Big Town. So the Grebo, feeling angry and betrayed, ceded the disputed land, but the pilfering did not stop.[31]

To make matters worse, in the midst of these negotiations Holmes began to show an open antagonism toward Snetter. He gave Snetter only navy bread to eat and some coffee to drink, and Snetter had to go to Fair Hope to eat regularly with Leighton and Jane. Leighton remonstrated with Holmes and said his actions sprang from "an unreasonable and unhallowed prejudice," but his strictures did no good, and the antagonism between the men grew more public and more troubling. Snetter became a member of the newly formed church at Fair Hope, and Leighton wrote to Latrobe in his defense. He noted that Holmes was trying to slander Snetter, but that the colonists held Snetter in much higher regard than the white agent. Echoing Dr. Hall's earlier evaluation of the Charleston barber, Leighton wrote: "I give it to you as an opinion founded upon a long and thorough acquaintance with Mr. Snetter that he is the *crown* of the American population in Africa. Nor do I think it possible for you to have added a more valuable member to your colony." And he added a note about Snetter's former patron in Charleston, Thomas Grimké, the brother of the two abolitionists Sara and Angelina Grimké: "If Thomas Grimké were alive he would listen with astonishment to any serious charge made against Mr. S for he enjoyed for many years a place in that worthy man's confidence and affection next to that of his own family."[32]

So tension grew in the colony not only between the settlers and the Grebo, but also between Holmes and Snetter, and the governor's disdain for the colonists was becoming blatantly obvious. Leighton found all of these developments distressing and became increasingly apprehensive about what was happening in Harper.[33]

BEFORE ALL OF these tensions erupted into open confrontations, Leighton and Jane had been making plans for the emancipation of the Bayard slaves. Early in the spring of 1836, Leighton wrote Nicholas Bayard and said that the time had come to free those who lived in the settlement on Hutchinson Island. In that letter, he recommended the Maryland colony as the best place for those who wished to come to West Africa. He subsequently wrote Latrobe that he and Jane were anxious that the soon-to-be emancipated slaves should make their new home at Harper. He confessed that he did not know how many of them would be willing to leave Savannah behind and choose a new life in a far country. But he and Jane wanted them to have a choice, and they wanted to prepare the way for them if they chose the little colony on an African cape. In this way, wheels were finally beginning to turn that would lead to the emancipation of Paul and the other Bayard slaves who lived by the waters of the Savannah.[34]

LEIGHTON HAD WRITTEN to Nicholas while he was still optimistic about what he saw happening with the colonists. But as the tensions with the Grebo grew, so, too, did Leighton's concerns. The Maryland board wrote asking him to give his honest evaluation of what was happening at Harper. Although he would later write the board about the need for decisive leadership by the colonial governor, he now responded to the board's request by once again emphasizing the need for immigrants who could sustain themselves in the demanding context of a new colony. Before he and Stephen Wynkoop had left on their exploratory trip in 1833, Leighton had written Jane saying that he did not think all blacks were suited to be colonists. What was needed were enterprising colonists who could face the hardships of providing their own food, housing, and clothing in a new environment. This conclusion had been reinforced when he and Wynkoop had visited Monrovia. They had reported to the mission board in Boston that they had seen settlers who were prospering in their new home, but they had also seen many who were in deep poverty, who were wracked by diseases, and who were struggling to support themselves. Leighton and Wynkoop had accused the colonization societies of being so eager to get settlers that they had deceived people, discounting the hardships and dangers they would face in a new colony.[35]

Now, in the summer of 1836, Leighton responded by insisting once again that the most critical issue was the selection of immigrants. He wrote that the challenges of a new colony at the Cape were real, and that to meet those challenges, settlers needed to have "steady, sober, industrious habits." The board needed to be honest with prospective settlers about the difficulties that lay ahead of them. The Maryland board, he said, had simply sent anyone who wished to go or could be persuaded to go out as settlers. Consequently, a significant number of settlers had become a burden to the colony, making demands on its meager resources. Leighton was articulating a concern that future leaders of the colony would express over and over again—care must be given in the choice of settlers so that they would aid in the development of Maryland in Liberia and not be a burden.[36]

In a letter to Anderson, Leighton wrote about what he perceived to be the particular burden of recently freed people: "All of them who have health might easily render themselves comfortable, happy, and independent, but they keep the chains which once bound them in slavery—and it is not an uncommon thing to hear them say that they would prefer bondage to freedom and this humiliating acknowledgement is made notwithstanding the comforts of life can be obtained with less cost of labour here than at home—I mean where they earn it under taskmasters." He compared these complaining settlers to the Israelites, who, when they were freed from their bondage in Egypt and were wandering in the Sinai wilderness, began longing for the "fleshpots of Egypt." Such base ingratitude, he thought now, marked many settlers as they faced the challenges at Cape Palmas. "From their children," he thought, "if they are brought under the influence of education and religion, much may be expected; but for the present generation, those who were once under the withering influence of slavery, but little ought to be anticipated."[37]

Leighton was convinced that the habits and dispositions of those raised under the "withering" social and psychological conditions of slavery were very difficult to discard. Slavery, he thought, left deep scars and made the careful selection of immigrants a fundamental ingredient for the success of the colony under the daunting challenges of a new settlement. Some settlers agreed with Leighton and reported that too many of them had firmly fixed in their minds the "idea that we cannot do without 'the fleshpots of the Egyptians.'" But other settlers objected, insisting that the difficulties they faced flowed not from the blight of slavery on their character, but from the way the colonization authorities in Baltimore had misled them in the United States and then neglected them once they reached West Africa.[38]

They were all entering an enormously consequential debate that was to last for generations: What were the legacies of slavery's oppression? Did slavery shape in any consistent way the character of African Americans? Were the habits and dispositions of Paul in Savannah, of the Gullah on General's Island, of Snetter in Charleston, shaped in any consistent way by slavery's chains? And what about the character of European Americans? What about Leighton and Jane, and what about Eliza Clay in Savannah and William Wilson by Boggy Gully, and what about Latrobe in Baltimore and Anderson in Boston? Did slavery shape in any consistent way their dispositions, their habits of thought, and their ways of seeing the world, and especially their ways of seeing African Americans and Africans? In the coming years, Leighton would change his mind on these questions—several times.[39]

Leighton was doing more, however, in his letters to Latrobe and Anderson than calling attention to what he regarded as the "withering" influences of slavery. He was also exposing the ideological foundation of the Maryland Colonization Society. The primary purpose of the society—for which it received substantial funds from the state of Maryland—was to whiten Maryland. The establishment of a healthy, thriving colony was secondary and incidental to this primary purpose. The society had as a clear objective the removal of slaves and those free blacks whom General Harper had called "a population for the most part idle and useless, and too often vicious and mischievous," and as a result the society was eager to send whosoever would or could be persuaded to go. Because of Leighton's increasing willingness to unveil this ideological foundation, the abolitionists used him as an ally in their attack on the colonization enterprise, and Latrobe and other leaders of the Maryland society began to see him as a troublesome and meddling missionary.[40]

If Leighton had growing concerns about the immigrants, he had growing admiration for the Grebo, notwithstanding his abhorrence of their fetishes and sassy wood ordeal. On his visits to Big Town, he was often invited into Grebo homes. The houses were circular, varying in diameter from twelve to thirty feet, with high-peaked roofs that looked like neat caps set on top of the walls. Fires were kept burning in the center of each house, and the smoke rose up through the thatch, keeping insects away from both the thatch and the grain stored directly underneath it. The floors, raised ten or twelve inches above the ground, were made of clay that was as smooth and hard as masonry. Some doorways were paved with palm nut shells and acquired in time an attractive metallic luster. The women swept the floors regularly and kept all in order—pots filled with water, wood stacked outside for fires, sleeping mats rolled up during the day and neatly stored, and decorative dishes and pots, obtained in trade from some passing ship, hanging on the walls. The women had, noted Leighton, "a place for everything and everything in its place."[41]

The Grebo women were industrious in other ways as well. They rose early and went laughing and talking in bands to a spring to get water, looked after the needs of their children, and tended their gardens. In certain seasons, they went several miles from Big Town to work their farms. Leighton found the women robust and strong and capable of carrying immensely heavy burdens on their heads, no doubt reminding him of the elegant stride of the Low-country slave women he had seen carrying, with apparent ease, bags of cotton from a Pine Grove field, sheaves of rice at Fair Hope plantation, or a basket of vegetables to the Savannah market. Now, in the evenings at Big Town, he watched women trudging home with large water-pots, or heavy bundles of wood on their heads—and perhaps a sleeping child slung to their backs. And he found, to his amazement, that they could walk this way for miles, without ever raising a hand to steady or adjust these heavy burdens. While Leighton thus admired the industry and strength of the women, he thought they regarded themselves "as little better than beasts of burden, and are much below the men in general intelligence." He and Jane were beginning to believe that part of their missionary challenge was to change the place of women in Grebo society and the women's understanding of themselves.[42]

As for the Grebo men, he found them "by no means indolent," even if they did not perform as much hard labor as the women. They spent much time preparing and planting the farms and harvesting their crops. And they were, of course, in much demand as seamen on the ships that sailed along the coast and, as Leighton knew from personal experience, knew how to handle a canoe with amazing skill. He noted that among European and American traders, the Grebo men had a reputation for being "active and obliging, if treated with justice and kindness; but sullen, obstinate, and perverse if imposed upon."[43]

Leighton was particularly impressed with the cleanliness of the Grebo.

"All classes," he wrote, "perform daily ablution with hot water, and the adults often twice in the day. After the thorough application of water and a coarse towel made of grass-cloth, they rub a small quantity of oil over their entire person, which imparts a bright and healthful appearance to the skin, and is no doubt greatly promotive of their general health." Leighton thought it was true that the women had little sense of "delicacy" in the way they dressed—they wore only a short cloth around their waists—but such light clothing, together with their frequent bathing and swimming in the surf, helped to keep them, and the men and children, too, free from what he called "those distressing odors" that could quickly arise from the body in hot, humid climates.[44]

As he learned more about the Grebo of Big Town, Leighton heard stories of the towns and villages in the interior, and on occasion he met someone from "the brush" who came to trade at Big Town, or to see the strange whites who had settled at Fair Hope. From his first visit to the Cape, Leighton had wondered if the interior, with its reported mountains, did not promise a location for a mission station far away from the danger of miasmas and removed from the influence of the colony at Harper. Four days after he wrote the Maryland board about his growing apprehensions in regard to the colony, he left on his first exploration of the interior. Jane, busy with her school, stayed at Fair Hope to manage its affairs while Leighton was away.[45]

William Davis, Freeman's brother, joined Leighton as a guide and translator. Davis had spent a number of years in Sierra Leone, where, according to Leighton, by his industry and economy he had accumulated a sufficient sum of money to purchase a small boat, which he loaded with a valuable cargo of goods. About three months before Leighton and Jane arrived at Fair Hope, he had left Sierra Leone on board his little vessel hoping to reach his home at Cape Palmas. His boat, however, had floundered in rough waters, and he had lost all the goods that he had so carefully accumulated during his years in Sierra Leone. When he came with Freeman to visit Fair Hope, Leighton found him dejected in spirits but interested in the work of the mission.[46]

Davis was, like Ballah, part of an Atlantic Creole world and felt a deep tension between the traditions of the Grebo and the modern Western world he had encountered, both on trading ships and in Sierra Leone's capital, Freetown. Before he and Leighton left for the interior, Davis had already placed his daughter in the mission school. She was fast becoming a favorite with Jane, who gave her the English name "Mary Clealand" after a Philadelphia friend and supporter of the mission.[47]

The settler blacksmith, Anthony Wood, joined Leighton and Davis for their exploratory trip. A native of the West Indies, Wood had been taken by his owner to Baltimore, where he had eventually gained his freedom. Restless and smarting from the racism that he felt permeated every aspect of US society, he had fled to Haiti, then to Monrovia, and finally, at Dr. Hall's urging, to Harper. Energetic, popular, and a leader among the settlers, he was already a thorn in the flesh of the white authorities in Baltimore and their agents at Harper—he did not hesitate to challenge the decisions of Hall or Holmes.[48]

In early June 1836, Leighton, Davis, and Wood—together with several Grebo porters—left Harper. They followed the little road that led northeast to the Big Town farms. After walking over rolling country for several miles, they came to the Grebo rice fields. Leighton had seen the rice fields at Fair Hope plantation and Richmond-on-Ogeechee as well as those that lined the Savannah and those along the Cooper and Ashley rivers near Charleston. And yet he was astonished by the extent of the cultivation here and the quality of the rice the fields produced. It was, he wrote, "as good as any I had ever seen in South Carolina or Georgia." It did not occur to him that the cultivation of Lowcountry rice might be deeply connected to West Africa, and that what he was seeing only a few miles from Big Town was part of a long and sophisticated tradition of rice cultivation that had been carried from many places along the West African coast to the slave markets of Charleston and Savannah.[49]

After leaving the Big Town farms, they followed a little foot trail through the bush. At about one o'clock, they came to a village, where they received an excited welcome and were invited to stay for the night. They decided to pass on after only a short visit, however, and soon came again to extensive rice fields that stretched out in every direction. At about four o'clock, they came to large groves of lime and orange trees loaded with fruit, whose beauty, Leighton thought, could be more easily imagined than described. Walking through the groves, they came to Gnambahda, a handsome town which Leighton found exceptional in its cleanliness and in the openness of its streets. Located on a hill, the town was surrounded by a high, spiked wall. They approached Gnambahda undetected by anyone, apart from a few children at play. They passed through a low gate in the wall, and suddenly there was a yell, and the whole town seemed to come pouring out of houses and running down the streets to press tightly around them in an enthusiastic greeting. Leighton felt cut off from fresh air and almost deafened by unrestrained shouts and the loud roar of many voices. The travelers made their way to the house of the headman, who greeted them warmly, provided a place for them to stay, and roasted a sheep for their breakfast. Leighton gave him a dash of trade goods—cotton handkerchiefs, razors, and beads.

The next day, they set off again through rich and verdant fields of rice before entering a dense bush of tall grasses, mud, and water, and then once again rice fields, as they began a gradual ascent. The country became hilly and exceedingly beautiful. At the top of each hill, the little band stopped to gaze at the grandeur of the surrounding countryside, its enchantment heightened by lush rice fields that crowned the hills around them. Leighton had difficulty believing that he was in the country of an uncivilized people.

In the early afternoon they came to their destination—Denah, the town of King Neh on the Cavally River. Dr. Hall had visited the town the previous year by traveling up the river and had brought back from Neh an invitation for Leighton to visit. Neh was not at home when they arrived, but his head wife welcomed them and dispersed the crowd that was pressing around them. She gave them a place to rest and had warm water brought for them to bathe their feet. The king soon joined them, and he gave them his own house for the night. The visitors found it decorated with much china-ware, an indication of Neh's wealth.

Leighton was particularly taken by Neh and his wife. He found her to be a remarkable woman—"in dignity of manners, energy and stability of character" she excelled, he thought, any Grebo woman he had met. And his feelings were moved when he saw how she and Neh related to one another with "kindly feeling and conjugal attachment which bound the pair together," a contrast, he thought, with what he had seen among the coastal Grebo, whose relationships seemed cooler and more dispassionate. So, once again, Leighton was encountering particular men and women who challenged his early impressions and powerful stereotypes about the character of the Grebo.[50]

The next morning, after more lavish dashes, Leighton and Neh discussed the possibility of establishing a school in the town. The proposal was eagerly accepted by Neh, although he seemed to Leighton to be more interested in trade than in the education of the children. Their business complete, the little party boarded canoes supplied by Neh and floated down the Cavally. As they approached the coast, Leighton wrote that he was "much reminded of my native Carolina—on both sides of the river there were large fields of beautiful rice—some unsurpassed, rather unequalled by any that I ever before saw." They reached Baphro's town, Grand Cavally, at sunset, spent the night there, and the next morning hiked the twenty miles back to Fair Hope and Big Town.[51]

Like his trip with Jane to Rock Town, the excursion to Denah opened new vistas for Leighton. Now he had caught a glimpse at least of the interior, with its rice fields and orchards and villages. And from hilltops he had seen in the distance cloud-covered mountains that seemed to beckon and invite him into their mysteries.

TOWARD THE END of the summer of 1836, Simleh Ballah returned from his visit to Baltimore. The trip had been a great adventure for him. He had proved something of a sensation in Baltimore, with his filed teeth and the blue tattoo running down his forehead and nose to his chin. He had stayed with Latrobe, who was writing, with other members of the colonization board, a "Code of Laws for King Freeman." Every evening Ballah met with his host, who explained to him the details of the document, and Ballah responded as the "king's mouth." He told the board that Freeman "send me dis country. I come for peak his word. . . . I come for look country and peak him words."[52]

In order to "look country," Ballah traveled around the city. In the harbor he saw sleek clipper ships and sloops and schooners. On city streets he walked into the shadows of tall buildings and church steeples and heard the roar and whistle of the astonishing engines of the Baltimore and Ohio Railroad Company. And everywhere he went he saw black slaves pushing carts or driving wagons or selling fish and vegetables, and he very well may have seen black men, women, and children being sold in the city's slave markets.[53]

When Ballah returned to Big Town, he brought with him a copy of the laws written in Baltimore for the Grebo living at Cape Palmas. Leighton wrote Latrobe that King Freeman had asked him to read the document to all of his headmen. The laws were reasonable and humane—criminals were to be tried before a judge, and if found guilty, punished according to the character of the crime. "If a man kill another man because he hated and wanted to kill him, he must be hung." But, "If a man kill another man, and did not hate him or want to kill him, but did not take care, and killed him, he must go to jail and be punished as the judge says." And so the laws went, just the kind of code one might expect from a group of well-meaning white men living in Baltimore trying to write a legal document for the Grebo living thousands of miles away. A Grebo, they said, was to be tried by a Grebo judge, and the "American men must be tried by the American judges, and when the dispute is between a native and an American man, there must be a native judge and an American judge, and if they don't agree, the American governor of the colony must settle the business."[54]

Leighton was clearly skeptical of the whole process. For white men who knew almost nothing about Grebo culture and society to write a code of laws for the Grebo seemed naive at best. Leighton was learning only too well the great distances between the world of Baltimore and the world of Cape Palmas. So Leighton was not surprised when he found that the laws "assailed habits and customs of longstanding." Moreover, he apparently thought that it was an attempt by the Maryland board to assert its authority over the Grebo. But he read the code to the gathered Grebo and explained the laws to them, he told Latrobe, "just as I found them." The Grebo listened and gave their assent to the code, which must have seemed exceedingly odd with its modern Western assumptions. But having accepted the code, they promptly ignored it—for accepting and ignoring did not seem odd to a Grebo way of thinking. So the Grebo kept to their traditional ways, and in the evenings around communal fires, Ballah no doubt told about the strange things he had seen in Baltimore as he tried to help his people as they encountered the power and aggression of the "Merica man."[55]

A few months after Ballah's return from his American adventure, Leighton asked him to go with him to visit a village in the interior. Teddah, a Grebo king from a village about thirty miles from Big Town, had come with some of his headmen to see the white couple at Fair Hope. They had never seen whites before and were eager to see Leighton and Jane with their own eyes and to see as well the buildings at Fair Hope. Leighton gave Teddah a calico gown, which delighted the king, and he asked Leighton to come visit his Bolobo people, who spoke a Grebo dialect.[56]

Leighton and Ballah set out in late October 1836 with four other men from Big Town. During the first part of the day, they followed the trail that Leighton had traveled the previous June with William Davis on their way to Neh's Town. Only the fields that then had spread out before them lush with rice were now overgrown with grass and weeds—so rapid was the growth of vegetation in a tropical climate. This startling change, Leighton noted, provided hints of the massive amount of labor required to clear the fields and raise the rice.

The group soon left the familiar trail and turned in a more northerly direction, passing through small villages as they entered a country marked by high hills, from whose summits they could see the distant, beckoning Kong Mountains covered with clouds. Late in the afternoon, they approached Teddah's town. Word of their presence raced before them and they were greeted by laughing, shouting children some distance from the town. As they drew near, they found the whole population waiting in an uproar. The group of travelers was, wrote Leighton, quickly "walled around by a solid mass of naked human beings" who led them to the center of the town. Only a few had seen a white man before, and Leighton's appearance caused a sensation. They urged him to take off his hat, and when he did so and they saw his straight hair, they gave out a loud shout, and he had difficulty keeping hands off his head. Fatigued from their long hike, the visitors were grateful when a chicken was supplied for their supper. They were given quarters with Teddah and his family.[57]

In the morning, they were awakened by a woman singing at their door and then the discharge of guns. They went out of the house and were greeted by the headmen, whom Teddah had summoned. A man led a bullock to them, and Leighton was asked if he wished it killed. He said yes, and immediately the man stepped forward and with a powerful slash of his knife cut the animal's throat. A bowl of steaming blood was brought to Leighton but he turned away, unable to show his gratitude for such hospitality. Ballah took over and ordered the bullock butchered with one portion for the visitors, one for Teddah's family, one for the headmen, and one for the rest of the people. Everyone seemed to think this was a good and wise distribution.

Later in the day, at Leighton's request, Teddah had the people assemble for a "God palaver." Leighton was determined to say at least something about the Christian gospel, but he trembled when he found himself, "a minister of the living God, surrounded by five hundred human beings, not one of whom had ever heard of the name of Jesus or the glad tidings of salvation." What was he to say to these people, whom he imagined saying to him: "What does the Lord have to do with us?"[58]

Leighton spoke to Ballah in Pidgin English, in the cadences Leighton had known since his childhood by Boggy Gully, and Ballah interpreted what he said and translated it into Grebo. Leighton told the people that what he had to say could make "he heart be glad plenty." Who, he asked, "make all dis man, dem bush, dem tree, dem riber; who make de sky, de sun, de moon, and all dem pretty star? He be God and he be he word I come you country for peak." Leighton then said: "First time no one man lib to dis world. Den God he make one man and one woman. Dat man and dat woman go hab pickerninny and dem pickerninny go hab more, bomby de world come up full people. Some go one country for lib, some go turer way." God then saw that all, in whatever country, had a "bad heart . . . dey no lub me, dey no do what thing I tell dem for do, all time dey go fight war." God wondered what to do and decided, because all had "done spile dat world I make for dem," God would send them to hell—"one bad place." Then Jesus said "to he father let me go down der to dat world. I go make he heart good. I go show him how for do all time; so bomby de world come up good again."[59]

Leighton was uneasy with what he had told the people—it was so simple, so limited, and so much of the gospel was missing—and he wondered about how Ballah was both interpreting and translating what he said. But Leighton felt he had to start somewhere, and he was gratified when the old men of the town asked him to stay longer and to tell them more. His sermon was an introduction for them of a strange story from a white man, but it was also part of an introduction for Leighton. Where was he to start when he sought to tell the Christian story to those who knew nothing about it? What assumptions could he make about what might interest them, and what connections could he make to their world that might provide a bridge of understanding?[60]

That night the people gave Leighton a sermon, in a very different form, about their world and their understanding of it. The rice harvest had been completed and it was time to dance. The drums began to beat and then a leader appeared. He ran, wrote Leighton, like a "wild horse" around the open space in the center of the town and was soon joined by forty or fifty men. They circled the space in a single line until the music quickened, and then every man seemed to try to outperform all the others by running, leaping, squatting, and jumping, always moving his whole body in rhythm with the music, each man's face reflecting first fear, and then contempt, and then the next moment laughter or anger. Only the men danced that night, except, noted Leighton, for "some old withered women" who, roused by the recollections of former days, rushed out to join the leaping men.[61]

The dancing seemed wild and chaotic to Leighton. Like the Grebo music that accompanied it, the dancing must have had a structure and a story to tell about the nature of the Grebo world, its social relations, and its deep assumptions about human life. But whatever that structure and story were, they remained hidden to Leighton, as strange to him as his sermon must have been to the Grebo. He found the whole performance amusing, but then thought of the dances he had seen in Charleston and Savannah. He wrote home: "Perhaps, however, if one of these children of nature were allowed to step into one of your own 'refined dances,' he would think his own equally as rational at least."[62]

The next day, Leighton discovered two men from a neighboring village who had a slave with them. The wretched man had been visiting in their village when, they told Leighton, they had learned that an order for a slave had arrived. They had waited until he was asleep, they said, and then "fell upon him in the night, bound him, and hurried away." Leighton rebuked them and said what they had done was wrong, but they replied that no white man had ever told them such a thing before. They wondered, "If we do not sell slaves how will we get cloth, musket power, etc." Ballah, who was translating, could not contain himself with this and leaped into the conversation, asking with feeling, "How do I get clothes and muskets and powder and everything I want!"[63]

What troubled Leighton the most, however, beyond the treachery of the men, was the influence of whites even in such distant villages. The influence of whites in Africa, he wrote in his journal, came mostly from the slave traders, whose footsteps were "to be traced in wars, in bloodshed, by tears, in tumults, in distress, in misery and by everything that can degrade and render savage the heart of man." So with such thoughts about the deceit and corruption of the human heart and the degrading role of whites in the bitter history of Africa, Leighton turned with his companions toward the coast and hurried back to Fair Hope and Big Town.[64]

BY THE LATE summer of 1836, Leighton and Jane were beginning to think of Fair Hope as home. In the evening, when the work of the day was done and their prayers said, they sat together on their piazza listening to the sounds of the African surf and enjoying the windborne feel of the sea. They watched the nighttime fires at Big Town slowly dim and heard in the distance the Grebo bringing an end to their day. Then, beneath the stars and the vast canopy of an African night, they retired to say their personal prayers and to put their heads down at a place they were coming to think of as their place—Fair Hope, this spot of earth jutting out into the rolling surf of the Atlantic on an African cape. This landscape where palms stirred in the night wind, this place with its surrounding towns and villages, its fetishes, rice fields, and funerals, was slowly beginning to shape how they saw the world and what they heard in the world and how they responded as sentient beings to a world as seen, heard, and experienced among the Grebo of West Africa. Perhaps nowhere was the newness and strangeness of this place more apparent than in their discovery of the complex humanity of the people they were encountering here—Freeman and Simleh Ballah, William Davis and little Mary Clealand, Neh and his wife, Baphro and Teddah, and all the others who, in one way or another, had touched Leighton and Jane, and who in turn were being touched by them.[65]

Yet always, even as Leighton and Jane worked and slept beneath an African sky, there rumbled far down in their memories another Fair Hope in distant

Georgia and a boyhood home at Pine Grove by the flowing waters of the Black River. These old home places held their own mysteries as they lingered in the recesses of their imaginations to shape and interpret what they saw, heard, and experienced. Everywhere they went in Africa, and everything they encountered that might challenge old assumptions and values, was being met, and would continue to be met, with the active tenacity of these unforgotten old homes and of former times. So Leighton and Jane knew the struggle between the old and the new, between the shaping dispositions of childhood and youth and a new world they were encountering when they saw a sassy wood ordeal or the richness and verdure of a vast Grebo rice field. No less than Simleh Ballah and William Davis, they were trying to find their way between two worlds, even as they believed that under the providence of God their world was the world of the future.

Not far from Fair Hope, in Harper, Charles Snetter and Anthony Wood and the other settlers also put their heads down at night beneath the stars and the vast canopy of an African night. They, too, were trying to create a new place, a new home—Maryland in Liberia—perched on an African cape jutting out into the Atlantic. How they saw the rolling Atlantic and how they interpreted the Grebo landscape was also being shaped by their daily experiences in this new space they were coming to call home. Yet they remembered, no less than Leighton and Jane, distant homes on another Atlantic coast and specific places where slaves labored and slaves were sold and where slave sorrows reaped rich rewards for whites. Their past, with all of its pain and hard struggles and surprising attachments, had not been left in Charleston or Baltimore or some slave settlement, but had crossed the Atlantic with them to live at Harper, and to live far down in their hopes and dreams and dispositions. So their deep memories and their African experiences mingled together, and out of the mingling there had begun to emerge a settler culture and the sometimes conflicted ways in which settlers interpreted life at Fair Hope and among the Grebo.

In Big Town, the Grebo also watched the evening come. Freeman and Davis and Ballah and all the others—they, too, inevitably heard the sound of the surf and felt the night wind gather and saw the stars of an African night appear one by one. As they sat around their fires, they knew that in Harper the settlers were preparing for the night, and they could see the oil lamps at Fair Hope begin to glow in the distance as the sun set over the Atlantic. They saw and heard and felt all of this not as those seeking a new home, but as those who had known this place from birth, and who felt around them the presence of ancestors who had inhabited and still did inhabit the land. Yet Freeman and Davis and Ballah and all the others must also have known, to varying degrees, that Harper and Fair Hope were now a part of the landscape at Cape Palmas, and that the world that they had known before Dr. Hall arrived with the first settlers was changing, and that some new day, not yet seen, was to follow.

And far away in Savannah, where the cotton was piled high on wharfs and where on a full moon the tide pushed hard against the flow of the river, Paul and his father, Charles, and his sister, Charlotte, and all of the other Bayard slaves went about their daily lives and no doubt wondered about the future and what they would have to face and what they would have to do when their white owners finally made known to them their decisions.

Chapter Eight

Sorrows and Conflicts

While Leighton and Jane were growing accustomed to life under an African sky, troubles were slowly building for all of those who lived at Cape Palmas. Oliver Holmes, the white dentist from Baltimore, had been a miserable appointment as agent and interim governor of the little colony. His public dispute with Charles Snetter—who had become the most respected member of the settler community—had undermined his authority, and neither the Grebo nor the settlers trusted him. Holmes returned their distrust with a vengeance and a deep contempt.

Fortunately for the colony, Holmes's tenure was short lived. After only seven months at the Cape, he received news in early September 1836 that a new agent and governor had been appointed. Holmes immediately resigned and announced that he was leaving the colony. "He returns in quite a bad humor with the colonists," Leighton wrote Rufus Anderson, "and says he will do all he can to injure them at home. I have only to say of him that his course and conduct has been boyish and puerile in the extreme—some abatement however is to be made for his youth and the fever in his brain."[1]

If Holmes's departure was good news for all who lived at the Cape, even better news arrived for Leighton and Jane—they learned in the late summer of 1836 that the mission board in Boston was sending out a young white couple and a young African American man to join them in their work at Fair Hope. Leighton and Jane were elated. While they had come to think of Fair Hope as their home and were happy in their work, they longed for colleagues, not only to help with the growing responsibilities of the mission, but also to be friends and companions. Leighton wrote Anderson that when they thought of the near arrival of the three colleagues, they felt "that our cup of happiness is not only full but running over."[2]

David White, a New Englander, was an earnest young graduate of

1. First African Baptist Church. Organized in 1788, First African was the most influential African American church in Savannah in the nineteenth century. During Andrew Marshall's long ministry (1826–1856) over four thousand African Americans joined the church. Jane Bayard was teaching Sunday School here when Leighton Wilson first met her. From Edgar G. Thomas, *The First African Baptist Church of North America.* Courtesy of the Georgia Historical Society.

2. Slave Settlement, Richmond-on-Ogeechee Plantation, outside of Savannah. The plantation was the home of Jane Bayard Wilson's friend Eliza Clay. The free woman of color Margaret Strobel spent time here when she was preparing to be a teacher at Cape Palmas. Pencil drawing by Edward W. Wells, May 1838. Courtesy of Carolyn Clay Swiggart.

3. Salem Black River Presbyterian Church. Founded in 1759 by Scottish families who had moved up the Black River from an earlier settlement at Williamsburg, South Carolina. Beginning around 1800, it became a congregation of increasingly wealthy cotton planters. In 1860 it had 100 white members and 610 African American slave members. Leighton Wilson spent time here visiting nearby slave settlements with his uncle the Reverend Robert James. Painting by Elizabeth White. Author's collection.

4. Mt. Zion Presbyterian Church. Founded in 1809 by Scottish families that had moved further up the Black River beyond the area around the Salem congregation. Like Salem, it became in the early decades of the nineteenth century a congregation of increasingly wealthy cotton planters. Leighton Wilson's Christian faith and commitments were first nurtured here. In 1860 the congregation had 77 white members and 120 African American slave members. Author's collection.

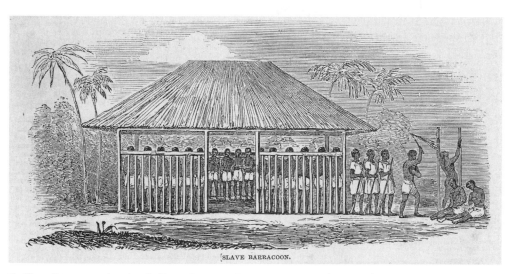

5. Slave Barracoon by the Gallinas River in Sierra Leone. Leighton Wilson visited in the area on several occasions and regularly saw slave ships of Pedro Blanco that operated out of the Gallinas. Wilson encountered a similar barracoon on his arrival in Gabon. *The Illustrated London News.* AP4 .I5. Special Collections, University of Virginia, Charlottesville, VA.

6. Enslaved Africans in Hold of Slave Ship Bound for Brazil. Most of the slaves the Wilsons and other missionaries saw being shipped from Gabon in the 1840s were being carried to Brazil. Johann Moritz Rugendas, Voyage Pittoresque dans le Bresil. Traduit de l'Allemand (Paris, 1835). *Viagem pitoresca altraves do Brasil.* F2513 .R925 1972. Special Collections, University of Virginia, Charlottesville, VA.

7. Slave Auction, Charleston, SC. Slaves in the older seaboard areas of the US were sold and carried in massive numbers to an expanding Cotton Kingdom in the west. Leighton Wilson would have seen such auctions during his stay in Charleston in 1830. *The Illustrated London News.* AP4 .I5. Special Collections, University of Virginia, Charlottesville, VA.

FAIR HOPE.

8. Fair Hope Mission Station, Cape Palmas, Liberia. This drawing reflects the village-like character of Fair Hope by 1841. Drawn in Boston by S. E. Brown, it does not show the beach as described in many of the Wilson letters. *The Missionary Herald,* 1841, p. 352.

9. Kroo Town. The Grebo were often identified simply as Kru or Kroo. Houses in Big Town at Cape Palmas would have looked much like this, although the town was much larger and the houses more compactly placed. Compare the houses in the drawing of the Fair Hope Mission Station and the mortar in photograph B. Drawing perhaps by a Dr. McDowell. *Drawings of Western Africa.* MSS 14357. Special Collections, University of Virginia, Charlottesville, VA.

TOKO, A GABUN CHIEF.

10. Toko. A much admired and sophisticated merchant who welcomed the Protestant mission to the Gabon estuary in 1842. He led in the 1840s the Mpongwe opposition to French control of the estuary. Leighton and Jane Wilson regarded him as their best friend among the Mpongwe, although he never converted to Christianity. Drawn by a Dr. McDowell and found as front piece in John Leighton Wilson, *Western Africa: Its History, Condition, and Prospects* (New York, 1856).

YANAWAY, A GABUN PRINCESS.

11. Yanaway. Most likely she was a daughter of King Glass in Gabon. Leighton Wilson thought that both Mpongwe men and women "display great taste in braiding their hair." He was particularly impressed by the skill women "display in selecting a given style for any particular face." Drawn by a Dr. McDowell and in John Leighton Wilson, *Western Africa: Its History, Condition, and Prospects* (New York, 1856).

Krooman

Slaver Cutter

12. Kroo (or Kru) were frequently sailors on European and American ships and were often in the Gabon estuary. The village in the drawing shows the typical arrangement of a Mpongwe village. The "slave cutter" reflects descriptions of Toko's *Waterwitch*, which he sold to Portuguese slavers. Leighton Wilson utilized the small cabin on the *Waterwitch* on his trip with Toko up the Como River. *Drawings of Western Africa*. MSS 14357. Special Collections, University of Virginia, Charlottesville, VA.

13. This medicine dance is from Corisco Island close-by the Gabon estuary. The drawing reflects the description in William Walker's diary of when a Mpongwe had a "devil in his belly." Drawing perhaps by a Dr. McDowell who drew many sketches while traveling along the West African coast with Captain Richard Lawlin and Leighton Wilson. *Drawings of Western Africa.* MSS 14357. Special Collections, University of Virginia, Charlottesville, VA.

Condemned as a witch!

14. The drawing shows a condemned witch being buried alive. His guilt was most likely established by the sassy wood or "red water" ordeal. Note in the foreground the two containers which may have held the red water. The man on the left appears to be a European or American observer, perhaps Dr. McDowell. *Drawings of Western Africa.* MSS 14357. Special Collections, University of Virginia, Charlottesville, VA.

MOURNING.

15. A scene similar to this followed King Glass's death. A woman, most likely the head wife, stretches out beside the body. Women sit around in lamentation. *Drawings of Western Africa.* MSS 14357. Special Collections, University of Virginia, Charlottesville, VA.

Leighton's alma mater, Union College, and of Princeton Theological Seminary. His wife, née Helen Wells, a lively young woman from New York, was deeply in love with her husband and committed with him to the mission in Africa. Benjamin Van Rensselaer James was a free black from New York who was to establish and run a printing press at the Cape. His primary responsibility would be to print materials for schoolchildren, religious tracts, hymns, and portions of the Bible—first in English, then in Grebo. Light skinned with dark, curly hair, James was to a remarkable degree a man without guile. To be sure, he was savvy about the ways of whites and knew the harsh realities of racism. But he confronted the white world out of a deep inner peace and a genuine piety and he was soon to win not only Leighton's and Jane's respect but also their affection.[3]

The trio arrived at the Cape on Christmas Day, 1836, as the surf thundered and rolled toward shore. With them was Thomas Savage, a white physician who was joining the new Episcopal mission that had been established by James Thomson on the far side of Harper. "When we reached the beach," wrote Helen White, "we found Mr. and Mrs. Wilson waiting with open arms to receive us." The Whites and James climbed the hill to Fair Hope and found it, Helen wrote home, a beautiful location and much more pleasant and delightful than they had imagined in their most sanguine moments. King Freeman and nine of his headmen called to pay their respects and to welcome them to their country. In this way the newcomers began their time at Fair Hope with warm welcomes, with the excitement of a new and exotic place, and with high hopes for their new work as Christian missionaries.[4]

But within a few weeks all three were struck with fever. Helen was first. Initially her symptoms were not severe, and David gave her constant, loving attention. James was next, but he recovered quickly with the careful ministrations of Leighton and Jane. Helen's fever, however, lingered, and her husband grew increasingly alarmed. They talked together about their decision to come out to Africa, and he said he had never enjoyed so much of life in so short a time as he had since his arrival at the Cape. She assured him of her love and how glad she was they had come.[5]

David, however, became depressed as he watched Helen struggle—her temperature rose and fell, rose and fell, and rose again. He began to say that he would die when the fever hit him. Walking out beyond the garden, he found a spot overlooking the surf, pointed it out, and told Leighton he wanted to be buried there. Soon the fever did strike him—with great intensity. Leighton and Jane did all they could to fight it—they gave him calomel, then laudanum, then morphine, trying to calm his agitation and ease the fever. They used "the cups" to bleed him, and then mustard plaster to blister him and rouse him when he sank. At one point he grew wild and frantic as his fever rose higher and higher. Fighting for his life, he threw off his bedcovers and tried to climb out the window of his room before Leighton was able to restrain him. A physician came from a visiting American naval vessel, but nothing availed as David sank into a coma and, Leighton wrote, "death laid his sceptre" upon him.[6]

A funeral followed quickly, though Helen was still ill and could not attend. Ballah, William Davis, and two other Grebo men served as his pallbearers, taking his coffin out to the selected spot. Freeman walked behind them, as did a large crowd of the people, who had come to join a grieving Leighton and Jane and to see and hear the funeral service for a white man. They saw a coffin without food or gifts carried to an open grave in the African soil. They saw deep grief that was restrained, heard hymns sung, and listened to Leighton read from the Bible. And they heard, through Ballah's translation, Leighton preach on those who die in the Lord and on the promises of the gospel for eternal life.[7]

When Helen had been told of her husband's death, she asked for prayer that God would give her strength to face her loss. Her only desire to live, she said, was to do good for the Grebo people. Leighton and Jane gave her constant, tender attention, but Helen's sense of being alone without the young husband whom she loved was overwhelming, and she felt far from the home she had known. She wept the tears of a broken and lonely heart. The ship's physician attended her; Dr. Savage came as well, after recovering from his own fever—they shaved her hair off and applied blisters to her head, her breast, and her feet. They gave her calomel and opium, but nothing stopped the raging of the fever, and in great pain and deep loneliness she joined David in death. Two weeks after her husband's funeral, she was buried beside him at Fair Hope at Cape Palmas on the West African coast.[8]

The agonizing deaths of such an attractive, lively young couple were a heavy blow for Jane and Leighton. "You can little imagine," Jane wrote her family in Philadelphia, "how desolate we are, and how this stroke has bowed us to the ground!" Leighton wrote Rufus Anderson in Boston that his and Jane's feelings were indescribable. He trusted, he wrote, that it had "humbled us more than any previous event of God's providence and has taught us to feel that there is no hope for Africa except in the Almighty arm of Jehovah." Leighton confessed that he found their deaths mysterious and inscrutable. He kept telling himself that somehow their deaths were a part of God's gracious providence and that the Judge of all the earth would do right. But such a confession was not easy. He and Jane had received the young couple with joyful but trembling hearts, and then their worst fears had been realized. The entire mission at Fair Hope seemed to be called into question—How could they go on, he wondered, or how could they encourage other young couples to join them in the work? He and Jane prayed and prayed again asking for strength and guidance. They talked together into the night and comforted one another and reminded each other of God's love and God's promise not to desert them. And slowly they gathered their courage and faith, and Leighton wrote Anderson that they would not lose heart. "There is hope for Africa," he told Anderson, "and we believe that God's mercy towards her will yet be disclosed in such a way as will make the hosts of Heaven and the inhabitants of earth wonder and adore." So Leighton and Jane—while knowing only too well that the fever had caused the deaths of the young couple—placed their deaths finally in the mystery of God's providence and put their own hopes in what they believed to be God's good and gracious purposes for Africa.[9]

Whatever their trust in divine providence and their hopes for Africa, Leighton and Jane were discouraged and felt beaten down. They had a fine new colleague in B. V. R. James, but their grief over the death of the young couple was intensified by what they began to regard as the deteriorating conditions of the young colony.

THE MAN CHOSEN to replace Oliver Holmes as governor, John Brown Russwurm, was a black man—a great surprise to all who thought blacks needed whites to govern them and keep them from descending into anarchy. At least he was perceived to be black by those whose eyes had been shaped by the racial assumptions of white America. With a white father and a light-skinned Jamaican mother, he was thought of as white by the Grebo until they were told he was black.[10]

What was certain was that Russwurm was a remarkable man, and that he had struggled against the racism of a white world all of his life. He was one of the first black graduates of an American college and was the cofounder of the first black newspaper in the United States, *Freedom's Journal*. And he was to be the single most important leader in the early history of Maryland in Liberia, a colony established by alarmed whites in order to help whiten America.[11]

Russwurm had graduated from Bowdoin College in Maine, where he had had as classmates Henry Wadsworth Longfellow, Nathaniel Hawthorne, and a number of men who would become US senators and congressmen. He had read Herodotus in Greek and Livy in Latin, had studied natural science and mathematics, and had shown a special interest in history. Deeply immersed in the cultural traditions of the West, he was nonetheless fully aware of his status as a black man in white America. A classmate remembered him as a "diligent student, but of no marked ability," as he compared him to Longfellow, Hawthorne, and a number of prominent political leaders—a high standard of "marked ability" for any college student. Russwurm was, he wrote, rather withdrawn and eager to avoid any situation that might embarrass him because of "his sensitiveness on account of his color." The tone of the comment and the assumptions it represented revealed the painful challenges faced by a brilliant young black man in antebellum America.[12]

Russwurm had launched *Freedom's Journal* with Samuel Cornish after moving to New York in 1827. The journal was intended to counter the harsh racist propaganda being published in several of the city's papers. The editors declared that their purpose was "to arrest the progress of prejudice" and to serve as a shield against the evils of such prejudice. But the paper was also intended to encourage a spirit of independence and community identity among the city's growing African American population.[13]

Russwurm had been particularly vehement in his attacks on the American Colonization Society and the Liberian experiment. What free blacks were committed to, he had insisted, was the emancipation of those in bondage. First must come the removal of slavery's chains; then the possibility of emigration could be considered. But after two years of such attacks on colonization, Russwurm had changed his mind. He had arrived at the conclusion that it was a "mere waste of words, to talk of ever enjoying citizenship in this country: it is utterly impossible in the nature of things: all those who pant for this, must cast their eyes elsewhere." As a proud and accomplished man, he simply thought that racism ran too deep in America for any black to find a true home in the land of slavery.[14]

The response to his change of heart had been swift and vociferous. Blacks burned him in effigy in New York and Philadelphia. He was called a traitor to his race. His old colleague Samuel Cornish later compared him to Benedict Arnold. When Russwurm announced that he had accepted a position in Monrovia as superintendent of schools, many believed he had been bought out. William Lloyd Garrison wrote, in *The Liberator*: "If his vanity had not been superior to his judgment, and his love of distinction greater than his regard for consistency, he would never have been seduced away to Liberia."[15]

Russwurm had first arrived in Monrovia in 1829 and came into almost immediate conflict with its white governor—it galled him to have a white man over a black colony in Africa. He founded the colony's first newspaper—the *Liberian Herald*—and used it to promote black pride and independence, and had also served as colonial secretary. He entered business partnerships with several successful merchants, including the Methodist minister George McGill from Baltimore, whose daughter he married in 1833. With his seemingly inexhaustible energy, Russwurm became a partner and friend of Dr. James Hall—before Hall's appointment as the first governor of Maryland in Liberia. In time, Hall—who was also a graduate of Bowdoin—became one of Russwurm's closest friends and supporters. In turn, Russwurm named one of his sons James Hall.[16]

Years later, the white physician provided an intimate and perceptive description of his friend. Russwurm, Hall said, was a tall man who carried himself in a dignified and gentlemanly manner. He had large eyes that were keen and penetrating. He had a good mind and was able to quickly judge the character of those around him. But Hall also thought his friend "was exceedingly sensitive, amounting even to jealousy, and having once lost confidence in a person, he seldom, if ever, re-acquired it." He was reserved, and, like many blacks, he did not, for good reason, reveal much of himself to whites—a reserve he also began to show toward blacks after being attacked so fiercely in New York. Hall found him, however, to be not only reserved but also sensitive about his status as "a colored man." He was particularly ready to take offense at anything said by a white. It required, Hall wrote, "the greatest delicacy in the choice of words to render even praise acceptable to him, when coming from a white man." Hall thought that few blacks had suffered so much from such causes.[17]

It was this brilliant, proud, and often conflicted man—who knew not only the deep indignities of American racism but also the hostility of many black Americans—who followed Holmes as governor and agent at Cape Palmas. And when he arrived at Harper in September 1836, he found at Fair Hope, on the outskirts of the settlement, a white missionary couple from South Carolina and Georgia.[18]

DURING THE MONTHS after his arrival at Cape Palmas, Russwurm discovered that the colony was facing a severe food shortage. Irregular rains had reduced the size of Big Town's rice crop. And the little gardens and farms of the settlers—often neglected for more profitable trade or lumbering—were not adequate to meet the needs of the colony. The Grebo, knowing the settlers' dependence on Grebo rice, cassava, and palm oil, had raised their prices dramatically, reducing some settlers to great want and distress. To add to their difficulties, ships were regularly arriving from Baltimore with new emigrants—but few supplies. Russwurm was distraught. Echoing Leighton's report to the Maryland board in the summer of 1836, Russwurm wrote that the emigrants had received extravagant promises in Maryland about what awaited them and had not been told "the dark as well as the bright side of the picture." When they arrived and found the hard realities of colonial life, they complained bitterly to Russwurm, demanding that their needs be supplied out of the fast dwindling resources of the colonial store. The fever also struck them hard—shortly after the arrival of one ship with eighty-three immigrants, ten of their children died. A number of despairing families turned to Fair Hope for help, and Leighton and Jane were besieged with requests for food and supplies.[19]

The mission at Fair Hope, however, was soon facing its own difficulties. Leighton received word in December 1837 that a financial panic, fueled in large measure by land speculation in the West and a banking crisis, had hit the United States. Supporters of the mission movement, now worried about their own finances, had cut back on their contributions to the American Board. In addition, the Presbyterian church, one of the primary supporters of the board, was in the midst of a bitter division between those who called themselves "Old School" and those who were known as "New School." A leader of the Old School was none other than Jane's cousin Charles Hodge at Princeton. And among the things he was advocating was the establishment of a Presbyterian board of foreign missions. Instead of the ecumenical American Board, governed by an independently elected board, the denomination, he said, needed its own board under the authority of the church's General Assembly. The church had split in 1837, leaving only the New School faction supporting the American Board. This had meant another sharp reduction in funds flowing to the board's offices in Boston.[20]

For all of these reasons, Leighton had to cancel plans for establishing schools in surrounding villages, and he and Jane were forced to reduce the number of boarding students at Fair Hope. They accepted the necessity of cutting back, but Leighton wrote Anderson that if they were required to make more cuts in their work, "we would be almost tempted to resemble ourselves to a parent in the act of strangling his own offspring."[21]

WHEN RUSSWURM HAD been appointed governor at Cape Palmas, Leighton had written him a letter of congratulation. He also wrote to Latrobe to say that he approved of the appointment—not that his approval was needed, but Leighton had apparently thought that it would be an encouragement to Latrobe to hear positive reactions from someone who was living at the Cape and not making decisions in far-off Baltimore.[22]

During the first months following Russwurm's arrival, Russwurm and Leighton developed a relationship of mutual respect. But having a black governor was clearly a new situation for Leighton. For some years, Leighton had been pushing himself, trying to move beyond the degrading stereotypes that whites had of Africans and their far-flung descendants. Many of his letters and reports to America were intended to challenge such stereotypes. His experiences with Freeman, Ballah, and William Davis had given him a deep respect for them along with other Grebo. More recently, he and James had established an immediate rapport with one another. The New York printer had written Anderson shortly after his recovery from the fever: "To dear Brother Wilson and wife I shall ever feel deeply indebted for their unvaried kindness and attention during my sickness and affliction. Their cordial feelings and friendly advice have very strongly endeared them to me."[23]

But for all of his struggles to overcome in his own heart and mind the racism of American society, Leighton could not fully overcome the world of deep assumptions that roamed far down in his memory. All of his earliest recollections of Pine Grove and Boggy Gully, all of his experiences in New York, Philadelphia, and Massachusetts, all that he had seen in Charleston and Savannah and Fair Hope plantation, had taught him that whites were to be ultimately in charge. So when Russwurm had been appointed governor, Leighton had written Anderson that, while he thought the appointment to be "judicious," he nonetheless felt "it quite a revolution in affairs that brings us under a *black government*."[24]

For his part, Russwurm had no doubts about the deeply bred racism of whites. His conviction, after all, about the pervasiveness of American racism had been a primary reason for his emigration to Liberia, where he hoped the burden of race could be lifted. And now, as governor at Harper, he found an influential white man at the Fair Hope mission station—it must have seemed that he was unable to escape even in Africa the oppressive presence of whites.

Leighton and Russwurm, though cordial enough toward one another, consequently found it impossible to establish a relationship of trust. Leighton wrote to Anderson that the reserved Russwurm "keeps quite at a distance from us and watches with a very suspicious eye—why I do not well know for no one has desired his administration to be successful more than I have." Leighton was experiencing what many well-meaning whites had learned, to their dismay—that many African Americans felt guarded around whites. It was dangerous for them to forget the power or the deep racial assumptions that lingered in even well-intended white minds.[25]

The governor, however, had other, more immediate concerns than Leighton and Fair Hope during his first year in office. Tensions intensified as supplies in the colony shrank—even as new immigrants arrived—and the price of Grebo rice continued to soar. The colonists, Russwurm wrote Latrobe, were "too dependent upon the natives for almost every kind of labor" and were not producing adequate supplies for themselves. And, he added, a number of colonists were longing to return to America. The idea, he said, "that we cannot do without 'the fleshpots of the Egyptians' is too firmly fixed in their minds."[26]

The settlers, for their part, were dismayed by their difficulty in obtaining rice and by the pilfering of the Grebo, which seemed to have no end. As tensions grew between the settlers and the Grebo, the settlers increasingly thought of the Grebo as "savages" and regarded them with growing hostility. Rather than identifying with the Grebo as African brothers and sisters, the settlers clearly regarded themselves as Americans, as a people distinct from the Africans around them. They were arriving by a different route at the same conclusion that abolitionists were coming to and that those who rejected the idea of colonization had been saying for some time—that African Americans were fundamentally Americans and not Africans. The settlers wanted to maintain this American identity, which was rooted in Western civilization and which built upon the skills and culture of the West—especially an ability to read. Their privileged position at the Cape in relationship to the Grebo was built on the power that flowed from Western culture. One leading settler wrote Latrobe that he was afraid that before the settlers could get a good school, the Grebo would be educated by the mission school, and "the natives would become our equals, and even surpass our youth in literary requirements." He insisted that the education of the Grebo was a cause of constant concern among the colonists. In regard to the Grebo, he thought the colony should adopt the opinion "of residents of the Southern States in relation to their blacks—'they had better remain in a happy state of ignorance.'"[27]

The settlers, of course, differed from the abolitionists and other opponents of colonization in that they thought they could practice their American culture more fully and completely in Liberia than in the United States with its powerful racism. The bitter irony was that the colony, as an extension of the United States, brought with it its own peculiar form of American racism in the settlers' disdain of the Grebo.[28]

In late 1836, the rising tensions between the settlers and the Grebo erupted. Someone broke into the colony's storehouse and stole some trade goods. The colonial authorities promptly arrested an old man, a much venerated leader among the Grebo, and put him in jail. The Grebo were enraged and determined to free the man and take revenge on the colonists.

A few days later, the authorities learned that a young boy was the real culprit. They went to arrest him, but this time the Grebo were ready. They chased after the arresting officers and a number of settlers, who all ran to Fair Hope, scrambled over the fence, and found refuge in the mission house. Four or five hundred armed Grebo with blasting war horns and ringing bells arrived at the gate of the mission, where Leighton had placed himself to meet them. Standing in the midst of the Grebo, Leighton found that "not one single individual offered the least disrespect." Leighton convinced them to sit and wait while he went to meet with Russwurm and Freeman.[29]

Leaving Jane to wait alone with those outside the gate, Leighton went into Harper, where Russwurm and Freeman joined him. Leighton asked the governor to release the old man to Freeman's care, and Russwurm agreed. Leighton, now joined by the king's brother William Davis, went into Big Town and arranged a palaver for the next day. When the palaver was announced, the Grebo at Fair Hope returned to Big Town, while more settlers came to the mission seeking refuge until the matter was settled.

The next day at the palaver Freeman was clearly furious at Russwurm. Freeman told him he should not remain at Cape Palmas—Russwurm later wrote that Freeman "has thrown it in my teeth that I am not a proper man for Governor—meaning that I am not a proper white man." The king consequently addressed Leighton—who found himself caught in the middle of the dispute—and not Russwurm, and Leighton had to use all the influence he had to get Freeman to give Russwurm a fair hearing. Russwurm, speaking through Leighton, said that the two people could live peacefully if the pilfering stopped. So the accusations and negotiations proceeded, with Leighton acting as a mediator, until an agreement was reached that satisfied the Grebo and the crisis came to an end.[30]

Russwurm was grateful to Leighton for his intervention. He wrote Latrobe that Leighton had played an important role in settling the dispute and that Jane had acted with equally commendable zeal. Leighton hoped that good might come of the confrontation. "There is a melancholy disposition," he told the American Board, "among the greater part of the Americans when set down in this country to be overbearing and to treat the natives as an inferior race of beings. This affair will teach them to respect their rights and to treat them with more kindness and decorum."[31]

ALTHOUGH THE GOVERNOR and the missionary were thus cordial to one another, and had acted together in defusing a crisis with the Grebo, they were soon to find that Cape Palmas was not large enough for both of them. They had brought across the Atlantic competing memories and visions that made the Cape contested ground. Russwurm remembered his struggles as a black man at Bowdoin; Leighton remembered Pine Grove and Boggy Gully. The governor remembered being burned in effigy by angry blacks because of his decision to go to Liberia; the missionary remembered the enthusiastic send-off he and Jane had received in Philadelphia. Russwurm envisioned Harper as a refuge from American racism and as a center for a proud new African American nation. Leighton envisioned Fair Hope as one of several launching spots for the conversion of Africa to the Christian faith and as a school to raise up indigenous leaders to accomplish that conversion. Both men brought strong wills and deep commitments to their respective visions. The consequence was conflict and the eventual abandonment of Fair Hope.

NOT LONG AFTER the palaver, Charles Snetter came to live and work at Fair Hope. He had been a thorn in Russwurm's side—he was strong-willed, popular with the settlers, and not above challenging the authority of the governor. The governor—worried that Snetter would become an agitator appealing to the passions and prejudices of the people—had removed him from his position as storekeeper. Certainly the dark-skinned former Charleston barber identified more closely with the settlers and their experiences than with the light-skinned, highly educated Russwurm. Snetter spoke the language of the settlers, Russwurm the language of a Bowdoin graduate. Russwurm's remarkable achievements and his deep internalization of Western culture had made him not only a favorite of the colonization board in Baltimore, but also a man well-prepared to challenge a pervasive white racism. But these achievements, and his internalized values and class assumptions, had a tendency to distance him from the very people to whom he was so deeply committed. He thought of the settlers as "ignorant and prejudiced," worried about their morals, and thought many of them ill-prepared for the responsibilities of colonists. He consequently tended to be autocratic—a trait the board in Baltimore thought of as firm and decisive. But critics later complained that the colony was "a large plantation [with its] governor acting as an overseer."[32]

Leighton had a house built at Fair Hope for Snetter's family. He employed Snetter to run the mission's secular affairs and hired his wife as a schoolteacher. Leighton had high hopes for Snetter. He proposed to the American Board that Snetter, although lacking formal education, could be prepared as a doctor for the mission. Dr. Savage had agreed to be his mentor, and Leighton hoped the board would agree to bring Snetter, after his apprenticeship with Savage, to New England to study for a year or two in a medical school there.[33]

Russwurm was understandably unhappy with Snetter's remaining at the Cape, for he represented the most serious challenge to his leadership. In this way, Leighton's long friendship with Snetter—reaching back to their days together in Charleston at the Circular Church—and his employment of Snetter became points of tension between the governor and the missionary.

The growing antagonism between Leighton and Russwurm broke into the open when one of Pedro Blanco's slave ships came limping into the harbor at Cape Palmas in April 1837. The ship had been trading along the coast, purchasing rice to provision a cargo of slaves. When Russwurm allowed the ship to stay in the harbor—and also allowed settlers to work on the ship, and its captain to buy supplies from the colony's store—Leighton became furious. On visits to Monrovia, he had learned that Russwurm, while still living in Monrovia, had sold a ship to Blanco, and that he had regularly supplied the slaver with provisions—essential food needed for the transatlantic passage of a slave ship. Leighton had thought such activities would cease when Russwurm became governor at Harper, but now, by letting the slave ship load provisions at Cape Palmas for a cargo of slaves, Leighton concluded, Russwurm was deliberately aiding the international slave trade. He wrote Rufus Anderson in Boston that the governor had "prostituted the character of the colony by rendering himself and the settlers accessory to this odious and nefarious traffic." He and Dr. Savage protested vigorously, but Russwurm ignored them. The two missionaries wrote Latrobe about the affair, warning that if such cooperation with slavers was not stopped, and Russwurm rebuked, they would not be able to keep quiet about what was happening in the colony.[34]

Differences between the governor and Leighton were also exacerbated by the presence of African American teachers connected with the mission. Russwurm complained to Latrobe that Leighton was hiring some of the most gifted settlers from Harper to work at the mission, drawing them away from work that might more directly benefit the colony. Latrobe wrote Leighton about the matter, and Leighton replied that the original agreement with the Grebo had stipulated that the mission would provide schools for the Grebo, and that the mission had spent considerable time and money educating those settlers who were now serving as teachers. Leighton agreed, however, that he would hire no more settlers as new teachers. Instead he would hire native Africans, Fanti who had been educated at Cape Coast by British missionaries.[35]

But this accord did not put an end to the tensions between Russwurm and Leighton. Russwurm insisted that the teachers should participate in the colonial militia. "My own opinion," Russwurm wrote to Latrobe, "is that all colored persons in the colony should perform public duties unless expressly sent out by the missionary society as preachers or teachers."[36]

Leighton insisted, however, that those who were teaching Grebo children could not be part of a militia organized to fight the Grebo. Teachers marching back and forth with the militia would make them look like the enemy of those they were seeking to serve. Furthermore—and this infuriated Russwurm—Leighton regarded the colony as a project of an American benevolent society, one among many such societies. One benevolent society could not impose conditions on the work of another, especially when it had been insisted from the first that the mission at Fair Hope was independent from the colony.

Leighton's stance presented a direct challenge to the colonial authorities, to the Maryland Colonization Society, and to their premise that Maryland in Liberia was a legitimate state. But Leighton was adamant—how, he wondered, could a group of men in Baltimore organize themselves into a benevolent society and then pretend they had the authority to establish a nation at Cape Palmas?

When one of the teachers was fined for not participating in the militia, Leighton sent an angry note to Russwurm and raised an American flag at Fair Hope to emphasize the mission's independence. Leighton immediately regretted the tone of his note, which called into question the governor's authority in the matter. He sent an apology the same day, but the damage was done. Russwurm was deeply offended. Although the missionary and the governor would find themselves having to cooperate with one another in the future, their relationship became one of mutual antagonism. They consequently referred the issue of militia participation to their respective boards.[37]

BACK IN THE United States, Anderson and Latrobe tried to defuse the growing antagonism between the governor and the missionary. The leader of the
American Board of Commissioners for Foreign Missions and the leader of
the Maryland Colonization Society's board of directors believed that it was
in the best interest of each organization for their agents to work in cooperation and harmony. The different objectives of their respective societies, they
believed, could be best promoted through collaboration. At first, however,
Anderson sided with Leighton, telling Latrobe that it was a great question
how far one incorporated benevolent society could assume jurisdiction over
the agents of another society. But when Latrobe insisted that Maryland in
Liberia was a state with authority over all who lived within its borders, Anderson backed off. He agreed that, just as any foreigner living in Maryland
was under the civil authorities of Maryland, so any nonsettler living in Maryland in Liberia was under the jurisdiction of its civil authorities. So Anderson
and Latrobe agreed that Leighton and Jane, the printer James, and the teachers at Fair Hope were to be under the lawfully established authority of the
colony.[38]

In his correspondence with Latrobe, Anderson also took up the question
of Leighton's angry note to Russwurm—Latrobe had sent him a copy. Trying
to respond in a diplomatic and delicate way, Anderson wrote asking Latrobe
to be patient with Leighton. "You will understand me, however, when I sug-
gest, in respect to the whole matter of jurisdiction, while the governors of
your colony are colored men, and our missionaries are Southern men, that
while all necessary care is taken to preserve the principle of *right* (which ought
not to be conceded by your agent)[,] difficulties which may arise, and which
threaten to be serious, should, as far as may be, referred for settlement to the
societies at home. I wish such a reference may never again be necessary." In
his polite but convoluted manner, Anderson was saying that African American governors and white Southern missionaries were going to clash, and that
when serious differences arose, it was best to have the two white executives—
one in Boston, the other in Baltimore—decide the issues.[39]

Whether Leighton learned of this comment by the Bostonian is unknown. But he almost certainly would have regarded such a comment as patronizing and a betrayal of his trust. Leighton accepted Anderson's rebuke
for the angry tone of his note to Russwurm, but he no doubt would have
been deeply offended by the white Bostonian's remark to the leader of Maryland's efforts to rid the state of free blacks—as if Anderson and Latrobe
had somehow freed themselves, in contrast to the Southerner Leighton, of

any racial prejudice. Russwurm—given his long experience with patronizing whites—would no doubt have found little that was surprising in Anderson's remarks.[40]

When Leighton was informed of Anderson's position that the mission was under the jurisdiction of the colony, he protested vigorously. Maryland in Liberia was not, he noted, recognized by the United States, Britain, or any other government in the world as an independent state. Moreover, Leighton warned Anderson, the Grebo, in their original agreement with the Maryland Colonization Society, had specifically refused to yield any of their independence to the colonial authorities. Maryland in Liberia, Leighton insisted, was an imperial incursion into West Africa, and the Grebo were facing the same assaults on their independence that other indigenous peoples were facing when confronted by colonists backed by Western military and cultural power. He compared the Grebo to the Cherokees in Georgia, noting how the American Board and its missionaries had denied the right of Georgia to extend its authority over them. Did the American Board not have the same responsibility, he asked, to deny the right of the Maryland Colonization Society to exert its authority over the Grebo? In all of this Leighton was utilizing arguments that abolitionists had been hurling at colonization projects. William Lloyd Garrison had been using the bitter example of the Cherokees to denounce colonization as a scheme rooted in racism. When the little colony at Cape Palmas was being established, abolitionists in Boston had called it a "scheme in cruelty and oppression." British abolitionists were not only organizing for "Aborigines' Rights" but had been waging a furious campaign against the intrusion of white settlers in South Africa into the lands of indigenous people. Leighton was soon to find that the abolitionists would be utilizing his reports of what was happening at Cape Palmas as a part of their anticolonization campaign. The mission's relationship to colonial authorities was consequently far from resolved.[41]

RUSSWURM HAD TO contend not only with a meddling missionary, but also with restless settlers who were frequently angry about his decisions and unhappy about what they perceived to be his autocratic ways. An explosive confrontation between the governor and the colonists took place in the summer of 1837. And the person who most directly challenged Russwurm was Charles Snetter.

The brig *Baltimore* arrived at the Cape on July 4, 1837, with a passenger whose brief experience in Harper would ignite the fury of the settlers against Russwurm and his father-in-law, George McGill. The passenger—a fourteen-year-old boy—had been discovered after the *Baltimore* had left port and was considered a runaway slave. The ship's captain was determined to return him to Maryland in order to avoid a heavy fine and possible criminal prosecution. While the brig was anchored in the harbor, the boy—with the help of a settler—managed to escape the ship. He "ventured his life for his freedom," a settler later wrote, in order to make it through the surf to shore. When the captain discovered that the boy had escaped, he came on shore looking for him. George McGill provided the captain with help, and the boy was captured.[42]

Charles Snetter, hearing the commotion when the boy was taken, tried to intercede with the captain, but to no avail. He appealed to McGill, the vice agent, but was dismissed as meddling. Standing with other settlers, Snetter wept as he watched the boy being carried back to the ship and slavery. The next day, Snetter wrote Latrobe. McGill, he said, had laughed at him for "his weakness" in protesting and weeping over the return of the young boy to the ship. "Never did I see a captive runaway in Custody since I left America untill I seen it in this colony," Snetter said. He wondered if this action meant that any slaver could come to Harper and capture settlers or Grebo and carry them off. He reminded Latrobe that the colony's constitution said there was to be no slavery in the colony, and he warned that he would not remain in the colony if such practices were allowed to continue.[43]

Snetter had strong settler sympathies on his side—a crowd had been with him when he pleaded that the boy not be returned. But Russwurm supported McGill, and they both thought of Snetter as a dangerous rabble rouser who had stirred up the settlers over an affair that was none of their business. And so they paid no attention to his protests and became even more determined to limit his influence among the colonists.[44]

Snetter's work at Fair Hope, however, also complicated matters. Leighton was in the midst of insisting that Fair Hope was separate from the colony, and he didn't want to add unnecessary fuel to his controversy with Russwurm. So he accepted without protest the return of the boy to the ship, and he wrote Latrobe and expressed his regret that an employee of the mission had become involved in a colonial issue. But only a few months earlier, he had protested vigorously when Russwurm had allowed the repair and resupplying of Pedro Blanco's slave ship. Perhaps a Maryland runaway came too close to his memories of Boggy Gully or Fair Hope plantation, to old Jacob the cook at Pine Grove, or Paul the carpenter in Savannah. Or maybe he reasoned that the international slave trade was illegal, but slavery in Maryland was not. For whatever reason, Leighton thought he could protest a slave ship being provisioned at Cape Palmas, but not the return of a boy on the run from slavery in Maryland.[45]

Leighton didn't know it at the time, but he was making an ominous distinction. The difference between his reaction to the Baltimore runaway and his reaction to the slavers traveling the Liberian coast must have seemed hypocritical not only to Russwurm and McGill but also to Snetter. But if Leighton was aware of the distinctions he was making—and his reasons for making the distinctions—he did not acknowledge these distinctions in his letters home.

A few months later, when Leighton was in Monrovia, he saw settlers engaged in extensive business dealings with six slave ships that visited the port for provisions. Fearing that Cape Palmas faced the same danger, he wrote Anderson that if the hopes of colonization societies were realized, it would be a disaster for Africa. Unless the Liberian colonies refused to support the international slave trade in any way, he said, Mother Africa "can never rejoice at the recovery of her lost and stolen children."[46]

But when Leighton looked at the relationship between the settlers and the indigenous people, he wondered if the colonies would themselves become slaveholding countries. He noted a proposal before the colonial assembly in Monrovia that would establish a fourteen-year apprenticeship for Africans, which he thought was a disguised attempt to establish slavery in the colony. He feared that whites in the colonization societies were "constructing a machine with their own hands that is destined only to scatter fire brands and death among the inhabitants of unhappy Africa."[47]

RUSSWURM FOUND ALL of Leighton's concerns about the international slave trade simply an example of another arrogant white trying to tell black Americans how to act. When Leighton had protested the provisioning of the slave ship, the governor had written his predecessor, Oliver Holmes, about Leighton's meddling in colonial affairs. Russwurm told the white Baltimore dentist—who was eager to hear the worst about Leighton—that the ship had been none of the missionary's business. It was his firm belief, Russwurm continued, that if the meddling didn't stop, colonial governors would have to deal with issues that distracted them from their primary responsibilities of governing. As governor, he said, he already had "to contend against the ignorance and prejudice of the colonists and these are enough for any one individual."[48]

Chapter Nine

The Bitter Cost of Freedom

Nicholas Bayard had received letters from Jane and Leighton in late 1836 asking him to make the final arrangements for the emancipation of their slaves. The letters had taken almost five months to make their way from Cape Palmas to Savannah, but Nicholas was very glad to receive them, for he was eager to bring the intentions of his sisters and their husbands to completion. He had discovered years earlier, while trying to develop the General's Island plantation, that the management of a plantation was no easy matter. And more recently he had been finding the management of his sisters' slaves to be burdensome even in Savannah and on nearby Hutchinson Island—shoes and clothing had to be provided; corn, pork, and other provisions had to be purchased; accounts had to be kept; doctors had to be summoned; and many small details of slave life seemed to need constant attention. As a banker preoccupied with what would become the financial crisis of 1837, he was ready to free himself of responsibilities for Paul and Charles and Charlotte and all those who lived in the settlement across the flowing waters of the Savannah.[1]

Nicholas wrote immediately to Latrobe asking about "all the privileges and inducements extended by your society to emigrants." He wanted the details before he talked to those in the settlement, for he anticipated that some who lived there would be reluctant to leave Savannah for what he called "the blessings of freedom and colonization." Moreover, the Hutchinson Island plantation itself needed to be sold immediately. Restrictions, Nicholas wrote, had been placed on the property in 1818. His father had entered a contract with the Savannah authorities that required him to abandon the rice fields with their regular flooding and draining. The authorities wanted to reduce the fever-causing miasmas that rose from any rice fields near the city, so Dr. Bayard had agreed to grow only "dry crops" on the land and to maintain the dams to keep out the tide. Now, in 1836, if the people in the settlement were suddenly removed, there was a real danger the land would be flooded and a heavy penalty incurred. Already there had been difficulty with the city authorities. Some years earlier, an inspector had found the plantation badly neglected when most of the people had been moved to General's Island—the dams of the old rice fields had been washing away, trunks regulating the flow of water were missing gates, and in many spots nothing prevented the ebb and flow of the tide. Alarmed that "noxious vapours" might arise from such neglected fields, the city had insisted on extensive work, and it had to be done in order for the estate to avoid a heavy fine. So Nicholas felt he could not proceed with the emancipation until the plantation was sold and he was freed from the responsibility of maintaining the dry culture of the island.[2]

In early 1837, Nicholas was finally ready to visit the settlement and tell those who were known as Bayard slaves about the plans for their emancipation. He had made the trip across the river to the island many times—to check on crops or the sick, to visit in the settlement, or talk with an overseer—but the familiar trip must have caused some anxiety for him every time, as he spent most of his days behind a desk. To get to the island, first he had to make his way carefully down the steep cobblestone dray-ways from the Savannah bluff to the waterfront, where a boatman would be waiting with his bateau—what the Gullah called a "Trus-me-Gawds." Nicholas would climb in, seat himself as the little boat was held in place against the lapping waters, hold on as the boatman pushed from shore—and trust in God that they would not be flipped suddenly into the river. With only the thin planks of the bateau between him and the dark waters, he must have felt the river's closeness and the power of its deep currents and its flowing tide. He knew only too well that the Savannah had claimed many victims, for some from the settlement had been caught by its waters. Now, in February of 1837, as the little boat moved out into the river and toward the island, Nicholas could see, through a small copse of winter woods, the settlement where the people were waiting.[3]

The slaves had gathered in the open space before the cabins. Here, over the years, in this communal space, fires had burned, food had been prepared and eaten, stories had been told, songs had been sung, and things had been said that could only be said in secret away from the ears of whites. Nicholas greeted them and then told them of the plans for their emancipation. He read letters from Jane and Leighton describing the colony at Cape Palmas and the Grebo people among whom they lived. Nicholas told them they were not to be forced to go to Africa—if they wished, they could go to a free state in the North and begin a new life there. But they could not be emancipated and remain in Georgia; the state's laws would not allow it. The decision was to be theirs.[4]

In this way, the slaves of Hutchinson Island finally learned what these missionary owners had planned for them and what options were being placed before them. Paul and his father, Charles, and his sister, Charlotte; Old Adam and young Clarissa; the driver, John, and the plowman, William; and all the others—they who had known so few options in their lives—were now being asked to make a choice. Each of them and all of them together had had to struggle under the weight of slavery's chains to find some small space to move around on their own and to make decisions that mattered in their own lives. And now they were being told they must decide about their own future. So they stood there before Nicholas, these black men and women, these Gullah people, and out of the experiences and circumstances of their individual lives and their life together they listened to Nicholas tell them about the choices they had to make. Some were old and enfeebled, some were young and strong, some were mothers with children in their arms, some were women who had husbands on other plantations or in the city, some were men with wives and children who—owned by others—would be left behind if their men chose freedom. As Nicholas laid out for them the choices they had to make, they knew only too well that even now, even the option to decide, even the opportunity for freedom, carried the deep sorrows of their history and revealed once again the pervasive, entangled oppression of their slavery. Nicholas told them they did not have to decide immediately—the plantation with their settlement home would first need to be sold, and they had time to consider their options. So their time of deciding, of choosing, began, there in the settlement where the waters of the Savannah murmured close by and white-bodied seagulls and terns called wildly to one another and flew back and forth above the river waters.[5]

NICHOLAS WAS UNSUCCESSFUL in his attempt to sell the Hutchinson Island plantation—real-estate values had plummeted because of the financial crisis, and he could find no buyer for the valuable riverfront property. He consequently decided to move ahead with the emancipation plans and to hire enough slaves to keep up the place and maintain its old rice dams and gates so that the land would be dry, free from noxious miasmas, and not liable to costly fines from the city authorities. In late October 1837, he wrote the Maryland Colonization Society board that he anticipated that most of the Bayard slaves would embark for Cape Palmas early in the next year.[6]

Some of the slaves were still struggling with their decision—Should they claim their emancipation and go to West Africa or to one of the Northern states, or should they remain in Savannah with their families in slavery? Isaac had a wife on an adjoining plantation. Juba was the mother of five-year-old Grace and the infant Hosa. Her husband, Renty, the children's father, lived on a nearby plantation. Jack, the son of carpenter Jack who had been Paul's teacher, had a wife on another plantation. And Paul himself—he had a wife and children in the city. They all had to struggle not only with their own conflicted feelings but also with what they were being told by family and others—that it was folly and madness to leave Savannah for the treacherous shores of Africa.[7]

For Paul, the struggle was apparently intense. On the one hand, he was deeply drawn to freedom. As a carpenter moving around the city, he had tasted a little freedom, and that taste had made the bitterness of slavery unbearable. On the other hand, he was deeply attached to his wife and children. In spite of his hard work as a carpenter and what he had earned for the Bayard estate, he did not have the money to purchase his own family. Moreover, Savannah itself was his home—he knew its streets and alleys and the sounds of the city and the peculiar feel of the wind as it blew inland over marshes and riverbanks. He knew by name many of its people—black and white—and how ships sailed proudly from its wharfs and how parks and gardens provided delight to the eye and relief from the sun. This space, this particular place among the places inhabited on the earth, was where he had been shaped as a man, a black man among the Gullah-speaking people of the Georgia Lowcountry. But what Paul also knew was that Savannah was a place of slavery and that Cape Palmas promised to be a place of freedom. So he chose to take the risk of freedom and go to his rightful inheritance. He chose freedom, but his choice was not free of history. His choice was the choice of a particular black man in Savannah who bore the physical marks of his people, who carried in the details of his life the larger story of what black men and women had experienced in America, and who consequently had to choose between the narrow and bitter options offered him as a black man. But he claimed what freedom he had and he chose Cape Palmas. And he told his wife and children that he would do all that he could as a free man in Africa to gain their freedom and bring them out to join him in his new home.[8]

NICHOLAS NOW MOVED rapidly to make the final arrangements with the Maryland board. He sent a check to cover the expenses of the transport of the freed slaves from Baltimore to Harper and enough funds to purchase supplies to last them for six months after their arrival. He purchased clothes and shoes for the emigrants in Savannah, provided them with bedding and other household goods, and had Paul make chests out of white pine boards, so that all of the people would have a way to carry their personal belongings. He booked passage for them on the brig *Opelousas* to carry them in April from Savannah to Baltimore. But as the time approached, Nicholas worried that some would not go. "Efforts have been made," he wrote the Maryland board, "and are still making by the acquaintances (both white and coloured) of these servants to prevent their embarking: with no success as yet that I know of, but the point cannot be fully tested till the last moment." In the end, all but two adults decided to go—Old Toby, who was sick, and Old Lucy, who was blind. Old Toby soon died, and Old Lucy lived out her last days in the quarters behind Nicholas's town home. The rest decided that they were finally strangers, foreigners on Hutchinson Island, who yearned for a homeland where they would be free.[9]

WHILE THOSE IN the settlement were making their decisions, and beginning to gather and pack their few possessions and the supplies Nicholas purchased, Leighton and Jane were becoming increasingly anxious—had they made a terrible decision when they had written Nicholas, encouraging the people of the settlement to join the colonists at Cape Palmas? When they had written the letter, they had thought that Maryland in Liberia was a promising colony. Now, in early 1838, with conditions in the colony rapidly deteriorating, and with their growing antagonism toward Russwurm and their deep doubts about his leadership, they wondered—Were they encouraging people to risk their lives in a floundering little colony with little promise? Moreover, they were becoming increasingly convinced that the colonization of African Americans was at its heart imperialistic. Leighton wrote Rufus Anderson in February 1838 about the impending emancipation and emigration: "We are not elated at the idea of them coming to this country, for we regard the colonization cause as a very doubtful one—yet as it is their choice, and as almost anything is better than indefinite slavery, we do not presume to control their choice." But Leighton had concluded that "if the Dutch Boors and English settlers in South Africa have oppressed and injured the Kaffers and Hottentots, then you may expect the American colonists to carry on the work of oppression here as soon as their numerical strength would warrant, with tenfold fury."[10]

At the same time, Leighton asked Anderson about the two young slaves Leighton had himself inherited. Could they be sent to Boston? Perhaps John, the older of the two, might be apprenticed as a bookbinder or trained in some other mechanical art, with the hope that he might join the mission someday. Thinking Jessie a girl, he asked if some woman in Boston might receive her and educate her. "My only desire," he noted, "is that she may be educated and set free where she would be happy and respectable." And he added, "I know nothing at all about this child," which was obviously true, since Jesse was a little boy. Leighton wrote his father at Pine Grove, telling him what he had written Anderson, and asked him to do what was necessary to have the children sent to Boston. But, he said, "I wish it distinctly understood however that neither of the children are to be removed without both their own and their mother's consent."[11]

Meanwhile, conditions in the colony continued to deteriorate. With food supplies greatly reduced, Russwurm asked Freeman in February 1838 to join him on a visit to the bush to see if provisions could be purchased directly from the interior towns, with their extensive rice fields. With a few other settlers and Big Town Grebo, they hiked to Grand Cavally, King Baphro's town, where they were strongly advised not to try to go up the river. The river Grebo were jealous of their trading privileges with the interior and did not want any competition from Harper or Big Town. Ignoring the advice, the travelers took canoes and headed up the river. They were soon attacked, robbed of all their possessions, stripped of all their clothes, and sent walking back completely naked and humiliated. The whole affair seemed to Leighton but another example of Russwurm's poor judgment and lack of leadership. The year before, Leighton and William Davis had made a trip up the Cavally and had met no hostility from the river Grebo. Russwurm's river fiasco, along with the continuing feud over missionary personnel being required to serve in the colonial militia, was the straw that broke the camel's back for Leighton and Jane. In April 1838, Leighton wrote Nicholas not to send the people to Liberia.[12]

Leighton wrote that he hoped the letter reached Nicholas before the people left Georgia. He assured his brother-in-law that the letter would not have been sent without the weightiest reasons. "Since the election of a colored man to the office of governor of this Colony," Leighton wrote, "and another for Liberia proper, the progress of colonization has been in a rapid and fearful decline; and I look upon it at this moment as on the verge of ruinous precipice." He and Jane had become convinced that "colonization as conducted at present is little else than a system of iniquity and oppression." He thought the colonists at Harper had become idle, vicious, and turbulent, and that they would soon starve to death unless they began to plunder and rob the Grebo. Indeed, he thought such an event probable unless the Grebo united and overwhelmed the colony. He noted that those who had arrived on a recent ship did not have adequate supplies, and that many of them had, according to the colonial physician, died from want of food. Leighton believed "the chief part, if not the whole of these evils, have arisen from the mismanagement and want of principle" on the part of Russwurm. And, he added, "the time has been when I felt that anything was better than unconditional Slavery: but I would now change the tone and say that anything is better than Colonization." He was confident that many colonists, if given the chance, would return to the United States, and he was convinced that if the Bayard people came to Harper, "*poverty, wretchedness, and discontentment* must be their portion." He and Jane believed that Nicholas would be able to find good alternatives to colonization for the emancipated people. If, however, the letter was too late and the people had already sailed, he and Jane, he assured Nicholas, "shall use our best efforts to place them on the best footing out here."[13]

However legitimate Leighton's fears about the deteriorating conditions in Monrovia and Harper, his almost casual comment—"Since the election of a colored man"—revealed a world of racial assumptions—assumptions he had brought with him from Pine Grove and from Union College in New York and from Columbia Theological Seminary in South Carolina. However much he had struggled against those assumptions and however much they had been challenged by his time with the printer James, with Freeman and Ballah and William Davis, old voices still spoke out of deep memories. These voices slipped out in casual comments, especially during times of stress, and let it be known that they would not, could not, be easily silenced. When Leighton wrote Nicolas, the old voices spoke their mind and revealed their power to shape what Leighton saw, to evoke what Leighton felt, and to guide what Leighton did.

IN FACT, THE letter arrived in the United States too late by several months. Early on the morning of April 29, 1838, the newly emancipated people from Hutchinson Island gathered on a Savannah wharf, said their painful goodbyes, and boarded the brig *Opelousas*. Then, when the tide was right and the morning wind was filling the ship's sails, anchors were raised, and the captain edged the ship into the flowing river. They moved with the current as Paul and the others from the settlement stood on deck. They watched as the city began to fade from sight. Savannah's tree-lined parks and slave markets, its sturdy warehouses and soaring church steeples, slowly disappeared into the horizon and drifted into their deep memories. Now the travelers looked out over the passing landscape of marshes and unhurried creeks and saw Tybee Island come into view and then the mouth of the river. Before them lay the rolling Atlantic and the hopes of an old dream—to live a life of freedom on the shores of Mother Africa.[14]

They first spent a week in Baltimore, where for the first time they publicly claimed family names. In Savannah they had had only first names—Paul or Belinda or Jack or Juba, the "servants of" the Bayards. Now they claimed family names and family histories that declared that they were people with their own memories and with their own identities. They listed their names as Adams, Jenkins, and Johnson, as Jackson, Jones, Mumford, and Ward—names that linked them to a more distant past, often to earlier owners who were remembered in secret traditions, and whose names had marked the beginning of an African American family tradition. Paul and his parents and his sister all took the name Sansay, after a white Haitian refugee family in Savannah. No one took the name Bayard, but almost a third took the name McIntosh after the old General. In this way they linked their past and their memories to their future and their hopes as free people.[15]

They sailed from Baltimore on May 15, 1838, on the schooner *Columbia* and arrived at Cape Palmas on July 2. There they passed through the crashing surf in Grebo canoes and, for the first time in their lives—after so many years of waiting and yearning—finally felt the African shore beneath their feet. Here at this place, on this African soil at Cape Palmas, they saw before them in the little town of Harper what they had seen only from afar—a homeland and a place of freedom. What awaited them, however, was not only freedom, but also hard times and a long road into a demanding and uncertain future.[16]

The difficulties they faced became immediately apparent when their supplies were brought off the ship—the pine chests that Paul had made were brought ashore, and their bedding and personal possessions were there, but the supplies that Nicholas had ordered to be purchased in Baltimore were nowhere to be seen. Leighton was furious. He wrote immediately to the Maryland board: "We are utterly at a loss to know what is to become of the new emigrants. The Captain has landed *one barrel* of cornmeal and says that this is all the bread stuff he has on board for them and Mr. Russwurm has not on hand one of rice that he can spare them nor is there any probability so far as I can see that he will be able to procure any for six weeks to come—besides it is a time of an unparalleled scarcity throughout the colony." Mr. Bayard had, Leighton said, sent funds to Baltimore for a six-month food supply, but what had arrived was not enough for ten days. Moreover, Leighton wrote, no provisions had been made for them to have materials for the construction of their houses. Leighton told the Maryland authorities that he was going to purchase the necessary provisions and materials from the first ship that arrived at the Cape. He would give the captain a money order that could be redeemed in Baltimore out of the funds sent by Nicholas. Fortunately—Leighton later regarded it as providential—they had at Fair Hope an extra twenty-five bushels of rice that had been purchased before it had become necessary to reduce the size of the school. Without this, Leighton later wrote Latrobe, "I do not see but they would have suffered extremely."[17]

Russwurm was also distraught. In addition to the lack of provisions, he worried about the composition of the immigrants, in particular the mothers with children who had left their husbands behind in slavery. "Can a woman with 2 or 3 children be expected to maintain herself for the first 2 or 3 years in a new country? An acquaintance with people just emancipated knows that it is with the utmost difficulty that males ever can be driven to make the requisite exertion to maintain themselves—how much greater then the difficulty where you have to deal with females without protectors."[18]

So in this way, under these demanding circumstances, those who had fled Hutchinson Island began their new life of freedom at Cape Palmas on the West African coast. There were thirty-one of them altogether. At Leighton's and Jane's request, they were given land on an island in the slow-flowing Hoffman River immediately north of Harper. Russwurm thought it a poor choice, because it was away from the security of Harper, but the soil was good, and Jane and Leighton evidently thought it wise for the new arrivals to be some distance from what they regarded as the corrupting influences of the older settlers. With Leighton and Jane helping to provide medical attention—they were learning more about how to treat malaria with quinine—the *Columbia* emigrants were, Russwurm wrote, "highly favored" and suffered relatively little from the fever. Two young children died, but in comparison to those who had come out on other ships, the new emigrants were thought healthy.[19]

Regardless of what Russwurm, Leighton, and others thought about the indolence of newly freed slaves, Paul and his father, Charles, began immediately to clear their land. Paul was thirty-five and his father sixty-nine, and they showed in their tough hands and strong bodies the hard labor of their years. They had each been allotted five acres, and the work ahead of them was arduous, but they set to work and cut trees and grubbed up stumps with axes and mattocks. With Paul's mother, Mary, and his sister, Charlotte, they used hoes to turn the land, because they had no mules or oxen to pull plows. And Mary, who was now sixty-six, planted a large garden, just as she had done for so many years on Hutchinson Island. When the building materials that Leighton secured arrived, Paul took them and, using his good skills as a carpenter, began to construct a neat house for himself. Within six months of his arrival, he could write: "I have got my farm partly cleared down and my house twenty by twenty six almost finished." Later, across the little set-tlement road from his house, he built another neat house for his parents and sister, who meanwhile lived with him.[20]

Next to Paul's five acres, John Johnson—he had been the driver on Hutchinson Island—cleared his land and with his wife, Catherine, also began to plant. And, no doubt with Paul's help, he, too, built his house, and he and Catherine began to make a new home for themselves. And so it went as others from the old settlement cleared land and began planting. Some of the women took up spinning. And one young boy became an apprentice to a blacksmith. In this way those who had left Hutchinson Island settled on an island in a West African river and named the place Bayard Island, a reminder—like the name Fair Hope—of a remembered past.[21]

The Savannah immigrants found, however, in their Grebo neighbors other reminders of their past. When Paul and the others heard the Pidgin English of the Grebo, its accents and grammar did not sound strange but familiar to those who were a part of the Gullah people and of a larger Atlantic Creole community. Grebo fetishes were not startling to those who had known the secret charms used in the slave settlements on General's Island and on the surrounding Lowcountry plantations. Grebo funerals, with their drums and gifts of food, china, and cloth, did not appear peculiar or exotic. Grebo fables and proverbs; Grebo witches and Grebo doctors; Grebo rice, benne seed, and okra; Grebo dancing and Grebo music—all no doubt evoked memories of life in the slave settlements of the Georgia Lowcountry. Yet such familiarity did not mean that Paul and the other Savannah immigrants identified, any more than the earlier settlers had, with the Grebo. For all of their familiarity with some aspects of Grebo life, those who moved from Hutchinson Island to Bayard Island saw themselves as African Americans, and not Grebo.[22]

Two weeks after their arrival, the Savannah immigrants made the startling discovery that Mother Africa and her returning children were at one another's throats—open hostilities broke out between the African American settlers and the Grebo. Already tensions had been rising as both sides had been steal-ing sheep and cattle from one another. In a dispute over a sheep, one settler shot a "bush" Grebo, seriously wounding him. Settlers and Grebo from Big Town gathered at the sound of the shot. The wounded man was carried into Harper for treatment. Tensions rose dramatically.[23]

The following night, a fire accidentally broke out in Big Town and with strong winds quickly consumed most of the town. Although no lives were lost and many possessions had been saved, the next morning was filled with confusion and much shouting and searching. In the midst of the confusion, a party of "bush" Grebo came to the home of the settler who had shot their kinsman. They killed him, brutally murdered three of his children, and escaped back into the bush.[24]

Word spread rapidly among the settlers. The militia was called out, led by Charles Snetter. Snetter was regarded as the most competent military leader in the colony, and he quickly led the militia to the edge of town, where the murders had taken place. Some Grebo from Big Town had taken refuge from the fire by running to their farms, and they were now returning. The militia, with no grounds to suspect that the men had anything to do with the murders, fired upon them and bayoneted the men. Two died and another was badly wounded. The Big Town Grebo then came out in force and except for the intervention of Freeman and Russwurm, war seemed inevitable.[25]

Russwurm acted quickly and decisively to calm the waters, convening a court with a handpicked jury. Although most of the settlers regarded Snetter as a hero, the court found that he had acted in a precipitous way in the confusion and excitement of the moment. They turned the case over to Russwurm for disposition. The governor, who had long regarded Snetter as dangerous, banished him from the colony—he was to leave as soon as he could get his affairs in order. With this action and payments to the Grebo, the tensions seemed to ease.[26]

Leighton, disillusioned by the actions of his Charleston friend, dismissed Snetter from his work at Fair Hope. Snetter joined the Methodist Church in Harper—where most of the settlers were members—and began preaching an apocalyptic message about war between the settlers and the Grebo and calling upon the settlers to drive out the Grebo, just like the ancient Israelites had driven the Canaanites from the promised land. "Fire! Fire! Fire from heaven!" he shouted as he went around the colony. Settlers flocked to Snetter's cause. A petition was drawn up denouncing Russwurm and proclaiming that Snetter's impeding banishment was the "first move to give the lives of our wives and Children into the hands of the Savages around us who thirst for our Blood." All of the men from Hutchinson Island sided with Snetter and signed the petition except for Paul and his father.[27]

Russwurm ignored the petition, and when it was posted, he had it removed. "I took no notice of it," Russwurm wrote, "because the whole proceedings from first to last were riotous and contrary to law." As for the colonists, he thought "all are ignorant, but those whose lives have been spent on plantations are deplorably so: they know nothing—and have to learn their social and political alphabet as much as a child does his ABCs." The Maryland board did not respond to the petitioners, by its silence making it clear that Russwurm had the power and support of the white authorities in Baltimore.[28]

In early 1839, Snetter, the former Charleston barber, finally left for Monrovia, where he was soon made captain of the militia's Rifle Corps. In March 1840, he was killed leading an assault against Gatoomba, a king who had been attacking surrounding towns in the interior.[29]

And at Cape Palmas, those who had once lived on Hutchinson Island by the flowing waters of the Savannah began a new life of freedom in an African colony. Now they had to contend with the harsh realities of Cape Palmas—with sickness, and want, and warring peoples.

Chapter Ten

Exploring Strange Worlds

By the time the settlers from Hutchinson Island arrived at Cape Palmas in the summer of 1838, life at Fair Hope had assumed a familiar routine. Leighton and Jane rose early and, after their private devotionals, they held family worship with their sixty boarding students and the printer B. V. R. James—prayers were said, scripture read, and hymns sung. Breakfast followed: a plate of rice and some cold bread. Like the students, Leighton and James ate their rice with some palm oil, what Leighton called African butter. Jane did not use the rich oil—not having acquired a taste for it—but did use molasses on her bread, which had been baked with flour shipped from Philadelphia. Jane then oversaw the students as they washed the dishes and put them away, Leighton did his morning exercises, and James prepared for his work at the printing press. At nine o'clock, Jane began her class with the students, while Leighton was joined by his Grebo teacher, William Davis, who was leading him into the intricacies of the Grebo language.[1]

At noon, dinner was served in Lowcountry fashion—vegetables from the garden that Leighton had started, rice, some corned beef or ham brought across Atlantic highways in barrels, or perhaps fresh fish or chicken, or occasionally the meat of a sheep or goat or slaughtered bullock. Much of this was familiar to the Wilsons. In the Lowcountry, rice had been a staple of their diets—they had eaten it at breakfast with eggs and topped with a little butter; at dinner, they had enjoyed it as a *pilau* with shrimp, or as a *bog* with chicken or steaming with a gravy; and at tea they had eaten it in a cake or pudding, all reflecting an African heritage in a rice-dominated Lowcountry cuisine.[2]

Many of the vegetables from Leighton's garden they had known at Pine Grove or Fair Hope plantation, and James had no doubt known most of them in his New York home. Leighton was proud of his garden, which he worked daily—he later claimed it was the best in Liberia—and it yielded year-round supplies of cabbages, tomatoes, okra, onions, beets, squash, guinea squash (eggplant), cucumbers, melons, corn, peas, sweet potatoes, and beans. With the regular flow of the vegetables into the kitchen, the costs for the boarding school were substantially reduced.[3]

An American woman from Harper was employed to cook meals at Fair Hope, and she prepared the food as it might have been prepared by the waters of the Black River or Savannah—a little salt pork with the vegetables, okra to make a thick gumbo, and sweet potatoes baked before a fire. The sight, aroma, and taste of such food no doubt evoked for the Americans deep memories of family and friends, of particular places and scenes of tables spread and meals shared.

But there were also unfamiliar foods that were beginning to find a place on the dinner table at Fair Hope—tropical fruits and palm oil, leafy green callalou, and, above all, cassava. This starchy, tuberous root had made its way generations earlier across the Atlantic highways from South America to become a staple of West African peoples. The Grebo pounded the root in a mortar and made it into a dough, which they rolled into a ball and dipped into a pungent, peppery soup seasoned with the region's famous melegueta pepper. A Grebo cook who helped with the preparation of meals for the growing number of schoolchildren brought the traditions of Grebo food preparation to the meals served at Fair Hope and no doubt helped to introduce a West African cuisine to Jane, Leighton, and James. The dinner table thus became not only a time evoking memories of distant homes, but also a time for the Americans to explore the world of the Grebo through their senses of smell and taste. As they bit into and felt in their mouths the textures and flavors of Grebo food, prepared in Grebo fashion, they had a taste of another culture that was for them a strange world. And they experienced as well an intimate encounter with physical elements of a West African environment—the fruits of its fields, gardens, and forests—mediated to them through the art of Grebo cuisine.[4]

King Freeman enjoyed joining them for the noontime dinner and was a frequent visitor at Fair Hope. He and his brother William Davis, together with Ballah, would sit at the table, and after Leighton had said a prayer of thanksgiving, they all ate the food placed before them. Some of what was spread on the table was familiar to the three men and to the schoolchildren who ate nearby: rice and okra and eggplant as well as palm oil and cassava. But there were also new items for them to taste and eat—at least items not regularly eaten by the Grebo: hams shipped from New York and Philadelphia, salt fish from Boston, corned beef from Baltimore, tea and coffee, and beets and cabbages and peas and beans distinctive to North America. So the Grebo who ate at Fair Hope were also exploring strange worlds. They were encountering products of a North American environment mediated through the practices and cuisine brought from distant places.

Freeman had learned shortly after the establishment of Fair Hope that if he wanted to eat at Jane's dinner table, he had to dress for dinner. This meant that the simple piece of cloth around his waist was not enough, and he had to put on a shirt and pants and sometimes a black coat and his favorite hat. And for all three men, there were questions of table manners. How do you eat at a table furnished in Western style with a knife, fork, and spoon? They were used to eating not at set times but when they were hungry, not at a table but seated on the ground.[5]

The eating customs of the Grebo, it was plain for all to see, were not the customs of the settlers. Leighton described what he observed when visiting in Big Town. After the men carefully washed, a Grebo woman put before them a large wooden bowl of rice whose preparation had been carried to what Leighton called "the highest perfection." She then poured over and mixed into the rice some fragrant palm oil. When all was ready, each man thrust his hand into the mixture, took up some rice, rolled it into a ball, threw back his head, popped the ball into his mouth, and then, with little chewing, swallowed the rice. Sometimes there was meat—beef, mutton, chicken or duck, fish, shellfish, or game of some kind, "from the leopard to the wood-rat." But the Grebo used meat sparingly, and when they did it was generally served in soups or stews seasoned with pungent, spicy peppers.[6]

For Freeman and other Grebo to eat at the table at Fair Hope consequently provided an experience of a distant, powerful culture. When they had first encountered forks, the men had been uncertain about how to use them and had watched carefully to see what strange ritual or practice was involved. When Jane and Leighton, for their part, each picked up a fork in a natural and unconscious manner; held it properly, as they had been taught in Savannah or Pine Grove; and used it to eat cabbage or a slice of ham, they were showing how deeply they identified with a distant culture and an elite class within that culture. And they, together with James, were also showing their Grebo guests a cultural tradition that was fast intruding into Grebo ways.[7]

Yet, in spite of all the cultural distinctions that asserted themselves when they sat down together, a bond was being created around the table at Fair Hope. Leighton, Jane, and James were eating with Freeman, Ballah, and Davis—and the simple physical act of breaking bread (or cassava) together, and talking together over food, drew them closer to one another and into a deeper recognition of their shared humanity. Such regular experiences were not unimportant when tension rose at Cape Palmas and when goodwill played its part in settling disputes.[8]

For a variety of reasons, however, Governor Russwurm was seldom a part of these shared meals at Fair Hope; nor was he often the host for such meals at the governor's home. In some ways, the distance between Fair Hope and Harper seemed greater than the distance between Big Town and Fair Hope, and the greater distance seemed to flow, perhaps ironically, from a shared history. Although James and the Wilsons ate together every day, Russwurm—a proud, reserved black governor from New York—and the white missionaries from South Carolina and Georgia did not find it easy to break bread together.

After dinner, the Wilsons read to one another for an hour, then Jane returned to her class and Leighton wrote, attended to the secular matters of the mission, and worked in the garden. James had his work with the press. At 4:30, Leighton and Jane took a long walk on the beach, where they gathered shells to send home to friends, discussed the events of the day, and listened to the steady thunder of the surf. Tea was at six, and afterward they assembled their students for devotionals and then conversation together.

Jane now had in the school not only Grebo but also some African American students, whom she was training to be teachers. The missionaries hoped that as the students studied together and learned from one another, the school would become a means of bridging some of the distance between the Grebo and the settlers. So Jane had their American students learning Grebo, and the Grebo students learning English. When they gathered in the evening, the Americans, Leighton wrote, were required to speak a sentence in Grebo, and each of the Grebo students spoke one in English. Every sentence, he noted, "is analyzed and understood by all present. We are by this amused as well as instructed; and I trust that this acquisition will be devoted to the glory of God." Evening devotions followed, then James went to his lodging, and Leighton and Jane had their quiet time together on the piazza to enjoy the night wind, to watch the slow dimming of the fires at Big Town, and to talk together beneath the beauty of the African sky.[9]

BY THE TIME the settlers from Hutchinson Island arrived at the Cape, several mission schools were flourishing. At Fair Hope, a school building had been erected on the far side of the garden, and day schools had been established at Rock Town and at Graway on the eastern end of Lake Sheppard. At Rock

Town, a young African American named William Polk was living and teaching, under arrangements that Leighton had negotiated during several visits to the town. At Graway, where Yellow Will was king, John Banks was the teacher. Yellow Will, a young man of about twenty-five, had already worked on the island of Fernando Po, hundreds of miles southeast of the Cape, where he had been the head of the Africans employed by the English. Like William Davis, Yellow Will was a Grebo who had already encountered the strange ways of Europeans and Americans. Banks, a native of Baltimore, had immigrated as a young boy to Monrovia in 1831. He had come to Harper as Dr. Hall's house servant and assistant in 1834. When Fair Hope was established, Hall placed him under Leighton's care to be educated as a teacher. A year and a half later, he and Leighton went to Graway to talk with Yellow Will about starting a school. Yellow Will, welcoming the idea, summoned all hands to work, and in twenty-four hours a comfortable new house for the teacher stood in an enclosed yard. None of those involved could have imagined the impact that a graduate of this little school would one day have on the religious life of West Africa.[10]

Unlike later boarding schools among Native Americans and Australian aboriginal people, which were linked to the power of the state, Grebo children were not forcefully removed from their families and placed in schools in the name of assimilation. Rather, Grebo parents, who had been interested from the first in having their children taught by the missionaries, were enthusiastic supporters of the schools, especially when they saw their children learning the mysteries of reading and writing. Soon, parents from surrounding villages and towns began bringing their children to Fair Hope, urging the Wilsons to admit them, but most had to be turned away for lack of room—a disappointing experience for the parents, and difficult reminders to Leighton and Jane of their limited resources.[11]

Jane was the heart of the school at Fair Hope, shaping its character and overseeing the details of its daily life. She used the "Lancastrian System," where the more advanced students helped to teach the less advanced ones—a method that not only provided more individual attention than Jane could have given to each student, but also helped the more advanced students advance even more. It was a system that assumed that the one who teaches learns.

With the exception of the young settlers who were being trained to be teachers, all of the students at Fair Hope were Grebo. They began their lessons with reading and writing, utilizing a Grebo primer that Leighton had written and James had printed. They were also introduced to English grammar and European history, and they had regular lessons in mathematics, natural science, and astronomy. Geography was popular—they had class-room globes and could find on them Cape Palmas and Maryland and England, see their relationships to each other, and see the continents and the oceans and the great expanse of Africa's interior. Leighton ordered books from America that Jane wanted to use in class—a dozen of Peter Parley's popular geography for children and of J. L. Comstock's *Youth's Book of Astronomy*; two dozen copies of Frances Fellows's *Astronomy for Beginners*; Miss Mary S. Swift's *Natural Philosophy*; Euclid's *Geometry*; and after a few years, for more advanced students, Ebenezer Porter's *Rhetorical Reader*. They soon had a telescope sent out from Boston so they could look at the craters on the moon, peer at the wonders of an African night sky, and learn that the earth circles the sun. They had a prism to see the colors of the rainbow, and Jane had a bell that announced a regular schedule and the rhythm of a clock. In all of this they were exploring new worlds and being taught new ways of seeing and experiencing the world around them, even as they were having old knowledge and old ways challenged. Once they saw Cape Palmas on a globe, once they learned of the Copernican Revolution, once they studied European history and natural science, their Grebo world was never the same for them. It was not, of course, that the traditions and ways of their people had no more power in their lives—the students were not passive, as if Jane and other teachers were simply pouring Western knowledge and ways into their heads. Rather, they were active interpreters of what they were being taught. Nevertheless, their Grebo world was being transformed by their school experience, even as the Western world they were studying was being interpreted by their experience as members of the Grebo community. They soon found themselves in the awkward position of having one foot in one world and one foot in another, and not being fully at home in either.[12]

At first the school at Fair Hope focused almost exclusively on boys—a dormitory had been built for them—but a few girls, such as William Davis's daughter, Mary Clealand, had also been admitted. The Grebo children under Jane's care were boarding students, as Leighton and Jane hoped to immerse them in the cultural traditions of Western Christianity. Their religious beliefs, their dispositions, their assumptions—all were to be shaped by the spirit and routines of Fair Hope. To lodge such beliefs and dispositions at the deepest level of their hearts and minds, the students needed to be removed, the missionaries were convinced, from the competing influences of Grebo culture in Big Town and its surrounding hinterlands. By establishing a boarding school at Fair Hope, they were drawing on a familiar strategy of Protestant missions worldwide, for they believed that it was only through such acculturation that a native ministry could be raised up and indigenous churches established. The Grebo parents, of course, were not unaware of what was happening in the school, but for their own varied reasons, many brought their children to Fair Hope and placed them under the care of the young missionary couple.[13]

Among the boys, Jane's most promising student was Wasa Baker. His father, a headman in Big Town, had brought him to Fair Hope as soon as the school was opened. Bright, articulate, with a ready smile and winsome ways, Wasa quickly won Leighton's and Jane's admiration and affection. He already spoke a Creole English when he came to the mission as a young teenager, so for a while, when Ballah was in Baltimore, he served as Leighton's translator. Leighton found him "a most amiable and worthy boy."[14]

As Wasa grew accustomed to the routines at Fair Hope and experienced Jane's quiet and kind ways, he slowly began to feel that it was his home. He loved to sing hymns, and he listened carefully to the Bible stories being taught and to the messages of Leighton's sermons on Sundays. As he became more at home at Fair Hope, he found that the mission and its church were becoming a new family for him as he began to develop a sense of identity as a Christian, with new assumptions and values. Still, he kept his Grebo name, Wasa, even as he accepted an English family name, Baker.[15]

After Wasa had been at the school for about eighteen months, he went one day to Leighton's study, taking with him a girl who was completely naked. In his Creole English, Wasa asked, "Misser Wilson, how you like disher gal?" Leighton responded, "Very well," and asked him what he meant. Wasa explained that her father wished to betroth her to him, and that if the Wilsons would take her, "learn her book and all Merica fash, my heart be very glad for dat palavar; for," he said, "bymby I be proper Merica man myself, den I no want dese here woman for my wife, cause he no sabby anything but for bring water and wood." Leighton told him they would take her if her father would request it, but that they "would not recognize any right on his part to control her, and would allow no connection between him and her until she became marriageable according to American usages." In addition, Wasa must also pledge himself never to have more than one wife. Wasa, eager to be a "proper Merica man," agreed to it all, as did the girl's father, and Leighton and Jane took the girl into their school family. They gave her the English name Maria, and she soon joined Mary Clealand and a few other girls at Fair Hope.[16]

Leighton and Jane were coming to the conclusion that they needed to make the education of girls a more formal part of the mission. The boys they were educating to become teachers would eventually need wives who could do more than "bring water and wood," as Wasa had put it. Young Grebo men who converted to Christianity needed Christian helpmates who would be fully a part of the mission effort. Moreover, the Wilsons came to believe that the education of Grebo girls was an important means of improving the relationship between the settlers and the Grebo. Leighton wrote the board in Boston that he and Jane had become convinced that colonization would be a deep and lasting curse to Africa unless there was a free amalgamation of African Americans and the Grebo. The colonists, he reminded the board, were bitterly prejudiced against the Grebo, and he thought they would remain so until the Grebo were raised, through religion and education, to equality with the African Americans. When settlers found Grebo men and women who were Christians and educated, then their prejudices against them would be mitigated, and the two peoples could begin to live together in peace as one community. He did not say, of course, whether he thought this same process would work with whites and African Americans in Savannah or along the Black River.[17]

One of the first things Jane had to do for Maria was provide her with some clothes. During her time at the Cape, Jane had grown accustomed to seeing not only naked children but also nearly naked men and women—and sometimes completely naked adults when they were bathing and swimming. For a Bayard woman raised in Savannah and Philadelphia, the sight of a Grebo man coming naked out of the surf, or of a naked Grebo woman bathing in the ocean, must have been startling at first. To be sure, Jane as a young white woman was at ease being surrounded by the Grebo—their dark complexions and numbers did not seem strange or threatening for one who had spent so much time among the Gullah at Fair Hope plantation and in Savannah. Unlike so many whites, she was not frightened or repulsed by black bodies. But the sheer physical reality of a naked body—with all of its emotional and inevitable sexual power for those who were accustomed to seeing only fully clothed men and women in public—must have been disquieting for Jane. What did she think when she saw these African bodies, these Grebo men and women famous for their handsome physiques? Whatever she thought, both she and Leighton were discovering that naked African bodies, like naked European bodies, came in all sizes and shapes, showed the inevitable marks of time, and exhibited the peculiarities of personal experience. Grebo bodies, no less than Grebo personalities, were varied. At any rate, Jane quickly adopted a kind of practicality about this aspect of Grebo culture and made little note of it. She did, however, have her expectations about dress at Fair Hope—as Freeman had experienced—and she insisted that her younger students always wear, in Grebo fashion, a single piece of cloth around their bodies, while the more advanced students began to adopt some aspects of Western dress.[18]

Shortly before Wasa brought Maria to Leighton, Margaret Strobel and her daughter, Catherine, returned to Fair Hope. The little school that Margaret had been running in Harper had been taken over by an African American Methodist minister—most of the settler children were Methodist—and Leighton had not objected. So Leighton had a small cottage built for the mother and daughter at Fair Hope, and Catherine joined Jane as a teacher in the boarding school. Margaret once again took up the vocation she had practiced in Savannah, becoming a seamstress. In this way, the mission was able to provide, along with food, clothing for all the Grebo students.[19]

The Wilsons did not intend to teach adult Grebo. The young couple thought the habits, temperaments, and ways of thinking among adults had been so deeply embedded since childhood that Jane's limited resources and energy could best be focused on teaching children. Adults, they hoped, could be reached through Leighton's preaching, once he learned enough of the Grebo language to undertake such a daunting task. But when Simleh Ballah and William Davis came to Leighton and asked to be taught to read and write in English, he and Jane thought they could not turn them down. Both men had spent time as Leighton's teacher, translator, and interpreter and had explained to him much about Grebo ways. So Leighton, in a spirit of mutuality, took on the responsibility of being their teacher, even as he remained their student—and they became his students, even as they remained his teachers.[20]

Both men impressed Leighton with their quick minds, but he was amazed by William Davis. On the day Davis began his lessons, he came into Leighton's study with his daughter, Mary Clealand. Sitting on her father's lap, she began to teach him the English alphabet. "In half an hour from the time the book was first opened to him," Leighton reported, "and having no other teacher than his own child, he *thoroughly* learned every character in the Alphabet. And in less than six months he could not only read, but wrote an intelligible note." Leighton, thinking no doubt of the trouble he was having learning Grebo, wrote Rufus Anderson, saying that Davis's "progress in learning so far is *unequalled* by anything I have ever known either in America or Africa." In a letter to the Johns Island Presbyterian Church, where Sunday by Sunday a small group of wealthy South Carolina slave owners gathered with their slaves to worship, Leighton wrote about Jane's students. "The progress of the children," he insisted, "in learning I would not say is *good* but *extraordinary*. A large proportion of the boys and girls can read the English testament with as much ease and facility as the children of similar ages and advantages in any school in the world. I am aware that many persons regard the inhabitants of Africa as a *stupid, dull race* of men, but I feel confident no one would who would look into the progress of these children." He then told the white Carolinians about Davis and his accomplishments and intellectual gifts. In this way Leighton found that the students at Fair Hope, whatever their ages, served to challenge deeply entrenched stereotypes and to refute claims that mission work among Africans was well-meaning but naive—an effort to reach those who were incapable of understanding or internalizing the Christian gospel. Leighton and Jane hoped and prayed that their work and their reports would stir the hearts and imaginations of those at home and kindle within some the courage to follow an ocean highway to Cape Palmas.[21]

SO THE WORK at Fair Hope was going forward, not only in the schools, but in other areas as well—even with the mission's restricted resources. Perhaps most remarkable was the work of the newly established press and of the African American printer B. V. R. James. Before James arrived in late 1836, Leighton and Jane had already discovered that the English alphabet contained some letters whose sounds were not used in Grebo—c, j, q, v, x, and z. They had also found that they needed some simple and suitable characters to denote Grebo sounds that were not contained in the English alphabet. But because there was no single way of ascribing a letter of the alphabet to an individual sound in the Grebo language, difficult decisions had to be made. Using the orthography developed by John Pickering for American Indian languages, Leighton had transcribed individual sounds in the Grebo language into Latin characters with a distinct Grebo alphabet, then ordered the necessary fonts for the press from Boston.[22]

With the proper materials in hand, James began to print an amazing number of books and pamphlets. In March 1839, the mission at Fair Hope reported what had been printed during the previous year. In 1838, James had printed 1,500 copies of a twenty-page Grebo "First Reading Book"; 1,370 copies of a Grebo vocabulary and dictionary; 382 copies of a Grebo grammar; and 600 copies each of pamphlets on "The Story of Joseph" and the Gospel of John. In addition to several thousand copies of other pamphlets, the Gospel of Matthew had been translated into Grebo, and 1,720 copies had been printed. Altogether, James had printed 181,532 pages in one year.

He had also started printing materials for the Episcopal mission at Cape Palmas and the Baptist mission at Basa Cove on the Liberian coast. The missionaries clearly hoped that literacy would flow rapidly from mission schools and that reading and writing would help to spread new information and perspectives. But literacy would also challenge older ways of remembering and the authority of old traditions.[23]

Leighton, in conversation with Jane and James, had to make decisions about what to print and in what order. Most critical was the decision to translate parts of the Bible from the Greek and publish them in Grebo. First came the Gospel of Matthew, and shortly thereafter the Acts of the Apostles. To undertake such translations and publications was a daunting task, and it involved critical judgments. The three missionaries at Fair Hope were committed to raising up a Grebo church as quickly as possible, and they envisioned it having Grebo leaders and a Grebo Bible. In this they were reflecting the broad commitments of the Protestant mission movement as well as the particular commitments of the American Board. But what books of the Bible to translate first? Should they start with Genesis or maybe Psalms, or what about Paul's Letter to the Romans? What was the best starting point for the Grebo journey into the strange world of the Bible? The missionaries apparently decided on Matthew and Acts because they believed that these two books conveyed the story of early Christianity and the essential message of the gospel in the most accessible possible way for the Grebo.[24]

Matthew begins with a genealogy and is marked by vivid stories and parables—the birth of Jesus and the visit of the Wise Men; the devil tempting Jesus in the wilderness; the Sermon on the Mount; the Lord's Prayer; the sick and the blind being healed and demons being cast out of afflicted people; the feeding of the 5,000; a parable about seeds and a sower; and the story of the Last Supper, of Jesus being betrayed and crucified, and of his resurrection from the dead. Acts provides the earliest history of the church and its missionary efforts, but it, too, contains memorable stories: the lame being healed, Stephen being stoned to death, the conversion of an African and other gentiles, Paul's conversion, exorcisms of demons, Peter breaking out of prison with the help of an angel, and Paul being shipwrecked.

These stories were well received by the Grebo, who were themselves great storytellers. They believed in the power of words and were concerned about healing and malevolent forces in their world. And the Grebo learned in Acts that the Greeks and Romans did not have to become Jews to be Christians, that they did not have to renounce most of their old culture to be followers of Jesus. They heard Paul announce to the Athenians that he had noticed that they had an altar "to an unknown god," and that he had come to tell them of the One whom they had been seeking.[25]

With these two books and their vivid stories, the Grebo encountered a Christian message that addressed important aspects of their everyday life. And they encountered a religious faith that seemed to allow them to add new beliefs and practices onto many of their traditional ways, which did not have to be discarded in order for them to become Christian. In this way, Matthew and Acts provided pivotal and foundational stories for an emerging Grebo Christianity; in time, as Christianity expanded rapidly across the continent, they became favorite books of the Bible across Africa.[26]

Leighton, of course, did not translate these books or write a Grebo grammar and dictionary on his own. First, Simleh Ballah was his Grebo translator and teacher, and then, for a short while, Wasa Baker, but it was Mworeh Mah—William Davis—who worked with him most intensely and for the longest time. Davis thus played a key role in what poured from James's press. Translation was a complicated process of reciprocity between missionary and Grebo teacher. What Grebo word was to be used for "God"? Could a Grebo deity's name be used? What about the word for "soul" or "righteousness," "sin" or "love"? What Grebo language was to be used to describe Jesus rising from the dead? Great care had to be taken, and Davis was no passive participant in the process. He spent long hours and several years with Leighton teaching him about the nuances of Grebo language and culture. In this way, the gospel stories began to be more than foreign imports by missionaries, or the reflection of some cultural imperialism—they began to be indigenized by Davis and other translators, and through them the gospel stories were carried by Grebo words and grammar deep into Grebo culture.[27]

Leighton did not fully realize it at the time, but by translating the biblical stories, he was setting the stories free from his control—the Bible was on its way to becoming a Grebo Bible. As the Grebo began their move from being an oral culture to a literate culture, first Matthew and Acts and then other biblical books carried great symbolic power and authority as written texts. Leighton himself found that the word "book" was a symbol of intelligence among Africans, and he once recounted an African fable that attributed the power of whites to their possession of the arts of reading and writing. Consequently, when literate Grebo began reading aloud from the Grebo Bible in Grebo towns and villages, it seemed an almost miraculous phenomenon that demonstrated a marvelous new power. A new divine word was coming to them in their own language, making the Grebo tongue, the vernacular language of the people, the bearer of the divine. Yet, because this new divine word was coming to them in their own language, the word was not simply new, but also old. A pre-Christian past with its religious life was being embedded in a Grebo Christianity through the conventions of speech. And the Grebo, like other peoples before and after them, began to identify with the people and stories of the Bible and to claim the Bible's message for themselves.[28]

Even the operation of the printing press itself was beginning to pass into Grebo hands. Shortly after James arrived, two young Grebo men from the school at Fair Hope—both recently converted to Christianity—became his apprentices. One, Francis Allison, was soon sent to New York to learn book-binding as a part of the mission strategy of the American Board. The board, wrote Rufus Anderson, wanted indigenous people around the world who were trained in the art of printing wherever the mission had presses. The hope was that gradually the books written by missionaries and the scriptures translated by missionaries would be replaced by those which were written, translated, and printed by indigenous peoples. The goal was to encourage Grebo and other indigenous authors and to incite their literary labors through the activity of their own presses.[29]

WITH THE APPRENTICES helping with his printing responsibilities, James was able to give some of his time to teaching at Fair Hope. He quickly established himself as a gifted teacher and won the affection and admiration of his students. Leighton and Jane greatly admired him and were secretly pleased when James began showing some romantic interest in Catherine Strobel. Catherine had been a young girl when she and her mother had lived in Savannah, and she had only fading memories of life in Georgia. She had quickly become bilingual after they had arrived at Cape Palmas. By early 1839, she was a bright and attractive nineteen-year-old. Both Leighton and Jane admired her and enjoyed her company. James, who was twenty-five at the time, was apparently as inept in courting her, however, as Leighton had been with Margaret Adger in Charleston, and he was soon to find himself in an awkward situation.

James and Catherine were both living at the mission, teaching at the mission, and having their meals at the mission with Leighton and Jane. But so was Catherine's mother. Leighton, who was largely oblivious to such matters, was apparently warned by Jane that Margaret, who was thirty-five, was taking an interest in James. So daughter and mother soon began to compete for James's attention. Leighton tried to warn James about "being entrapped by the mother while he was seeking the hand of the daughter." Although Leighton worked well with Margaret, he and Jane thought her a much less attractive person than her daughter—they did not think they could always rely on her and found her fickle and preoccupied with herself. Moreover, wrote Leighton, "she renders herself personally offensive by the free use of tobacco"—she liked her pipe and snuff and simply ignored the Wilsons' objections.[30]

When Leighton talked to James about Margaret, James seemed surprised and assured Leighton that she would be the last person in the world that he would think of marrying. But perhaps the suggestion caused James to take note of the mother, for shortly thereafter, James announced that they were engaged. The Wilsons were obviously disappointed in his choice. Leighton wrote Anderson: "Mr. James has been exemplary in a very remarkable degree for piety, industry, and devotion to the missionary work, and there is scarcely an individual of his acquaintance who has not loved and esteemed him." When Leighton and Jane had learned of the engagement, Leighton wrote, matters had gone so far that they did not feel that they could express any reservation. "We had no right and we felt no inclination to interfere," Leighton said, and so they tried to be supportive in the face of the announced engagement. "We therefore showed them," he told Anderson, "all the attention on the occasion of the marriage which the circumstances of the case and Christian propriety would allow."[31]

Leighton had a house built for them at Fair Hope of approximately the same size and design as his and Jane's, and he recommended that his own annual salary be reduced from $500 to $400 so that James, as a married man, might receive the same amount as Leighton. As for Catherine, she was left feeling very little respect for James, and Leighton feared she would become a thorn in James's side. She apparently lived with the Wilsons for a while before moving in with her mother and new stepfather, reconciling herself to the marriage. They became a family of three, and in four years, when Margaret had a child, Catherine became a loving aunt. She never married, and the Wilsons' fears never materialized. The James/Strobel family settled down to a long, happy, and influential life together as missionaries on the coast of West Africa. And James and Paul Sansay became friends, and during the coming years, the printer from New York and the carpenter from Savannah worked together to build up what they increasingly regarded as their African homeland.[32]

Chapter Eleven

The Conversion of William Davis
(Mworeh Mah)

Tensions, perhaps inevitably, continued to build between the mission at Fair Hope and the colony at Harper, between the white Wilsons from Georgia and South Carolina and the African American settlers seeking to escape American racism and the bitter legacies of slavery. In the midst of these tensions stood not only Big Town and the surrounding Grebo people but also the African Americans—especially B. V. R. James—who were a part of the mission and deeply committed to its life and purposes.

For his part, Leighton thought that his early fears were being realized—that the proximity of the mission to the colony had turned out to be an impediment to the work at Fair Hope. The disdain the colonists had for the Grebo, their imperialistic intentions toward Grebo land, and their readiness to go to war with the Grebo were not just distractions; they were a genuine threat to the work at Fair Hope and the other recently established schools in neighboring towns. Leighton consequently began to look around and to wonder: Did they need to give up all the work they had done at Fair Hope and all their study of the Grebo language and culture, to abandon the Grebo of Cape Palmas, and establish a new mission far from the influence of the African American colonists and their white sponsors in Baltimore? It increasingly seemed to Leighton a bitter and infuriating necessity.

Yet from the outset, Fair Hope had been considered a launching spot for missions to the interior and to the large populations known to exist in many other parts of West Africa. Leighton's explorations in 1835 and 1836 had been early attempts to get some idea of the countryside and the people who lived beyond the immediate vicinity of the Cape. In the spring of 1837, however, he made his most extensive exploration of the interior in the hope of finding in the fabled Kong Mountains some suitable location far beyond the influence of the colonial settlement.[1]

With William Davis as his guide and interpreter and several other Grebo men as companions and porters, Leighton set out for the Pah country far up the Cavally River. The Pah, reported to be a numerous people, were said to live in the Kong Mountains—those distant peaks that Leighton and Simleh Ballah had seen on their excursion to Bolobo. Leighton now hoped to find on their high slopes a promising land far from settlers that might have a healthier landscape than the coastal regions with their mangrove swamps and miasmas.[2]

The travelers spent their first night at Grand Cavally near the mouth of the river. King Baphro provided them with lodging, but Leighton found himself sharing quarters with a Portuguese slaver employed by none other than Pedro Blanco. The man was trading rum for rice in order to secure provisions for Blanco's slave ships—he told Leighton, to the missionary's astonishment, that the ships numbered almost a hundred. Leighton was troubled by finding a slave trader at Grand Cavally, and the slaver himself must have been less than happy to find a well-known American missionary as his roommate for the night. "Our meeting," Leighton noted, "was not very cordial."[3]

What was particularly distressing for Leighton was that Baphro was trading with the man. But Baphro was following an old practice. The European and American captains of slave ships had to keep their wretched captives alive during the long transatlantic passages, and the Grebo and other people along the coast had sold rice and various provisions to them for generations. The agricultural skill and prowess of Africans had consequently helped to fuel, in a bitter irony, the international slave trade. Moreover, by trading New England rum for Baphro's rice, Leighton thought the slaver was inflicting curse upon curse. It all seemed a vicious circle, for the rum was addictive, and its widespread use, Leighton was convinced, led to a growing decadence, to sickness, and to the impoverishment of coastal communities. He talked to the man and tried to show him the wickedness of the business in which he was engaged, but to no avail—the rice was secured and the rum traded.[4]

The next day, Leighton and his companions set off up the river in several large canoes. Baphro had recently concluded a treaty with the Pah that encouraged trade between the interior and the coast, and the travelers were hopeful that the treaty would help to ease their way into Pah country. Leighton also made clear that he was not interested in trade; thus, they avoided the hostility that greeted those trying to establish new trading patterns.

About twenty miles from the coast, Leighton and his companions passed one of the most sacred places of the region—Haidee, the home of the "Grand Devil Oracle." They found a group of pilgrims there who were from Cape Lahu, far to the south on the Ivory Coast—they had come, like ancient Greek pilgrims to Delphi, to hear from the priests and to learn the wisdom of the oracle. The pilgrims had brought sacrifices and offerings and heard a strange echo at the mouth of the Haidee cave as the priests spoke into the cave's recesses and the echoing voice gave answers to their questions.[5]

The travelers from Cape Palmas quickly passed this sacred place and its pilgrims and pushed up the river to Denah, the place where Leighton and Davis had been so warmly welcomed in 1836 by King Neh. Arriving in the evening, they found that the old king had lost his favorite wife, the one whom Leighton had so admired, and with whom the king had had such an affectionate and mutually respectful relationship. The grieving Neh was in great distress and even seemed to Leighton to be deranged. Neh's once prosperous and happy home was now in great disarray and filled with melancholy, and Leighton felt the deep sadness of the scene.

The travelers spent the night in Denah, but rather than linger for a day, as Leighton had intended, they left the old king and his town early the following morning. For the next several days, the travelers continued up the river, spending their nights in different villages and receiving everywhere an enthusiastic welcome.

In one village they met a headman from Pah whose short stature, fine physique, and courtly manners convinced Leighton that the Pah were a people entirely distinct from those along the seacoast. Leighton had bowed to him as he ascended the hill to the village, and the Pah, Leighton noted in his journal, "returned the compliment with as much grace and ease as if he had spent all of his days in the most refined and polished society." The encounter made Leighton more eager than ever to reach the Pah country, so they hurried on, leaving the river and turning north to travel through country where the people had never before seen a white man.[6]

As the travelers approached a village or town, the people seemed astonished and with much commotion ran toward the strangers, leaping and shouting and impeding their way until Leighton stopped and turned toward them to satisfy their curiosity. As the travelers moved further away from the river, Davis and the other Grebo began to regale Leighton with Grebo stories and fables and to entertain themselves with Grebo jokes. Now, with his comrades, Davis was Mworeh Mah the Grebo, remembering and delighting in the traditions and culture of his people as he teased Leighton with the complex meaning of seemingly simple stories and amusing fables and the distinctive humor of Grebo jokes. Leighton enjoyed this part of the trip greatly and the glimpses it provided into deep parts of Grebo life. Later he wrote of the astonishing number of Grebo fables and their importance for the Grebo people.[7]

The travelers, following a beautiful stream, entered a forest of enormous trees and climbed mountains whose grand vistas reminded Leighton of the Catskills he had seen as a college student. After several days of travel, they finally reached Grabbo, the head town of the Yabo people. They immediately noticed that the town lacked the neatness of the earlier towns they had passed through, and that the people did not flock around them or give them a warm welcome. More ominous still, the entrance to the town was marked by human skulls, and they remembered that they had been told that the Yabo were cannibals. Leighton had not been alarmed by this report, since it was a common ploy for those on the coast and along the river to say this about inland villages. Eager to keep their trading privileges with the interior, traders spread the rumors of cannibalism in an effort to frighten anyone seeking contacts that bypassed established trading patterns. However, as Leighton entered the town and looked around Grabbo at the hanging skulls—what he called "trophies of their skill and power"—he saw evidence of their cruelty and ferocity, and confirmation, he believed, of the reports of their cannibalism.[8]

Leighton gave presents to the Yabo and told the people he was a man of God and not a trader; they seemed pleased and gave the travelers a house for the night. As the tired travelers sought refuge in the house, the people came crowding around so that Leighton and the others felt almost suffocated, as if the circulation of air was cut off in the stifling heat. Then, in midst of this crowd, Leighton and several others were struck by "bilious fever," with severe diarrhea and nausea. The palaver drums began to beat and a noisy assembly was convened that lasted through the night. The next morning Leighton was extremely weak; at one point he collapsed under a tree. People pushed close to see the strange white man, and Leighton, thinking that he would die there, fell asleep. For a while it appeared the Yabo would not let the travelers leave, but finally, through the efforts of Davis and a man sent along by Baphro, and because of their fear of the Pah, they allowed them to depart.

Now began an excruciating trip back toward the river. The afflicted could walk only a short distance before they collapsed, and only with great difficulty did they arouse themselves to stumble forward. They took several wrong turns but eventually reached a friendly village, where they rested and tried to recuperate. During the next few days, with the help of other villages and with Davis's leadership, they struggled on, and finally they made their way back to the river. Davis, after some hard negotiations, secured canoes for the trip down river to Grand Cavally, and from there they made their way along the beach to Fair Hope and Harper.

Leighton came away from the trip feeling that their lives had been providentially saved, but their failure to reach Pah country and the painful difficulties they had encountered meant that hopes for a station deep in the interior had to be put aside. They needed to find, he concluded, some new place along the coast, away from the influence of the colonial authorities in Harper.[9]

LEIGHTON WAS INCREASINGLY convinced that the mission must do more than think about alternatives to Cape Palmas—specific plans needed to be made to leave Fair Hope and to establish the mission in a new location. Wars between colonists and Africans in other parts of Liberia were, he thought, a warning of what was to come at Cape Palmas. Almost from the beginning of the settlement at Monrovia, there had been warfare between the colonists and the surrounding peoples, and tension seemed always in the air. Moreover, Leighton was chafing at the assertions of authority by Russwurm, and he worried about the hostility some settlers felt toward Fair Hope, because of the mission's work among the Grebo, and especially toward those Grebo who had become Christians. The hostility toward William Davis was particularly intense.[10]

Davis's conversion and admission into the church had been a long process. When he first came to Fair Hope in 1835, he had already had some exposure to Christianity in Sierra Leone, where he had lived for several years. He spoke the Pidgin English of African traders on the coast and believed in the importance of education as the source of white power. As soon as Jane had opened her school, he had placed his daughter, Mary Clealand, under Jane's care. He had himself become a star student of Leighton's and had played, as Freeman's influential brother, an important role in the ongoing negotiations between settlers, Grebo, and the mission. With Freeman and Simleh Ballah, he had been a frequent dinner guest at Fair Hope, and he had become Leighton's primary teacher of Grebo and interpreter of Grebo culture. Most days he had opportunities to observe life at the mission and to watch Leighton and Jane as they went about their work. He was also frequently present for their times of prayer and Bible reading, and he, along with Freeman, was regularly a part of the congregation that gathered at Fair Hope on Sundays to hear Leighton preach. In the early days, he was, with Ballah, a translator of Leighton's sermons.[11]

At first, Leighton had been reluctant to preach often, because he feared he might not be understood, given his poor grasp of the language, and also his concern that the translator would convey the wrong message. But as he grew more confident in his use of the language and learned to trust Davis's translations, he began to preach more regularly. It was a demanding task. The Grebo were not passive, but asked hard questions of the preacher. Early in his preaching Leighton reported that some old men, evidently leaders among the Grebo, asked him to address what he called "the evidences of the authenticity of the Bible and the circumstances and manner of its communication to mankind." Sometimes there was open opposition to his preaching, but mainly there were questions about the strange message Leighton was delivering. Leighton believed that there was a natural repugnance in the human heart to the message of the gospel, and that the repugnance was as much among the Grebo as anywhere else, but he was encouraged by the "open-heartedness and cordiality" of the Grebo and what he regarded as the spirituality that marked their understanding of the world.[12]

Leighton had no power to coerce Davis or other Grebo into becoming Christian. Indeed, if he had had such power, its use, or the use of bribery, would have betrayed his fundamental convictions about the nature of conversion. As a Calvinist, he had worried as a young man in Charleston about the depth and sincerity of his own conversion. "Outward signs"—daily Bible reading, prayer, and regular church attendance—were not enough. What was needed was an inward experience that produced outward signs of faithfulness. Sincerity and authenticity, Leighton believed, were the marks of such an inward experience and of true conversion, and this was what he looked for in the Grebo. Such marks could not be administered in a ritual—to think, as Catholics were said to think, that baptizing a person would make that person a Christian was for Leighton nothing less than a belief in magic. But conversion, he was convinced, was also more than a warm feeling in the heart—although it was certainly that. Nor was it simply a public confession of Christian faith—although it was certainly that as well. For Leighton, conversion was finally and completely an act of a gracious God. It was not a matter of simply making up one's mind to accept Jesus as Lord and Savior—Who, he wondered, could do that with the human will so entangled with selfishness and sin? Nor was conversion simply believing certain doctrines, as if it were only a matter of intellectual assent to a creed. No, for Leighton, conversion came as a mysterious and wonderful gift of God. What else, he thought, could change the dispositions and inclinations of the human heart? To be sure, one had to hear the gospel preached and to know the gospel story as a prelude to receiving the gift of conversion. And that preaching and that teaching was what the mission was about—and so Leighton and Jane and James and the other Christians at the mission attempted to do their part even as they prayed for the outpouring of God's Spirit upon the Grebo in a gift of conversion. "We preach the Gospel," wrote Leighton, "plainly and faithfully to them, and rely entirely upon the grace of God for any success which we may be permitted to realize."[13]

A question remained, however: How was the little church at Fair Hope— it had been organized with Leighton as its pastor—to know if Davis had been converted and was ready to be baptized and admitted into its fellowship? In 1837, Leighton had written his family at Pine Grove about Davis. "He is attentive to religious instruction," he wrote, "but has not as yet given evidence of a renovated heart." And if the providence of God was a mystery, so, too, was the human heart. Who could know the interior life of another, or discover sincerity and authenticity by probing another's soul? Only God knew what was in a person's heart. Leighton was too well aware of the deceitfulness of his own heart, and he daily sought self-knowledge through prayer and Bible reading in his struggles against his own illusions and self-deceptions. Moreover, he was acutely aware of how difficult it was for him to know anything about the inner life of a Grebo, with all of the great differences that separated their world from his. "The interior life of the people," he later wrote, "their moral, social, civil, and religious condition, as well as their peculiar notions and customs, have always been a sealed book to the rest of the world." All of this meant that the church at Fair Hope, with Leighton as its pastor, could only look at William Davis's life—at the performance of his sincerity—to test the authenticity of his conversion and decide about his application for church membership. Did the outward signs of Davis's life, they asked, bear the marks of an inward sincerity? A trial period of many months was required in which the church tried to discern if the Lord had really touched his heart and given him the gift of conversion. But of course, during the testing period, what Leighton was looking for were patterns of piety and behavior that European and American Protestants had long expected among the converted.[14]

A lot was being asked of Davis in his conversion. He was Freeman's brother and one of the most respected leaders among the Grebo of Big Town. He had to give up the protection of the fetishes and abandon many of the basic assumptions of Grebo life—a belief in divination and witchcraft and their accompanying convictions about what caused pain or death; a Grebo understanding of time in which the spirits of the dead mingled with the living and the souls of the dead often inhabited the bodies of animals; and the rituals of the Grebo, such as funerals and the sassy wood ordeal, which united the Grebo in a coherent community. His deepest assumptions, his dispositions and inclinations nurtured since his childhood in Big Town, were being challenged, and he was being invited to change his world and much of the way he understood himself and others.[15]

But Davis apparently had discovered much that attracted him to Christianity. His own experience and his own perspectives played important roles in his conversion. He knew, like many a European and American, how to be skeptical toward traditional beliefs, and he found in Christianity new, more satisfactory answers to questions presented by ordinary life at Cape Palmas, perhaps especially the causes of sickness and death. Christianity promised him a freedom from the fear of malevolent powers. It placed him in a new narrative that was rooted in the biblical stories and that had him moving from birth, to life, to death, to resurrection and eternal life with God. He came to confess that Jesus was his friend, and if he was to walk with his friend, Davis understood, he was to live a life of love and service.[16]

No doubt part of what attracted him to Christianity was his close observation of Leighton and Jane and the other Christians at Fair Hope. In spite of all of their weaknesses and failures, Leighton, in particular, must have seemed to him more powerful than the fetish priests, and conversion most likely seemed a move toward what whites called "civilization" and the power it possessed. Still, why did he become a Christian when so many other Grebo did not? What made him, during the coming years, seek to live out his life as a Grebo Christian, a Grebo follower of Jesus?[17]

Whatever the answer, what was clear was that he did not stop being Mworeh Mah, a Grebo, when he became a Christian. Even as he struggled to leave behind specific aspects of Grebo life, he also carried with him many of the traditions and much of the world of the Grebo. He had, after all, grown up in Big Town. His earliest memories were marked by life in his father's compound with his father's wives. He, no less than his brother, Freeman, knew the daily routines of Grebo life—the way the women went for water early in the morning, how they stirred the fires, swept the floors, and prepared rice and various stews. He knew what was required to prepare Grebo fields for planting, how to harvest rice and cassava, and how to protect cattle and goats from a marauding leopard. His memories and sense of himself were intertwined with the history and culture of his people—the meaning of palaver drums, the intricacies of Grebo political organization, who was related to whom, and what the relationships meant in Grebo society. Moreover, the specific landscape of Cape Palmas had insinuated itself into his most elemental senses—the constant, distant sound of the surf; the smell of dry thatch; the texture of boiled cassava; and the way palms bent and their fronds rattled when the wind came hard off the ocean. This particular place on the high banks of Cape Palmas, with its view of things seen and unseen; this world, with its sounds, scents, and tastes, its hopes and fears—this place and this world, these home voices, continued to live and rumble deep within him. He was a Grebo Christian and not a Christian who had been raised in Savannah or near the waters of the Black River. And while he carried with him into Christianity part of the world of Grebo religion—particularly a quest for protection against natural and spiritual enemies—what he most clearly and obviously wanted to carry with him into his new faith were his four Grebo wives.[18]

For Davis, as a Grebo man, wives represented status and wealth. Like their Kru relatives, Grebo men often spent years working on the ships that traded along the West African coast, and the wages they earned were largely spent to secure wives. To find a wife, however, was not a simple matter, as if a Grebo man could simply go out looking for one. Rather, the securing of a wife involved careful negotiations by the headman of a man's family (the headman controlled the wages earned on ships by the men in the family) with the headman of a young girl's family. Leighton found at Big Town that the girl's family generally received three cows, a goat or a sheep, and a few articles of crockery-ware or brass rods. In this way polygamy as practiced among the Grebo was deeply intertwined with the larger economic and cultural systems of the people. While these systems were in constant flux, to radically change any major part of them—such as the practice of polygamy—threatened the whole way of life of the Grebo. How, for example, would a man's wealth and status be determined if not by the number of his wives? And what would happen to the role of the headman and his control of a family's wealth if he no longer had to negotiate for many wives? And what about the women— how would their lives and their work change if a wife were not one wife among several working a man's garden and fields, preparing his food and raising his children? Davis's conversion and the question of his four wives was consequently more than a question about the content and character of Christian faith and morals. His wives linked him to the cultural assumptions and intricate social structures of his people. Did he have to give up three of his wives, in the same way that he had to give up his fetishes and his participation in the sassy wood ordeal, in order to become a Christian and a member of the church at Fair Hope?[19]

Davis and his four wives lived in Big Town in a fenced compound with a small house for each wife and her children. One of the women was his head wife, and all four apparently lived in general harmony with one another, sharing work and looking after each other's children. Leighton had visited the compound, and while he shared the common Western commitment to monogamy, he could see in the Davis compound that it would be a great injustice to insist that three of the wives and their children be suddenly turned out on their own without a protector. He wrote Rufus Anderson in Boston and asked about the position of the American Board "on men who have more than one wife being admitted to church." "It is generally agreed that the missionary ought not to dissolve existing connections," Leighton said. "And if so, are we to deprive of church communion and fellowship a man whose conduct in one particular we could wish to have amended?" Later, he asked Charles Hodge at Princeton the same question, wondering if a convert should be required to give up his wives. This requirement would cause "the disruption of an existing union without the mutual consent of the parties by whom it was formed." Such a disruption, he added, would also allow the converted man's children to be scattered out of the reach of parental influence and control.[20]

Before he received a response from the American Board, Leighton had already made up his mind—Davis should be admitted into the fellowship of the church without having to give up any of his wives, but he could not take a new wife and remain a church member in good standing. The missionary was impressed with how Davis himself was handling the issue. Shortly after his return from the trip to Grabbo, Davis assembled his wives and told them that he intended to live a new life. None of them, however, were to be sent away. He would continue to provide for them and would instruct them in the Christian faith, but they must, he said, "set aside every species of immortality, observe the Sabbath, etc."[21]

Davis told Leighton that Freeman and others strongly opposed his becoming a Christian and had done everything they could to stop him except making him go through the sassy wood ordeal. Already there had been ten or twelve conversions, but they had mostly been young people, like Wasa, who had been in the school at Fair Hope. But Davis's conversion was particularly alarming to the other members of the Grebo community. It must have seemed to them not only an abandonment of ancient ways by a leader, and consequently a threat to the social order of the Grebo—intertwined as it was with powerful religious beliefs and practices—but also a provocation to the world of spirits and ancestors. Who knew what retribution might be visited not only upon Mworeh Mah but also upon the whole Grebo community?[22]

In spite of such opposition, Davis was baptized in April 1838. Standing before Leighton and the congregation, which included Freeman and other Grebo, Davis watched Leighton dip his hand into a bowl of water and then felt—as generations of Christians before and after have felt—the water poured over his head as he heard the words, "I baptize thee in the name of the Father, and the Son, and the Holy Ghost." As a part of the liturgy of baptism, Leighton told Davis that the water represented the cleansing from sin by the blood of Christ, which "takes away all guilt of sin" and signifies a "rising to newness of life" in Christ. Davis was admonished to remember that by his baptism he renounced and was "bound to fight against the devil, the world, and the flesh." Leighton then gave Davis the right hand of Christian fellowship as he welcomed him into the membership of the church.[23]

After his baptism, Davis sat with Leighton and Jane, with James and Margaret, with Wasa and his young wife, and with the other church members at the Lord's Table as the sacrament of the Lord's Supper was celebrated. A long, thin table was set in the front of the little church at Fair Hope, and Leighton invited the church members to come forward and sit together around the table, like those members at Mt. Zion near the Black River had done when Leighton was a boy at Pine Grove. With Freeman and other Grebo watching, Leighton prayed, read scripture, and gave those at the table bread, a common loaf on a plate, and wine in a single cup. Then those sitting at the table passed to one another the bread and wine, elements confessed to be holy signs and seals of the covenant of grace, a commemoration of Christ's offering up of himself upon the cross, once and for all. Christ, said Leighton, was the Host at the table, and they were all Christ's guests.[24]

A bond was being created among them—no one sitting around the long table was an alien or stranger, but all were bound to one another in the social act of eating and drinking together as the guests of Christ. In this way, Davis, as a new member of a community that reached far beyond the pounding surf at Cape Palmas, received the holy meal in anticipation of a Heavenly Banquet. Only, unlike the congregation at Mt. Zion, in the congregation at Fair Hope there was no separation of white and black members—all sat together around the table as they received from Christ and one another the bread of life and called upon the name of the Lord.[25]

Soon after his admission to the church, Davis began a night school in Big Town for Grebo men and women who wanted to learn how to read and write in their own language, and thus he began to be a Christian teacher among his own people.[26]

However, Davis soon began to feel bitter opposition to his conversion—and to his teaching—from the African American settlers in Harper. For an influential Grebo like Davis to become a Christian seemed to many settlers a dangerous step toward Grebo equality with the settlers. "Natives," they wrote in a petition to the Maryland Colonization Society board, are "beginning to be admitted into church and say they are civilized." The petitioners expected that "soon there will be application made for citizenship." They called specific attention to "one W. Davis" who had several wives and as a member of the church was now able to take his oaths in the courts of the colony. "We," they wrote, "born in a civilized country, instructed by our superiors, yet we have to submit to be brought down with Heathens, their oaths taken with ours what would not be done in America under our masters." Davis, though he had become a Christian and had been admitted into the fellowship of the church, was still regarded as a heathen because he was a Grebo. Like their masters in America—and like the white members of Mt. Zion—the settlers wanted to be certain that church membership did not mean any social equality or rights of citizenship for those whom they regarded as their inferiors. The unity confessed at the Lord's Table was being challenged at Cape Palmas no less than at Mt. Zion.[27]

For Leighton and Jane, the settlers' opposition to Davis's conversion and baptism seemed the strongest possible confirmation of their deep hostility to the mission. The work of the mission was, he thought, demanding enough. Those who worked at Fair Hope did not need antagonistic settlers complaining that "Heathen" were being admitted into the church and might claim equal rights with the colonists. So, in spite of their years of building up Fair Hope and their deep commitments to the Grebo, Leighton and Jane felt they must leave this place—this place where they had known so many sorrows and hopes, where in the evenings they had sat together beneath an African sky listening to the sounds of the surf.

SHORTLY AFTER DAVIS'S admission into the church, Leighton and Jane sailed south on the *Emperor* with their old friend Captain Lawlin who had brought them out in 1834. They wanted to explore other areas of the West African coast in the hopes of finding a new place and a new start for the mission. As they sailed along the coast, they passed Spanish and Portuguese slavers carrying their stunned, struggling cargoes to the slave markets of Cuba or Brazil. Lawlin was trading for camwood, palm oil, and ivory and knew the coast well from his many trips along its shores. Everywhere they dropped anchor, canoes came rushing out and the deck of the *Emperor* was quickly covered with men trading their goods for American products. Leighton noted that while whites generally thought the Africans "stupid," the Africans knew how to drive a clever bargain and turn the tables on the whites. He thought that for every case in which a white trader outsmarted an African, five cases could be found where an African trader outsmarted the captain of an American or European ship. Lawlin, as an experienced trader, knew and trusted some of the chief merchants along the coast, and with some he left considerable goods, to be paid for when he returned. Leighton and Jane were generally impressed with these merchants. One Leighton described as a "square" man about six feet tall with a jet black complexion and a sober and dignified demeanor. He dressed in European clothes and lived in a large house filled with European furniture. Others, especially those hardened by the slave trade, the young missionaries found to be cruel and treacherous—even intrepid Kru and Grebo sailors sought to avoid them.[28]

At Cape Lahu on the Ivory Coast, the Wilsons found a large population and an inviting opportunity for a mission. But it was Cape Coast and its surrounding region that captured their imaginations the most. Here the coast was lined with old forts where slaves brought from the interior were once held in dark and stinking dungeons before being led out into the light and to a rolling surf and waiting slave ships. Now some of the old forts were crumbling, as if the weight of their history was bearing down on them in revenge. But others—Dixcove, Cape Coast, Elmina, Accra—were now committed to what was called "legitimate trade," trade that was not involved in the buying and selling of slaves or the supplying of provisions for slave ships.[29]

At Cape Coast Castle, with its dungeons and bitter memories of slaves waiting for they knew not what, the English governor, George MacLean, gave Leighton and Jane a warm welcome. He urged them to consider establishing a mission in nearby Accra. Already there were British missionaries along the coast, and the Americans could work in cooperation with them. The governor told them of the Ashanti and Dahomey kingdoms, of their wealth and military prowess and also of their cruelty—a number of slaves, he said, in a nearby town had recently been buried alive following an eclipse of the sun.[30]

With such reports ringing in their ears, the missionaries went back aboard the *Emperor*, and in eight days of clear sailing far out to sea, they were back at Cape Palmas and Fair Hope. Their visit had been too brief to make any decision about an alternative to Fair Hope, but Leighton sent his journal to

Anderson and urged that missionaries be sent to take advantage of the opportunities he and Jane had seen all along the coast.[31]

IRONICALLY, THE QUEST for a new location came at a time when the mission at Fair Hope was prospering. The little congregation was slowly growing as more students began to join and an occasional adult like William Davis was converted. The press, with its two Grebo printers, was humming under B. V. R. James's direction. A school at Rock Town was doing well, as were two in the interior with young Grebo teachers. At Sarekeh, a town about twelve miles from the Cape, Wasa Baker and his wife, Maria, had recently established a school. Maria, whom Wasa had brought naked to Leighton three years earlier, had finished her studies with Jane and had become a Christian, and she and Wasa had been married by Leighton. In addition to their school for the children at Sarekeh, Wasa and Maria opened their home morning and evening for prayer and scripture reading. Growing crowds joined them as they heard the young couple sitting at their door singing hymns. The people loved the singing and also the Bible stories they heard—the story of the Old Testament patriarch Joseph was a great favorite, perhaps because he had once been a slave in Egypt and had, by interpreting the Pharaoh's dreams, been set over all the land of Egypt—and so the biblical stories began to be a part of the storytelling tradition in the village. In this way, and with a number of night schools in Big Town, the work of the mission at Fair Hope was expanding.[32]

The mission was expanding in other ways as well. From the beginning of their time at Fair Hope, Leighton and Jane had been pleading for more missionaries. The arrival and then the tragic deaths of David and Helen White had been a heavy blow to the mission, but in early 1839 word arrived that Dr. and Mrs. Alex Wilson were being sent to the Fair Hope mission. Leighton and Jane were elated. Dr. Wilson, who was from South Carolina, was no relation to the Wilsons of Pine Grove, but he and Leighton's father were close friends. He had already spent some years as a missionary doctor in South Africa and had finally left because of the wars between the white settlers and the native peoples. He and his new wife (his first wife had died of fever in South Africa) began a mission at Fish Town, a large and prosperous town beautifully located about twenty miles north of the Cape. He liked the Grebo and soon found them to be largely a peaceful people. "Perhaps," he wrote, "there is no heathen nation less blood thirsty than the Grebo. They are palaverous and noisy enough, but they shirk from the shedding of blood. They have wars it is true, but sometimes they continue from 5 to 10 years, and there will not be 20 lives lost." He noted that they used guns, but not very effectively, and he compared them to the "brave Zulu who assegai in hand, rushes down on his adversary; and fights hand to hand, until the death of one party puts an end to the combat."[33]

The arrival of these new missionaries was a great encouragement to Leighton and Jane. Although the doctor and his wife lived some distance from Fair Hope, there were regular opportunities for them to visit the Cape and for Leighton and Jane to enjoy their company. They called him Dr. Wilson, and his young wife they called Mrs. Dr. Wilson. The Dr. Wilsons also became friends with James, Margaret, and Catherine and, like most others, they quickly grew to admire James and his work as a printer and teacher. At mealtimes at Fair Hope, they were frequently joined by William Davis, Freeman, and Ballah. While Fish Town was well beyond the bounds of any colonial claims to authority, the Dr. Wilsons must have heard of the Grebo and missionary concerns about the settlers, who seemed to want more and more land. The doctor had watched the Boers in South Africa intrude on the lands of indigenous people, and he had arrived with little sympathy for settlers of any complexion. So it was not surprising that he soon joined Leighton in warning the American Board about the colony and about Russwurm's attitude toward the mission.[34]

WHILE THE MISSION was thus prospering in a variety of ways, Leighton was also encouraged by what he perceived to be important changes among the Grebo. In December 1839, an extended palaver debated the continued use of the sassy wood ordeal. Encouraged by Freeman and Davis, the Big Town Grebo decided to abolish the ordeal. In celebration of the decision, Leighton prepared a great feast, inviting Freeman and all of the leading men of Big Town. The meal, Leighton thought, was a way of confirming the decision and sealing it for the future. He wrote Anderson that the ordeal had been one of atrocious cruelty. Although its chief victims had been the elderly, all the people had begun to realize that it was an extremely cruel and oppressive practice, a practice from which no one had been exempt. But Leighton had been at the Cape long enough to know that deeply held practices were not easily discarded. He consequently wrote Anderson that he wanted to be guarded and not encourage exaggerated expectations. Still, he thought the decision indicated a "desire on the part of the people to extricate themselves from the cruelties of heathenism." He was wise to be guarded.[35]

A number of the younger men were in fact resistant to the decision and insisted that the ordeal was the only way to discover and punish those who caused harm. Not long after the palaver, a great thunderstorm swept across the Cape and lightning struck a house in Big Town, killing three young boys. Some said it was because of the abandonment of the ordeal; others said it was the work of a witch. Messengers were sent to an oracle at Grand Sesters north of the Cape. The oracle, located at a large and imposing tree, apparently sent word back that the ordeal must be continued.[36]

A month after the palaver, a woman was accused of witchcraft in the death of her stepson, and the ordeal was demanded. Her accusers sought to keep Leighton ignorant of what was happening, but someone—most likely William Davis—told him. Leighton went early in the morning to Freeman and had a palaver called with the headmen. He insisted that they release her, saying the ordeal had been abolished and its end sealed with a feast. But his arguments were to no avail. After various evasions, Freeman finally told Leighton to go back to Fair Hope and not to interfere. The woman, he said, had already been taken to the woods and given the red water concoction. It was a bitter and distressing moment for the missionary.[37]

Meanwhile, Dr. Samuel McGill, the son of the Methodist minister and trader George McGill and Russwurm's brother-in-law, had learned what was going on. McGill—who had recently returned from studying medicine in the United States, where he had endured the racism of his fellow students—had joined the crowd, in order, he later said, to "note the effects" of the concoction on the struggling woman.[38] She was young and robust, but her eyes already were glazed when he arrived. He took her pulse—it was soft, and her skin was dry. She could not hold up her head, and it rolled on her shoulders and breast. She tried to walk but stumbled and fell. Members of the crowd, infuriated when they learned of Leighton's opposition, took hold of her feet and began dragging her, cutting her badly. She finally freed herself from them, and McGill, thinking her near death, pleaded with the crowd to let him take her, offering to treat also the man whom she was accused of bewitching. He was pushed away in the fury of the moment. Still she struggled. They held her arms and legs, and one man put his foot on her head as they tried to pour more red water down her throat and then down her nose. Somehow she found the strength to resist. They put sand in her eyes and mouth, but she fought them off. Finally they overwhelmed her by pouring water in her nostrils and clapping strong hands over her mouth, then they buried her head under the sand. In this way she died, and with her died the hope that the ordeal had been abolished.[39]

For Leighton, the woman's horrifying death was a painful reminder that old ways die slowly and not without a great struggle. The way forward for the mission was to be long and arduous, and hopes for the conversion of the Grebo had to be tempered by a realization of the strength and resilience of Grebo traditions.

WHILE THE PLANS to relocate were being discussed at Fair Hope, and while life in Big Town was showing a growing strain between old traditions and new ways, the settlers at Bayard Island were struggling to establish a new life in a demanding environment. After all but two children had passed successfully through the initial fevers, the hard realities of life in a young colony soon began to be felt. The supplies Leighton had provided upon their arrival were exhausted in six months, and recurrent fevers and other illnesses began to take their toll. Names began to disappear from the colonial records—eighteen-year-old Diana McIntosh died the first year; twenty-seven-year-old Juba McIntosh died the next, as did seventy-year-old Belinda Mumford and Juba's little three-year-old, Hosa McIntosh, whose father, Renty, was in Savannah.[40]

But others were surviving and making a new life for themselves where the surf pounded around a West African cape and where night fires in Big Town could be seen in the distance. Charles and Mary Sansay, in spite of their age, were working hard on their little farm, as were John and Catherine Johnson on theirs. Some on Bayard Island were employed as sawyers and laborers, and one was learning to be a blacksmith. Several of the women were working as spinsters and needlewomen, and among both the men and the women there were those who were finding marriage partners in Harper and who came out to Fair Hope for Leighton to marry them.[41]

As a skilled carpenter, Paul Sansay was in the best position to prosper in the young colony. Now what he had learned in Savannah he put to use at Cape Palmas—his knowledge of saws, augers, gimlets and chisels; his understanding of how a joist was connected to a beam and how a window could be framed or floorboards tightly laid. After he had built his own neat house, and had gotten his parents and his sister settled in their new home, he found plenty of work to do in Harper. Leighton hired him to do some work at Fair Hope, where Paul met and became friends with Wasa and William Davis. His sister, Charlotte, who had been Jane's personal maid in Georgia, also came out to Fair Hope, but only occasionally, and she and Jane, who had spent so much time together in Savannah and at Fair Hope plantation, renewed in only limited ways their complicated relationship. Charlotte was now a free woman in West Africa. The distance between Bayard Island and the Fair Hope mission was apparently a help as Charlotte sought to avoid being caught in any remnant of slavery's web that had once entangled her and Jane.[42]

Paul did not forget his wife and children in Savannah. Six months after he arrived at Cape Palmas, he wrote Latrobe asking for help in freeing his family. "I do feel myself," he said, "very happy that my lot has fell were it is. But in one thing only I can Say that I am not Satisfied in that is my wife and children that I have left behind me being Slave as I was but has not the chance that I had of getting them freedom there is one thing I should like you to write me about that is if I could not make it convenient for me to come over next fall to see if I could not do something for them perhaps with a few friends I may be the means of getting them out of bondage by next fall expedition." If any of his friends asked about him, he told Latrobe, he should "tell them I am under my own vine and fig tree none dare molest nor make me afraid and doing well as I can expect."[43]

Paul wrote his wife as well, sending the letters to Nicholas and asking him to read them to her. But slowly his letters began to grow more infrequent. In 1841, Nicholas wrote Latrobe that Paul's wife had not heard from him in some time and that she was anxious to do so, as her master was moving her and the children to Macon in the middle of the state. Was there any chance that she and the children might be freed? Had Paul, she wondered, reached Baltimore? If he had, Nicholas told Latrobe, it was important to warn him not to return to Savannah. Georgia law was clear—he would be arrested and sold back into slavery.[44]

But Paul never made it back to Baltimore, and while he prospered and became a leader in the colony, he never married again. So he made a life for himself in the new land far from his place of birth and slavery, and far from his wife and children. And more than most of the settlers, he made friends among the Grebo—especially the newly converted Christians Wasa and William Davis.[45]

Chapter Twelve

Rose-Tinted Glasses

In 1841 the Maryland legislature asked the Maryland Colonization Society for a full report on the progress of its colony at Cape Palmas. Having appropriated $20,000 a year for the work of the society, the legislature was asking how successful the project had been in furthering the effort to whiten Maryland.[1]

Latrobe wrote a glowing report. The colony, he said, was intended to make the American settlers the means of civilizing and Christianizing their ancestral homeland. He reported a happy relationship between the society and the missionaries and acknowledged that the missionaries had played an important role in preserving peace and goodwill between the Grebo and the colonists and in the improvement of both. He asserted that the Maryland Colonization Society board had authority over the colony and that the colonial authorities at Cape Palmas governed on behalf and in the name of the board. The board, he said, was building a new nation in Africa, and when the time came for the board to transfer its power to the settlers, then Maryland in Liberia would stand as a nation among the family of nations. And to make clear that the Maryland Colonization Society did not regard itself as one US benevolent society among many, Latrobe insisted that all persons residing in the colony who were not citizens of it were like strangers residing in any other civilized country. They had to obey the laws of the colony. Latrobe was clearly claiming that the Baltimore board had authority over the missionaries connected with the Boston board and the Episcopal mission society.[2]

In regard to the Grebo, they were, Latrobe said, clearly "savages," and by implication their country was not "civilized" and those residing in it were not bound to pay obedience to Grebo laws. Latrobe informed the legislature that Maryland in Liberia had experienced a total exemption from native wars in spite of the savage ways of the Grebo. He acknowledged that many

opponents to colonization believed that civilized settlers inevitably encroached upon and finally exterminated the indigenous people around them.
But Latrobe insisted that the black settlers at Cape Palmas would eventually
absorb the Grebo into colonial society and in this way become a blessing to
Africa. For Latrobe, such an amalgamation was nothing less than striking
proof that the contact of civilized people and savages was only fatal for savages "when the barrier of colour interposes an obstacle to amalgamation
which can never be overcome." In conclusion, Latrobe and the Baltimore
board boasted that the prosperity of their colony at Cape Palmas was unparalleled in the history of colonization. They proudly announced that the
inhabitants of Maryland in Liberia had "proved an honor to their race."[3]

Latrobe and the Maryland board must have known that their report was
a view of the colony as seen through rose-tinted glasses manufactured in
their own offices. Indeed, anyone who read the *Maryland Colonization Journal*,
edited by Dr. James Hall, must have known the same. At the time of the report, only 453 emigrants had been sent to the colony and approximately
107 had arrived from Monrovia and Liberia proper. Of these 560, the
board's report said, only a little over 200 were in the colony in January 1841.
Some had returned to the United States, and others had left for Monrovia,
but many, very many, had died within a year or two of their arrival. With the
colonists often weakened by severe food shortages and poor housing, the
death rate, especially among children, had been staggering. Moreover, Russwurm and Samuel McGill had been regularly reporting the intense hostility
of the settlers toward the Grebo while reflecting their own disdain for the
settlers themselves. As for the missionaries, both those of the American Board
and those of the Episcopal mission were preparing to leave the bounds of
the colony because of what they perceived to be the opposition of the colonial authorities to their presence there and the opposition of the settlers to
the education of the Grebo.[4]

But rose-tinted glasses seemed necessary in Baltimore in 1841. The census
of 1840 had sent a deep tremor through the white Maryland establishment
because it had revealed the expansion of the American frontier in the south.
Ambitious and aggressive whites were pouring into a black belt of rich and
promising land that stretched from Georgia to the Mississippi Valley. The
settlers, seeking their fortunes, had created a huge demand for slaves to clear
the land and plant and harvest cotton. As a consequence, slave traders had
been busy in Baltimore, as well as in Richmond, Charleston, Savannah, and
many points in between. They had been buying black men, women, and children and marching them to the lucrative markets of an expanding Cotton

Kingdom. Some planters on the old Atlantic seaboard had joined this exodus, taking their slaves to the beckoning lands of Alabama and Mississippi, of Louisiana, Arkansas, and Texas. For the slaves, the westward movement was like a Second Middle Passage, a terrible uprooting and often agonizing separation from family and friends. For many whites in the old seaboard areas, however, this removal of slaves presented threatening demographic shifts. In Maryland, in particular, the westward movement of slaves appeared to be creating a grave danger for the state—while slaves were leaving, free blacks were staying and having large families.[5]

In circulars sent throughout the state, Latrobe spelled out the alarming census returns and their implications for Maryland. The state was becoming, wrote Latrobe, a place inhabited by two distinct races of free people—one white and one black. Each race, he said, had widely differing characteristics. Latrobe pointed out what seemed obvious to him—free whites and free blacks could not live together in harmony on the same soil. Never in history had they done so, he insisted, and the inherent and unchangeable principles of human nature would keep them from doing so in the future. If whites and free blacks ended up living together in Maryland in anything like equal numbers, Latrobe predicted, one of two alternatives would be the result. One was intermarriage and equality of political rights. The other was the oppression of free blacks, their rebellion, the repression of the rebellion in a bloodbath, and the final expulsion of what Latrobe called "the weaker and less energetic race."[6]

Latrobe dismissed the first alternative as impossible. Intermarriage and political equality could not be considered, Latrobe said, because of "the degraded condition of the coloured race, and the fact that the marks of their degradation are distinct, indelible and perpetual; and will ever prevent those who have been their masters, from receiving them as equals, in the social or political relations." In addition, such an amalgamation between the two races would lead to the humiliation of whites as they lost their identity in what Latrobe called a "mongrel posterity." But the other alternative also seemed unthinkable. Many whites, Latrobe thought, would object to a bloody expulsion of free blacks, because whites had as one of the principles of their nature an "aversion to discord and violence." There was only one way to avert such impending and dreaded calamities, he said: African colonization. Latrobe clearly believed that perceived racial differences between whites and blacks were insuperable, while the cultural differences between the African American settlers and the Grebo were not. Amalgamation was desirable in Cape Palmas, but would be an unthinkable calamity in Maryland.[7]

Governor Russwurm apparently made no written response to the report or to the circulars sent out by Latrobe and the board. Perhaps it was simply what he had come to expect.

The seismic demographic shifts reflected in the census of 1840, however, sent ripples racing out of Baltimore harbor to hit the shores of Cape Palmas. Latrobe and his colleagues, in an atmosphere of near panic, were determined to meet the perceived threat of free blacks, to do all they could to whiten Maryland, and to be strong and resolute in their management of their West African colony—and this included how they dealt with troublesome missionaries who might raise questions about the assumptions, purposes, and results of colonization.[8]

WHILE LATROBE WAS writing his report and sending out circulars, Leighton and Russwurm continued to glare at one another across the distance that separated Fair Hope from the governor's house in Harper. Each man carefully watched the other for any action or any report that would confirm his worst suspicions. Yet each of them also knew that the other had an important role to play at the Cape. Leighton acknowledged and grudgingly admired Russwurm's concern for the Grebo. He thought that the governor, unlike almost all of the settlers, took the interests of the Grebo seriously, even if he naturally put the interests of the colony first. Moreover, Leighton knew that Russwurm and Freeman had been able to reach a *detente* in regard to conflicts between settlers and Grebo, and that they generally worked well together to oil the relationship between Harper and Big Town. Russwurm, on his part, knew that Leighton was regarded by the Grebo as their friend and that he had played, and could again play, an important role in helping to settle disputes.[9]

So the two men watched one another. And the attitudes and the actions that followed their watching reflected the world that Leighton had known at Pine Grove and the world that Russwurm had experienced in Maine and New York—the bitter burden of race seemed to have come across the Atlantic to Cape Palmas like a rat hidden in the hold of a ship.

In spite of their differences, Russwurm and Leighton found themselves once again working carefully together in May 1841 to settle a boundary dispute between the Grebo of Big Town and the Grebo of Rock Town. Through their joint efforts, a settlement was reached between the rival communities and war was avoided.[10]

But open conflict soon erupted between the governor and the missionary—and once more, as in 1838, the conflict was over the question of mission personnel serving in the colonial militia. Mission teachers had been secured from Cape Coast and Sierra Leone, and the colonial authorities imposed fines on them when they did not report for duty in the militia. Leighton and Russwurm exchanged notes on the matter—the notes were civil in tone but clear in articulating their different positions. Leighton quoted a letter from Anderson giving "the official" conclusion of the correspondence between Anderson and Latrobe in 1838 about missionary personnel and the militia: "As the missionaries and assistant missionaries we send from this country in the colony are to be regarded and treated as foreigners, so also are the native Teachers we may bring from tribes not subject to the colony to be regarded." Foreigners in the colony, said Anderson, "as well as in all other parts of the world, are exempt from military duty, serving as jurors, etc."[11]

Russwurm wrote back defiantly: "I can say nothing about Dr. Anderson's letter to you, as I receive instructions only from Md. Col. Soc." And in those instructions he found nothing that exempted the "civilized" Africans at Fair Hope from military duty.[12]

The two men agreed to submit the question once again to their respective societies in the United States. When Russwurm wrote the board in Baltimore, he said, after giving his interpretation of the situation, that he intended to resign at the end of the year. He gave no reasons for his decision, but it was clear he was tired of dealing with recalcitrant settlers and troublesome, presumptuous white missionaries—or perhaps his announcement was a considered attempt to provoke a strong response from the board.[13]

At this point Dr. Alex Wilson and B. V. R. James leaped into the fray. They wrote a joint letter to the American Board in Boston. The colonists, they said, believed the Grebo and the settlers had opposing interests—the settlers were said to regard anything advancing the interests of the Grebo as detrimental to the colony. Because the missionaries were trying to elevate the Grebo, many settlers had begun to resent the work of the mission and to see the missionaries as a threat to the colony. The white physician with years of experience in South Africa, and the black printer and teacher from New York, wrote, "We would by no means condemn colonization because the Colonists are Colored persons. We believe that white Colonists of the same character and under the same circumstances would trample down and drive out the natives just as soon." They concluded, however, that the missionaries could no longer carry on their work in the colony in peace and comfort. And they noted that the Episcopal missionaries had already decided to move their work beyond the bounds of the colony and of Russwurm's authority.[14]

Russwurm wrote again to his board as well. The missionaries, he said, in their relationship with the colonists, "acted like men, who were dealing with beings of an inferior order, and by their speeches only tended to widen the breach." He reported that invidious comparisons were being drawn between the missionary boards and the Maryland Colonization Society. The missionaries, he said, were telling the Grebo that the mission societies were rich and the colonization society was poor. And what was worse, said the governor, the missionaries were telling the Grebo that the colonists wanted the missionaries out of the way so that they could drive Freeman and his people away from Big Town.[15]

And so it went as each side made its accusations against the other, and the divisions hardened.

RUSSWURM'S LETTERS, AND especially his announcement that he intended to resign, caused alarm in Baltimore. The colonization society board was already in crisis, in spite of Latrobe's glowing report several months earlier. The society was deeply in debt, was under constant attack by abolitionists, and was losing support from conservatives associated with the mission societies. It had done little, in spite of substantial state aid, to rid Maryland of what whites regarded as the state's dangerously increasing free black population. And now the board's star, John B. Russwurm, the brilliant governor and anchor of the board's troubled colony, was announcing his intention to resign.[16]

Latrobe and his colleagues acted quickly. They said that Russwurm clearly understood the laws of the colony—any civilized African at Fair Hope was required to perform military duty. They wondered how the Reverend Leighton Wilson or anyone else who had examined the laws of the colony could think otherwise. They pointed to a need for a strong defense, since the colony was surrounded by "barbarians." And they pleaded with Russwurm "to continue the exercise of functions that have been exerted so honorably to himself and so beneficially to the colony." They communicated their decision to both the American Board and the board of the Episcopal Domestic and Foreign Missionary Society.[17]

In Boston, Rufus Anderson and his colleagues received communications from Baltimore and from the missionaries at Cape Palmas. They protested the Maryland Colonization Society's action, pointed to the correspondence between Latrobe and Anderson in 1838, and wondered how teaching Africans the skills of modern warfare would add to the security of the colony. They asked for a reconsideration and resolved that requiring African teachers to do military duty would be injurious, if not destructive, to the mission. They noted that the mission had been established by the American Board with the consent and approbation of the Maryland Colonization Society. When they had established a mission at Fair Hope, Anderson and his colleagues said, they had had no reason to anticipate the enforcement of a law so repugnant to the principles that guided their missions around the world. Any attempt by the Maryland society to reverse its earlier position and require military duty would be regarded, they said, as oppressive to the mission. They asked Latrobe and the Baltimore board to send Russwurm instructions that would prevent any agitation of the subject in the future. And they warned the Baltimore board not to take any action that might make mission and colonization in West Africa appear incompatible with one another. The Christian public, they said, would be watching, and if a confrontation took place, the Bostonians made clear, colonization would be the loser.[18]

Latrobe and the Baltimore board were adamant—they were going to support Russwurm, and they were not going to be instructed by anyone in Boston. Latrobe wrote Anderson that the Baltimore board saw no reason to modify the action it had already taken.[19]

WHEN LETTERS REACHED Cape Palmas stating the decision of the colonization society board, the missionaries knew that the time had come for them to act. They closed the school at Fair Hope and moved the center of their educational mission to Fish Town, beyond the colony's borders. Dr. Wilson, who had started the school at Fish Town, had died of dysentery in the fall of 1841, and a grieving Mrs. Dr. Wilson was staying at Fair Hope. So James went to Fish Town to head the school and to teach with Margaret and Catherine. Some of the African teachers at Fair Hope joined them while others went to other outlying schools, and in this way they avoided having to participate in the colonial militia. At the same time, the Episcopal mission was moving the center of its operations to Yellow Will's town at Half Cavally as well as to Grand Cavally, where Baphro was king. In this way the Episcopal mission also moved beyond the authority of Russwurm and the colonial government.[20]

WHILE THE MISSIONARIES at Cape Palmas were seeking to extract themselves from what they regarded as Russwurm's interference, both the American Board and the Episcopal mission board were making plans to increase their West African efforts. Both Leighton and his Episcopal colleagues had been pleading for help. The challenges before them, they had acknowledged, were great, but they had insisted that the opportunities for mission in West Africa were far greater. In early 1842, more missionaries finally arrived—three for the Episcopal mission and three for Fair Hope.[21]

Benjamin Griswold, William Walker, and William's wife, Prudence Walker, arrived at Fair Hope in February 1842. They were all Vermont Yankees who had grown up under the shadow of the Green Mountains among an independent people of small farms and villages. Two of the three were to influence the West African mission in important ways, and one was to become Leighton's closest colleague during the coming decade.

Griswold had been born and raised in the little village of Randolph in central Vermont. After graduating from Dartmouth College in 1837, he had spent some time at Andover Theological Seminary before transferring to Yale to complete his theological education. While a student at Yale, Griswold had been deeply moved by his encounter with the prisoners from the Spanish slave ship *Amistad*. He spent time with Cinqué, the leader of the captive Africans who had revolted off the coast of Cuba and gained control of the ship, and who had, guided by two Spanish crewmen, sailed along the US coast until being taken by an American revenue cutter. Griswold had gone regularly to the jail in New Haven to assist one of his instructors, George E. Day, in teaching the prisoners English and the Bible. There, with the Africans crowded around, he had learned that Cinqué was one of the thousands that had passed through the slave factories of Pedro Blanco on the Gallinas River before being carried along Atlantic highways to Cuba.[22]

The trial of the *Amistad* mutineers had attracted intense national interest, becoming a rallying point for abolitionists. It nurtured in Griswold both abolitionist sympathies and an antipathy for any colonization schemes. On the day the district court ruled that the Africans were to be freed, January 13, 1840, Griswold had decided that he wanted to be a missionary to West Africa. On December 6, 1841, after a year of medical studies—he hoped eventually to receive a medical degree for his mission work—he sailed from Boston, and he came ashore through the surf at Cape Palmas on February 3, 1842. Riding in the canoe with him was a skeleton that he anticipated using in any medical practice he had in Africa and in preparation for his hoped-for return to medical school in the United States.[23]

William Walker grew up near the tiny village of Vershire, where farmers who tried to make a living off of the rocky Vermont soil came for supplies, and where on Sundays they came to worship at the white-framed Congregational church. A tall, lanky farm boy, he had been raised by his parents in modest Yankee fashion at the foot of mountains where summer days were long and green and winter days were short and white. Here year round, morning sun came first to mountain tops, and here young Walker learned to rise early, before roosters stirred in January or sleek crows came sailing out of maples in late spring into fields of sprouting corn. In the summer and fall he split and stacked wood, so that fires could burn and glow on winter nights when the wind howled or when quiet snow built a white world. He learned to plow a straight furrow behind a strong horse, and to turn a tight circle for neat rows, but he also learned a little carpentry, and during summer vacations he became a skilled blacksmith. In this way and in this place he began to carry himself in his own distinctive fashion, to look at the world through eyes shaped by the daily scenes and routines of his life, and to understand himself as a man in such a world. He was blunt, straightforward, and fearless. But he was also restless, for he knew the narrowness of creek-bed roads and of his valley home, and he felt the confining power of hill and ridge and mountaintop. Years later, after going through deep personal sorrows, he developed an introspective and tender heart that tempered the Yankee steel in his character that had been forged on a Vermont farm.[24]

When he was eighteen, William Walker left his valley home for a wider landscape, and for Amherst College in Massachusetts. He carried with him not only his Latin grammar, but also calloused hands and a strong, angular physique. While he was a student at Amherst, his parents gave up on farming Vermont soil and left with his younger brothers and sisters for the rich and abundant lands on the Wisconsin frontier. Years would pass before he saw them again. After Amherst, he went to Andover Theological Seminary, and after Andover he married a young Vermont woman with the good Yankee name of Prudence. A few weeks after their marriage, they sailed from Boston with Griswold.[25]

The three young Vermonters received from Leighton and Jane a warm and anxious welcome. The newcomers moved into the upstairs rooms at Fair Hope and waited for the fever to strike. They did not have to wait long. All three were soon struggling as the malarial parasites entered their bloodstreams and invaded their red blood cells. Their fevers raged and then dropped, raged again, and seemed intent on bringing them all down to the grave. But with the careful nursing of Leighton and Jane, Griswold and William Walker began to recover. Prudence, however, after some hopeful signs, began to sink toward death in spite of all that her desperate husband and friends could do. With her husband and Jane at her side, Leighton finally told her that death was near. She was buried in the little cemetery at Fair Hope beside David and Helen White, who five years earlier had also come to Cape Palmas in love and with faith and hope. A grieving William Walker made a simple marker for the grave of his Prudence.[26]

Two weeks later, in May 1842, Leighton and Griswold—together with a number of former students and teachers at Fair Hope and from outlying schools—sailed for the south with Captain Lawlin on the *Atalanta*. They were determined to establish a new station far removed from any colonial authorities. Jane stayed at Fair Hope with the still weak and grieving William Walker and with Mrs. Dr. Wilson. The plan was that once the travelers found a spot for the new mission, Leighton and all but Griswold would begin the work of establishing a new station. Griswold was to return to Fair Hope to help with the closing of the mission at Cape Palmas. Then Griswold, Walker, and Mrs. Dr. Wilson—together with the James family and the African teachers at Fish Town—would sail south to join Leighton. Jane in the meantime would sail to the United States for a visit with family before returning to Africa and the new mission station. The plan was complicated, and, as might be anticipated, unexpected developments would shape what actually happened.[27]

Two months later, Griswold and Captain Lawlin returned to Cape Palmas with the news that the travelers had found a place for the mission by the waters of the Gabon estuary. Leighton and the Grebo students and teachers were already preparing a place for the new station on a hillside above the great estuary. Work was now to proceed for the closing of Fair Hope and for the transfer of the station to Gabon.[28]

The following week, Captain Lawlin prepared to sail directly for New York with Jane as a passenger. She and Leighton had been talking for some months about the possibility of her returning to the United States on furlough. She had suffered a terrible bout with dysentery during an epidemic in the fall of 1841—an epidemic that had killed not only Dr. Wilson but also many Grebo and settlers. She and Leighton had decided that a furlough would allow her to recover her health more fully, to have a thorough exam by a Philadelphia physician, and to see friends and family.[29]

So in July 1842, Jane said her painful goodbyes to the other missionaries, to her Grebo friends and former students, and, no doubt, to Paul and others from Bayard Island. With her luggage already on board, Grebo canoe men carried her through the surf and held steady as she boarded the *Atalanta*. Captain Lawlin then raised anchor and the ship began to move toward the north. Jane stood on the deck and watched a place she had come to love begin to disappear into the horizon—the tall palms of Cape Palmas swaying in the morning wind, the smoke from Big Town and the settler houses curling skyward, waves heaving and crashing on a wide beach. But of course it was Fair Hope, a cottage and cluster of buildings in the distance, that held her attention. There in that fading spot was the place closest to her heart and deepest in her memory. Seven years had passed since singing boatmen had brought her as a young bride through the rolling surf to an African home. She and Leighton had been welcomed ashore by King Freeman and a tumultuous crowd of singing, dancing Grebo and led up the hill to the newly built cottage overlooking the Atlantic. Later she had become the much loved teacher of many Grebo children—what deep pleasure she had found in teaching them and watching them discover a world beyond Cape Palmas. She had welcomed Freeman and Ballah and Davis to her dinner table and had listened to their stories and had tried to understand something of their lives. And there at Fair Hope she and Leighton had sat together on its piazza and looked out in the evenings into the wonders and beauty of an African sky and African nights.[30]

The leaving was not easy for Jane, nor had it been for Leighton. So many hopes and so much effort had been concentrated in this place they had come to call home. While they both thought they had made the right decision to leave, Leighton later wrote Jane that "there are scenes, associations and events connected with that place and people which will ever endear them to me, and there are many there for whom I shall continue to pray as long as I frequent the throne of grace." They had spent years learning the Grebo language, studying Grebo ways, and teaching Grebo students. And during the course of those years they had come to admire much about the Grebo and to call some of them friends. Now they felt they had to leave behind the fruit of their labors because of the opposition of the colonists.[31]

The Grebo had watched Leighton leave in May, and now, two months later, they saw Jane leave as well. So Leighton and Jane, who had come among them with such high hopes, who had eaten with them, and who had brought so many changes with them—they had now abandoned them. Jane had been a cheerful and winsome spirit among them and had taught some of their children how to master the mysteries of reading and writing. Leighton had been their friend, had doctored many of them, had helped to settle many disputes among them, and had spoken for them in their conflicts with the colonists. They had called him "true man" because "he never changes his word." And Dr. James Hall, Governor Russwurm's close friend and supporter, observing Leighton's way with the Grebo, said of Leighton, "We know him to have possessed the confidence of the native Africans to a greater degree than any other white man we have ever met with on that coast."[32]

In this way those whom the Grebo had counted on and trusted left them. The missionaries of the American Board turned over their remaining students and schools to the Episcopal mission, which had moved beyond the control of the colonial authorities. So while the work of Fair Hope was to be continued by the Episcopal mission, the loss of Fair Hope was a blow for the Grebo. Leighton had been a consistent and influential voice on their behalf, and Jane had been their friend in the ordinary comings and goings of life at Cape Palmas.

For Governor Russwurm, however, the departure of Leighton and Jane did not seem an abandonment, but rather a relief. Leighton, in particular, had been so confident that he knew what was best for the settlers; he had assumed such a self-righteous attitude toward Russwurm's dealing with slavers, and had been so ready to interfere in matters that were none of his business. And Leighton had always been watching the governor, looking for some false step, some wrong turn, some mistake that was the inevitable lot of a leader in a demanding new situation. And then when Russwurm did make some poor calculation or some error of judgment, the white missionary could say—but of course he is a colored man.[33]

A ғɪɴᴀʟ ᴅʀᴀᴍᴀᴛɪᴄ chapter of Fair Hope's history, however, remained to be played out during the months following Jane's departure. Four days after the *Atalanta* sailed, thieves broke into Fair Hope and took most of the trading goods that Griswold and the Walkers had brought out with them. They even took the skeleton Griswold had brought for his medical work. The theft was much more serious than the earlier pilfering—that had simply been a regular annoyance—and represented a major shift in the Grebo's relationship to what remained of Fair Hope. Griswold was furious, especially about the loss of his skeleton.[34]

Word soon circulated that the thieves were four headmen from Big Town. Walker wrote in his diary: "The whole people are engaged in this matter, and it leaks out." What soon leaked out was that Freeman was a recipient of some of the stolen goods. Griswold, as a young abolitionist, abhorred the colonization movement, and he, like most other abolitionists who knew of Russwurm, had little respect for him. Furthermore, he thought the colonial government had no authority over him or over the Grebo. So he ignored the governor and sent a note by Wasa asking for a palaver about the stolen goods. Freeman agreed, and the next day the king came to Fair Hope with a number of Grebo leaders. When Freeman arrived, Griswold immediately proceeded to read a statement from one of the Grebo leaders saying that Freeman had received some of the stolen goods. The king flew into a great rage and stormed away, threatening Griswold and the mission with a "heavy palaver" and violence. Dr. Savage, hearing reports of what had happened, sent word to Freeman saying that what they had done to Fair Hope they had done to him, that he was one with Fair Hope, and if Freeman touched Fair Hope, he was hurting the Episcopal mission as well.[35]

That evening there was a great palaver for Wasa, who was accused of giving information to the missionaries about the theft, but William Davis and Kra, another of the king's brothers, stood up for Wasa and there was a decided majority in his favor. Nevertheless, when Wasa returned to Fair Hope, he gathered all of his possessions and sent them to Paul Sansay on Bayard Island to keep for him, for he feared he would be heavily fined.[36]

The next day, Griswold and Walker went to Big Town for another palaver. Freeman explained how he had been insulted by the charges, saying they had made his heart burn. Then he said to the young Vermonters: "American black man was all the same as himself," implying that as white men they did not have the same relationship to the Grebo as the black settlers. Freeman told Griswold and Walker that as they had just arrived at the Cape and were soon going away, they did not understand the way a palaver worked. You "make this palaver wrong," said the king. Freeman then stood, said the palaver was settled, and went off greatly pleased with himself. The missionaries believed that Russwurm had been acting behind the scenes to encourage Freeman to ignore them and walk away from the palaver.[37]

The matter thus rested for the next two weeks while the men went about their business. Walker and Griswold began negotiations with Russwurm's father-in-law, George McGill, who was eager to purchase the buildings at Fair Hope and get control of the Fair Hope land. In spite of the dispute with Freeman, Griswold was busy treating ill Grebo, even amputating a hand that had been badly mangled by the explosion of a gun.[38]

Then the dispute suddenly entered a dangerous new phase. Word arrived that a US man-of-war, the *Vandalia*, was approaching Cape Palmas to avenge the plunder of an American trading ship and the murder of its crew by a non-Grebo village some fifty miles south of Cape Palmas. Rumors spread that the navy would come to the aid of the missionaries and force the return of the stolen goods. William Davis came out to Fair Hope and reported that a settler had told him that the navy could not offer the mission any help unless the governor requested it. Russwurm, Davis said, was incensed that Griswold had not followed the protocol of asking him to negotiate the palaver with Freeman. Russwurm seemed determined to make the missionaries acknowledge the authority of the black colonial officials in any dealing with the Grebo.[39]

When the *Vandalia* arrived, its captain, William Ramsay, invited Walker and Griswold on board together with Lancelot Minor, an Episcopal missionary. Griswold, not feeling well, declined, and Walker and Minor spent a seasick day on the ship. Ramsay wanted to learn if they had heard any details about the plundered American ship. They had little to add to what Ramsay already knew, but during the course of their conversation, Walker told the captain of the difficulties the mission was having with Freeman and the Grebo. Minor then told how both the Episcopal mission and the mission of the American Board felt constantly harassed by the colonial authorities. Both missions, he said, had moved their work beyond the boundaries of the colony. Ramsay apparently found it very strange that the colony should take such a stand in regard to the missions. But more significantly, he said that since the colony was not recognized by the United States, he would act as if there were no colony or colonial authority at Cape Palmas.[40]

If Ramsay had no authority to recognize the settlement at Cape Palmas as a legitimate state, he did have the responsibility of protecting American citizens and their property. He consequently told the missionaries that he would send his first lieutenant to talk with Freeman and the Grebo headmen. The lieutenant would tell them that restitution must be made immediately or the captain would fire on them and destroy all their towns.[41]

Later in the day, Russwurm and George McGill came on board. For the first time in the seven months he had been in Africa, Walker met the governor. There had been no welcome from him when the missionaries had arrived. And when Russwurm had failed to attend Prudence's funeral or to send condolences, Walker had made no effort to visit the governor. Their relationship was thus strained even before their first meeting on the *Vandalia*.[42]

Ramsay, trying to gather whatever information he could about the plundered ship, asked Russwurm and McGill if they knew any details about what had happened. Russwurm went over what he had heard and then made the mistake of telling Ramsay how he should retaliate. The captain responded coolly, apparently thinking the governor presumptuous, and said he would act as he chose. Russwurm and McGill left the ship late in the afternoon without the captain saying a word to them about the colony and its relationship with the missions or his plans for dealing with the Grebo. The captain of an American merchant ship anchored at Cape Palmas told Walker the next day that the governor was not satisfied with his reception on board the *Vandalia* and that Captain Ramsay was as little satisfied with the governor.[43]

Several days later, Ramsay followed up on his promise to help the missionaries recover their stolen goods. The lieutenant whom he sent ashore, a

"Lt. Ring," came with some marines. Ring immediately sent for Freeman to meet him at Fair Hope. The king delayed and then said that Ring should come to Big Town for the palaver. Ring sent word again that the king should come to Fair Hope or he would have him brought there. Finally Freeman arrived with his headmen. He told Ring how such matters had been handled in the past—the governor had called on the king to return the stolen goods or make restitution, and then had waited on him to do so. The lieutenant took no notice of this earlier protocol but proceeded to enumerate the stolen goods. He then asked Freeman if they would have the goods returned to Fair Hope. The king said the same thing over again—how in the past the governor had asked Freeman for the return of the goods and then had waited for the king to make restitution. Ring told him he had heard that once and would not hear it again. He must say yes or no very quickly. Ring reported his instruction from Captain Ramsay: he was "requiring the return of the goods and promise of good conduct in the future, or he should proceed to punish them by destruction of their town and by hanging up the King and headmen." This, noted Walker, "cut the old King dreadfully. He found himself in close quarters. He then said, 'We will pay it.'" Ring had Freeman and his headmen put their marks on an agreement to have the stolen goods returned. After inscribing their marks, they left, saying, "Them be too big men. We fraid of them."[44]

Walker and Griswold found themselves agreeing with the Grebo. Ring, although a pleasant man in their estimation, had looked savage, Walker wrote, because of his irritation with Freeman's delays. What worried the missionaries was their fear that Ramsay and Ring had put themselves in a difficult situation. If the Grebo failed to return the goods, would Ramsay actually fire on them? The missionaries, having raised the issue with the navy, now found that they had unleashed the possibility of a violent military response. The guns of the *Vandalia* might end up destroying Big Town and killing some of the very people the mission had been established to serve. Having long taken the stand that the mission could not participate in any military action against the Grebo, they now faced the embarrassing and potentially disastrous possibility of having instigated a naval bombardment of Big Town! Meeting with the Episcopal missionaries, they sent a joint note to Captain Ramsay insisting that they could recommend only peaceful measures.[45]

When Russwurm learned of the palaver at Fair Hope, he was outraged that he had been bypassed. He sent a protest to Ramsay and included documents asserting his authority. The captain ignored the documents, except to ask why they had been sent. Russwurm then sent a note to Ramsay, which the captain, in disgust, sent to Fair Hope for Griswold and Walker to read. In it, Russwurm pointed out that the colonial government was the legally established government of the colony and had responsibility for dealing with the Grebo. He said that as governor of the colony, he had not been treated with all due respect by the missionaries in their palaver with Freeman. For their conduct, he concluded, "the government can assign but one cause— *bitter prejudice*, which as Christian missionaries, should be laid aside for the time being, at least, while they continue in the black man's country." Moreover, wrote Russwurm, there had been a want of courtesy on Ramsay's part in his dealing with the colonial government—the captain had failed to consult the colonial authorities before sending Lt. Ring to Fair Hope and holding the palaver with Freeman. The captain thought the governor impertinent and did not reply to his note.[46]

At this dangerous point, William Davis became a critical player in the negotiations, serving as a middleman between the various factions. Freeman was still delaying the return of the stolen goods. Davis called a palaver with his brother and the other Grebo leaders and told them they must act quickly to return what had been stolen; if the goods could not be returned, they would have to pay for them. Freeman and the leaders protested, saying that Russwurm had said they did not have to pay; indeed, they believed they would be fools to do so. But Davis persisted, saying that he had heard that Ramsay was planning to send a boat to take Freeman and some headmen on board the *Vandalia* and keep them there until the stolen goods were returned or restitution made.[47]

Nothing was settled by the palaver, but Freeman was clearly growing anxious. The Grebo were realizing that Ramsay was serious and intended to use his naval power to secure some compensation for the missionaries. Davis sent a note to the captain asking for twenty-four hours to try to settle the matter. Ramsay responded positively and asked Davis to write to him and tell him what he knew. Had Russwurm, the captain wondered, tried to interfere behind the scenes in the negotiations between the missionaries and the Grebo?

Davis wrote the captain and gave him details that went back before the arrival of the *Vandalia*. Immediately after the goods had been stolen, Griswold had sent a letter to Freeman via Wasa. The king had gathered the headmen and had had Davis read the letter to all of them. Griswold said in the letter that he didn't want to hurt the Grebo and had urged Freeman to return what had been stolen before the man-of-war arrived. The king, Davis wrote the captain, responded to Griswold's letter by saying that he did not believe the US Navy would act on behalf of the missionaries. Davis had persisted and had asked his brother and the people "how much rice you gone to pay." They responded by saying that the governor and some leading settlers told them that "we must no pay anything to these ministrys." But, Davis wrote Ramsay, he was now hearing the people say, "Gov. tell no truth." After I heard this, Davis said, "I feel sorry because I fear them to get heavy palaver."[48]

In the end, under Davis's leadership, a palaver was settled, the goods were paid for in rice and cattle, the guns of the *Vandalia* were not fired, and Freeman was soon back at Fair Hope eating dinner and going to church. Russwurm, however, sent a protest to the naval authorities in Washington. Ramsay informed the colonization board of Russwurm's interference with the missionary's palaver. The naval authorities cleared Ramsay—he was doing his duty to protect Americans, and the US government did not recognize Maryland in Liberia as a state.[49]

Latrobe and his colleagues, however, were outraged. A year earlier they had given their rose-tinted report to the Maryland legislature, claiming that a happy relationship—"in every way satisfactory"—existed between the colonization society and the missionaries. Now, in December 1842, they wrote the mission boards that if the missionaries ignored the colonial government again, the missions would have to leave immediately. Anderson replied apologizing for Griswold, saying that he was young and did not understand the established protocol; if Leighton had been there, things would have been different. And he wrote a scolding letter to Griswold which the Vermonter vigorously rejected. If placed in the same situation again, Griswold wrote back, he would pursue precisely the same course. Moreover, if he had been wrong, then he was the one to make an apology, and he was sorry that Anderson had presumed to apologize for him. The US government, he reminded Anderson, did not recognize the authority of the colonial government; the Grebo had not submitted to the authority of the colonial government; and Russwurm did not have even the shadow of authority over the Cape Palmas Grebo. Griswold pointed out that he had not become a citizen of the colony, and Anderson and the American Board were not to attempt to settle his civil relations; nor should they pretend to have the power to surrender him to any foreign government. The young Vermonter and Yale graduate, who had stood with the *Amistad* prisoners, was not going to be intimidated by a mission board in Boston![50]

Later, when he learned of the whole affair, Leighton backed him up. In a more restrained and diplomatic manner, he wrote to Anderson that he would have done the same as Griswold, as Russwurm had no authority over the Grebo. James, who had been at Fish Town during the controversy, was even more circumspect. As an African American missionary, he wrote as well, quoting the part of Russwurm's letter in which he accused the white missionaries of ignoring him and of being prejudiced against him as a black man. "With regard to W and G refusing to ask Gov R.'s assistance I have nothing to say," he wrote. "Your decision on the matter will be perfectly satisfactory to my mind knowing as you do the state of affairs between the colony and the mission." And the mission board itself—much to the delight of abolitionists—finally publicly declared that the missionary movement and colonization were not compatible.[51]

But it was all, of course, already a settled matter as far as the mission at Fair Hope was concerned. A few weeks after the Grebo had made restitution with rice and cattle, Griswold and Walker, together with the widow Mrs. Dr. Wilson and some more teachers and students, sailed for Gabon. James, Margaret, and Catherine, however, stayed behind at Fair Hope. Margaret was pregnant, and they didn't want to leave the old mission cottage until the baby had been born and had passed safely through the seasoning fever. They planned to stay until Leighton returned for a short visit to close up the affairs of the mission in 1843; at the same time, Leighton would be meeting Jane upon her return from the United States.[52]

The days of Fair Hope mission thus drew close to a conclusion. The mission was leaving behind as its legacy a Grebo grammar, dictionary, hymn book, school books, and part of a Grebo Bible. It was also leaving behind William Davis and a cluster of other Grebo Christians. The converts were already beginning to attach themselves to the Episcopal mission and its schools and stations, which lay beyond the colony's borders. None of those leaving and none of those staying could have imagined that in the years ahead a Grebo Christian leader would emerge who would transform the religious life of a great multitude of West African people.

Chapter Thirteen

"The Liberty of Choosing for Themselves"

A s Jane sailed toward New York through the rolling waters of the Atlantic, she no doubt thought of her sister, Margaret, and Margaret's
husband, James Eckard. She was eager to see them and had learned shortly
before leaving Fair Hope that they, too, were returning to the United States.
Already in the summer of 1842 they were on board some ship moving
through the waters of a distant ocean toward home and a reunion with family
and friends.[1]

The Wilsons had kept up with the Eckards through letters from home
that conveyed news of them, as well as by reading missionary papers that
gave reports from scattered but rapidly growing mission stations around the
world. But there had also been letters from Margaret and James that had
made their way across oceans to Cape Palmas. Sometimes they arrived as a
surprise when a ship sailing from Ceylon or India stopped at Cape Palmas.
But most often they came doubling back, having been received by some friend
in England who forwarded them to Fair Hope. These carefully folded pieces
of paper with their messages in ink—often smudged or blotted—arrived as
welcomed news after their long journeys and as indicators that the ocean
highways of an Atlantic world were connected to other highways that crossed
other oceans in great circular networks. Traveling along these highways were
people, animals, plants, and pathogens; cloth and spices; guns; and any other
article of trade that promised a profit. And along these highways and their
connecting dusty or muddy roads, Protestant missionaries had been traveling
and sending letters and reports in increasing numbers for several decades.[2]

The missionary journals and religious papers that had arrived at Cape
Palmas in carefully packed bundles had been reminders to Leighton and Jane
that their mission at Fair Hope was part of a worldwide mission effort
among Protestants. The *Missionary Herald* from Boston, the *Missionary Register*

and the *Missionary Herald* from London, the *Charleston Observer* from South
Carolina, and the *Home and Foreign Record* from New York—these and other
journals and papers had come to Fair Hope as manna from heaven and had
been slowly and lovingly consumed. Leighton and Jane had carefully paced
themselves in order to spread over as many days as possible the pleasures of
reading about a world beyond the surf at Cape Palmas. They had read about
Leighton's friend John Adger, who was working among the Armenians in
Turkey, translating the Bible into modern Armenian while being protected
by the Turkish government. They had read of J. L. Merrick, Leighton's classmate at Columbia, and his work in Persia, and about missions in southern
Africa and in India and China and on the islands of the Pacific and
Caribbean. But most of all, they had read with intense interest the reports
on the life and work of the Eckards in Ceylon among the Tamil people.[3]

James Eckard had been teaching at Batticotta Seminary on the Jaffna
Peninsula, where a strong educational system was being rapidly developed
by Protestant missionaries from the United States and Britain. He had taught
in both English and Tamil and had assisted in the production of thousands
of tracts and books pouring from four missionary presses on the peninsula—
13,289,000 pages had been produced in 1839 alone! Cholera was the great
scourge among the people there, and James often had to act the role of physician. He later told Charles Hodge that he gave cholera sufferers a mixture
of calomel and opium, and that if the potion was retained, it usually resulted
in a cure.[4]

But Margaret and James had not been immune themselves to the diseases
of a tropical environment, and after nine years in Ceylon, they were headed
home in 1842 in the hope that Margaret would regain her health. Jane's return to the United States was timed in part for her to see her much-loved
sister. But neither Jane nor Leighton had realized how difficult their separation would be, how much they would miss one another, and how anxious
they would be as month after month passed with no communication between
them.

JANE ARRIVED IN New York in the early fall of 1842 and hurried south to
be reunited with her Pennsylvania family. Eight years had passed since she
and Leighton had sailed for Cape Palmas, and she was eager to see her Bayard
cousins—Theodosia Bayard and Elizabeth Bayard Henry were like sisters to
her, and she regarded James Bayard as a brother. But Jane was also eager to
see and consult with her cousin Hugh Hodge, a prominent Philadelphia
physician and professor at the Medical College of the University of Penn-

sylvania. In addition to her recurrent spells of fever, she had never fully recovered from her bout with dysentery in the fall of 1841. The attack had left her weak, and some of its symptoms still lingered when she arrived in Philadelphia. Dr. Hodge insisted that she stay in the city under his care for several months, so she stayed in the fine home of James Bayard on Washington Square in Philadelphia, and Theodosia and the Henrys visited her there. She told them about life at Cape Palmas and the work and adventures she and Leighton had had among the Grebo people.[5]

During her absence, the Bayards and Henrys and their church friends had read not only Jane's letters but also Leighton's reports, which had been published in the *Missionary Herald*. They must have had a thousand questions for Jane: What did a greegree look like? Did the Grebo still leave bodies on the island of the dead? Had she seen a sassy wood ordeal herself? Could the children really learn to read and write in English?

Jane surely faced these questions and also many more, for she had been to a distant land and had lived among "savages." Missionaries—even missionary wives—were expected to tell stories of such exotic places and exotic peoples and to report on the spread of the gospel in foreign lands. And much to James Bayard's distress—he had been secretary of the Philadelphia branch of the American Colonization Society—Jane had to explain why they were leaving Cape Palmas after so many years there and after all of their efforts to learn Grebo and work among the Grebo people. There had been conflicts with Russwurm and Latrobe, and she and Leighton and the other missionaries had come to believe that colonization was a type of imperialism that hindered their work as missionaries. They had finally decided to leave Cape Palmas because of the hostility of the settlers and the colonial authorities. The papers were already reporting extensively on the controversy and stating the charges and countercharges between the missionaries and the colonial authorities.[6]

Jane, of course, could not speak at a public meeting or during a church service, for she was a woman, and her sphere was confined by polite society to that which was private and domestic. Besides, Jane was shy and did not even want her name to appear in print. So she spoke quietly in elegant parlors and drawing rooms, in carriages rumbling down busy Philadelphia streets, and at dinner tables loaded with familiar food, and in this way and in these circumscribed situations she conveyed images of Africa to family and friends. She told them of the Grebo and of life on a mission station overlooking the Atlantic. She told stories of King Freeman and his remarkable brother William Davis, and of Simleh Ballah with his filed teeth and tattoo. She told of how the men had been frequent guests at her dinner table, and how they had taught the missionaries much about the ways of the Grebo. And she had, as well, much to tell about the settlers at Harper—about Governor Russ-wurm and Paul Sansay; about Charlotte, Paul's sister, who had once been Jane's personal servant; and about all the others who had once lived on Hutchinson Island across from Savannah and who now lived on Bayard Island across a little river from Harper and Big Town.

And she had much to say about Fair Hope—how it had become like a little village, with its houses and garden, with its school and church, and with even its own cemetery on a bluff above the Atlantic. She and Leighton had lived there in their cottage, and there she had taught in her school, with students such as Wasa and Maria, Mary Clealand, and other sons and daughters of the Grebo. Now, in Philadelphia, she described Fair Hope as a remem-bered place, a habitation filled with purpose and anchored in her imagination. She and Leighton had been happy there, in spite of illness and grief and dis-appointment, and they had been full of hope there; they had felt at home there even as they had known Fair Hope was not their home. And in spite of her reticence and her restricted sphere as a woman, her narratives began to be reported in papers as the experiences of a highborn woman in Africa. In this way Jane became an interpreter of Africa—a vast continent—and through family and friends and papers her stories and her interpretations be-came for many a window into an imagined world.[7]

In late November 1842, Jane was able to leave Dr. Hodge's care and sail for Savannah. After a short trip down the coast, her ship moved slowly up the Savannah River until the little tree-covered city came into view, and then the ship came to anchor across from Hutchinson Island. As she looked around her, Jane now saw Savannah and its waterfront with the eyes of one who had seen an African coast and had come ashore at an African cape in an African canoe with singing Grebo boatmen. Familiar scenes greeted her as she made her way from the riverfront up to the Savannah bluff—slave porters pushing heavy carts up the steep cobblestone dray-ways, slave women walking elegantly with baskets of vegetables on their heads, slave fishermen hawking mullet and shrimp, crabs and oysters. Jane now saw all of this as one who had sat at table with King Freeman and William Davis and Simleh Ballah, who had taught Wasa and Maria and Mary Clealand. And she saw it all as one who knew free people living on Bayard Island who had once lived as slaves across the Savannah.

Jane had a happy reunion with Nicholas and his family. He had been through deep waters himself—he had been married twice and twice widowed. He was now married a third time—to a widow with three children—and he and his large family welcomed Jane back to her old Savannah home. Jane went out to Richmond-on-Ogeechee and saw her friend Eliza Clay, who was still conducting her classes for the religious instruction of her slaves. But Eliza's brother Thomas Clay had died a young man, and Eliza was now running the large plantation while looking after her brother's children and his rather helpless widow. In Savannah, Jane went and sat once again in the pew where she had once sat with her parents at the Independent Presbyterian Church. There, as she sang familiar hymns, she could look into the high balcony that surrounded the elegant sanctuary and see slaves sitting in their place. And when communion was celebrated, and the slaves came out of the balcony, they sat at the long table by themselves after the white members had been served. How different from Fair Hope, where she had sat at the communion table with William Davis and Wasa and the other worshipping Christians.[8]

Then, in the late fall 1842, Jane was at last reunited with Margaret, who finally arrived from Ceylon with her husband. Jane and Margaret had been inseparable as young sisters, and now, after eight years apart, they had much to share. Margaret had suffered greatly from cholera and showed in her worn looks how desperately sick she had been. But she was recovering, and she had happy memories of Ceylon and the Tamil people on its north coast. The Batticotta school where James had taught was thriving—many wealthy Hindus were sending their sons to the mission school to be prepared for a changing world. Few, it was true, had converted—they seemed more interested in receiving a Western education than in becoming Christian—but some had been drawn to Christianity and had been baptized. Already some of the school's former students had become teachers and pastors, and they were laying, it was hoped, the foundation for a Tamil church. But the Eckards had already decided that Margaret's health would not allow them to return, so their years of mission work had come to an end. James had agreed to spend the next year in Savannah raising funds for the American Board.[9]

Nicholas told the sisters how he had managed their property while they had been away. Most of the land on Hutchinson Island had been sold for the handsome price of $8,000. Nicholas, prudent man that he was, had invested the money in insurance and railroad stock. Both stocks held promise for the future—especially the stock in the Central Railway, which was soon to connect Savannah with Macon in the middle of the state. A transportation revolution was sweeping the country, and Nicholas was glad to be able to transfer some capital from land to railroads. Already the stocks were providing a good return on their money, better than what was received from land still owned by the sisters. Altogether a substantial fund had been accumulated for them during their years abroad.[10]

Margaret learned the details of the emancipation of their slaves, and from Jane she no doubt learned about those who had once lived on Hutchinson Island. Jane reported that Paul Sansay was doing well and had become a friend to some of the Grebo converts, but he had been in a major dispute with a newly arrived Catholic missionary (who would stay only a short time at the Cape) over some work Paul had done for him. Paul's sister, Charlotte, had adopted two orphaned children, but had seldom come out to Fair Hope to visit Jane, her former mistress. John, who had been the driver on Hutchinson Island, and his wife, Catherine, had gone with John's younger sister, Rhina, to work with Presbyterian missionaries some miles north of Cape Palmas at Sutra Kru and were as hard working and reliable as always. But it had been a mistake, Jane no doubt said, to send them all to the Maryland colony, with its deep hostility toward the Grebo—it would have been better to have made arrangements for them to settle in a Northern state.[11]

The sisters made a quick trip to Fair Hope plantation to see their McIntosh relatives, who had been so kind to them as orphaned girls. For both of them, but especially for Jane, the plantation was a place of deep memories. Here she had learned to love the quiet of a Lowcountry landscape, and here she had experienced the love of her McIntosh family. Once again she saw Gullah people working in rice and cotton fields and saw their evening fires in the plantation settlement, and she heard once again their distinct Creole intonations, which evoked memories of Big Town and another Fair Hope.[12]

Jane needed to see not only her own family but also Leighton's, so after her time in Savannah and at Fair Hope she made her way to Pine Grove shortly before Christmas 1842. There she found the Wilsons waiting to see their dear Jane and hear reports from Africa. Now, as she had with her family and friends in Pennsylvania and Georgia, she told her stories of Africa and of Leighton and of their work among the Grebo people. After church and at the dinner table, and later sitting on the piazza on balmy winter afternoons, questions were asked and answers were given that built a missionary narrative and painted an image of Africa as seen through the eyes of one who had lived in a cottage at Cape Palmas. There she had taught bright, eager Grebo children not only to read and write, but also geography and math and natural science. There in that distant place she had regularly welcomed to her dinner table black men and women—Margaret and Catherine Strobel from Savannah; Mr. B. V. R. James from New York; and King Freeman, Simleh Ballah, and William Davis from Big Town. How strange and exotic—and not a little threatening—it must have all seemed to those whites who lived their settled lives close to the Black River and not far from the cabins at Boggy Gully.[13]

And what did old Jacob the cook and those who served meals and cleaned rooms and brought tea to the piazza, what did they hear when they heard these stories told to the Wilsons and their friends? Did they have their own questions to ask Jane? How did those who had sent Leighton off with such a tumultuous outpouring of emotion and prayer respond to Jane's stories of Africa? How, in the evenings around communal fires by Boggy Gully, did they retell what they had heard and overheard about black men eating at the same table with a white woman, about black children learning to read and write so quickly, about the Grebo William Davis helping Leighton to translate whole books of the Bible?[14]

THE SLAVE SETTLEMENT at Boggy Gully presented its own questions to Jane. How was she, a missionary teacher among the Grebo, a missionary host to Grebo men, a missionary wife who had sought to demonstrate a Christian life to Grebo people—how was she to react to those who lived in bondage at Pine Grove? In particular, what was this missionary going to do about her husband's two slaves? Leighton had inherited them through his mother, and he knew little about them. He had asked Jane, before she left for the United States, to visit with them and to try to get to know a little about them. Perhaps, he said, she could prevail on them to accept an offer of freedom and move to one of the free states.[15]

Jane met with John and Jesse and found that John, the older of the two, had married and did not wish to leave his wife. Jesse, still a young boy, was attached to his mother—she was in poor health and increasingly feeble—and he did not wish to leave his Black River home either.[16]

Leighton had never received a reply from Rufus Anderson in Boston or a friend in New York when he had written them in 1838 about the possibility of John's going north and learning some "mechanical art" or becoming a bookbinder. Nor had Leighton had a reply from his request that Jesse be educated in Boston. Leighton had only the vaguest memory of Jesse and had thought the young slave a girl. "My only desire is that she may be educated" Leighton had written Anderson in 1838, "and set free where she would be happy and respectable."[17]

While nothing had come of Leighton's efforts to find a place for the young men in Boston or New York, his continuing ownership of them had not gone unnoticed by abolitionists. He was accused of being "a man stealer," and the American Board was being increasingly attacked for employing a "man stealer" as a missionary. Anderson had written letters to both Jane and Leighton about the matter. Jane responded after her return to Philadelphia, explaining that the Bayard slaves had been freed, but both John and Jesse refused to leave their Black River home. She wrote Anderson: "These young men know fully, for I have spoken to them myself, that they can go to Africa or one of the northern states at any time they please. We can compel them to do either. Shall we do it?" And from Gabon Leighton wrote, telling the story once again of Paul Sansay and the others who had lived on Hutchinson Island and who now lived as free people in West Africa. He rehearsed one more time the story of his inheritance of John and Jesse, of how he had tried to free them and make arrangements for them to go to the North, and of how he had received no replies to his inquiries and how he had heard from his sister that they were "decidedly opposed to leaving the place of their nativity," and that their family and "others thought the proposition unkind." He told how he had asked Jane to try to get them to go north, and said that if she failed, he could think of only one thing to do—present a petition to the South Carolina legislature to allow them to be freed and remain in the state. He and Jane both emphasized that Leighton had never received any money that came from John's and Jesse's labors. Indeed, he said, "so far as I have had funds to dispose of in the cause of humanity, they have been appropriated *chiefly* to promote the happiness and comfort of those who have been in bondage." And then he added a jab at the abolitionists who had been attacking him: "I have no desire nor have I had for years to see any of my fellow men in bondage, and perhaps when the secrets of eternity are revealed, it may be seen that I have not done less for the cause of freedom than some of my fellow men who think I have been remiss."[18]

Leighton, in his letter to Anderson, addressed what he regarded as the underlying assumptions of those who had attacked him. He did not understand their reasoning, he wrote Anderson—Was it his duty to use *force* with his slaves? He thought it better to use moral means, to try to persuade them to claim their freedom and leave the state. John and Jesse, he insisted, "have the liberty of choosing for themselves, and I have endeavored to communicate such light and information as will enable them to choose wisely. And this seems to me, if not the highest liberty they are capable of enjoying, it is the best that is in my power to confer. If I take away this liberty of choice, and coerce them, then it seems to me I would be guilty of exercising that arbitrary authority over them which is one of the worst and most prominent features of slaveholding."[19]

Leighton admitted that there may be situations where it would be proper for a person to act for the good of another, even against the will of the other. But Leighton did not think this was such a case—for if he exerted his right to act for John and Jesse, he would sacrifice their rights. Nor did he think it would be for the general good of the slaves of the South if he protected himself from the attacks of abolitionists by freeing John and Jessie without moving them out of the state. They would then become public property and would be auctioned to the highest bidder. That, at best, he said, would amount to "the doubtful principle of sacrificing the private rights of individuals to the general good of mankind."[20]

Leighton was revealing in his letter to Anderson how deeply he was rooted in the physical, social, and intellectual world of Pine Grove—in spite of his travels and broad interests and commitments. He valued the concrete, the particular, the given, and he sought to avoid abstractions like "the general good of mankind." He was willing to consider the general good of slaves in the South, but what he was really concerned about were not abstract slaves, but slaves with names—John and Jesse—and their right to make decisions for themselves.

This deep commitment to the concrete and the particular, together with his strong sense of place, would lead Leighton and Jane in 1861 to make a surprising choice of their own. But, of course, their choice—like the choices made by John and Jesse and the bitter choices made earlier by those who lived on Hutchinson Island—was not going to be simply a choice reflecting the private rights of individuals. Leighton and Jane were going to find themselves having to make a choice not as lonely individuals, but as a couple deeply enmeshed in family and rooted in a Southern landscape and entangled in the web of slavery.

In the end, Leighton sent his father certificates of freedom for John and Jesse. "If John and Jesse," he said, "would go to one of the free States, I would be greatly pleased. But if they prefer to remain on the plantation and work as heretofore, then let them do so, with the understanding that they may leave whenever they choose to do so." Leighton thought that if the whole matter were not "noised abroad," then only family would know that he had freed them, and no one in the neighborhood would feel disposed to disturb them. If, however, word got out that they had been freed, then they could be sent out of the state. "I feel assured," he wrote his father, "that you will do the best for them that you can." And he added: "I commend them to the care of the Lord."[21]

So at Leighton's instructions, both men continued to live at Boggy Gully, only now as free men. They received a small income from their work plus their board and clothing. They had their taxes paid by Leighton's father. John became what Leighton's brother Sam called "something of a carpenter" and made extra money for himself by building kitchen furniture, flour boxes, and other household items, which he readily sold. Young Jessie did what brother Sam called "light labour" for a few years and lived in the cabin with his mother. Later he took up the hard labor of a farmhand, married, and lived with his wife close to the waters of Boggy Gully.[22]

PART III

Life Among the Mpongwe

Chapter Fourteen

Toko and the *Waterwitch*

When Leighton had left Cape Palmas in the spring of 1842, he did not know what lay ahead of him or what the future of the mission might be. He only knew that he and Benjamin Griswold had to find an alternative to Fair Hope, and that Captain Lawlin had told them that Gabon was a good possibility. From the start of the trip south, however, Leighton had been restless, worried about what lay ahead, and he had missed Jane terribly. Except for Leighton's short trips into the interior, they had been together constantly since their marriage eight years earlier.

As Lawlin had sailed the *Atalanta* further and further south, Leighton had poured out his heart in letters to Jane, who was then waiting at Cape Palmas for Lawlin to return and take her to the United States. "My dear wife," Leighton wrote, "I was little aware how severe a duty I was imposing both upon you and myself when I proposed a separation of nine months or a year." He said his time with her had been the eight happiest years of his life, happier than all the rest of his life put together. He wrote that while their early years together had been all "fervor and glow, the longer and more matured part of our life has been the season of a steadily growing affection." He felt overwhelmed when he remembered how as a young bride she had cared for him during his long and deranged bout with malaria. She had been a lonely woman on the coast of Africa watching over what she thought was a dying husband. He told her that her name and image were constantly in his mind, and that, thinking of her, he was encouraged, even though he was sailing toward an unknown destination. Standing on the *Atalanta*'s deck and watching mile after mile of African coastline passing slowly before him, Leighton had felt his world shifting and its foundations shaking, and only his sense of a guiding providence, of a higher purpose for their lives, had kept him from becoming seriously depressed.[1]

To help keep his melancholy in check, Leighton turned his attention to the passing African coastline. He took careful note of its rivers and lagoons, and noted the changing contours of the land—from the high tableland of the Ivory Coast to the hills of the Gold Coast to the mountains of Cameroon. When Captain Lawlin went ashore, Leighton and his traveling companions accompanied him. They spent a few days at Elmina and a week at Cape Coast, and Leighton had time to visit once again the sites where years earlier so many slaves had been kept in wretched dungeons before being shipped to Jamaica or Cuba or Charleston or some other place of waiting slave markets. With him on these visits was not only Griswold but also a Dr. McDowell. The doctor was an artist of sorts, who kept busy throughout the whole trip drawing scenes of a passing mainland and of West African life. On his return to Cape Palmas, McDowell would give Jane a collection of his sketches.[2]

When they had finally reached Gabon, Lawlin had taken the *Atalanta* slowly into the wide estuary—about fourteen miles across where it met the Atlantic. They sailed along the north shore past Point Clara and Qua Ben's Town before the *Atalanta* came to anchor off King Glass's Town. Glass—his Mpongwe name was R'Ogouarouwé—was the "Big Man" of the Agekaza clan of the Mpongwe people, and his town was the most important trading center in the region (although it, along with the other Mpongwe towns, was small in comparison to Big Town). Glass had immediately come out to greet them in a neat sailing boat. With him was Lawlin's trading partner and old friend Toko. They had been wanting an English school to be established for their children, and they said they would build a school if Leighton and Griswold established their mission at Glass's Town. Toko invited all of the Cape Palmas newcomers to stay in his home—a large and comfortable house with a number of rooms and European furniture. Dr. McDowell drew a handsome sketch of Toko and of Yanaway, most likely a daughter of Glass, and Leighton and Griswold quickly concluded that they had found the place for the new mission.[3]

Griswold wrote the mission board to give the reasons for their decision. There was, he said, no other mission in the estuary, so there would be no duplication of mission work. The Mpongwe were eager to have schools and they were, Griswold thought, among the most civilized people they had encountered on the West African coast—he was most impressed by their sailboats, which were far more sophisticated than the dugout canoes he had seen used by others. Yet, in spite of their sophistication, they were a people, he said, deeply in need of the Christian gospel—they were unmistakably pagan, with their greegree houses at the entrances to their towns and with charms that covered their bodies to "preserve themselves from sickness, defend themselves from danger, and deliver themselves from the evil spirit." Griswold wrote that the location of Glass's Town by the shores of the estuary was also a reason he and Leighton had selected it as the place for the new mission—the rivers that emptied into the estuary provided easy transportation into the interior and promised access to people far removed from the coast. And finally, Gabon seemed—for Africa—a healthy place, although Griswold was quick to say that "no one must come to Africa who will shrink from suffering or who is afraid of death."[4]

Leighton wrote Jane that "The Gaboon," as he called the Gabon region, "is a new chapter in my African experience. Things are greatly different from anything we have ever before seen in Africa. The river itself (I think it should rather be denominated a bay) is a noble one, and opposite the place where we are to live is greatly enlivened by beautiful sailboats flying in every direction." The place they were to live was just outside of King Glass's Town, about half a mile from the shore on a hill called Baraka. In earlier years there had been a Portuguese slave barracoon there, and one of the first tasks before the missionaries was clearing away the bones of slaves whose bodies had simply been dragged away and left in the bush—an ominous sign of things to come.[5]

While Lawlin was still in the estuary trading and negotiating with Toko, Leighton and Griswold hurried to learn as much as they could about the area. One day they secured a boat and sailed across the estuary—almost twenty miles—to the south shore to visit the town of King William, who was also called King Denis by the French and Antchouwe Kowe Rapontchombo by the Mpongwe. Both Leighton and Griswold were immediately impressed. Leighton described the king as a man of medium stature, with a compact and well-formed frame and great muscular power. He was about sixty years old and had a very black complexion that contrasted wonderfully with his large, snow-white beard. Leighton thought he had mild and expressive eyes and a gentle and persuasive voice that was friendly and dignified. He was, Leighton thought, the most king-like man he had ever met in Africa. Griswold also found him to possess a remarkably pleasant face. Seldom, Griswold remarked, had he "seen a man more agreeable in his manners. His intercourse with his people seemed marked with kindness, mildness, dignity and authority." The king showed them his Legion of Honor medal, which he had received from the French for his aid to French sailors, and a gold medal from Queen Victoria for rescuing four British sailors. He spoke French and Pidgin English and most likely some Portuguese and Spanish. He was clearly an impressive person, but the missionaries would later learn that he was also a much more complicated person than they at first perceived.[6]

William received them warmly and invited them to dinner. Unlike the Grebo, who would have had Leighton and Griswold sit on the ground with them to eat, William ushered them to chairs at a table set with silver knives, forks, and spoons. The king had a fine meal served to his guests—including wine and champagne, which the missionaries politely refused. Afterward, he took them to see some of his town. They saw manacled slaves, many of whom belonged to the king, and learned to their mortification that most of the slavers used ships built in New England for the slave trade. They were told the ships had been sailed to Cuba, where slavers had purchased them at a handsome price.[7]

The missionaries, in spite of their positive impressions of the king, were clearly disturbed by what they perceived to be his engagement with the slave trade. They had every right to be. William took them a short distance from town and showed them a barracoon kept by a diseased and short-tempered Spaniard. Leighton wrote Jane telling her what they found. "Think of four hundred and thirty naked savages of both sexes, of all ages, sizes and conditions, brought together in one enclosure chained together as gangs of twenty, thirty and forty and all compelled to sleep on the same platform, eat out of the same tub, and in almost every respect live like so many swine. More than this, on the *middle passage* they must have still more circumscribed quarters and live on much scanter fare. But God reigns and this vile trade in human beings must come to an end."[8]

But more horrors were to come. A few days after their visit, the missionaries were informed that two men had escaped and had been recaptured. Brought back, they were tied up in the center of the barracoon, while all the people were made to stand around them and watch the terror that was to follow. The enraged Spaniard went into the midst of the people with his gun. While the two men watched, he charged it with powder and balls, and then walked within a few feet of the first man and fired directly into him. In his fury he recharged his gun and fired again and again, blowing the man apart as his terrified companion watched. He then turned to the second man, who, wrote Griswold, "stood by waiting a similar fate, which he received so soon as the Spaniard had glutted his vengeance upon his companion."[9]

Neither Leighton nor Griswold had been so close before to such degradation or witnessed such sickening violence as that done by the Spaniard.

Even the terrors of the sassy wood ordeal did not compare to such brutality. Leighton wrote Jane that he hoped never again to "visit a similar scene of human degradation." Griswold had his abolitionist's commitments strengthened. He wrote up what had happened and sent it back to Boston for publication and for the stirring of public outrage.[10]

NOT LONG AFTER Griswold departed with Lawlin and Dr. McDowell to return to Cape Palmas and his confrontation with King Freeman over stolen goods, Leighton began traveling regularly around the estuary. He was eager to visit various towns and talk with kings or the local Big Men about the establishment of schools. Toko was his primary guide. As the leading trader on the north shore, he had extensive contacts and an intimate knowledge of the region. Leighton estimated that he did $12,000 or $15,000 of business each year. The missionary was amazed that Toko could manage a business of this extent "in the smallest fractions and driblets, without the aid of any written accounts." Yet it was done, Leighton wrote in his journal, with the utmost accuracy, without any other aid than that of Toko's memory. The result was that Toko lived, it seemed to Leighton, in a respectable style and associated with foreigners on terms of a general equality.[11]

Leighton developed an almost immediate affection for Toko. The Mpongwe trader was hospitable, humorous, drank only a little rum, and was, above all, honest and dependable. About forty years old when Leighton first met him, Toko was of medium height with a dark black complexion. He possessed, Leighton wrote, "a very remarkable and intelligent countenance, strongly marked with the deep vein of natural humor which pervades his whole composition." Although wealthy, he was careless in his dress and unpretentious in his manners, but, Leighton noted, "his shrewdness and unbounded humor, almost in spite of himself, peer out at every turn in conversation." A great talker and storyteller, Toko on his frequent visits to Baraka could keep Leighton laughing late into the night—not an easy task with the serious missionary.[12]

Leighton compared Toko's storytelling with that of King William on the south shore. Both men, Leighton wrote, were familiar with all the traditional stories of their ancestors and had their minds amply stored with fables, allegories, and proverbial sayings. Leighton thought the king, who was more formal in his deportment, was precise and very cautious in all his statements. When telling a story to white men, Leighton wrote, "he is careful not to state anything too hard for their credence. He keeps his own fancy under restraint and is much more apt to take from than to add to the current stories of the country." Leighton thought William's stories more reliable than Toko's, as the king "deals more in actual facts than fictitious representations." So Leighton listened carefully to what William said in order to learn what he could about the history of the Mpongwe and the customs of the people.[13]

But if Leighton tried to learn from William's stories, he loved and delighted in Toko's. Toko, he said, knew nothing of William's restraint. "When he sets out to rehearse one of his favorite fables, all his humor is at once stirred up, and he yields himself to the spirit of his story. He is all glee himself, and the hearer cannot for his life avoid being carried along with him. The wild animals of the woods are summoned before his audience, they are endued with all the cunning and shrewdness of man, and before you are aware of it, you have before your imagination a perfect drama." Leighton found that Toko had no misgivings about exceeding the credulity of his hearers—his humor was constantly prompting him to test just how far he could take someone into the world of his imagination, and Leighton thought that he sometimes purposely stretched his points so far as to turn the whole story into outright burlesque. Toko's humor was clearly infectious. When he laughed, his whole body shook—he began to abandon himself to his laughter and to bend slowly to his right as his laughter overflowed from deep within him, spilling onto his hearers the surprises and inconsistencies of his story. He seemed to know instinctively that his humor and laughter came from uncovering, with a surprising twist in a story, the often hidden ambiguities and pretensions of life. Things were not always what they seemed, especially for white men. Toko told of Engena, the "largest and most powerful of the monkey tribe, and of Telinga, the smallest." Telinga, a shrewd and funny little fellow, tricked the powerful Engena into giving him his daughter for a bride. But the powerful animals of the forest, indignant that such a little monkey as Telinga should win the hand of the belle of the forest, drove Telinga away. So he "sprang into the nearest tree, and, ascending to its highest boughs, vowed never again to live on the ground, where there is so much violence and injustice." If Toko ever gave any hint that he thought Telinga might reflect something of his own experiences and hopes or those of someone else, Leighton never noted it.[14]

In time, Leighton came to realize that such fables and Toko's laughter and humor were deeply linked to love—to Toko's love for the Mpongwe people and for their traditions and ways. And Leighton, almost in spite of himself, found, as his listened to Toko and laughed with him, that he was in fact learning something from Toko, not only about the Mpongwe—the character and habits of the people and the geography of the country—but also about what it means to be human, with all of the hopes and fears, ironies, and deep ambiguities of human life.[15]

SHORTLY AFTER HIS arrival in Gabon in the summer of 1842, Leighton went with Toko to his plantation, which was a short distance from Glass's Town. When they arrived, they found Toko's wives working with his slaves as they prepared fields for planting plantains, cassava, yams, sweet potatoes, groundnuts, corn, pumpkins, and beans. Most of Toko's slaves lived on the plantation in the *ompindi*—a slave settlement close to the fields. Largely isolated from free people during most of the year, the slaves were joined by Toko's wives during planting and harvest time. Toko, like other rich Mpongwe men, only visited his plantations occasionally, giving most of his time to his work as a trader. When Leighton and Toko arrived, the women prepared a rich feast whose main course was fufu, made of green plantains mashed and shaped into long rolls and wrapped in plantain leaves. Leighton found it softer and more spongy than what he had usually eaten at Cape Palmas, but nevertheless tasty. A sauce, the consistency of butter, was made of parched peanuts pounded and baked with dried fish and was served with the fufu. It, too, was tasty, but Leighton found it rather rich. The man who had grown up by the waters of the Black River was being introduced to the particular flavors and textures of Mpongwe cuisine and to the particular character of Mpongwe slavery. They were distinct and different from what he had known before, but they were also familiar and pointed toward links in an Atlantic world.[16]

Toko, a man deeply rooted in the traditions of his people, was part of a world that stretched far beyond the waters and shoreline of the Gabon estuary. English and American merchants knew him well—especially those in Bristol and New York. And Toko knew them—their ways of doing business and the character of the merchandise they sent out to be traded along the African coast. He spoke English with ease and could also conduct business in Spanish, Portuguese, and French. He knew that the American captains who sailed into the estuary were in competition with the English, and that both were in competition with the French, and he had become only too well aware that distant politics influenced trade—especially who could buy slaves and who could not. Perhaps, above all, he was deeply aware of the power of Western culture and how it was beginning to transform life around the estuary. On one occasion, not long after William Walker arrived at the new mission station, Toko found him hard at work on some blacksmithing project and said to Walker that the "white man is a Devil." Walker told him "that was not a very good name." "Well," said Toko, "he is good Devil. He sabba [knows] everything." Toko saw in the white man's ability to "know every-thing" the root of the white man's power and wealth—power and wealth that were demonstrated every time a great ship came proudly sailing into the es-tuary from some distant place loaded with exotic goods, and often with large cannons. So the white man with his knowledge, the white man who "sabba everything," was a devil—he seemed a good devil who had come into the es-tuary with the tempting fruit of new knowledge that gave power and wealth. What Toko was beginning to realize, perhaps more than any other Mpongwe, was that there were fearsome costs to be paid for taking this fruit and eating this fruit and having this fruit of Western knowledge become a part of a Mpongwe man or woman and of Mpongwe society. But the temptation to take and eat was real, and Toko felt its attraction.[17]

It was not surprising, therefore, that Toko wanted his children educated by the missionaries so that they, too, might "sabba everything." Like the Grebo William Davis before him, Toko brought his daughter to the mission school as soon as it was established to live there and to learn the ways of the whites. Leighton had written Jane in the United States saying that he had given the young girl the English name "Jane Bayard," the name he said "I love so much, and with which she is not a little pleased." She was, Leighton said, "a beautiful and remarkably sprightly child." But the name did not stick, and even the missionaries soon came to call her by her Mpongwe name—Wâwâ—and they, along with her father, would learn in a few years just how "sprightly" she was. Toko also sent two sons to the school—Renjogo and Ntâkâ Truman. They were to be deeply immersed in the world and the West-ern knowledge of Baraka, but always as the children of the Mpongwe and of their father, Toko, who loved the traditions and ways of his people.[18]

WHEN A TRADE dispute broke out between the Mpongwe of Glass's Town and the Shékiani (a "bush people" who lived along the tributary rivers of the estuary), Toko was given the task of trying to settle the matter. He invited Leighton to join him. They would travel, he said, in fine style on his *Waterwitch*, the largest Mpongwe boat in the estuary, and would visit numerous towns in the interior. The missionary readily agreed. He was eager to learn what he could of the area while he and Jane were separated by so many miles.[19]

The *Waterwitch* was a wonder to Leighton. Built out of one enormous log, it was fitted with bulwarks, painted, and propelled by neat sails with elaborate rigging. A small, comfortable cabin made of thatch and saplings provided some protection from the tropical sun and from any rain squall that might come suddenly upon those sailing it on open water. Leighton could see that its sleek lines and careful construction revealed a high level of craftsmanship and made it fully capable of sailing on the open ocean. He took his mattress on board—he had the little cabin pretty much to himself—along with provisions for five or six days and medicines he might need. Several Mpongwe went along to serve as the crew, carrying their guns with them. Leighton was anticipating a great adventure, and he was not to be disappointed.[20]

They left Glass's Town around ten in the morning with sails set. A good breeze and strong tide turned the *Waterwitch* into a thing of life that raced over the waters. In the front of the boat the crew relaxed and huddled around a few smoldering embers to smoke their pipes. Later they stretched out to nap in the sun. The helmsman sailed the boat close to the north shore and Leighton saw thick tropical forests, grassy fields, and the wide streets of Mpongwe villages almost buried in plantain trees. He looked and he saw the water reflecting the forest and the sky, and he felt the steady movement of the boat and the breeze that carried them along, and he thought the whole scene one of transcendent beauty.

Late in the afternoon they approached the confluence of two rivers that poured their waters into the estuary. The smaller of the two—the Remboué—flowed from a southeasterly direction. At its mouth, it was about a mile across, and near its western bank stood an important Mpongwe town—Nghaga, or King George's Town. The people there were much engaged in the slave trade, being well located to buy slaves brought down the river from the interior and to sell them to Spanish or Portuguese traders who made their way up the estuary. King George himself owned hundreds of slaves, who worked his plantations and lived in the slave settlements.[21]

Toko turned the *Waterwitch* up the larger river, the Como, which was about two miles across at its mouth. As night began to come on, the men slackened the ropes on the sails, loaded their guns, and placed them so that they could be seen by anyone who might be thinking of attacking the boat. They were entering the "bushmen's country," Toko told Leighton, the land of the Bakèlè and Shékiani peoples, and Toko laughed and teased Leighton saying that he wanted the "bushmen" to know that Mpongwe could shoot as well as they. Toko sailed the *Waterwitch* into a moonlit night as the river waters lapped at the bow of the boat and shadows crept across the river. At about 9 p.m., they approached an island, ran the boat close to its sandy shore, anchored, and got out to stretch and rest for a while before sailing again into the night.

Several hours later, as the first hints of dawn began to touch the eastern sky and shadows began their retreat through morning mists, the *Waterwitch* reached the village of King Passall—a miserable place on marshy land over-run with mangroves and their tangled roots. They anchored and came ashore. Passall was not there, but Leighton thought the surprised inhabitants looked diseased and wretched, just as one might expect any people to look who lived in such a swampy, miasma-rich location. He didn't see a single healthy-looking person in the village, and he thought that it was "questionable whether another settlement could be found on this river, or anywhere else in the world, where there was a greater concentration in so small a compass of all sorts of diseases." The travelers rested, visited with the people, and waited for the Big Man of the village.[22]

Just before dark, Passall arrived. A short, stocky man, he looked healthier than the other inhabitants of his village, and Leighton thought him to be a good-natured, jolly old man. Toko, however, told the missionary that the year before, a British man-of-war had sent a boat up the Como in pursuit of a slave vessel. The officer on the boat had failed to take the necessary precau-tions, and three of the sailors had been killed at Passall's house. The others had been held until ransomed. Passall now invited those on the *Waterwitch* to stay in the same house—and they did so without fear, apparently because Toko was with them.

For the next several days they remained there while Toko engaged in pre-liminary negotiations. The dispute that Toko had come to settle had arisen between the Shékiani of a nearby village and the Mpongwe of Glass's Town. The Mpongwe had failed to pay a debt they owed the Shékiani, and the Shékiani had retaliated by capturing several Mpongwe. They were threatening to sell them into slavery if the debt was not paid.[23]

After a few days, Toko and his companions went to the town that had the claim against the Mpongwe. The travelers arrived in the evening, and Leighton was impressed by the beauty of the place—he saw before him a neat village located above a flowing river and surrounded by enormous trees. Shortly after they entered the village, a full moon rose, spread a luminous light over the scene, and evoked a sense of wonder and mystery. Leighton stood by a fire and watched the negotiations proceed—Toko took a plantain leaf, cut it into strips, and used the strips to demonstrate what had been owed and what had been paid and what was still owed. Leighton was moved by what he saw before him. Here, he wrote in his journal, was "man, that active, restless being," under the canopy of a tropical forest, by the banks of a flow-ing river, in the light of a full moon, in the midst of the wonders of God's creation. Here in this place man, "though unknown to all the world besides," was "nevertheless urging forward his little interests with the same earnestness and intensity of feeling, which are experienced in the most exalted stations." Yet, however beautiful the scene, Leighton felt an encompassing melancholy for what he, a missionary from Pine Grove, saw as the circumscribed world of those who stood before him. As he looked at Toko and the others sitting and negotiating before a fire and in the light of the moon, he thought of them as the living representatives "of innumerable generations, who have lived on the same spot, engaged in the same pursuits, and gone down to the grave in the same moral midnight." For the men and women before him were all "profoundly ignorant of Jesus Christ and the way of salvation!" Still, in the midst of his melancholy, Leighton was hopeful. In his imagination he saw a rapidly approaching time when such scenes would be redeemed. "Is there any extravagance," he wrote, "in thinking that the voice of strife and discord, the song of the nocturnal dance, and the cry of war, which have resounded along the banks of this river from generation to generation, shall be turned into anthems of the most exalted praise to God and the Lamb?"[24]

A little after midnight, Toko signaled that they were to leave, although the negotiations were still incomplete. Back on board the *Waterwitch*, they sailed further up the river until, a little after dawn, they reached the town of King Kobangai. Leighton was once again delighted with what he found— the town was well situated, and the houses were new, commodious, and built with taste and skill. In contrast with the people of Passall's village, Leighton thought, the people here appeared to be healthy, comfortable, and cheerful. Kobangai himself was impressive—six feet six inches tall, he was a man of great authority in all the towns along the river. He wore European clothes, including a marvelous beaver hat with an enormously broad brim whose edges were bound with gilt braid. The tall hat, sitting like a crown on the head of such a large man, must have made Kobangai appear almost like a giant to many. Because of the respect shown to him up and down the river, he was being asked to help with the unfinished negotiations. He welcomed the travelers with kindness and hospitality to his large house—sixty to seventy feet long and twenty feet wide. He gave Toko a goat and a small tusk, and to Leighton he gave a goat and, in response to the missionary's curiosity, various articles made by the people. Leighton saw furniture—chairs, tables, settees— which he thought at first were European imports, but they had been made by skilled local craftsmen. Leighton saw as well a number of musical instruments, some of which were exceedingly sweet-toned—especially one brought from far in the interior that had been intricately made and was much like a guitar. But he also saw empty barrels of rum scattered around, and he knew that two worlds were intersecting even here by the banks of the Como.[25]

Of most interest to Leighton were visitors from the interior who had journeyed many days to reach Kobangai's Town in order to trade for goods brought up the river from the coast. They were Fang, called Pangwe by Leighton and other missionaries. Leighton saw immediately that they were entirely different from the coastal tribes in their features and general appearance, and he thought them, both men and women, "vastly superior in their personal appearance." Like the Pah, who lived far in the interior from Cape Palmas, and whom Leighton had sought to find on one of his explorations when at Fair Hope, they appeared uncorrupted and free from the vices that afflicted those in long contact with whites. "Their form," he later wrote, "is indicative of strength and energy rather than grace or beauty. Their stature is of medium size, but compact and well-proportioned, and their gait is alike manly and independent." They had, he wrote, soft hair usually plaited into four long braids, two of which they wore in front and two in the back. They smeared their bodies with a red ointment that quickly identified them as Fang, and Leighton noted that they wore "no clothing except a narrow strip of bark cloth between their legs." Leighton was told that the Mpongwe had known of the Fang for only about twenty years. From what he learned, he thought the Fang were migrating in large numbers toward the coast, and from what he saw of their strength and vigor, he thought that the Shékiani, weakened as they were by the slave trade, would soon be overrun and largely supplanted by them. Leighton did not realize—nor apparently did Toko—that the missionary was anticipating what was to happen not only to the "bushmen," but also to the Mpongwe.[26]

WITH THE NEGOTIATIONS dragging on, Toko laughed and dared Leighton—this white man from Pine Grove—if he wished to go with him to a nearby village and "see the devil raised." Leighton, his curiosity stirred by Toko's laughter and description, accepted the challenge, and soon he and Toko were walking a narrow path that wound its way into the jungle beneath the high canopy of a tropical forest on a moonlit night. Several Fang quietly accompanied them, carrying iron spears forged and sharpened by blacksmiths in their mountain homeland. After making their way along the path for a while, they heard the sound of drums, and then excited voices, and soon they saw light flickering ahead of them. Emerging from the shadows of the path, they walked into a village square illumined by nighttime fires. Anxious spectators stood around the edges of the light, and in the center, twelve or fifteen haggard old women were engaged in what seemed to Leighton "some conjurations." In their midst, a young woman, clothed in green leaves, frantically dashed around in the grip of some frenzy. Startled by the sudden appearance of strangers with a ghostly white man, the old women ran with the young woman into a house. But the young woman could not be contained. She broke free, rushed from the house, ran across the square, and disappeared into the darkness of the surrounding forest. The drums continued to beat until suddenly she reemerged, a leafy phantom, carrying in each hand a long green vine. She began running around the square in what Leighton thought was a state of wild, uncontrolled delirium. Toko told Leighton that she had been given a powerful narcotic, the decoction of the bark of a tree, and it appeared she had been given too much. Finally her footsteps slowed, her frenzy eased, and she collapsed on the ground in a stupor.[27]

Now the time had come for "calling up the devil." All became quiet—the drumming ceased and many ran into houses, including Toko and the drummers, to peer through the bamboo toward the shadows of the forest. Leighton and the Fang remained at the edge of the circle of light. Leighton described in his journal what he saw. From the darkness there appeared a giant figure—"his infernal majesty," Leighton called him—a man on stilts, his body completely concealed except for what appeared to be black cloven feet. Wearing over his face an intricately carved but hideous mask, he began moving around the open square in a terrifying manner. Then, out of the shadows and into the light and the silence of the village, rushed another figure—he was, wrote Leighton, "another devil, a dwarf in size," and he carried a glittering sword. Now in a furious and menacing manner he approached those who had dared to remain in the presence of the giant. But Leighton did not flee; nor did the Fang, who held their ground grasping their spears. The giant and the dwarf moved slowly away, fading back into the shadows of the forest, apparently to prepare for a second appearance. But it was enough for Toko. He came out of the house to which he had fled and indicated that they had seen enough. They all hurried back down the path through the shadows of a moonlit night to Kobangai's Town.[28]

Leighton wrote that what they had seen was precisely what whites "would suppose to be an African's idea of the devil." And of course it was that—what Leighton saw, he saw through white eyes that already had embedded in them powerful images, eyes that saw preconceived notions of "an African's idea of the devil." But what Leighton saw was also more. He saw with eyes that had been shaped by biblical stories; by images of Satan in Milton's *Paradise Lost* and of Mephistopheles in Goethe's *Faust*; by folktales and ghost stories told on the piazza of Pine Grove; and by the enlightened, scientific world that was behind the ships that came sailing proudly into the Gabon estuary. The

English word "devil" that Toko had learned and that Leighton used carried with it a world of memory and meaning for Leighton, a different world from the world of a young woman racing around a village square under a nighttime African sky, and different, too, from the world of the figures who emerged from the shadows to dance and threaten. By using the word "devil" to describe what he was seeing, Leighton was ushering into the village square a sinister resident of his own world—Satan, Lucifer, Mephistopheles, the father of all lies, the great master of hell—to dance and to threaten all who dared to look upon him. What Leighton saw that night as he stood beside the Fang was nothing less than an "African devil" as seen and interpreted by a white man from Pine Grove, a "white devil" who was said to "sabba everything."[29]

What Leighton didn't sabba, however, what he didn't know, was what the "devil raising" meant to the Shékiani gathered around nighttime fires. He knew that Toko had been amused at the prospect of showing the white man such a scene, but once they entered the circle of light in the village, even the wise and sophisticated Toko had been frightened by what he saw. Later, Leighton wrote about initiation rituals for young Mpongwe women and about the Shékiani having a Great Spirit whom they called Mwetyi. This Mwetyi lived in the "bowels of the earth" and came "to the surface of the ground at stated seasons, or when summoned on any special business." Perhaps it was Mwetyi who had been raised and before whom the people had fled. But if so, Leighton didn't recognize him or understand what the racing young woman was racing from, or racing toward, or racing for.[30]

In coming years, African Christians, in all of their diversity, would see this introduced figure that Leighton saw—Satan—in light of those familiar and terrifying figures that came out of the shadows to dance and threaten on moonlit nights. But in this new devil, this Satan, they would see personified not only a terrifying figure on stilts, not only a part of their old religion, but the personification of *all evil* that threatens to hurt or destroy human life. And against this devil, this Satan, whatever his disguise, they would engage in "spiritual warfare," trusting the gospel of a powerful new African Christianity to protect believers and to cast out all fear.[31]

Toko FINALLY FINISHED his negotiations, and the *Waterwitch* returned to Glass's Town. Shortly thereafter, Toko sold his handsome boat for a handsome price to a Spanish slave trader at King William's Town. It was the same trader who a few months earlier had blown apart the two slaves who had escaped his barracoon. The Spaniard wanted to use the *Waterwitch* to ferry slaves out to waiting ships.[32]

And Leighton wrote up his adventure with Toko on the *Waterwitch* and sent the story to Rufus Anderson, who published it in the *Missionary Herald.* Then, in parlors in Boston, Philadelphia, and Savannah, on the piazza at Pine Grove, and all across the country, white men and women—Bayards, Henrys, and Hodges; Clays and Wilsons; and a host of others—read of Toko and the *Waterwitch*, of Passall and Kobangai, of Fang moving toward the coast, and of a "devil raising" in a tropical village in far-off Africa. And in the reading and in the telling of such a missionary narrative, many no doubt had their images of Africa both reinforced and challenged.[33]

But such narratives were not confined to whites. On some plantations in the Lowcountry, pious plantation owners on Sunday afternoons read to Gullah slaves stories from a white missionary who had grown up by the Black River not far from Boggy Gully. Whatever the purposes of whites in reading such stories to slaves, the hearing of such stories provided a reminder to Gullah people—a reminder that the way life was ordered in the Lowcountry was not the way life was ordered everywhere, that whites were not always owners and blacks were not always slaves. In unintentional ways, stories about Toko and African kings, about the handsome *Waterwitch* and even a "devil raising," may have helped to undercut on some plantations white attempts to control the imaginations of slaves. It is, of course, impossible to know, but perhaps when some Gullah heard of Toko, they imagined new and subversive alternatives to white power and white rule.[34]

Chapter Fifteen

A Sophisticated, Hospitable, and Heathen People

In late winter 1843, Leighton went to Cape Palmas to wait anxiously for Jane's return from her visit to the United States. Although she had written a number of letters, none of them had reached him in Gabon, so he was uncertain that she had even arrived safely in New York. To his immense relief, when he reached Cape Palmas he found that a letter from Margaret Eckard had arrived—Jane was well, had been busy visiting family, and expected to sail in the spring with Captain Lawlin. Leighton consequently turned his attention to the final details of closing what remained of the Fair Hope mission and to the publication of several small tracts in Mpongwe. He had with him a Mpongwe interpreter who was helping him prepare the tracts and who was working with him on the details of the language. Leighton had spent less than a year in Gabon and he was already preparing a simple publication in the local language. He had already found Mpongwe a much easier language to master than Grebo.[1]

He stayed with B. V. R. James and Margaret and Catherine at Fair Hope. Margaret had recently given birth to a little girl, and the James family was staying at the old mission station until the child safely passed through the seasoning fever. So Leighton worked on completing the Mpongwe tracts, and James printed them. First came a sixteen-page "Colloquial Sentences in English and Gaboon," followed by "Scripture Questions," "Scripture Precepts," and then "Hymns in Gaboon"—five hundred copies of each. After the printing was completed, Leighton and James carefully boxed the press. They made preliminary arrangements for the cottage to be sold to George McGill and for the little cemetery to be kept neat and cleared of grass and underbrush.

Final arrangements had to be made as well for former students. Most had already been placed in the Episcopal mission at Half Cavally, but there were some who were eager to join the new mission in Gabon. Among these were Wasa and Maria. They had had good success with their little mission at Sarekeh and they wanted to go and establish a school among the Mpongwe.[2]

Leighton also talked with William Davis about his daughter, Mary Clealand. Davis had brought her to Jane when the school had first opened at Fair Hope, and she had quickly become one of Jane's star students. Now, in 1843, Davis agreed to her request that she go with Jane and Leighton to join the mission among the Mpongwe. Neither Davis nor Jane nor Leighton could have imagined the important role this beautiful young Grebo woman would have in the early history of the church in Gabon.[3]

WHEN JANE FINALLY arrived at Cape Palmas, she and Leighton had a wonderful, happy reunion, and both vowed there would never again be such a voluntary separation. Jane brought with her Jane Cooper, a free woman of color from Savannah, who had agreed to come out and help Jane and be a teacher at the new school at Baraka. She was not officially under the American Board—the Wilsons paid all her expenses themselves and provided her salary—but for the next seven years she would be an important part of the mission. Also on the ship was the Grebo printer Francis Allison. He had spent six months in New York studying bookbinding and was to become the printer in Gabon.[4]

After a short stay at the Cape, Captain Lawlin pulled anchor and sailed the *Atalanta* once again for Gabon. With him were twelve who had come on board from Fair Hope—Grebo, African American, and European American men and women. Their destination was Baraka.[5]

WHEN THE *ATALANTA* disappeared on the southern horizon, Russwurm wrote Latrobe that the abandoned land at Fair Hope should not be given to any other mission. It was, he said, too valuable and too contiguous to Harper to be deeded to any other society. Shortly thereafter, Russwurm's father-in-law, George McGill, who had already bought and dismantled most of the Fair Hope buildings, took possession of the former mission land. There, where in the evenings the fires of Big Town could be seen glowing in the distance and night winds stirred tall palms, McGill set about building warehouses for the little settler community at Harper. And Russwurm wrote Latrobe to let "the name of Fair Hope die."[6]

Ten days after leaving Cape Palmas, Captain Lawlin ran the *Atalanta* toward a long, low cape on the south side of the Gabon estuary, then tacked sharply and headed for the north shore. The travelers saw stretching out before them a magnificent body of blue water that mirrored the tropical sky. To the north and to the south, shorelines of dense forests appeared to hold the waters of the estuary in place like giant pincers. Lawlin sailed the *Atalanta* along the high and rolling north shore toward King Glass's town. Watchful eyes spied the brig and the captain's familiar insignia. William Walker and some Mpongwe quickly launched a little sailboat and came alongside. After a brief reunion on deck, the travelers climbed down the ship's ladder and were soon headed for the beach.[7]

When the sailboat hit sand some twenty or thirty yards from the beach, Mpongwe men came splashing through the water to carry Jane and the other women ashore. As Jane was lifted by strong black arms, perhaps she remembered her first arrival at Cape Palmas. Then, singing Grebo canoe men had taken her through the crashing Atlantic surf to the beach, where King Freeman and a multitude of shouting, largely naked Grebo had greeted her and her young husband.

Now, as she set her feet on the shore at Glass's Town, Jane found a crowd of Mpongwe, handsomely dressed, many in European fashion, waiting to shake the hand of each traveler in a gentle manner and to say to each: "Mbolo"—"May you live to be old." Leighton knew many of the Mpongwe already, and their greetings to him were warm and enthusiastic. The travelers made their way up from the shore through the crowd and into the town—a single street ran before them and up a hill toward the mission at Baraka. As they entered the town, they saw bamboo houses set close together on both sides of the street—they were larger than any Jane had seen at Big Town or elsewhere along the coast.[8]

At the upper end of the town, at the highest point, they came to the king's house. King Glass, as was his custom, was waiting for the newcomers. Seated in a chair in front of his house, he wore a coat and stovepipe hat and held in his hand a staff. He, too, gave a warm welcome to Leighton, for they had spent much time together during Leighton's first stay. The king extended his welcome to Jane and the others from the *Atalanta*. For his own reasons, Glass was pleased that the Americans had established their mission at the edge of his town.[9]

Jane could see that the king was a rheumy-eyed old man, probably in his early nineties when they met, but still a shrewd trader and political leader. His once dark and shiny skin was deeply wrinkled and had taken on an increasingly crusty, ash-colored look. He still claimed he was "the greatest rum drinker in the River," and William Walker agreed, thinking "there is no one who will dispute his claim to this distinction." He had many wives and even more slaves—Leighton had earlier estimated that he owned at least two hundred.[10]

The headman of his village since 1839, Glass—R'Ogouarouwé was his Mpongwe name—traced his ancestry back through four or five generations to Re-Ndoukoue, the man who had first led the Agekaza clan of the Mpongwe down the right bank of the Como River to the estuary, where they had settled at Glass's Town and other villages along the north shore. Here they had prospered. Glass's Town had become the most important trading center on the estuary, rivaled in the 1840s only by King William's Town on the south side.[11]

The slave trade and slaves had been a part of Mpongwe society from deep in their history. By the seventeenth century, the Mpongwe were buying slaves and iron from the Dutch—they needed, a Dutch trader wrote, "men for their wars and iron for weapons." In the early years of the eighteenth century, while some slave trading continued, the Mpongwe had wanted primarily European iron, clothes, furniture, guns, French brandy, and then New England rum. During the closing decades of the eighteenth century, however, the slave trade had become increasingly important. Now the Mpongwe were not buying slaves from Europeans, but selling slaves to them. Primarily middlemen, the Mpongwe bought slaves from different parts of the interior and sold them to Portuguese and Spanish, Dutch, English, French, and American slavers. But not all slaves were sold—many were kept by the Mpongwe, and by the beginning of the nineteenth century slavery had come to dominate much of Mpongwe society. Ownership of slaves had become a sign of wealth and prestige. In time, as the harsh realities of slavery among the Mpongwe and surrounding peoples became more apparent, Jane and Leighton found distressing parallels to what they had known in Georgia and South Carolina.[12]

After being warmly welcomed by Glass, who spoke to them in the familiar Pidgin English of Atlantic Creoles, the travelers went further up the hill, where, about half a mile from the beach, they found the mission station at Baraka. An African American carpenter and his apprentice (they had been hired to come down with the first group from Cape Palmas) had built a large and attractive white frame cottage reminiscent of many a Lowcountry home—it had green shutters and a wide front porch intended to provide shade and a place to sit and visit and enjoy any breeze coming off the water.[13]

When Jane entered the cottage, she found familiar furniture from Fair Hope all neatly arranged, with woven Mpongwe mats on the floor. Overhead there was no ceiling—only open beams and the underside of the roof. Such an arrangement made the house cooler than it would have been with ceilings and allowed the walls and exposed roof to be swept and kept clear of insects and reptiles—although not altogether successfully. One missionary later said that missionaries used mosquito netting over their beds to keep lizards and centipedes from dropping upon them when they were asleep. William Walker killed a large snake, a deadly Green Mamba, in his room in 1844 and noted that another had disappeared somewhere in the cottage.[14]

From the front porch of the cottage, Jane and Leighton had a fine view of the estuary and could see it dotted with the white sails of Mpongwe boats. Frequently they and other missionaries could see the sails of European or American ships, such as the *Atalanta*, trading in the estuary for dyewood and other forest products. But all too often they could also see Portuguese and Spanish slavers—frequently American-made ships—across the estuary, or sometimes close by, anchored off Glass's Town to buy slaves for the highly profitable Brazilian markets.[15]

By the time Jane arrived at Baraka in July 1843, Mpongwe workers had already built a library house and a workshop out of bamboo for Walker, who—Yankee farm boy that he was—was always busy with some carpentry or blacksmithing project. Other buildings were soon to be added to the station—a second cottage, this one made of bamboo; a little clapboard church in meetinghouse style; a metal storage building shipped from New York; a bamboo schoolhouse and bamboo dormitories; a bamboo chickenhouse and a bamboo shed for goats and sheep and a few cows; and, immediately behind the main cottage, a bamboo kitchen. Already a handsome hedge of lime trees had been planted around the perimeter of the mission. With their long and dangerous thorns, the trees were soon to provide—it was hoped—some protection against leopards and against any coming or going except through the gate. In a few years, a fine orchard was growing—with native mangoes and palms as well as varieties imported from New York—over the area where slave bodies had once been dumped.[16]

So the mission station at Baraka was in the process of becoming a mixture—southern cottage next to Mpongwe bamboo buildings next to an iron building from New York all situated among imported fruit trees growing among mangoes and palms and thorny limes. Over the coming years, this growing, evolving physical landscape, with all of its incongruities, reflected the growing, evolving social landscape of Baraka, where Americans and Grebo and Cape Coast Fanti and Mpongwe were living and working together. Here, visitors—Mpongwe, American, and European traders and explorers, Kru and

Grebo sailors—often found Baraka a pleasant and welcoming place, but it was not to be a place without tensions, jarring cultural contradictions, and deep sorrows.

ON THE DAY the *Atalanta* arrived at Glass's Town, William Walker wrote in his diary that the arrival of the twelve travelers "makes a large addition to our family, our cares, and our labors." It also made possible the rapid expansion of the mission to other towns on the estuary. But first the mission had to organize itself. Within a week of the arrival, Walker had drawn up a covenant and a few rules for the regulation of a church, and Leighton had been elected pastor. Leighton, with a committee of four, was to administer the government of the church, for all was to be done decently and in order, mixing Presbyterian and Congregational polities to suit the needs of a mission church.[17]

But organizational concerns did not take all of their time—romances had thrived while Leighton had been away. Benjamin Griswold came to him and said that he and the widow Mrs. Dr. Wilson had decided to marry. She was an attractive young woman and had been married to Dr. A. E. Wilson only a short time before his death at Fish Town—his first wife had died in South Africa. Leighton, still naive about such matters, had thought when they first came to Baraka that she and William Walker had some interest in one another—but he had added in a note to Jane, "I have no penetration in such matters and may be mistaken in my suspicions." He was mistaken, and so he was surprised when Griswold told him the news. Walker was not surprised. "This is what I have long been expecting," he wrote in his diary, "though they have both more than once positively denied any such intention. Probably at that time they had no such intentions, and I suppose that they were then deceiving themselves and did not know their own hearts so well as I could read them in their actions."[18]

But theirs was not to be the only wedding. John Edwards, a Fanti from Cape Coast who had been a teacher at Cape Palmas, announced that he and the widow Mrs. Brent wished to be married. She was a Grebo, a graduate of the school at Fair Hope, and had been married for a short while to Thomas Brent, a native of Sierra Leone and a teacher at Fair Hope. On their voyage to Gabon, Thomas had drowned in a capsized canoe off Cape Lahu on the Ivory Coast.[19]

So the two widows took on new husbands and joined them in their work as the missionaries at Baraka organized themselves for their teaching and evangelistic efforts among the Mpongwe and surrounding peoples.

Leighton was deeply impressed by the Mpongwe during his early years at Baraka. He had seen much of the West Coast of Africa, from Sierra Leone in the north to the Gabon Estuary in the south. He had met the tall and handsome Mandingos and Vai in the north; he knew and admired the Kru, with their knowledge of sailing and their reliable character; he had gone ashore through the heavy surf at Cape Lahu on the Ivory Coast and had walked its city streets and talked with its leading merchants; he had visited the old slave fort at Elmina, and had seen its surrounding town and fishing fleet from atop its high walls; and he had spent time at Cape Coast among the Fanti. He knew about the Ashanti and Dahomey kingdoms, with their astonishing military and political power, and had talked with those who had visited their capitals; and he had seen Accra and visited the islands of Fernando Po, St. Thomas, and Corisco. And, of course, he knew the Grebo— King Freeman and Ballah and William Davis and all the others among whom he and Jane had lived and worked for seven years. Yet when he thought of all of these different places and these different peoples who lived along the coast with their different languages and different traditions and customs, he thought the Mpongwe were the most sophisticated and hospitable.[20]

Not long after first stepping ashore at Glass's Town, he wrote that from a social point of view, the Mpongwe were elevated far above any people he had yet encountered or heard about along the whole West Coast of Africa. They were, he said, decidedly civil and kind, and he thought them remarkably generous. "There is seldom a day," he said, "when I do not receive a present of a basket of groundnuts, sugar cane, fufu or something of the kind." For someone who had lived for years among the Grebo and who had sailed with sea captains trading along the coast, he was pleasantly surprised that the gifts were given without any expectation of a return. Not that the Grebo and others had been stingy, but when gifts were given by them, gifts were expected in return.[21]

Leighton was impressed as well by the linguistic abilities of the Mpongwe—some Mpongwe traders knew not only the languages of surrounding peoples but also several European languages. Leighton noted that one trader, named Cringy, "speaks English, French, Portuguese, and at least half a dozen native languages with wonderful ease. He is perfectly familiar with the peculiar habits, feelings, and customs of all these nations, and he can act the Frenchman, the Spaniard, or the Englishman, just as circumstances may demand, without any apparent effort." William Walker and Benjamin Griswold expressed in their letters and journals similar positive perceptions of the people of the estuary.[22]

Leighton, Walker, and Griswold had good reasons to praise the Mpongwe—they wanted, after all, the decision to establish a new mission at Baraka to appear wise and prudent. But their perceptions and sentiments were widely shared by European and American ship captains and explorers. Indeed, Captain Lawlin's enthusiasm for the Mpongwe was what had first encouraged Leighton to explore the idea of starting a mission among them.[23]

All the Americans at Baraka were perplexed by this level of Mpongwe sophistication and amiability. Why, they wondered, did the Mpongwe have such a character, when other peoples along the coast did not? It was true, they admitted, that the Mpongwe had had much contact with "civilized" Europeans and Americans, but no more than many others who still seemed to be as fierce and barbarous as ever. Moreover, the missionaries believed that contacts with white sailors and traders—especially slave traders—had been a deeply corrupting influence on coastal peoples. Whites almost always left behind more vices than virtues. "Many of the vices of heathenism," William Walker reported to the American Board, "have not only been sanctioned and encouraged by the example of Europeans, but a great many peculiar to civilized countries have been grafted upon their character." So how did the Mpongwe come by their virtues?[24]

The answer seemed to lie in the traditions of the people—however carefully the missionaries thought those traditions needed to be evaluated—and in the role of an extraordinary man, Râgombe, who had lived many generations earlier. He held, wrote William Walker, "the same rank in the estimation of this people that Confucius does in the regard of the Chinese." His sayings had been handed down by oral tradition and "magnified by ten thousand rehearsals, until they are truly wonderful." The Mpongwe, said Walker, gave Râgombe credit for making their language and their laws, and they ascribed to him superhuman wisdom and power. Walker concluded that some remarkable man had exerted a powerful influence upon the character of the people, and it was this influence that had guided the Mpongwe over the generations and that had created in the towns and villages of the estuary such a polished, hospitable, and sophisticated people.[25]

If the Mpongwe were polished, hospitable, and sophisticated, they were also, in the view of the missionaries and other Europeans and Americans, unmistakably heathen. They were, wrote Leighton shortly after his arrival, heathen in the full force of that word. He had quickly found that witchcraft and polygamy and a thousand other kindred vices were "as common and as inveterate as at Cape Palmas or any other place in the world." William Walker wrote to the American Board that they never forgot they were in a land of heathenism, and he did not want the board to forget it. He wrote that among the Mpongwe, slavery, polygamy, and intemperance were universal and dreadful. But, he added, "a history of intemperance here would be precisely the history of the same vice in America. So also of slavery." Nevertheless, the missionaries insisted that the Mpongwe's universal belief in witchcraft, their participation in rituals that seemed particularly repulsive to the missionaries, their use of fetishes and charms, together with their ignorance of Christian faith and life, provided unequivocal proof of heathenism. European and American explorers, after praising the Mpongwe, also emphasized a shadow side—the Mpongwe drank far too much rum; the women, with the encouragement of their husbands, often acted as prostitutes for visiting sailors; and the men were dishonest and effete and were generally obsessed with trade and the wealth it brought.[26]

These competing perceptions of the Mpongwe helped to shape the work of Leighton and his colleagues. Their primary strategy for the mission—it was the grand strategy of the American Board—was to develop an indigenous Christian leadership as quickly as possible, to provide that leadership with translations of the Bible and religious tracts, and to nurture that leadership so that it would soon be producing its own literature for its own people. The intent was to prepare the way for an indigenous, self-sustaining, self-governing church to evangelize its own people. In order to carry out this grand strategy around the estuary, Leighton and the other missionaries knew they had to learn about the distinctive social structures of the Mpongwe and take these structures into account, especially their underlying assumptions about the world and the routine practices of their daily lives. Leighton later wrote that missionaries must study the "character of the people" and adapt "their instruction to their wants." This meant that at Baraka and at the other outpost soon to be established, the mission's grand strategy had to be adapted to the particular and apparently conflicting character of the Mpongwe.[27]

On the one hand, the missionaries had to acknowledge and honor the strength and winsome nature of many Mpongwe habits and deeply internalized traditions and to acknowledge Mpongwe familiarity with and participation in a broader Atlantic world. On the other hand, the missionaries were there, risking their lives, in order to challenge the heathenism of the people and to present them with a Christian message, an alternative to the ways in which they understood the world and lived their lives. The challenges the missionaries faced—both the Americans and their Grebo and Fanti coworkers—were real, and their work over the coming years was to be demanding, deeply challenging them all. Disappointment and depression, homesickness and loneliness—and on occasion hysteria—together with almost constant illness often threatened to overwhelm them, and sometimes did. Moreover, they were going to be contending not only with the strength of Mpongwe ways and traditions, as well as the attractions of a nascent capitalist economy built on Atlantic trade, but also with the difficulties of living and working closely together, where their own peculiarities, eccentricities, and pettiness could blossom and flourish.

And there were questions of authority—Who was to make what decisions and how were they to be made? Clearly, the Americans were going to be in charge, and among the Americans the men would have the commanding voices. And among the men, the white ministers would carry the most authority—although the nonordained African American B. V. R. James would have a respected voice, receive a larger salary than William Walker, and play a key role as printer and teacher. So tensions could and did simmer and sometimes come out into the open, revealing sensitivities and vanities, weariness and doubts, prejudices and power structures among "civilized" Christians. What kept this little disparate band going, what encouraged most of them to persevere, was their shared confidence in the providence of God, their belief that God was the Lord of history whose purposes were being worked out as year followed year, and their conviction that God's purposes—seen most clearly in the Bible and in Jesus—were good and gracious and included a future Christian Africa. And not least in keeping them going was their hope that they had a part to play in that future.[28]

AT BARAKA, JANE took primary responsibility for the development of a boarding school for boys and young girls. Working with her from the first were Miss Jane Cooper, the free African American woman from Savannah who had come out with Jane on her return from the United States, and a Mrs. Stocken, the widow of a Methodist missionary in Monrovia. Wasa and Maria were there as teachers, as was young Mary Clealand. They were soon joined by the James family, who finally arrived from Cape Palmas after their infant daughter had safely passed through the seasoning fever. James was to help set up the printing press, but his gifts for teaching meant he also had important responsibilities for the boys' school. Margaret James was busy at first with their daughter, but the former seamstress from Savannah was soon teaching sewing in the afternoons to the schoolgirls, who were learning how to make Western-style clothes. Catherine Strobel was with them—she had apparently put behind her any resentment she had had about the way James had first courted her and then married her mother, and she had become an excellent teacher. As a single woman, she had a degree of freedom in her life, but she also was greatly dependent on her mother and stepfather. She lived with them—as a family they had their own cottage at Baraka—helped to look after Anna, and had her identity closely tied to the James household.[29]

Jane had learned much at Fair Hope about what was needed to run a mission school, and she and her coworkers therefore put schedules and pedagogical strategies they had developed among the Grebo into practice among the Mpongwe. The day began early with morning prayers; after this, students drew water from the mission well for use during the day and then swept and cleaned their bamboo dormitories. Breakfast was next around a long table— a simple affair of fufu and cassava and water from the well. A little before nine, the school bell rang. The bell, brought from Fair Hope, was the voice of a scheduled day. It marked off periods, assigned activities to each passing hour, and taught a new way of thinking about time. On its first ringing, the bell called the day-students who lived in Glass's Town to come up the hill to Baraka. There they would join the boarding students in the bamboo schoolhouse. They came running and walking, alone and in groups, and entered the shade of the mission school. One of the teachers prayed, read a passage from the Bible, and led the singing of one of the hymns that Leighton had translated into Mpongwe. The lessons that followed were in English—precisely what the parents of the students wished for their children, since English was the language of trade at Glass's Town. So the students learned the English alphabet and practiced English sentences—"Good morning teacher." "Thank you." "God is love." And they memorized English vocabulary—a *nk ma* was a "monkey"; a *mboni* was a "goat"; *mbe* was "bad"; and *kamba* was "to speak."[30]

In later years, when the missionaries were more fluent in Mpongwe, entering students first learned the Mpongwe alphabet developed by Leighton and then proceeded to learn to read one of the Mpongwe booklets prepared by Leighton—"Scripture Questions" or "Scripture Precepts"—or, later still, one of the books of the Bible translated into Mpongwe. Then students plunged into English, and as the students advanced, they were introduced, as at Fair Hope, to other books—including the English Bible—and to arithmetic, geography, astronomy, and natural history.

Again, as at Fair Hope, the more advanced students helped to teach the less advanced ones. This system allowed not only for more attention to be given to beginners but also encouraged in the older students a sense of responsibility and an ownership of what was being taught.[31]

What was taught in the classroom, of course, was only the most formal part of the education at Baraka. The school bell had its part to play, but so did other factors, perhaps especially the food that was served at the mission station and the ways in which it was served. Peter Edwards, a Fanti from Cape Coast, was with his wife the cook and the steward, the majordomo, at Baraka. A young Mpongwe man was employed to purchase local foods. Each morning he went into Glass's Town and surrounding villages to meet women who were hawking sweet potatoes and pineapples, yams and groundnuts, sweet bananas and sugar cane, Indian corn and pumpkins, peas, beans, tomatoes, and eggs. These Peter and his wife prepared in the distinctive Fanti ways that they had brought with them from Cape Coast—they liked to fry the fish in palm oil, fix groundnut soup, use okra and tomatoes together, and when rice was available, they prepared rice balls. With these and other dishes they extended the students' world through the tastes and textures of food.[32]

Plantains and cassava were, however, the staples for all the meals, and most likely Peter bought them already prepared. Mpongwe women took green plantains and either boiled or roasted them before a fire. When boiled, they had something of the look of a peeled Irish potato and were bland and starchy. When roasted, they became very white and had the flavor of breadfruit. Either way, when mashed and rolled out into a baton or a ball they became fufu to be eaten with some rich soup or sauce, as Leighton had done when he had first visited Toko's plantation.[33]

The cassava required more work. The women who sold the prepared roots first soaked them for about a week until they became soft. Then, after drying the roots in the sun, they pounded them in a mortar, added a little water, and made a dough, which they molded into long loaves about the size of a man's arm. After wrapping the dough in long, tough plantain leaves, they tied the loaves with vines and steamed them for an hour or two by suspending them over pots of boiling water. When the cassava loaves—which were now called "hanky"—were ready, the women took them, still wrapped in their leaves, to Baraka. And when the leaves were unwrapped, the hanky emitted a pungent, sour aroma that the Mpongwe loved but the missionaries found offensive. Leighton noted that when the cassava was prepared in this way it was preferred to almost any other food by those who had grown up eating it. But he thought that with its odor and its bland and starchy taste, the cassava was far from tempting to foreigners—himself included. He called it an "apparently indigestible mass."[34]

Peter got fish from a young Mpongwe boy who was hired to catch or secure a daily supply. The estuary was a rich fishery, and fish—both fresh and smoked—was a regular item for the Mpongwe and for those who ate their meals at Baraka. Sometimes the fish was used in soups, and sometimes, when dried, its smoky flesh was mashed and made into a sauce to be eaten with fufu or hanky. Chickens—gaunt and tough from scratching around sandy yards—were also regularly available. Goats were as well. They seemed to wander everywhere around Glass's Town and nearby villages and were also kept at Baraka, where an occasional leopard would snatch one. On special occasions, Peter would kill a goat, barbecue it, and chop it into many pieces, then serve it with fufu and fruit and vegetables grown in the mission garden or bought from the women who with baskets on their backs hawked squash, beans, okra, and greens.[35]

Supplementing these familiar foods were imported items from distant places. Rice was regularly ordered from Cape Palmas and brought down by ships in the West African trade. For the Grebo who had come from Fair Hope, rice was an essential part of their diet, and it was soon being planted at Baraka. Corned beef, hams, and sea biscuits came from the United States, and cows were imported from Cape Palmas, although they did not thrive in the tropical climate of Gabon. These imported foods, however, played only a minor role in the diets of the schoolchildren, not only because they were intended primarily for the Americans and newly arrived West Africans, but also because the students preferred fish, fufu, and hanky.[36]

Two meals were served at Baraka—breakfast and then dinner at three o'clock, in Lowcountry style and according to Mpongwe custom. Here the traditional foods, often prepared in Fanti style, together with Grebo rice and occasional European or American dishes, were served at long tables where the children sat in chairs. Jane and the other teachers taught and expected the children to use Western manners—to use a knife and fork with ease, to say "please" and "thank you," and to sit up straight and not interrupt each other when talking. The hope was that such daily practices would help the children to internalize European and American ideas of domestic order and hygiene and to develop an inner life that was receptive to a Christian message. But, of course, much of this way of sitting at a table was not new or strange to the children. Like the food that was served, the manners that were taught were a mixture of the familiar and the new. Unlike the Grebo, the Mpongwe had been using knives and forks for years—the missionaries knew this from the hospitality they received over and over again in Mpongwe homes. Leighton had written shortly after his first arrival at Gabon that he was "invited two or three times a week to breakfast, dinner or tea, and that not served upon a dusty old chest, but on a table and in good European or American style." He later wrote that the Mpongwe "take their meals at table, and use knives and forks as gracefully and naturally as any other people in the world." And

William Walker found that in even more distant Mpongwe villages the people were accustomed to eating in this way. Such a way of eating, such polished table manners, reflected the Mpongwe's long contact with Europeans and Americans and the degree of their adaptation to European and American styles as well as their traditional Mpongwe politeness and hospitality.[37]

IF THE FOOD that was eaten and the way it was eaten at the Baraka school indicated the sophistication of the Mpongwe and their long engagement with an Atlantic world, the food also embodied aspects of Mpongwe life that the missionaries found deeply troubling. Most of the food produced around the estuary was grown by the slaves of the Mpongwe who were living on the surrounding plantations. A few months after he arrived at the estuary, Leighton wrote that the Mpongwe character was more seriously stained by their participation in the slave trade than he had at first imagined. He and the other missionaries were dismayed by the size of the trade in the estuary—it was so much more than anything they had seen at Cape Palmas.[38]

But of course the slave trade was not simply a matter of Mpongwe character. The Mpongwe needed trading partners, and they were a part of a great and complex transatlantic economic system. Leighton noted that the Mpongwe participation in the trade "should not occasion surprise so long as white men are concerned in it and place before them the strongest inducements to take part also." Ironically, the Mpongwe's increased participation in the transatlantic trade flowed in part from the good intentions of anti-slavery forces in Europe and the United States. After the British and Americans had outlawed the international slave trade in 1807, the British navy had begun vigorous and often successful patrols to capture slavers in areas north of the equator. Much of the trade had then moved south, and the estuary had gained in importance for slavers. Planters in Brazil and Cuba still had an insatiable appetite for imported slaves—the total number imported into Brazil alone during the long history of the trade exceeded by ten times the total number ever imported into the United States—and the sailing time from the estuary to Brazil was relatively short. This meant that most of the slavers were Portuguese or Spanish, although, to the missionaries' continuing mortification, they knew that many of the slave ships had been built in New England or Baltimore for the trade.[39]

Although most of the slave trade was conducted across the estuary on its southern shore, slavers came regularly to Glass's Town. The old king himself did not hesitate to sell slaves and was particularly glad to receive rum in exchange.[40]

The slavers occasionally came to Baraka to have a visit with the Americans as well. During their first year in the estuary, the missionaries were, wrote William Walker in his diary, "honored with a call" by one of the Spanish slavers. "He looked," noted Walker, "just as I should suppose a man would who is engaged in such an infernal business"—he was thin, disheveled, and afflicted with some skin disease. The missionaries remonstrated and warned him about the wrath to come—the consequences of such an "infernal business"—but such lectures made little impression on him or on other slavers. They were glad to have a meal with the missionaries and to enjoy a little "civilized" company, even if it meant having to listen to a lecture by Walker or Leighton—or Griswold, with his intense hatred of slavery. The slavers responded by saying that slave trading was simply a business—and a very profitable one, too—as if this meant all judgments against it could be dismissed. Leighton was later to write vehemently against such claims by some very "civilized" white Christians in Savannah and Charleston.[41]

Mpongwe treatment of their own slaves seemed to Leighton and the other missionaries to reflect the dual character of the people. On the one hand, compared to working in a Brazilian sugar-cane field or on a Lowcountry rice or cotton plantation, the work of Mpongwe slaves did not appear to the missionaries particularly onerous. The slaves lived some distance from their owners, did not suffer the distinctions of race found in the Americas, and were able, over time, to become more fully integrated into their society than a Gullah slave in the Georgia or South Carolina Lowcountry could ever hope to be in theirs. On the other hand, slavery was still slavery, and among the Mpongwe it had its own cruelties that the missionaries thought penetrated and hardened the hearts of the Mpongwe. They saw signs of this almost from the beginning of their time at Baraka.[42]

Six months after his arrival in the estuary, Leighton was walking on the beach reviewing Mpongwe vocabulary words, which he had carefully written on notecards. As he walked along flipping the cards and memorizing words, he came to a small crowd of Mpongwe who were laughing. Looking to see what was amusing them, he saw a young child who was sick and emaciated. The child, a slave of a man who came regularly to Baraka to study English, was being dragged off by a boy to the bush to be left to die. Leighton rebuked the people for their cruelty and laughter and had the child carried to Baraka, where it was given medicine and nourishment. William Walker, on seeing the child and hearing the story, thought it a good thing to rebuke the inhumanity of the people. But, he said, "this barbarity to slaves has been induced by the white slave trader. He whips them to death, shoots them, and drags them off to die." Such, he concluded, "is the brutalizing influence of slavery the world over." Walker thought the spirit of God alone could soften their hearts and that the decision to bring the dying child to Baraka demonstrated a Christian alternative to what Leighton had seen on the beach.[43]

What became increasingly clear to the missionaries was what appeared to them to be the tangled relationship between slavery, the food the slaves produced, and the deep beliefs and ritual practices of the Mpongwe. Like the Grebo, the Mpongwe thought that illness and death were the result of someone's malevolence, and, not surprisingly, the people thought to have the most enmity toward the Mpongwe were their slaves. Mpongwe slaves, like slaves in South Carolina and Georgia, were in a particularly good position to poison their owners. They were the ones who raised the food, and some of them cooked food for their owners. They had access to powerful toxins, secret herbs and poisonous roots that could be quietly mixed into fufu or hanky or slipped into a sauce or soup. The use of such poisons was regarded as a kind of sorcery—the Mpongwe word for a sorcerer was the same as the word for using a poison—and the act of eating was a dangerous, vulnerable moment, a way of opening oneself to malevolent forces. A missionary later wrote that the distinction between a fetish and a poison was vague among the people. "What I call a 'poison' is to them only another material form of a fetich power," he wrote. Both poison and fetishes, he wrote, were thought to be made powerful by the presence of a spirit.[44]

So slaves came to be regarded as dangerous, and eating was dangerous, and slave owners—not unlike white Georgians and South Carolinians—were constantly suspicious about the intentions and activities of their slaves. For the slaves of the Mpongwe, this fear and suspicion were weapons of the weak, weapons that could be used to restrain abusive owners and make them think twice about angering a slave. Leighton thought that the way a Mpongwe master treated a slave was much modified by a dread of witchcraft. If a slave owner acted cruelly, the slave could retaliate with "all the machinations of witchcraft which that slave may be able to command." But such weapons carried a fearful price for the slaves, as Leighton and the other missionaries soon learned.[45]

One day in November 1843, William Walker was returning to Baraka from a nearby village. As he approached the mission station, he saw three slaves dragging a young slave woman through the brush. She had been killed by her owner, and the slaves were being made to dispose of the body. They had a rope around her neck and were pulling her along as her warm blood laved the ground and as rough branches and brambles scratched and tore her body. The men were pulling her toward a little clearing, where they could leave her to decay in an open place. Walker asked why she had been killed and was told she had been accused of bewitching—of poisoning—a Mpongwe child that had died. Walker went to Baraka, got some Mpongwe boys at the school, and returned to bury the young woman in the sandy soil above the estuary.[46]

The next week, he was walking on the beach not far from Glass's Town when he "smelt a horrible stench." He left the beach and entered the bush to investigate. There he saw what he called a "slave wasting fire," and in it, another slave woman, perhaps about twenty years old, who had been killed, "a human body half consumed, which appeared to have been recently in the full vigor of life." He asked what had happened and learned that another Mpongwe child had died; the father had killed the slave woman on suspicion of her having poisoned the child. Once again Walker wrote in his journal: "Surely the dark places of the earth are full of the habitations of cruelty." That evening he preached at Baraka, and the man who had killed the young woman and had her burned was in the congregation. Walker said nothing about what he had seen, as he had not yet learned all the circumstances. But he vowed in his diary: "If my life is spared I intend to speak at large on the subject."[47] He would have ample opportunities during the coming years.

Chapter Sixteen

Rainforest Lessons

As Leighton and the other missionaries began to learn more about the Mpongwe and their many scattered villages and towns, they quickly decided that they needed to move beyond Baraka and to establish schools at certain critical points around the estuary and the surrounding rainforest. By the end of 1843, they had another station and five day schools.

Benjamin Griswold and his young wife—the former Mrs. Dr. A. E. Wilson—moved three miles up the estuary near the town of Prince Glass, old King Glass's nephew. The young couple called the station after the ancient name of the place, Ozyunga, which they were told meant "benevolent friend." They had a comfortable bamboo house built in Mpongwe style on a hill about three hundred yards from the estuary and were charmed by its location, by the beauty of its surroundings, and by the wide vista that stretched out before them. The house was large enough for a small boarding school for girls, which Mrs. Griswold ran. She had caused a sensation when she first arrived at the estuary—she had come as a young widow from Cape Palmas—since she was the first white woman most Mpongwe had ever seen. Women had crowded around her and had been eager to touch her hair, and she had soon won the affection of many. At Ozyunga, the schoolgirls came to regard her as "Mama Griswold," and, with her earlier experience at Fish Town, she showed herself to be a good and accomplished teacher. The Griswolds found that the Mpongwe had little concern for the education of girls, but the young missionaries were committed to the task—they hoped not only that the girls would convert to Christianity, but that, as educated young women, they would be suitable matches for the boys who were being educated and converted at other mission schools. In this way Christian couples could be raised up among the Mpongwe to become teachers and preachers for their people.[1]

In the late afternoons, when her teaching was done, the young bride visited surrounding villages to talk with the women. The talking itself must have been very limited, since at first she did not speak Mpongwe, and most of the women knew, at best, only a little English. But in her own limited fashion, she was doing the work of a pastor and evangelist, work that would have been forbidden her in her US home. She had a kind and gentle disposition and soon began to be trusted to help arbitrate disputes among village women. She therefore began to learn a little more about Mpongwe women with their hospitable ways, and they began to learn a little more about this kind but strange white woman who had come to live in a Mpongwe house on a hill above the estuary.[2]

WHILE THE GRISWOLDS were establishing the station at Ozyunga, two former students from Fair Hope were setting up day schools nearby. The Grebo George Coe was at Case's Town about a mile from Baraka. B. B. Wisner, another Grebo, was at Prince Glass's Town about two miles from Baraka and close to Ozyunga. Both men lived and taught in Mpongwe homes until a school could be built at each location that had a room in the back where they would live. Because they were young and inexperienced, it seemed wise to have them close to the mission stations at Baraka and Ozyunga.

Older and more experienced teachers went to more distant and demanding locations. At King George's Town, where the Remboué River flowed into the estuary about twenty-five miles from Baraka, the Fanti John Edwards and his Grebo wife established a school. Some ten miles up the river, at the most distant location, the African American teacher Josiah Dorsey had a school at King Duka's Town. At both of these places the Mpongwe built houses for their schools and their new teachers. Each house had one large room where the children gathered for their lessons and for scripture reading, prayer, and singing, and two rooms in back where the teacher lived. Meanwhile, across the estuary from Glass's Town, the Grebo Francis Allison set up a temporary school at Tom Larsen's Town, where he would teach until he could begin the printing and bookbinding he had been trained to do during his time in New York.[3]

WHILE THE SCHOOLS were being established, Leighton, Walker, and Griswold were hard at work studying the Mpongwe language. They each had a Mpongwe teacher—to be sure, they were teachers who carried less authority than Simleh Ballah or William Davis had among the Grebo, but they were nevertheless men who helped Leighton and his colleagues gather vocabulary and understand the grammar and some of the nuances of the language.

The missionaries were all amazed by the beauty of Mpongwe—a beauty that invited delight in the language and a relatively quick mastery of it. At Cape Palmas, Leighton had studied for four years before he had dared to preach in Grebo. But at Baraka, he started preaching in Mpongwe only nine months after arriving in the estuary. A year later, he wrote Charles Hodge at Princeton of his admiration for the language: "How a language so complicated in construction, so pliant in inflection, so perfect in the classification of its words and at the same time so invariably harmonious could have originated with an uncultivated people is truly inexplicable." Later still he wrote that the language was soft, pliant, and flexible to an almost unlimited extent. He found the grammatical principles of the language to be systematic, the vocabulary to be large and easily expanded, and the nuances of the language to be subtle and able to express many shades of thought and feeling. And he thought that "perhaps there is no language in the world which is capable of more definiteness and precision of expression." Through correspondence and through conversations with merchants and missionaries from eastern and southern Africa who stopped briefly in the estuary, Leighton began to sense that Mpongwe was part of a great language family that stretched across the southern part of the continent. The more he learned about the native tongue of his friend Toko and of King Glass and the children who came to Baraka to learn English, the more intensely he began to explore this possibility. [4]

WILLIAM WALKER WAS Leighton's closest colleague, and he was destined to be the longest-serving missionary in Gabon under the American Board. He was, in good Yankee style, a Jack-of-all-trades. He kept a diary—in the early years with almost daily entries—and he recorded in passing how he repaired rigging for a visiting American vessel, helped Toko with the construction of one of his boats, built a boathouse and then a henhouse, constructed a fence at Baraka, and used his blacksmith's hammer and anvil to repair an iron stove and for innumerable other projects. But he was also a serious language student and a careful recorder of the ways of the Mpongwe—often with ironic observations about the supposed superiority of "civilized" Americans and Europeans. Above all, however, he was a missionary from New England, a man who committed his life to bringing the Christian gospel—a gospel he had first learned in a Vermont valley—to the people of Gabon.[5]

Tall and lanky, Walker was the most intrepid of all the missionaries. A colleague later called him "utterly fearless," and it was true that he carried within him a kind of Yankee steel that had been nurtured on a valley farm. He was also utterly blunt—perhaps a part of his fearlessness—for he said and wrote just what he thought without the cushion of good manners. Leighton and Jane—who also said what they thought but in more oblique and diplomatic ways—loved the young Yankee, and he had a deep and abiding affection for them. Perhaps it was because they had been together when his Prudence had died, and because they had stood beside him when she had been buried in the little cemetery at Fair Hope as the wind had come strong off the ocean. Leighton and Jane certainly knew Walker's continuing melancholy and loneliness, even as he tried to banish them with work and prayer and commitment to a mission vision that he and Prudence had shared.[6]

Walker shared the cottage at Baraka with Leighton and Jane, and his room there was his home base. But in the early years of the mission he was constantly on the move, often staying for months at a time at some distant village. At first, he began simply going out from Baraka to visit the "bush people," the Shékiani, in inland villages that were within walking distance of Baraka. The Shékiani language was closely related to Mpongwe, and Walker managed to communicate with them enough to try preaching. But what he communicated apparently seemed extremely odd to the Shékiani, and the results were modest, at best. Walker, however, persevered, and during the coming years, even as the number of Shékiani began to shrink dramatically under pressure from the Fang, he continued his interest in and concern for them—especially those who were slaves of the Mpongwe.[7]

Walker also had special responsibility for visiting and encouraging the teachers who were located some distance from Baraka and Ozyunga. He had already begun visiting the key towns before the schools had been established and had done the primary work of making arrangements for them.[8]

Walker was glad for these trips to the distant towns—they got him away from Baraka where English was spoken and pushed him to be constantly using his Mpongwe. They also gave him time to be alone, even in the midst of the Mpongwe, and to reflect and to remember and to think about the future. But the trips were demanding and he was sick most of the time, suffering recurrent bouts of fever and all too often dysentery.

And yet, despite the illnesses that plagued him, Walker could not be bound to the relative comfort of Baraka. He continued his rigorous program of visits, particularly to King George's Town, which was the most important of the interior towns. His habit was to leave Glass's Town in the morning in a Mpongwe boat outfitted with sails and oarsmen. If wind and tide were favorable, they reached King George's Town by late in the afternoon—although, all too often, night came on when they were on the water, and even the moon and stars had disappeared by the time they turned up the narrow Abäaga Creek that they needed to follow to get to the town. Then they had to push their way along—the mangroves were so thick and tangled that the oars were of no use except as poles to be shoved into the dark mud of the creek—and overhanging branches made for what Walker called an "Egyptian darkness." Thick spider webs draped the narrow passage, often entangling those in the bow of the boat, and mosquitoes descended upon them in hungry battalions. When they reached the head of the creek, they scrambled up a slippery bank and walked for several miles through the rainforest along the narrowest of paths—it was barely visible by the light of their torches. But when they finally reached the town on its high hill, King George—Rassondji was his Mpongwe name—always gave them a warm welcome, and the people were affable and kind, as might be expected among the Mpongwe.[9]

The king was old, wrinkled, and gray and showed the signs of his age by his slow and stiffed-legged movements and by the way his skin hung loosely from his once-muscular arms. But he was, like Toko, a great storyteller and could tell the history of the Mpongwe. The Ndiwa were, he said, the first people on the estuary. The Mpongwe had then lived far in the interior and had been taught to believe that if a Mpongwe man saw the salt water, he would soon die. But the Ndiwa people had slowly dwindled in number, and the Mpongwe had moved town by town and village by village down from the headwaters of the rivers that emptied into the estuary until they had finally settled in their present locations.[10]

The old king, for all the difficulty of reaching his town, obviously knew of a wider world. George said he remembered when he was a boy how English and American ships, as well as Spanish and Portuguese, had come up the estuary and anchored off the Remboué to trade with his father for slaves, who had been brought down from the interior. He had also traveled much in the interior when young; he had then followed in his father's footsteps, doing business with the white traders for many years. He knew their ways of bargaining, and he was familiar with the varying quality of the products they offered in exchange for ivory and slaves, dyewood and beeswax. He knew as well how time was on his side in dealing with Europeans, how anxious they were to complete their transactions and get away from the sickly climate that left so many of them dead.

George, however, was not the only one in the town who knew of a world beyond their rainforest home. Years earlier, two young men in his town had been sent to France, where they had spent eight years. They came back speaking and writing fluent French, telling of their adventures, and describing the wonders they had seen. But having seen Paris and Bordeaux, they found that life in a Mpongwe town had little appeal. They had been anxious to return to France—and perhaps they did. (Walker gave no indication in his diary whether he ever met them, or whether their stories of European cities and marvels had excited much curiosity in their hometown.) Because of such contacts, those who lived in George's Town knew of a world far beyond Abaäga Creek and the Remboué River and its broad estuary. They consequently possessed, as did their Mpongwe relatives around the estuary, polished manners and sophisticated ways. They ate with knives and forks and dressed in stylish fashions, and some spoke several European languages.[11]

George's Town had been, earlier in the century, the most prosperous of the Mpongwe towns because of its key role in the slave trade, but signs of decay and decline were clear by the time Walker began visiting. George, for all of his hospitality, had become a drunkard—a wily drunkard, to be sure, but still a drunkard—and the people seemed to be slipping into a deep morass from all the rum that had been pouring in on them with the slave trade. On one of his early visits, Walker found George "and nearly all the people drunk. In such circumstances the king, of course, was very glad to see me, and told me of his delight a dozen times at least." After observing the people drinking and fighting throughout the day, Walker noted in his diary that "rum kills in Africa as well as America." What was particularly galling for him was that most of the rum in this and the other Mpongwe towns came from Walker's own New England, where its use as a currency in the slave trade was adding to the wealth of many.[12]

George's Town, despite its many signs of decay, was nevertheless an important town, and the people had been eager for a school and had soon built one. There, the Fanti John Edwards lived with his wife and taught Mpongwe children. The work was demanding, was far from the friendships and support available at Baraka, and required great commitment. Such isolation made Walker's visits important occasions for the Edwardses that were much welcome.[13]

By spending time at George's Town and at Duka's Town further up the Remboué where Josiah Dorsey had a school, Walker was able to study more intensely not only the Mpongwe language but also the social structures and the religious and cultural traditions of the people. He learned about the different clans of the Mpongwe—the Agoulamba, the Assiga, and the

Agekaza—but he and the other missionaries didn't make too much of them. People were moving about from one location to another—especially toward Glass's Town, with its profitable trade with the English and Americans— and the missionaries usually lumped all the clans together and simply called everyone Mpongwe.[14]

In a similar way, the missionaries had adopted the convenient use of the word "king" that had long been used by European and American traders. Walker and Leighton and the other missionaries had quickly learned that Glass and William and George and the other "kings" were not kings like Louis Philippe of France, or the powerful Gezu, who was king and absolute monarch of Dahomey. They were, rather, *aga*—Big Men or Head Men, as the missionaries called them—men who exercised leadership not only over their own towns but also over clusters of surrounding villages. They had, wrote Walker, "but very limited authority, and no power to exact money or inflict punishment, unless in accordance with the expressed opinion of the principal men—that is, all the old men." Nevertheless, the missionaries— following the example of the traders—referred to them as "kings," implying more power and authority than George or any of the others ever possessed.[15]

Walker often stayed for extended periods at George's Town and paid shorter visits to Duka's Town and to Tom Larsen's. He worked hard on his study of the language, which for all of its beauty nevertheless required intense effort to master. His diary recorded the hard work involved: "Began writing at the imperative mood, negative and affirmative of the verbs in my vocabulary," he wrote one day. And the next: "Writing still on the verb and find great irregularity in the formation of the imperative mood, but shall soon be able to reduce it to order and deduce the principles of its formation and I hope that by the time that is accomplished I shall have most of them fixed in my mind."[16]

While he sat at the door of the school poring over his notebooks and vocabulary cards, he observed the comings and goings of the people around him. Coffles of slaves frequently passed before him chained together by their necks, and Portuguese slavers were often there making purchases. When he remonstrated with them, they simply repeated their familiar storyline—"It is our living." And a profitable living it was. According to their account, they could expect a shipload of slaves to bring $350,000 in a Brazilian market— and $300,000 of that would be their profit.[17]

Nights at George's Town were often interminable for Walker. Mosquitoes kept him awake with their infernal buzzing, and the noise of the town was often loud and raucous—especially when the slavers brought fresh supplies of rum. And when someone was sick—had a "devil in the belly" or in the head—drums were beat all through the night. Drummers, said the New Englander, placed one end of the drum on the ground, took the other between their knees, and with little sticks eight or ten inches long they pelted away with might and main. "With half a dozen of these drums, and 50 or 100 women screaming at the top of their voices, they manage to scare up quite a noise." If they did not manage to drive away the troubling devil, they did come close to driving the missionary crazy.[18]

Women were often called from different towns to help drive out a devil. On one occasion when Walker was staying at King George's, a man came down with a devil in his belly. Women were called to come from Glass's Town to make fetishes for him and to drink his rum—for the rum was the price of their help. All through the night they wailed—they seemed to Walker to be themselves possessed of the demon rum. In his diary he quoted an expression among the Mpongwe—"The women are Devils for drinking rum"—and indeed, Walker and Leighton and the others in the mission were discovering that Mpongwe women had a much more complex role in Mpongwe society than they had at first imagined.[19]

The missionaries had sensed conflicting images of Mpongwe women from the first—sometimes they appeared to be treated with great respect, but at other times they seemed little more than chattel. Leighton had written Jane shortly after his arrival at Glass's Town that the women were treated with a great deal of kindness and attention. He noted that the head wife was seated by her husband in all important palavers and took part in the deliberations. A few months later, however, Benjamin Griswold watched as old Glass gave a troublesome young wife to a man for a jug of rum. Griswold concluded, "Wives are exchanged here as horses and oxen are in America." Some years later, Leighton wrote Rufus Anderson that a husband did not have "even the right of property in his wife." She was regarded only as a sort of loan from her father, a loan that could be withdrawn at will. And what was worse, wives thought that they had fulfilled their destiny only if they enriched their husbands with a few children. In this way, Leighton thought, "the entire female population of the country is fully engrossed and no man can get a wife except so far as he may succeed in enticing her away from someone else."[20]

The missionaries were clearly struggling in their attempt to understand the relationship between husbands and wives among the Mpongwe. And the relationship was made more complex and confusing to the missionaries by the differences between Mpongwe husbands and their Mpongwe wives, on the one hand, and between Mpongwe husbands and their non-Mpongwe wives, especially slaves, on the other. Elaborately constructed laws regulated who could be married to whom and the different roles of children of the different types of marriages—the child of a Mpongwe father and a free non-Mpongwe mother, the missionaries found, was considered a Mpongwe, but the child of a Mpongwe father and a non-Mpongwe mother who was a slave was considered an outsider.[21]

One thing, however, became increasing clear to Walker and Leighton and the others in the mission—women had an independence and authority in Mpongwe society that exceeded anything they had at first imagined. An unhappy woman often simply ran away from her husband or took up with a man from another town or village. To be sure, such independence was not without its dangers. On one occasion, when Walker was staying at George's Town, a woman who had run off with another man was caught and brought back by her furious husband. Throughout the night, Walker listened to her screams as her husband beat her. The next morning, the man put a chain around her neck and was in the process of staking her before his door in order to continue the flogging when Walker was finally able to secure her release, presumably through his authority as a visiting white man. She was badly bruised, and Walker wondered how she and other women could survive the outrageous fury of a husband's wrath.[22]

Still, many women were successful in escaping their husbands and over a period of time might move from husband to husband. Following such escapes, the abandoned husband might seek revenge not on the wife but on the new husband. If he could not be found, then several kin of the new husband could be killed in his stead. And that killing often resulted in the revenge killing of the first husband, or some of his kin, until a palaver finally settled the matter. Walker wrote to a friend in New England that when a Mpongwe man ran away with another's wife, his action would typically set off a process of retaliation and revenge. Here, he said, were both the causes of war among the Mpongwe and their manner of carrying them on. He thought it all seemed very stupid and unreasonable, but he added: "If you could strip the wars of Christian nations of their sophistry and pomp, and great swelling words of vanity, where is the mighty difference?" He could see none, he said, except that in Gabon, only three or four people perished, whereas with the refinements of civilization and the impulsive energy of Christianity, many thousands, or tens of thousands, or hundreds of thousands perished.

"Is there after all," he asked, "any difference in the hearts of men, unless grace has made it? Or will Downing Street or the White House sanctify deeds that are utterly detestable coming from an African hut?" And then, remembering what the State of Georgia had done to the Cherokees, he concluded that the people around him in Gabon were no more enlightened or Christian than the governor and legislature of Georgia. Both the Georgians and the revenge-seeking Mpongwe were barbarians. The lanky New Englander tried to restrain himself as he recoiled from the evil he saw in the world. He did not wish to moralize, he wrote his friend. He knew that he would be accused of not understanding the circumstances, of not taking into account the particular ways of the Mpongwe or the complexity of the situation in Georgia. He said he had been told that many times, but he insisted that he understood "enough of one to see its stupidity and of the other to see its unmitigated wickedness and barbarity."[23]

AS WALKER LIVED among the people of George's Town and as he walked narrow trails to nearby villages and slave settlements, he began to have a growing awareness of the great depths of the rainforest and the ways in which its massive trees and lush vegetation shaped the life of the Mpongwe. The surrounding rainforest apparently did not carry for the Mpongwe the dark and hostile jungle images it had for many whites, but it did have poisonous snakes that frequently slipped into town looking for a rat; herds of elephants that sometimes destroyed a grove of plantains overnight, along with much of the people's food supply; and driver ants that moved in long columns, consuming any living thing that could not get out of their way. But perhaps most of all for the Mpongwe, the rainforest was home to leopards—solitary hunters, symbols of power and authority. Traditionally closely associated with village leaders, leopards were also animals of deep mystery, embodiments of evil intent.[24]

On one of Walker's earliest visits to George's Town, word came that a leopard had carried off a slave on one of the plantations. But everyone thought a man had changed into the leopard and had made the attack, and George, wrote Walker, "did not seem disposed to do anything about it, unless it was to try the people with poison and see who it was." Three days later, news came that a leopard had carried off a woman from a house on the plantation during the night. Her young son was with her in the house when the leopard entered, but apparently he had been frozen in terror, and in the morning the people found him crying. Walker urged George to send men with him to the plantation to try to find either leopard tracks or the bodies of the man and woman. But the king was fearful and would not consent to Walker's going. "I find the king," wrote Walker, "with all his amiability and hospitality, very superstitious." This people, wrote Walker in his diary, "suffer almost incredibly from fear. They fear witches, and poison, and leopards, and each other. O blessed day when they shall be delivered from this bondage. Satan now rules them with a rod of iron."[25]

So Walker found that King George and the people of his town possessed both an admirable hospitality and brutal, superstitious ways that left the missionary dismayed. Over and over again he found George "as pleasant as ever, and just as heathenish. Sometimes drunk, sometimes sober." Yet, when sober, George impressed Walker and the other missionaries with his thoughtfulness and with his ability to engage them in the most serious theological conversations. George said that he believed "God made the world and all things and all people and now had left them not regarding their actions nor caring for the characters of men." Like the ancient Hebrew poets, George said he often saw bad men prosper and live to be old, while just as often good men were poor and soon died. How is this, the old king asked, "if God is good and just and cares for the actions of men?" And George utterly rejected the missionaries' assertions about heaven and hell, about "the future state," and insisted—like some Gullah storyteller—that he did not believe that at death the soul went to another world. Instead, he believed that one remained nearby, able to wander about from place to place, and with the power to inflict evil upon the sons and daughters of the earth.[26]

The king's thoughts on these matters seemed to reflect not only the religious traditions of the Mpongwe but also the wisdom that flowed from his own experience—and perhaps also from the disillusionments of advancing age and from what he saw going on around him. Even he, perhaps especially he, could see that his town was losing its former strength and self-confidence and was clearly in decline. George thought the suppression of the slave trade by the British was the cause of the growing poverty of the people. But Walker reached a different conclusion: "Nothing can be plainer than the fact that the slave trade has made them drunkards, almost obliterated their sense of right and wrong, and now the people are reaping a terrible harvest of sorrow, and no one can tell where it will end." Nevertheless, the New Englander felt a growing affection and commitment to the people and their amiable, hospitable, and often thoughtful ways: "Still there is no place in the world where we are more cordially received and better entertained, as far as they have the means of doing anything for us."[27]

WALKER OFTEN MADE the trip back to Baraka at night in order to catch the tide and a favorable wind and to avoid getting stuck on the large sandbar where the Remboué emptied its waters into the estuary. He and his Mpongwe companions would walk the narrow trail through the rainforest that led to Abaäga Creek, each carrying an *ojo*—a torch made of impure beeswax and other inflammable materials rolled together and wrapped in plantain leaves. They walked quietly in a single file as they listened to the disparate sounds of the night—the wind in the trees, the buzz of insects, the call of some bird or the cry of some forest creature. The travelers peered into the darkness that surrounded them and that gave way only briefly to the light of their passing torches before quickly closing in behind them. And the darkness listened to them and peered back at them as they moved along their path—occasionally some startled creature stirred the brush in flight, and sometimes rainforest eyes caught the light of an *ojo* and glowed within the engulfing night.[28]

When they had reached their boat and had made their way down the creek into the river and out into the estuary, Walker found deep satisfaction in being on the open water and feeling the land wind that filled the sail and moved the boat along. When the moon was bright, it built its own world of light and shadows across the estuary, and the trees of the shoreline stood out against their forest background in ways never seen during the day. But when the night was dark or overcast, then the waters seemed part of the sky, and the Mpongwe helmsman used ancient skills to navigate toward Glass's Town. Walker sometimes stretched out and listened to the sound of water lapping against the boat and to the crew talking as their pipes glowed in the dark. He often dozed until the first hints of the morning began to appear—the sky in the east paled, and through the morning mist egrets flew from their roosts in long, slow lines, and it was day.[29]

ON HIS RETURN to Baraka from one of his trips to George's Town in July 1844, Walker learned that his friend and colleague Benjamin Griswold was very sick. Griswold had himself been on a trip far up the Como River—he had been to Kobangai's Town, where Leighton had gone with Toko on the *Waterwitch*. Griswold had come down with a fever and had returned to the mission station at Ozyunga suffering hard chills and a dangerously fluctuating fever. The young abolitionist was expecting to return soon to the United States to continue his study of medicine—he wanted, he said, to be better prepared to serve the mission as a physician. But he did not take care of himself on his return from Kobangai's Town, and he got up too quickly from his sickbed.

When a man was brought to the mission badly cut up from a drunken fight, Griswold had spent the night standing over him and sewing him up. It was too much, and the fever came roaring back with a vengeance. In spite of Leighton's desperate efforts to treat him, Griswold never recovered.[30]

Shortly after he had first arrived in the estuary, Griswold had written that "no one must come to Africa who will shrink from suffering or who is afraid of death." The young New Englander—who as a student at Yale had been so moved by the prisoners of the slave ship *Amistad* that he had committed his life to Africa—died on July 7, 1844. He was thirty-three.[31]

Griswold's body was brought to Baraka, where Walker and Leighton made his coffin and laid their friend in it. A large crowd of Mpongwe began to gather for his funeral—Toko and old Glass, schoolchildren and the curious, and those who came out of a polite respect for one who had for a time lived among them. They walked up the hill through the wide street of Glass's Town to the newly marked off cemetery at Baraka. There they heard Leighton preach the strange message of Christian faith and the hope of a heavenly home, and there they heard the little cluster of Christians—whites and blacks, Americans, Grebo, and Fanti—sing a hymn, and they saw a wooden coffin lowered into the ground and covered with the soil of an African hillside.[32]

Chapter Seventeen

The French: "The Most Dishonest and Shameless People"

In 1842 when Leighton and the others from Cape Palmas had first sailed around Cape Clara into the broad and beautiful Gabon estuary, they had thought they were entering a region far removed from the colonial interests of Europeans or Americans. They knew that trading vessels from Bristol and London, from New York and Salem, visited the north shore regularly, but the ship captains had no trading houses or permanent presence in the estuary—Captain Lawlin of the *Atalanta* being a case in point. Leighton and the other travelers also knew from what Lawlin had told them that French merchants—primarily from Bordeaux—had established important contacts and trade with King William on the south shore. What the travelers from Cape Palmas did not know, however, was that the French had larger ambitions for Gabon. For several years, they had been eyeing the estuary and thinking of the important role it could play in their commercial and military plans for West Africa. Merchants in Bordeaux were eager to expand their Africa trade, and the French navy saw the estuary as a fine harbor for a protected naval base. The navy needed such a base in their efforts to intercept any French vessels carrying slaves—the French had outlawed participation by their ships in the international slave trade and would soon abolish slavery in their Caribbean colonies. But the French also wanted such a base for military reasons in case of some future war with the British or the Americans and for their assertion of control over selected regions of West Africa.[1]

With these interests in mind, two French warships had sailed around the bar at Cape Clara in March 1838 and had slowly moved along the south shore as its officers and crew observed the terrain and the broad waters of the estuary. Anchoring near King William's Town, they saw a Portuguese ship loading slaves they had bought from the Mpongwe for the Brazilian market. Since the French navy was primarily concerned with intercepting slavers flying the French flag, they did not disturb the Portuguese, who went about their business of ferrying their wretched captives out to their ships.[2]

The French captain went ashore, where he was greeted warmly in French by the king. William was eager for more trade with the French and indicated that he could provide large quantities of ivory and ebony. The king had a brother who had served in the French army, and William, while always ready to trade with any ship that sailed into the estuary, was particularly partial to the French, who had given him the French name "Denis." The captain was impressed by the king and wrote a report that stressed not only the possibility of trade with him but also the potential of the estuary as a naval base.[3]

The French navy returned the next year under the command of Edouard Bouët-Willaumez. He found King William's Town already occupied "by a population eminently French in language, manners, habits, and sentiments." He was astonished by the "civilized" ways of the Mpongwe and attributed their sophistication to the long influence of French traders—including French slavers who had once frequented the estuary. Bouët-Willaumez signed a treaty with the king on February 9, 1839, that ceded to the French a strip of low, sandy land along the south shore. As a consequence, George was nominated and made a chevalier of the French Légion d'Honneur. The wily king, however, while wearing his handsome medal, had in fact thwarted French efforts to build a fort on the south shore by ceding them poor and unhealthy land.[4]

Three years later, Bouët-Willaumez returned to the estuary, focusing his attention this time on the north shore with its higher ground and healthier climate. On March 18, 1842, he signed a treaty with Louis, the headman of a village that lay between Glass's Town and the mouth of the estuary. Louis conveyed to the king of France "full and entire" sovereignty and placed his village under the protection of the French, who were about to begin in earnest their move to control the estuary. The treaty alarmed neighboring towns, whose leaders immediately perceived what the intentions of the French really were.[5]

Leighton and Griswold arrived three months later. They made their decision to establish their mission at Baraka without any knowledge of the looming threat to Mpongwe independence. But Glass and Toko knew the threat—they were outraged by Louis's actions—and their invitation to the

Americans to establish a mission was apparently motivated not only by their desire for a school but also by the hope that the Americans might provide some protection from French intrusions.[6]

In June 1843, a year after the establishment of Baraka, the French began building a fort at Louis's village. Toko and Glass saw the fort as an ominous sign of things to come. After talking with them, Walker noted in his diary that they understood the strategic importance of a fort at any one of the towns—it would give the French control of the whole estuary and end the independence of the Mpongwe. The missionaries were themselves soon alarmed by the French move and by its implications for their mission. They had abandoned their work at Cape Palmas because of the interference of the colonial government and their belief that the settlers were hostile to the Grebo and hungry for their land. But any aggression by the little American colony seemed tame compared to the potential for French imperialism in West Africa and the Gabon estuary. Moreover, the missionaries anticipated that the French would bring Catholic missionaries with them, and they believed that the deep and shared hostilities between Catholics and Protestants would quickly become an inescapable part of the mission effort in the estuary. The question that Leighton and Walker and the others at Baraka consequently faced was how the missionaries of the American Board should respond to the French efforts to take control of the estuary.[7]

On the one hand, they knew only too well that they could be accused of meddling in politics if they became directly involved in any conflict between the Mpongwe and the French. This had been the bitter complaint lodged against Leighton and the Episcopalian missionaries at Cape Palmas when they had accused the settlers of unjust treatment of the Grebo. To take a stand on behalf of the indigenous people against powerful external forces invited the charge of intruding into affairs that were none of the business of missionaries, who were supposed to be there solely to evangelize the heathen. On the other hand, they regarded the French moves as the first steps toward an oppressive colonial regime that would overwhelm the people to whom the missionaries were committed and for whom they felt a responsibility.[8]

Leighton and the other missionaries tried to avoid any direct confrontation with the French by seeming to be scrupulously neutral in disputes between the Mpongwe and the French. At the same time, however, they provided detailed accounts of French actions to American and British readers and authorities. They hoped to appeal to Christian audiences in America and Britain that were deeply committed to missions, to ending the international slave trade, and to the protection of "the rights of aborigines" who were facing—from the Americas to South Africa, Australia, and New Zealand—the aggression of white settlers.[9]

William Walker led the way in implementing this strategy. Two weeks after the French began building their fort at Louis's village, Walker wrote to the British evangelical abolitionist Thomas Fowell Buxton. A leader of the second generation of British abolitionists, Buxton had skillfully directed the efforts that had led in 1833 to the abolition of slavery within British domains. He had then turned his great energies to "Aborigines' rights" and had chaired a parliamentary committee to investigate the treatment of indigenous peoples in British overseas settlements. Utilizing missionary reports, he had won some important protections for indigenous peoples of Australia and New Zealand and in particular for the Xhosa and Khoi of South Africa.[10]

In his letter to Buxton, Walker described the situation in the estuary and declared that the French were clearly attempting to gain control of the whole area. Glass and other leaders, Walker wrote, "are anxiously enquiring whether England can protect them." The missionaries could not answer their inquiries, Walker said. He was consequently writing Buxton to ask if the British government could give any protection to the Mpongwe, if they requested it, to ensure that their rights and territory would not be encroached upon.[11]

Walker's concern about the intentions of the French had been heightened when he had spoken to some French officials. They replied to his inquiries by saying they were only doing in Gabon what the American settlers were doing in Liberia! Walker was appalled by the French arrogance. "I once thought," he wrote in his diary, "that the French had at least a show of honor and manliness. But in their intercourse with this people they have shown themselves the most dishonest and shameless of any people I ever met." And then he revealed his own deep Protestant prejudices: "But I suppose they are just like all Papists."[12]

While the Mpongwe and the missionaries awaited some word from British friends, the French began to put pressure on Glass and Toko. Gifts were offered to induce them to sign treaties in November 1843, but the old king and the wise Toko refused the enticements and sent them back. So the French waited and made their plans.[13]

In March 1844, while Leighton and Walker were visiting King George's Town, a French trader came to Glass's Town, spent the night drinking with the old king, and got Glass to sign what Glass thought was a letter of friendship to the French king. The next day, the French commander came to Baraka and told Jane that Glass had signed a treaty ceding sovereignty to the French—the mission, he said, was now under French protection. Toko and the other Mpongwe of Glass's Town protested vigorously. Glass had been tricked, they said, and anyway, the old king had no right to sign such a document on behalf of his town without the approval of a public assembly. When Leighton and Walker returned, they found the people in an uproar. After listening to the excited accounts of Toko and Glass and others, the missionaries thought the king's mark had been "obtained by the blackest villainy." They nevertheless counseled a peaceful protest.

At the request of the old king and their friend Toko and other headmen, they wrote letters to King Louis Philippe and to Queen Victoria. A British trader, Toko's friend Captain Samuel Dyer, took the letters and got the marks and wrote the names of over a hundred men in Glass's Town. When the French commander was shown the letters, he simply dismissed them and said nothing would be retracted. Walker wrote again to Buxton and the Aborigines' Protection Society, and Leighton wrote the American Board. He asked Rufus Anderson to make some inquiries about American and British attitudes toward French moves in the estuary. But the French were adamant, and when Bouët-Willaumez arrived back in the estuary and was given a letter of protest written by Leighton and Walker at the request of Glass and Toko, he simply tore it up and threw it into the wind and waves. Leighton and Walker went on board Bouët-Willaumez's ship and told him that since Glass's Town refused to accept the treaty, they regarded Baraka as under the protection of Glass and not the French. They insisted they were not fomenting resistance but only responding to the request of the people to act as their intermediaries. Bouët-Willaumez was polite but said the treaty was signed and in force. Two days earlier he had signed treaties with all of the other major kings around the estuary acknowledging the sovereignty of France over the two banks of the estuary and all the waters that lapped at their shores. King William and King George were among those who signed. They had all been given many gifts.[14]

Still Glass and Toko held out, refusing to give up the independence of Glass's Town. They were waiting for help from the British and had been encouraged by the arrival of the *Decatur*, a US sloop-of-war commanded by Walker's friend Joel Abbott. The commander and some of his officers visited Baraka and dined with the missionaries, and Leighton and Walker, together with Toko, were invited on board the *Decatur* and sailed with it until it passed the bar at the mouth of the estuary. The Americans seemed to be taking an interest in French moves to control the estuary, and their presence seemed to offer some hope that American warships would act as a brake on French aggression.[15]

There had also been a visit from Commodore Josiah Tattnall, a native of Savannah and a friend of Jane's family. He had refused to "intermeddle in any manner in the affairs of the French and natives," but he did call on the French commander, who assured him that he had the kindest intentions toward the missionaries. Tattnall also listened closely to what Leighton and Jane told him and reported his conclusions to his commanding officer, Commodore Matthew C. Perry, who wrote the secretary of the navy that France intended not only to control the estuary, but also to prepare the way for a colonial settlement. The estuary, Perry thought, was to be a French naval base, and it would be well situated in the event of any future war with England or the United States.[16]

So Glass and Toko stood their ground, hoped they would get some help from the British or Americans, and watched every move by the French. And at Baraka, on the hill above Glass's Town, the missionaries looked out over the estuary, with its darting Mpongwe sailboats and canoes, its trading ships flying American or British or French flags, and its Portuguese and Spanish slavers. Leighton and the other missionaries once again wondered and worried about how their missionary efforts would be influenced by imperial incursion into West Africa. Meanwhile, the French completed their fort at Louis's Town, continued to strengthen their presence in the estuary, and planned their next attempt to get Glass and Toko to accept French authority over the Mpongwe.[17]

IN AUGUST 1844—with matters apparently at a stalemate between Glass, Toko, and the French—William Walker left Gabon for a furlough to try to recover his health. He had been suffering repeated bouts with fever, he was lonely and struggling with depression, and he was outraged by the French moves in the estuary.[18]

Walker sailed for the United States by way of England. Arriving in Bristol in December, he was quickly invited to stay in the home of the city's mayor, Richard King, whose business had extensive trade relations with the Mpongwe. Walker found that the mayor and his brother were trying to help the Mpongwe preserve their independence, but the brothers were finding no encouragement from the British Foreign Office. The tall, gangly New England missionary spoke with merchants in the city, went to antislavery meetings, and attended meetings of the Aborigines' Protection Society. Everywhere he went he spoke about his experiences in Gabon and about the French aggression, and his remarks, he thought, "caused considerable sensation." He traveled to London with Governor George MacLean of Cape

Coast—who had been so kind to Leighton and Jane on their visits to the former slave fort and its surrounding town—and together Walker and MacLean spoke of Africa and the efforts of the British to end the international slave trade. Walker called at the Foreign Office and had an interview with Lord Canning, undersecretary of state for foreign affairs. He gave Canning a full report of how the French were taking control of the estuary and how they had obtained King Glass's mark through trickery.[19]

Everywhere there was much interest in what he had to say, and often outrage over the French aggression, but the official British response to the French moves in the African estuary were cautious. British commercial interests in Gabon did not merit a confrontation with the French. A British warship sailed to the estuary to investigate the situation, but the ship's officers only promised to use the good offices of their government with the French on behalf of the Mpongwe.[20]

After three months in England, Walker sailed for Boston, where he continued to speak on behalf of the Mpongwe and to warn against French aggression in the estuary. He met with Anderson and leaders of the American Board; visited Yale, Amherst, and Dartmouth and spoke with their students; met with local pastors; and spent time with the family of his dear Prudence. He even traveled by train, boat, and stage to far-off Wisconsin to see his family and other Vermonters who had settled frontier lands, which had their own history of bloody Indian Wars and of French, British, and American colonization. Everywhere he went, he once again told about the mission in Gabon, about the slave trade and the bitter role of New England rum and ships in the nefarious business, and about the aggression of the French. He also met and dined in Washington with George Bancroft and his family. Bancroft, the recently appointed secretary of the navy, was, Walker thought, "one of the most amiable men living," and the secretary no doubt had his ears filled by the young missionary's reports on the slave trade and French moves to control the estuary.[21]

Walker, who continued to grieve the death of Prudence, found his visit with her family particularly painful. He was lonely, and his depression seemed to follow him wherever he went. He began to think of finding a wife who was committed to the church's mission in faraway places and who would return with him to Baraka and to his work among the Mpongwe and Shékiani. After visiting his family in Wisconsin, he returned to New England, and there he met Zephiah Shumway. She and Prudence had been girlhood friends, and she shared Prudence's commitment to missions. A rather plain young woman, she was kind and compassionate and ready to go beyond the valleys of her Vermont home. So when Walker began to talk to her about marriage, she said she was willing to go with him to Africa. She knew the dangers, and she knew the fate of her friend Prudence, whose grave was on a hillside at Cape Palmas. But the life of a missionary was a great adventure, too, and for Zephiah it was a high calling that involved the giving of self to a great purpose. She and Walker were engaged in August 1845 and married in October. They expected to sail for Gabon the next month.[22]

But as they waited in New York for their passage, Rufus Anderson hurried from Boston to tell them of news he had just received from Leighton. The newlyweds, Anderson told them, must delay sailing. There had been "serious collisions between the French and natives of the Gaboon," and the mission station at Baraka had been bombarded by a French warship and fired upon by French troops.[23]

WHILE WALKER WAS traveling in Britain and the United States, the French began to put increased pressure on Glass and Toko to acknowledge French authority over the estuary. When persuasion had failed, and when what Leighton called French "sophistry" had been recognized and rejected by Glass and Toko, the French had established a naval blockade hoping to deny provisions to Glass's Town. Any canoe or Mpongwe boat leaving the town was confiscated or sunk, and even the mission boat was seized when it was sent to bring a newly arrived and sick missionary, Albert Bushnell, back from Ozyunga. But the blockade did not bring compliance with French demands. Glass and Toko remained defiant and refused to raise the French flag according to a flag protocol insisted upon by the French. The frustrated and disdainful French—they called Toko a "bushman of no consequence"—decided that force was necessary.[24]

As tensions grew, Leighton, in conversations with French naval officers, continued to insist on the neutrality of the mission. Since Glass's Town was asserting its independence, and the mission was there at the invitation of the town's leaders, Leighton said, he could not acknowledge French authority. If, however, the town agreed to accept French rule, or if the French took the town by force, the mission would "obey the powers that be." He also told the French that he had been informed by Commodores Abbot and Tattnall—as well as other US naval officers—that in the case of hostilities, he should raise the American flag as an indication of the mission's neutrality and to rely upon the US flag for protection. The French insisted he was not the political representative of the United States and had no right to raise the American flag; they simply dismissed the opinion of the US naval officers who had advised Leighton.[25]

The French began their assault by firing blank cartridges toward the shore for several days. They evidently hoped that the sounds of shots would intimidate Toko and the old king and warn them of what was to follow if they did not concede to French demands. When this pyrrhic display failed, the French began a coordinated assault on the Mpongwe town. First they began an intermittent bombardment from ship cannons. But by the time the bombardment began, the people had already largely abandoned their homes and had fled to their plantations in the bush. The missionaries and their boarding students remained at Baraka and it soon came under attack. A thirty-two-pound shot crashed into the church, "where," wrote Leighton, "the Commander had every reason to suppose that our school was assembled."[26]

Leighton immediately raised the American flag over the mission house where children and teachers and missionaries all huddled. "This," he wrote, "if it had any effect at all, caused the fire to become more intense, and brought the balls still nearer to our dwelling." He lowered the flag, thinking it might be "construed as an act of resistance," but still the bombardment continued, with shells passing over the house—one shell landed in the yard in front of the mission house, throwing debris onto the porch and badly frightening those huddled inside. When the naval shelling finally stopped, a company of French marines landed on the beach, and African troops from Senegal approached the town by land. Then, in a coordinated attack, they stormed into the town, firing into the bamboo houses and up the hill into the yard and buildings at Baraka.[27]

Fortunately, no one was killed or injured, either at Glass's Town or in Baraka, and a serious diplomatic incident was narrowly avoided with the Americans. The French commander soon left the estuary, and the new commander made apologies to Leighton for the attack. US naval ships then arrived in the estuary. Their commanders received assurances from the French that the missionaries were welcome and that, indeed, the mission was seen as doing good. Leighton himself was reported to be held in high regard by the French as a man of integrity and goodwill. But Glass's Town was now under French control, and the French could be safely generous in their assessments of Leighton and the mission.[28]

Leighton was disappointed with the American response. He had hoped that the US naval commanders would take the Mpongwe's resistance to the French seriously and listen carefully to Glass's and Toko's accounts of what had happened. He wrote Henry Bruce, commander of one of the American warships, "I regret that you do not feel authorized to benefit from the testimony of the natives." That refusal, of course, lay close to the heart of Western power and arrogance—How could any proud white naval officer, French or American, on board a marvelous ship-of-war with all of its indicators of a superior civilization, possibly benefit from the testimony of Africans? What could a Mpongwe, a black man, possibly say that would make a white naval officer willing to risk breaking established protocols among Western nations?[29]

Glass and Toko, however, remained defiant. They rejected the annual gifts of the French to Mpongwe leaders, for they knew the acceptance of such gifts would be regarded as an acknowledgment of French authority and legitimacy. The king and Toko were trying to maintain the independence and traditions of their people even as they realized that independence was now a thing of the past. Their traditional ways faced a steady assault not only from the French but also from their friends who had stood with them at Baraka. For those friends at Baraka—white and black Americans, Grebo and Fanti—were all laboring to transform the world of the Mpongwe, to lead them away from their old ways into a new world of Christian faith and life.[30]

Chapter Eighteen

Home Visit

After the French bombardment and assertion of control over the estuary, life at Baraka returned to its more familiar routines. The Protestant mission, however, now had competition from a Catholic mission established near the French fort and supported by the French authorities. While the Mpongwe watched and wondered, the missionaries of the two missions eyed one another across the gulf of their histories and their competing understandings of Christian faith and life. But when the Catholic missionaries also suffered the deadly fevers and other illnesses that hit the Protestant missions, both missions began to reach cautiously beyond their differences and to engage one another. Their common struggles and a commitment to civility allowed them—in spite of their deep animosities—to visit one another, to help one another in times of illness, and to cooperate as they both worked on understanding Mpongwe language and customs. Nevertheless, the animosities were real—the Protestants thought the Catholic rituals and religious images reflected a belief in magic not far from the fetishes of the Mpongwe. And the Catholics were amazed by the egalitarianism among the Protestant missionaries, who had no bishops or archbishops or pope. They made, Leighton wrote, "a vigorous effort to convince the people that we [Protestants] are not the true ministers of the Gospel." But a kind of truce was established between them, and Leighton thought the truth would finally be known by its fruits. He hoped that the Protestant mission would be able to appeal to the witness of its life—the fruits of a Protestant faith—with confidence. And he prayed that life at Baraka and at the other stations and schools would not bring shame to the gospel they preached.[1]

THE SCHOOL AT Baraka was full in 1845, and the little congregation received some recent converts, who were an encouragement to the missionaries. But the mission was badly understaffed. The James family had left earlier for furlough in the United States; Walker and his new bride were still waiting in New England for passage; and Wasa and Maria, badly homesick for their Grebo homeland, had returned to Cape Palmas to work for the Episcopal mission.[2]

Even the arrival of a new missionary from the United States turned out to be a disappointment. Albert Bushnell, a rather frail man possessed by a nervous restlessness, had arrived shortly before the French attack on Baraka. Soon afterward he had married the widow Mrs. Stocken, and they had taken over the station at Ozyunga that had been left vacant by the death of Benjamin Griswold. Bushnell, however, had been hit hard by fever, and after he was finally able to get back to Baraka, the French had begun to fire on the mission. The whole experience had left him shaken, and he and his new wife soon left for a furlough in the United States. Leighton was troubled by Bushnell's response to the trauma of the French attack and what he called "the extreme derangement" of Bushnell's nerves. Leighton wondered if Bushnell had the emotional strength needed to face the demands of mission work in Africa. He later wrote Rufus Anderson that the young man needed to be carefully examined by a competent doctor to see if he should return to the estuary. Leighton had, he confided to Anderson, serious apprehensions that Bushnell suffered from hypochondria—apprehensions later shared by William Walker.[3]

So Leighton and Jane found themselves at Baraka without the companionship of other white Protestant missionaries, not unlike their early years at Fair Hope. But mission friends were now nearby. The Fanti John Edwards and his Grebo wife were living and conducting school at George's Town; George Coe and B. B. Wisner, both Greboes, were teaching nearby; and the Grebo Francis Allison and his Grebo wife, a former student of Jane's at Fair Hope, were still at Tom Larsen's Town across the estuary. They would soon return to Baraka, where Allison would take over the work of the printing press while B. V. R. James was away.[4]

Leighton and Jane, however, felt their closest attachment to Mary Cleland and Josiah Dorsey. In many ways Jane looked on Mary as her child, or at least a student who occupied a bright and lively place within Jane's quiet heart. When William Davis had brought Mary to Fair Hope in early 1836 to be educated at the mission, Jane had recently had a miscarriage, and then she had been in a great struggle with death as she had nursed a delirious Leighton back from an African grave. Mary had come into their lives as a gift to their hearts and as a beautiful young girl—vivacious, affectionate, and smart like her father. As the daughter of Davis and the niece of King Free-man, Mary was part of the most influential Grebo family at Big Town. And when she had sat on her father's lap and quickly taught him the English alphabet, and had later encouraged him in his conversion to Christianity, she had become a shining example of mission hopes for Africa. It was no wonder that Jane and Leighton had such admiration and affection for her. And she apparently admired and loved them back. When the decision was made to leave Fair Hope for the new mission at Baraka, she gladly decided to go with them and join them in their work. Although she would return to Cape Palmas from time to time to see her father and family there, she had cast her lot with Jane and Leighton and the mission at Baraka.[5]

Mary and Josiah Dorsey had known one another at Cape Palmas but became better acquainted as they visited together at Baraka. Dorsey had been born a slave in Maryland and freed by his owner in order to immigrate to Cape Palmas. Shortly after Dorsey's arrival at the Cape in late 1836, Leighton had hired him to help with the school at Fair Hope; at the same time, Dorsey would receive some additional education. In 1838, he had become the American Board's teacher at Rock Town, and when Leighton and Griswold had sailed in 1842 looking for a new mission location, he had gone with them. By 1844, he was established as the teacher at Duka's Town far up the Remboué River, where he soon became fluent in Mpongwe. He made, however, regular trips back to Baraka, where he and Mary saw one another. By 1846, they had known each other for years, but now Mary was in her late teens and he in his mid-thirties, and they were clearly in love. Leighton married them in the little mission church, and they were soon settled in a comfortable bamboo home and conducting school at Prince Glass's Town a short distance from Baraka. In 1848 Mary gave birth to a little boy, whom they named William Leighton Dorsey. So a young Grebo woman and a freed African American immigrant to Maryland in Liberia named their first child after his Grebo grandfather William Davis from Big Town and after their friend and mentor Leighton Wilson from Pine Grove. Other children followed, and all would have important roles to play in the early history of the church in Gabon.[6]

WALKER AND HIS young bride—he called her Zeniah—were finally able to sail with Captain Lawlin for Gabon in early September 1846. B. V. R. James and his family were with them, although they had decided not to return to Gabon. The news of the French attacks and of the bombardment of Baraka had been deeply distressing to them, and James had accepted a call by the

Presbyterian Mission Board to teach and manage a school in Monrovia. When they arrived in Monrovia, they moved into a handsome two-story stone house—it had bedrooms for visiting missionaries, a room they called "Captain Lawlin's Room," and a piazza that ran along the front of the second story, where they could sit in the evenings and watch the comings and goings in the little town.[7]

Margaret was no doubt glad to get away from the paternalistic eyes of Leighton and Jane and to claim her own respectable place in Monrovian society. Before long she was entertaining many visitors and overseeing a prosperous household with the watchful eye of a careful matron. Catherine lived her own quiet life with them, under the shadow of her mother and stepfather, giving herself to her teaching in the Presbyterian school and contributing to its growing reputation as the best in Liberia. For his part, James began to identify himself as a settler, a Liberian patriot. He abandoned the antagonism toward colonization that he had earlier shared with Leighton, and in a few years he was elected the clerk of the Liberian senate. The Wilson and James families, however, did not end their close relationship. During the coming years, regular correspondence flowed between the families, and extended hospitality and mutual affection were shared.[8]

After leaving the James family in Monrovia and conducting his business there, Captain Lawlin sailed for Cape Palmas, with William Walker and his bride once again aboard. When Lawlin anchored off the cape, William went ashore. He was filled with conflicting emotions as the ship's boat neared the land. The Cape, he thought, looked like home, but it was a home of hard memories. He called on Governor Russwurm and had a pleasant visit—the old animosities apparently put aside. But Walker was depressed by what he found as he walked the streets of Harper and visited in Big Town. War between the Grebo and the settlers had only been narrowly avoided a few years earlier by the intervention of Commodore Matthew Perry and his Africa Squadron, and deep tensions and animosities were being held in check only by the diplomatic skills of Russwurm and King Freeman. The Episcopal mission, it was true, was doing good work, but the African fevers had been unrelenting as they did their own destructive work among the missionaries. Some missionaries had died, and others were largely incapacitated. The mission, like Baraka, was badly understaffed. Walker returned to the ship in a melancholy mood.[9]

The next day, he and Zeniah went ashore through the rolling surf. As the wind and the surging power of the waves lifted the ship's boat and carried it toward the shore, Walker pointed out to his young wife the outlines of

Harper and Big Town and the little island where the Grebo left their dead. Back to the right they could see the hilltop where once there had been a mission station called Fair Hope. They visited the Episcopal mission, and Zeniah saw the mission and its cemetery firsthand and saw on the faces of the missionaries the effects of the fevers. Walker met with old friends and saw former students among the Grebo, then went by himself out to Fair Hope, where, he wrote, "I spent my first nine months in Africa. But how changed the place! Everything looked desolate." The tall New Englander walked out to the little mission cemetery past the graves of David and Helen White, who had died so shortly after their arrival, and stood by the grave of Prudence.[10]

If he had later walked to the northern edge of Harper, Walker would have seen Bayard Island, although the name Bayard had now been dropped and largely forgotten. Paul Sansay was still living there by himself and was a leading member of the settler community. He remained a thorn in Russwurm's flesh, always taking the side of the settlers when there were conflicts with the governor. The carpentry skills that Sansay had first learned in Savannah as an apprentice to the slave carpenter Jack had served him well in Harper. He had been appointed "Measurer of Lumber" and "Measurer of Buildings" and had his hand in many things—too many, Russwurm thought. His father, Charles Sansay, had died a few years before, and his mother was living with his sister, Charlotte, who had once been so close to Jane as her personal "servant" in Savannah and at Fair Hope plantation.[11]

Charles McIntosh was the most prominent of the other citizens of Harper who had once lived in the Hutchinson Island slave settlement by the waters of the Savannah. He still carried the name of General Lachlan McIntosh, had been elected constable, and had recently returned from a long exploratory trip to the interior. His party had followed inland routes traveled by Leighton in 1836 and 1837 when he had tried to reach Pah country. Like Leighton's party, McIntosh and his party had experienced illness and difficulties, but they had learned that the Pah—like the Fang in Gabon—were moving toward the coast, and they were eager to establish direct trade relations with Harper without Grebo middlemen.[12]

So the former Bayard Island, with all of its links to Savannah, was becoming a part of Harper. Those who lived there were putting old ways and old memories behind them, and they were assuming new identities as free men and women, citizens of Maryland in Liberia. And Fair Hope—it was becoming a receding memory for those who had once lived there, who had hoped there and had grieved there. Walker finished his visit and left the place where he had buried his Prudence, where once ocean winds had filled his days and the sounds of the surf had echoed through long, sleepless nights.

CAPTAIN LAWLIN SAILED from Cape Palmas on December 1 and, after stops along the way, reached the Gabon estuary on December 26, 1846. At about 3 p.m., they anchored off Glass's Town and met Jane and hundreds of Mpongwe on the beach. "I can barely describe the sensation I felt," he wrote in his diary, "in again meeting the people who have so long been waiting and despairing of my return."[13]

Leighton and Jane had been awaiting the arrival of the Walkers in order to be free to return to the United States on furlough. It had been thirteen years since Leighton had sailed out of New York Harbor with Jane, and he was long overdue for a rest for the good of his health. He wanted to promote the mission among various constituencies while in America, but he and Jane were simply ready for a visit home. So, four months after the Walkers arrived, the Wilsons sailed with Captain Lawlin for New York. With them were the Episcopal missionaries Dr. and Mrs. Thomas Savage, who had arrived with Captain Lawlin from Cape Palmas.[14]

Sometime before Savage arrived at Baraka, Leighton had learned that an enormous ape—called a *njina* by the Mpongwe—had been killed by a hunter. When he went to a nearby village and saw the skull of the animal, Leighton wrote that he "knew at once, from its peculiar shape and outline," that it belonged "to an undescribed species." He purchased the skull and some of the animal's bones, intending to send them to Rufus Anderson in Boston. When his friend Dr. Savage from Cape Palmas arrived, Savage encouraged him to try to secure as well the bones of another *njina*. Leighton, with his many contacts around the estuary, was able to buy a second but smaller skull.[15] Leighton carried these two skulls, together with their accompanying bones, to New York, where he turned them over to Savage to take to Boston. Leighton later wrote Rufus Anderson, "The skulls and bones of the African *ourangs* [the common name used for large apes], which I loaned to Dr. Thomas Savage and which he has informed me have been left with the Society of Natural History, Boston, were intended for the Missionary Rooms." If, however, Leighton wrote, they will serve "the cause of science better by remaining where they are, I am willing that you should make such disposition of them."[16]

The skull and bones, in fact, caused an immediate sensation in the scientific community and among the general public. Savage, together with Jeffries Wyman, professor of anatomy at Harvard, rushed to write an article for the

Boston Journal of Natural History: "Notice of the External Characters and Habits of Troglodytes Gorilla, A New Species of Orang from the Gaboon River." The gorilla quickly burst into the awareness and imagination of the Western world. Most ominously, the Harvard professor wrote in the Boston journal that "it cannot be denied, however wide the separation, that the Negro and Orang do afford the points where man and the brute, when the totality of their organization is considered, most nearly approach each other." In this way the *njina* Leighton first saw in a Mpongwe village was on its way to becoming, in the imagination of the Western world, a terrifying beast of the jungle—a beast often associated with the most degrading images of Africans.[17]

While Savage was meeting with Professor Wyman, Leighton and Jane were busy visiting friends and family. They went first to Lawrenceville, New Jersey, for a happy reunion with Jane's sister, Margaret, and her husband, James Eckard, who were staying briefly with the Bayard cousins. James Eckard had recently accepted a call to become pastor of the New York Avenue Presbyterian Church in Washington. In Lawrenceville, Leighton saw two-year-old John Leighton Eckard for the first time. His nephew, like William Leighton Dorsey in Africa, bore the name of the missionary from Pine Grove.[18]

Leaving Jane with the Bayard and Hodge relatives in New Jersey and Philadelphia, Leighton hurried south. He was eager to see his father, who was now in his seventies and in poor health. But Leighton also needed to see his sisters and brothers and make his position on slavery clear to them. When he had sent his father documents freeing his two slaves—John and Jesse—it had caused, his sister Sarah wrote, much grief and perplexity in Leighton's family. They wondered if he had been "influenced by a desire to appease the abolitionists." He had responded by writing that he had never intended to cause pain, and that he didn't know how they could think he was influenced by a desire to appease the abolitionists when he had made his own position on slavery clear to the family long before the abolitionists had begun to attack him. So Leighton hurried south, back to Pine Grove, back to the place he called home and to the people who were family, in order to reiterate what he had already said to them. He had written Sarah in a language and with sentiments he thought most likely to persuade her and other members of the family.[19]

He began by saying that slavery was not necessarily sinful. Since the Bible nowhere directly condemned slavery, he thought—at least theoretically— that "a conscientious Christian *may* hold slaves without committing a sin." But American slavery, he insisted, was opposed to the spirit of the gospel. Leighton told Sarah that while there were many objectionable features to

American slavery, he would select two to describe in order to clarify his views for his family. We cry out with one accord, he wrote, against the pope for denying Catholics the use of the Bible. But the pope could respond by saying that we deny the slave the use of the Bible. Moreover, it was not simply a matter of having a personal right to own slaves: "I, as a conscientious Christian," he told his sister, "may hold slaves and not abuse my authority. I may conduct myself towards them in such a way as to secure their and my highest happiness. But remember I am lending the influence of my example to others who may and will abuse their power. For the sake of others therefore, I cannot hold slaves." Leighton knew his sister would recognize the reasoning of his argument—the same sort of argument was being used by the temperance movement. A person had the moral freedom to drink alcoholic drinks in moderation, but for the sake of others who might abuse alcohol, a Christian was to refrain from drinking. "I, as a conscientious Christian," wrote Leighton "abstain from the use of ardent spirits (chiefly) for the sake of others. For the same reason I wish to rid myself of slaves." He told Sarah that when he had sent bills of freedom for his slaves John and Jessie, all he had expected or desired was that they know that they could choose to go north to freedom or remain at Boggy Gully under the guardianship of Leighton's father or one of his brothers. The choice was to be theirs. "And this," he wrote Sarah, "is still my wish."[20]

In this way, Leighton talked to his family about slavery, about John and Jessie, and about all the slaves who lived by Boggy Gully and the other growing slave settlements that now marked the homes where Leighton's brothers and sisters lived. He told them that he was no "ultra-abolitionist," but that slavery was doomed to die. It was best if white Southerners led the way for the emancipation of their slaves. The family must have listened carefully to Leighton—or at least politely—for they were very proud of him. Already a brother and sister had named sons for him. But the Wilsons of Pine Grove and surrounding plantations knew something Leighton apparently had not realized—slavery was prospering all along the Black River and throughout Sumter County, and the Wilsons were prospering along with their neighbors. The slave population of the county had more than doubled since Leighton had been away, and the county would soon be the wealthiest in the state and one of the wealthiest in the nation. Helping to fuel that growing wealth was the developing technology of modern, Western civilization and the arrival of a railway in Sumter County. Trains could carry with great efficiency cotton, the product of slave labor and sorrow, to humming mills in far-off England and New England.[21]

So Leighton tried to explain his opposition to slavery in ways that he thought his family would be most likely to hear and appreciate. He was trying to be clear and forceful without alienating them or causing their support of slavery to harden. He was clearly no William Lloyd Garrison or Frederick Douglass furiously denouncing slaveholders as "man stealers," or calling for the immediate abolition of slavery. Nor did he write as a slave who daily suffered the degradations and oppression of slavery. Rather, he wrote as a much-loved child of Pine Grove, and he used the language, manners, and piety of his home to try to persuade his family that slavery must finally be abolished. He did not seem to comprehend the entrenched power of slavery or its growing strength. Nor did he anticipate what would become clear only later—the inability of civil discourse to bring slavery to a peaceful end. But more than any of this, what he could not see, or would not see, was the seductive power of his Black River home. Already in the 1840s this home ground was calling to him to come over to the side of slavery, beckoning him to join the people he loved and the place he loved, reminding him of the obligations of gratitude for a generous love that had been given him since his birth.

AFTER THIS QUICK visit with family, Leighton returned to New Jersey, bringing sister Sarah with him. He spoke with students at Princeton as well as in New York, at Yale, and at Andover about Africa and the great need for more missionaries. And he wrote and published an article in the *Journal of the American Oriental Society* on the "Comparative Vocabularies of Some of the Principal Negro Dialects of Africa." He noted the differences between the languages of the northern coast and those of the southern. He pointed out the ways that coastal peoples had incorporated new words into their vocabularies through their trading activities with one another and with Europeans. And he spoke of their use of pronouns, verbs, and adjectives and how the different languages made gender distinctions. But most important of all, he called attention to the common ancestry of the dialects spoken across the vast region of southern Africa. He said that although a common ancestry had been suggested some years earlier, sufficient evidence had been lacking to establish it as a fact. In order to provide such evidence, he gave parallel vocabularies and details of grammar from the dialects of people from Cameroon in West Central Africa to Mozambique in East Africa and south to the Cape. After many pages of comparisons, he concluded that his study showed a degree of resemblance between these dialects sufficient to prove that they were related to one another and that the numerous peoples who inhabited an enormous swath of southern Africa must be of one great family. The article was an important early contribution to the identification and study of what came to be called the Bantu language and peoples of southern Africa.[22]

IN DECEMBER 1847, Leighton and Jane traveled south to spend the winter months with family. They visited Charleston, where Leighton spoke and preached at Circular Congregational Church, the church where he and the barber Charles Snetter had once worshiped together. They traveled to Savannah and met old friends, and Leighton preached on missions and the effort in Gabon. Jane's McIntosh cousins had sold Fair Hope plantation and were now living in Savannah, but her brother, Nicholas Bayard, had moved to the village of Roswell in the former Cherokee nation of upcountry Georgia. The twice-widowed Nicholas had married Eliza King, daughter of Roswell King, who had founded Roswell near the new city of Atlanta shortly after the Cherokees had been violently forced from their lands. The Kings had been joined by other Lowcountry families who had largely divested themselves of their slaves and had used the income from the sale of their slaves and plantations to invest in new textile mills in Roswell and in the railroads spreading across Georgia. Perhaps Leighton thought of the Grebo when he looked around at the handsome mansions that had been built in Roswell, and perhaps he remembered how he had compared the imperialism of the settlers at Cape Palmas to what Georgia was doing to the Cherokees. And maybe he remembered how he had had at least a little taste of what it was like to be on the receiving end of Western military power and aggression when the French had bombarded Baraka. But perhaps he didn't remember any of this, or if he did, maybe he simply didn't talk about it with his in-laws and friends.[23]

IN JANUARY 1848 Leighton and Jane went to Pine Grove, where they enjoyed its balmy winter days. Now they had time to walk sandy roads through open pine forests and down to the Black River swamp; time to feel the warmth of a winter sun; and time to rest. They visited those who lived by Boggy Gully, saw and talked with John and Jessie, and attended church at Mt. Zion, where Leighton preached in the afternoons to the growing number of slaves who were members of the congregation. And though Leighton was eager to return to Baraka and to his work among the Mpongwe, he knew—and Jane also knew—how deeply he was attached to this place. Here he once again experienced the light of the morning sun pouring through his old bedroom window bringing a new day. Here in the late afternoons as he walked well-known trails by fields he had worked as a boy, the land itself triggered memories—

the evening air would stir, bring the fragrance of earth fresh turned by late winter plowing, and offer an irrepressible sense of well-being. And here by the Black River and Boggy Gully, at Pine Grove and Mt. Zion, the sound of familiar voices told him he was home, where whites were owners and blacks were owned. He was a child, an offspring, of this place, and no amount of travel would free him from the ways in which this Black River home had shaped his inner life and bound him to this particular landscape where settlement cabins stood close to plantation houses.[24]

In the spring, Leighton and Jane returned to Philadelphia to be with Jane's Bayard family, and for Leighton to promote the mission cause in churches and schools throughout the Northeast. In June they went to New York to prepare for their departure and to attend the annual meeting of the American Board. A large and influential membership packed one of the city's largest churches. The Honorable Theodore Frelinghuysen, former US senator and a Whig candidate for vice president in 1844, presided. Leighton was asked to speak, and he told of French aggression and spoke at length in order to "correct errors and misapprehensions in relation to Africa." He described the landscape of West Africa and its varied and often beautiful scenery. He told of the many different peoples and traditions there and of how they were far from the stereotype of "an African." He spoke of the need for the Christian gospel among the different peoples and nations and described fetishes and the fears that he believed lurked beneath them.[25]

But most of all he tried to respond to the question he had been asked over and over again during his time in the United States, the question "about the capabilities of the African race for intellectual improvement." He acknowledged what almost all whites firmly believed as they looked at white power spreading around the world—that there was little chance that an African or Chinese or Indian could be "made what the white race is" intellectually. But he insisted that Africans had remarkable intellectual capabilities that would astonish most whites. And he told stories of what students had accomplished—students whose "intellectual capabilities were most marvelous"—and once again told stories about the brilliance of the Grebo William Davis and his daughter, Mary Clealand. In contrast to the images that were to gather quickly around the *njina* bones that he had turned over to the Society of Natural History in Boston, he painted images of Africans as individuals with histories who were part of gripping stories, who had minds and a human spirituality to be deeply admired.[26]

But in all of this, Leighton never mentioned Toko—Toko who had sailed the handsome *Waterwitch*, who had amazed Leighton with his ability to conduct extensive and complex trading, and whose humor and storytelling had been a gift and a guide for Leighton. For Toko had not been converted to Christianity and did not fit the mission narrative that Leighton wanted to convey.

Chapter Nineteen

"He Worships with Sincere Devotion the Customs of His Ancestors"

While Leighton and Jane were in the United States, Toko continued his resistance to the French. He faced, however, daunting challenges. He knew the French possessed overwhelming economic and military power, and that they were using it in systematic ways to extend their domination over the estuary. At the same time, as he looked around at the towns and villages of the estuary, he could see, to his distress, that his people were losing much of their vitality. Most obvious was a rapid decline in the Mpongwe population. When Leighton had first arrived at Baraka in 1842, Toko and other Mpongwe had told him that the Mpongwe had once been much more numerous and that their numbers had been steadily falling during the past half-century. No one, Leighton noted, seemed to be certain about the causes of the decline. But by 1848 it was clear that the rate of decline was increasing rapidly. It was also clear that the rapid decline was directly related to the arrival of more and more ships from Europe and the United States. The ships brought with them goods to trade, especially rum, and also pathogens that devastated the population in periodic epidemics—in particular, smallpox and measles. And the ships also brought sailors, sailors who spent time ashore with Mpongwe prostitutes, whose husbands encouraged them to earn a little money. So syphilis and gonorrhea, together with a growing alcoholism, had spread widely among the Mpongwe, and Mpongwe birthrates had fallen below what was needed to maintain their numbers.[1]

The ships arriving in the estuary were bringing, however, not only diseases and rum and eager sailors from far places, but also challenges to the old traditions of the Mpongwe. Toko had felt this challenge deeply, saying that the white man was a devil who "sabba everything," a devil who had come into the estuary with the tempting fruit of new knowledge that gave power and wealth. And, of course, among those who arrived on ships from far places with new ways of thinking, and new answers to old questions, were Toko's friends at Baraka, with their schools and books and strange message about Christian faith and life. So Toko had to struggle against the political domination of the French as the strength of the Mpongwe population was eroding. And he had to struggle to maintain the old ways and traditions of the Mpongwe as they were being called into question, and often regarded with revulsion, by the whites who had taken up residence along the shores of the estuary.[2]

BOTH TOKO AND Glass had continued to refuse the annual gift from the French in order to symbolize their independence, but people around the estuary began to complain that Toko was the real cause of tension with the French. The French commander visited William Walker at Baraka and offered him any assistance he needed if Walker "would only reconcile Toko to the French." "*Simple Man!*" Walker wrote in his diary. "He probably did not know that he was asking impossibilities." Once again the French offered Toko the annual gift in early 1848, but they found him, Walker proudly wrote, "incorruptible and no wise inclined to receive the price of his country's freedom."[3]

But Glass was another matter. The king was old—very old, almost one hundred—and tired, and he was still traumatized by the French bombardment of his village. So a short while after Toko refused the annual gift, Glass went to the French blockhouse, had dinner with the French officials, and accepted their gift. The old king seemed resigned to the fate of his people and to his own approaching death. "From the day on which the gift was put into his hands," Walker sadly noted, "he neither ate nor drank, but went down at once to his grave."[4]

On the day of his death Glass's wives and other women sat around his body and wailed before his door the ancient Mpongwe laments. Then, as their voices grew hoarse and the shadows of night began to reach across the estuary, a drum began to beat and a peculiar moan filled the air and engulfed the old king's town. Indâ, a mysterious spirit of the forest, emerged from the shadows, a man in disguise wrapped in dried plantain leaves. "No female must see him," Walker wrote. So the women fled Glass's house with fear and "ran as from death itself." Indâ entered the town followed by young men, who danced to the plaintive melody flowing from a Mpongwe flute. The spirit moved slowly and in a threatening manner. Then, suddenly, his followers scattered throughout the town and seized all the goats, sheep, and fowl they could find, killing them and carrying them off into the forest for what was reported at Baraka to be a great feast. Walker noted in his diary that the ritual seemed to be performed by a kind of secret society, sarcastically adding that it was probably "quite as sensible and useful as the Odd Fellowship or Free Mason societies" in New England.[5]

The next day, Walker arrived at the king's house shortly before they closed the coffin. Beside the shriveled and stiff corpse the people had placed cloth, a looking glass, the old king's pipe and some tobacco, and an uncorked bottle of rum and a tumbler. Walker saw around the coffin a number of jugs, pitchers, and pans to be deposited in the grave, together with some balls and a board so that Glass could play in death a Mpongwe game he had loved in life. Walker conducted a short funeral service. "In the presence of about one hundred people," he wrote in his diary, "we sang a hymn and made a prayer in Mpongwe, then sang another hymn and pronounced the benediction. During this there was the most profound silence, and had I had perfect command of the Mpongwe language, I would have made some remarks, but I feared lest I should by a blunder destroy the impression already made, and so left." Glass was carried out of his house, where he had welcomed so many and had drunk much rum. They did not take him to the cemetery at Baraka but buried him on another hillside a short distance from the waters of the estuary.[6]

Toko was now alone in resisting the French. Then, in the summer of 1848, word reached the estuary that the French king, Louis Philippe, had abdicated. Hopes soared that the French would leave. Toko went to the grave of an ancestor—a former Big Man of a nearby town—and sacrificed a goat, calling on him and other ancestors to help in the struggle for independence. But it was to no avail. The French did not budge but rather began to consolidate their control of the estuary. Toko grew increasingly despondent. He was suffering greatly from asthma, and to make matters worse, his daughter Wâwâ had become stubborn and rebellious.[7]

Shortly after Leighton had first arrived in the estuary, Toko had taken Wâwâ to Baraka and asked that she be educated in the mission school. A beautiful and remarkably sprightly child, she had been a good student. And yet the fact that she had become acculturated to Western ways made her more attractive to the traders who came and spent time in the estuary. She had been married as a young girl, according to Mpongwe custom, but Toko still had authority over her. Several months before Glass's death, she had taken up with an unscrupulous Englishman, the captain of one of the trading ships then in the estuary. Toko, who was famous for not being able to control his children, sent word for her to return to shore, but she refused. He went to the ship to try to persuade her, but she still refused. The Englishman was

A. John Leighton Wilson and Jane Bayard Wilson shortly after their return from Africa in 1852. Courtesy of the Presbyterian Heritage Center, Montreat, NC.

B. Gullah women in the Georgia Lowcountry hulling rice with mortar and pestle. This effective African method removed the hull with little grain breakage. Compare the mortar in drawing 9. Courtesy of Georgia Archives, Vanish Georgia Collection, sap93.

C. Gullah man driving ox cart on Sapelo Island, Georgia. The use of such ox carts continued into the twentieth century. Note the sandy road. Courtesy of Georgia Archives, Vanish Georgia Collection, sapo74.

D. John H. B. Latrobe (1803–1891). Latrobe was president of the Maryland State Colonization Society and oversaw the establishment of Maryland in Liberia at Cape Palmas. Like most white supporters of colonization, he thought free blacks constituted a grave danger to white America and saw colonization as the only humane way to avoid a catastrophic collision of the races. Courtesy of the Maryland Historical Society.

E. Dr. James Hall, first governor of Maryland in Liberia. He negotiated with the Grebo the right to establish the Maryland colony at Cape Palmas. While he and Leighton Wilson clashed when Wilson began to oppose colonization as a form of imperialism, Hall later said of the missionary "we know him to have possessed the confidence of the native Africans to a greater degree than any other white man we have ever met with on that coast." Courtesy of the Maryland Historical Society.

F. John B. Russwurm (1799–1851). One of the first African Americans to graduate from college and co-founder of the first African American newspaper. He emigrated to Liberia and became governor of Maryland in Liberia. He and Leighton Wilson worked together to maintain peaceful relations between the colony and the Grebo, but came to regard each other with suspicion. Courtesy of the George J. Mitchell Dept. of Special Collections and Archives, Bowdoin College Library, Brunswick, Maine.

G. "Fetish Magician in Gabon." The night following King Glass's death, a low moan filled his town. Then *Indâ*, a mysterious spirit of the forest, emerged from the shadows wrapped in dried plantain leaves. This photograph shows a similar figure. From Robert Hamill Nassau, *Fetichism in West Africa*.

H. Njembe. A secret society of women that involved rites of passage as young girls were initiated into its carefully guarded mysteries. Mpongwe women are shown here. They were said to discard any western dress and put on native cloth during the rite. Note the white paint on the face showing participation in a Njembe ceremony. From Robert Hamill Nassau, *Fetichism in West Africa*.

I. Mpongwe Mother and Child. This handsome picture shows a traditional way for a Mpongwe mother to carry a child. From Robert Hamill Nassau, *My Ogowe*.

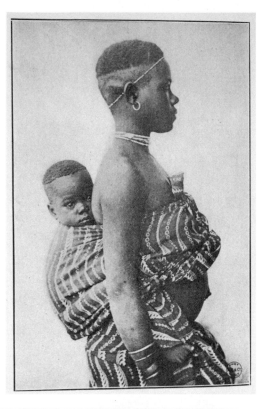

J. Missionaries at Baraka around 1870. William Walker is the tall man, center back. His diaries provide a daily account of the early days of the Gabon mission. Cornelius DeHeer is seated in the front holding a hat. When his wife died, he sent his young daughter Cornelia to Leighton and Jane Wilson, then living in New York. With his permission, the Wilsons adopted her as their own child. Courtesy Presbyterian Heritage Center, Montreat, North Carolina.

K. Baraka. This photograph from the late nineteenth century shows the first cottage built at Baraka. The house was built in 1842 by African American carpenters from Cape Palmas. Leighton and Jane Wilson lived here until their return to the US in 1852. This was also William Walker's primary residence. Courtesy Presbyterian Heritage Center, Montreat, North Carolina.

L. Fang Warrior. Beginning in the 1840s, the Fang began to move from the Gabon interior toward the coast. Leighton Wilson encountered Fang warriors in 1843 during a trip up the Como river with Toko. Wilson thought the Fang appeared free from the vices that afflicted those in long contact with whites. The Fang were soon to overwhelm other peoples living closer to the coast. From Robert Hamill Nassau, *My Ogowe*.

M. Fang Woman. This woman by her stance and look shows the strength and energy of the Fang so much admired by Americans and Europeans. From Robert Hamill Nassau, *My Ogowe*.

N. Village Preaching, around 1880. A missionary from the Baraka mission is addressing a gathering of men in an interior village. Note the varied expressions on the men's faces. From Robert Hamill Nassau, *My Ogowe*.

O. "Fetish Doctor." This man is seated in the middle in the "Village Preaching" photograph. The triangular patch of hair is described by a missionary as "the professional tonsure" of a "Fetish Doctor." From Robert Hamill Nassau, *Fetichism in West Africa*.

P. Ruins of Columbia, SC, 1865. This photograph looks down Columbia's Main Street. Shortly after the departure of Sherman's troops, Leighton Wilson and the African American John Wilson each drove a wagon of supplies into the city from Wilson's home some fifty miles away. They delivered them to refugees at Columbia Theological Seminary, which had not been burned. Courtesy of National Archives, photo no. 165-SC-53.

paying her twelve dollars a day, she said, and her husband was glad for the income. "This is the example," wrote Walker in disgust, "of most of the Captains who visit the coast. Better bring the small pox or any other plague than such vile plagues of body and soul as are left here by these dregs of civilization." Wâwâ stayed with the Englishman and traveled with him as he traded along the coast until he sailed for home some months later.[8]

Weakened by his asthma, Toko's good humor was not able to keep at bay a deep discouragement that flowed from the French aggression, Glass's death, and Wâwâ's disobedience. Several months after Glass died, Toko took a gun, pointed it at himself, and pulled the trigger. It misfired. He tried again, and again it misfired. And "so he supposed," he told Walker, "that God was not pleased to let him die so," and that he should not try again.[9]

A chastened Toko continued to come to Baraka. He attended church faithfully, listening carefully to what the missionaries had to say, but although his children became Christians—eventually even Wâwâ—he did not. He was a Mpongwe at the deepest level of his self-awareness in spite of his cosmopolitan ways and knowledge of distant lands. He would not leave the world of his ancestors and the land that they inhabited, nor would he try to silence their voices, which spoke deep within him and around him and through him. As a boy and young man he had learned the moods of the estuary, its currents and tides, its coming in and going out, and he had seen moon rise and star rise over its waters. He had listened by glowing fires as the old ones told stories of ancestors and recounted fables rich and refined with years of telling. He had watched his elders enact ancient traditions and teach the young ones how to go about their work according to long-established custom. Here, among his own people, as a young one himself, he had learned how to carry himself, how to think about himself, and how to live in the presence of his ancestors. Now, as an old man, being of this place, being one with the landscape of his home and the traditions of his people, he did not find the message of the missionaries convincing—even if he came to believe that some of the traditions of his people were foolish and embarrassing. And so, just as he resisted the imperialism of the French, he resisted the appeals of his friends at Baraka and their calls to him to change his heart and to adopt new ways of seeing the world and being in the world.

LEIGHTON AND JANE returned to Baraka in late August 1848. With them were the twice-widowed Mrs. Griswold and the Bushnells—Albert Bushnell was returning despite continuing reservations about his mental health. But most encouraging was the presence of three new missionaries, or at least two of three new missionaries. Ira and Jane Preston were from Ohio and were a particularly gifted young couple. He would quickly prove himself the best linguist among all the missionaries, and she would be a lively and thoughtful teacher much loved by her students. Years later she would write *Gaboon Stories*, a little book intended for American children but full of careful observations about school life, the Mpongwe, and the "bush people." In contrast, W. T. Wheeler, the third new missionary, was a disaster. From the first, Leighton and others wondered how the board in Boston could have sent to Gabon a man who found some dreadful disease in every ache and pain he felt.[10]

On their arrival, however, they found, much to their distress, that Zeniah Walker had died. The young bride had become pregnant during the long voyage to Baraka. The preceding February, she had given birth to a son, who had gasped a few times and then closed his eyes in death. For two months afterward she had fought for her own life while bleeding internally. William Walker had tried desperately and lovingly to do what he could for his ailing wife with the aid of a French doctor. Zeniah died in late March, confessing her faith in a "precious Redeemer" and her love for her distraught husband. Walker buried her beside their son, and he built a fence and planted flowers around the grave. But he was devastated. "The reality and greatness of my loss," he confided to his diary, "presses upon me with increasing force. I want to ask someone to wake me, so that I may escape from this dreadful suffocating feeling and look once more upon the face of my dear Zeniah." He felt alone and surrounded by darkness: "If I sit in the house, all is desolate and if I go out double desolation meets me on the threshold as I return." Later he wrote that he believed she was in a better world, "but I weep because I have a human heart. But I pray for reconciliation and try to school my heart into submission. I am not conscious of cherishing my grief, though I know there is great danger of it. I feel the obligations of duty to the living around me. I hardly know my own heart now. The violent repression of grief as well as pain, only makes it more intense. I desire to lie passive in God's hands. The furnace is hot indeed. May God give strength according to my day."[11]

Walker was not alone in his agony. Jane Cooper, the free woman from Savannah who had come out with Jane Wilson in 1843, had become close to Zeniah and had helped to care for her as she battled for her life. Exhausted by the loving attention she had given Zeniah, she felt overwhelmed when her friend died. A profound loneliness pressed in upon her, and she became deeply depressed. She began to suffer from hysteria, beginning with faintness and ending in violent laughing and crying. Walker gave her an antispasmodic, but it seemed to do little good. Finally she was calm enough to take a sea voyage—she and all her friends at Baraka hoped it would help her recover. So she was not at Baraka when the returning and new missionaries arrived.[12]

But there was encouraging news to greet Jane and Leighton as well. Upon their return they learned that some of the students at Baraka "had a new heart" and were seeking membership in the church. Several sons of prominent Mpongwe had announced that they wanted to be baptized, that they were rejecting the ancient ways and beliefs of the people and were ready to assume a new identity as Mpongwe Christians. This news caused much excitement among the Mpongwe, and opposition was immediate. The parents of one boy sent for him and locked him in their house to keep him from being baptized. The parents of another beat him and shut him up in their house. The missionaries feared that Toko was at the bottom of all the opposition. He was certainly deeply troubled by the conversions. Walker concluded that "there are hearts that hate all these things and perhaps no one more than Toko, our first and firmest friend."[13]

Leighton preached a sermon before a large congregation of Mpongwe in which he tried to address the opposition directly. In the audience were many of the Mpongwe who had said that no Mpongwe should abandon or alter the traditions of the ancestors. He told them that they had already left some old traditions behind and had changed others. He pointed out how they had adopted new rituals from Cape Lopez south of the estuary, and had embraced new spirits and new fetishes from other places. Walker worried about the results of such an open attack upon their most cherished beliefs, but he later learned that the people had called Leighton's sermon "truth and reason." If they thought it "truth and reason," that did not, however, lessen their opposition.[14]

The missionaries were learning that much of the opposition was organized in secret societies, some of which were apparently part of ancient Mpongwe traditions and others of which reflected traditions and practices of the "bush people" around them and of slaves brought from deep in the interior. The Mbwiri—or Ombwiri—was a secret society among the men. It had political and economic functions and also played a central role in initiating young men through rites of passage into adulthood and into the traditions of the Mpongwe. When Indâ had come into town dressed in thick layers of plantain leaves and brandishing a sword after King Glass died, he was apparently a part of this secret society. "Mbwiri" was also the name of an ancestor spirit—Leighton thought it was a class or family of spirits—who was the author of everything mysterious or marvelous.[15]

Indeed, ancestors seemed to inhabit every hill, every hidden place of the forest, every village and town, every house and heart. In trying to understand the nature and social sources of Mbwiri and related societies among "bush people," Leighton noted that all the different peoples and clans had extraordinary regard for the elderly, which he thought naturally turned to a veneration of the dead. When a man died he was not divested of his power and influence and could be called upon for aid in times of conflict or trouble. Leighton knew that the bones of ancestors were kept in small boxes or reliquaries, which were often hidden away and frequently were of exquisite workmanship. The skulls of distinguished persons were especially valued and preserved with care. Often the skulls were taken out of their reliquaries and cradled in the arms of a grieving relative, who might sing lullaby-like songs while pouring into the ear of a revered parent or ancestor all the sorrows of a troubled heart. When a skull was cut from the corpse of an important man, it was sometimes hung in a way that the decomposing brain—the seat of wisdom—dripped upon chalk that could later be applied to a man's forehead in order for him to absorb the wisdom of the ancestor. These ancestor spirits often spoke in dreams that, Leighton found, were received with "the most deferential attention."[16]

When young men entered the ranks of the secret Mbwiri society, they were consequently entering the world of their ancestors and of the people who had originally inhabited the land. Women, children, and slaves were strictly forbidden to see the secret rituals of the Mbwiri. Leighton thought that the Mbwiri and similar societies among surrounding peoples were intended to keep the women, children, and slaves in a state of subordination to Mpongwe men. When the missionaries saw the public aspects of the Mbwiri rituals, they saw singing, dancing, and behavior they regarded as especially repugnant—especially what they thought of as a kind of wanton sexuality. "The vileness of their songs and actions," Walker thought, "are beyond description, and what must the hearts be from which they proceed." But then, as often happened, such reflections made him think of home, and he wondered if "many in Christian lands, whose external morality is fair, are viler in heart than these dark minded people."[17]

On his part, Leighton thought that however much these beliefs and secret societies involved superstitions, they also exerted some positive influence on the character of the people. Although he was repulsed by some of the traditions and practices of the people, he recognized that they served a social function. They established a bond of affection between parent and child, taught the child to "look up to the parent not only as its earthly protector, but as a friend in the spirit-land," and provided a lively impression that life extended beyond death.[18]

Women had their own secret society—Njembe—a kind of parallel to the Mbwiri. It, too, involved rites of passage as young girls were initiated into its carefully guarded mysteries. Because the Njembe was feared by men for its knowledge of powerful magic and poisons, Leighton thought that the society provided some protection for women. But, more fundamentally, it provided an introduction for young girls into the traditions and secret ways of Mpongwe women. Long and elaborate ceremonies were involved—including the catching by hand of a snake that lived among tangled mangrove roots. Some ceremonies were public, but many were held in secret, often within a sacred circle that contained a cone-like mound in the middle.[19]

On one occasion, when men were forbidden to be present, William Walker stumbled upon some of the women's secret rites. The women were furious and, he wrote, "raised a great storm about my ears. They wanted plenty of money because they said I cursed Njembe." They followed him home, beating with a stick the *orĕga*—a kind of crescent-shaped board used only in Njembe ceremonies. When Walker refused to pay their fine, they followed him the next day, singing a curse and saying he would die. Walker and the other missionaries dismissed the Njembe curses, but they knew its power in the life of Mpongwe women. They regarded the mysteries of Njembe as "more vile and polluting than civilized man can imagine," especially because of what a missionary later called its "indecent ceremonies and phallic songs," which often ridiculed specific men. Perhaps such ridicule was one of the defenses women had against male abuse, but the missionaries were convinced that even Mpongwe men "were overwhelmed with shame at the shamelessness of the women."[20]

Leighton knew that there was much that he and the other missionaries did not know or understand about these secret societies. They were, after all, secret, and they were also exceedingly complex and fluid, as the rituals and names of spirits from one clan or people overlapped and influenced the religious beliefs and practices of those around it. What he did know was that the secret societies were powerful means of transmitting and maintaining traditional beliefs and practices and of resisting the work of the missionaries in their attempts to convert the peoples around the estuary. Leighton later speculated, in pondering the influence and character of the societies, that perhaps there was a danger of looking too much at their dark side, at those aspects of the societies that seemed particularly impure, vicious, and dissolute to the missionaries. If so, he wondered—perhaps thinking of himself and his colleague William Walker—if it were a danger "into which the older missionaries are most likely to fall."[21]

So most of the Mpongwe resisted the appeals of the missionaries at Baraka, struggling to follow the ways of their ancestors even as their political and economic independence was being swallowed up by the French. And Toko, who refused to sell his birthright for a French gift, also resisted the appeals and challenges that flowed from Baraka. But even as he continued to make sacrifices at the graves of ancestors, and to call on fetish doctors to cure illnesses, and to believe in witchcraft, he was uneasy. He knew that changes, deep changes, were coming, and he could see the changes in the conversions of his children. Still, he persevered as he struggled between competing worlds. "He worships with sincere devotion the customs of his ancestors," wrote Walker, "and every day breaks and changes them blindly because self rules."[22]

WHILE THE MISSIONARIES at Baraka struggled against the resistance of the Mpongwe, they continued to face the devastations and sorrows of African fevers. Those who came to the mission came knowing that the fevers awaited them and that the mission cemetery lay patiently waiting as well. Those who survived their first bout with the fevers found their joints aching, their ears buzzing from quinine, and, all too often, their bodies racked by recurrent fevers. But the fevers were not the only afflictions of such a tropical environment. Strange funguses appeared on their backs. Boils sometimes covered their bodies—William Walker and the Grebo teachers from Big Town were frequent sufferers. An ulcer ate up the ankle and life of a young Mpongwe student and convert. And among the parasites that could invade the body and leave a person weak and debilitated were worms—including hookworms, tapeworms, and, above all, guinea worms, which had to be slowly removed from an open wound over a period of several weeks as the worm was wound around a stick.[23]

Five months after she returned with Leighton and Jane from the United States, Mrs. Griswold died after a short and violent attack of fever. She had survived when her first husband, Dr. A. E. Wilson, had died at Rock Town of the dysentery that was raging among the Grebo. And she had survived when her young husband Benjamin Griswold had succumbed to the fever at Ozyunga. So in early 1849, everyone at the mission thought she had passed through the necessary African seasoning to live without fear of a deadly attack. When the fever had struck, it had seemed to be the usual recurrent fever—debilitating for a while but ultimately not dangerous. Leighton had given her quinine and calomel, but she had suddenly grown worse. To the dismay of all, none of the familiar treatments learned over their years of fighting the fever had worked. She died quickly and quietly. Leighton was distraught. He felt inadequate to the task of caring for the sick, and he struggled with God's purpose in taking one who, as he wrote, was "so cheerful, so energetic, so useful, so obliging," one who had seemed to be the least likely among them to become the victim of disease. He wrote Rufus Anderson that her death was "one of those dispensations of Providence which cannot be explained; and we must be dumb before the Lord, until he himself shall be pleased to disclose to us the reason for the trying event."[24]

At the same time that Leighton was trying to care for Mrs. Griswold, he was being confronted with the many ailments of W. T. Wheeler, the young man who had also come with the Wilsons on their return to Baraka. Wheeler, staggered by the illnesses he saw around him, came to believe that he was suffering from dyspepsia, neuralgia, a disordered urinary tract, and possibly some irregularity in his heart. Leighton believed that Wheeler had quickly become a great hypochondriac; the new missionary, he wrote, was "forever *tinkering* upon his system" with different medical approaches. Wheeler refused to take quinine, saying he could not possibly bear the effects of tonic medicines. Walker, in his straightforward way, told him that in that case he could not live in such a tropical climate. So the mission quickly bundled Wheeler off on the first ship headed to New York and wrote euphemistically that his "constitution is not adapted to the missionary work in Africa."[25]

Leighton and Walker grieved deeply over those who were being buried in the Baraka cemetery, and they felt almost overwhelmed by the weight of caring for the sick. Walker in particular suffered great distress over the death of Zeniah. "I have not yet got rid of the feeling," he wrote a friend in New England, "that I was responsible to the Board and the Church and the Mission and more than all to her friends for the death of my dear wife. You cannot imagine the unutterable agony I have endured from this feeling and often thought it would be a relief to me if I could cry out to them all and say, 'I could not save her.' . . . What a terrible name is this *Africa*. Are all who tread her soil forever to cry from the dust in agony of spirit? I fear that Bro. Wilson has much of that same feeling in regard to Mrs. Griswold's death. Do find us a physician, or we shall die." And Leighton wrote, "Send us a doctor," and "let him be a man of promise and ability."[26]

In the midst of such illnesses and sorrows the work of the mission continued. Walker and the newly arrived Ira and Jane Preston began stations far up the Como River among the Bakèlè. While Jane Preston opened a little English school, her husband astonished his colleagues with his language abilities. Leighton wrote Charles Hodges at Princeton that Preston was "the only missionary we have ever had who was gifted with a decided talent for language. In one year he made himself sufficiently acquainted both with the Mpongwe and [Bakèlè], to preach in either, and they are not very nearly related as dialects." Both Walker and Preston were working hard on preparing a Bakèlè grammar that could be used for translations, in schools, and by future missionaries. And they were also watching the Fang, who were moving steadily toward the estuary—Preston was soon to become the first Westerner to study the Fang language.[27]

At Baraka, Leighton and Jane were busy not only with their familiar responsibilities but with nursing the sick. Leighton continued his work on Mpongwe, translating portions of scripture and various religious tracts. He and Bushnell worked together on a translation of the Gospel of John. But what a challenge it was! How could they translate from the original Greek text into Mpongwe something more than a rigid, literal rendering of John? How could they help the Mpongwe catch in their own language a world and message that spoke of the Logos, of the Word made flesh? "In the beginning was the Word, and the Word was with God, and the Word was God. . . . And the Word became flesh and dwelt among us . . . full of grace and truth." No less than translating such a message into English, translating it into Mpongwe was a daunting task. What were they to use for "λόγοσ" (Logos, or Word)? Should they use the Mpongwe word for "one word," or should they use the Mpongwe word for "message"? Was there a Mpongwe word that had a suitable likeness for "λόγοσ" rather than a simple equivalent? Or, when the text declared, "The light shines in the darkness, and the darkness did not overcome it," were there special nuances or associations in Mpongwe that needed to be taken into account in rendering "the light" and "the darkness"? And how were they to take into account other dimensions of the text, such as its rhythm and the cadences that helped to shape the meaning of the text? Time and again they had to ponder such questions and ask Mpongwe helpers to explain and sometimes demonstrate what was meant by a particular word or phrase, or how those words and phrases were used in everyday conversation. Translation was a work of interpretation and creation as the missionaries and their Mpongwe helpers struggled together over a text. When the time came to have the gospel printed, Leighton wrote Anderson: "It will no doubt have its imperfections, but it will nevertheless be as good and correct as any we could prepare with our present knowledge of the language."[28]

Jane continued her work teaching and overseeing the work of the school. Jane Cooper—who seemed to have recovered from her attacks of hysteria and to be more stable—taught the girls. On one occasion she went with the Wilsons and Jane Preston to visit Josiah and Mary Clealand Dorsey at their school a few miles from Baraka. When they arrived, they found that about twenty Mpongwe elders had also come to see what the children were learning. Josiah examined the boys in English while Mary—who had become quite fluent in Mpongwe as well as English and her native Grebo—examined the girls in reading and spelling in Mpongwe. Then all the students recited in concert from the Mpongwe catechism that Leighton had written.

All the visitors were impressed, and all were invited to stay for lunch at the Dorsey cottage. They went in together—Mpongwe elders, African American and Grebo teachers, and white American missionaries—and sat down together at a long table. Mary had overseen the preparation of the meal and the setting of the table. Roasted and boiled plantains were served together with yams, sweet potatoes, rice, and different kinds of fresh fish, besides salt beef and sea-biscuit from the mission store. The dinner was apparently a great success, with much enthusiasm for the various dishes and lively conversation. When the meal was over, two little boys quietly took away the plates and brought out coffee and roasted peanuts. Jane Preston thought that Mary had managed such a fine meal very well, especially with so many guests, and the young missionary felt that she needed to "take a lesson" from her in hospitality and hosting. Mrs. Wilson, she said, "came away quite proud of Mary. She said she did not think a Philadelphia lady could have managed it better." Perhaps Mary's Grebo father, William Davis, would have been proud of his daughter as well. She had certainly entered deeply into the world of Fair Hope and Baraka.[29]

THE MISSION'S RELATIONSHIP with the French authorities was steadily improving during the late 1840s, although the missionaries had a deep dislike of much of French culture and an abhorrence of the decadence they saw in many of the French traders who were beginning to settle around the estuary. Still, the French and the missionaries visited one another regularly and sought to avoid any open conflict. Leighton and Jane welcomed into their home Paul Du Chaillu, the son of one of the traders. He studied English with them, and they hoped they would have a good influence on him. Years later, when he had become a famous explorer, he would remember them with affection.

For their part, Leighton and Jane could not have imagined that one day a great mountain range in Gabon would bear the name of their young student—Massif du Chaillu—and that he would be the first Westerner to see a live *njina* and contribute mightily to the reputation of the gorilla as a ferocious monster of the jungle.[30]

Toko remained the one Mpongwe leader who continued to resist the French. The French tried various strategies to get him to acknowledge their sovereignty over the Mpongwe—they invited him to official dinners, they offered him gifts, and they left presents at his house when he was away. Finally, their patience exhausted and their power in the estuary clearly established, they prepared to arrest the aging Toko on the charge that he refused to provide the French authorities with the names of those who had robbed an English trading house. Toko apparently thought that the traditional Mpongwe procedures should be used to handle the manner, and he had resisted French authority in the case. The French commander insisted that the French were in control and sent seventy armed men to take the old man and bring him to the jail at the blockhouse. Leighton was asked to help negotiate, and an extended palaver followed. Finally, Toko, apparently depressed by his confinement, gave the names and was released from jail. But to go free he had to sign an acknowledgment of French sovereignty. Leighton may have helped to persuade him to do so, since he had become convinced that French control of the estuary was the unavoidable reality that they all had to acknowledge. At any rate, the Mpongwe believed that Leighton had saved Glass's Town and the other villages in the area from being destroyed by the French. So Toko surrendered to French power, but he did not surrender his heart and mind to Western ways and Christianity. He remained, much to Leighton's sorrow, an unconverted Mpongwe.[31]

ONE OF THE BENEFITS of their newly established authority over the Mpongwe, according to French claims, was the end of the slave trade in the estuary. With their warships in the estuary, the French announced that no slaver would dare to sail around Cape Clara and risk the confiscation of his ship.[32]

The missionaries at Baraka thought such claims not only an illusion but also a deliberate deceit. They saw the coming and going of slave ships to towns around the estuary while the French pretended that the ships were nowhere to be seen. And the Mpongwe were as eager as ever to engage in the trade. Everywhere the missionaries went they saw slaves being bought and sold, often within sight of the French. Two slave factories at King William's Town—directly across the estuary from the French fort—sent fifteen or twenty slaves on their way to Brazil every week. Moreover, Spanish slave ships regularly visited towns on the north shore that were right under the nose of the French. To their continuing dismay, the missionaries knew that many of the slave ships had been built for their brutal business by Americans in New York, Salem, and Baltimore. Walker thought "the accursed traffic treads out every avenue of this country for the bones and sinews of men." When he saw Mpongwe buying slaves in Shékiani and Bakèlè towns, they seemed to him "more like vipers than like men." And when he watched a Mpongwe man leave a son as security for some ivory and take a slave to King William's Town to be sold, he felt overwhelmed by the human capacity for evil. "There is," he wrote in his diary, "more degradation in this world than my philosophy ever dreamed of."[33]

While they watched the continuing operations of slave traders in the estuary, the missionaries at Baraka became alarmed when they learned in 1851 that the British were considering ending their efforts against the international slave trade. The expense of keeping a British squadron patrolling the coast of West Africa was, some were saying, too much. Besides, it was being claimed that the squadron was not particularly successful and that the good done by the fleet was the concern of only a few. Parliament had already taken the first legislative steps to have the squadron withdraw from the coast of Africa. Leighton immediately wrote an article emphasizing what had been accomplished during the previous twenty years. He sent the article to England, where it was published, and a copy was given to the foreign secretary, Lord Palmerstone, who had it widely distributed. Drawing on his years of experience as a missionary and traveler, Leighton asked the British public to look carefully at the situation; the Royal Navy, he insisted, had ended the slave trade along large swaths of the West African coast. Leighton urged the British to continue their efforts on behalf of Africa and all humanity. He later received copies of his pamphlet, which were sent "in the name of Lord Palmerstone," and then welcomed word that Parliament had voted to continue the operations of the squadron. Leighton wrote to the *Missionary Herald* in Boston and declared that American Christians ought to be thankful for what the British had accomplished with their African squadron. Their efforts, he predicted, would come to be regarded "as one of the most noble achievements of the nineteenth century."[34]

EVEN AS THE missionaries went about their varied work, illness and death continued to undermine the strength of the mission. Mrs. Bushnell died of a liver ailment in January 1850. Then the Prestons were struck with liver problems; William Walker became largely debilitated by fevers; and Jane Cooper had a recurrence of her hysteria. The four of them sailed for New York in June 1850, hoping to recover their health. Walker hoped as well to overcome his depression and move beyond his grief for Zeniah. Leighton and Jane, together with a distraught Albert Bushnell, remained at Baraka with the newly arrived missionary Jacob Best. Then, in October 1850, the prayers of the mission seemed answered with the arrival of Dr. C. A. Ford, a man whom Leighton called a "real physician." But even a real physician was no match for the African fevers and other tropical diseases that stalked the mission compounds. Shortly after Dr. Ford began his practice, another young couple arrived—Roland and Nancy Porter. She was pregnant, and within a year—in spite of Dr. Ford's efforts—mother, father, and infant daughter were dead.[35]

William Walker and Ira and Jane Preston returned to Baraka in January 1852—Jane Cooper had remained in the United States and was living with the Eckards in Washington. With Walker was his third wife—Kate Hardcastle Walker of New York. She had accepted his proposal for marriage even though she knew the dangers that awaited her in Africa. Leighton and Jane received her warmly, as they had received Prudence at Fair Hope and Zeniah at Baraka.[36]

But after the welcome had been extended and the newly arrived missionaries had gotten comfortably settled at the mission station, Leighton and Jane told them of their own decision to return to the United States. Leighton's health had been undermined first by measles, then by influenza, and now by a serious liver ailment that appeared to be the result of accumulating illnesses. Jane had had difficulty recovering from an attack of fever, and she was struggling to regain her strength. Dr. Ford insisted they must return to the United States, warning that their lives were at risk. So Leighton and Jane quickly packed what they needed to take with them—they expected to return in a year—and sailed for New York on March 1, 1852.[37]

PART IV

Homeward Journey

Chapter Twenty

An Unsought and Unexpected Appointment

Leighton and Jane had a painfully slow voyage along the West African coast, stopping regularly at various ports for the captain to dash and barter, buy and sell with African tradesmen and merchants. Still, however tedious the voyage, the stops were opportunities for them to visit new places and to revisit places they had known on earlier trips. Everywhere they went, Leighton made notes about the slave trade, about the influence of the British squadron, and about the various peoples, cultures, and environments of the coast.[1]

At Cape Palmas they rode once again the high and crashing swells of the surf to visit Harper and Big Town. Landing at the beach, they went ashore. Here, so many years before, they had been greeted by King Freeman and a great crowd of shouting, dancing Grebo. Now, the beach was "McGill's Landing," named after Governor Russwurm's father-in-law, the merchant George McGill. No crowd welcomed them. They climbed the hill to the place where Fair Hope had once been their home. Looking around, the couple saw thick-walled and sturdy warehouses and a blacksmith shop owned by Anthony Wood—he and Leighton had once trekked together far into the interior through verdant fields of rice. The now veteran missionaries walked through the cemetery of deep memories to the place where their cottage had stood. For seven years they had worked and dreamed and prayed at this place. On the cottage's piazza, Freeman and Simleh Ballah and William Davis had joined them in the late afternoons to sit and talk as the surf pounded and as the evening lights of Harper and Big Town flickered and then glowed in an African night falling quickly across the landscape. Now, as they stood at this place of memories, Leighton and Jane could see not only Harper and Big Town but also the island of the dead, recently renamed Russwurm Island.

Within a few months, Freeman, as Pah Nemah, king of the Grebo at Big Town, would be carried to the island and placed beneath a canoe tipped on its side. There under an African sky he would become a part of a landscape that had been his home. And in Big Town, the people would pour out their ancient laments for one who had led them safely through a dangerous time of great transition.[2]

Russwurm had died in 1851 after a protracted illness. His had been a remarkable life of brilliant accomplishments amid disappointments and deep contradictions. Having found America a choking, oppressive place, he had sought freedom and dignity in a struggling colony on the African coast among settlers who identified themselves as Americans and representatives of American culture. Often disdainful of the settlers, Russwurm had nonetheless poured out his life for them and their cause. The leader of a colonial enterprise, he had been a friend of the Grebo, and with Freeman he had managed to keep the peace between Harper and Big Town. The settlers had been eager for him to be replaced as governor, but when he died, they knew that a difficult future awaited them without his leadership.[3]

So Jane and Leighton found Cape Palmas a changed place. And because it was changed and because they were changed by their years at Baraka, leaving the Cape was not difficult or painful. They were to continue to remember their time there, and they were to continue to pray for the Grebo and the Episcopal mission among them. But Fair Hope and Big Town and Harper and even Bayard Island were now a part of a memory receding into the chambers of their hearts and into scenes of their imaginations.

IN MONROVIA LEIGHTON and Jane stayed in the comfortable home of the James family. B. V. R. James had become an ardent patriot of Liberia and had put his earlier reservations about colonization behind him. In 1847, Liberia had become an independent nation. Its independence had been prompted in part by the old question that had so troubled Russwurm and Leighton—Did a colony have the authority as a state to enforce its laws, or was it just the project of one benevolent or philanthropic society in the United States? In 1845, the governor in Monrovia had ordered the seizure of a British vessel for refusing to pay port fees. In response, the British had sent a gunboat to retaliate by taking a large vessel owned by a prominent resident of Monrovia. And the British government had informed the US government that it "could not accept the slightest assumption of any sovereign powers being present in a commercial experiment of a Philanthropic society." The settlers' desire for independence consequently grew more intense, and with the strong encouragement of the American Colonization Society, independence had been declared in 1847. James had grown to love this independent Liberia, and he was deeply committed to its prosperity and progress.[4]

When Leighton and Jane visited with the James family in 1852, they learned that their old colleague and friend had recently participated in a military campaign against a powerful African king. Tensions, always simmering between colonists and the surrounding Africans, had exploded in an open war. In a long letter to a friend in the United States, James had joyfully compared the resulting settler victory to the biblical story of the Israelites entering the Promised Land and defeating the Canaanites. A few months earlier, in December 1851, William Walker had learned, while visiting Monrovia, how the African American settlers, in retaliation for a brutal attack, had killed a number of Africans and had nailed their heads and hands on settler houses.[5]

LEIGHTON AND JANE arrived in New York in early summer 1852. They went immediately to Washington for a happy reunion with Margaret and James Eckard. From there they went to Philadelphia to visit Jane's cousins Theodosia Bayard and Elizabeth Bayard Henry, and for Leighton to see Jane's cousin Dr. Hugh Hodge. Hodge advised them not to go south during the summer months, but for Leighton to have a time of quiet recovery in the New England mountains. So Leighton and Jane, together with Theodosia and the Eckards, found accommodations with a farming family in the Berkshires of western Massachusetts.[6]

By the end of August, Leighton was feeling stronger. They went to Washington, and while they were staying with the Eckards, Leighton began making speaking trips and buying supplies in New York for the mission, including an iron fence for the cemetery at Baraka. In October they finally headed south to Pine Grove. Sisters and brothers and cousins and friends welcomed them home and drove buggies down sandy roads to hear their stories about life in a distant and exotic place. But William Wilson had died in 1850, and the death of the old patriarch and the absence of his voice made Pine Grove more than ever a place of memories, and in that absence Leighton and Jane put their heads down at night on the rope-strung bed where Leighton had once dreamed as a child.[7]

They left for Charleston in November and stayed in the handsome Adger mansion on Spring Street. Leighton's old college friend John Adger had returned from his missionary labors in Armenia, where he had worked to translate the Bible into modern Armenian. In Charleston, Adger had started a new work among the city's slaves—in the face of much white opposition.

But under Adger's leadership, and with the financial support of his father, the largest church building in the city would soon be erected for the use of slaves, who had already named the new church "Zion." John Adger and his young colleague John Lafayette Girardeau had worked out a plan whereby only a few white families would belong to Zion, and while they would provide the church officers, in good paternalistic fashion, they and not the slaves would have to sit in the balcony of the church, and they would listen to sermons that addressed black slaves and not white owners. Already, large numbers of blacks—slave and free—were finding in the deeply oppressive atmosphere of Charleston a little free space to breathe at Zion. They had begun joining the church in large numbers, turning Zion into one of the centers of African American life in Charleston.[8]

Leighton and Jane also visited with John's sister, Margaret Adger, to whom Leighton had once proposed. Margaret's husband, Thomas Smyth, was the scholarly pastor of the city's Second Presbyterian Church, and he was rapidly building in his mansion on Meeting Street what would become the largest private library in the South and one of the largest in the nation. He had recently completed a major book defending the unity of the human races in which he had attacked a rising scientific racism. The focus of Smyth's attack was Harvard professor Louis Agassiz, who had described what he insisted were the differences between the African and Caucasian brains: "A peculiar conformation," Agassiz had written, "characterizes the brain of the adult negro. Its development never gets beyond that observable in the Caucasian in boyhood. And besides other singularities, it bears a striking resemblance, in several particulars, to the brain of an ourang-outang." Leighton's old *njina* had become a key player in the attempt of white scientists to prove a dual origin for and fundamental physical differences between "Negroes and Caucasians." In response, Smyth had called on the testimony of the Bible to defend the fundamental and essential unity of the races. But he had also challenged Agassiz and other scientists by emphasizing the history and culture of African civilizations. In three chapters on the "Former Civilizations of Black Races of Men," he had presented a wide range of historical and anthropological evidence showing that "dark or black races, with more or less of the negro physiognomy, were in the earliest period of their known history cultivated and intelligent, having kingdoms, arts, and manufacturers." There was no indication, he had insisted, that the enslavement of Africans was other than of modern origin. "The degradation of this race of men therefore, must be regarded as the result of external causes, and not of natural, inherent and original incapacity." Smyth's cause was one Leighton had long championed and would soon take up once again.[9]

After their visit in Charleston, Leighton and Jane sailed for Savannah. There Leighton preached at the Independent Presbyterian Church and addressed large and apparently interested audiences on the subject of African missions. The Wilsons no doubt had occasion to look across the flowing river to Hutchinson Island, where Paul Sansay and the other Bayard slaves had once lived. In less than two years, a great hurricane would come roaring up from the Caribbean and send a twelve-foot tidal surge across the island, killing almost a hundred men, women, and children who lived in its old settlements.[10]

From Savannah they went to visit Nicholas Bayard and his family in the little village of Roswell, not far from Atlanta. There amid humming new textile mills and handsome Greek Revival homes—built from the proceeds of Lowcountry plantations—they talked with family and many friends. The missionaries told about Toko and their dear Mary Clealand Dorsey, who was now teaching Mpongwe students, and about life at Baraka and the sorrows that surrounded its cemetery. And no doubt they told Nicholas what they knew of Paul Sansay and the other former slaves whom he had once sent to General's Island by the waters of the Altamaha. Perhaps Nicholas remembered the day those who were called Bayard slaves had gone on board the *Opelousas*, and how they had stood on deck as they had sailed slowly away from Savannah on their way to Baltimore and Cape Palmas and freedom.

In Roswell, Leighton and Jane had time to reflect on what they were seeing and learning from their travels. All around were signs of the great transformations sweeping across their homeland—especially the trains that were already reaching out in every direction and that had made their trip from Savannah to Roswell so quick and comfortable. The missionaries home from Baraka were experiencing the results of a transportation revolution and of new ways of investing capital. As they rode in cars behind powerful new engines, they were participating in a new mobility for people and cotton and cattle, for lumber and corn, and for all the products of human ingenuity. With other riders, they felt a powerful rumbling beneath them and looked out on a world rushing by train windows. Such an experience invited new ways of seeing the world and new ways of thinking about the future as the sound of the train whistle cried out across the land.[11]

But Leighton and Jane heard another kind of rumbling in their conversations with family and friends. Political positions about slavery were becoming more inflexible as massive numbers of slaves continued to be carried to an expanding southern frontier. The vast new territories of the far west, taken by military power from Mexico in 1848, had created a crisis. Were the recently conquered territories to be open to slavery, or were they to be free from slavery and open for white pioneers of modest means? The Compromise of 1850 had finally seemed to settle the question, promising stability for the nation. California had been allowed to enter the Union as a free state. In other territories, the slavery question was to be decided by popular sovereignty. The slave trade was abolished in Washington, DC. And a harsh new fugitive slave law was established. While Leighton and Jane were in Roswell, the presidential election of 1852 appeared to confirm the Compromise and to indicate the desire of the nation for peace and stability. Franklin Pierce, a strong supporter of the Compromise, was elected president by an overwhelming majority in the electoral college. "We trust," Leighton had written his sister Sarah, "that God has some higher destiny for our Country" than a division of the nation.[12]

But Leighton had not only been listening, he had also been talking to family and friends and to any who would listen to him. Writing from Roswell, he told Rufus Anderson about the conversations he was having with white Southerners. He had been endeavoring with some success, he told the Bostonian, "to show that the African race are capable, when placed in suitable circumstances, of a high grade Christian civilization and that a higher destiny awaits them than slavery or heathenism." He had, he said, discussed the whole subject of slavery with every man of intelligence and influence whom he had met in South Carolina and Georgia. As far as he knew, he wrote, the conversations had not caused the slightest ill feelings. He had tried to make four points. First, that slavery could not be permanent in the United States. Second, Southerners had the duty of facing the subject realistically and addressing it before it became unmanageable. Third, Christians had the duty to impart religious knowledge among slaves in preparation for their emancipation. And fourth, the consequences of emancipation would not be as disastrous as white Southerners supposed. He found that almost everyone he talked with agreed that slavery could not be permanent in the United States. White Southerners, he thought, were willing to address the question of slavery in a realistic manner "as soon as their excited feelings have been sufficiently calmed"—he had apparently found them greatly agitated by the attacks of abolitionists and by the debates that had resulted in the Compromise of 1850. He also thought, in his own attempt at realism, that the price of cotton needed to fall if white Southerners were to think about ending slavery. He had, after all, seen the enormous growth of wealth among his own family members and friends in South Carolina from the labor of their slaves. In regard to the religious instruction of slaves, he had found—perhaps thinking especially of the work of John Adger and John Girardeau in Charleston—that Southern whites were more engaged in such a "deed of benevolence" than the people of the North knew. But there was resistance on his fourth point about the consequences of emancipation not being disastrous. "They are," he said, "as yet very skeptical. The idea of emancipation is not half so formidable as the continuance of the blacks among them after they are liberated."[13]

In this way Leighton drew on his years in Africa, on his experience with King Freeman and Russwurm, with Toko and Mary Clealand Dorsey, to raise and press the question of slavery with Southern whites. He was trying to translate his African experiences, his encounters with living, breathing men and women—Grebo and Mandingo, Kru and Fanti, Mpongwe and Fang— into the language and idiom of white Americans, especially white Americans who spoke with the distinct accents of affluent and proud South Carolinians and Georgians. He did so as one who was both an outsider and an insider, one who had seen and known an African world and one who was a Wilson from Pine Grove married to a Bayard from Savannah and Philadelphia.

IN SPITE OF his returning strength, Leighton's old ailment still troubled him. He and Jane returned to Washington to spend the winter with the Eckards and for Leighton to see Dr. Hodge in Philadelphia as well as other doctors in New York. They all came to the same conclusion—returning to Gabon would jeopardize his life. Still, Leighton and Jane hoped to return to Baraka. And while they waited, Leighton began to prepare a manuscript on West Africa. He ordered books from New York and Boston, sent to London for missionary reports and travel accounts, and gathered any papers or journals he thought might be helpful. Then he had a serious attack of his liver ailment—worse than any he had had before—and he and Jane became convinced that the doctors were correct and that he should not return to Baraka.[14]

In May 1853, shortly after he had recovered enough from this last attack, Leighton went to Philadelphia to attend the Presbyterian General Assembly. He was, to his surprise, nominated for a professorship at Princeton Theological Seminary—a position he quickly turned down, saying he was not qualified. But when he was elected one of the three secretaries of the Presbyterian Board of Foreign Missions located in New York, he accepted. The decision was difficult—he and Jane loved Africa and their work at Baraka, and they longed to return to what they had come to regard as their home.

But the serious nature of his illness seemed to stand in the way of their returning, and the election seemed a providential event, an opening door for them to continue their mission work. He wrote to his family in South Carolina: "The appointment was unsought and unexpected, and therefore, I suppose it ought to be considered as providential. I can do more for African missions at this post than at any other in the country."[15]

And so their life as missionaries came to an end. As a young couple they had committed themselves to beginning a new work in Africa. They had ventured out along Atlantic highways as voyagers, not knowing what awaited them, going in faith and hope, and carrying with them the worlds they had known in Savannah and Philadelphia, at Pine Grove and Fair Hope plantation. And they had found at Cape Palmas and Baraka other worlds and they had sought to learn what they could of those worlds—their landscapes and languages, their stories and traditions, their hopes and fears. They sought to learn what they could of these other worlds—and even grew to appreciate much that was in these worlds—because they thought something better awaited Africans. They believed that the Christian gospel was good news for all people, that it brought freedom from fears of malevolent forces and from death itself. They believed deeply that King Freeman and William Davis, Wasa and Mary Clealand, Toko and his children all deserved to hear the Christian gospel and to decide for themselves if it was good news. To tell this good news and to raise up Africans who would spread this good news had been the focus of their lives. In all of this, Leighton and Jane were confident that in the gracious providence of God a great future awaited Africa. So in 1853, as they made this transition in their life from Baraka to New York, they did not think of their life in Africa as simply a great adventure, and certainly not a great misadventure. Rather, they thought that they had been a part of God's strange but loving intentions for the Grebo and the Mpongwe and for all the sons and daughters of a great continent.

BY THE END of the summer 1853 the Wilsons were settled in a large and comfortable home in the upper part of Manhattan. Here they immediately began to welcome regular guests—missionaries home on furlough or preparing to leave for some distant port; friends and relatives from the South and from Philadelphia and Princeton; and an occasional convert sent from some distant place to study or learn some trade in the United States. As at Fair Hope and Baraka, the Wilsons were generous in their welcome, and Jane found in overseeing such hospitality a way to make her own contribution to the mission effort. She provided a hospitality, one visitor wrote, that reflected her character—"unaffected, simple, and elegant."[16]

In the mornings, Leighton walked to the mission office in Manhattan. His two colleagues were cousins of Jane's—Walter Lowrie, former US senator from Pennsylvania, and his son the Reverend John Lowrie. Together the three men divided the work of the board. Each took primary responsibility for a region of the world as they corresponded with an ever growing number of missionaries in India and China, in southern Africa and Siam, in Liberia and the Middle East and a variety of other scattered places. The Protestant mission effort had rapidly expanded during the time that the Wilsons had been in Africa. Missionaries in increasing numbers were traveling to distant lands establishing "foreign missions," their work supported by missionary agencies in Britain and Germany; in Switzerland, Holland, and Scandinavia; and in the United States and Canada. In the Presbyterian offices in New York, Leighton had primary responsibility for Africa, but he also assumed increasing responsibility for the work among the "Indian Nations" of the southwestern United States.[17]

Leighton's work was demanding and took much discipline. He wrote to encourage and comfort missionaries in distant places. He ordered supplies, made arrangements for them to be shipped, worked on budgets, and kept a careful eye on finances. Every Monday the board met, and Leighton served as the board's recording secretary while participating in the board's decisions about personnel, relations with other mission agencies, and finances. He edited the foreign department of the board's magazine, *Home and Foreign Record*, carefully selecting letters and reports from missionaries in order to create missionary narratives of Protestant Christianity advancing around the world—in 1856, an unprecedented sixty missionaries were sent by the Presbyterian Board alone to various mission fields. And Leighton began to travel widely and to speak at Synod meetings around the country as well as to the General Assembly, going one year to St. Louis and another year to Kentucky and another year to Cincinnati. He made an extensive tour of the Native American Nations of the old Southwest, visiting missions and schools in Oklahoma among the Cherokee, Creek, Choctaw, and Chickasaw, peoples forced from their homes by the land-hungry imperialism of American whites.[18]

In all of his travels, Leighton saw evidence of a rapidly expanding country. He experienced once more the radical changes taking place in transportation, and he observed the restless energy, the cultural resources, and the technological sophistication that were allowing white Americans to have their brutal way with native peoples and the landscape of America. Yet what he was seeing was not only the expansion of white America, not only the knitting together of a nation with railroad tracks and steamboat paddles and telegraph wires, but also the building forces of division, the growing differences between an expanding, slaveholding South and an expanding, free North.

IN THE EVENINGS in New York Leighton completed his manuscript on West Africa, which was published by Harper and Brothers in 1856 as *Western Africa: Its History, Condition, and Prospect*. The book gathered together and greatly expanded what he had already written in letters, reports, and articles in learned journals, and it drew much from notes he had taken over the years as he had sailed along the West African coast, visiting its towns and talking to its people. The purpose of *Western Africa* was to provide "information about a portion of the world of which very little is truly known," he wrote, and beneath that purpose was his always pressing desire to break open old stereotypes about Africa and Africans.[19]

Leighton discussed the geography of West Africa with great care—its diverse natural scenery, its rivers and lagoons, its seasons, winds, and surfs, and how this varied geography influenced the character of different West African societies. He told of European explorations of the coast, the rise of the transatlantic slave trade, and the misery and oppression that followed Europeans wherever their ships sailed along the coast. He wrote of three principal divisions of West African peoples and culture—Senegambia in the far north, Northern Guinea, and Southern Guinea—and made careful distinctions between the Mandingo and the Wolof, the Kru and Ashanti, the Yoruba and the Mpongwe and the "interior tribes." He displayed his interest in anthropology and the different cultures of West African peoples, describing in detail diverse family and political structures, marriage customs and domestic habits, and the various African practices of agriculture, architecture, and trade. He wrote of polygamy and how degrading he found it for women, and how deeply entrenched it was in West African societies. He explained how the Ashanti had an absolute despotism built upon the massive ownership of slaves and a formidable army, told of their cruel human sacrifices, and explained why the Kru did not practice slavery and had a more democratic polity. He pointed out that Africans did not all look alike. Some were light and some were dark and some were in between, just as some were tall and slender and others were short and muscular. As could be expected, he paid special attention to language. One chapter compared and contrasted the languages of the Mandingo, the Grebo, and the Mpongwe. When he turned to religion, he once again pointed to differences, but he also pointed to certain continuities, especially the important role of ancestors; the apparent universal belief in the power of fetishes, witches, and sorcerers; and a widespread confidence in the efficacy of the sassy wood trial. But he was cautious, noting, "It is not an easy task to give a full and satisfactory exposition of the religious creed of the pagan tribes of Africa."[20]

Leighton obviously wrote *Western Africa* as an outsider, a stranger who had lived among some West Africans and visited among many others. As an outsider he was claiming to be an authority on West Africans and their cultures, interpreting them to a Western world. He had, as a stranger, made a massive effort to compose dictionaries and grammars, to codify some of their languages and customs, and to understand the interior life of the Grebo and Mpongwe. He had, as an outsider and stranger, moved from simply observing and trying to understand them and convert them to an identification with them. He had joined the Grebo in their struggles with the colonists at Harper, and he had sided with the Mpongwe in their resistance to the French in Gabon. But he was nevertheless an outsider, and he knew it. He knew he was from Pine Grove and not Big Town or Glass's Town and that he had come to West Africa as a messenger and an advocate of Christian faith and Western ways. And that knowing finally made him not only confident as a stranger intent on conversion and transformation, but also cautious. So he cautioned when he described some characteristic that it was "said to be" such and such and he warned that the "interior life of the people, their moral, social, civil, and religious condition, as well as their peculiar notions and customs, have always been a sealed book to the rest of the world."[21]

For all of its focus on the history and cultures—and natural history, too—of West Africa, Leighton's book, like his life, was intended to support and encourage a Christian mission to Africa. He was trying to present Africa and Africans in a new light, as a place and peoples deserving the attention and commitment of American Christians. The last chapter—"The Agency Devolving on White Men in Connection with Missions to Western Africa"—revealed most clearly this intent. While Leighton acknowledged and affirmed that the growth of the church in Africa was necessarily the work of African Christians, he thought that—as in the early days of the church in Europe and America—the church in Africa needed missionaries in its early days. And because he believed that the work of missionaries involved sophisticated engagement with new languages and cultures, he insisted on the need for white Christians, those with all the advantages of a classical education, to be deeply involved in the work. He knew and acknowledged the role of

African Americans—remembering, no doubt, B. V. R. James and Josiah Dorsey and others doing their important work—but he thought that, given the place of African Americans in US society, too few of them had been able to secure the education necessary for the demanding work of translating, teaching, and preaching in another language and culture. For this reason, and because whites had a responsibility to Africa for all of the death and destruction they had caused, white Christians, he said, must take up the challenge of presenting the Christian gospel to Africans.[22]

Leighton believed, at least he hoped, that Africa had a bright future. He had found, he wrote, that the "African is social, generous, and confiding; and, when brought under the benign influence of Christianity, he exemplifies the beauty and consistency of his religion more than any other human being on the face of the earth." So when the missionary from Pine Grove looked to the future, he thought that the time might come when Africans "may be held up to all the rest of the world as examples of the purest and most elevated Christian virtues."[23]

LEIGHTON'S NEW YORK office was well situated for him to receive regular reports and correspondence from Liberia and Gabon. Among the missionaries in Liberia, B. V. R. James was Leighton's most important correspondent. The two old colleagues had confidence in one another and apparently genuine affection. They signed their letters "yours truly and affectionately," and sent their warmest regards to one another's families. Margaret came and spent some months with the Wilsons in New York as a way to try and improve her health, and Catherine later came and stayed with Leighton and Jane because her health was greatly impaired. And when her health was better, they saw her off to Monrovia, to her home with her mother and stepfather, and to her work as a faithful missionary teacher.[24]

Although Leighton believed that whites were needed to give organizational direction to the Liberian mission, and that African Americans faced the difficulty of proving they could manage a school efficiently, he made James the real head of the mission in Liberia, giving him—and not recently arrived white missionaries—responsibility for the finances of the mission and for the oversight of much of the mission's work. And James, in turn, supported Leighton when Leighton insisted there was a need for white missionaries to go to Liberia, and not simply black missionaries. When some African Americans attacked Leighton for this, James had written: "Well, all I have to say is, let all the good, faithful, and deeply pious *white missionaries* come to Liberia that can be induced to come, and means can be raised to support them; here is work enough for them and the colored missionaries too."[25]

IN 1857, WORD arrived that a long-expected war had finally erupted between the Grebo at Big Town and the settlers at Harper. The governor—Boston Jenkins Drayton—was, like Charles Snetter, a free man from Charleston who had had powerful friends among influential Charleston whites. Sent as a missionary to Cape Palmas by Southern Baptists, Drayton was imprudent and implacable in his hatred of the Grebo and stood in marked contrast to the cautious and conciliatory Russwurm. He ordered a surprise bombardment of Big Town that left the town in ashes and its inhabitants scattered and impoverished. Altogether, eight Grebo towns were burned. But the Grebo rallied, burned a number of settler homes, destroyed the Episcopal mission outside of Harper, and threatened, at one point, to destroy Harper and kill or drive off the American settlers. Only the intervention of the authorities and troops from Monrovia brought the war to a conclusion. The Liberian government and the Grebo signed a treaty acknowledging that Big Town was no more—the long-held dream of the settlers to take over the town was finally accomplished. One of the three Grebo leaders who signed the bitter treaty was Simleh Ballah, who had been Leighton's teacher, who had sat with King Freeman and William Davis on the piazza at Fair Hope, and who had once visited Baltimore and had stayed in the hospitable home of Benjamin Latrobe.[26]

Dr. James Hall, who by odd circumstances happened to arrive at the Cape at the time of the treaty, walked through the ruins of Big Town. The founder and first governor of Maryland in Liberia looked around and saw the blackened ruins of what he remembered as old King Freeman's Town. The town, he lamented, had once had been thickly covered with circular thatched houses, running up to a point like haystacks, containing some 1,000 or 1,200 men, women, and children. Here, in 1834, with Leighton watching, he had negotiated with Freeman over the sale of land to the Maryland Colonization Society. Now, he wrote, not a vestige of Big Town remained except for a few blackened coconut trees, the circular hearths and hard-beaten earthen floors of Grebo houses, and masses of broken crockery, items which once had constituted their principal wealth. Hall believed that "those who first gave us a right to set foot in the land" had been "divested of their natural right guaranteed to them again by solemn treaty." They had been "driven from their homes and the homes of their fathers by an unjust war."[27]

Among those who had participated in the war was Paul Sansay. He had survived the conflict, but two years later, James wrote Leighton, the carpenter had died. He had once made, under the harsh demands of slavery, an agonizing decision for freedom. He had hoped that he would be able to find a way to bring his wife and children to Cape Palmas, but the cost of their purchase and transport had been too much for him, and he had lived out his days on the African coast as a free but single man. With his death, the record of those who had once lived in the slave settlement on Hutchinson Island, by the flowing waters of the Savannah, came to an end.[28]

Big Town's destruction must have evoked many memories for Leighton and Jane. It no doubt appeared a confirmation of their worst fears—that colonization was an act of imperialism, and that the colonists at Cape Palmas were intent on subjugating the Grebo and taking their land.

REPORTS AND CORRESPONDENCE also arrived regularly in New York telling of developments at Baraka and outlying schools and stations. William Walker wrote his old colleague faithfully, and letters and annual reports from the mission were printed in Boston's *Missionary Herald*, where Leighton and Jane could read the latest news of friends and places they remembered with such affection.[29] Moreover, Leighton had official responsibilities that kept him in touch with Rufus Anderson in Boston, as the Presbyterian Board in New York and the American Board in Boston had occasions to cooperate in their mission efforts. But the most regular letters and reports came from the Presbyterian missionaries on the island of Corisco, which lay off the coast a short distance from the estuary. Because of their proximity and shared commitments, the missionaries on the island and those at Baraka were in regular touch with one another and frequently visited each other. To Leighton's and Jane's surprise, one letter from Corisco arrived accompanied by a little girl— seven-year-old Cornelia DeHeer. Cornelia had been born in Ohio and had gone with her missionary parents to Corisco. When her mother had died of a malignant fever, her grieving father had sent her to New York, asking Leighton and Jane to take her into their home as their own daughter. This they gladly did, for she came as a happy gift to their hearts and lives. They quickly loved her as their own child, and she, in turn, grew to love them as her adopted parents.[30]

Some of the news that arrived from Baraka was encouraging, but much of it was not. The hard work of translation was proceeding, the press was turning out a steady stream of books and pamphlets, and the schools were often full of promising students. But death continued its steady assault on the mission. New missionaries arrived, and many soon died. Most discouraging was the death of Dr. C. A. Ford. The missionaries had hoped that as a well-educated and accomplished physician, he would stand between them and the raging fevers, debilitating parasites, and all the many other ailments that hardened their livers and threatened their lives. And they hoped as well that his medical work among the Mpongwe would help break up their superstitions, since many of their beliefs were intimately related to their diseases. The doctor had cured some and eased the pain of others, but he had been no match for death, and after several years, he, too, had succumbed to a tropical fever. Still, the work went ahead, and from time to time the missionaries saw encouraging signs that their work was not in vain. They hoped that "perhaps the seeds sown in tears during these years past are about to spring up and bear fruit to the glory of God."[31]

DURING THESE YEARS, the French continued to consolidate their power around the estuary. The little town of Libreville was growing up around the Catholic mission and around the military post, which had now been moved to higher ground on what was called "The Plateau." French and other European traders were aggressively replacing the Mpongwe as the middlemen who bought lumber and ivory and other goods from the interior to sell to traders who came on ships now crowding into the estuary. Even more alarming for the Mpongwe was their own rapidly declining numbers. When Leighton had first arrived in 1842, he had estimated that 6,000 Mpongwe, plus another 6,000 of their slaves, lived around the estuary. By the closing years of the 1850s, the number of Mpongwe had dropped to only 3,000. Introduced diseases—especially smallpox, measles, and syphilis—had done their work, as had New England rum. Birthrates had plummeted, and pregnancy had come to be viewed by many as an economic drag on the earning capacity of young women—especially in their relationship with visiting seamen—and therefore something to be avoided. For all of these reasons, the Mpongwe found themselves in an ever-deepening crisis as the demographic foundations and economic base of their society steadily eroded.[32]

Toko, who worshiped "with sincere devotion the customs of his ancestors," felt deep in his old bones this shaking of foundations. He had been the premier trader in the estuary, the most respected man among the Mpongwe, because of his honesty, his business acumen, his irrepressible good humor, and his knowledge of the stories and ancient ways of his people. But by the late 1850s, he saw his trade being taken over by Europeans. He could see the crumbling and abandoned places and the decline of his people all too clearly. He wondered about the cause of such ruin, and as a Mpongwe, he thought it must be the result of some malevolent intent and act of sorcery. Toko exacted his revenge. One day, a slave of his was discovered who had made a fetish to keep trade away. Toko had the man bound, taken out into the estuary, and dropped overboard, to drown struggling against the waters.[33]

A few months earlier, Toko's son Ntâkâ Truman—who had been a student at Baraka—showed that he had not abandoned the ways of his ancestors in spite of his having listened for years to the lessons and sermons of Jane and Leighton and Walker and the other missionaries. When Truman's young wife died, he—like his father—looked around in Mpongwe fashion for some sorcery that must have caused her death. One of his slaves, Awĕmĕ, was caught and accused of bewitching her. William Walker knew Awĕmĕ—he called him "a poor, sickly, stupid fellow"—and did not believe Truman when he said that the slave had confessed. Walker questioned Awĕmĕ, and he could get no such confession out of him. Then Truman had Awĕmĕ tortured to make him confess to a fetish or some poison, but the frightened slave endured, and his torturers said his endurance was sure proof of his guilt. Walker confronted Truman and, using both Mpongwe traditions and Christian belief, angrily warned him against killing Awĕmĕ. He told Truman that if he killed the man, the slave's image would hound him in dreams and in waking visions of the night, and Truman would meet Awĕmĕ and Walker at the judgment seat of God. Truman winced and writhed, and the women who sat by howled with rage, but Walker's threats did no good, wrote Walker, and so they murdered him.[34]

So the customs of the ancestors persevered and showed their strength as Toko's slave struggled against the waters of the estuary and as the blood of Truman's slave laved the ground near Baraka. But neither the water nor the blood arrested the decline of the Mpongwe or the steady erosion of a Mpongwe world that had once been praised for its sophistication and hospitality.

TOKO DIED ON December 3, 1858. He had long suffered with asthma and had finally given up struggling for breath. He had first welcomed Leighton to the estuary, and he had been the great friend of the missionaries at Baraka even as he maintained the remembered ways of his people. The French, in honor of the old man who had so long opposed them, fired several can-nons—one blew up as if in protest, killing one man and seriously injuring another.

Two days later, about daylight, Walker conducted a private service as Toko was buried in the little cemetery at Baraka among the missionary graves. The English sea captain Samuel Dyer had a tombstone erected for his old friend, and in the surrounding towns and villages the women wailed the ancient Mpongwe laments.[35]

A Patriot's Choice

For years Leighton and Jane had wondered about and worried about the growing tensions between the North and the South, and they had experienced in their own lives the charges and countercharges that swirled around American slavery. During their engagement in 1832 they had written one another about the Nullification Controversy and what dangers it might hold for the future of the Union. When they had joined with abolitionists in opposing the colonization movement during their years at Cape Palmas, they had been called racists by settlers and colonization officials. And when they were in the midst of trying to free their slaves in the 1830s and 1840s, Leighton had been attacked by abolitionists as a "vile slave-holder" and "man-stealer." Then, once Leighton and Jane had freed their slaves, Leighton's family and friends had questioned his loyalty to the South. They wondered if he had become "a rampant abolitionist." Following the Mexican-American War, Leighton and Jane had been alarmed by reports they received in Baraka about the bitter debates over slavery and its expansion. And when they learned of the Compromise of 1850, they had felt greatly relieved "for the safety of the Union of the states." At least all of this was how they remembered and thought of their experiences of the great questions that were threatening to shake the foundations of the nation's life.[1]

During the 1850s, Leighton and Jane had ample opportunity to see the growing differences between the North and the South. As they went about their daily lives in New York, they could see a steady stream of new immigrants arriving from distant ports. These new arrivals brought with them old ways, new hopes, and no memories of an earlier America. In his travels around the country, Leighton saw the rapid swelling of cities in the North and the constant push of the frontier in the West. In soot-covered Pittsburgh, he saw the glow of iron furnaces and heard the noise of new factories. In far-off St. Louis—already in the 1850s larger than Charleston and Savannah combined—he saw the mixing of peoples from many places and the strength and restless energy of a river city on the edge of opportunity. And everywhere people seemed to be moving, creating, destroying, apparently cut loose from their pasts, yet trying to carry remembered ways into new places and new landscapes.[2]

If Leighton saw new immigrants and booming cities and industries in the North, when he traveled to the old southwestern and southern frontiers—places such as Mississippi and Texas—he encountered the explosive energy of slavery. The contrast between North and South seemed stark. Young black men and women in massive numbers were being marched over land or packed onto trains to labor in Alabama, Mississippi, and Arkansas, or carried by steamers down the Mississippi from the Upper South to New Orleans's booming slave market, or to new cotton fields in Texas. In the years since Leighton had been a boy by the Black River and Boggy Gully, more than a million slaves had experienced a Second Middle Passage from the seaboard South to the southern interior as the Cotton Kingdom spread and sent down deep roots. By the time Leighton began his travels around the country in the 1850s, this Second Middle Passage already far exceeded in numbers the total number of Africans brought in the transatlantic slave trade to the United States. Yet Leighton, who had been so horrified by the international slave trade, and who had worked so hard against it, did not see or recognize this massive deportation of slaves, this forced uprooting of African Americans, this astonishing expansion of slavery across the South, as an intolerable scandal that cried out for him to join with those who were condemning it and who were fighting its power and arrogance. Or, if he saw and recognized the scandal, and if he heard the call to protest, he turned his eyes away and rejected the call.[3]

Yet, at the very time Leighton was ignoring this Second Middle Passage, he reacted with alarm and forthrightness to calls by some white Southerners to reopen the international slave trade. White radicals in the South were rejecting, with angry defiance, any claim that slavery was an evil and that it must be abolished. Rather than give an inch to any hint of antislavery sentiment, they had been marshaling for years every argument they could discover or concoct—including a rising scientific racism—to justify slavery. Slavery was, after all, an ancient institution known in all societies and supported by all religions. And an advancing scientific knowledge, they said, demonstrated that Africans unmistakably constituted an inferior race with smaller brains. Slavery was, they consequently announced, a positive good, the best possible way to manage a labor force and utilize the untamed energy of Africans and their uncivilized descendants.[4]

Now, in the 1850s, these proslavery radicals were snarling with increased intensity as they insisted that no moral sentimentality or Northern hypocrisy should be allowed to block slavery's expansion. And in this context they made their most arrogant claim—they stood against the tide of the nineteenth century, commanded it to roll back, and demanded the reopening of the international slave trade. They dreamed of slave ships once again sailing boldly and legally into Charleston harbor and up the flowing waters of the Savannah and into the port at New Orleans. Leighton knew these dreamers and the noxious night air from which their dreams emerged only too well. As a young man, he had written Jane about "my native *Carolina*" and the radical spirit that lurked beneath polished manners, an ostensible piety, and profound isolationism. Moderates in the state had been trying for years to temper the radicals, and Leighton had tried to do his part even from a distance. He had written letters to the *Charleston Observer* about African students who would astonish whites with their quick mastery of languages and Western learning. And he had written about the brilliant William Davis and his daughter, Mary Clealand, and about Wasa, and about the beauty and flexibility of the Mpongwe language, and about Toko and his ability to master complex trading responsibilities, and Toko's marvelous *Waterwitch*. But although moderates seemed to be keeping the peace, the radicals in the state, and their fellow "fire-eaters" in other Southern states, had kept up their agitation, waiting for their moment. The call to reopen the international slave trade was a shameless expression of their contempt for any antislavery sentiment and a part of their strategy to divide the nation and create a slaveholding confederacy. Among other things, the fire-eaters hoped that a reopened international slave trade would incense the North, and that Northern outrage would cause white Southerners to unite and move toward secession.[5]

In 1858, the South Carolina legislature received a report, initiated by the governor, advocating a proposal that the state, on its own, reopen the international slave trade. Leighton was horrified. He wrote a long and scathing article for the *Southern Presbyterian Review* that was republished and distributed as a pamphlet in the summer of 1859—"The Foreign Slave Trade: Can It Be Revived Without Violating the Most Sacred Principles of Honor, Humanity, and Religion?" He did not need, he wrote, to address the impact such a trade would have upon the South. His friend John Adger had already shown the "extreme folly and danger of such a measure." Leighton's intention was to show that the "South cannot countenance the revival of this traffic without dishonoring herself, and inflicting renewed and incalculable misery and wretchedness upon the inhabitants of Africa." Such a trade, he insisted, never had been, and could not be, carried on except by fraud, by violence, and by perpetual warfare and bloodshed. And so, once again, he rehearsed the history and bloody consequences of the trade, citing European travelers who had recounted the horrors of African wars for slaves and the rapacious appetite of whites for slaves and for the wealth that slaves brought. In addition to pointing to the cruelties involved in capturing slaves, Leighton described the cruelties of the journey from the African interior to the coast, the cruelties of detention on the coast, and the cruelties of the Middle Passage, which, Leighton wrote, "is but another term for the grossest cruelties ever practiced upon any portion of the human race." Leighton insisted that the number of Africans who would die in slave wars, detentions, and Middle Passages would far exceed the number who would survive to labor in the cotton and sugar fields of the South. "Is the South," he asked, "prepared for this? Will she forego her honor, her sense of justice, and her religion, so far as to associate herself with the vilest men that have ever disgraced the annals of humanity, and once more apply the torch of discord and war for the purpose of obtaining slaves?" It seemed inconceivable to him that the South he knew could be so blind as to accept such a course, or that South Carolinians could be so full of insane arrogance, so devoid of Christian compassion, and so confined to their own little world that its leaders would propose such a course.[6]

Leighton knew that, in addition to the cruelty and inhumanity of the international slave trade, what made the proposal to reopen it so full of madness and blind hubris was the fear whites had of blacks. White advocates of colonization had been fueled by a belief that there was no place in America for blacks, that there was a great need to whiten not only Maryland but other states as well. Blacks needed to be sent back to Africa, Latrobe and others had argued, not brought from Africa to America! Leighton knew only too well the disdain and disgust many whites felt toward Africans and their descendants. He knew that respectable scientists were questioning the full humanity of Africans, insisting on the dual origin of the races and comparing Africans to the *njina*, the newly discovered gorilla. In his travels around the South, Leighton had heard over and over again how whites feared the consequences of emancipation, that with emancipation they would find themselves living among a freed but barbarous people. Given the racism of white Americans, what madness suggested the importation of more Africans? Writing from New York, Leighton clearly saw how the Southern radicals were deepening the existing divisions between the North and the South, and he felt the prospects of war growing more ominous.[7]

In the midst of this turmoil, Leighton hoped that the more intelligent and conservative people of the nation would prevail, that they would quell the agitations and preserve the Union. He believed and hoped, he wrote his old colleague B. V. R. James, that the majority of the American people would keep to a sound and prudent path. He clearly hoped that extremes could be avoided, that passions could be cooled, and that, in the providence of God, slavery would die a slow and gentle death under the influence of the gospel and the progress of civilization. And in Monrovia, James, seeing the clouds gathering over his old homeland, wrote to a friend: "How true it is, the greater injury done to the injured, the greater the hatred of those that have done the injury! And such is emphatically the feelings and treatment of the American white man towards the black race. They know they have done him the greatest possible injury, therefore they hate him and despise him!"[8]

ABRAHAM LINCOLN WAS elected president in November 1860. There had been four major candidates, but Lincoln, the Republican candidate, had won, with a resounding 59 percent of the electoral college vote. The election showed that a united North was able to decide the nation's future, and the white South responded with rage. "The Northern people," wrote a New Orleans newspaper editor, "in electing Mr. Lincoln, have perpetuated a deliberate, cold-blooded insult and outrage on the people of the slaveholding states." In Columbia, the *Southern Presbyterian* called on the South to defend its rights and to resist Northern aggression. Disunion was better than subjugation and being ruled by the Northern fanatics who had elected Lincoln. Better to live as a free people, eating only cornbread and wearing only homespun, than remain in the Union as a subjugated province governed by a foreign imperial power.[9]

A month after Lincoln's election, South Carolina voted to secede from the Union. Among those who attended the Secession Convention was Leighton's kinsman the Reverend Thomas Reese English, a son like Leighton of the Mt. Zion Presbyterian Church. He joined in making the vote for secession unanimous, and after the vote he led the convention in prayer.[10]

Leighton and Jane were distraught by these developments. They had family in both the North and the South—Eckards, Bayards, Henrys, and Hodges in the North, and Bayards, McIntoshes, Wilsons, and a host of other relatives along the Black River in the South. In New York, they were part of a large circle of friends and colleagues and were greatly loved and admired by many. They attended the Brick Presbyterian Church, whose pastor, Gardiner Spring, was a prominent member of the Presbyterian Foreign Mission Board and a close colleague of Leighton's. In Charleston, Columbia, and Savannah, they had old friends—Adgers, Smyths, and Clays, to name only a few.

So Leighton and Jane felt divided as the nation's divisions deepened, but their sympathies were clearly with the South. Leighton believed that the question of liberty was at the heart of the crisis. The election of Lincoln appeared a sure sign that the North was claiming its liberty to impose its will on the South. Like the settlers at Cape Palmas and the French in Gabon, the North, by electing Lincoln, was acting in an arrogant, imperialist manner. If the white South had its radicals, the North had its radicals as well—abolitionists who had been calling year after year for the immediate freeing of the slaves in the South. They were ready, Leighton believed, to ignore the laws of the land in order to assert their liberty to follow their own conscience. Now, with the election of Lincoln, Leighton thought, the abolitionists had the power of the federal government behind them as they claimed the liberty to abolish slavery.[11]

But Leighton believed the white South had its inalienable liberty, too— the liberty to decide for itself the fate of Southern slaves. Leighton hoped that the South would take the issue of slavery in hand and work out a way for slaves to be eventually liberated. But the white South, not the abolitionist North, was to do the liberating and to make the decisions about when and how the slaves were to be freed. Leighton had been raised on stories of how his grandfather and great-grandfather had resisted British aggression during the American Revolution. They had ridden with Francis Marion, the Swamp Fox, to defend their homeland against foreign imperialism, and they had fought for the liberty of those who had settled along the Black River. Now, once more, it seemed, the liberty of his people was being threatened—this time by the tyranny of a Northern majority.[12]

So liberty was the issue for Leighton, but even the meaning of the word was contested. Lincoln saw the contest clearly. "We all declare for liberty," he said, "but in using the same *word* we do not all mean the same *thing*. With some the word liberty may mean for each man to do as he pleases with himself, and the product of his labor; while with others the same may mean for some men to do as they please with other men, and the product of other men's labor." Here, declared Lincoln, "are two, not only different, but incompatible things, called by the same name—liberty."[13]

For Leighton, liberty resided in moderation—it could be found only between the extremes of tyranny, on the one hand, and anarchy, on the other.

Many of his friends in the North shared such a view and hoped that moderation would prevail against both tyranny and anarchy and keep war from erupting. But like the word "liberty," the words "tyranny" and "anarchy" meant different things in the North and in the South. The tyranny that Leighton feared was the tyranny of an aggressive North imposing its will on the South. The anarchy he feared was the anarchy of an imposed liberation of slaves who no longer had their true friends, Southern whites, guiding them. But the tyranny that increasing numbers in the North saw was the tyranny of a slave system—the arbitrary power of a slave master to whip and beat, and to buy and sell, black men, women, and children. And while many in the North feared the anarchy that could result if there were an immediate emancipation of slaves, they feared more directly the anarchy of secession, and of a lawless disregard for the Constitution. So in the midst of rising anger, and in the face of incompatible and competing interpretations of liberty, tyranny, and anarchy, Leighton hoped for moderation. But the moderation he hoped for could not bridge the chasm that separated the South from the North, or halt the formation of a Southern confederacy. Leighton's colleague, James Henley Thornwell, professor of theology at Columbia Theological Seminary, wrote: "Two Governments upon this continent may work out the problem of human liberty more successfully than one."[14]

Leighton had an opportunity to spell out his understanding of these issues a few days after South Carolina seceded, when he exchanged a series of frank and painful letters with Jane's cousin Charles Hodge in Princeton. Leighton and Hodge had been correspondents when the Wilsons were at Fair Hope and Baraka, and during the years the Wilsons were in New York, the Princeton professor had become Leighton's closest friend and confidant. But, in spite of family ties and deep friendship, the national crisis divided them.

Leighton knew that Hodge was heart and soul a conservative. The Princeton professor believed in tradition and he believed in order. And although he thought slavery was a great blight on the nation's life, what troubled him the most was not the slave's bondage but what he saw as a coming wave of disorder and anarchy and the looming threat of war and its chaos and bloodshed. Hodge had long viewed abolitionists as a radical fringe in the North, and he had condemned their disregard for the orderly processes of law and civil society. But he thought secessionists were not only radical but also criminal, traitors who were threatening to bring down on the nation all of the terrors of a civil war. He longed, like his friend Leighton, for moderation, for conservative people in the North and the South to bridge their differences, to find compromises, and to restore order and peace to the land.[15]

Shortly after South Carolina seceded, Hodge wrote an article on "The State of the Country," and sent a copy to Leighton before he had the article published. Hodge condemned what he regarded as the extremism of the abolitionists and the way they were treading on the South's liberty; the South, he said, should be able to work out its own answer to slavery. But in even stronger language he condemned the "absurdities, abnormities, and evils which flow from secession," likening those who would support it to Benedict Arnold.[16]

Leighton replied in a long letter. Hodge's article, he wrote, had much that would irritate both the North and the South. Leighton acknowledged that there was wisdom in what Hodge had written, but he strongly disagreed with much that was in the article. Leighton confessed to his old friend the deep grief he felt over their disagreements and his inability to bridge the differences that separated them. This inability did not stop Leighton, however, from making his arguments as he sought to show that the South was the injured party and the North the aggressor. White Southerners felt oppressed, he wrote, because the North was seeking to impose its will on the South and was "planting her heel upon the neck of the South." Leighton said he prayed most earnestly for the preservation of the whole Union. And, he added, "if the North will concede what is just, and what the South imperatively needs, the Union may be saved. Otherwise, we go to pieces." What Leighton obviously believed the South needed was to be left alone, free from Northern domination. The South, he thought, was only claiming its inalienable right to work out its own answer to the slave question and its liberty to forge its own destiny.[17]

Hodge replied: "My dear, precious friend. Your letter fills me with despair. That a man so wise, so gentle, so good as you are, one whom I unfeignedly regard as one of the best men I ever knew, should evidently approve of what I consider great crimes and disapprove of what I understand the plainest principles of truth and justice, shakes all confidence in human convictions. I never felt so deeply before that opinions are not thoughts, but feelings." Hodge had come to the conclusion that carefully constructed arguments were not shaping responses to the crisis in either the North or the South. Feelings, rooted in the deepest memories and associations people had, were shaping what they were seeing in the unfolding drama of secession. Hodge and Leighton, who shared so much in outlook and affection, were looking at the same developments in the nation's life, and yet, Hodge wrote, "we are almost as far apart as though we did not believe in the same God and Saviour or recognize the same moral law." If we, wrote Hodge, "who love each other and who sincerely desire that truth and justice should prevail, thus differ, what must be the case of those who are not thus united, or who are animated by feelings of mutual enmity!"[18]

Leighton wrote back: "My dear friend and brother. If the differences of views between you and myself on the general state of the country is the cause of despondency on the one side, it is of real heartfelt grief on the other." He reiterated and expanded once again his belief that the South was the aggrieved party, that it had been abandoned by the conservative men in the North who had stood with it against the attacks of the abolitionists, and that, with the election of Lincoln, the North was acting in an imperialistic and aggressive manner toward the South. He concluded: "I do not expect to pursue this correspondence further. I am afraid that the time for argument is gone by, but whatever may happen, I trust I shall always regard yourself as one of the dearest friends I have had. God save us all from terrible times and scenes."[19]

So the correspondence between the old friends came to an end. Each wanted compromises to preserve the Union. But the distance between the North and the South was too great to be bridged by well-meaning moderates seeking understanding. One had to be on one side or the other; one had to mean one thing or the other; one had to make a decision for Union or secession.

DURING THE COMING months—from January to early April 1861—as many people in both the North and the South struggled to avoid a war, Leighton and Jane stayed in their New York home and agonized about what they were to do. Was it possible for them to stay in their comfortable Manhattan home, and for Leighton to continue his work with the Mission Board? Could they abandon their family members in the South, leaving them to face the horrors of a looming civil war and the wrath of a powerful and aggressive North? What was the path of duty, of Christian love and discipleship? For the moment, an answer did not have to be given. Leighton continued his work at the Mission Board and was busy writing the annual report for the May meeting of the Presbyterian General Assembly to be held in Philadelphia. His hopes rose and fell for the Union as he watched the developments around him. His letters to the missions in Africa told how he looked for every promising sign of compromise, and how he grieved every failed attempt to find some way to avoid bloodshed. At the end of December 1860, he wrote the mission on Corisco saying that with the election of Lincoln, the nation was in the greatest distress. Southerners, he said, regarded Lincoln as an abolitionist. Florida, Alabama, Mississippi, Louisiana, and Georgia were preparing to follow South Carolina out of the Union unless they received guarantees protecting them from the aggression of the Lincoln administration. On February 1, 1861, he wrote James in Monrovia that he expected that two nations would be formed, but hoped that, after tempers cooled, they might be reunited in a stronger union. By March he was feeling encouraged. When he wrote again to the Corisco mission, he said that the fear of civil war was passing away. A Southern confederacy had been established, and people North and South were waiting to see if it would include all or only a part of the slave states. On April 9, James wrote Leighton: "I greatly rejoice and thank God for the favorable intelligence which our last papers bring and truly hope during the lull of the fearful storm of passions which the inauguration of the new President has produced, the people of all classes will take time to consider and again come to their right senses." Three days later, on April 12, 1861, Confederate forces fired on Fort Sumter in Charleston Harbor. The Civil War had begun.[20]

LEIGHTON AND JANE knew that the time to act had arrived. They sold their New York home and its furnishings and purchased a house in Savannah from a Georgia family that had moved to New York. The Savannah house was a handsome townhouse located a short distance from the old Bayard home in the heart of the city. But it was bought sight unseen, so anxious were they to transfer the proceeds of the New York house to an investment in the South. After saying their goodbyes to many friends, Leighton and Jane, together with eleven-year-old Cornelia, left the city for the Eckard home in Pennsylvania, where Margaret and James Eckard now lived with their children. There the Wilsons awaited the meeting of the Presbyterian General Assembly, which was to be held in Philadelphia in the middle of May. Leighton hoped that the church, which had not become divided along North-South lines, would somehow stay united, and that it might contribute in some way to the efforts that many were still making to pursue peace and reunion. And he wanted to give his reports on the mission in Africa and among the Native American nations of the Southwest.[21]

The waiting was painful and awkward. Not only were Leighton and Jane facing a separation from those they loved, but they also found themselves among family members who were strong supporters of Lincoln. Most distressing was their relationship with the Bayards in Philadelphia. Jane had long regarded her cousins Theodosia Bayard and Elizabeth Bayard Henry as sisters, and Leighton had a close and affectionate relationship with them and other members of the family. In 1861, however, Elizabeth's son, Alexander Henry, was serving as mayor of Philadelphia, and he was strongly identified with the Union cause and Lincoln's commitment to preserve the Union. Jane was particularly distressed by the resulting tensions and felt great reluctance to leave those whom she loved, whatever their political positions. And Margaret was torn as well. Both sisters had deep ties North and South and divided hearts. And both sisters were wives, committed by love and a sense of wifely duty to remain with their husbands. So out of the swirling, turbulent power of conflicting loyalties and emotions, they faced the bitter realities of a divided nation and family.[22]

The Presbyterian General Assembly met the third week in May. Leighton attended as a member of the Board of Foreign Missions and not as a voting member of the assembly—his South Carolina presbytery refused to send any commissioners. This meant that, except for his reports on missions, he had no voice or vote. He spent most of his time watching the proceedings.[23]

These conservative Old School Presbyterians meeting in Philadelphia had been able to remain together while other denominations—most dramatically, Baptists and Methodists in the 1840s—had split North and South over the question of slavery. The Presbyterians had been able to maintain their unity by clinging to the doctrine of the spirituality of the church. The church, it was said, was to deal with spiritual matters and not political ones. So, for a generation, slavery had been banned from the debates of the church—except when the Presbyterians had been forced to defend themselves from the attacks of Scottish Presbyterians, who were demanding that the American church denounce slavery and slaveholders. But now, the guns around Charleston harbor had fired on Fort Sumter and its Federal troops. In Philadelphia, it seemed all too clear that Southern whites had plunged into anarchy, sedition, and rebellion. As soon as the assembly convened, there were demands that it make a statement supporting the Union. Gardiner Spring, Leighton's friend and New York pastor, moved that "this General Assembly . . . do hereby acknowledge and declare our obligations to promote and perpetuate, so far as in us lies, the integrity of these United States, and to strengthen, uphold, and encourage, the Federal Government in the exercise of all its functions under our noble Constitution: and to this Constitution in all its provisions, requirements, and principles, we profess our unabated loyalty." The motion passed by a large majority.[24]

Charles Hodge and a number of conservatives protested. While emphasizing their own commitments to the Union, they insisted once again that the church had no right to decide a political question. During the American Revolution, they said, many Christians in Great Britain had regarded the Americans as rebels. But neither the Church of Scotland nor the Church of England had issued mandates of loyalty to King George. They did not declare it to be obligatory for Christians in America to do all that lay within them to strengthen, uphold, and encourage the king in the exercise of the prerogatives of his crown.[25]

The assembly rejected the protest and issued a stinging rebuke to the Princeton professor and those who supported his position. Did they expect the assembly to sanction by its silence the treason of white Southerners?

> Would they have us recognize, as good Presbyterians, men whom our own government, with the approval of Christendom, may soon execute as traitors? . . . What, when "a crime, the heinousness of which can be only imperfectly estimated" . . . is already committed; when thousands of Presbyterians are likely to be seduced from their allegiance by the machinations of wicked men; . . . when armed rebellion joins issue with armed authority on battle-fields, where tens of thousands must perish; when it remains a question, whether our national life survives the conflict . . . is it uncalled for, unnecessary, for this Christian Assembly to renew . . . respect for the majesty of law, and a sense of obligation of loyalty? Let posterity decide between us.[26]

Leighton immediately resigned from the Board of Foreign Missions. He crossed into Virginia at Alexandria the day before travel was closed. Jane and Cornelia stayed behind in Pennsylvania for a conflicted Jane to say her tearful goodbyes to family and friends. In New York, Walter Lowrie wrote to B. V. R. James that "our dear brother J. Leighton Wilson" had resigned his position with the board and had returned to South Carolina. And far off in Monrovia, James responded with "deepest regret." "This information," he wrote Lowrie, "gives great pain and great disappointment. Yet I must say again, I believe Mr. Wilson's motives are pure and holy." Your country, he wrote, "is truly in a sad and awful condition, and all to effects of slavery. I have foreseen this sad calamity for many years. *God is true and just*, and I believe what he has said in his Holy Word!"[27]

Other friends in the North grieved Leighton's departure, too, for few men in the church were as greatly admired or loved as he. But not many of his friends were surprised. Years later, a colleague in New York remembered visiting Leighton before his departure for Pennsylvania. Leighton had told him that he prayed that God would save the nation from civil war, "but if it comes, my mind is made up, I will go and suffer with my people."[28]

LEIGHTON HURRIED SOUTH toward Columbia. In Richmond and everywhere south of Richmond, he could see the gathering of troops as white men responded to the call to defend their homeland and new nation. In Columbia, he stayed at the home of his old professor George Howe, a few blocks from the seminary where thirty years earlier Leighton had begun his formal theological education. Together with Howe and other church leaders who were clustered around the seminary, Leighton joined in conversations about the formation of a Presbyterian Church in the Confederate States of America. Presbytery after presbytery in the South was withdrawing from the assembly, and there was, they thought, a clear need for a distinct national church for the new nation.[29]

In late June, Leighton left for Louisville, Kentucky. There he met Jane and Cornelia for a joyful but tearful reunion. With great difficulty, Jane had said her goodbyes to Margaret and other loved ones, but Leighton was committed to a Southern home, and so, with the help of influential family members, she and Cornelia had made their way across the Ohio River into Southern territory. Now together again, the little family hurried south to Columbia, and from Columbia to Pine Grove. Leighton rented a house nearby, not too far from the old family place and Boggy Gully, not too far from the Black River and Mt. Zion. So Leighton cast his lot with the South, with home, with a specific place he believed to be his homeland, and with a people he believed to be his people. And Jane joined him, and she, too—this child of Savannah and Philadelphia—cast her lot with the South.[30]

Leighton's return to the South was, he believed, an act of patriotism—of local patriotism—of devotion to a particular and remembered place and to a particular and greatly loved people. But the return was not simply a reflection of a local patriotism for Leighton, for it was also an act of national patriotism, of patriotism for a remembered national life. He was joining, he believed, those who were defending an older America against the imperialism of the Yankees, and against perceived threats to the ordered ways of the nation and the ways the nation had been governed. He had painfully concluded that if he remained in the North, if he took his stand not with Dixie but with New York and Philadelphia, with Princeton and Boston, with a Yankee idea of the Union, he would be deserting a people and a place he loved. If this was to be the cost of freedom for those who lived by Boggy Gully and in the other settlements and slave quarters of the South, then the cost was too high. So he took his stand with Dixie, with Pine Grove and Mt. Zion, and with a white South.

Although Leighton accused the North of an aggressive imperialism, he knew only too well that the South was hardly free from such a charge. He had compared the actions of the colonists at Cape Palmas to the imperialism of Georgia and Andrew Jackson in the removal of the Cherokee, and he knew that the calls for the reopening of the international slave trade were linked to a grand vision of some Southern whites for a slave nation that included not only captured Mexican territory but also Cuba. But what Leighton now perceived as Yankee imperialism was directed against his own people, his home, where all of his deepest emotions had been shaped and where his affections were still rooted.[31]

To be sure, Leighton had been willing to leave father and mother, brothers and sisters, and a landscape of deep memories. When he and Jane had heard the call to be missionaries, they had left home, and they had sought to free themselves from its peculiar institution. They had moved far beyond their home and far beyond most white Americans in their regard for Africans and their descendants. But even though they had freed their slaves, and even though they thought they had freed themselves from slavery, they had not freed themselves from their history, and they had not realized how their love for home—and for one another—had continued to entangle them in the web of slavery and racism. For racism was a part of their Southern home, and for them to love a white Southern home and family had come to mean, in some diabolical way, that they had to support slavery and its underlying racism. Slavery was who they were in spite of their manumissions, in spite of their fighting the slave trade, in spite of their years away from Pine Grove and Savannah and Fair Hope plantation. They could not, finally, separate slavery from home or from themselves, because they could not find the freedom to transcend the contingencies of their lives, and they could not abandon the loyalties of their hearts.

Leighton and Jane thought, of course, that they had the freedom to make a choice between the North and the South, between those who were committed to restricting and eventually abolishing slavery and those committed to defending it. They did not believe in some kind of social determinism—that the deep influences of home finally limited their freedom or their range of choices. They were, after all, missionaries. They had spent years trying to convert the Grebo and the Mpongwe, King Freeman and Simleh Ballah, Toko and King Glass. They had called on them to give up the traditions of their people, to abandon old practices and social arrangements, and to see the world and act in it in new ways. And though not many had converted, some had—above all, William Davis, who as an adult had defied the contingencies of his own life, given up many of the deepest assumptions of his people, and freely decided to be a Grebo Christian. Yet Leighton and Jane and their missionary colleagues believed that their best strategy for the conversion of the Grebo and the Mpongwe was to focus on the children, to remove them as much as possible from the influences of home and the surrounding culture, and to have them internalize at an early age certain assumptions, dispositions, and ways of seeing the world. What they had difficulty seeing were the ways in which their own childhood homes, their own histories, had created within them certain assumptions, dispositions, and ways of seeing the world, and how, out of the chaos of many feelings and conflicting motives, they had made their decisions.[32]

Certainly, Leighton and Jane themselves knew a broader world than their Southern homes. Their dispositions and their ways of seeing the world had been challenged by their varied experiences. Odysseus-like, they had sailed on strange seas far from home and had seen what was, for them, strange sights, some abhorrent, and some marvelous. They both had sailed on many occasions along the West Coast of Africa, had seen Sierra Leone, Cape Coast, and Accra, and they knew the sound of the surf at Cape Palmas and the wide expanses of the Gabon estuary. Leighton had trekked far from the coast with William Davis and other Grebo, trying to reach the Pah and the Mountains of Moon, and he had sailed on the *Waterwitch* far up the Como to see distant villages with Toko. King Freeman and King Glass, B. V. R. James and Josiah Dorsey, Margaret Strobel James and Mary Clealand Dorsey, Toko and William Davis—they all in one way or another had allowed Leighton and Jane to catch at least important glimpses of other worlds and to transcend some of the assumptions that had shaped their lives. So it was not that they were provincial, or that they had not changed and had their visions broadened. Nor had their abhorrence of the slave trade been a sham. Rather, the love of home and the demands of loyalty and the power of early memories had finally been stronger than an alternative vision that could be seen on the horizon with Lincoln's election.

Home was consequently the siren voice that seduced them on their odyssey, that called out to their spirits in the familiar accents of their youth and of their dreams and enticed them south. To follow this beckoning voice, Leighton and Jane had to silence other voices, voices that they had heard on their journey across a surging Atlantic and beneath an African sky. They had to say to James and King Freeman, to William Davis and Mary Clealand, to Toko and Wasa and Maria—be silent.

Like Toko, Leighton was rooted in a place and being of that place, being one with the landscape of his home and the traditions of his people, Leighton did not find the message of Lincoln to be convincing. Leighton could not, or would not, abandon his people or their ways for to do so would be a rejection of his own deepest identity. And Jane, though deeply divided between a Northern and a Southern home, between greatly loved family in Pennsylvania and greatly loved family in South Carolina and Georgia, turned south finally because Leighton turned south, and to be with Leighton was to be home. So Leighton and Jane set their faces toward home, followed its familiar voice, and made their homeward journey after their long wanderings. They gave themselves to the white South, to a history and people committed to maintaining slavery and its deep oppression. And this giving of themselves was both an act of deep love and the desertion of a moral vision, both a commitment to a place and an abandonment of their long struggle to escape the web of their Southern home and the demands of their deepest, most insistent memories. [33]

Civil War

In August 1861, a few weeks after the Confederate victory at Bull Run, Leighton went to Atlanta to help plan the formation of a Presbyterian Church in the Confederate States of America. Already a Confederate government had been organized, and most white Southerners saw themselves as now living in a new nation with Richmond as its capital. Presbyterians in the South moved quickly to organize a Presbyterian church for the new nation. Throughout the spring and summer of 1861, presbyteries in the Southern states had withdrawn their connection with the Presbyterian Church in the United States of America. They had expressed outrage that the General Assembly meeting in Philadelphia had meddled in politics, had called for support of the federal government, and had declared secession to be treason. Those meeting in Atlanta intended to draw together these now independent presbyteries into a new church under a new General Assembly.[1]

Leighton listened to the plans being formulated for a meeting of a General Assembly, but his heart was not in the issues of polity that were being debated in Atlanta. What he wanted to do was to make sure the new church would be deeply committed to missions, and especially to foreign missions. So he kept raising the question of missions, and he insisted that if the new church was to have integrity as a Christian church, it must have a missionary heart. Federal ships, of course, were already making it unlikely that any missionaries would be sailing out of Charleston or Savannah, or from Mobile or New Orleans. But those who gathered in Atlanta saw missions as a noble cause—a cause that lifted their eyes beyond the troubled waters of the Confederacy. Commitment to missions, they believed, would help to legitimize the new church and would provide a marker for its self-understanding and identity.[2]

As a result of his appeal, Leighton was commissioned to visit the Indian Nations in the Southwest, where a number of schools and churches had been established by the Board of Foreign Missions in New York. The Indian Nations had been a part of his responsibilities in New York, and during the previous seven years he had visited them on several occasions. Now, in late September 1861, he left his Black River home and traveled to the Southwest Indian Territory, in what would later become Oklahoma. There on horseback and in wagons, and sometimes on foot, Leighton followed rough roads to visit the Cherokees, the Creeks, and the Chickasaw, and he met with the Choctaw Council in Doaksville, the Choctaw capital. Everywhere, he found the people in turmoil and often divided between those who supported the North and those who supported the South. All of the communities he visited were beginning to suffer the ravages of war. Eight boarding schools, with more than five hundred pupils, had been abandoned, as most of the missionaries had returned to their homes in the North. Many congregations were also scattered. But Leighton found encouraging signs as well—treaties were being signed with the Confederate government, and the people were eager for missionaries to return and join native preachers and teachers. Leighton promised that the churches of the South would not abandon them and that he would work to have the schools reestablished and teachers and missionaries settled once again among them.[3]

In early December, Leighton was back in Georgia, attending the first meeting of the General Assembly of the Presbyterian Church in the Confederate States of America. The assembly met in the First Presbyterian Church of Augusta, whose pastor was Joseph R. Wilson (his son, Woodrow Wilson, was too young to pay much attention to the proceedings). The commissioners were a distinguished group of white Southerners—brilliant, affluent, well-traveled, and pious—who for years had been pouring out their powers in defense of slavery and a Southern homeland. Among them were the men who were to become Leighton's closest friends and colleagues— James Henley Thornwell, former president of the South Carolina College and now professor of theology at Columbia Theological Seminary; John Adger from Charleston; Benjamin Morgan Palmer from New Orleans; Charles Colcock Jones, known among whites as the "Apostle to the Negro Slaves"; George Howe from the seminary in Columbia; and James Woodrow, who, having received a PhD in chemistry from the University of Heidelberg, had come to Columbia to teach theology. Thornwell and Jones would live only a few more years, but the others were to join Leighton in working to create a Southern Presbyterian Church that in war and in humiliating defeat would strive to defend a Southern homeland and its traditions against the onslaught of the North and a modern world.[4]

The assembly's most important act was to adopt "An Address to the Churches of Jesus Christ Throughout the World." Written by Thornwell, the address was intended to justify the creation of a new church and to demonstrate that the Southern church was not guilty of schism. Thornwell argued that it was desirable for churches to be organized along national lines, and that such organizations did not disrupt the spiritual unity of the universal church. But there was an equally pressing reason for a Southern Presbyterian Church. The Gardiner Spring Resolution at the Philadelphia assembly had been a deeply political act, he wrote, overstepping the bounds of the church's responsibilities. Church and state, Thornwell argued, were two separate spheres—the church was the sphere of grace and the state the sphere of justice. The state had no right to intrude into the church's sphere, and the church had no right to intrude into the sphere of the state. Thornwell acknowledged that there was a point at which the respective jurisdictions of church and state seemed to meet—and that was in the idea of duty. When, he said, "the State makes wicked laws, contradicting the eternal principles of rectitude, the Church is at liberty to testify against them; and humbly to petition that they may be repealed. In like manner, if the Church becomes seditious and a disturber of the peace, the State has a right to abate the nuisance." This bold statement must have appeared extreme to Leighton, if he remembered how he had been accused of "meddling in politics" at Cape Palmas and Baraka, when he had taken the side of the Grebo and the Mpongwe.[5]

But the question, of course, remained: Was slavery one of those "wicked laws, contradicting the eternal principles of rectitude," requiring the church to testify against it? Thornwell and the Southern assembly—unlike later defenders of the South—readily admitted that slavery "lies at the root of all the difficulties which have resulted in the dismemberment of the Federal Union, and involved us in the horrors of an unnatural war." The fundamental question for Thornwell thus became, Do the scriptures directly or indirectly condemn slavery as a sin? Thornwell's answer was to look at the scriptures themselves. Is not, he asked, the institution of slavery recognized and accepted in both the Old and New Testaments? And, if you try to appeal to the genius and spirit of Christianity and the Golden Rule to "love your neighbor as yourself," did not Moses and the apostles sanction slavery while accepting the Golden Rule? So Thornwell and the assembly—including Leighton—did not condemn slavery. They insisted that the responsibility of the church was not to address the system of slavery as an institution governed by the state, but rather, to speak to the relationship between masters and "servants." The church was to call masters to be kind and benevolent in their treatment of their slaves, and to be concerned for the salvation of those committed to their care by a mysterious providence. And the church was to teach slaves to be obedient to their masters. In this way, the doctrine of the "spirituality of the church" became a powerful theological and ideological weapon for the defense of slavery and in the years to come became a defense for a "Southern way of life." Now the church could stand in silence and say that it had no authority to adjudicate political issues or to address the great social questions of the day. When Leighton signed the "Address," he indicated anew that he had returned home to the world he had known as a youth.[6]

Leighton reported to the assembly on his trip to the Southwest Indian Territory, and the assembly enthusiastically adopted his recommendation that the Southern church assume responsibility for mission work among the people of the territory. He urged the assembly to adopt, as the "great end of her organization," the mission of the church "into all the world." Once again, the assembly enthusiastically approved his recommendation.[7]

Southern Presbyterians, who had been far behind Northern Presbyterians in their concern for missions, thus committed themselves to foreign missions as never before. For the next one hundred years, Southern Presbyterians—with other white Christians in the South—were to be marked by a new passion for foreign missions, to be equaled only by their passionate insistence that the church not meddle in politics or social issues. The assembly elected Leighton as its secretary for foreign missions, a position he was to hold for the next twenty-three years. But of course with the federal blockade of the South, and with the devastations of war, there was little he could do other than work to support the struggling mission among the Indian Nations of the Southwest until the war came to its bloody end.[8]

FROM THEIR HOME near the Black River, Leighton and Jane watched the progress of the war, and their hopes rose and fell with reports from distant battles. In 1862, battle followed battle, with victory on one side and then another—Union victories at Fort Donelson in Tennessee and Pea Ridge in Arkansas, at New Orleans and at bloody Shiloh in Tennessee. But the Confederates had their victories as well—Stonewall Jackson's successes in the Shenandoah Valley, the defeat of a Union attack on Charleston, and Lee's victory at the Second Battle of Bull Run. But the loss of life on both sides was staggering, more than anyone had anticipated. Antietam in Maryland turned out to be the bloodiest single day of battle of the war—and in American history—and although its outcome was said to be inconclusive, it was enough of a Union victory for Lincoln to announce that he intended to issue an Emancipation Proclamation on January 1, 1863, freeing slaves in any Confederate state not under Union control.[9]

As the reports of battles lost and battles won arrived at their Black River home bloody year after bloody year, so, too, did the news of young men dying. The little community of whites who worshiped at Mt. Zion was hard hit. Leighton's brother Sam lost two sons, including young Leighton Bayard Wilson. Families began traveling to Virginia to bring back the bodies of their men and boys from some distant battlefield or hospital burying ground. Leighton helped to conduct some of the services as sons and husbands were committed to the ground of the Mt. Zion cemetery, earth to earth, ashes to ashes, dust to dust, while the community confessed its sure and certain hope of the resurrection to eternal life, through Jesus Christ their Lord. But the grief was intense, and whatever consolations came from their Christian faith, the bitter losses remained and were long remembered.[10]

Distant battles had a direct impact on Leighton's work for the new church. New Orleans had been the location of the church's office of domestic missions. When the city fell to the Union navy, Leighton was given the responsibility of domestic missions—to add to his responsibility for foreign missions—and in this way the work of supplying Presbyterian chaplains for the Confederate Army became his primary responsibility. In this task, Leighton showed himself to be a skilled administrator. He worked out a system whereby more than a quarter of the Presbyterian pastors in the South spent some time as army chaplains. They worked in hospitals among the wounded, wrote letters home for the dying, and preached to and counseled troops who knew they were facing death or terrible wounds. Leighton went to Virginia, and there, crouching with troops in the muddy trenches around Petersburg, he talked and counseled and read scripture and served the Lord's Supper. He visited in hospitals and tried to comfort those who were suffering the traumas of wounds. And he sat by the beds of those who were inflicted by the scourges of the battlefield trenches and army camps—pneumonia or dysentery or typhoid or a rotting gangrene or some terrible combination of them. Leighton met with Robert E. Lee, and together they spoke about the "spiritual wants of the army" and the need for chaplains among the troops.[11]

At home, Leighton and Jane established regular routines as they sought to build a new life in the midst of so much death and destruction. Jane saw after the house and the education of Cornelia, and she joined other women at Mt. Zion in an "Association for Relief." They made blankets, quilts, and uniforms; washed and boiled old clothes and cut them into strips for bandages; and gathered food from gardens, barns, and smokehouses to be sent to hospitals and to loved ones in muddy trenches.[12]

Leighton worked in his study, writing letters to pastors and securing chaplains and preparing addresses and sermons for different church groups. Early on Sunday mornings, he preached to large congregations of blacks, who gathered in a little grove of trees at Mt. Zion before they all went in the church for a worship service with the whites.[13]

When not in his study or traveling, Leighton once again took up gardening, the pastime he had enjoyed so much at Cape Palmas. John, Leighton's former slave, whom Leighton had freed but who still lived by Boggy Gully, came and worked with Leighton, and the two men finally became acquainted with one another. They worked together in the garden soil—a white man and a black man whose lives had been intertwined across the great distances that had separated them, and that still separated them. Who knows what they thought as they unavoidably looked at one another working this Black River garden? When John saw Leighton digging, planting, and reaping, what did he think of this Wilson from Pine Grove, this missionary to Africa, who had freed him and offered him the choice of leaving home for the North or for Africa? Did he wonder about this tall white man who had come back to his Black River home to take his stand on the side of slavery? And when Leighton saw John digging, planting, and reaping, what did he think of this strong black man, a carpenter, whose mother had been inherited by Leighton's mother, this black man who also claimed the name Wilson and a Black River home? Did he wonder about John, about what he thought and felt, this black man who loved his own family and his own people and the landscape of his home so much that he would not abandon them even for a fuller freedom in a distant place? But perhaps neither man thought much about the other, and perhaps neither looked at the other and wondered. Perhaps they simply worked the soil together and assumed that all was already known that needed to be known about the other.[14]

WHILE LEIGHTON AND Jane struggled to keep some order in their lives and to be of service to the church and their young nation, battle continued to follow battle, and Confederate territory and hopes shrank. In May 1864, news arrived that General William T. Sherman had taken Rome, Georgia, in the northwestern part of the state. Nicholas Bayard and his family had moved to the little city in 1859, and Nicholas had invested heavily in the railroads, steamboats, and ironworks that were making Rome a prosperous city in the old Cherokee territory. When Sherman's troops withdrew to join the attack on Atlanta, Nicholas's investments were largely destroyed and left in smoking ruins. So the banker who had once sent Paul Sansay and the other Bayard slaves off to Africa with their pine chests of belongings now found himself and his family largely destitute.[15]

In early September, Atlanta fell, and with its fall there soon came fire and great destruction—the train depots and sheds, the rolling mills and machine shops, and the foundries and the arsenals were all put to the torch, and with them going up in the flames were hotels, churches, and businesses as well as somewhere between four thousand and five thousand homes. In the middle of November, Sherman plunged into middle Georgia on a brilliant and daring march to the sea. Cutting his supply lines and all communications with the North, he moved his great army toward Savannah, declaring that the army would live off the land. Foragers were organized to plunder a large swath of Georgia, and to bring corn, peas, and bacon; cows, pigs, and chickens; horses and mules to the rumbling army. Behind them the foragers left burning barns and the ruins of smoldering homes, and following them came newly liberated black men, women, and children.[16]

By early December, Sherman was near Savannah. On December 10, Richmond-on-Ogeechee, the plantation home of Eliza Clay, went up in flames. Jane had often visited the plantation, one of the most beautiful in the South, and here her friend Eliza had helped to prepare Margaret Strobel for her role as a teacher at Cape Palmas. Already to the south, Darien had been destroyed, and among the surrounding plantations that had been raided and had buildings burned was Fair Hope, where Jane had spent so many happy days with her McIntosh relatives, and where she and Leighton had made plans for their life together as missionaries.[17]

On December 20, the mayor of Savannah surrendered the old city so that it would not suffer the fate of Atlanta. The next day Sherman telegraphed Lincoln: "I beg to present you as a Christmas-gift the city of Savannah." Now Union troops marched through the streets where Paul Sansay had once hurried to his carpentry work, and they marched past wharfs where stunned Africans had once come out of the wretched holds of slave ships into the light of a Georgia sun and into the life of Georgia slaves. The marching troops brought with them freedom for the black slaves in the city, and it seemed to many of the liberated slaves nothing less than miraculous, the bold act of a liberating God. "I'd always thought about this, and wanted this day to come, and prayed for it and knew God meant it should be here sometime," an enslaved woman declared as she looked around at the troops and shook her head in disbelief. "But I didn't believe I should ever see it and it is so great and good a thing, I cannot believe it has come now; and I don't believe I ever shall realize it, but I know it has though, and I bless the Lord for it." The historian of First African Baptist Church remembered in the cadences of a black preacher the jubilant scene: the Yankees "had come for our deliverance, and the cry went around the city from house to house among the race of our people, 'Glory be to God, we are free!' Shout the glad tidings o'er Egypt's dark sea, Jehovah has triumphed, his people are free!"[18]

Sherman soon crossed the flowing waters of the Savannah into South Carolina. Before leaving the city, he told a South Carolinian, who was seeking to return home, "You will be going out from the frying pan into the fire." He did not believe he could control his troops as they entered the state that was believed to have started all of the death and destruction of the war. "You have heard of the horrors of war," Sherman warned. "Wait until my army gets into South Carolina and you will see the reality." And he told a Union officer that the time had come to punish the people of South Carolina. In a surprise move, Sherman marched toward Columbia and not Charleston. Town after town went up in flames, as did any barn or plantation house that lay in the path of the army. Soon it was Columbia's turn. Shortly before Sherman moved his army out of the fallen city toward North Carolina and the final surrender of Confederate forces, Columbia went up in flames. By the morning of February 18, 1865, substantial parts of the city were smoldering ruins.[19]

As Sherman's army moved toward the north, foragers and small detachments of Union troops rode along the Black River road, raiding the surrounding plantations. But the destruction they left behind was not as severe as that which followed Sherman's main army. Leighton, learning of the disaster that had swept over Columbia, organized a relief effort. Members of Mt. Zion gathered meal and bacon from their own dwindling supplies. Leighton secured two four-horse wagons, and he and John loaded them with the gathered supplies. With John driving one wagon and Leighton the other, the white man and the black man made their way together over the fifty miles to the city, where they found that the seminary had escaped the fire and was now housing many hungry refugees. After unloading what they brought and visiting among those crowded into the seminary's dormitories and classrooms, the two men returned with their empty wagons to their Black River homes.[20]

A FEW MONTHS before Columbia's destruction, B. V. R. James wrote Walter Lowrie from Monrovia and spoke of the furious storm of human passions now raging across an unhappy America. Leighton's old colleague and friend believed that God "thoroughly holds in his hand the vial of wrath that is now being emptied upon the nation." For James, the cruel war would only come to an end when God was "satisfied with the measure of wrath to be meted out to a people who have for more than one hundred years been treasuring up iniquity for this day of his vengeance." Until then, James said, "all must bow to God's holy will and say 'It is the Lord, let him do whatsoever seemeth to him good!'"[21]

Lee surrendered at Appomattox Courthouse on April 9, 1865. On Good Friday, April 14, Lincoln was assassinated.

Home Ground

Seven months after the fighting had reached its bloody conclusion and civilians could make their way through the desolate landscape of the South, Margaret Eckard set out from Pennsylvania to reach Jane and Leighton. She was determined to reach her sister as quickly as possible, even though travel was demanding and dangerous—rails and bridges had been destroyed, Richmond and other cities and towns were in ruins, soldiers and refugees were still trying to get home, and Freedpeople were on the move, desperately looking for husbands or wives, parents, or children who had been carried away or sold to some distant or unknown place.[1]

Margaret spent a month struggling southward until she finally reached the little village of Mayesville, not far from the Black River. An early winter storm had swept in from the west and covered the landscape with ice—young pines were bent over, and the branches of large pines threatened to snap with a loud crack and fall to the forest floor from the weight of the ice. Exhausted by her travel and its anxieties, she rode out early in the morning to the farm Leighton had rented. Jane heard the sound of the buggy and then saw her sister. Hurrying to one another over the frozen ground, the sisters fell into each other's arms as waves of emotion and the deep grief of the war washed over them. They had parted with much anguish four years earlier, each following her husband and what she believed to be the path of duty. Now they held tightly to one another in a silent embrace, their voices choked by mingled sorrow and joy. Margaret's daughter later remembered her mother's description of the reunion and how she could see in Jane's "white hair, bent form, wrinkled face, shabby dress, the want of comforts about the house, what that loved one had gone through and suffered." Yet Jane knew that her own suffering and want were not to be compared to that of many others, and she spoke not a word of complaint, either then or afterward.[2]

Margaret apparently brought what was most immediately useful—US dollars. Leighton and Jane also had US dollars from the sale of the house they had bought in Savannah in early 1861. With these funds they bought the old Pine Grove house from Leighton's sister Sarah, together with fifty acres that immediately surrounded it, and they purchased an adjacent forty acres from a cousin. Here, they thought, was land enough for a large garden, some corn, an expanded orchard, a wood lot, and pasture for a few cows and horses—a place where they could live happily and simply while they sought to be faithful to the responsibilities that lay before them in a defeated and devastated South.[3]

Included in the fifty acres they had bought from Sarah were the former slave cabins by Boggy Gully. When Sherman's army shook the land, those who lived in the old settlement had to discover, like other Freedpeople across the South, the meaning of their emancipation and the place they would call home. They had to learn the limitations now being placed on whites, and they had to find the boundaries of their new freedom—to decide where they were going to live, now that they could move around, and how they were going to make a living, now that they no longer had to plow and cook for "master and missus." At the war's end, many Freedpeople across the South had hoped that they would receive some land in compensation for their years of slave labor, perhaps even forty acres and a mule. But such hopes had quickly faded, and they were left with questions about how to respond to whites who were determined to keep them in their place of subordination.[4]

For most of the men and women who lived by Boggy Gully, the old settlement had been the only home they had ever known. Year after year, Sharper and Ben, Nelly and Sabrina, Abraham and Matilda—together with husbands and wives, parents and children, cousins and settlement neighbors—had gone out early in the morning from their smoky cabins to plow with mules, to hoe and pick cotton, to wash clothes and cook meals, to sweep and scrub, to butcher hogs and milk cows, and to do all that they were told to do by the white Wilsons. After the work of the day, they had returned to the settlement, to the packed and swept ground before their cabins, where evening after evening they had gathered around communal fires to cook and eat their suppers, to hear old Jacob and others tell their stories, and to say what they could not say before whites. Then, as fires had slowly died, they had gone night after night into dark cabins, where they had stretched out on simple beds and had fallen asleep surrounded by the sounds of Boggy Gully creek flowing toward river swamps where dark waters swirled and emptied into the Black River on its way to the Atlantic and a broader world. Over time, this place, with its sights, sounds, and memories, had insinuated itself into their sense of themselves and of their place in the world. The settlement and their life at Pine Grove had shaped the ways they walked and the ways they told stories and jokes, what they cooked and what they dreamed, how they saw the morning sky and how they imagined what might lie beyond the horizon. But because Boggy Gully had been not only their home, but also a place of exhausting labor and deep oppression, the familiarity of such a home had also evoked resistance and called forth visions of new places—places where a man could keep what he had raised by the sweat of his brow and where a woman could gather eggs, milk a cow, churn butter, and cook for herself and her own family. So when freedom came, some had left to find a new home on some other plantation or in some town or village. They wanted to get as far away from Boggy Gully as possible. They wanted to distance themselves from the Wilsons, those whom they had called master or mistress, and find in a new place some new freedom.

Among those who left was Jessie, who, along with John, had been freed by Leighton years earlier, and who had known, even as a free person of color, the weight and burden of the place. He headed to the little village of Mayesville, where he lived with his wife, Tisba, and their daughter, Patience, and sought to make a new home and a new life. He did not, of course, find in Mayesville a place free from the racism and oppressions of a defeated white South; nor did he leave behind the dispositions and deep assumptions that had been nurtured in him over his years by Boggy Gully. But the move to Mayesville was nevertheless an act of freedom, an attempt to break some of the constraints he had known and to declare both his ability and his right to make choices within the confines of his world.[5]

If some had left the old settlement, others had decided to stay, and some had arrived at Boggy Gully fleeing their own memories of other places, seeking a new place to live and work away from the old authorities who had controlled so much of their lives. So those who stayed and those who were newly arrived lived in the old settlement and worked under contract as hired hands, either around the house or on the remnant of land that had been part of Pine Grove plantation.[6]

Among those who stayed was John, who with his wife and children called the Boggy Gully settlement home. No less than Jessie's decision to leave, John's decision to stay was a decision he made in freedom within the confines of his world. Yet it was also a decision in deep continuity with his past. Unlike Paul Sansay, who had decided to leave his family in Savannah and go to Cape Palmas and its promised freedom, John had decided twenty-five years earlier to stay with his family at Pine Grove, rather than go north, or to Liberia, as Leighton had urged him. This "liberty of choice" Leighton had called John's "highest liberty," the most fundamental freedom John could enjoy. So John now chose to stay in the old settlement, and he kept busy with his carpentry work around the place and on neighboring plantations. As the years passed and his hair grayed, he became known as "Uncle John." Leighton gave him responsibility for overseeing the place, especially when Leighton was away. And "Uncle John" became for the whites who knew him an example of the good and faithful servant, and he carried as a deep burden of his freedom a powerful image among whites—the black man who stayed in his place.[7]

In this way, Pine Grove plantation became for Leighton and Jane "Old Homestead," as gradually the new name replaced the old. The gangly old house still stood above the settlement cabins as a reminder of old times that were not forgotten. Within its walls and on its piazza Leighton and Jane lived in the presence of earlier times, and they heard voices that still spoke out of deep memories, as the past displayed its vitality and pressed its legacies deep into the present. But Old Homestead was also a reminder of how much had changed. It was no longer the seat of many acres and much cotton and many slaves, but of few acres and a cluster of freed families. So it was from here, from this particular place with its old voices and new circumstances, that Leighton and Jane looked to the future.[8]

HANGING OVER OLD Homestead at this intersection of the past and the future was an inescapable and almost unbearable question for many Southern whites: How was it possible that the white South lost the war? White Southerners had thought they were invincible, and yet the Yankees had beaten them. They had believed their cause was just, and yet Union armies had devastated a once rich and prosperous Confederacy. How was it possible to suffer such a crushing defeat in a morally coherent universe? How could such evil come to a people who were so sure they were following God's way and will? Had God abandoned the Confederacy and all the plantation homes along the Black River, or was God simply asleep and indifferent? Had God acted in infidelity and unrighteousness toward the white South? Or had the South— and the church, in particular—been terribly wrong about slavery? Had a white Southern heart been hardened, like Pharaoh's toward the Israelite slaves, and had white Southern ears been simply deaf to the cries of black men, women, and children? The Presbytery of South Carolina confessed shortly after the end of the war that "the faith of many a Christian is shaken by the mysterious and unlooked-for course of divine Providence."[9]

These questions, so pressing for so many Southern whites, did not seem to preoccupy Leighton and Jane. Perhaps they had experienced too many sorrows at Fair Hope and Baraka, had seen too many hopes dashed, and had struggled too often with the mysterious providence of the Lord as they had watched one young missionary after another die a painful death. And perhaps they thought themselves somehow innocent, freed from the burden of slavery because they had freed their slaves, had fought the international slave trade, and had in earlier years denounced Southern slavery. But whatever their reasons for not being preoccupied with these questions of slavery and defeat, the questions were in the air they breathed, and the answers given to these questions by white Southerners were to shape Leighton's and Jane's world for the rest of their lives.[10]

Of all Leighton's close associates, John Adger responded most vigorously to this crisis of faith. Writing in the *Southern Presbyterian Review* in early 1866, Adger confessed that God was at work in the victory of Union armies and in the defeat of the Southern nation. The South's cause was just, Adger declared, but it had nevertheless lost the war. The Yankees had larger armies and much greater material resources, but these were only the instruments of the Almighty. The deeper meaning of the South's defeat could only be found in the gracious providence of God, who chastened those whom He loved. Because God loved the South, God was disciplining the South for God's own good and gracious purposes. But Adger warned the North that it should tremble if all the slaughter and destruction "has taught her only pride and self-confidence, censoriousness and severity towards brethren." He insisted that even if the South's defeat was the work of God, the South was not ashamed of the war, or penitent for her noble, but unavailing, defense of constitutional liberty. And he refused to acknowledge that white Christians in the South had been wrong in regard to slavery. "We retain," Adger wrote, "all of our former opinions respecting slavery," as he defiantly asserted slavery "was a kindly relation on both sides." Nevertheless, emancipation had come and was an accomplished fact. Southern Christians, he said, had been preoccupied with the slavery question for decades, and had conscientiously studied its duties and had sought to solve the problem of its future. But "our Northern brethren" claimed "a commission from the Almighty to solve the great problem, and they accordingly have abolished the institution. We cannot dispute their claim, nor are we so disposed." Now, said Adger, the burden of the emancipated slaves fell upon those who had freed them. The North had assumed a great new responsibility for the Freedpeople. On its part, the white South could pray for the success of the emancipators—*if* the North worked for what was in the *true* interest of the former slaves and not some Northern agenda. And, Adger added, white Southerners "still love the negro."[11]

Building on reflections such as these, the little world that Leighton and Jane now inhabited committed itself to a new world not so very different from the old one—except in its bitter defeat and poverty, its growing provincialism, and its haunting awareness that others regarded their Southern Zion as backward and unrepentant. Here, in this new but old world, a familiar creed was adopted and once again asserted—the best way for the North to fulfill its obligations to the black men, women, and children of the South was to leave them in the kindly care of Southern whites. Southern whites, it would be said with little sense of irony, knew and understood Southern blacks much better than distant Yankees did.[12]

As MIGHT BE expected, when Leighton and Jane looked at the desolation that surrounded them, they saw a need for a school, especially one for the daughters of planters. The schools that had previously existed for them had been broken up by the war, and with the poverty that now pervaded the Black River communities, it appeared the girls would be left with only the most meager education. Jane was also restless after her years of domestic life in New York and on a rented farm during war, and she was eager to take up her old vocation again, to teach as she once had taught at Fair Hope on an African cape and at Baraka, where the sounds of Mpongwe life had drifted up from Glass's Town.

Jane still owned some property in Georgia—it had belonged to her grandfather General Lachlan McIntosh—and it was not far from General's Island, where Paul Sansay and other Bayard slaves had once lived and worked among the Gullah people of the area. This land she now sold, and with the proceeds, she and Leighton had a small, neat school built at Old Homestead—not unlike the school that had been built at Fair Hope for Grebo children.[13]

The school was associated with Leighton's name, but it was in fact Jane's school, built with her money and directed by her. At first there was enough room in the old house for all the girls to live there with Leighton and Jane and Cornelia. But as the reputation of the school grew, rooms were found for more students at neighboring homes—with the family of Leighton's brother Robert, with brother Sam's family, with the Andersons and Scotts and Bradleys. Soon there were too many students for Jane to teach by herself, and so teachers were hired, eventually five in all, and girls began to arrive from other states to study under Jane's direction. One was a recently orphaned child—Alice Johnson—whom Leighton and Jane adopted as their own, and from whom they received much love and affection for the rest of their lives.[14]

The curriculum at Old Homestead must have included much that Jane had once taught to Grebo students at Fair Hope and to Mpongwe students at Baraka—perhaps especially geography, to show Lowcountry girls a broader world than what they knew. And no doubt the pedagogy used by the Black River was not so distant from the one Jane had used above the pounding surf at Cape Palmas and by the broad waters of the Gabon estuary.

Leighton had John build a study in the yard, where Leighton could write his letters, reports, and articles for missions, foreign and domestic, and where he could have his private devotions and get away from the noise of many young voices. But he joined students and teachers for their main meal. They all ate their dinner together at the old house—vegetables from the garden, meat from the smokehouse, eggs from the henhouse, milk and butter and clabber from the milk house—all prepared in the kitchen house by black women who lived by Boggy Gully. And before those boarding in nearby homes left for the evening, Leighton had devotions with them, and often they sang together hymns of the mission movement. Years later, former students remembered Jane and Leighton fondly. They had been, it was said, kind and thoughtful and warmhearted. And it was remembered that Leighton had frequently said that the "great want of the world was grace and common sense."[15]

The daughters of planters were not, however, the only ones who needed an education. Those who lived in the surrounding settlements needed to learn to read and write, and they needed to receive an education that would help to prepare them for the responsibilities of their new freedom. So a night school was opened for the Freedpeople, who came after the labors of the day to learn the mysteries of reading and writing. And Leighton wrote, only a few months after Lee's surrender, to his local representative, urging that in a new state constitution black men who could read and had a little property be given the right to vote. Nothing, he wrote, "would exert a more salutary influence upon their general character than the prospect and possibility of their being raised to the privilege of the elective franchise." White South Carolinians, of course, rejected such a proposal. Yankee power and the Fifteenth Amendment were necessary to secure the franchise for black men across the South—a right that even then lasted for only a few years before being crushed by a resurgent white South determined to keep blacks in their place.[16]

ALMOST AS SOON as the war ended, Leighton turned his attention to the devastated and struggling churches of the South. Church buildings had been destroyed, congregations had scattered, and many pastors had been left with the most meager resources to maintain themselves in their ministries. As the secretary for domestic missions for the Southern Presbyterian Church, Leighton used his considerable administrative skills to organize the church to respond to the crisis. With the General Assembly's approval, he established a sustentation fund. Churches with some resources contributed to the fund, and Leighton traveled monthly to Columbia to meet with the committee charged with allocating funds to those churches and pastors most in need. To encourage support of the fund, Leighton began to travel widely— especially to Baltimore, Louisville, St. Louis, and New Orleans, where the devastations of the war had not been as severe, and where there were large and affluent Southern Presbyterian congregations. Through the careful management of the collected funds, churches began to be rebuilt, pastors were sustained in their ministries, and new churches were established. But the work was slow, and the demands were great.[17]

Part of the work of domestic missions was to encourage what whites still referred to as "the religious instruction for colored people." The General Assembly insisted in December 1865 that the abolition of slavery had not altered the relation in which "our Church stands to the colored people nor in any degree lessened the debt of love and service which we owe them." The assembly insisted that long experience had invariably proved the advantage of blacks and whites worshiping together in one church. There was no reason, the assembly declared, for anything to be otherwise, now that blacks were free and not slaves.[18]

Although Leighton began receiving some reports that Freedpeople were leaving churches where they had worshiped with whites, he was at first encouraged by the number who remained. This was perhaps especially true at Mt. Zion and at the Salem Black River Church, where his uncle Robert James had once worked as a pastor among the growing number of slaves who lived nearby. Many of the six hundred blacks who had been members at Salem were still worshiping there with whites in 1866—and at Mt. Zion, not only were many black members continuing to be a part of the congregation, but other Freedpeople had begun to join. But all of this was soon to change. White church leaders were determined to remain in control, insisting that the congregations were white congregations no matter how many blacks attended. And blacks, seeing that little had changed, were increasingly unwilling to sit in balconies, sing hymns selected by whites, and remain under the authority of white elders. By 1868, most blacks had gone out from the white-controlled churches to establish their own. They generally did not go out one by one, but together as coherent black congregations that had existed for years within the confines of white-controlled congregations. And as they went, they took with them a sense of being a part of these particular black congregations—a church within a church. They had sat together in the balconies, had often worshiped together outside before they went into the white-dominated service, and had their own informal leaders. So they went out together from the white churches and took with them a history and a memory of walking together as a black church during the hard days of slavery.[19]

For Leighton, the most distressing departure of Freedpeople was from the Salem congregation, where as a young man he had worked for a season with his uncle Robert James. Leighton was convinced that the Freedpeople had left because they had been enticed away from their old church by Northern Presbyterians with promises of financial support. The black congregation had gone a mile down the road from Salem to establish their new church, which they named "Good Will Presbyterian." For Leighton, the establishment of this congregation and its call of a pastor supported by the Northern Presbyterian "Committee on Freedmen" was nothing less than an outrageous intrusion into his own home ground, another example of Northern aggression. Northern Presbyterians, it appeared to Leighton, were following Sherman's army with their own ecclesiastical imperialism.[20]

Not long after the establishment of Good Will, Leighton received a letter from S. C. Logan, the secretary of the Northern church's Committee on Freedmen. Logan had been a great admirer of Leighton before the war, and he had taken up his work for the Freedmen because of one of Leighton's missionary addresses. Now he wrote Leighton asking about possible cooperation between Northern and Southern Presbyterians in the building of churches and schools for the Freedpeople. He asked for Leighton's views about such cooperation and for any suggestions he might have about ways that the two churches could work together. Logan's letter provided Leighton with an opportunity to express in a candid manner just what he thought.[21]

Blacks, Leighton wrote, had been a happy part of congregations with white Southerners until the Southern country had been "deluged with Northern agents of every hue and stripe, the great mass of whom seemed to regard themselves as heaven-commissioned to fill the minds of the negroes with hatred and animosity toward their former owners." He insisted it "was utterly untrue to say there was any marked bitterness between the whites and blacks of the South, either before or subsequent to the war, save what was called into existence" by these Northern agents. Leighton used Good Will as an example and claimed black members had left Salem because they believed that Northern Presbyterians would give them more financial support than impoverished Southern whites could provide. Blacks would quickly become, Leighton claimed, dependent on this Northern largess and expect the North to continue these favors indefinitely. Providence, Leighton insisted, had appointed the Southern church as the chief agent for the great work of enlightening and improving the condition of the Freedmen. Northern men had nothing but a theoretical knowledge of the African character, while Southern men had been familiar with the race all their lives.[22]

Logan responded in a respectful but forceful manner. The alienation Leighton described between Southern whites and blacks was not the result of Northern inference, he said, but rather flowed from the "grand idea of *liberty*." Liberty and the "assertion of their manhood" had led blacks out of the gallery of Salem and down the road to establish Good Will. The Freedpeople had not been seduced by Northern promises; nor were they relying on Northern charity. Rather, they had left on their own and had made great sacrifices in the effort to build their own church and establish their own school. As for white Southerners knowing blacks better than Northerners, Logan reminded the former missionary to Cape Palmas and Gabon that the church had been sending missionaries with great success beyond their home ground into other regions of the world. Furthermore, he said, Leighton was simply misreading providence. Once the Southern church did have responsibility for the nurture and care of blacks in the church. "But that time has passed, and circumstances have changed; this people have changed also." And then Logan made his most telling point—"while you have been studying them, they have been as busily engaged in studying you." Logan was respectfully but clearly making his point—blacks had been watching white Southerners for a long time. And because of their watching and what they had learned about white assumptions, intentions, and actions, they had gone out from the white-controlled congregations to form their own congregations, to worship in the ways the Spirit moved them, and to call their own leaders and to organize in freedom their own congregational life.[23]

Perhaps nothing revealed Leighton's blindness and deafness—his inability to transcend the world of his Black River home—more than this correspondence with Logan. All around him were black men and women whom he thought he knew, but whom he saw only partially and opaquely. He had grown up with them and had come back to live among them after his years in Africa, yet he failed to hear the depth of their yearning for freedom and their rejection of any white claim to own them body and soul. Perhaps even more fundamentally, Leighton failed to hear their insistence that whites did not own an exclusive claim to a Black River home. This home ground was as much theirs as it was Leighton's. They had worked the land, and their labor had brought forth the land's riches. In all the radical insecurity of slavery, they had lived here, raised their families here, and buried their loved ones here. They, too, heard the deep voices of this landscape with its cotton fields and sandy roads and swirling dark waters. They, too, remembered what life had been like on its plantations and in its settlements, and their memories contested the claim that only "kindly relations" had existed between masters and slaves. So they had the freedom to invite, if they wished, Northern help to establish black churches and schools on their own home ground. The arrival of such help was not some Yankee imperialism intruding on white Southern territory, but Yankee help in response to the invitations of Southerners—black Southerners—to come to the place they called home. But Leighton could acknowledge only one memory of what life had been like at Pine Grove, and he could see as he looked out across the landscape only a white South, a South where blacks were seen not only as laborers, but also as a responsibility and burden for well-meaning white Christians.

FOR LEIGHTON AND his colleagues, as for other white Southerners, the challenge was how to keep the South white and how to suppress any competing memories of old times. Leighton's young colleague John Lafayette Girardeau gave a brilliant articulation of their strategy. Girardeau had followed John Adger in his work among the blacks of Charleston, and it had been Girardeau who had built Charleston's Zion church into a center of African American life in the city, with over 2,000 blacks worshiping weekly at Zion in the years before the war. When the Carolina dead from Gettysburg were brought home after the war to be reinterred in Charleston's Magnolia Cemetery, Girardeau was chosen to address the 6,000 whites who gathered for the occasion.[24]

How were white Southerners to maintain, Girardeau asked, the principles and traditions for which so many had died? How were they to resist an alien culture, the "ruthless, leveling Spirit" and "democratic license" that had arrived with Yankee armies and gunboats? Quoting Stonewall Jackson's dying words, Girardeau declared, "Hold your ground, Sir!" And the way the ground was to be held, the way the white South was to meet the cultural imperialism of the North, was by maintaining the heart of Southern white culture, what Girardeau called "the inalienable, indestructible power of thought and language—the faculty by which we form our opinions, and that by which we

express them." The preservation of a white Southern homeland could be accomplished, he said, by "scrupulously adhering to the phraseology of the
past—for making it the vehicle for transmitting to our posterity ideas which
once true are true forever. . . . We may do it by the education we impart to
the young; by making our nurseries, schools and colleges channels for con-
veying from generation to generation our own type of thought, sentiment
and opinion, by instamping on the minds of our children principles hallowed
by the blood of patriots." Those hallowed principles included states' rights
and freedom from any outside interference as whites sought to maintain a
"Southern way of life." In this way a white Southern identity could be created
for the future through the careful control of its memory and language.[25]

So now it was the white South's turn to try to maintain what it came to
think of as the traditions of the past and the ways of ancestors. White Southerners could define themselves as standing against an invading culture, a modern world of Yankee material power and Yankee ideas that seemed to have
let loose the anarchy of black self-assertion and black freedom to move beyond the place assigned to them by whites. In this struggle, the "phraseology
of the past," a coherent body of shared images and ideas, and the education
imparted to children, could provide both a sense of identity for white Southerners and a guide to the future. The ways in which whites spoke of "the
South," the words they chose to describe "kindly" black and white relations,
and the images they created of happy plantation homes could provide a unity
to the white South not only in *space*, claiming a geographical region, a home
ground, as its own, but also in *time*, linking white memories of the way things
were to how things could be in the future. If the South could keep its language, its symbolic system and way of seeing the world, then its cause would
not be lost.[26]

Because Leighton was to participate in Girardeau's strategy, he was to find
himself in a position not unlike that of his old friend Toko, who had struggled so mightily to maintain the identity and traditions of the Mpongwe
against a modern Western world. But however much Southern whites wanted
to claim a distinctiveness for "the South," it, too, was an inescapable if sometimes reluctant and odd part of that modern Western world. A white Southern identity overlapped in powerful ways with the identity of the
enemy—Yankees, American patriots, modern people. White Southerners
were soon to think of themselves as patriotic Americans—perhaps, they
thought, the most patriotic people in the nation. And, not incidentally, the
white South knew how to use—even in defeat—the power and violence of
the modern world to protect its "phraseology of the past" and to keep blacks

"in their place." Modern organizational skills, modern means of communication, modern propaganda, and modern weapons were turned on blacks. Paramilitary and vigilante groups—most notably the Ku Klux Klan—quickly organized across the South after 1865, drawing recruits from men who had served in the Confederate Army. Using strategies they had learned from the old slave patrols and local militias, white secret societies brutalized and murdered blacks and sometimes their white sympathizers—shooting them, hanging them, cutting them up, and sometimes burning them alive. Disguising themselves in terrifying dress and robes, these secret societies practiced on their victims rituals of degradation, and often emasculation, with the intent of maintaining a "Southern Way of Life." The language of white Southerners—its words, expressions, and phrases—was not ethereal. The "phraseology of the past" did not hang suspended in the air above a Southern landscape, but was a language that emerged from, and then reinforced, violence and brutality.[27]

Distant Voices

W hile white Southerners went about their often bloody work of keeping the South white, crushing as best they could any black independence or self-assertion, Leighton's heart continued to be drawn to what he
regarded as the great work of foreign missions. Many Southern Presbyterians
believed that the church had to focus on building up its Southern Zion as it
struggled to recover from the devastations of war. But Leighton insisted that
if the church was to have any claim to be regarded as a true church of Jesus
Christ, then even in its weakest hour it must engage in foreign mission. Everywhere he traveled around the South—and especially when he visited theological seminaries—he spoke of Jesus's "Great Commission" to "go and
make disciples of all nations." Soon—sooner than anyone had anticipated—
theological students and others began to volunteer for mission, more than
the church could send or maintain. But some could be sent, and were sent,
as a Southern Presbyterian mission movement began to grow, aided especially
by women and their missionary associations in local churches.[1]

The mission among the Choctaw and Chickasaw that had struggled
through the war years began to show promise. Missionaries began to establish
new schools and churches, and Choctaw and Chickasaw pastors and teachers
began to take increasing responsibility for the life of the church among their
people. And with the federal fleet no longer blockading Southern ports, missionaries could once again go abroad. Soon there were growing numbers of
missionaries and teachers in China, missionaries in Mexico and Colombia—
and even in Italy, working in cooperation with Italian Protestants, and in
Greece, working in cooperation with Greek Protestants. But the mission that
captured Leighton's imagination most fully, and that stirred his deepest memories, was the mission to Brazil—a mission that had a direct and bitter link
to Baraka, and to King Glass, King William, and King George.[2]

When Leighton had first arrived in the Gabon estuary and had visited the slave barracoon at King William's Town, he had seen four hundred naked men, women, and children who were being forced "to live like swine" before being shipped to Brazil through the horrors of the Middle Passage. During Leighton's time at Baraka, he had watched ship after ship leave the estuary bound for the slave markets of Brazil. If Leighton did not know exactly how many people had been shipped to Brazil from throughout Central Africa during the nineteenth century, he knew nonetheless that the numbers were massive. In fact, the number of Africans carried to Brazil between the years 1791 and 1856 alone—2,343,000—far exceeded the number carried to the North American mainland from 1619 to 1860—388,000. Unlike the overwhelming majority of African Americans by the time of the Civil War, many of the newly arrived Africans in Brazil had had little contact with Christianity, and for Leighton they presented a great mission field. As the number of Southern missionaries in Brazil began to grow, Leighton decided to see the country for himself and to visit the young mission.[3]

So Leighton sailed on the *South Carolina*, a steamer whose home port was not Charleston but New York. To embark, he had to return to the great city that had once been his home, and from which he had departed in 1861, in order, it was said, "to cast his lot with his own people." In New York he had an opportunity to see the city's amazing growth and to talk once again with his old colleagues in the mission office. They had all once shared much mutual affection, so that even the bitterness of the war had not alienated them from one another. And they had much to discuss. Whatever tensions existed between Northern and Southern Presbyterians at home, they were eager to cooperate in the work of foreign missions that was now expanding rapidly around the globe. Nowhere was their cooperation clearer than in Brazil, where the missionaries of the two churches regarded each other as friends and colleagues.[4]

Leaving New York in late November 1874, the *South Carolina* steamed rapidly south, soon passing St. Thomas and Martinique and other islands of the Caribbean. Leighton was amazed by the ship's speed and by the comforts of his cabin. He remembered his first trip across the Atlantic in 1832, when he had shared a tiny cabin with five others as the little ship rolled and tossed its way across the open ocean for two months. Now, he believed the comfort and speed of the steamers had been "brought about by the providence of God for the advancement of the Redeemer's kingdom."[5]

When they reached the northern coast of Brazil, he spent several weeks in Recife and other cities that had once received slave ship after slave ship.

Leighton visited with missionaries, took careful note of the environment, and thought, as he visited markets and rode streetcars, and went out into villages, that it would be difficult "to find anywhere else in the world a more thorough admixture of races. The European, the Indian, and the Negro are compounded in every conceivable proportion." Sailing south along the coast, he was moved by the beauty of the landscape, and when the ship reached Rio de Janeiro, he thought that nothing he had ever seen could compare to its beauty and grandeur. Sailing south again, this time on a French steamer, he disembarked at Santos, and then he took the train to São Paulo, where there was a thriving Northern Presbyterian school that was already being praised in the Brazilian papers for its high standards and progressive American ways. In a few decades, the "American School" would become MacKenzie Presbyterian University, one of the premier universities in Brazil. From São Paulo, Leighton went by train to Campinas in the heart of coffee country, where Southern Presbyterians had established a congregation and the well-respected International School.[6]

Everywhere Leighton went he was hosted by missionaries, and from them he received his primary impressions of the country and the prospects for Protestant missions. The Catholic Church, he was told, though present everywhere throughout the country and deeply connected with the feast days and folkways of the people, was under increasing attacks from progressive sectors of Brazilian society, especially for what was said to be the corruption of the clergy. So perhaps it was not surprising to Leighton that when he visited Protestant congregations, he found not so much the poor or the enslaved as the "respectable": liberal Brazilians—lawyers, engineers, and doctors and their families—who were reading the Bible for themselves and rejecting what they regarded as the hierarchical assumptions of Catholicism. Whatever Leighton's hopes about the mission reaching the sons and daughters of West Africa—many of whom were still enslaved—the reality he found was a mission that in its early days was attracting people primarily from the more progressive and professional elements of Brazilian society.[7]

After three months in Brazil, Leighton sailed for New York—this time on a large and handsome English steamer. He took with him powerful images of Brazil as a great mission field and a deep commitment to raising up more missionaries for the mission and more money for its support. And he took with him as well an awareness that he could not stay at Old Homestead and conduct the work of foreign missions. However much he loved his Black River home, and however much Jane loved her school, he needed to be located in a major port, a place where great steamers of many nations came, and from which they went forth, carrying goods, people, and news from around the world. So, shortly after his return to Old Homestead, he and Jane began making plans to move to Baltimore, where Benjamin Latrobe was a prominent citizen and now president of the American Colonization Society.[8]

WITH THE MOVE to Baltimore in 1876, Leighton could more easily supply the needs of the Southern Presbyterian missionaries—sending them letters and papers, medicines and food, drafts of money and bills of exchange—and could stay in closer contact with the leaders of other US mission agencies. But Baltimore also provided Leighton and Jane with the opportunity to hear distant voices from far-flung mission fields. Among these voices were voices from Liberia. In regular reports sent to mission boards in the United States, they told of life in the young republic—including Cape Palmas, where so many of Leighton's and Jane's early hopes had been focused and where their memories still lingered over scenes from Fair Hope, Harper, and Big Town.

B. V. R. James had died a few years earlier at his home in Monrovia. Their old friend had not only been an outstanding teacher and leader of the mission in Liberia, but had also been called to fill high stations of trust in the government, and had been greatly respected by all classes of people. His highest honor, said his obituary, "was that of being an exemplary follower of Christ and a devoted laborer in his service."[9]

Margaret and Catherine were still in Monrovia, far from Savannah and the world they had once known. During the years following James's death, they had been watching as growing numbers of immigrants arrived in Liberia. The old dream of an African Motherland was once again stirring the imagination of some African Americans as they faced the violence of the Klan and the collapse of hopes released by emancipation. Liberia now seemed to be a welcoming place for African Americans, beckoning weary blacks who yearned to be free of US racism. They looked to the young Liberian republic for their deliverance, seeing it as a promised land, a land flowing with milk and honey, a land of new opportunities.[10]

A friend and missionary colleague of the James family—the brilliant West Indian Edward Wilmot Blyden—was encouraging this renewed interest in colonization, insisting that African Americans and West Indian blacks were to be the means of civilizing Africans. Leighton, while working at the Presbyterian Foreign Mission Board in New York, had been instrumental in sending Blyden to Liberia as a Presbyterian missionary, and Blyden's younger brother had stayed with Leighton and Jane before going out to Liberia, so the Wilsons had a personal interest in Blyden and his work. In 1876, Blyden was teaching at James's old school and was writing influential essays, which in time would be regarded as foundational for African nationalism and a "Pan-Africanism" envisioning the unity of the continent and its scattered children. Africans and blacks of the African diaspora all shared, Blyden wrote, a distinct African culture that drew them together as an authentic people.[11]

As in the past, many whites were supporting this "Back to Africa" movement. They pointed to a growing body of "scientific evidence" that encouraged the belief that there was no place in the United States for people of African descent. No one was a more fervent cheerleader for these developments than Benjamin Latrobe, the former leader of the Maryland Colonization Society, who had come to regard Leighton in the late 1830s as a troublemaking missionary at Cape Palmas.

The year Leighton and Jane moved to Baltimore, Latrobe was invited by King Leopold of Belgium to a conference in Brussels in preparation for what was touted to be a colonization project in the Congo. Latrobe was unable to attend the conference—and of course he did not know that Leopold would soon begin a brutal exploitation of the Congo—but Latrobe wrote the Belgium ambassador of his own enthusiastic support for the king's project and of his own deep commitment to the colonization of African Americans in Africa. He wrote that, as head of the Maryland Colonization Society, he had superintended vessel after vessel embarking for Cape Palmas believing that "the day would come when two races that will not intermarry must separate, *if both are free*," and he proudly noted that he had worked for colonization, seeing it as a refuge for the "weaker race." He regarded Liberia as an entry point for the continent, and its colonists as the agents for the civilizing mission that the king claimed he envisioned for the Congo. For Latrobe, if a great emigration of the weaker black race took place, "so as to give America a homogenous white population, Liberia will have fulfilled a grand destiny as the noblest missionary enterprise that the world has ever known."[12]

So when Leighton and Jane arrived in Baltimore, they found that the old claims for colonization that they had so vigorously opposed were being strongly advocated in a postemancipation America. Now, colonization was being promoted as a way to remove the very men, women, and children who had been freed by the war. For many whites, North and South, Freedpeople were an alien element on the home ground of whites—the United States of America. Even Lincoln, the Great Emancipator, had entered into secret negotiations with the British—*after* he had issued the Emancipation Proclamation—to secure a place in the Caribbean for the colonization of the

Freedpeople. In this way the new immigrants to Liberia represented not only their own efforts to escape the deep racism of American society by returning to an African Motherland, but also the encouragement and support of that same racism.[13]

For many of the indigenous people of Liberia, however, the colonists did not seem like returning brothers and sisters. For the Mande and the Gola, the Kru and the Grebo, and other indigenous peoples, the colonists were outsiders—outsiders who were advancing a settler intrusion into their home ground. The year before Latrobe wrote his glowing letter to the Belgium ambassador, the Grebo at Cape Palmas and the surrounding countryside had risen in protest of settler expansion and authority. Having acquired Western arms and military strategies, the Grebo had quickly defeated an army of the Liberian republic and had threatened to overrun and destroy Harper. They had found that in order to defend themselves from the power of the Western world represented by the African American colonists, they had to utilize the material resources and military strategies of the West. They showed in other ways as well that Grebo culture was itself in the midst of great changes— changes brought about by their contact with settlers and missionaries from the United States. They had consulted a traditional oracle before the war and had made one of their leaders drink the sassy wood "red water" concoction to prove he had not collaborated with the settlers. Yet, as the Liberian Army had retreated, the Grebo had begun to sing Christian hymns—perhaps some first translated into Grebo and published by Leighton—and had chanted the *Gloria in Excelsis*. Many young Grebo educated by the Episcopal mission had become Christians, and Grebo Christians, such as William Davis, and Wasa and Maria Baker, had established mission outposts in the interior. So even as the Grebo sought to defend themselves from outside intrusions, and even as they continued to remember and practice many of the ways of their ancestors, they were transforming themselves by their engagement with and appropriation of Western ways and Christian faith.[14]

Once again, the arrival of the US Navy with its huge naval guns—a vivid reminder of Western power—was necessary to bring peace between the settlers at Cape Palmas and the Grebo. A US Navy captain came ashore and called the Grebo leaders together and asked them if they wanted peace or war. He showed them the USS *Alaska*, a well-armed sloop-of-war, anchored not far from Russwurm Island—the Grebo's island of the dead. The captain said that there were many more ships with such guns, and that they, too, could come to Cape Palmas. He said that the Grebo had been paid more for their land than the American Indians had been paid for theirs, and that if the Grebo did not acknowledge the right of the settlers to the land, he would proceed to destroy their towns. The Grebo could see the *Alaska*, and they heard the captain's words, and they said they wanted peace. And so they surrendered more land and agreed to come under the authority of the Liberian government. But the war of 1875 would not be the last war between the Grebo and the Americo-Liberians as they struggled over what each considered their own home ground.[15]

LEIGHTON HAD LONG believed that newspapers were critical for the success of the mission movement. So shortly after the end of the Civil War, he established *The Missionary* as a means of encouraging Southern Presbyterians to support missions. In addition to publishing letters and reports from the church's missionaries, he published reports from other missionary agencies in order to provide a picture of Christian expansion to the "far corners of the world." And of all the reports he published, none were more extensive or of more interest to Leighton than the reports from Baraka.[16]

William Walker was still at Baraka when Leighton began publishing *The Missionary* in 1866. Walker's third wife, Kate Hardcastle, had survived the fevers, and the couple had had a happy life together. He had continued his work translating the Bible into Mpongwe and supervising the boys' school, while Kate had taken up Jane's old work of teaching in the girls' school. Walker had made several important exploratory trips—especially an early trip far up the Ogowe River south of the estuary—and he had continued to make notes in his journal and write missionary narratives about the life and practices of the Gabonese people he encountered. Most surprising to Leighton, however, were the published letters of Albert Bushnell. When Bushnell had experienced "the extreme derangement" of his nerves after the French bombardment of Baraka in 1845, Leighton had thought that Bushnell would never survive as a missionary. But thirty years later he was still at work preaching, translating, and teaching.[17]

The reports coming from Baraka told of the continuing consolidation and extension of French control around the estuary and of the arrival of the Fang as they pushed steadily toward the coast from the interior. All the kings whom Leighton had known had died except for King William on the south shore. A strong supporter of the French and their cultural influence, he had nevertheless kept to the traditions of the Mpongwe. When his chief wife died in 1865, he had had two slave women buried alive with her, as one of the women struggled for her own life. Two years later, when the king discovered that a slave had made a fetish against him, he had had the man chained to a log, where driver ants began to devour him. The French admiral who was visiting the king saw the man and, after hearing him confess, ordered that he be shot. Walker, on being told the story by the admiral, had been completely disgusted. Such confessions could not be trusted, he insisted, especially when the translator was the king's son. "There is nothing," Walker wrote, "that so confirms these people in their superstitions and cruelties as the *Solmonic* judgments. The Admiral's bowels of compassion yearned over the poor victim, and he took a short method of relieving him. This is French civilization." As for the cruel treatment of slaves by the Mpongwe, Walker thought, "Slave holding is the same over all the earth."[18]

For years the French had done little to interfere with the domestic slavery of the Mpongwe, but by the 1870s they were trying to end the killing of slaves by masters. In 1875, the French banned capital punishment of slaves, and the Mpongwe system of slavery began to crumble. As Mpongwe men began to lose control over their slaves and former slaves, they began to try to control them through a series of brutal murders. Slave men and women were found beheaded, their bodies split open, their internal organs removed, and their corpses mutilated with what appeared to be the claw marks of leopards. Men, it was said, were turning themselves into leopards, and these leopard men were spreading their terror throughout Mpongwe society, especially among slaves. Although there were disagreements among the French authorities and missionaries about the perpetrators and their purposes, the secret societies of the leopard men and their bloody rituals functioned to intimidate slaves and the newly freed and to support the weakening authority and wealth of Mpongwe men. If Walker knew of the brutal activities of the Klan in the United States, perhaps he would have also written that the struggle of masters to intimidate slaves and former slaves was "the same over all the earth."[19]

The missionaries at Baraka were distressed by the decline of the Mpongwe and their lack of strong leadership. No less than the Mpongwe, the missionaries missed Toko—his humor, friendship, and wisdom. "The successors of Toko have become very small," Walker noted as he looked at Mpongwe leaders in the 1860s. Nevertheless, new leaders were emerging, but none of them were more important to the mission than Toko's son, Ntâkâ Truman. He had repented of the 1857 murder of his slave Awĕmĕ — in fact, when Walker had told him he would be haunted by Awĕmĕ and would meet him before the judgment seat of God, Truman had been badly shaken. Turning to Christ for forgiveness, Truman had confessed that Christ was his only savior from his sins. In 1863, after more than a year of observation by the church at Baraka, he had been baptized.[20]

Truman's conversion—his passage from being a Mpongwe to being a Mpongwe Christian—had been, however, a long time coming. Toko had sent him to the school at Baraka when he was a young boy, and he had spent eleven years there under the tutelage first of Jane and Leighton and then of the other missionaries and teachers. He had followed in his father's footsteps, becoming a trader, but after his conversion he began to study theology and church history with Walker. In 1870 he was ordained as the first Mpongwe Protestant pastor. His wife, Emma, was also a graduate of the school at Baraka, and she, too, was a Christian. They settled at a mission station at the upper end of the estuary, where they worked among the Bakèlè and the Fang. But just as his father, Toko, had had to face the imperialism of the French, Truman had to face a growing paternalism among the missionaries. He was not treated as an equal partner in the mission, and his salary was never the equivalent of what the white missionaries received. He protested vigorously and wrote the Mission Board in the United States. When he didn't receive a prompt reply, he wrote again, saying, "If I was a white man, you would answer my letters." What Truman was experiencing was the weakening in the mission movement of an earlier hope that indigenous people would quickly assume leadership of newly established Christian churches. Some missionaries and mission boards were beginning to view Western imperialism as an asset for the mission movement, believing that a continuing paternalism in mission stations was but a part of the "white man's burden."[21]

Still, Truman persisted in his work, and in 1878, and again in 1883, he spent time in the United States to help with the publication of a Mpongwe Bible. He and Emma spent years among the Fang, whose language they had mastered, as the Fang continued their expansion around the estuary. In this way Toko's son and daughter-in-law struggled against the growing paternalism of the white missionaries. Truman continued to write letters to the Mission Board in New York saying he was not being treated fairly; he insisted that as an ordained minister he had an equal voice with the missionaries in the life of the church, and he refused to follow instructions from white missionaries about what he should wear and how he should spend his salary. In all of this, he helped to lay the foundation for what became the Église évangélique du Gabon.[22]

The children of Josiah and Mary Clealand Dorsey also played an important role in the establishment of the church in Gabon. Josiah, who had been born a slave in Maryland, and who had taught at Cape Palmas and then at various places around the estuary, had died in 1860. He and Mary had had three children. Their son, William Leighton Dorsey, had become a

Roman Catholic and was the first Mpongwe to study for the priesthood. He died in Senegal in 1869 before being ordained. One daughter, Sarah, married the Mpongwe pastor at Baraka, Owondo Lewis, and became affectionately known as Ma Sarah—or Masera—as a teacher in the girls' school and a leader in the church at Baraka. Another daughter, Celia, married an African American from New England—a trader at Glass's Town, now part of Libreville—and together they were also influential members of the Baraka congregation.[23]

A few years after Josiah's death, Mary married—in the church at Baraka— a wealthy Scotsman, a trader in Libreville, and then accompanied him on some of his extensive travels along the West Coast of Africa and to Britain. She had been a bright and beautiful little girl when her Grebo father, William Davis, had brought her to the mission station at Fair Hope, committing her to the care of Jane and Leighton. They had surrounded her with much affection, and she had returned the affection and had followed them to Baraka. There she lived out her remarkable life as a teacher, a Grebo Christian in Gabon who had been loved and nurtured as a child and young woman by a couple from Savannah and Pine Grove.[24]

So the hopes for an indigenous leadership—hopes that had arrived with the early missionaries to Gabon—were not empty hopes, but hopes that began to be slowly fulfilled in spite of the failures, idiosyncrasies, and paternalism of the missionaries who came to Baraka with its waiting cemetery. The missionaries brought with them to the estuary the deep assumptions and dispositions of another world with its seemingly inescapable racism. They made their way up rivers and through rainforests, often traveling at night and enduring the pain of fevers, dysentery, and parasites. Often living among the people for years—the Mpongwe, the Bakèlè, the Shékiani, and the Fang—they tried to understand their ways, even those that they found abhorrent, and they sought to catch glimpses of their worlds even as they were trying to transform those worlds. In these efforts of transformation they were most successful with the young who came to the schools they established. But it was, above all, the missionaries' translations of the Bible that had the most profound effect. These translations broke the missionaries' control of the Christian message and laid the foundations for an indigenous expression of the faith—a Gabonese Protestant Christianity.[25]

LEIGHTON AND JANE remained in Baltimore until the fall of 1884. During these Baltimore years, Leighton was busy with many things, especially traveling and raising funds for foreign missions. He had an able assistant to help with the correspondence and finances, but gradually his strength began to ebb and he felt more and more the burden of his work. Jane, having given up her much-loved school in order to move to Baltimore, was busy hosting visitors and working with women's groups in local congregations. But she was also troubled by recurrent bouts of malaria that seemed to flare up suddenly for no apparent reason. Her sister, Margaret, had died in 1872 during a visit to Old Homestead. She had been buried at Mt. Zion, far from her home in Pennsylvania, next to the plot set aside for Jane and Leighton in the soil of South Carolina. Her death was a deep grief for Jane, who loved her dearly.[26]

Leighton and Jane spent several winters at Old Homestead—they hated the cold of Baltimore—and some summers they spent a few weeks in the Virginia mountains to try and recover their strength. Their adopted daughter Cornelia had married a prominent planter who lived not far from Mt. Zion, and they would see her on their visits home. And they would see as well Alice Johnson, whom they had also adopted, and who was now living with Leighton's sister Sarah near Old Homestead. But old friends and family members were dying. Charles Hodge died in Princeton in 1878. When his son sent Leighton a copy of his *Life of Charles Hodge*, Leighton wrote back that when he had read it he had felt that he "had lived over again" all the pleasant friendship they had once enjoyed.[27] Nicholas Bayard died in 1879 and was buried in Upper Mill Cemetery, McIntosh County, not far from Fair Hope plantation, where Jane, surrounded by McIntosh relatives, had once learned to love the sights and sounds of a Lowcountry home, and where Charlotte Sansay had once been kept busy as Jane's "personal servant," seeing after the needs of an earnest young white woman.[28]

LEIGHTON AND JANE returned to Old Homestead in 1884 to live out their last days together in their Black River home not far from Boggy Gully. Leighton preached regularly at Mt. Sinai Presbyterian Church, where the former black members of Mt. Zion generously welcomed him. And he discovered that the Good Will congregation and school were thriving under the leadership of their pastor, with more than 350 students enrolled in the school. The school had quickly gained a reputation for the discipline it imparted to its students. The teachers insisted that students leave behind their African American dialect and adopt "standard" English. They were to learn through grammatical structure, syntax, and vocabulary new ways of understanding the modern world they were entering as free people. Like the Grebo and other non-Western peoples, they were having to learn the ways and adopt much of the culture of those who were intent on keeping them in their place. If they were to escape their oppression and move toward an improved material well-being, they had to internalize the sources of white power—in particular, literacy, an ascetic self-discipline, and highly developed organizational skills. Yet the Good Will school was also committed to nurturing in its students an African American story, a story of the way things had been in the settlements and at slave sales, a story that challenged and contradicted the story being taught to white children about the way things had been in "the South." And so the students heard the stories of older people and learned their history as it had been experienced by black men and women who had once sat in the evenings around settlement fires to eat and to talk together beneath a Carolina sky.[29]

FRIENDS AND RELATIVES were regular visitors to Old Homestead. Young nieces and nephews especially enjoyed hearing Leighton tell stories about Africa. In the evenings they sat on the piazza—or in the yard, if no breeze was stirring and the air was muggy—while katydids and tree frogs provided the music of the country and sheet lightning occasionally lit the sky. Then Leighton told stories of Fair Hope, where an ocean wind stirred palms on an African cape, and of Baraka and his friend Toko, and of a trip on the *Waterwitch* far up an African river. The stories had been polished by years of telling, the rough edges of memory smoothed in the mind of an old man.[30]

As Leighton looked back over his life, the providence of God became both more real and more mysterious. For years he had confessed, especially in times of perplexity or sorrow, that human history had a purpose and a direction guided by God. But with old age, he seemed to rest more easily in such a confession. Looking back over his own life, he marveled at the deep mystery of what he had experienced and how far it was beyond anything he could have planned or chosen for himself. But it was finally not an idea or a doctrine that he confessed and trusted, but a person. "We are timid and fearful about the approach of death," he wrote his sister Mary, "but simple trust in Jesus Christ as our savior is all the preparation that any of us needs."[31]

As the shadows of his life lengthened and as he saw death approaching, Leighton began to wonder if he had loved his Black River home too much, if he had made an idol of this Southern landscape, this place where morning had first greeted him and where family and friends had first loved him and where the church had first taught him about God's grace and providence. He had long believed—this missionary who had so vigorously opposed African fetishes—that the heart of sin was idolatry. Leighton was convinced that all sin and all the deep alienations of the human heart had their ultimate source in worshiping not the Creator but what was created, in making a god out of that which was not God, in the breaking of the First Commandment of the Holy One of Israel—"Thou shall have no other gods before me." As his life drew toward its close, Leighton came to see that his greatest temptation had been the worshiping, the making of an idol, of that which was good—even a Black River home and landscape. He had every reason to be thankful for those who had loved him as a child and for the particular attachments of a people and the peculiar beauty of a landscape that entwined his heart. Yet he came to see, however partially, that this good, this home ground that had come to him as a gift, had seduced him. This idol had blinded him to the deep oppression and injustice that were bound up with Pine Grove and Mt. Zion and Old Homestead and that seemed an inescapable part of his life. In a moment of feeling broken and wounded, he confessed to a friend that "perhaps God sees that I idolized my country and then my church. Perhaps he means to teach me that I should have no object but him, should trust none but him, have nobody but him to work for, and nothing else to love."[32]

JANE DIED LESS than a year after their return to Old Homestead. Her illness was brief, and Leighton was constantly by her side. She did not blink when she saw death coming toward her, but confessed her faith in Christ and held Leighton's hand as her breathing slowly came to an end. She was buried beside Margaret in the Mt. Zion cemetery.[33]

Leighton knew that he would soon join her in death, and he believed that he would be united in heaven with her, and with all those whom he loved. But he grieved deeply for Jane. Now when he reached for her hand it was not there, and when he turned in bed, her familiar place was empty. His companion, his Jane, was gone. Still, he tried to carry on—writing letters to missionaries and friends and preaching to the black congregation at Mt. Sinai. Their adopted daughter Alice was with him, and Cornelia came as well, and they did all they could to make his last days easy and comfortable. When he was finally confined to his bed, his brother Robert and a male cousin came and cared for him. He lingered for several weeks sleeping or semiconscious. He died in the seventy-eighth year of his life, a year almost to the day after Jane's death.[34]

The funeral was held at Mt. Zion. The congregation was large and flowed out of the sanctuary onto the grounds and beneath the trees Leighton had known as a child. When the service was over, the pallbearers lifted his casket and carried it slowly down the aisle and out into the bright sunlight of a Southern cemetery. They laid him in a grave next to Jane's, earth to earth, his native home, and then they sang with choked voices the missionary hymn:

> *From Greenland's icy mountains,*
> *From India's coral strand;*
> *Where Afric's sunny fountains*
> *Roll down their golden sand:*
> *From many an ancient river,*
> *From many a palmy plain,*
> *They call us to deliver*
> *Their land from error's chain.*[35]

EPILOGUE

Today not far from Mt. Zion and its cemetery, dark waters stir almost imperceptibly in cypress swamps as they gradually form the headwaters of the Black River. Meandering slowly toward the coast, the river gathers the waters of Boggy Gully and other creeks and flows past white sandbars and forests of tupelo, black gum, and water oaks. A few miles from the coast it joins the waters of the Great Pee Dee River before emptying into Winyah Bay and then the Atlantic.

If you went about four miles—as the crow flies—southeast from the point where the river waters enter the bay, you would come to Friendfield plantation, one of the great rice plantations of the Lowcountry, where for generations Gullah people lived and labored and produced great wealth for whites. Still standing on the plantation are six whitewashed slave cabins, remnants of what was once a large slave settlement. In about 1850, in one of the cabins of the settlement, a little boy, Jim Robinson, was born into slavery. After the Civil War he was one of those who decided to stay in the old settlement, and with his wife, Louiser, they raised their family, while he sharecropped and no doubt kept his eye out for the Klan and other vigilante groups. In about 1880, they moved to a place close to the slow-moving waters of the Black River. As the old rice culture began to collapse and as other opportunities beckoned, their children and grandchildren began to move away. In 2008, Jim Robinson's great-great-granddaughter, a Princeton University and Harvard Law School graduate, returned and spoke at the African Methodist Episcopal Church, where her ancestors had once worshiped. Her name was Michelle Obama, and she was campaigning for her husband, Barack Obama, who would shortly be elected president of the United States. "Things get better when regular folks take action to make change happen from the bottom up," she said. "Every major historical moment in our time, it has been made by folks who said, 'Enough,' and they banded together to move this country forward—and now is one of those times."[1]

If the forty-fourth First Lady of the United States represents startling changes in the nation's life, even more startling changes of global significance can be seen in a nearby white congregation in the resort and retirement community of Pawley Island, where slave owners had once spent the summer away from the miasmas of their rice plantations. All Saints Anglican Church is a congregation of largely affluent whites who have withdrawn from the Episcopal Church and have placed themselves under the ecclesiastical and spiritual authority of the Anglican Province of Rwanda in Central Africa. The African archbishop, Emmanuel Kolini, had launched in 2000 a "Mission in the Americas" as a missionary outreach of the Anglican Church of Rwanda. The mission was designed to reach the "130 million people" in the United States who do not "presently know Jesus Christ." South Carolina Episcopalians at All Saints wanted to be under what they considered a more conservative and orthodox church leadership—especially in regard to the ordination of women and gay and lesbian persons. Whatever irony may be seen in Lowcountry whites seceding and placing themselves under the authority of Africans, it was clear that some African Christians had identified the United States as a great mission field.[2]

The growth of Christianity in Africa throughout the twentieth century—with the continent's terrible wars, natural disasters, and pandemics—had been nothing less than phenomenal, with the number of Christian Africans increasing from fewer than 9 million in 1910 to more than 516 million in 2010. A multiyear study by the Pew Foundation released in December 2011 found that the number of Christians in sub-Saharan Africa had grown exponentially, from 9 percent of the population in 1910 to 63 percent in 2010. "If that is not, quantitatively, the largest religious change in human history in such a short period," wrote the distinguished historian Philip Jenkins, "I am at a loss to think of a rival." While missionaries such as Leighton and Jane, B. V. R. James, and William Walker helped to lay the foundation for this great transformation—especially through schools, translations, presses, and, later, hospitals—the growth of Christianity in Africa had been primarily through the preaching and teaching of African Christians themselves. And the first of the great African itinerant preachers was a Grebo—William Wadé Harris.[3]

Harris was born at Graway, at the eastern end of Lake Shepard, where in 1836 Leighton had established a school at the request of King Yellow Will. The young African American John Banks had been the teacher of the school until it was turned over to the Episcopal mission. As a young boy, Harris had gone to live and study with an uncle, a Methodist minister at Sinoe between Cape Palmas and Monrovia. The uncle had apparently been educated at the local Presbyterian mission school, for he bore the name of Leighton's old colleague in New York, John C. Lowrie.

A year before Leighton died, Harris joined the Episcopal Church at Graway, and he soon became a teacher and catechist for its mission. He began to be influenced, however, by the writing of Edward Blyden, who had followed B. V. R. James as a teacher in Monrovia, and by the apocalypticism of the new movement of Jehovah's Witnesses. In 1910, when the Grebo once again went to war against the Americo-Liberians, Harris had been deeply sympathetic to the Grebo and had been arrested and imprisoned. There he had a powerful religious experience—the angel Gabriel, he said, had visited him and had anointed him a prophet, a Black Elijah. Released from jail, Harris put on a white robe and turban and took up a staff in the shape of a cross. Living simply, he began walking and preaching and drawing great crowds. He denounced witchcraft and the fetishes of the people, and he began baptizing great numbers of people. When he went to the Ivory Coast, multitudes were converted; more than 100,000 people were said to have destroyed their fetishes, and in Ghana many followed suit. Although Harris preached against many traditional beliefs and practices, he was himself an exorcist and faith healer, and he accepted polygamy as compatible with Christian faith and life. Many of his converts joined Methodist and Catholic churches, but many others began to form their own indigenous Christian communities. In this way he helped to lay the foundation for the rapid growth of independent African churches, which brought together Christian and traditional African practices, and which helped to fuel the astonishing growth of Christianity in Africa during the twentieth century.[4]

WHEN LEIGHTON was commissioned as a missionary for the American Board in 1834, Rufus Anderson stressed that the objective for the mission was to raise up African leaders for an African church. Such a church would be self-supporting, self-governing, and self-propagating. And Leighton had later written, after reflecting on the diverse peoples and cultures of Africa, that a mysterious providence seemed to be guiding a people who had experienced so much suffering toward "some important future destiny." Anderson caught a glimpse of the great transformations that were to come to Africa in the twentieth century. Leighton could not have imagined, however, that African church leaders would one day regard his own beloved Lowcountry—and, in particular, affluent whites in the Lowcountry—as a part of a great mission field, and that the demographic center of Christianity would shift from Europe and North America to the "Global South"—to Africa and South America, to the Pacific Rim, and even to China, which seemed poised in 2013 to become, in a few decades, the nation with the largest Christian population in the world. Perhaps Leighton would have wondered if these new Christians were being called, in the words of the old missionary hymn, to deliver his beloved homeland and his long-reunited country "from error's chain."[5]

ACKNOWLEDGMENTS

By the Rivers of Water was long in the making and thanks are owed to many people and several foundations who helped along the way. In 2005 a sabbatical spent as a Visiting Fellow at Clare Hall, Cambridge, provided not only rich library resources on West Africa but also opportunities to be in conversation with Visiting Fellows in a variety of disciplines. Among those who discussed in helpful ways my work on the Wilsons were Judith and David Kohn, Robert Ackerman, Daksh Lohiya, Alisa and Howie Shvrin, and Jim and Peg Utterbeck. Liz Ramsden and Ann and Nichol Thompson were generous in the hospitality shown to my wife Nancy and me during our time in Cambridge.

Ron Hoffman of the Omohundro Institute of Early American History and Culture, College of William and Mary, made possible my participation in the 2007 conference at Elmina, Ghana, on the first governmental efforts to abolish the Atlantic slave trade. The conference allowed me to hear many voices speaking on the slave trade—especially the voices of African scholars—and introduced me to the social and physical landscape of Elmina and Cape Coast. I was able to discuss my research project over meals with US scholars Ira Berlin, Philip Morgan, David Blight, Daina Berry, Lonnie Bunch, and Oliver Patterson. Beatriz Mamigonian from Brazil, Walter Gam from Cameroun, Zagba Oyortey of the British Museum, and Akeem Akinwale from Nigeria were all very helpful in providing interpretations and observations related to my study. Walking through the slave castles at Cape Coast and Elmina—both places visited by Leighton Wilson—was important and deeply moving, as were visits to markets and fishing villages.

The Lilly Foundation, through a grant administered by the Association of Theological Schools, provided an opportunity for me to spend time in Gabon. Ted Maris-Wolf of the Omohundro Institute gave good advice and made helpful contacts for my visit to Gabon. In Libreville, Kathleen Dahir of the Université Omar Bongo graciously organized my visit and made many contacts for me. Thierry Alan Frejus was translator, guide, and storyteller for me. Mary Cloutier, unofficial historian of the early Protestant missionaries in Gabon, was my chauffeur and source of much information about the Baraka mission. She was, and continues to be, an indispensable interpreter of early mission history in Gabon. Professor Atoz Ratanga, Department of History, and Professor Bridget Bikah, Department of Psychology, at the Université Omar Bongo, kindly spent time with me discussing the history and culture of the Mpongwe. Dr. Emile Mbot, anthropologist, and former Director, Ministry of Culture, invited me to spend a day with him at his beautiful plantation outside Libreville. He discussed with me traditions of the Mpongwe and issues of interpretation. Dr. Fuka Bananga Jomain and Dr. Wayne Fricke of the Bongolo Evangelical Hospital, Bongolo, reviewed diseases and health problems that have traditionally afflicted the people of Gabon. Madame Pauline Nabang spoke with me about the history of the Baraka congregation and about the present life of the Protestant church in Gabon. When I found myself in need of a room in Libreville, Cheryl and Arnie Solvig welcomed me to the Guest House of the Christian and Missionary Alliance. Steve Straw, a pilot with Aviation Médicale de Bongolo, went out of his way—after I had left Gabon—to secure pictures for me.

The Griffith Foundation provided a grant that greatly assisted my research in Atlanta and Savannah. Joe Evans, Buz Wilcoxon, Katelyn Gordon, Nancy Yao, Adam Copeland, and Andrew Whaley copied from microfilm several thousand letters, personal papers, and newspapers. Sara Myers, Richard Blake, Griselda Lartey, Erica Durham, Mary Martha Rivere, Chris Paton, and Jeff Vaughn of the John Bulow Campbell Library, Columbia Theological Seminary, all provided help in securing books, papers, and photographs. President Laura Mendenhall and Dean Cameron Murchison of Columbia gave much encouragement during the early stages of my research.

In Savannah, the staff of the Georgia Historical Society was always helpful as I explored the society's rich collection of materials on the Georgia Lowcountry. I am especially grateful to Stan Deaton and Christy Crisp, whom I now regard as friends. I spent much time while in Savannah observing the character of the Savannah River and visiting Hutchinson Island, where the Bayard slave settlement had been located. Paul Pressly, director of the Ossabaw Island Education Alliance, invited me to participate in its 2008 symposium on "African American Life in the Georgia Lowcountry: The Atlantic World and the Gullah Geechee." This wonderful gathering allowed me to be in conversations about the Lowcountry with Phil Morgan, Betty Wood, and Allison Dorsey. Paul Pressly also invited me to join in a consultation,

2009–2010, with the Ossabaw Island Foundation about the people who had once lived and worked on Ossabaw as slaves and then as freed people. The consultation meetings, held on the island, involved not only vigorous discussions about African American life in the Lowcountry, but also the experience of moving around an island landscape. All of the consultants brought insights from their various disciplines, but particularly important for my work were the contributions by Nichole Greene, curator of the Old Slave Mart Museum in Charleston; George McDaniel, director of Drayton Hall Plantation, Charleston; and Emory Campbell, chair of the Gullah-Geechee Commission with the National Park Service. I spent several days at Hog Hammock, Sapelo Island, in conversation with Cornelia Bailey discussing African American life in the Lowcountry and listening to traditional island stories. Buddy Sullivan of the University of Georgia's Research Center on Sapelo provided much information about the history and environment of the area around Darien. He was particularly helpful in regard to both Fair Hope Plantation where Jane Bayard Wilson spent much time and General's Island where Paul Sansay and other Bayard slaves once lived.

I spent time on the inland waterways of the Lowcountry with Townsend Warren, Joe Dobbs, and Danny Bacot, who readily shared their knowledge of tides, marshes, and saltwater creeks. Joe Dobbs and Paul Pressly described for me their experience of the Savannah River with its changing moods. Some years earlier I spent time on Lowcountry rivers with the crabber Buddy Smith, whose knowledge of old rice fields and of all the living creatures that swim in Lowcountry waters or fly above them or walk beside them left me astonished. For almost fifty years I have floated, from time to time, Lowcountry rivers in canoes or bateaus or kayaks with various friends. During these float trips I have tried to be a good observer of the world of cypress-stained rivers and swamps.

In South Carolina, Archie and Anna Chandler provided wonderful hospitality and opened the archives of the Mt. Zion Presbyterian Church for me. They took me for my first visit to the site of Leighton Wilson's home, pointed out where they remembered the remains of the slave settlement by Boggy Gully, and drove me to various old home places along the Black River. Robert and Jerry Law invited Nancy and me to dinner in their beautiful antebellum home in Bishopville, SC, talked with us about the history of the Mt. Zion church, and provided me with a map showing the locations of plantation homes along the Black River. Sally Wilson, Bill Holmes, and Dick Dabbs of the Salem Black River Presbyterian Church welcomed me and talked with me about the history of the congregation. The Reverend Ella

Busby and the Reverend Frank Colcough gathered a group of older members of the Good Will Presbyterian Church who had attended the Good Will School, Sumter County, South Carolina. They spoke of African American memories of the Black River region and about their experiences as students during the 1920s and 1930s at the Good Will school. Particularly memorable were their stories of school life with its discipline and high standards, and of old-time root doctors who knew how to heal a cut or cure a stomachache, and of ghosts and hags who were said to linger about swamps and dark corners. Mary Crockett of the South Carolina Department of Natural Resources canoed the Black River with me and my colleague Lee Carroll and talked about the river's natural and social history.

Mary Jo Fairchild of the South Carolina Historical Society, Steve Engerrand of the Georgia Archives, Iris Bierlein and Damon Talbot of the Maryland Historical Society, Ron Vinson of the Presbyterian Heritage Center, and Harry Miller of the Wisconsin Historical Society all went out of their way to provide me with needed materials.

John Ellington, a linguist who spent years translating portions of the Bible into various Bantu languages, discussed with me the challenges of translation. Justo Gonzalez and Carlos Cardoza-Orlandi, historians of Christian missions, asked hard questions about the Wilsons and their colleagues and encouraged me in my efforts to understand early Protestant missions in West Africa.

I have been privileged to work directly with several people at Basic Books. Katy O'Donnell was both cheerful and ready to offer help along the way, as was Alex Littlefield. Rachel King organized a production schedule that took into account my schedule. Kathy Streckfus was careful with many details as copyeditor and saved me from much embarrassment.

I am deeply grateful to Lara Heimert, publisher at Basic Books. She enthusiastically received the proposal for this book and she took upon herself in 2012 the demanding task of line editing the manuscript. No one has done more to encourage me in my work as a historian than Lara Heimert—first when she was at Yale University Press and now at Basic Books. I can only say that I am deeply indebted to her and that I have learned much from her.

Because this book was eight years in the making, my family has had to persevere as I have disappeared most mornings into the nineteenth century. This perseverance has been especially true of my wife Nancy. While going about her own busy life—so full of generosity, love, and vitality—she has been a genuine partner in the writing of this book.

The book is dedicated to my sister and brother-in-law: Judy and Will

Hair. Over many years they have welcomed Nancy and me, our children, and now our grandchildren, into their home and lives. They have been as a couple models of faithfulness to one another, and they, together with their children and grandchildren, have taught us much about the amazing gift of a life lived together in joy and gratitude.

NOTES

The following abbreviations have been used in the notes.

Individuals and Institutions

BVRJ	Benjamin Van Rensselaer James
JB	Jane Bayard until marriage
JBR	John Browne Russwurm
JBW	Jane Bayard Wilson
JH	Dr. John Hall
JHBL	John Hazlehurst Boneval Latrobe
JLW	John Leighton Wilson
MEW	Martha Elmira Wilson
MMW	Mary Margaret Wilson
RA	Rufus Anderson
SEW	Samuel Ervin Wilson
SSW	Sarah Susanna Wilson
WW	William Walker
WTW	William Thomas Wilson

Document Sources

ABCFM	American Board of Commissioners for Foreign Missions papers, Houghton Library, Harvard University, microfilm copies at Columbia Theological Seminary, Decatur, Georgia
CCR	Chatham County Records, Savannah, Georgia
CO	*Charleston Observer*
CTS	John Leighton Wilson Papers, Columbia Theological Seminary, Decatur, Georgia
GHS	Georgia Historical Society, Savannah
GLD	Georgia Legislative Documents, Georgia State Archives, Atlanta
MGAPCUS	*Minutes of the General Assembly of the Presbyterian Church of the United States*
MSCS	Maryland State Colonization Papers, Maryland Historical Society, microfilm copies at Columbia Theological Seminary, Decatur, Georgia
MZPC	Archives of Mt. Zion Presbyterian Church, St. Charles, South Carolina
PCCC	Probate Court, Chatham County, Georgia
PCSC	Probate Court, Sumter County, South Carolina
PHS	Records of the Board of Foreign Missions, Presbyterian Church in the United States of America, Presbyterian Historical Society, Philadelphia
SCCC	Office of the Clerk of Superior Court, Chatham County, Georgia
SCHS	South Carolina Historical Society, Charleston
SCL	South Caroliniana Library, University of South Carolina, Columbia
SCSC	Office of the Clerk of Superior Court, Sumter County, South Carolina
WHS	Wisconsin Historical Society, Madison
WWD	William Walker Diary, Wisconsin Historical Society, Madison

Chapter One: A Slave's World

1. For Paul and the slave settlement on Hutchinson Island, see Estate of N. S. Bayard in account with N. J. Bayard, Administrator, 1822–1838, SCCC.

2. For the history of Savannah, see Walter J. Fraser, Jr., *Savannah in the Old South* (Athens, GA, 2003); Betty Wood, *Women's Work, Men's Work: The Informal Slave Economies of Lowcountry Georgia* (Athens, GA, 1995), 78–163; Whittington B. Johnson, *Black Savannah, 1788–1864* (Fayetteville, AR, 1996); and especially, for the Civil War era, Jacqueline Jones, *Saving Savannah: The City and the Civil War* (New York, 2008).

3. For Paul as a carpenter, see Estate of N. S. Bayard, 16 January 1830, 6 April 1831, SCCC. For the Savannah River, see Francis Harper, ed., *The Travels of William Bartram: Naturalist Edition* (Athens, GA, 1998), 19–22; J. T. Henderson, *The Commonwealth of Georgia: The Country; the People; the Productions* (Atlanta, 1885), 174–177; Thomas L. Stokes, *The Savannah* (New York, 1951); Wood, *Women's Work, Men's Work*, 77–79.

4. For Charles as Paul's father, see Inventory of Slaves, Estate of N. S. Bayard, 1822, PCCC. For Charles as porter, see Estate of N. S. Bayard, 18 January 1826, 15 January 1827, SCCC.

5. For slave ships arriving in Savannah and for the *Mary*, see Voyages Database, 2009, Voyages: The Trans-Atlantic Slave Trade Database, www.slavevoyages.org (accessed 1 September 2010). Although the Georgia legislature outlawed slave imports in 1798, the law was largely ignored, as the *Mary's* arrival made clear. More than 9,000 slaves were landed in Georgia, almost all in Savannah, during the first few years of the new century. See James A. McMillin, *The Final Victims: Foreign Slave Trade to North America, 1783–1810* (Columbia, SC, 2004), 48.

6. For the *Flora*, see Voyages Database. For the transatlantic "Middle Passage," see Colin A. Palmer, "The Middle Passage," in *Captive Passage: The Transatlantic Slave Trade and the Making of the Americas*, Smithsonian Institution (Washington, DC, 2002), 53–75.

7. For the congressional action ending the legal importation of slaves into the United States, see Hugh Thomas, *The Slave Trade* (New York, 1997), 499–502. There is a rapidly growing literature on the international slave trade. For an overview, see David Eltis, "A Brief Overview of the Trans-Atlantic Slave Trade," Voyages Database. For the US transatlantic slave trade and the numbers illegally arriving in the United States after 1808, see David Eltis, "The U.S. Transatlantic Slave Trade, 1644–1867: An Assessment," *Civil War History* 54 (2008): 347–380.

8. For Charlotte as Paul's sister, see Inventory of Slaves, Estate of N. S. Bayard, 1822, PCCC. For Charlotte as a domestic, see Estate of N. S. Bayard, 2 January 1837, SCCC; Emigrant Roll, Schooner *Columbia*, 15 May 1838, MSCS. For Charlotte as JB's personal servant, see JLW to JB, 21 June 1833, 11 July 1833, CTS. For the role of domestic slaves as conveyors of information to slave communities, see Eugene D. Genovese, *Roll, Jordan, Roll: The World the Slaves Made* (New York, 1974), 328–365.

9. For quotations and the Scots' antislavery petition, see Harvey H. Jackson, "The Darien Antislavery Petition of 1739 and the Georgia Plan," *William and Mary Quarterly* 34, no. 4 (1977): 618–631. For McIntosh, see Harvey H. Jackson, *Lachlan McIntosh and the Politics of Revolutionary Georgia* (Athens, GA, 2003 [1979]), esp. 6–9. For the opening of the transatlantic slave trade to Georgia, see Betty Wood, *Slavery in Colonial Georgia, 1730–1775* (Athens, GA, 1984), 98–104.

10. Lachlan McIntosh, Account Book, 1799–1812, GHS; Lachlan McIntosh, Letters and Papers, GHS; Lachlan McIntosh, Memorandum Book, GHS; Inventory of Slaves, Estate of N. S. Bayard, 1822, PCCC. For McIntosh land, see Buddy Sullivan, *Early Days on the Georgia Tidewater: The Story of McIntosh County and Sapelo* (Darien, GA, 2001), 760. For McIntosh County lands, see also Estate of N. S. Bayard, 11 November 1823, 10 November 1825, 24 January 1831, SCCC, and 28 March 1823, *Savannah Republican Gazette*. For Cumberland Island, see Estate of N. S. Bayard, 21 March 1822, SCCC. For Lottery Hall Plantation on the Ogeechee River, see Estate of N. S. Bayard, 18 June 1816, SCCC.

11. For marriage contracts and the role of husbands in regard to a wife's property, see Brenda E. Stevenson, *Life in Black and White: Family and Community in the Slave South* (Oxford, 1996), 79–81. For examples of slave divisions at the marriage of a slave owner's daughter, see Erskine Clarke, *Dwelling Place: A Plantation Epic* (New Haven, CT, 2005), 100, 378–382.

12. For obituary of the girls' father, Nicholas Serle Bayard, see *Savannah Republican Gazette*, 30 October 1821.

13. For Paul receiving carpenter's tools, see Estate of N. S. Bayard, 16 January 1830, SCCC. For slave carpenters, see Ira Berlin, *Many Thousands Gone:*

The First Two Centuries of Slavery in North America (Cambridge, MA, 1998), 84–85, 168; Philip Morgan, *Slave Counterpoint: Black Culture in the Eighteenth-Century Chesapeake and Lowcountry* (Chapel Hill, NC, 1998), 214–218, 227–228, 349; Wood, *Women's Work, Men's Work*, 47, 105.

14. For slaves moving freely around the city, see Johnson, *Black Savannah*, 55–83; Wood, *Women's Work, Men's Work*, 80–95; Jones, *Saving Savannah*, 87–88. For slaves hiring themselves out, see Morgan, *Slave Counterpoint*, 352–353; Johnson, *Black Savannah*, 100–121; Fraser, *Savannah in the Old South*, 94–96, 144, 286–287. For slave housing, see Richard C. Wade, *Slavery in the Cities: The South, 1820–1860* (Oxford, 1964), 58–62; Wood, *Women's Work, Men's Work*, 129–131. For the punishment and jailing of Bayard slaves, see Estate of N. S. Bayard, 3 April 1823, 16 March 1824, 12 June 1826. For slave jails and punishments in Savannah, see Johnson, *Black Savannah*, 50–53; Wood, *Women's Work, Men's Work*, 113, 117–118; Fraser, *Savannah in the Old South*, 203–205.

15. For free blacks in Savannah, see Index of Free People of Color, Chatham County, 1817–1839, GHS; Wade, *Slavery in the Cities*, 249–252; Johnson, *Black Savannah*, 85–132, 185; Jones, *Saving Savannah*, 47–49.

16. For a Bayard runaway, see Estate of N. S. Bayard, 3 March 1823. For examples of runaways in Savannah, see *Savannah Republican*, 18 July 1816, 3 January 1820, and Clarke, *Dwelling Place*, 347–348. On runaways generally, see John Hope Franklin and Loren Schweninger, *Runaway Slaves: Rebels on the Plantation* (New York, 1999); John W. Blassingame, *The Slave Community: Plantation Life in the Antebellum South* (New York, 1972), 104–131.

17. Quotations: Charles Lyell, *A Second Visit to North America*, vol. 2 (London, 1849), 3; James M. Simms, *The First Colored Baptist Church in North America* (Philadelphia, 1888), 247. For Andrew Marshall and First African Baptist Church, see Emmanuel King Love, *History of the First African Baptist Church, from Its Organization, January 20th 1788, to July 1, 1888* (Savannah, 1888), 7–34; Simms, *The First Colored Baptist Church*, 76–106; Whittington B. Johnson, "Andrew C. Marshall: A Black Religious Leader of Antebellum Savannah," *Georgia Historical Quarterly* 69 (1985); Johnson, *Black Savannah*, 11. For Protestant Christianity and slave religion as found at First African, see Albert J. Raboteau, *Slave Religion: The "Invisible Institution" in the Antebellum South* (Oxford, 1978), 189–193; Vincent L. Wimbush, "The Bible and African Americans: An Outline of an Interpretative History," in *Stony the Road We Trod: African American Biblical Interpretation*, ed. Cain Hope Felder (Minneapolis, 1991), 81–97; Sylvia R. Frey and Betty Wood, *Come Shouting to Zion: African American Protestantism in the American South and British Caribbean to 1830* (Chapel Hill, NC, 1998), 80–148; Janet Duitsman Cornelius, *Slave Missions and the Black Church in the Antebellum South* (Columbia, SC, 1999), 103–123.

18. For the ways in which social spaces influence dispositions while individual agency is maintained, see the work of Pierre Bourdieu, especially *In Other Words: Essays Towards a Reflexive Sociology*, M. Adamson, trans. (Cambridge, UK, 1994).

19. For General's Island, see Sullivan, *Early Days on the Georgia Tidewater*, 760.

20. Estate of N. S. Bayard, 15 February 1825, 10 November 1825, 3 January 1826.

21. For the passage down the coast to Darien and for the character of the landscape, see Charles Lyell, *A Second Visit to North America*, vol. 1 (London, 1849), 307–351. For intercoastal water schooners and their coastal trade, see William C. Fleetwood, *Tidecraft: The Boats of South Carolina, Georgia and Northeastern Florida, 1750–1950* (Camden, SC, 1995).

22. Quotation: Fanny Kemble Wister, *Fanny: The American Kemble* (Tallahassee, FL, 1972), 164. For map and description of General's Island, see Malcolm Bell, Jr., *Major Butler's Legacy: Five Generations of a Slaveholding Family* (Athens, GA, 1987), 117–120. For the general environment, both physical and social, see William Dusinberre, *Them Dark Days: Slavery in the American Rice Swamps* (Athens, GA, 2000).

23. The most comprehensive treatment of the black culture of the South Carolina and Georgia Lowcountry is Morgan, *Slave Counterpoint*. See also Philip Morgan, ed., *African American Life in the Georgia Lowcountry: The Atlantic World and the Gullah Geechee* (Athens, GA, 2010); Margaret Creel, *"A Peculiar People": Slave Religion and Community-Culture Among the Gullahs* (New York, 1988); William S. Pollitzeer, *The Gullah People and Their African Heritage* (Athens, GA, 1999); and Dusinberre, *Them Dark Days*. For the population of McIntosh County, see Sullivan, *Early Days on the Georgia Tidewater*, 782.

24. For the survival of the mentioned African words and phrases and for the development of Gullah language and its role as a bearer of culture, see Morgan, *Slave Counterpoint*, 560–580. See also Sidney W. Mintz and Richard Price, *An Anthropological Approach to the Afro-American Past: A Caribbean Perspective* (Boston, 1992), 20–22; Michael Montgomery, *Essays in the Development of Gullah Language and Culture* (Athens, GA, 1994); Frederic G. Cassidy, "The Place of Gullah," *American Speech* 55 (1980): 3–16;

Lorenzo Dow Turner, *Africanisms in the Gullah Dialect* (Chicago, 1949). I have used "Gullah" for the African Americans of the Lowcountry of both South Carolina and Georgia, rather than the term "Gullah-Geechee," which is often used today. The name "Geechee," from the Ogeechee River, refers to African Americans from the Georgia Lowcountry. Since "Gullah" was used in the nineteenth century and most of the twentieth by both blacks and whites to refer to Lowcountry African Americans in both states, I have simply avoided an anachronism by using "Gullah" rather than "Gullah-Geechee." For an example of the use of "Gullah"—or "Golla"—by blacks in the Georgia Lowcountry to refer to themselves, see Georgia Writers Project, Savannah Unit, Works Projects Administration, [Mary Granger], *Drums and Shadows: Survival Studies Among the Georgia Coastal Negroes* (Savannah, GA, 1940), 113.

25. Quotation: Georgia Writers Project, *Drums and Shadows*, 187. For Atlantic Creole, see Berlin, *Many Thousands Gone*, 25–27. For recognition of the similarities between the language of the Gullah and the Pidgin English spoken in a Creole world of West Africa, see JLW to JB, 28 January 1834, CTS; Georgia Writers Project, *Drums and Shadows*, 123, 127.

26. Quotations: Charles C. Jones, Jr., *Negro Myths from the Georgia Coast, Told in the Vernacular* (1888; reprint, Columbia, SC, 1925), 50, 37; Georgia Writers Project, *Drums and Shadows*, 176. For boatmen's songs, see Charles Lyell, *A Second Visit to North America*, vol. 1, 244–245; vol. 2, 1–2; Dena J. Epstein, *Sinful Tunes and Spirituals: Black Folk Music to the Civil War* (Urbana, IL, 1977), 166–172; Morgan, *Slave Counterpoint*, 591–594. For the purchase of supplies, see Estate of N. S. Bayard, 10 November 1825. For Anansi stories in the wider Atlantic world, see Philip Sherlock and Hazel Bennett, *The Story of the Jamaican People* (Kingston, 1998), 197. For Buh Rabbit and other Gullah stories, see Jones, *Negro Myths*.

27. Quotation: Charles C. Jones, *Thirteenth Annual Report of the Association for the Religious Instruction of the Negroes, in Liberty County, Georgia* (Savannah, GA, 1848), 22. For Gullah dances, see Georgia Writers Project, *Drums and Shadows*, 133, 161. For the cultural significance of slave dancing, see Morgan, *Slave Counterpoint*, 581–588, 592–593. Cf. the indigenization of dance forms in the Caribbean, drawing from African and European sources to create a distinct Caribbean dance. See Rex M. Nettleford, *Caribbean Cultural Identity, The Case of Jamaica: An Essay in Cultural Dynamics* (Kingston, 1979), 27–30.

28. Quotation: Bell, *Major Butler's Legacy*, 151–152.

29. Georgia Writers Project, *Drums and Shadows*, 176. For the development of the banjo, See Dena J. Polachek Epstein, "The Folk Banjo: A Documentary History," *Enthnomusicology* 19, no. 3 (1975): 347–371; Morgan, *Slave Counterpoint*, 585.

30. For the reach of the drums' sound out to the sea islands and back, see Georgia Writers Project, *Drums and Shadows*, 118.

31. Quotation: ibid., 160; cf. ibid., 122, 140. For slave use of drums, see Morgan, *Slave Counterpoint*, 582–587.

32. Quotations: Georgia Writers Project, *Drums and Shadows*, 146, 131. For slave funerals, see Raboteau, *Slave Religion*, 71–72, 83–85; Frey and Wood, *Come Shouting to Zion*, 51–54; David Hurst Thomas, et al., "Rich Man, Poor Men: Observations on Three Antebellum Burials from the Georgia Coast," American Museum of Natural History, *Anthropological Papers* 54 (1977): 393–402.

33. Quotation: Georgia Writers Project, *Drums and Shadows*, 142. See also pp. 147, 183.

34. For witches among whites, see Diane Purkiss, *The Witch in History: Early Modern and Twentieth-Century Representations* (New York, 1996). For the continuing white experience of hags in the Lowcountry, see Chapter 3, note 9. For leopard men, see Chapter 24, note 19. For Gullah witches, see Georgia Writers Project, *Drums and Shadows*, 124, 179, 139.

35. Quotation: Georgia Writers Project, *Drums and Shadows*, 143. For other examples of Gullah charms, see ibid., 132, 155. Cf. "Journal of a Missionary to the Negroes in the State of Georgia," *Charleston Observer*, 21 September 1833. See also Theophus H. Smith, *Conjuring Culture: Biblical Formations of Black America* (New York, 1994), 140–158; Michael Mullin, *Africa in America: Slave Acculturation and Resistance in the American South and the British Caribbean, 1736–1831* (Urbana, IL, 1992), 68–92; John Thornton, "On the Trail of Voodoo: African Christianity in Africa and the Americas," *The Americas* 44 (1988): 261–278.

36. A massive anthropological literature seeks to understand or explain witchcraft, conjurers, and magic. A good entry point into the literature is Brian Morris, *Religion and Anthropology: A Critical Introduction* (Cambridge, UK, 2006). For the story of a slave conjurer in the Georgia Lowcountry, see Erskine Clarke, "They Shun the Scrutiny of White Men: Reports on Religion from the Georgia Lowcountry and West Africa," in *African American Life in the Georgia Lowcountry: The Atlantic World and the Gullah Geechee*, ed. Philip Morgan (Athens, GA, 2010),

131–150. For Dr. Joseph Habersham's visits to the Hutchinson Island settlement, see, for example, Estate of N. S. Bayard, 1 January 1825. The Bayard estate records contain no expenses for medical treatment for those on General's Island. For root doctors and healing, see S. B. Abbott, *The Southern Botanic Physician* (Charleston, SC, 1844); Julia F. Morton, *Folk Remedies of the Low Country* (Miami, FL, 1974); Georgia Writers Project, *Drums and Shadows*, 147–148; Morgan, *Slave Counterpoint*, 624–629.

37. See James C. Scott, *Domination and the Art of Resistance: Hidden Transcripts* (New Haven, CT, 1990), 142–143, and for slave use of poisons in the Lowcountry, see Morgan, *Slave Counterpoint*, 614–618.

38. Estate of N. S. Bayard, 21 February 1827.

39. "Indenture Between the City of Savannah and Nicholas S. Bayard, Doctor," 6 November 1819, CCR; *Georgian* (Savannah), 3 June 1822. For the death of Esther Bayard with note on death of her husband, Nicholas S. Bayard, see *Georgian* (Savannah), 6 June 1822. For the history of malaria in the Lowcountry, see Randall M. Packard, *The Making of a Tropical Disease: A Short History of Malaria* (Baltimore, 2007), 55–61; Peter H. Wood, *Black Majority: Negroes in Colonial South Carolina from 1670 Through the Stono Rebellion* (New York, 1974), 87–88; Christian Warren, "Northern Chills, Southern Fevers: Race Specific Mortality in American Cities, 1730–1900," *Journal of Southern History* 63, no. 2 (2000): 274–277; H. Roy Meterns and George D. Terry, "Dying in Paradise: Malaria, Mortality, and the Perceptual Environment in Colonial South Carolina," *Journal of Southern History* 50, no. 4 (1984): 533–550. For a history of yellow fever epidemics in the nineteenth-century South, see Margaret Humphreys, *Yellow Fever and the South* (Baltimore, 1999), 5, 45–76. J. R. McNeill has written about the ways in which deforestation on sugar plantations created ideal conditions for mosquitoes, what he calls a "creole ecology." The same is said of Lowcountry rice plantations. See J. R. McNeill, *Mosquito Empires: Ecology and War in the Great Caribbean, 1620–1914* (Cambridge, UK, 2010).

40. See Estate of N. S. Bayard, 1827–1836. For "Old Adam and Old Toby," see ibid., 25 January 1832, 10 January 1834. For Charles as a porter, see ibid., 18 January 1826, 15 January 1827. For garden and market, see ibid., 31 October 1825, 16 March 1836, 30 August 1836. For Paul, see ibid., 2 April 1831, 6 April 1831, 24 May 1831, 1 August 1832, 13 June 1833.

41. For special treatment of Paul, see ibid., 1830–1836.

42. For Paul's wife and family, see Paul Sansay to JHBL, 16 January 1839, MSCS; Nicholas Bayard to JHBL, 18 September 1841, MSCS. For slave marriages in Savannah, see Johnson, *Black Savannah*, 115–118; cf. Wade, *Slavery in the Cities*, 117–121.

43. For slave housing patterns, see Wade, *Slavery in the Cities*, 58–62; Wood, *Women's Work, Men's Work*, 129–131.

Chapter Two: Many Mansions

1. For Dr. Nicholas Serle Bayard, see "Died: Nicholas S. Bayard," *Savannah Republican Gazette*, 30 October 1821. For a quick view of Bayard connections, see "Bayard Family" in Wikipedia. For an extended description of the family, see A. A. Hodge, *The Life of Charles Hodge D.D. LL.D: Professor in the Theological Seminary, Princeton, NJ* (New York, 1880), esp. 1–19.

2. For son Nicholas, see "Bayard, Nicholas James," in *The Children of Pride: A True Story of Georgia and the Civil War*, ed. Robert Manson Myers (New Haven, 1972), 1462–1463. For Jane Bayard's birth on Cumberland Island, see Hampden C. DuBose, *Memoirs of Rev. John Leighton Wilson, D.D., Missionary to Africa, and Secretary of Foreign Missions* (Richmond, VA, 1895), 42–43.

3. For a brief history of the Independent Presbyterian Church, see "A History of IPC," n.d., Independent Presbyterian Church, www.ipcsav.org/our-church/a-history-of-ipc/.

4. Quotation: "Died: Nicholas S. Bayard," *Savannah Republican Gazette*, 30 October 1821.

5. Quotation: "Died," *Georgian* (Savannah), 6 June 1822.

6. For passenger list of the ship *Garonne*, see "Port of Savannah," *Georgian* (Savannah), 4 July 1822.

7. For Nicholas's stay with the Hodge family and details of the Hodge/Bayard family, see Hodge, *The Life of Charles Hodge*, 1–19.

8. Ibid., 5.

9. For examples of the close relationship with Bayard cousins, see JLW to JB, 20 July 1833, CTS; JLW to JB, 3 September 1833, CTS; JLW to B. B. Wisner, 2 September 1834, ABCFM.

10. Estate of N. S. Bayard in account with N. J. Bayard, Administrator, 2 July 1822, 12 February 1824, 11 November 1824, 25 February 1825, 17 June 1825, 7 February 1826, SCCC.

11. The Bayards were part of the "Old School" Presbyterian tradition and church. See Hodge, *The*

Life of Charles Hodge, 1–19, for examples of the practices of their piety. For the most thorough statement of "Old School" theology, see Charles Hodge, *Systematic Theology* (New York, 1873), vols. 1 and 2. For an introduction to "Old School" Presbyterians and their place in nineteenth-century religious life in the United States, see Sydney E. Ahlstrom, *A Religious History of the American People* (New Haven, CT, 1972), 455–471.

12. For the understanding of vocation, see Hodge, *Systematic Theology,* vol. 2, 639–723. For the roots of this understanding in Calvinist thought and practice, see Charles Taylor, *Sources of the Self: The Making of the Modern Identity* (Cambridge, MA, 1989), 211–233. For its place in a Lowcountry slave society, see Erskine Clarke, *Our Southern Zion: Calvinism in the South Carolina Low Country* (Tuscaloosa, AL, 1996), 165–181; Erskine Clarke, *Dwelling Place: A Plantation Epic* (New Haven, CT, 2005), 82–96, 278–280.

13. For the role of human agency, see Hodge, *Systematic Theology,* vol. 2, 280–312. See, for comparison, Pierre Bourdieu, *The Logic of Practice,* Richard Nice, trans. (Palo Alto, CA, 1990 [1980]), for a sociological approach to the relationship between a person's social location and personal agency.

14. Cf. Catherine Beecher, *A Treatise on Domestic Economy for the Use of Young Ladies at Home* (Boston, 1841); Catharine E. Beecher and Harriet Beecher Stowe, *The American Woman's Home, or Principles of Domestic Science; Being a Guide to the Formation and Maintenance of Economical, Healthful, Beautiful, and Christian Homes* (New York, 1869). Cf. for women in the South, Michael O'Brien, *Conjectures of Order: Intellectual Life and the American South, 1810–1860* (Chapel Hill, NC, 2004), 253–284.

15. For the complex relationship between domesticity and women's involvement in US Protestant missions, see Jane Hunter, "Women's Mission in Historical Perspective: American Identity and Christian Internationalism," in *Competing Kingdoms: Women, Mission, Nation, and the American Protestant Empire, 1812–1960,* ed. Barbara Reeves-Ellington, Kathryn Kish Sklar, and Connie A. Shemo (Durham, NC, 2010), 19–42.

16. Estate of N. S. Bayard, 7 February 1826, 1 February 1830.

17. Ibid., 1827–1832.

18. For their growing questions about slavery, see JLW to JB, 24 October 1834, CTS; JLW to JB, 20 October 1834, CTS.

19. Estate of N. S. Bayard, 1826–1833, passim.

20. Quotation: Ernest Trice Thompson, *Presbyterians in the South,* vol. 1 (Richmond, VA, 1963), 429.

21. "Centennial of the Independent Presbyterian Church, Savannah, Georgia," *Journal of the Presbyterian Historical Society* 10, no. 3 (1919): 126–130.

22. For the words of the hymn, see "From Greenland's Icy Mountains," n.d., NetHymnal, www.cyberhymnal.org/htm/f/r/fromgrim.htm. For Lowell Mason, see Carol A. Pemberton, "Lowell Mason," in *American National Biography,* eds. John A. Garraty and Mark C. Carnes (New York, 1999), vol. 14, 656–657.

23. For Eliza Clay and Clay family, see "Clay, Eliza Caroline," in Myers, ed. *The Children of Pride,* 1491.

24. Carolyn Clay Swiggart, *Shades of Gray: The Clay and McAllister Families of Bryan County, Georgia During the Plantation Years* (Darien, CT, 1999), 1–33. For Clay involvement in the religious instruction of their slaves, see Thomas S. Clay, "Detail of a Plan for the Moral Improvement of Negroes on Plantations. Read Before the Georgia Presbytery. [Continued]," *Charleston Observer,* 2 February 1834. For the opposition to the Clay efforts, see Lacy K. Ford, *Deliver Us from Evil: The Slavery Question in the Old South* (Oxford, 2009), 463–470.

25. For JB's regular visits to Fair Hope, see JLW to JB, 21 June 1833, CTS.

26. For Fair Hope plantation and the route from Darien to Fair Hope, see Buddy Sullivan, *Early Days on the Georgia Tidewater: The Story of McIntosh County and Sapelo* (Darien, GA, 2001), esp. 34–36, 257–258.

27. For the slave population at Fair Hope and its surroundings, see ibid., 242. For the widespread use of carriages by whites in the Lowcountry, see Clarke, *Dwelling Place,* esp. 174–175, 216, 272–273. For the use of carriages generally, see The Museums at Stony Brook, *19th Century American Carriages: Their Manufacture, Decoration and Use* (Stony Brook, NY, 1987), 34–65.

28. For JB's growing concern for the emancipation of her slaves, see JLW to JB, 29 January 1833, CTS; JLW to JB, 24 October 1833, CTS; Records of Superior Court, Chatham County, Georgia, 5 October 1838, Record Book 2W-2, SCCC. For JB's heart being "fixed upon that *injured and neglected* people" of Africa, see JLW to JB, 29 December 1833, CTS.

29. For JB at Fair Hope, see JLW to JB, 21 June 1833, CTS. For the landscape, see Charles Lyell, *A Second Visit to North America,* vol. 1 (London, 1849), 307–351. See William Bartram, *Travel Through North and South Carolina, East and West Florida* (New York, 1988 [1791]), 36–40, for descriptions of flora and fauna and for Bartram's visit to a McIntosh planta-

tion. For a map showing details of the immediate landscape around Fair Hope, see Sullivan, *Early Days on the Georgia Tidewater*, 722.

30. Ahlstrom, *A Religious History of the American People*, 422–424; Andrew F. Walls, "The American Dimension in the History of the Missionary Movement," in *Earthen Vessels: American Evangelicals and Foreign Missions*, eds. Joel A. Carpenter and Wilbert R. Shenk (Grand Rapids, MI, 1990), 1–25.

31. DuBose, *Memoirs*, 43. For Protestant mission societies not accepting single women in the early years of the mission movement, see Elizabeth E. Prevost, *The Communion of Women: Missions and Gender in Colonial Africa and the British Metropole* (Oxford, 2010), 1–27; Deborah Kirkwood, "Protestant Missionary Women: Wives and Spinsters," in *Women and Missions, Past and Present: Anthropological and Historical Perceptions*, eds. Fiona Bowie, Deborah Kirkwood, and Shirley Ardener (Providence, RI, 1993), 23–42.

32. Quotation: Georgia Writers Project, Savannah Unit, Works Projects Administration, [Mary Granger], *Drums and Shadows: Survival Studies Among the Georgia Coastal Negroes* (Savannah, GA, 1940), 176. For a word about the Bayard sisters seeking husbands in order to become missionaries, see JLW to SSW, 27 October 1832, CTS.

Chapter Three: A Black River Home

1. Hampden C. DuBose, *Memoirs of Rev. John Leighton Wilson, D.D., Missionary to Africa and Secretary of Foreign Missions* (Richmond, VA, 1895), 14–15. For Major John James, see George Howe, *History of the Presbyterian Church in South Carolina* (Columbia, SC, 1870), vol. 1, 407–409; Steven D. Smith, "John James," in *The South Carolina Encyclopedia*, ed. Walter Edgar (Columbia, SC, 2006), 493. For Francis Marion, see Robert Bass, *Swamp Fox: The Life and Campaigns of General Francis Marion* (New York, 1959).

2. For a vivid account of the first settlement, see excerpts from the diary of Robert Witherspoon found in Howe, *History of the Presbyterian Church in South Carolina*, vol. 1, 213–214. For the settlement, see Alexander Hewat, *An Historical Account of the Rise and Progress of the Colonies of South Carolina and Georgia* (London, 1779), vol. 2, 63–64. For the historic character of the Black River, see Mary Crockett and Elise Schmidt, "Black River Eligibility Study for the South Carolina Scenic Rivers Program," June 2001, South Carolina Department of Natural Resources. Mary Crockett of the South Carolina Department of Natural Resources accompanied the author and Leon Carroll during a day's float of the

river on 12 May 2011, providing an account of the river's social and natural history.

3. James A. Wallace, "Historical Discourse, 1856," in W. J. Cooper, *History of Williamsburg Church* (Kingstree, SC, 1981), 12–24; Howe, *History of the Presbyterian Church in South Carolina*, vol. 2, 250–251; James F. Cooper, *History of the Indiantown Presbyterian Church, 1757–1957* (n.p., 1957). The Indiantown congregation was on Black Mingo Creek, often called the Northern Branch of the Black River.

4. DuBose, *Memoirs*, 11. For a picture of the Wilson house, see bulletin, "Centenary Exercises: John Leighton Wilson," Mount Zion Church, March 24–25, 1909, CTS.

5. Wilson "Births" and "Marriages" in Wilson Family Bible, CTS. See also Session Records and Deacons' Book, MZPC; Hugh R. Murchison, "John Leighton Wilson," 2, CTS; Jerry Fox Law, *A History of Mt. Zion Presbyterian Church, 1809–2009, St. Charles, South Carolina* (n.p., 2009), passim.

6. For expansion of Wilson lands, see County Record D 127, 9 February 1812; EE 341, 1 September 1819; F 561, 6 March 1821, SCSC; and Last Will and Testament of William Wilson, Will Records 1 A, 13 May 1850, PCSC.

7. For Wilson slaves, see Last Will and Testament of William Wilson. In 1844, after making gifts of slaves to his various children, William Wilson had thirty-six slaves, and his single daughter, Sarah, had twenty-six, all living at Pine Grove. See "Mt. Zion Church Bond for the Year 1844," Deacons Book, MZPC. The Mt. Zion congregation had the unusual practice of taxing members according to the number of slaves they owned rather than through pew rents.

8. Quotation: JLW to RA, 12 June 1836, ABCFM.

9. Dubose, *Memoirs*, 20–21; John Miller Wells, *Southern Presbyterian Worthies* (Richmond, VA, 1936), 51–52. For JLW's acknowledgment of the secret world of black slaves, see J. Leighton Wilson, *Western Africa: Its History, Condition, and Prospects* (New York, 1856), 215. This secret world continued in the local African American community for a number of generations. Interviews by the author with older members of the African American community organized by the Reverend Ella Busby, Goodwill Presbyterian Church, Sumter County, South Carolina, 13 May 2011. Most striking were the memories of root doctors and the experience of having hags take the breath away. William Warren of Charleston said that he and other whites had had similar experiences. Following his experience, black friends told him that

it was a hag who had ridden his chest. Interview on 15 May 2011.

10. "A List of Colored Members of Mt. Zion Church," Session Records, MZPC; "Mt. Zion Church Bond for the Year 1844," Deacons Book, MZPC; Howe, *History of the Presbyterian Church in South Carolina*, vol. 2, 250–251, 347–348, 484.

11. JLW to MMW, 4 January 1832, SCL; Murchison, "John Leighton Wilson," 5. For the character of the plantation kitchen with its equipage, see John Michael Vlack, *Back of the Big House: The Architecture of Plantation Slavery* (Chapel Hill, NC, 1993), 43–47. For the best account of foods prepared in the plantation kitchens of the South Carolina Lowcountry, see Karen Hess, *The Carolina Rice Kitchen: The African Connection* (Columbia, SC, 1992).

12. DuBose, *Memoirs*, 13; Murchison, "John Leighton Wilson," 6. Cf. C. Van Woodward, *Thinking Back: The Perils of Writing History* (Baton Rouge, LA, 1986), 14.

13. Wilson later spoke of the "less open form" of slave life in the American South. See Wilson, *Western Africa*, 215.

14. Older blacks in Sumter County have vivid memories of the ways in which whites sought to control blacks. Interviews at Goodwill Presbyterian Church, Sumter County, South Carolina, 13 May 2011.

15. For a review of scholarly discussions of slave day-to-day resistance, see Robert William Fogel, *Without Consent or Contract: The Rise and Fall of American Slavery* (New York, 1989). See also, for slave resistance, Philip Morgan, *Slave Counterpoint: Black Culture in the Eighteenth-Century Chesapeake and Lowcountry* (Chapel Hill, NC, 1998); John Hope Franklin and Loren Schweninger, *Runaway Slaves: Rebels on the Plantation* (New York, 1999).

16. For the "Pine Grove" name, see JLW to JB, 30 April 1833, CTS. For small farms of the Lowcountry, see Stephanie McCurry, *Masters of Small Worlds: Yeoman Households, Gender Relations, and the Political Culture of the Antebellum South Carolina Lowcountry* (Oxford, 1995).

17. DuBose, *Memoirs*, 20–21; Wells, *Southern Presbyterian Worthies*, 51–52.

18. For the role of landscapes in shaping human perspectives and emotions, see Benjamin Z. Kedar and R. J. Zwi Werblowski, *Sacred Space: Shrine, City, Land* (New York, 1998); Frederick Turner, *Spirit of Place: The Making of an American Literary Landscape* (San Francisco, 1989); and Wendell Berry, *What Are People For?* (Berkeley, CA, 1996). For the role of place, history, and tradition among many white Southern-

ers, see Robert H. Brinkmeyer, Jr., *The Fourth Ghost: White Southern Writers and European Fascism, 1930–1950* (Baton Rouge, LA, 2009), 24–70. For the relationship of memory to place and identity, see Paul Ricoeur, *Memory, History, Forgetting*, trans. Kathleen Blamey and David Pellauer (Chicago, 2004), 41, 56–92.

19. JLW to RA, 12 June 1836, ABCFM; JLW to RA, 23 January 1843, ABCFM; JBW to RA, 1 April 1843, ABCFM; "Report on Slavery," *The Liberator*, 30 September 1842, 154. For slaves' attachment to the places where they "were born and brought up," and the reasons for such attachments, see Frederick Douglass, *Life and Times of Frederick Douglass* (1881; reprint, New York, 1962), 97.

20. JLW to MMW, November 1828, SCL; DuBose, *Memoirs*, 11, 22–27; Murchison, "John Leighton Wilson," 5; John Adger, *My Life and Times* (Richmond, VA, 1899), 58–69.

21. Quotations: JLW to "Dear Sisters," 1 March 1828, SCL.

22. JLW to MEW, 1 August 1828, SCL.

23. Quotation: ibid.

24. DuBose, *Memoirs*, 24–25. For comparison of the Catskill region to distant places, see J. Leighton Wilson, "Journal of a Tour to Grabbo," 3 March 1837 to 5 April 1837, ABCFM.

25. For the Wilson family, see Wilson "Births," "Deaths," and "Marriages," Wilson Family Bible, CTS.

26. Quotation: Howe, *History of the Presbyterian Church in South Carolina*, vol. 2, 651–652. For JLW's deepening concern over slavery and his own ownership of slaves, see JLW to RA, 29 December 1832, CTS; JLW to RA, 12 June 1836, ABCFM; JLW to RA, 23 January 1843, ABCFM.

27. Quotation: DuBose, *Memoirs*, 29. On the Adgers, see Adger, *My Life and Times*, 34–40; Tom Downey, "Adger, James," in *The South Carolina Encyclopedia*, ed. Walter Edgar (Columbia, SC, 2006), 4–5.

28. For Palmer as a progressive church leader, see Lacy K. Ford, *Deliver Us from Evil: The Slavery Question in the Old South* (Oxford, 2009), 254. For the membership of Circular Congregational Church, see Circular Congregational Church, Independent C. Church Register, 1796–1824, Book of Church Records, 1825–1850, and the 1818 Statement of Faith and Constitution with List of Signatures, Circular Congregational Church archives. For the social profile of the congregation, see Erskine Clarke, *Our Southern Zion: Calvinism in the South Carolina Low Country 1690–1990* (Tuscaloosa, AL, 1996), 142–164.

29. Good entry points for the Second Great Awakening are Sydney E. Ahlstrom, *A Religious History of the American People* (New Haven, CT, 1972), 385–510; Nathan O. Hatch, *The Democratization of American Christianity* (New Haven, CT, 1989); Mark A. Noll, *A History of Christianity in the United States and Canada* (Grand Rapids, MI, 1992), 163–244. For Palmer and those joining Circular Congregational Church, see Benjamin Morgan Palmer, "Pastor's Book," SCHS; Circular Congregational Church, Membership Records, SCHS. Note that Snetter left for Liberia before his formal preparation for church membership was completed. His wife was already a member. See JLW to JHBL, 6 September 1836, MSCS.

30. Quotations: JLW to MMW, 2 August 1830, SCL.

31. This understanding of his conversion and conversion in general developed over the years. At first the focus was on turning his heart over to God and being accepted by God. But from the first there was also the experience of Jesus as his redeemer and savior. See JLW to MMW, 2 August 1830, SCL; JLW to "My Dear Sisters," 9 September 1830, SCL; JLW to MMW, 30 October 1830, SCL; JLW to SSW, 14 January 1831, SCL.

32. Quotations: JLW to MMW, 30 October 1830; hymn "Amazing Grace." For JLW's reflections on the death of a Christian, see JLW to RA, 28 January 1837, ABCFM; JLW to "Dear Parents, Brothers, Sisters and Friends," 27 October 1841, CTS. For JLW's comparison of the death of a Christian with that of one "with no hope," see J. Leighton Wilson, "Journal of a Tour to Grabbo," 3 March 1837 to 5 April 1837, ABCFM.

33. For JLW's commitment to self-knowledge and reflection, see JLW to MMW, 2 August 1830, SCL; JLW to "My Dear Sisters," 9 September 1830, SCL; JLW to MMW, 30 October 1830, SCL. For an example of praise for JLW's character and integrity—by one who differed strongly with him in regard to colonization and missions and who was in frequent conflict with him—see James Hall, *Colonization Journal*, 2nd ser., vol. 2 (1843): 3.

34. Benjamin Morgan Palmer, "Pastor's Book," SCHS. For Snetter as a barber, see State Free Negro Capitalization Tax Book for 1823, 1826, and 1827, SCHS; and "93 Market Street," Directory for the City of Charleston, 1829, SCHS. For the important place of black barbers in Southern society, and Charleston in particular, see Douglas Walter Bristol, Jr., *Knights of the Razor: Black Barbers in Slavery and Freedom* (Baltimore, 2009), 104–105, 126–127, 137–

138, 160–162. For Snetter's relationship to Grimké, see JLW to JHBL, 6 September 1836, MSCS. On Thomas Grimké, see Adrienne Koch, "Two Charlestonians in Pursuit of Truth: The Grimké Brothers," *South Carolina Historical Magazine* 69 (1968): 159–170.

35. Quotation: James 1:23. For the reform impulse stirred by the Second Great Awakening, see Ahlstrom, *A Religious History of the American People*, 415–428.

36. For the debate over colonization in Charleston, see Ford, *Deliver Us from Evil*, 318–322. In recent years historians have engaged in a vigorous debate about Denmark Vesey and the alleged insurrection associated with his name. For helpful summaries and judicious reflections on the debate, see ibid., 207–298; and David Brion Davis, *Inhuman Bondage: The Rise and Fall of Slavery in the New World* (Oxford, 2006), 221–225.

37. For the American Colonization Society, see P. J. Staudenraus, *The African Colonization Movement, 1816–1865* (New York, 1961). For a sympathetic contemporary interpretation of colonization by a Princeton Seminary professor, see Archibald Alexander, *A History of Colonization on the Western Coast of Africa* (Philadelphia, 1846). See also below, Chapter 4, note 22, on the colonization movement.

38. Henry and his family had lived with Gregorie on Anson Street in Charleston in the 1820s. See State Free Negro Capitalization Tax Book for 1822, SCHS. Quotations: *The Friend* 5 (1832): 283.

39. Henry and his family sailed on the *Hercules* and landed on 6 January 1833. For Snetter, see *The Friend* 5 (1832): 384. For the death of Charles Henry and family members from fever, see http://ccharity.com/shiperculess1833.htm.

40. Quotation: Minutes, Charleston Union Presbytery, 1 March 1830, PHS. Note that this was before JLW's conversion experience.

41. For the democratic impulse in the Western revivals, see Hatch, *Democratization of American Christianity*, esp. 49–66. Cf. Clarke, *Our Southern Zion*, 165–166.

42. Quotation: Howe, *History of the Presbyterian Church in South Carolina*, vol. 2, 416–417. See also Clarke, *Our Southern Zion*, 119–121.

43. Quotation: JLW to MMW, 4 January 1832, SCL. For the students enrolled, see Louis C. LaMotte, *Colored Light: The Story of the Influence of Columbia Theological Seminary, 1828–1936* (Richmond, VA, 1937), 298.

44. For the formation of the American Board of Commissioners for Foreign Missions, see Joseph

Tracy, "History of the American Board of Commissioners for Foreign Missions," in *History of American Missions to the Heathen, from Their Commencement to the Present Time* (Worcester, MA, 1840), 27–33; Ahlstrom, *A Religious History of the American People*, 423–424.

45. Quotation: JLW to MEW, 6 January 1832, SCL.

46. Quotation: Howe, *History of the Presbyterian Church in South Carolina*, vol. 2, 416–417. See also JLW to JB, 29 December 1832, CTS; "Letter of J. L. Wilson," *Charleston Observer*, 5 August 1837; DuBose, *Memoirs*, 40.

47. JLW to SSW, 27 October 1832, SCL. LaMotte, *Colored Light*, 70–73.

48. Quotations: JLW to SSW, 27 October 1832, SCL; Thomas Smyth, *Autobiographical Notes, Letters and Reflections*, ed. Louisa Cheves Stoney (Charleston, SC, 1914), 79.

Chapter Four: A Place Seen from Afar

1. Quotations: JLW to SSW, 27 October 1832, SCL.

2. JLW to JB, 1 December 1832, CTS; Hampden C. DuBose, *Memoirs of Rev. John Leighton Wilson, D.D., Missionary to Africa and Secretary of Foreign Missions* (Richmond, VA, 1895), 43–44. For the Joseph Cumming family, see "Cumming, Sarah Wallace," in *The Children of Pride: A True Story of Georgia and the Civil War*, ed. Robert Manson Myers (New Haven, CT, 1972), 1499. For the Sunday school at First African Baptist taught by members of Independent Presbyterian Church, see James M. Simms, *The First Colored Baptist Church in North America* (Philadelphia, 1888), 91–92; Whittington B. Johnson, *Black Savannah, 1788–1864* (Fayetteville, AR, 1996), 25. For descriptions of JB, see JLW to JB, 13 September 1833, CTS; DuBose, *Memoirs*, 69. For descriptions of JLW's appearance and "remarkable physical strength," see *Minutes of the Synod of South Carolina at Its Annual Sessions, October 20–22, 1886* (Spartanburg, SC, 1886), 21–22; DuBose, *Memoirs*, 21; John Miller Wells, *Southern Presbyterian Worthies* (Richmond, VA, 1936), 51–52.

3. Quotations: JLW to JB, 1 December 1832, CTS; JLW to JB, 10 December 1832, CTS.

4. JLW to JB, 10 December 1832, CTS.

5. For James Eckard, see A. A. Hodge, *The Life of Charles Hodge D.D. LL.D: Professor in the Theological Seminary, Princeton, NJ* (New York, 1880), 18; *Missionary Register* (London), 1 January 1834, 63; "Eckard, James Reed," in *Encyclopedia of the Presbyterian*

Church, ed. Alfred Nevin (Philadelphia, 1884), 207–208. For the early history of the Ceylon and South India mission, see Clifton Jackson Phillips, *Protestant America and the Pagan World: The First Half Century of the American Board of Commissioners for Foreign Missions, 1810–1860* (Cambridge, MA, 1969), 32–56. For the context of the Tamil mission, see T. Sabaratnam, "Sri Lankan Tamil Struggle: Growth of Nationalisms," September 2010, Association of Tamils of Sri Lanka in the USA, www.sangam.org/2010/09/Tamil_Struggle-8.php.

6. Quotations: JLW to JB, 18 December 1832, CTS. JLW quotes from JB's letter.

7. JLW to JB, 28 December 1832, CTS. For an important analysis of the nullification controversy, see William W. Freehling, *The Road to Disunion: Secessionists at Bay, 1776–1854* (New York, 1990), esp. 213–286.

8. For the comparison of imperialism in Africa with white imperialism against the Cherokees, see JLW to RA, 25 September 1838, ABCFM. For the Cherokee removal, see Gary E. Moulton, *John Ross, Cherokee Chief* (Athens, GA, 1978); and Michael D. Green, ed., *The Cherokee Removal: A Brief History with Documents* (Boston, 1995).

9. Quotation: JLW to JB, 21 June 1833, CTS.

10. Ibid.

11. Quotations: JLW to JB, 3 July 1833, CTS. See also JLW to JB, 28 December 1832, CTS, for opposition in Savannah. Perhaps the single most influential dismissive statement about the character of Africans was by Hegel: "The Negro, as already observed, exhibits the natural man in his completely wild and untamed state. We must lay aside all thought of reverence and morality—all that we call feeling—if we would rightly comprehend him; there is nothing harmonious with humanity to be found in this type of character." For Hegel, sub-Saharan Africa "is no historical part of the World; it has no movement or development to exhibit." Georg Wilhelm Friedrich Hegel, *The Philosophy of History* (New York, 1956), 93, 99. For examples of other such images, see George M. Fredrickson, *The Black Image in the White Mind: The Debate on Afro-American Character and Destiny, 1817–1914* (New York, 1971); James Brewer Stewart, "The Emergence of Racial Modernity and the Rise of the White North, 1790–1840," *Journal of the Early Republic* 18 (1999): 181–217; Chinua Achebe, "An Image of Africa," *Massachusetts Review* 18, no. 4 (1977): 782–794; Philip D. Curtin, *The Image of Africa: British Ideas and Action, 1780–1850* (Madison, WI, 1964), esp. 28–

57. For an important analysis of these images, see V. Y. Mudimbe, *The Invention of Africa: Gnosis, Philosophy, and the Order of Knowledge* (Bloomington, IN, 1988), esp. 1–23. For a powerful visual presentation of degrading stereotypes of Africa and Africans, see Jan Nederveen Pieterse, *White on Black: Images of Africa and Blacks in Western Popular Culture* (New Haven, CT, 1995).

12. JLW to JB, 3 July 1833, CTS; JLW to JB, 7 July 1833, CTS.

13. Quotations: JLW to JB, 20 July 1833, CTS.

14. Quotation: Simms, *The First Colored Baptist Church in North America*, 88. On Clay, see JLW to JB, [?] August 1833, CTS.

15. Quotation: JLW to JB, [?] August 1833, CTS. For other plans involving Margaret Strobel, see JLW to JB, 1 September 1833, CTS. In 1817, Savannah had outlawed schooling for both slaves and free people of color. See Jacqueline Jones, *Saving Savannah: The City and the Civil War* (New York, 2008), 54.

16. Quotation: JLW to JB, 1 September 1833, CTS. For an angry response to the "rabble" who attacked Pinney and for details of his address, see "So Persecuted They the Prophets Before You," *Charleston Observer*, 28 September 1833. For the context of the attack on Pinney and for the "infidel party" in South Carolina, see Lacy K. Ford, *Deliver Us from Evil: The Slavery Question in the Old South* (New York, 2009), 449–480; Erskine Clarke, *Dwelling Place: A Plantation Epic* (New Haven, CT, 2005), 169–172. For background on Pinney, see *The Missionary Herald*, [?] July 1844, 222; James A. Cogswell, *No Turning Back: A History of American Presbyterian Involvement in Sub-Saharan Africa, 1833–2000* (Philadelphia, 2007), 6–7. For the American Colonization Society, see P. J. Staudenraus, *The American Colonization Movement, 1816–1865* (New York, 1961); Tom W. Shick, *Behold the Promised Land: A History of Afro-American Settler Society in Nineteenth-Century Liberia* (Baltimore, 1977); Lamin Sanneh, *Abolitionists Abroad: American Blacks and the Making of Modern West Africa* (Cambridge, MA, 1999), 182–237. For the history of the colony and the Liberian state from an African perspective, see Amos J. Beyan, *The American Colonization Society and the Creation of the Liberian State* (Lanham, MD, 1991). For the larger picture of African Americans and the attraction of Africa, see James T. Campbell, *Middle Passages: African American Journeys to Africa, 1787–2005* (New York, 2006).

17. JLW to JB, 8 September 1833, CTS; JLW to JB, 13 September 1833, CTS; "Ordination of a Missionary," *Charleston Observer*, 28 September 1833.

18. Quotation: JLW to JB, 13 September 1833, CTS.

19. For the challenges and hardships facing Liberian settlers, see Antonio McDaniel, *Swing Low, Sweet Chariot: The Mortality Costs of Colonizing Liberia in the Nineteenth Century* (Chicago, 1995); Svend E. Holsoe, "A Study of Relations Between Settlers and Indigenous Peoples in Western Liberia, 1821–1847," *International Journal of African Historical Studies* 4, no. 2 (1971): 331–362; and cf., Wilson Jeremiah Moses, ed., *Liberian Dreams: Back-to-Africa Narratives from the 1850s* (University Park, PA, 1998).

20. For the Maryland Colonization Society and its colony, see Richard L. Hall, *On Afric's Shore: A History of Maryland in Liberia, 1834–1857* (Baltimore, 2003); Penelope Campbell, *Maryland in Africa: The Maryland State Colonization Society, 1831–1857* (Champaign, IL, 1971); Jane Jackson Martin, "The Dual Legacy: Government Authority and Mission Influence Among the Glebo of Eastern Liberia, 1834–1910" (PhD diss., Boston University, 1968); Eugene S. Van Sickle, "A Transnational Vision: John H. B. Latrobe and Maryland's African Colonization Movement (PhD diss., West Virginia University, 2005). For JLW's reception by Latrobe, see JLW to JB, 21 September 1833, CTS. For James Bayard's response to Latrobe, see James Bayard to JHBL, 22 October 1833, MSCS.

21. Quotation: *African Repository* 53, April 1877, 60. For the effort to "whiten" the upper South, see Ford, *Deliver Us from Evil*, 359–389. For the shifting demographics of slavery in Maryland, see T. Stephen Whitman, *The Price of Freedom: Slavery and Manumission in Baltimore and Early National Maryland* (Lexington, KY, 1997), esp. 10. For Latrobe's promotion of black leadership at Cape Palmas, see *African Repository* 53, April 1877, passim. Latrobe's complexity is seen not only in his life and writings but also in the varying responses of historians to him. Cf., for example, the treatment of Latrobe in Amos J. Beyan, *African American Settlements in West Africa: John Brown Russwurm and the American Civilizing Efforts* (New York, 2005); and in Winston James, *The Struggles of John Brown Russwurm: The Life and Writings of a Pan-Africanist Pioneer, 1799–1851* (New York, 2010). Van Sickle's dissertation, "A Transnational Vision," has the best and fullest treatment of Latrobe and explores the competing impulses in Latrobe's colonization efforts.

22. Quotations: Ira Berlin, *Slaves Without Masters* (New York, 1974), 204; *Liberator*, 4 June 1831. For a helpful summary of black responses to colonization,

see Leonard I. Sweet, *Black Images of America, 1784–1870* (New York, 1976), 35–68.

23. Quotation: Christopher Phillips, *Freedom's Port: The African American Community of Baltimore, 1790–1860* (Urbana, IL, 1997), 215.

24. Quotation: JLW to JB, 9 October 1833, CTS.

25. B. B. Wisner to JHBL, 5 October 1833, MSCS.

26. Quotation: JLW to JB, 24 October 1833. See also JLW to JB, 9 October 1833, CTS; JLW to JB, 13 October 1833, CTS; JLW to Henry Hill, 22 October 1833, ABCFM; JLW to JB, 15 November 1833, CTS.

27. JLW to RA, 12 May 1833, ABCFM; JLW to JB, 24 October 1833, CTS.

28. JLW to JB, 24 October 1833, CTS.

29. Quotation: ibid.

30. Quotation: ibid. Georgia law required any slave freed by an owner to leave the state; otherwise, the freed person could face re-enslavement. See Jones, *Saving Savannah*, 49.

Chapter Five: Testing the Waters

1. For details of the embarkation, see JLW to JB, 28 November 1833, CTS; John H. B. Latrobe, *Maryland in Liberia: A History of the Colony* (Baltimore, 1885), 36–37, 133; Richard L. Hall, *On Afric's Shore: A History of Maryland in Liberia, 1834–1857* (Baltimore, 2003), 3–5.

2. Quotation: Latrobe, *Maryland in Liberia*, 133–134.

3. Quotation: James Hall, "Cape Palmas," *African Repository* 60, no. 4 (1884): 102. For life on shipboard, see JLW to JB, 28 November 1833, CTS.

4. For a map of Atlantic currents, see David Eltis and David Richardson, *Atlas of the Transatlantic Slave Trade* (New Haven, CT, 2010), 8. The concept of an "Atlantic world" with an "Atlantic history" has become a rapidly developing field of historical study. For overviews of themes and issues and important interpretive studies, see John Thornton, *Africa and Africans in the Making of the Atlantic World, 1400–1800* (Cambridge, UK, 1998); David Eltis, "Atlantic History in Global Perspective," *Itinerario* 23, no. 2 (1999): 141–161; Bernard Bailyn, *Atlantic History: Concept and Contours* (Cambridge, MA, 2005); Jack P. Greene and Philip D. Morgan, eds. *Atlantic History: A Critical Appraisal* (Oxford, 2009).

5. Quotation: Hall, "Cape Palmas," 102.

6. For the launching of the sailboat and the

pursuit by "Guineamen," see J. Leighton Wilson, "Journal of J. Leighton Wilson on a Missionary Tour to Western Africa," 22–26 January 1834, ABCFM. Cf. JH to JHBL, 29 January 1834, MSCS. For Pedro Blanco, see Theodore Canot, *Captain Canot; or Twenty Years of an African Slaver*, ed. Brantz Mayer (New York, 1854).

7. Quotations: Wilson, "Journal," 27 January 1834, ABCFM.

8. For the arrival in Monrovia, see JLW to JB, 28 January 1834, CTS.

9. Quotation: Stephen Wynkoop, "Journal of S. R. Wynkoop to Western Africa," 1–5, ABCFM. For the language ability of the schoolchildren, see JLW to JB, 28 January 1834, CTS; Wilson, "Journal," 29–30 January 1834, ABCFM.

10. Quotations: Wynkoop, "Journal," 6, ABCFM; Hall, *On Afric's Shore*, 22. See also Wilson, "Journal," 31 January 1834, ABCFM.

11. JLW to JB, 28 January 1834, CTS.

12. Quotations: Wilson, "Journal," 3 and 6 February 1834, ABCFM. The Mandingo man was later discovered to be a slaver. See Wynkoop, "Journal," 9, ABCFM.

13. For introductions to the nature of West African religions and to the debates among scholars about the character of African religions and encounters with missionaries, see Sidney W. Mintz and Richard Price, *The Birth of African-American Culture: An Anthropological Perspective* (Boston, 1992 [1976]), esp. 44–45; Robin Horton, "On the Rationality of Conversion," *Africa* 45 (1975): 219–235; V. Y. Mudimbe, *The Invention of Africa: Gnosis, Philosophy, and the Order of Knowledge* (Bloomington, IN, 1988); Rosalind Shaw, "The Invention of 'African Traditional Religion,'" *Religion* 20 (1990): 339–353; J. D. Y. Peel's review article, "Historicity and Pluralism in Some Recent Studies of Yoruba Religion," *Africa* 64 (1994): 150–166; Sean Hawkins, "Disguising Chiefs and God as History: Questions on the Acephaloussness of Lodagaa Politics and Religion," *Africa* 66 (1996): 202–247; J. D. Y. Peel, *Religious Encounter and the Making of the Yoruba* (Bloomington, IN, 2000); Paul S. Landau, "Hegemony and History in Jean and John L. Comaroff's *Of Revelation and Revolution*," *Africa* 70 (2000): 501–519; David Maxwell, "Writing the History of African Christianity: Reflections of an Editor," *Journal of Religion in Africa* 36 (2006): 379–399; Patrick Harries, *Butterflies and Barbarians: Swiss Missionaries and Systems of Knowledge in South-East Africa* (Oxford, 2007). For a vivid first-person account of conversion and of an African Christian's sense of conti-

nuity with pre-Christian religious beliefs and practices, see Lamin Sanneh, *Summoned from the Margin: Homecoming of an African* (Grand Rapids, MI, 2012), esp. 82–121.

14. For the continuity in African religion in its pre-Christian and Christian forms, see Andrew F. Walls, *The Cross-Cultural Process in Christian History* (Edinburgh, 2002), 116–135.

15. Quotations: Wilson, "Journal," 1 February 1834; J. Leighton Wilson, *Western Africa: Its History, Condition, and Prospects* (New York, 1856), 208. See also Robert Hamill Nassau, *Fetichism in West Africa* (New York, 1904). Nassau was a young associate of JLW's. For a critical evaluation of missionary descriptions of fetishes, see John M. Cinnamon, "Missionary Expertise, Social Science, and the Uses of Ethnographic Knowledge in Colonial Gabon," *History in Africa* 33 (2006): 413–432. The term "fetish" is rarely used today to describe African greegrees—the physical bodies that embody spiritual power.

16. Hall, *On Afric's Shore*, 35.

17. Wynkoop, "Journal," 16–17, ABCFM. For the size of the Atlantic slave trade between 1820 and 1880 and its character, see Eltis, "Atlantic History in Global Perspective," esp. 151–152.

18. Quotation: Wynkoop, "Journal," 7, ABCFM.

19. Quotation: Wilson, "Journal," 7 February 1834, ABCFM. Later, after JLW had spent years among the Grebo—whom he designated under the general term Kru—he wrote, "they are as capable of intellectual improvement as any other race of men"—a clear challenge to derogatory Western stereotypes of Africans. See Wilson, *Western Africa*, 105. For the Kru, see George E. Brooks, *The Kru Mariner in the Nineteenth Century: An Historical Compendium* (Newark, DE, 1972); George E. Brooks, *Yankee Traders, Old Coaster and African Middlemen: A History of American Legitimate Trade with West Africa in the Nineteenth Century* (Boston, 1970), esp. 222–225; Francis Bacon, "Cape Palmas and the Mena or Kroomen," *Journal of the Royal Geographical Society* 12 (1842): 196–206; Esu Biyi, "The Kru and Related Peoples, West Africa," *Journal of the African Society* 29 (1929–1930): 71–77, 181–188.

20. Wilson, "Journal," 10 February 1834, ABCFM; Hall, *On Afric's Shore*, 38.

21. Wynkoop recorded the conversation between Joe Wilson and Freeman as Wilson related it the next morning. Wynkoop, "Journal," 21, ABCFM. See also Hall, *On Afric's Shore*, 40–41.

22. Wilson, "Journal," 10 February 1834,

ABCFM; Brooks, *Yankee Traders*, 222–233, 313–326. Cf. "Yali's Question," in Jared Diamond, *Guns, Germs, and Steel: The Fates of Human Societies* (New York, 1997), 3–32. "Why," Yali asked Diamond, "is it that you white people developed so much cargo and brought it to New Guinea, but we black people had little cargo of our own?" By "cargo," Yali meant the material goods of the West, such as that brought to West Africa in the nineteenth century. Ibid., 4.

23. On the political structures of Grebo society, see Wilson, *Western Africa*, 128–139; Hall, *On Afric's Shore*, 85–88; Jane Jackson Martin, "The Dual Legacy: Government Authority and Mission Influence Among the Glebo of Eastern Liberia, 1834–1910" (PhD diss., Boston University, 1968), 14–24.

24. Quotations: Wilson, "Journal," 11 February 1834, ABCFM.

25. Quotation: ibid., 12 February 1834.

26. Ibid; Martin, "The Dual Legacy," 74–75. See also Wynkoop, "Journal," 22, ABCFM.

27. Quotation: Wilson, "Journal," 12 February 1834, ABCFM.

28. Ibid; JLW to JB, 13 October 1833, CTS.

29. For Clay as a possible business manager, see JLW to JB, 30 November 1833, CTS.

30. Quotation: Wilson, "Journal," 13 February 1834, ABCFM.

31. For Baphro, see Hall, *On Afric's Shore*, 53, 55, 528n27; JLW to RA, 26 May 1837, ABCFM; JBR to JHBL, 1 November 1838, MSCS.

32. Wilson, "Journal," 13 February 1834, ABCFM.

33. For Simleh Ballah, see JLW to RA, 7 March 1836, ABCFM; Martin, "The Dual Legacy," 100, 270; Latrobe, *Maryland in Liberia*, 49–51.

34. Quotations: Hall, "Cape Palmas,"105. For the procedure of a palaver, see Wilson, *Western Africa*, 131–133.

35. For the treaty between the Grebo and the Maryland Colonization Society, signed by Freeman, Baphro, Weah Bolio and James Hall, see Martin, "The Dual Legacy," 422–423. For the list of goods given for the land, see Wynkoop, "Journal," 28, ABCFM. See also Hall, *On Afric's Shore*, 45–46, for the estimated value of $1,200.

36. Wilson, "Journal," 13–15 February 1834, ABCFM; JLW to JB, 13 April 1834, CTS.

37. For the promised land imagery, see Tom W. Shick, *Behold the Promised Land: A History of Afro-American Settler Society in Nineteenth-Century Liberia* (Baltimore, 1977).

38. Quotation: Wilson, "Journal," 28 February 1834, ABCFM.

39. Wilson, "Journal," 28 February–7 March 1834, ABCFM.

40. Quotation: Wilson, "Journal," 7 March 1834, ABCFM. For a report on Gomas [Gomez], "well known for his atrocities in the slave trade," see "Sierra Leone," in *The Morning Chronicle* (London), 4 September 1826.

41. Quotation: Wilson, "Journal," 7 March 1834.

42. Quotations: J. Leighton Wilson and Stephen Wynkoop, "Report of the State of the Colony of Liberia," 24 March 1834, ABCFM, passim.

43. Quotations: ibid.

44. Quotation: ibid, 8.

45. Quotation: ibid., 19.

Chapter Six: Fair Hope Among the Grebo

1. Quotations: JLW to JB, 13 April 1834, CTS.

2. JLW to RA, 13 April 1834, ABCFM; JLW to JB, 25 April 1834, CTS.

3. Clay returned to a divided First African Baptist Church. For his leadership as a deacon in the congregation, see James M. Simms, *The First Colored Baptist Church in North America* (Philadelphia, 1888), 49, 88, 92–105.

4. "Extracts from the Journals of Messrs. Wilson and Wynkoop," *Missionary Herald*, August 1834, 288–292; J. Leighton Wilson and Stephen Wynkoop, "Report of the State of the Colony of Liberia to the Prudential Committee of the American Board of Commissioners for Foreign Missions," 24 March 1834, ABCFM; J. Leighton Wilson and Stephen Wynkoop, "To the Prudential Committee of the ABCFM," 18 April 1834, ABCFM.

5. JLW to JB, 25 April 1834, CTS. On Wynkoop, see "Stephen Rose Wynkoop," in *Encyclopedia of the Presbyterian Church*, ed. Alfred Nevin (Philadelphia, 1884), 1049–1050.

6. Quotation: JLW to RA, 12 May 1834, ABCFM.

7. JLW to JB, 25 April 1834, CTS; JLW to RA, 12 May 1834, ABCFM.

8. For time at Fair Hope plantation, see JLW to RA, 12 May 1834, ABCFM; JLW to Henry Hill, 26 September 1834, ABCFM; JLW to Henry Hill, 23 October 1834, ABCFM.

9. "Marriages," in Wilson Family Bible, CTS. For the Eckards, see "American Board of Missions," *Missionary Register* (London), 1 March 1835, 141.

10. JLW to RA, 12 May 1834, ABCFM; JLW to Henry Hill, 16 October 1834, ABCFM. For Southern women organizing mission and other benevolent societies, see Ernest Trice Thompson, *Presbyterians in the South*, vol. 1 (Richmond, VA, 1963), 287–301. For the larger picture of women and missions, see Elizabeth E. Prevost, *The Communion of Women: Missions and Gender in Colonial Africa and the British Metropole* (Oxford, 2010), 1–27; Fiona Bowie, Deborah Kirkwood, and Shirley Ardener, eds., *Women and Missions, Past and Present: Anthropological and Historical Perceptions* (Providence, RI, 1993).

11. Hampden C. DuBose, *Memoirs of Rev. John Leighton Wilson, D.D., Missionary to Africa and Secretary of Foreign Missions* (Richmond, VA, 1895), 60.

12. JLW to RA, 12 May 1834, ABCFM; JLW to B. B. Wisner, 21 July 1834, ABCFM; JLW to B. B. Wisner, 9 August 1834, ABCFM; JLW to JB, 29 December 1832, CTS; JLW to RA, 12 June 1836, ABCFM.

13. JLW to B. B. Wisner, 21 July 1834, ABCFM; JLW to B. B. Wisner, 2 September 1834, ABCFM; JLW to Henry Hill, 18 September 1834, ABCFM; JLW to Henry Hill, 16 October 1834, ABCFM; JLW to Henry Hill, 5 November 1834, ABCFM. For trade goods and trading generally, see George Brooks, *Yankee Traders, Old Coasters and African Middlemen: A History of American Legitimate Trade with West Africa in the Nineteenth Century* (Boston, 1970); Tom W. Shick, *Behold the Promised Land: A History of Afro-American Settler Society in Nineteenth-Century Liberia* (Baltimore, 1977), 102–121; George E. Brooks, *The Kru Mariner in the Nineteenth Century: An Historical Compendium* (Newark, DE, 1972).

14. JLW to RA, 12 September 1834, ABCFM; JLW to RA, 21 September 1834, ABCFM; JLW to RA, 7 October 1834, ABCFM.

15. Quotation: "The Rev. John Leighton Wilson Received the Instructions of the Prudential Committee in the Central Presbyterian Church, Philadelphia," *Missionary Herald*, 19 October 1834.

16. For the distinctive American character of the ABCFM and other American mission societies and boards, especially as articulated by Rufus Anderson, see Andrew F. Walls, *The Missionary Movement in Christian History: Studies in the Transmission of Faith* (Edinburgh, 1996), 223–227.

17. Quotations: "The Rev. John Leighton Wilson Received the Instructions of the Prudential Committee in the Central Presbyterian Church, Philadelphia," *Missionary Herald*, 19 October 1834. For additional details of the commissioning service, see "Mission to Western Africa," *Charleston Observer*,

8 November 1834; "Cape Palmas of Maryland," *Missionary Register* (London), 1 January 1835. The mission strategy of developing indigenous leaders was a part of the ABCFM's larger strategy of initiating, in mission fields, "self-governing, self-supporting, and self-propagating" churches. See Paul Harris, "Denominationalism and Democracy: Ecclesiastical Issues Underlying Rufus Anderson's Three Self Program," in *North American Foreign Mission, 1810–1914: Theology, Theory, and Policy*, Wilbert R. Shenk, ed. (Grand Rapids, MI, 2004), 61–85.

18. Quotation: Records of Superior Court, Chatham County, Georgia, 5 October 1838, Record Book 2W-2, SCCC. The reason for Clay's delay in having the document recorded in Savannah is not clear, but it was most likely an attempt to keep the pending manumission secret.

19. See letter of JBW in Archibald Alexander, *A History of Colonization on the Western Coast of Africa* (Philadelphia, 1846), 423.

20. JLW to Theodosia Bayard, 14 December 1834, CTS; JLW to RA, 13 December 1834, ABCFM.

21. For the description of their arrival at the Cape, see JLW to RA, 10 January 1835, ABCFM.

22. Quotations: JLW to "Father, Mother, Sisters and Brothers," 26 January 1835, CTS; Alexander, *A History of Colonization*, 423. Cf. JLW to RA, 7 January 1835, ABCFM.

23. Quotation: JLW to JB, 13 October 1833, CTS. JLW designed the house while in Baltimore in preparation for his exploratory trip. For the replication of American architectural styles in Liberia, see Svend E. Holsoe and Bernard L. Hermand, with photographs by Max Belcher, *A Land and Life Remembered: Americo-Liberian Folk Architecture* (Athens, GA, 1988).

24. JLW to RA, 10 January 1835, ABCFM; JLW to "Father, Mother, Sisters and Brothers," 26 January 1835, CTS.

25. Quotation: Richard L. Hall, *On Afric's Shore: A History of Maryland in Liberia, 1834–1857* (Baltimore, 2003), 98. For Leighton's description of their arrival, see JLW to "Father, Mother, Sisters and Brothers," 26 January 1835, CTS. Cf. JLW to RA, 7 January 1835, ABCFM.

26. Alexander, *A History of Colonization*, 425.

27. Ibid.

28. Quotations: Alexander, *A History of Colonization*, 424, 429. For comments on their early interactions with the Grebo, see JLW to RA, 10 January 1835, ABCFM; JLW to "Father, Mother, Sisters and Brothers," 26 January 1835, CTS.

29. For descriptions of Davis, see JH to JHBL, 15 October 1834, MSCS; JLW to RA, 3 November 1836, ABCFM; "West Africa," *Charleston Observer*, 8 September 1838.

30. For Simleh Ballah, see JLW to RA, 7 March 1836, ABCFM; JLW to RA, 3 November 1836, ABCFM; JHBL, *Maryland in Liberia: A History of the Colony* (Baltimore, 1885), 49–51. For Baphro, see J. Leighton Wilson, "Journal of J. Leighton Wilson on a Missionary Tour to Western Africa," 12 February 1834, ABCFM; JLW to RA, "Journal of a Tour to Grabbo," 6 April 1837, ABCFM.

31. Quotation: Lacy K. Ford, *Deliver Us from Evil: The Slavery Question in the Old South* (Oxford, 2009), 71. See also Eric Robert Papenfuse, *The Evils of Necessity: Robert Goodloe Harper and the Moral Dilemma of Slavery* (Philadelphia, 1997); and Carey M. Roberts, "Harper, Robert Goodloe," in *The South Carolina Encyclopedia*, ed. Walter Edgar (Columbia, SC, 2006), 429–430. Hall, *On Afric's Shore*, 26–27.

32. For the character of the "tornados," see Brooks, *Yankee Traders*, 81. For weather patterns at Cape Palmas, see JLW to RA, 7 January 1835, ABCFM.

33. For mosquitoes and malaria, see Andrew Spielman and Michael D'Antonio, *Mosquito: A Natural History of Our Most Persistent and Deadly Foe* (New York, 2003); James L. A. Webb, Jr., *Humanity's Burden: A Global History of Malaria* (Cambridge, UK, 2009), 3–9; Randall M. Packard, *The Making of a Tropical Disease: A Short History of Malaria* (Baltimore, 2007), 19–31. Cf. Erskine Clarke, *Dwelling Place: A Plantation Epic* (New Haven, CT, 2005), 55.

34. Webb, *Humanity's Burden*, 4–5.

35. For a nineteenth-century physician's description of the course of malaria, see J. Hume Simons, M.D., *Planter's Guide, Family Book of Medicine: For the Instruction and Use of Planters, Families, Country People, and All Others Who May Be Out of the Reach of Physicians, or Unable to Employ Them* (Charleston, SC, 1848), 72–82.

36. For the evolutionary history of malaria in West Africa and for the development of some immunities by West Africans, see Webb, *Humanity's Burden*, 18–41.

37. Quotations: JLW to RA, 4 March 1835, ABCFM; JLW to RA, 23 November 1835, ABCFM. For malaria and pregnant women, see the World Health Organization's "Malaria: Fact Sheet," January 2013, www.who.int/mediacentre/fact sheets/fs094/en/.

38. JBW to RA, 15 June 1835, ABCFM. For the use of opium to treat malaria, see Webb, *Humanity's Burden*, 123–124.

39. Dr. J. Hall to B. B. Wisner, 19 March 1835, ABCFM; JBW to RA, 15 June 1835, ABCFM; JLW to RA, 7 July 1835, ABCFM. For the use of cinchona bark, the development of quinine, and the uncertainties of when and how to use quinine, see Webb, *Humanity's Burden*, 95–98, 102–110, 127–128.

40. Quotations: JBW to RA, 15 June 1835, ABCFM.

41. Quotations: JLW to RA, 4 August 1835, ABCFM. For the African role in the slave trade, see John Thornton, *Africa and Africans in the Making of the Atlantic World, 1400–1800*, 2nd ed. (Cambridge, UK, 1998). For US-made ships, especially those constructed in Baltimore for the slave trade, see Donald L. Canney, *African Squadron: The U.S. Navy and the Slave Trade, 1842–1861* (Washington, DC, 2006), esp. 21–22.

42. Quotations: JLW to RA, 30 September 1835, 7 November 1835, 19 November 1835, ABCFM. Letter written on different dates but sent as one letter.

43. For the role of missionaries in creating "standard" languages, see Dmitri van den Dersselaar, "Creating 'Union Ibo': Missionaries and the Igbo Language," *Africa* 67 no. 2 (1997): 273–295, esp. 273–275. For missionary dictionaries as "the point of contact" between missionary "linguistic power" and the discourse of an indigenous people, see Derek Peterson, "Colonizing Languages? Missionaries and Gikuyu Dictionaries, 1904 and 1914," *History in Africa* 24 (1997): 257–272. Jean Comaroff and John L. Comaroff have argued that missionaries "colonised the consciousness" of Tswana people of South Africa. See their influential two-volume *Of Revelation and Revolution*, vol. 1, *Christianity, Colonialism and Consciousness in South Africa* (Chicago, 1991), and vol. 2, *The Dialectics of Modernity on a South African Frontier* (Chicago, 1997). For a critical review article on the Comaroffs, see Paul S. Landau, "Hegemony and History in Jean and John L. Comaroff's *Of Revelation and Revolution*," in *Africa* 70, no. 2 (2000): 501–519.

44. For the ways in which missionary and African encounters involved a dialogue in which Africans were not passive, see J. D. Y. Peel, "The Pastor and the *Babalawo*: The Interaction of Religions in Nineteenth-Century Yorubaland," *Africa* 60 (1990): 338–369; Paul Landau, *The Realm of the Word: Language, Gender and Christianity in a Southern African Kingdom* (Portsmouth, NH, 1996). For the effects of the dialogue on missionaries, see Lamin Sanneh, *Encountering the West: Christianity and the Global Cultural Process. The African Dimension* (Maryknoll, NY, 1993).

45. Quotations: JLW to RA, 13 December 1834, ABCFM.

46. Quotation: ibid.

47. Quotation: ibid.

48. JLW to RA, 7 March 1836, ABCFM; JLW to RA, 1 January 1839, ABCFM; Alexander, *A History of Colonization*, 423; "Western Africa," *Missionary Herald*, November 1836, 409–413; JLW to RA, 7 February 1836, ABCFM; JLW to RA, 28 June 1836, ABCFM. For Margaret Strobel's relationship with JLW and JBW, cf. Elizabeth Fox-Genovese, *Within the Plantation Household: Black and White Women of the Old South* (Chapel Hill, NC, 1988), esp. 291–292; Deborah Gray White, *Ar'n't I a Woman? Female Slaves in the Plantation South* (New York, 1985), 27–51; James C. Scott, *Domination and the Art of Resistance: Hidden Transcripts* (New Haven, CT, 1990), 17–44.

49. Quotation: JLW to RA, 23 November 1835, ABCFM. For acquired immunities to malaria, see Webb, *Humanity's Burden*, 9–10, 33.

Chapter Seven: Beneath an African Sky

1. For details of the trip to Rock Town, see JLW to RA, 19 November 1835, ABCFM. Cf. for early description of Rock Town, J. Leighton Wilson, "Journal of J. Leighton Wilson on a Missionary Tour to Western Africa," 11 and 14 February 1834, ABCFM.

2. JLW to RA, 19 November 1835, ABCFM. For other descriptions of how the Grebo handled canoes in the surf, see Wilson, "Journal," 28 February 1835, ABCFM; Robert Smith, "The Canoe in West African History," *Journal of African History* 11, no. 4 (1970): 515–533.

3. For the history of swimming generally and especially by West Africans, see Kevin Dawson, "Enslaved Swimmers and Divers in the Atlantic World," *Journal of American History* 92 (2006): 1327–1356.

4. Quotation: JLW to RA, 19 November 1835, ABCFM.

5. Quotation: J. Leighton Wilson, *Western Africa: Its History, Condition, and Prospects* (New York, 1856), 214. Cf. also Wilson, "Journal," 14 February 1834, ABCFM. The term "fetish" is rarely used today to describe African "greegrees." Wyatt MacGaffey, for example, used "charm" for the physical bodies that embody spiritual power. See Wyatt MacGaffey, *Religion and Society in Central Africa* (Chicago, 1986).

6. Quotation: Wilson, *Western Africa*, 215.

7. JLW to RA, 19 November 1835, ABCFM; Wilson, "Journal," 14 February 1834, ABCFM; Wilson, *Western Africa*, 211–216. See also Erskine Clarke, "They Shun the Scrutiny of White Men: Reports on Religion from the Georgia Lowcountry and West Africa," in *African American Life in the Georgia Lowcountry: The Atlantic World and the Gullah Geechee*, ed. Philip Morgan (Athens GA, 2010), 131–150.

8. Quotation: JLW to RA, 19 November 1835, ABCFM.

9. Ibid.

10. Ibid.

11. Quotation: JLW to RA, 1 April 1836, ABCFM; cf. Dr. Thomas Savage, "Death of a Chief—Funeral Ceremonies," *The African Repository and Colonial Journal* 15 (1836): 107–110; John Clarke, "Letter from Cape Palmas," *The Baptist Magazine* (London), 1 May 1841, 247.

12. JLW to RA, 1 April 1836, ABCFM; cf. Stephen Wynkoop, "Journal of S. R. Wynkoop to Western Africa," 31, ABCFM; Savage, "Death of a Chief"; Clarke, "Letter from Cape Palmas," 247.

13. JLW emphasized "the agency" of the fetish. See Wilson, *Western Africa*, 211–216. For the issue of causality and agency, see Webb Keane, *Christian Moderns: Freedom and Fetish in the Mission Encounter* (Berkeley, CA, 2007), 1–13; Sidney W. Mintz and Richard Price, *The Birth of African-American Culture: An Anthropological Perspective* (Boston, 1992 [1976]), esp. 44–45; Patrick Harries, *Butterflies and Barbarians: Swiss Missionaries and Systems of Knowledge in South-East Africa* (Oxford, 2007). For an early and influential discussion of the issue of causality among non-European peoples, see E. E. Evans-Pritchard, *Witchcraft, Oracles and Magic Among the Azande* (Oxford, 1937). For a helpful summary of the issues, see Brian Morris, *Anthropological Studies of Religion: An Introductory Text* (Cambridge, UK, 1987), 186–203.

14. Quotation: "The Rev. John Leighton Wilson Received the Instructions of the Prudential Committee in the Central Presbyterian Church, Philadelphia," *Missionary Herald*, 19 October 1834.

15. An increasingly secular West would largely abandon a belief that some transcendent being acts with purpose in the details of history to move creation and human life toward a final goal. For introductions to the immensely complex story of secularization and its implications for Christian thought, see Herbert Butterfield, "God in History," in *God, History, and Historians: Modern Christian Views of History*, ed. C. T. McIntire (Oxford, 1977), 192–204; Reinhold Niebuhr, "The Foolishness of the Cross and the Sense of History," in ibid., 68–80;

Arnold Toynbee, "The Christian Understanding of History," in ibid., 176–191. Cf. also Paul Ricoeur, *Memory, History, Forgetting* (Chicago, 2006), esp. 293–342.

16. Quotations: Isaiah 55:8–9; John 1:14. Cf. JLW's reflections on death of young missionary couple, JLW to RA, 28 January 1837, ABCFM.

17. For "missionary hubris," see Michael O'Brien, *Conjectures of Order: Intellectual Life and the American South, 1810–1860* (Chapel Hill, NC, 2004), 180. For missionaries and cultural imperialism, see Andrew Porter, "'Cultural Imperialism' and Protestant Missionary Enterprise, 1780–1914," *Journal of Imperial and Commonwealth History* 25, no. 3 (1997): 367–391.

18. Quotation: Wilson, *Western Africa*, 215. For the question of the fear of "forces of evil" in the contemporary African churches and the role of Christian faith in reducing that fear, see Philip Jenkins, *The New Faces of Christianity: Believing the Bible in the Global South* (New York, 2006), 124–125.

19. Quotation: Romans 8:21. For the dynamics of conversion, see Robert W. Hefner, "Introduction: World Building and the Rationality of Conversion," in *Conversion to Christianity: Historical and Anthropological Perspectives on a Great Transformation*, ed. Robert W. Hefner (Berkeley, CA, 1993), 44; Humphrey J. Fisher, "Conversion Reconsidered: Some Historical Aspects of Religious Conversions in Black Africa," *Africa* 43 (1973): 27–40. Cf. Keane, *Christian Moderns*, esp. 6–9, 37–82, 176–196.

20. JH to JHBL, 15 October 1834, MSCS; Richard L. Hall, *On Afric's Shore: A History of Maryland in Liberia, 1834–1857* (Baltimore, 2003), 95–97. For early accounts by Europeans of the "red water ordeal," see John Thornton, *Africa and Africans in the Making of the Atlantic World, 1400–1800* (Cambridge, UK, 1998), 241. Cf. the competing interpretations of the death of a slave woman in Virginia in Sharla M. Fett, *Working Cures: Healing, Health, and Power on Southern Slave Plantations* (Chapel Hill, NC, 2002), 84–85.

21. Quotation: JLW to RA, 4 August 1835, ABCFM. Cf. JH to JHBL, 15 October 1834, MSCS.

22. Quotation: JLW to RA, 4 August 1835, ABCFM. *Missionary Herald*, January 1836, 65–66. For the widespread publication of such a narrative, see *Missionary Register* (London), 1 August 1836, 360. The missionary narrative that pitted the heroism and faith of the missionary against some terrifying African practice was perhaps most firmly established by the Swiss missionary Fritz Ramseyer.

He and his wife were held captive by the Asante in present-day Ghana for four years. They observed widespread human sacrifice, and at the death of a prince the sacrifice of six hundred slaves and the strangulation of three wives. See Fritz Ramseyer, *Quatre Ans Chez les Achanties* (Paris, 1876). Such narratives played a key role in establishing images of Africa and in encouraging the mission movement. See Patrick Harries, "Anthropology," in *Mission and Empire*, ed. Norman Etherington (Oxford, 2005), 238–246. But see also J. D. Y. Peel, "For Who Hath Despised the Day of Small Things? Missionary Narratives and Historical Anthropology," *Comparative Studies in Society and History* 37 (1995): 581–607.

23. Hall, *On Afric's Shore*, 113–115; JLW to JHBL, 6 September 1836, MSCS.

24. Anna M. Scott, *Day Dawn in Africa; or, Progress of the Prot. Epis. Mission at Cape Palmas, West Africa* (New York, 1858), 25–26.

25. Quotation: JH to JHBL, 1 May 1836, MSCS.

26. Quotation: JLW to RA, 18 March 1836, ABCFM.

27. Quotation: JLW to RA, 23 November 1835, ABCFM.

28. Quotation: "Minutes of a Public Meeting," 5 September 1838, MSCS. For settler antagonism toward the Grebo, see JLW to RA, 7 March 1836, ABCFM; JLW to RA, 3 November 1836, ABCFM; JBR to JHBL, 12 February 1837, MSCS; JBR to JHBL, 22 September 1841, MSCS.

29. Hall, *On Afric's Shore*, 118–124.

30. Wilson, *Western Africa*, 138. For a helpful summary of the differences between the Americans and the Grebo on landownership, see Hall, *On Afric's Shore*, 46–55.

31. Oliver Holmes to JHBL, 13 July 1836, MSCS; Jane Jackson Martin, "The Dual Legacy: Government Authority and Mission Influence Among the Glebo of Eastern Liberia, 1834–1910" (PhD diss., Boston University, 1968), 88–89.

32. Quotations: JLW to JHBL, 6 September 1836, MSCS.

33. For Holmes's disdain of the colonists, see Hall, *On Afric's Shore*, 195; JLW to RA, 3 November 1836, ABCFM; JBR to Oliver Holmes, 27 December 1837, MSCS.

34. JLW to JHBL, 25 May 1836, MSCS. See also JLW to RA, 12 June 1836, ABCFM.

35. JLW to JB, 24 October 1833, CTS; J. Leighton Wilson and Stephen Wynkoop, "Report of the State of the Colony of Liberia," 24 March 1834, ABCFM.

36. JLW to Ira Easter, 2 June 1836, MSCS. See also JBR to JHBL, 12 February 1837, MSCS; JBR to Oliver Holmes, 27 December 1837, MSCS.

37. JLW to RA, 1 April 1836, ABCFM.

38. Quotation: JBR to JHBL, 12 February 1837, MSCS. For settler complaints about being misled and neglected, see, for example, "Afflicting News from the Colony at Cape Palmas," *The Liberator* (Boston), 10 January 1835; "Memorial of Colonists to the Board of Managers," 15 June 1836, MSCS; "Petition of Colonists," 24 October 1844, MSCS. Cf. William E. Allen, "Rethinking the History of Settler Agriculture in Nineteenth-Century Liberia," *International Journal of African Historical Studies* 37, no. 3 (2004): 435.

39. These issues and the historiography around them are brilliantly analyzed in David Brion Davis, *In the Image of God: Religion, Moral Values, and Our Heritage of Slavery* (New Haven, CT, 2001), esp. 123–136. See also "Black Memory and Progress of the Race," in David W. Blight, *Race and Reunion: The Civil War in American Memory* (Cambridge, MA, 2001), 300–337.

40. Quotation: Lacy K. Ford, *Deliver Us from Evil: The Slavery Question in the Old South* (Oxford, 2009), 71. For the society's efforts to whiten Maryland, see ibid., 359–389. For abolitionists' use of JLW's reports on colonization, see, for example, "Colonization," *The Liberator* (Boston), 8 July 1842; and cf. "The Scheme of the Maryland Colonization Society," *The Liberator* (Boston), 9 August 1834; "Immediate Abolition," *The Liberator* (Boston), 24 January 1835; George M. Fredrickson, *The Black Image in the White Mind: The Debate on Afro-American Character and Destiny, 1817–1914* (New York, 1971), 1–42.

41. Quotation: Wilson, *Western Africa*, 126. For Grebo houses, see ibid., 107–109.

42. Quotation, ibid., 126. For the work of Grebo women generally, see ibid., 107–109, 125–126. For the elegant stride of West African and African American women carrying large burdens on their heads, and for how this walking technique conserves energy, see Philip D. Morgan, *Slave Counterpoint: Black Culture in the Eighteenth-Century Chesapeake and Lowcountry* (Chapel Hill, NC, 1998), 200–201.

43. Quotations: Wilson, *Western Africa*, 126–127.

44. Quotations: ibid., 125.

45. J. Leighton Wilson, "Journal of a Tour to King Neh's Town on the Cavally River," 6 June 1836, ABCFM.

46. For William Davis, see "Extracts from

Letters of Mr. Wilson, at Cape Palmas," *Charleston Observer*, 8 September 1838; Martin, *The Dual Legacy*, 101. Davis was serving as JLW's translator while Simleh Ballah was in Baltimore.

47. For Mary Clealand, see "Extracts from Letters of Mr. Wilson, at Cape Palmas," *Charleston Observer*, 8 July 1837; JLW to RA, "List of Students," 6 December 1839, ABCFM.

48. Hall, *On Afric's Shore*, 265–266.

49. Quotation: Wilson, "Journal of a Tour," 6 June 1836, ABCFM. For the African traditions of rice cultivation and the influence of rice on the development of the Lowcountry rice economy and cuisine, see Judith A. Carney, *Black Rice: The African Origins of Rice Cultivation in the Americas* (Cambridge, MA, 2002); Morgan, *Slave Counterpoint*, 33–46; Karen Hess, *The Carolina Rice Kitchen: The African Connection* (Columbia, SC, 1992). For the debate among historians about the extent of African influence in the development of Lowcountry rice plantations, see David Eltis, Philip Morgan, and David Richardson, "Agency and Diaspora in Atlantic History: Reassessing the African Contribution to Rice Cultivation in the Americas," *American Historical Review* 112 (2007): 1329–1358. The authors concluded that "the rice regime owed much to improvisation; it was a hybrid, synthetic rather than European or African in character" (1354). For responses to Eltis et al., see *American Historical Review* 115 (2010): 123–171.

50. Quotations: Wilson, "Journal of a Tour," 7 June 1836, ABCFM.

51. Quotation: ibid., 7 June 1836.

52. Quotation: John H. B. Latrobe, *Maryland in Liberia: A History of the Colony* (Baltimore, 1885), 48.

53. For Ballah's time in Baltimore, see ibid., 48–52.

54. Quotations: Latrobe, *Maryland in Liberia*, 130–133.

55. Quotations: JLW to JHBL, 6 September 1836, MSCS.

56. For Grebo dialects, see Sue Hasselbring and Eric Johnson, "A Sociolinguistic Survey of the Grebo Language Area of Liberia," SIL Electronic Survey Reports 2002-074: 100, www.sil.org/silesr/abstract.asp?ref=2002-074.

57. Quotation: J. Leighton Wilson, "Excursion to Bolobo," 25 October 1836, ABCFM.

58. Quotations: ibid., 26 October 1836.

59. Quotation: ibid.

60. For the active role of the African as a translator and interpreter of the Christian message, see Lamin Sanneh, *Translating the Message: The Missionary*

Impact on Culture (New York, 1989); Porter, "'Cultural Imperialism.'" Cf. Keane, *Christian Moderns*, esp. 6–9, 37–82, 176–196.

61. Quotations: Wilson, "Excursion to Bolobo," 26 October 1836, ABCFM. Cf. Hilary M. Beckles, "Crop over Fetes and Festivals in Caribbean Slavery," in *In the Shadow of the Plantation: Caribbean History and Legacy*, ed. Alvin O. Thompson (Kingston, 2002), 246–263.

62. Quotation: Wilson, "Excursion to Bolobo," 26 October 1836, ABCFM. For the relationship of music—and by implication dance—to social structures and deep cultural assumptions, see Kofi Agawu, "John Blacking and the Study of African Music," *Africa* 67 no. 3 (1997): 491–499. For dance, see Rex M. Nettleford, *Caribbean Cultural Identity, The Case of Jamaica: An Essay in Cultural Dynamics* (Kingston, 1979), 27–30; Morgan, *Slave Counterpoint*, 581–588, 592–593.

63. Quotations: Wilson, "Excursion to Bolobo," 27 October 1836, ABCFM.

64. Quotation: ibid.

65. Daily routines at Fair Hope are described in letters from the Wilsons. See, especially, JLW to RA, 28 June 1836, ABCFM; letter from JBW to "a friend in Philadelphia," published in Archibald Alexander, *A History of Colonization on the Western Coast of Africa* (Philadelphia, 1846), 423; and JLW to RA, 1 April 1836, ABCFM.

Chapter Eight: Sorrows and Conflicts

1. Quotation: JLW to RA, 6 September 1836, ABCFM. Holmes arrived at Cape Palmas on 4 February 1836 and announced his resignation in early September 1836. See Richard L. Hall, *On Afric's Shore: A History of Maryland in Liberia, 1834–1857* (Baltimore, 2003), 118–122, 134–135.

2. Quotation: JLW to RA, 3 November 1836, ABCFM.

3. For the Whites' background, see Joseph Tracy, "History of the American Board of Commissioners for Foreign Missions," in *History of American Missions to the Heathen, from Their Commencement to the Present Time* (Worcester, MA, 1840), 322; "West Africa," *Missionary Herald*, December 1836; Hampden C. DuBose, *Memoirs of Rev. John Leighton Wilson, D.D., Missionary to Africa and Secretary of Foreign Missions* (Richmond, VA, 1895), 89–91. For James, see Tracy, "History of the American Board," 322; JLW to RA, 16 April 1836, ABCFM; JLW to "My Dear parents, Brothers and Sisters," 21 April 1837, CTS; BVRJ to RA, 11 May 1837, ABCFM; Nancy Sikes

Porter to "Dear Mother," 30 June 1851, in the Mary Coultier private collection of Gabon mission letters.

4. Quotation: Dubose, *Memoirs*, 72. For the arrival of the Whites, see David White to RA, 28 December 1836, ABCFM.

5. JLW to RA, 28 January 1837, ABCFM.

6. Quotation: ibid.

7. Ibid.

8. Ibid.

9. Quotations: Dubose, *Memoirs*, 89; JLW to RA, 28 January 1837, ABCFM. For a full exposition of the doctrine of providence as understood by "Old School Calvinists" such as the Wilsons, see the work of JBW's cousin Charles Hodge, *Systematic Theology* (New York, 1873), vol. 1, 575–616.

10. Hall, *On Afric's Shore*, 149; JBR to JHBL, 21 August 1838, MSCS.

11. See Winston James, *The Struggles of John Brown Russwurm: The Life and Writings of a Pan-Africanist Pioneer, 1799–1851* (New York, 2010).

12. Quotation: Horatio Bridge, *Personal Recollections of Nathaniel Hawthorne* (New York, 1893), 30. For the period of JBR's time at Bowdoin, see ibid., 16–32. See also Nehemiah Cleaveland, *History of Bowdoin College with Biographical Sketches of Its Graduates, from 1806 to 1870* (Boston, 1882); James, *The Struggles of John Brown Russwurm*, 16–17, 352–353.

13. Quotation: James, *The Struggles of John Brown Russwurm*, 29. For the history and context of *Freedom's Journal*, see Jacqueline Bacon, *Freedom's Journal: The First African-American Newspaper* (Lanham, MD, 2007).

14. Quotation: James, *The Struggles of John Brown Russwurm*, 31. See also ibid., 44.

15. Quotation: ibid., 51. For the bitter response to Russwurm's decision, see ibid., 49–53.

16. Ibid., 60, 77.

17. Quotation: James Hall, "Monument to Governor Russwurm," *Maryland Colonization Journal*, March 1853, 352. See also James, *The Struggles of John Brown Russwurm*, 18–19, 261n61.

18. Russwurm's life and his role as governor of Maryland in Liberia has been the subject of significant scholarly debate. On the one hand, Winston James, for example, in *The Struggles of John Brown Russwurm*, provided a thoughtful and enthusiastic picture of Russwurm from a Caribbean and "back to Africa" tradition. Amos J. Beyan, on the other hand, in *African American Settlements in West Africa: John Brown Russwurm and the American Civilizing Efforts* (New York, 2005), presented a highly critical portrait from the perspective of the indigenous Liberian people.

Beyan tellingly dedicated his study "in memory of the more than 250,000 Liberians who died in the Liberian Civil War in the 1990s."

19. Quotation: JBR to JHBL, 7 July 1838, MSCS. See also, for the food crisis, JBR to JHBL, 26 April 1838, MSCS; JBR to JHBL, 28 April 1838, MSCS; JBR to Oliver Holmes, 28 April 1838, MSCS; JLW to Ira Easter, 5 July 1838, MSCS. William E. Allen has argued that complaints such as Russwurm's about the "Indolent Americo-Liberians" who "abhorred agriculture because it evoked unpleasant memories of slavery," and who "misinterpreted their new freedom as an excuse from work," is "actually a variant of the popular nineteenth-century stereotype of the lazy African slave of the Atlantic World." If so, it was a view fully articulated by African American leaders at Cape Palmas such as Russwurm and Samuel McGill. See William E. Allen, "Rethinking the History of Settler Agriculture in Nineteenth-Century Liberia," *International African Historical Studies* 37, no. 3 (2004): 435–462, esp. 435. For ships arriving with new immigrants from 1836 to 1838, see Richard L. Hall, *On Afric's Shore*, 452–473. For the high mortality rates among African American immigrants to Liberia, see Antonio McDaniel, *Swing Low, Sweet Chariot: The Mortality Costs of Colonizing Liberia in the Nineteenth Century* (Chicago, 1995).

20. For the financial panic of 1837, see Alasdair Roberts, *America's First Great Depression: Economic Crisis and Political Disorder After the Panic of 1837* (Ithaca, NY, 2012). For the split in the Presbyterian church, see Sydney E. Ahlstrom, *A Religious History of the American People* (New Haven, CT, 1972), 455–471.

21. Quotation: JLW to RA, 26 February 1838, ABCFM. See also JLW to RA, 29 December 1838, ABCFM.

22. JLW to RA, 25 August 1836, ABCFM.

23. BVRJ to RA, 11 May 1837, ABCFM.

24. Quotation: JLW to RA, 25 August 1836, ABCFM.

25. Quotation: JLW to RA, 16 April 1837, ABCFM.

26. Quotation: JBR to JHBL, 12 February 1837, MSCS. See also JBR to JHBL, 14 November 1836, MSCS.

27. Quotations: Samuel McGill to JHBL, 8 June 1840, MSCS. For the settlers' increasing hostility toward the Grebo and for settler identification of themselves as Americans and Grebo as savages, see "Remonstrance of Citizens of Maryland in Liberia," 12 September 1838, MSCS. See also JLW to RA, 3 November 1836, ABCFM; JBR to JHBL,

10 October 1841, MSCS; S. F. McGill to JH, 22 August 1844, MSCS. Cf. also Svend E. Holsoe, "A Study of Relations Between Settlers and Indigenous Peoples in Western Liberia, 1821–1847," *International Journal of African Historical Studies* 4, no. 2 (1971): 331–362. For settler opposition to education of the Grebo, see JLW to JHBL, 16 January 1836, ABCFM; JLW to RA, 3 November 1836, ABCFM; Hall, *On Afric's Shore*, 174.

28. Cf. James Sidbury, *Becoming African in America: Race and Nation in the Early Black Atlantic* (New York, 2007). Sidbury argued that, beginning in the 1820s, Northern free African Americans began to regard themselves as "colored Americans" and not Africans. Much of the use of "African," as in Savannah's First African Baptist Church, was from an earlier period.

29. Quotation: JLW to RA, 7 February 1837, ABCFM.

30. Quotation: JBR to JHBL, 21 August 1838, MSCS. For details of the confrontation, see JBR to JHBL, 12 February 1837, MSCS; JLW to RA, 7 February 1837, ABCFM.

31. Quotation: JLW to RA, 7 February 1837, ABCFM. For JBR's praise of JLW and JBW, see JBR to JHBL, 12 February 1837, MSCS. See also Hall, *On Afric's Shore*, 147–150; Jane Jackson Martin, "The Dual Legacy: Government Authority and Mission Influence Among the Glebo of Eastern Liberia, 1834–1910" (PhD diss., Boston University, 1968), 105–106.

32. Quotations: JBR to Oliver Holmes, 27 December 1837, MSCS; Martin, "The Dual Legacy," 179. Russwurm had already been in conflict with settlers in Monrovia. The settler-dominated colonial assembly had removed him from his position as colonial secretary in 1835. The white American Colonization Society board had reinstated him. See Beyan, *African American Settlements in West Africa*, 79.

33. JLW to RA, 7 February 1837, ABCFM.

34. Quotation: JLW to RA, 16 April 1837, ABCFM. For JLW's protest to JHBL, see JLW to JHBL, 18 April 1837, MSCS. For the critical role of African provisions in the international slave trade, see Judith A. Carney and Richard Nicholas Rosomoff, *In the Shadow of Slavery: Africa's Botanical Legacy in the Atlantic World* (Berkeley, CA, 2009), esp. 53, 57, 65–79. For the conflict between Methodist missionaries and colonial authorities in Monrovia during this period, see Tom W. Shick, *Behold the Promised Land: A History of Afro-American Settler Society in Nineteenth-Century Liberia* (Baltimore, 1977), 37–41; Eunjin Park, *White Americans in "Black" Africa: Black*

and White American Methodist Missionaries in Liberia, 1820–1875 (New York, 2001), 136–143.

35. JLW to JHBL, 6 July 1837, MSCS; RA to JHBL, 28 June 1837, ABCFM and MSCS.

36. Quotation: JBR to JHBL, 22 June 1837, MSCS.

37. JLW to JHBL, 5 July 1837, MSCS; JLW to JHBL, 6 July 1837, MSCS; George McGill to JHBL, 25 December 1837, MSCS; JLW to JHBL, 16 January 1838, MSCS; JBR to Oliver Holmes, 28 April 1838, MSCS.

38. RA to JHBL, 28 June 1838, ABCFM and MSCS; RA to JHBL, 11 July 1838, ABCFM and MSCS.

39. Quotation: RA to JHBL, 11 July 1838, ABCFM and MSCS.

40. Cf. JLW to RA, 11 October 1837, ABCFM. For the deepening sectional crisis in mission work, see Sydney E. Ahlstrom, *A Religious History of the American People* (New Haven, CT, 1972), esp. 649–669, and for the Congregationalists and Presbyterians, 455–471.

41. Quotation: "The Scheme of the Maryland Colonization Society," *The Liberator* (Boston), 9 August 1834. Cf. also "Immediate Emancipation," *The Liberator* (Boston), 24 January 1834; "Colonization," *The Liberator* (Boston), 8 July 1842. For JLW's protest to RA, see JLW to RA, 14 January 1839, ABCFM; and see also JLW to RA, 25 September 1838, ABCFM. For William Lloyd Garrison on the Cherokees and colonization, see Henry Mayer, *All on Fire: William Lloyd Garrison and the Abolition of Slavery* (New York, 1998), 137–139. For British abolitionists and their efforts to protect indigenous people from white settlers, see Alan Lester, "Humanitarians and White Settlers in the Nineteenth Century," in *Mission and Empire*, ed. Norman Etherington (Oxford, 2005), 64–85. Cf., for abolitionist parallels with JLW's arguments, G. B. Stebbins, *Facts and Opinions Touching the Real Origin, Character and Influence of the American Colonization Society* (Boston, 1854), esp. 155–189.

42. Quotation: Charles Snetter to JHBL, 9 July 1837, MSCS.

43. Quotation: ibid.

44. JBR to Oliver Holmes, 27 December 1837, MSCS.

45. JLW to JHBL, 6 July 1837, MSCS.

46. Quotation: JLW to RA, 25 October 1837, ABCFM.

47. Quotation: ibid. See also JLW's report on colonization sent to RA, 13 March 1838, esp. # 5, ABCFM. For abolitionists' summaries of charges

against Liberian settlers in regard to the slave trade, see Stebbins, *Facts and Opinions*, esp. 160–165; William Goodel, *Slavery and Anti-Slavery: A History of the Great Struggle in Both Hemispheres, with a View of the Slavery Question in the United States* (New York, 1852), esp. 341–352.

48. Quotations: JBR to Oliver Holmes, 27 December 1837, MSCS.

Chapter Nine:
The Bitter Cost of Freedom

1. The letters from JLW and JBW to Nicholas Bayard have not been found but are referenced, with excerpts, in JLW to RA, 12 June 1836, ABCFM; JLW to JHBL, 25 June 1836, MSCS; and JLW to RA, 28 June 1836, ABCFM. For the management of the Hutchinson Island settlement, see Estate of N. S. Bayard in account with N. J. Bayard, Administrator, 1832–1838, SCCC.

2. Quote from earlier letter to JHBL found in Nicholas Bayard to Ira Easter, 8 February 1837, MSCS. For the neglect of the dams and trunks of the former rice fields, see "Report of Richard Rowell," *Georgian*, 3 June 1822. See also Estate of N. S. Bayard, 15 February 1825, 10 November 1825, 3 January 1826.

3. For management of the estate, see Estate of N. S. Bayard, 1832–1838. For the bateau, a plank version of a dugout canoe, and its use on the rivers of the Lowcountry, see William C. Fleetwood, *Tidecraft: The Boats of South Carolina, Georgia and Northeastern Florida, 1750–1950* (Camden, SC, 1995), esp. 145–147, 316–321. For the dangers associated with using such a small boat on a powerful river, and for the Gullah name for the bateau, see ibid., 146, and Ambrose Gonzales, *The Black Border* (Columbia, SC, 1964), 335. For the drowning of Bayard slaves, see Estate of N. S. Bayard, October 1830 and June 1838, SCCC.

4. JLW to JHBL, 25 June 1836, MSCS; Nicholas Bayard to Ira Easter, 8 February 1837, MSCS; JLW to RA, 26 February 1838, ABCFM; Nicholas Bayard to Ira Easter, 2 April 1838, MSCS. For the communal spaces in Lowcountry slave settlements and activities there, see Philip D. Morgan, *Slave Counterpoint: Black Culture in the Eighteenth-Century Chesapeake & Lowcountry* (Chapel Hill, NC, 1998), 104–122; Theresa Ann Singleton, "The Archaeology of Afro-American Slavery in Coastal Georgia: Regional Perception of Slave Household and Community Patterns" (PhD diss., University of Florida, 1980); cf. James C. Scott,

Domination and the Art of Resistance: Hidden Transcripts, (New Haven, CT, 1990), 1–16.

5. Nicholas Bayard, "List of Slaves Belonging to the Estate of the Late Doc. N. S. Bayard of Savannah, Georgia, Who Would Probably Emigrate to Cape Palmas," 4 October 1836, MSCS.

6. Estate of N. S. Bayard, 1836–1838; Nicholas Bayard to Ira Easter, 26 October 1837, MSCS. See also Nicholas Bayard to Ira Easter, 1 November 1837, MSCS; Nicholas Bayard to Ira Easter, 20 November 1837, MSCS; Nicholas Bayard to Ira Easter, 14 December 1837, MSCS.

7. Bayard, "List of Slaves."

8. Ibid. Cf. Whittington B. Johnson, *Black Savannah, 1788–1864* (Fayetteville, AR, 1996), 150–153; Jacqueline Jones, *Saving Savannah: The City and the Civil War* (New York, 2008), 44–46, 49; Lacy K. Ford, *Deliver Us from Evil: The Slavery Question in the Old South* (Oxford, 2009), 321–324. For Paul's hopes to eventually bring his family to Cape Palmas, see Paul Sansay to "Dear Sir" [Latrobe?], 17 January 1839, MSCS.

9. Quotation: Nicholas Bayard to Ira Easter, 2 April 1838, MSCS. For funds sent to the Maryland board, see Nicholas Bayard to Ira Easter, 26 April 1838, MSCS. For provisions provided in Savannah, see Estate of N. S. Bayard, 1837–1839. For "Old Toby" and "Old Lucy," see "Indenture Between James R. Eckard and Margaret Bayard," 15 June 1833, SCCC; Bayard, "List of Slaves"; JBW to RA, 1 April 1843, ABCFM.

10. Quotations: JLW to RA, 26 February 1838, ABCFM; JLW to RA, 28 March 1838, ABCFM.

11. Quotations: JLW to RA, 26 February 1838, ABCFM; JLW to William Wilson, [?] March 1838, SCL.

12. For the Cavally River disaster, see JBR to JHBL, 26 April 1838; King Freeman to JHBL, 27 April 1838, MSCS; Hall, *On Afric's Shore*, 171–172. For JLW's early trip, see Chapter 11.

13. JLW to Nicholas Bayard, 26 April 1838, copied in letter from Nicholas Bayard to Ira Easter, 10 July 1838, MSCS. JLW had asked Bayard to "give the letter no needless publicity," but Bayard copied the letter and sent it to the Maryland Colonization Society, apparently not realizing it would increase the tension between the missionary and the colonial officials in Baltimore. For Russwurm's acknowledgment that many settlers wanted to return to the United States, see JBR to JHBL, 12 February 1837, MSCS.

14. Nicholas Bayard to Ira Easter, 30 April 1838, MSCS.

15. For the adoption of family names by freed slaves, see Leon F. Litwack, *Been in the Storm So Long: The Aftermath of Slavery* (New York, 1979), 248–251; Ira Berlin, *Many Thousands Gone: The First Two Centuries of Slavery in North America* (Cambridge, MA, 1998), 285–286; Christopher Phillips, *Freedom's Port: The African American Community of Baltimore, 1790–1860* (Urbana, IL, 1997), 88–91.

16. Cf. Paul Sansay to "Dear Sir" [Latrobe?], 17 January 1839, MSCS. See also Nicholas Bayard to Ira Easter, 30 April 1838, MSCS; Hall, *On Afric's Shore*, 467–470. Hall mistakenly has the Bayard people sailing directly from Savannah to Cape Palmas.

17. Quotations: JLW to Ira Easter, 5 July 1838, MSCS; JLW to JHBL, 15 January 1839, MSCS.

18. Quotation: JBR to JHBL, 7 July 1838, MSCS.

19. Quotation: JBR to JHBL, 1 November 1838, MSCS.

20. Quotation: Paul Sansay to "Dear Sir" [Latrobe?], 17 January 1839, MSCS.

21. For allotted tracts on Bayard Island, see "Revey Map," MSCS. For the occupations of the new immigrants, see Hall, *On Afric's Shore*, 467–470.

22. Cf. Morgan, *Slave Counterpoint*, esp. 560–580. See also Philip Morgan, ed., *African American Life in the Georgia Lowcountry: The Atlantic World and the Gullah Geechee* (Athens, GA, 2010).

23. JLW to RA, "Copied from Mr. Wilson's Journal," 13 August 1838, ABCFM.

24. Ibid.

25. Ibid.; JBR to JHBL, 6 August 1838, MSCS. Because Snetter was responsible for the secular affairs at Fair Hope, JLW had apparently not objected to his serving in the militia.

26. JLW to RA, "Copied from Mr. Wilson's Journal," 13 August 1838, ABCFM; Hall, *On Afric's Shore*, 183–191.

27. Quotations: JBR to Oliver Holmes, 24 May 1839, MSCS; "Petition from the Citizens of Maryland in Liberia," 12 September 1838, MSCS.

28. Quotation: JBR to JHBL, 1 November 1838, MSCS.

29. *The African Repository and Colonial Journal* 17 (1841): 41; Hall, *On Afric's Shore*, 557–558; Svend E. Holsoe, "A Study of Relations Between Settlers and Indigenous Peoples in Western Liberia, 1821–1847," *International Journal of African Historical Studies* 4, no. 2 (1971): 349–351.

Chapter Ten: Exploring Strange Worlds

1. JLW to RA, 28 June 1836, ABCFM.

2. Karen Hess, *The Carolina Rice Kitchen: The African Connection* (Columbia, SC, 1992).

3. JLW to RA, 28 June 1836, ABCFM. For provisions sent from the United States, see JLW to H. Hill, 18 March 1836, ABCFM. For JLW's garden and for the food eaten at Fair Hope, see JLW to RA, [?] January 1839, ABCFM; JLW to "Dear Parents, Brothers, and Sisters," 18 May 1840, SCL.

4. JLW to RA, 28 June 1836, ABCFM; JLW to RA, [?] January 1839, ABCFM. For West African foods and the history of cassava, see Judith A. Carney and Richard Nicholas Rosomoff, *In the Shadow of Slavery: Africa's Botanical Legacy in the Atlantic World* (Berkeley, CA, 2009), esp. 54, 108–111. For the ways in which European and African eating habits intersected and borrowed from one another, see Carney and Rosomoff, *In the Shadow of Slavery*, esp. 46–64; and Jeremy Rich, *A Workman Is Worthy of His Meat: Food and Colonialism in the Gabon Estuary* (Lincoln, NE, 2007), 22–44.

5. "Cape Palmas," *Charleston Observer*, 7 May 1836. For discussions of European clothes and various African cultural practices, see Hildi Hendrickson, ed., *Clothing and Difference: Embodied Identities in Colonial and Post-Colonial Africa* (Durham, NC, 1996). For the history of the knife, fork, and spoon and how they were used in the West, see Bee Wilson, *Consider the Fork: A History of How We Cook and Eat* (New York, 2012). Cf. Nancy Rose Hunt's description of a "knife and fork" education used by missionaries to promote European domestic order and ideas of hygiene, in *A Colonial Lexicon of Birth Ritual, Medicalization, and Mobility in the Congo* (Durham, NC, 1999), 118–123, and Carole Counihan and Penny Van Esterik, eds. *Food and Culture: A Reader* (New York, 1997).

6. Quotations: J. Leighton Wilson, *Western Africa: Its History, Condition, and Prospects* (New York, 1856), 122.

7. Stephen Wynkoop, "Journal of S. R. Wynkoop to Western Africa," 33, ABCFM.

8. Cf. Sidney W. Mintz, *Sweetness and Power: The Place of Sugar in Modern History* (New York, 1985), 3–5.

9. Quotation: JLW to RA, 28 June 1836, ABCFM.

10. For William Polk and the school at Rock Town, see JLW to RA, 24 August 1836, ABCFM; 3 November 1836; 26 May 1837, ABCFM. For Yellow Will, see Jane Jackson Martin, "The Dual

Legacy: Government Authority and Mission Influence Among the Glebo of Eastern Liberia, 1834–1910" (PhD diss., Boston University, 1968), 99; JLW to RA, 24 August 1836, ABCFM. For John Banks and the school at Graway, see RA to JHBL, 28 June 1837, ABCFM and MSCS. For the graduate, see Epilogue.

11. JLW to RA, 25 June 1836, ABCFM. Cf. Margaret D. Jacobs, *White Mother to a Dark Race: Settler Colonialism, Maternalism, and the Removal of Indigenous Children in the American West and Australia, 1880–1940* (Lincoln, NE, 2010), esp., xxi–xxxii.

12. JLW to RA, 3 November 1836, ABCFM; JLW to H. Hill, 18 March 1836, ABCFM; JLW to RA, 8 June 1839, ABCFM; West Africa, "Annual Report," 1839, ABCFM. For the dialectical tensions between the Grebo world and the world being introduced in the mission school, cf. Jean Comaroff and John Comaroff, *From Revelation to Revolution: Christianity, Colonialism, and Consciousness in Southern Africa* (Chicago, 1993); Robert W. Hefner, "World Building and the Rationality of Conversion," and Terence Ranger, "The Local and the Global in Southern African Religious History," in *Conversion to Christianity: Historical and Anthropological Perspectives on a Great Transformation*, ed. Robert W. Hefner (Berkeley, CA, 1993).

13. JLW to RA, 7 March 1836 and 3 November 1836, ABCFM; JLW to "Dear Parents, Brothers, and Sisters," 18 May 1840, SCL. For the role of boarding schools in nineteenth-century Protestant missions, see "Annual Report," *Missionary Herald*, January 1835, 12–16; Clifton J. Phillips, *Protestant America and the Pagan World: The First Half Century of the ABCFM, 1810–1860* (Cambridge, MA, 1969); Jon Rehner and Jeanne Eder, *American Indian Education* (Norman, OK, 2004).

14. Quotation: JLW to RA, 6 August 1836, ABCFM.

15. JLW to RA, 24 August 1836, ABCFM.

16. Quotations: JLW to RA, 20 July 1836, ABCFM.

17. JLW to RA, 3 November 1836, ABCFM.

18. For Grebo customs of dress and the physique of Grebo bodies, see JLW to RA, 5 July 1836, ABCFM; JLW to RA, 7 February 1839, ABCFM. JLW makes many observations in *Western Africa* about the variety in size, complexion, and general appearance of different African peoples. See comments on this in Michael O'Brien, *Conjectures of Order: Intellectual Life and the American South, 1810–1860* (Chapel Hill, NC, 2004), 181. Cf. Alexander Butchart, *The Anatomy of Power: European Constructions*

of the African Body (London, 1998). See also, for white images of African bodies, George M. Fredrickson, *The Black Image in the White Mind: The Debate on Afro-American Character and Destiny, 1817–1914* (New York, 1971); Philip D. Curtin, *The Image of Africa: British Ideas and Action, 1780–1850* (Madison, WI, 1964), esp. 28–57; Jan Nederveen Pieterse, *White on Black: Images of Africa and Blacks in Western Popular Culture* (New Haven, CT, 1995). For an important analysis of these images, see V. Y. Mudimbe, *The Invention of Africa: Gnosis, Philosophy, and the Order of Knowledge* (Bloomington, IN, 1988), esp. 1–23. Cf. the reflection of the Victorian explorer Samuel White Baker about the "educational advantages" for "young ladies" in being exposed to scenes of African nudity. See Tim Jeal, *Explorers of the Nile: The Triumph and Tragedy of a Great Victorian Adventure* (New Haven, CT, 2011), 243.

19. JLW to RA, 10 July 1836, ABCFM; JLW to RA, 16 March 1837, ABCFM.

20. JLW to RA, 3 November 1836, ABCFM.

21. Quotations: JLW to RA, 3 November 1836, ABCFM; JLW to Elipha White, 8 July 1837, in "Fair Hope, Cape Palmas," *Charleston Observer*, 21 October 1837.

22. JLW to RA, 20 July 1836, ABCFM. For a succinct summary of the difficulties in developing an orthography for a language, see Patrick Harries, *Butterflies and Barbarians: Swiss Missionaries and Systems of Knowledge in South-East Africa* (Oxford, 2007), 157.

23. For the operation of the printing press, see JLW to RA, 2 February 1839, 7 June 1839, ABCFM. For an introduction to the complex philosophical problem of the relationship between reading and memory and the challenge that reading presents to oral cultures, see Paul Ricoeur, *Memory, History, Forgetting* (Chicago, 2004), 141–145. For the issue of "literacy and religion" in the conversion of Africans to Christianity, see Terence Ranger, "The Local and the Global in Southern African Religious History," in *Conversion to Christianity: Historical and Anthropological Perspectives on a Great Transformation*, ed. Robert W. Hefner (Berkeley, CA, 1993), esp. 85–88.

24. For the focus on indigenous leaders and the Bible being translated into the vernacular of the people, see *Missionary Herald*, January 1839, 30.

25. Quotation: Acts 17:23.

26. See Andrew Porter, "'Cultural Imperialism' and Protestant Missionary Enterprise, 1780–1914," *Journal of Imperial and Commonwealth History* 25, no. 3 (1997): 367–391. For the important role in African Christianity of the Gospel of Matthew and

the Acts of the Apostles, see Philip Jenkins, *The New Faces of Christianity: Believing the Bible in the Global South* (New York, 2006), 53–54.

27. See "Missionary Translation in African Perspective," in Lamin Sanneh, *Translating the Message: The Missionary Impact on Culture*, rev. ed. (New York, 2009), 191–228. For missions as "cultural imperialism," see Comaroff and Comaroff, *From Revelation to Revolution*, esp. 8, 88; William R. Hutchison, *Errand to the World: American Protestant Thought and Foreign Missions* (Chicago, 1987); Brian Stanley, *The Bible and the Flag: Protestant Missions and British Imperialism in the Nineteenth and Twentieth Centuries* (Leicester, UK, 1990). For a counteremphasis on the agency and activism of indigenous peoples in mission efforts, and for the fluidity of cultures generally, see Sanneh, *Translating the Message*; Paul S. Landau, *The Realm of the Word: Language, Gender, and Christianity in a Southern African Kingdom* (London, 1995); Porter, "'Cultural Imperialism.'" The insistence that indigenous peoples have not been passive in the face of various imperialisms can be found with increasing frequency in a variety of studies. Cf., for example, on the slave trade, John Thornton, *Africa and Africans in the Making of the Atlantic World, 1400–1650* (Cambridge, UK, 1992); and for the fur trade, John R. Bockstoce, *Furs and Frontiers in the Far North: The Contest Among Native and Foreign Nations for the Bering Strait Fur Trade* (New Haven, CT, 2010).

28. Wilson, *Western Africa*, 229. For the history of Bible translations into various Grebo dialects, see Sue Hasselbring and Eric Johnson, "A Sociolinguistic Survey of the Grebo Language Area of Liberia," SIL Electronic Survey Reports 2002-074: 100, www.sil.org/silesr/abstract.asp?ref=2002-074. For the vernacular language as the bearer of the divine, see report on the work of Wasa Baker in a Grebo village near Big Town, in J. Leighton Wilson, "Annual Report of the Mission," JLW to RA, 30 December 1840, ABCFM. See also Kwame Bediako, "Epilogue," in Ype Schaaf, *On Their Way Rejoicing*, trans. Paul Ellingworth (Carlisle, UK, 1994); Sanneh, *Translating the Message*, 142–163, 191–228; Jenkins, *The New Faces of Christianity*, esp. 21–31. For the way a pre-Christian past was embedded in Grebo Christianity, see Andrew F. Walls, *The Cross-Cultural Process in Christian History* (Edinburgh, 2002), 119–122. Cf. the way African Americans made the Bible their book and identified with many of the stories in the Bible in Allen Dwight Callahan, *The Talking Book: African Americans and the Bible* (New Haven, CT, 2008). Perhaps the most vivid example of Africans today claiming their own interpretation

of the Bible is in the Anglican Communion, where African Anglicans are challenging North American Episcopalians over the issue of ordination of gay and lesbian people. See Jenkins, *The New Faces of Christianity*, esp. 18–21.

29. *Missionary Herald*, January 1837, 30. See also JLW to RA, 8 September 1837, ABCFM; JLW to RA, 7 February 1839, ABCFM.

30. Quotation: JLW to RA, [?] January 1839, ABCFM.

31. Quotation: ibid.

32. Ibid.; B. V. R. James to RA, 3 October 1842, ABCFM; JLW to RA, 15 October 1843, ABCFM; WW to RA, 16 September 1846, ABCFM; JLW to B. V. R. James, 1 November 1853, PHS; B. V. R. James to JLW, 15 March 1856, PHS; B. V. R. James to JLW, 20 December 1859, PHS; B. V. R. James to JLW, 9 May 1861, PHS; "Twenty-Seventh Annual Report of the Board of Foreign Missions of the Presbyterian Church in America, New York, 1864," PHS; William Rankin, "Mr. B. V. R. James," in *Foreign Missionaries of the Presbyterian Church* (Philadelphia, 1895).

Chapter Eleven:
The Conversion of William Davis
(Mworeh Mah)

1. For Cape Palmas as a launching place for the mission to West Africa, see "Mission to West Africa: The Prudential Committee of the American Board of Commissioners for Foreign Missions to the Rev. John Leighton Wilson," *Charleston Observer*, 8 November 1834; "Western Africa," *Missionary Herald*, January 1837, 28.

2. They left on 27 March 1837, and JLW completed his journal and marked it 6 April 1837. See JLW to RA, "Journal of a Tour to Grabbo," 6 April 1837, ABCFM. The Kong Mountains, or the Mountains of Kong, appeared on almost all nineteenth-century maps of West Africa. Late in the century they were found to be an illusion. What JLW saw in the distance were mountains of the Nimba Range.

3. JLW to RA, "Journal of a Tour to Grabbo," 6 April 1837, ABCFM.

4. For the important role of African agriculture in providing supplies for slave ships and making the international slave trade possible, see Judith A. Carney and Richard Nicholas Rosomoff, *In the Shadow of Slavery: Africa's Botanical Legacy in the Atlantic World* (Berkeley, CA, 2009), esp. 53, 57, 65–79. For the role of rum in the trade for rice and slaves, see also

JLW to RA, 26 May 1837, ABCFM; J. Leighton Wilson, *Western Africa: Its History, Condition, and Prospects* (New York, 1856), 151.

5. For Haidee, or the "Grand Devil Oracle," see James Hall to JHBL, 6 November 1835, MSCS; Wilson, *Western Africa*, 217–218; Anna M. Scott, *Day Dawn in Africa; or, Progress of the Prot. Epis. Mission at Cape Palmas, West Africa* (New York, 1858), 68–70; Richard F. Burton, *Wanderings in West Africa: From Liverpool to Fernando Po* (London, 1863), 284–285. For the continuing role of "sacred places" in African Christianity, see reflections of John Mbiti in Philip Jenkins, *The New Faces of Christianity: Believing the Bible in the Global South* (New York, 2006), 52–53. For a comparable development, cf. the continuing role of sacred places in Britain—from pagan Britain to Post-Reformation Britain, see Alexandra Walsham, *The Reformation of the Landscape: Religion, Identity and Memory in Early Modern Britain and Ireland* (Oxford, 2011).

6. Quotation: JLW to RA, "Journal of a Tour to Grabbo," 6 April 1837, ABCFM.

7. Wilson, *Western Africa*, 228–229. For some Grebo proverbs, see Edward Sapir, assisted by Charles G. Blooah, "Voice of Africa: Some Gweabo Proverbs," *Africa* 2 (1929): 183–184.

8. Quotation: JLW to RA, "Journal of a Tour to Grabbo," 6 April 1837, ABCFM. For the controversial subject of cannibalism, see Peggy Reeves Sanday, *Divine Hunger: Cannibalism as a Cultural System* (Cambridge, UK, 1986); Paula Brown and Donald Tuzin, eds. *The Ethnography of Cannibalism* (Washington, DC, 1983). For widespread reports of the consumption of human flesh during the Liberian Civil War, see Stephen Ellis, *The Mask of Anarchy: The Destruction of Liberia and the Religious Dimension of an African Civil War* (New York, 1999), esp. 221–224, 230–237.

9. JLW to RA, "Journal of a Tour to Grabbo," 6 April 1837, ABCFM.

10. JLW to RA, 14 January 1839, ABCFM. For the warfare between the settlers around Monrovia and the indigenous peoples, see Svend E. Holsoe, "A Study of Relations Between Settlers and Indigenous Peoples in Western Liberia, 1821–1847," *International Journal of African Historical Studies* 4, no. 2 (1971): 349–351. For the hostility of Cape Palmas settlers toward the conversion of Grebo, see JLW to RA, 14 January 1839, ABCFM.

11. Robin Horton, in two influential essays, pointed to the ways in which conversion to Christianity involved the experience of a broader social world and practical and cognitive adjustments to that world. See Robin Horton, "African Conver-

sion," *Africa* 41 (1971): 85–108; and "On the Rationality of Conversion," *Africa* 45 (1975): 219–325, 373–399. Davis's experiences in Sierra Leone and at Fair Hope were apparently important elements in his conversion.

12. Quotations: JLW to RA, 7 February 1837, ABCFM; JLW to Elipha White, 8 July 1837, in *Charleston Observer*, 21 October 1837. For JLW's early reluctance to preach in Grebo, see JLW to RA, 28 June 1836, ABCFM.

13. Quotation: JLW to RA, "Annual Report of the Mission," 30 December 1840, ABCFM. On the lack of power to coerce a conversion, see Andrew Porter, "'Cultural Imperialism' and Protestant Missionary Enterprise, 1780–1914," *Journal of Imperial and Commonwealth History* 25, no. 3 (1997): 367–391; J. D. Y. Peel, "For Who Hath Despised the Day of Small Things? Missionary Narratives and Historical Anthropology," *Comparative Studies in Society and History* 37, no. 3 (1995): 581–607. Porter and Peel argued that Protestant missionaries throughout much of the nineteenth century had little power to coerce conversions. For sincerity and authenticity in the conversion process, see Webb Keane, *Christian Moderns: Freedom and Fetish in the Mission Encounter* (Berkeley, CA, 2007), 1–13, 197–222. On images of Catholic understanding of baptism, see JLW's reflections on baptism and the early Catholic mission in the Congo and the later collapse of the church there in Wilson, *Western Africa*, 327–337; cf. Keane, *Christian Moderns*, 216. JLW's understanding of conversion, an orthodox Calvinist perspective, was being challenged in the United States by many, but especially by the evangelist Charles G. Finney, who insisted that all one had to do to be converted was to make up one's mind to accept Jesus as savior. For Finney's position and the response of his critics, see Keith J. Hardman, *Charles Grandison Finney, 1792–1875: Revivalist and Reformer* (Syracuse, NY, 1987); and for the ways Finney reflected the individualism and egalitarian impulses in US society, see Nathan O. Hatch, *The Democratization of American Christianity* (New Haven, CT, 1989), esp. 95–201. For a full exposition of JLW's theological position, especially as it opposed nineteenth-century ideas of personal self-determination, see the work of JBW's cousin, Charles Hodge, *Systematic Theology* (New York, 1873). For a succinct statement of this theological position, see Eberhard Busch, *Drawn to Freedom: Christian Faith Today in Conversation with the Heidelberg Catechism*, trans. William H. Rader (Grand Rapids, MI, 2010), 299–300.

14. Quotations: JLW to "My Dear Parents,

Brothers, and Sisters," 21 June 1837, SCL; Wilson, *Western Africa*, iii. For the organization of a church at Fair Hope, see "Western Africa: Exacts from letters of Mr. Wilson, at Cape Palmas," *Charleston Observer*, 8 September 1838. The church was organized as an adaptation of Presbyterian polity, with JLW as pastor and James as a lay elder. Together they formed the church session, which examined and received church members. For the "performance of sincerity," see Keane, "Conversion and the Performance of Sincerity," in *Christian Moderns*, 197–222.

15. Religious conversion raises demanding questions about human agency and the cultural construction of reality. See Robert W. Hefner, ed., *Conversion to Christianity: Historical and Anthropological Perspectives on a Great Transformation* (Berkeley, CA, 1993), esp. "Introduction: World Building and the Rationality of Conversion," 3–44. See also Andrew Buckser and Stephen D. Glazier, eds., *The Anthropology of Religious Conversion* (Lanham, MD, 2003), esp. xi–xviii.

16. See Peel, "For Who Hath Despised the Day of Small Things?"

17. Cf. Sean Hawkins, "Disguising Chiefs and God as History: Questions on the Acephalousness of Lodagaa Politics and Religion," *Africa* 66, no. 2 (1996): 202–241, esp. 241.

18. For the continuity in African religion in its pre-Christian and its Christian forms, see Andrew F. Walls, *The Cross-Cultural Process in Christian History* (Edinburgh, 2002), 116–135; Terence Ranger, "The Local and the Global in Southern African Religious History," in Hefner, ed., *Conversion to Christianity*, 65–98. Cf. also Kwame Bediako, *Christianity in Africa: The Renewal of a Non-Western Religion* (Edinburgh, 1995), and for continuity in British religion, see Walsham, *The Reformation of the Landscape*.

19. For Grebo wives, see Wilson, *Western Africa*, 112–119; JLW to RA, 1 April 1836, ABCFM; Scott, *Day Dawn in Africa*, 49–50; Richard L. Hall, *On Afric's Shore: A History of Maryland in Liberia, 1834–1857* (Baltimore, 2003), 87–88.

20. Quotations: JLW to RA, 26 February 1838, ABCFM; JLW to Charles Hodge, 1 December 1844, CTS.

21. JLW to RA, 18 April 1838, ABCFM.

22. Ibid.

23. For the liturgy and character of baptism at Fair Hope, see "Of Baptism," in *The Westminster Confession of Faith* (1645), the governing confessional document for Presbyterians in the nineteenth century. Cf. Erskine Clarke, *Our Southern Zion: A History*

of Calvinism in the South Carolina Low Country, 1690–1990 (Tuscaloosa, AL, 1995), 135–137.

24. For the theology behind this simple celebration of the Lord's Supper, see "Of the Sacraments," in *The Westminster Confession of Faith* (1645). The Calvinist theology of the Fair Hope mission insisted that the supper was not the sacrifice of a Catholic Mass but a "commemoration" of Christ's once and for all sacrifice. The bread and wine were regarded as remaining "truly, and only, bread and wine," in contrast to the Catholic confession that the bread and wine, through the mystery of transubstantiation, were the actual body and blood of Christ. Cf. Clarke, *Our Southern Zion*, 62–69.

25. Cf. the discussion of eating together as a social act, "a bond, created simply by partaking of food, linking human beings with one another," in Sidney W. Mintz, *Sweetness and Power: The Place of Sugar in Modern History* (New York, 1985), 3–5.

26. JLW to RA, 18 April 1838, ABCFM.

27. Quotation: "Petition from the Citizens of Maryland in Liberia," 12 September 1838, MSCS.

28. Wilson, *Western Africa*, 247. For the role and character of American traders such as Richard Lawlin on the West Coast of Africa, see George E. Brooks, Jr., *Yankee Traders, Old Coasters and African Middlemen: A History of American Legitimate Trade with West Africa in the Nineteenth Century* (Boston, 1970), esp. 3–5, and for the Leeward Coast, 222–290.

29. Cf. Robert Harms, *The Diligent: A Voyage Through the Worlds of the Slave Trade* (New York, 2002), 141; Kingsley Kofi Yeboah, *A Guide to the Cape Coast Castle* (Cape Coast, Ghana, 2007).

30. George MacLean to JLW, 31 December 1839, ABCFM; JLW to RA, "Visit to the Leeward Coast," 2 April 1839, ABCFM. See also Yeboah, *A Guide to the Cape Coast Castle*, 43–44.

31. JLW to RA, "Visit to the Leeward Coast," 2 April 1839, ABCFM.

32. JLW to RA, 6 December 1839, ABCFM; "Board of Missions," in *Missionary Register* (London), 1 January 1842.

33. Quotation: Dr. Alexander Wilson to William Armstrong, 24 September 1840, ABCFM. For Alexander Wilson's friendship with JLW's father, see JLW to William Armstrong, 29 January 1839, ABCFM. For Alexander Wilson's time in South Africa, see Dr. Alexander Wilson, "Journal," 15 June 1836 to 20 March 1837, ABCFM; William Ireland, *Historical Sketch of the Zulu Mission in South Africa* (Boston, 1865), 14–17. There are many letters from Dr. Wilson in South Africa to the American Board in ABCFM.

34. For Dr. Alexander Wilson's perspectives on the Cape Palmas colony, see Alexander Wilson to RA, 9 December 1839, ABCFM.

35. Quotation: JLW to RA, 6 December 1839, ABCFM. For the role of Freeman and Davis in the palaver that decided to abandon the ordeal, see JBR to JHBL, 8 December 1839, MSCS. See also Samuel F. McGill to Moses Sheppard, 3 January 1839, MSCS.

36. For the oracle, see Dr. Alexander Wilson to RA, 9 December 1839, ABCFM.

37. JLW to RA, 15 January 1840, ABCFM.

38. For Samuel McGill's experiences in the United States, see Hall, *On Afric's Shore*, 130–133, 194–197.

39. Samuel F. McGill to Moses Sheppard, 3 January 1839, in *Maryland Colonization Journal*, November 1843, 74–77. Parts of the letter had been published earlier as well.

40. "Census," Maryland in Liberia, 1839, MSCS; "Census," Maryland in Liberia, 1840, MSCS.

41. "Marriages in the Colony, 1839," MSCS; "Marriages in the Colony, 1840," MSCS; Hall, *On Afric's Shore*, 467–470.

42. Hall, *On Afric's Shore*, 469–470; WWD, 25 July 1842–11 November 1842, WHS.

43. Quotations: Paul Sansay to JHBL, 16 January 1839, MSCS.

44. Nicholas Bayard to JHBL, 18 September 1841, MSCS.

45. Paul Sansay's name does not appear on colonial marriage registries; nor do the census records of the colony list him as married.

Chapter Twelve: Rose-Tinted Glasses

1. Richard L. Hall, *On Afric's Shore: A History of Maryland in Liberia, 1834–1857* (Baltimore, 2003), 25; Jane Jackson Martin, "The Dual Legacy: Government Authority and Mission Influence Among the Glebo of Eastern Liberia, 1834–1910" (PhD diss., Boston University, 1968), 55–57; Lacy K. Ford, *Deliver Us from Evil: The Slavery Question in the Old South* (Oxford, 2009), 387–389.

2. "Ninth Annual Report, Board of Managers," 28 January 1841, MSCS.

3. Quotations: ibid.

4. For colonial statistics, see ibid.; Hall, *On Afric's Shore*, 475, 505–515. For mortality and food shortages in the colony, see Dr. Samuel McGill to JHBL, "Medical Reports on Illnesses, Deaths, and Births," 1 January 1842, MSCS. Cf. Antonio Mc-

Daniel, *Swing Low, Sweet Chariot: The Mortality Cost of Colonizing Liberia in the Nineteenth Century* (Chicago, 1995). For reports from colonial officials about the hostility of settlers toward the Grebo, see, for example, JBR to JHBL, 12 February 1837, MSCS; JBR to Oliver Holmes, 27 December 1837, MSCS; JBR to JHBL, 9 April 1839, MSCS; JBR to JHBL, 22 September 1841, MSCS; Samuel McGill to JHBL, 4 January 1840, MSCS; Hall, *On Afric's Shore*, 197, 207, 583n7. For the preparation of the missions to move beyond the borders of the colony, see Dr. A. E. Wilson, "Report of the ABCFM Mission," to RA, 24 August 1841, ABCFM; "Resolution," signed by Episcopal and ABCFM missionaries, 1 January 1842, ABCFM; Hall, *On Afric's Shore*, 232; Martin, "The Dual Legacy," 144–145.

5. For the impact in Maryland of the 1840 census, see Penelope Campbell, *Maryland in Africa: The Maryland State Colonization Society, 1831–1857* (Urbana, IL, 1971), 211–237; Christopher Phillips, *Freedom's Port: The African American Community of Baltimore, 1790–1860* (Urbana, IL, 1997), 180–188; Ford, *Deliver Us from Evil*, 388. For the massive movement of slaves from the Chesapeake to the Deep South, see Ira Berlin, *Many Thousands Gone: The First Two Centuries of Slavery in North America* (Cambridge, MA, 1998), esp. 358–365; Adam Rothman, *Slave Country: American Expansion and the Origins of the Deep South* (Cambridge, MA, 2005), esp. 45–54.

6. Quotation: "Circular Sent to the Counties" and "Circular Sent to the Prominent Friends of the Cause in This City," contained in "Minutes of the Meeting of the Board of Managers, Maryland Colonization Society," 13 March 1841, MSCS.

7. Quotation: ibid.

8. The removal of Maryland slaves to the black belt of the South illuminates one of the challenges of "Atlantic history"—how to discern the boundaries of an Atlantic world. How far west into the American continents does an Atlantic world extend? See Peter H. Wood, "From Atlantic History to a Continental Approach," in Jack P. Greene and Philip D. Morgan, eds. *Atlantic History: A Critical Appraisal* (Oxford, 2009), 279–298. Cf. also Alan Huffman, *Mississippi in Africa: The Saga of the Slaves of Prospect Hill Plantation and Their Legacy in Liberia Today* (New York, 2004); Walter Johnson, ed., *The Chattel Principle: Internal Slave Trades in the Americas* (New Haven, CT, 2005); Daniel K. Richter, *Before the Revolution: America's Ancient Pasts* (Cambridge, MA, 2011), esp. 346–368.

9. For JLW's and JBR's mutual suspicion, see, for example, JLW to RA, 14 January 1839, ABCFM; JBR to JHBL, 12 February 1837, MSCS; JBR to JHBL, 22 September 1841, MSCS. Cf. JLW to RA, 3 November 1836, ABCFM; JLW to JHBL, 15 January 1839, MSCS. For Russwurm's relationship with Freeman, see Samuel McGill's complaint about the governor's confidence in "old Freeman" in Samuel McGill to JHBL, 17 December 1843, MSCS.

10. JBR to JHBL, 31 May 1841, MSCS.

11. Copies of the correspondence between JLW and JBR are in the "Minutes of the Board of Managers," 12 November 1841, MSCS.

12. Ibid.

13. JBR to JHBL, 10 October 1841, MSCS.

14. Dr. A. E. Wilson and BVRJ to RA, 24 August 1841, ABCFM.

15. Quotations: JBR to JHBL, 22 September 1841, MSCS.

16. For abolitionist attacks on the colony at Cape Palmas, see, for example, "Liberia and the Slave Trade," *Morning Chronicle* (London), 28 August 1841; "The American Board and the African Colonies," *The Liberator* (Boston), 14 October 1842.

17. Quotations: "Minutes of the Board of Managers," 1 October 1841, MSCS.

18. RA to JHBL, 9 December 1841, ABCFM.

19. "Minutes of the Maryland Colonization Board," 13 December 1841, MSCS.

20. For the closing of the school at Fair Hope, see JLW to RA, 28 January 1842, ABCFM; JLW to RA, 7 April 1842, ABCFM. For details of Dr. A. E. Wilson's death, see "Decease of Doct. A. E. Wilson," *Missionary Herald*, May 1842, 1–2; *Missionary Register* (London), 1 April 1843, 209–210.

21. Hampden C. DuBose, *Memoirs of Rev. John Leighton Wilson, D.D., Missionary to Africa and Secretary of Foreign Missions* (Richmond, VA, 1895), 92–93.

22. "Benjamin Griswold," *Missionary Herald*, January 1844. On Griswold and the *Amistad* captives, see "Amistad and Yale: The Untold Story," n.d., *The Yale Standard*, March 3, 2012, www.yalestandard.com/histories/amistad-and-yale/. For George E. Day and Yale divinity students during the trial, see Howard Jones, *Mutiny on the Amistad: The Saga of a Slave Revolt and Its Impact on American Abolition, Law, and Diplomacy* (New York, 1987), 85, 119, 125, 203, 210.

23. "Benjamin Griswold," *Missionary Herald*, January 1844; JLW to RA, 25 July 1842, ABCFM.

24. William Walker's background and character are vividly portrayed in his diaries, which are lodged at the Wisconsin Historical Society.

25. WWD, passim.

26. JLW to RA, 14 April 1842, ABCFM; BVRJ to RA, 24 May 1842, ABCFM; "West Africa," *Missionary Herald*, October 1842, 412–413; WWD, January–June 1842, WHS.

27. JLW to RA, 25 June 1842, ABCFM.

28. "West Africa," *Missionary Herald*, December 1842.

29. JLW to RA, 25 June 1842, ABCFM; JBW to RA, 20 October 1842, ABCFM.

30. Cf. JBW to RA, 20 October 1842, ABCFM.

31. Quotation: JLW to JBW, 7 August 1842, CTS. Leighton expressed their grief over leaving Fair Hope to a Methodist missionary, Thomas Freeman at Cape Coast. Freeman wrote to Britain about how the "heartless colonists" had opposed the work of the mission. The letter was copied by a visiting US Methodist bishop and read before the US Methodist Mission Board. The letter added much fuel to the fire of controversy between missions and colonization and between abolitionism and colonization. See Thomas Freeman to John Beecham, 25 June 1842, MSCS; and Martin, "The Dual Legacy," 150–152.

32. Quotations: Archibald Alexander, *A History of Colonization on the Western Coast of Africa* (Philadelphia, 1846), 424, 429; James Hall, "White and Colored Missionaries in Africa," *Maryland Colonization Journal*, July 1847.

33. See, for example, JBR to Oliver Holmes, 27 December 1837, MSCS; JBR to JHBL, 22 September 1841, MSCS; JBR to JHBL, 26 June 1843, MSCS.

34. Benjamin Griswold to RA, 5 September 1842, ABCFM.

35. Quotations: WWD, 25 July 1842. William Walker's diary provides daily details of the events surrounding the theft and its repercussions. See WWD, July–November 1842, WHS.

36. Ibid., 25 July–28 July 1842. See also Benjamin Griswold to RA, 9 September 1842, ABCFM; JBR to JHBL, 26 September 1842, MSCS; Martin, "The Dual Legacy," 146–150; Hall, *On Afric's Shore*, 214–218. Hall's book has an important account of these events, but unfortunately it does not give references.

37. Quotations: WWD, 30 July 1842, WHS.

38. WWD, 24 August 1842, WHS.

39. For the plunder of the American ship and the arrival of the *Vandalia*, see Hall, *On Afric's Shore*, 215–216. For Davis's report, see WWD, 13 August 1842, WHS. For JBR's anger, see JBR to Dr. James Hall, 26 September 1842, MSCS.

40. WWD, 3 September 1842, WHS.

41. Ibid.

42. WWD, 3 September 1842, WHS. Cf. JBR to JHBL, 26 September 1842, MSCS; Hall, *On Afric's Shore*, 215–216.

43. WWD, 5–6 September 1842, WHS.

44. Quotations: WWD, 8 September 1842, WHS.

45. WWD, 8, 24 September 1842, WHS.

46. Russwurm's letter to Ramsay, 26 September 1842, is copied in Walker's diary, WWD, 3 October 1842, WHS. See also JBR to JHBL, 28 September 1842, MSCS; JBR to JHBL, 26 September 1842, MSCS.

47. WWD, 8 September 1842, WHS.

48. Davis's letter to Ramsay is copied in Walker's diary, WWD, 3 October 1842, WHS.

49. Ibid; Martin, "The Dual Legacy," 146–157.

50. Quotation: "Circular Sent to the Counties," in "Minutes of the Meeting of the Board of Managers, Maryland Colonization Society," 13 March 1841, MSCS. JHBL to RA, 8 December 1842, MSCS; RA to JHBL, 28 December 1842, ABCFM; Benjamin Griswold to RA, 29 June 1843, ABCFM.

51. Quotation: BVRJ to RA, 3 October 1842, ABCFM. For JLW's response, see JLW to RA, 18 July 1842, ABCFM. See, for a summary of the controversy, "Connection of the Mission at Cape Palmas with the Maryland Colony," *Missionary Herald*, November 1842. A special panel, headed by Chancellor R. H. Walworth, a distinguished New York jurist, reviewed the history of the conflict between the missionaries and colonists and concluded that there was a fundamental conflict of interests between the two parties and that the colonists were "hostile both to the native inhabitants of the coast and to the missionaries who are laboring for the spiritual welfare of such natives." See ibid. In *The Liberator*, William Lloyd Garrison published a detailed account of the conflict, giving examples from JLW's earlier letters, as a part of the abolitionist attack on colonization. See "The American Board and African Colonies," *The Liberator*, 14 October 1842.

52. JLW to JBW, 18 July 1842, CTS; JLW to JBW, 29 July 1842, CTS.

Chapter Thirteen: "The Liberty of Choosing for Themselves"

1. JLW to JBW, 24 May 1842, SCL.

2. For Eckard letters sent through England, see ibid. For letters traveling Atlantic highways and the ways in which they closed spatial gulfs, see Sarah Pearsall, *Atlantic Families: Lives and Letters in the Later 18th Century* (New York, 2011). For an Atlantic world being a part of larger networks of travel and communication, see Peter A. Coclanis, "Beyond Atlantic History," in *Atlantic History: A Critical Appraisal* (New York, 2009), eds. Jack P. Greene and Philip D. Morgan, 337–356.

3. See, for example, "Western Asia," *Missionary Herald* (Boston), January 1836, 7; "Mission to the Mohammedans of Persia," *Missionary Herald* (Boston), January 1837, 10; "Southern Africa," *Missionary Herald* (Boston), January 1839, 3–4; "Mission to the Cherokees," *Missionary Herald* (Boston), January 1839, 12–13; "Appeal of the Mission in Turkey," *Charleston Observer*, 21 August 1841; "Jamaica," *Missionary Herald* (London), November 1839, 86.

4. For the Tamil mission, see, for example, "Tamul People," *Missionary Herald* (Boston), January 1835, 13–16; "American Board of Missions," *Missionary Register* (London), 1 April 1839, 185; "American Board of Missions," *Missionary Register* (London), 1 April 1840, 208; "American Board of Missions," *Missionary Register* (London), 1 May 1843, 233. A. A. Hodge, *The Life of Charles Hodge D.D. LL.D: Professor in the Theological Seminary, Princeton, NJ* (New York, 1880), 18.

5. For JBW's illness, see JLW to "Parents, Brothers, Sisters and Friends," 27 October 1841, CTS; "Decease of Dr. A. E. Wilson," *Missionary Herald* (Boston), May 1842, 177–179; JLW to JBW, 18 July 1842, CTS. For JBW's treatment by Hodge, see JBW to RA, 20 October 1842, ABCFM; JBW to RA, 19 November 1842, ABCFM.

6. For James Bayard's role in the colonization movement, see James Bayard to JHBL, 22 October 1833, MSCS. For JBW's views on colonization, see JBW to RA, 20 October 1842, ABCFM; JBW to RA, 19 November 1842, ABCFM. For published accounts of the conflict between the missionaries and colonial authorities, see, for example, *Missionary Herald* (Boston), November 1842, 424–427.

7. For public comment and reports on JBW following her trip to the United States, see, for example, "Anti-Slavery Selections," in *Emancipator and Free American*, 10 August 1843. See as well her reports in Archibald Alexander, *A History of Colonization on the Western Coast of Africa* (Philadelphia, 1846), 425–426. For the role of the missionary home on furlough as "the great American window on the non-Western world," see Sydney Ahlstrom, *A Reli-*

gious History of the American People (New Haven, CT, 1972), 865–866. Cf. also Patrick Harries, "Anthropology," in *Mission and Empire*, ed. Norman Etherington (Oxford, 2005), 238–246.

8. JBW to RA, 10 February 1843, ABCFM.

9. For JBW being with the Eckards in Savannah, see JBW to RA, 19 November 1842, ABCFM; JLW to JBW, 15 March 1843, CTS. For details of the Eckards' time in Ceylon, see *Missionary Herald* (Boston), January 1835, 13–16; January 1836, 13; January 1837, 12–14; January 1838, 8–9; January 1839, 9–10; January 1840, 10; January 1841, 9; January 1843, 9. The Eckards had spent their early years in Ceylon at Panditeripo and later at Tillipally.

10. Estate of N. S. Bayard, 1837–1843, passim, SCCC. For the rapid development of railroads in Georgia, see George White, *Statistics of the State of Georgia: Including an Account of Its Natural, Civil, and Ecclesiastical History; Together with a Particular Description of Each County, Notices of the Manners and Customs of Its Aboriginal Tribes, and a Correct Map of the State* (Savannah, GA, 1849), 87–93.

11. For Paul Sansay and his dispute with the Catholic mission, see JLW to RA, 7 April 1842, ABCFM; Richard L. Hall, *On Afric's Shore: A History of Maryland in Liberia, 1834–1857* (Baltimore, 2003), 250. For Charlotte Sansay's adoption of two children, see Hall, *On Afric's Shore*, 470, 478; BVRJ to JLW, 8 July 1859, CTS. For the Catholic mission, see Edmund M. Hogan, *Catholic Missionaries and Liberia: A Study of Christian Enterprise in West Africa, 1842–1950* (Cork, Ireland, 1981), 12–22. For John, Catherine, and Rhina Johnson working at Sutra Kru, see JLW to JBW, 15 January 1843, CTS; JBW to RA, 1 April 1843, ABCFM.

12. JBW to RA, 10 February 1843, ABCFM; JLW to JBW, 15 March 1843, CTS.

13. JBW to RA, 19 November 1842, ABCFM; JBW to RA, 10 February 1843, ABCFM.

14. For slaves overhearing conversations among whites, see Erskine Clarke, *Dwelling Place: A Plantation Epic* (New Haven, CT, 2005), 149–151, 263, 321–322.

15. JLW to RA, 23 January 1843, ABCFM and CTS.

16. JBW to RA, 1 April 1843, ABCFM.

17. Quotations: JLW to RA, 26 February 1838, ABCFM; JLW to RA, 23 January 1843, ABCFM. See also "Report on Slavery," *The Liberator*, 30 September 1842, 154.

18. Quotations: on JLW being called a "man stealer," JLW to JBW, 25 February 1843, CTS;

from JBW, JBW to RA, 1 April 1843, ABCFM; from JLW, JLW to RA, 23 January 1843, ABCFM and CTS; JLW to RA, 23 January 1843, ABCFM and CTS. For the difficulty of emancipation in South Carolina after Denmark Vesey's attempted revolt, see Lacy K. Ford, *Deliver Us from Evil: The Slavery Question in the Old South* (Oxford, 2009), 196.

19. JLW to RA, 23 January 1843, ABCFM and CTS.

20. Quotations: ibid. The letter was published in a number of newspapers. See, for example, "Rev. J. L. Wilson's Letter," in *Emancipator and Free American*, 8 October 1843.

21. Quotations: JLW to William Wilson, 17 July 1843, CTS.

22. S. E. Wilson to JLW, 19 July 1847, copy in ABCFM. For Jessie's marriage, see Chapter 23.

Chapter Fourteen:
Toko and the *Waterwitch*

1. JLW to JBW, letters bundled together from 21 May 1842 to 19 June 1842, CTS.

2. Ibid. See also "Journal of Benjamin Griswold," 16 July 1842, ABCFM.

3. JLW to JBW, 23 June 1842, CTS. For the technical term "Big Men" in anthropology, see Jan Vansina, *Paths in the Rainforests: Toward a History of Political Tradition in Equatorial Africa* (Madison, WI, 1990), 73–74. For King Glass, see K. David Patterson, *The Northern Gabon Coast to 1875* (Oxford, 1975), esp. 31; Henry H. Bucher, Jr., "The Village of Glass and Western Intrusion: An Mpongwe Response to the American and French Presence in the Gabon Estuary, 1842–1845," *International Journal of African Historical Studies* 6, no. 3 (1973): 363–400, esp. 376. For Dr. McDowell's sketches of Toko and Yanaway, see JLW to JBW, 23–25 June 1842, ABCFM; JLW to [?] Treat, 24 September 1847, ABCFM. Yanaway was later given the name DuSausa.

4. Quotations: Benjamin Griswold to RA, 18 July 1842, ABCFM.

5. Quotation: JLW to JBW, 23 June 1842, CTS. On Glass's Town, see Bucher, "The Village of Glass," 382.

6. Quotation: "Journal of Benjamin Griswold," 16 July 1842, ABCFM. For JLW's description of the king, see JLW to JBW, 18 July 1842, CTS. For King William, or Denis, see Patterson, *The Northern Gabon Coast*, 30–31, 49, 90–92.

7. "Journal of Benjamin Griswold," 16 July 1842, ABCFM; JLW to JBW, 18 July 1842, CTS. Cf. Jeremy Rich's description of this encounter and

its implications for understanding Mpongwe culture. See Jeremy Rich, *A Workman Is Worthy of His Meat: Food and Colonialism in the Gabon Estuary* (Lincoln, NE, 2007), 22–23.

8. Quotation: JLW to JBW, 18 July 1842, CTS.

9. Quotation: "Journal of Benjamin Griswold," 26 June 1842, ABCFM. JLW's account of the visit to the barracoon was published in American, British, and French newspapers. See Henry Hale Bucher, Jr., "The Mpongwe of the Gabon Estuary: A History to 1860" (PhD diss., University of Wisconsin–Madison, 1977), 226.

10. Quotation: JLW to JBW, 18 July 1842, CTS.

11. Quotation: J. Leighton Wilson, "Extracts from the Journal of Mr. Wilson," *Missionary Herald*, June 1843, 234. For Toko's role in the estuary during the 1840s and 1850s, see Bucher, "The Village of Glass," esp. 376–377; David E. Gardinier, *Historical Dictionary of Gabon* (Metuchen, NJ, 1981), 186; Patterson, *The Northern Gabon Coast*, 56, 96–106; WWD, 16 April–22 June 1847, WHS.

12. Quotations: J. Leighton Wilson, *Western Africa: Its History, Condition, and Prospects* (New York, 1856), 294. See also JLW to JBW, 20 July 1842, CTS; Benjamin Griswold to RA, 22 June 1842, ABCFM.

13. Quotation: Wilson, *Western Africa*, 294–295.

14. Quotation: ibid., 382–384.

15. Ibid. See also, for Toko as a storyteller, WWD, 9 February 1843, WHS. For Gabonese folktales, see Robert Hamill Nassau, *Where Animals Talk: West African Folk Lore Tales* (London, 1914). For an evaluation of collections of Gabonese folklore, see Henry H. Bucher, Jr., "Mpongwe Origins: Historiographical Perspectives," *History in Africa* 2 (1975): 88.

16. JLW to JBW, 20 June 1842, CTS. Cf. for use of plantains, Rich, *A Workman Is Worthy of His Meat*, 24–25, 27–35; Vansina, *Paths in the Rainforests*, 61–62.

17. Quotation: WWD, 3 March 1843, WHS. For Toko's knowledge of Western merchants and politics, see Wilson, *Western Africa*, 294.

18. Quotation: JLW to JBW, 7 August 1842, CTS. On mission schools, see David E. Gardinier, "The Schools of the American Protestant Mission in Gabon (1842–1870)," *Revue Française d'Histoire d'Outre-Mer* 75, no. 2 (1988): 177; WWD, 17 October 1847, WHS; WWD, 20 September 1868, WHS.

19. Wilson, "Extracts from the Journal of Mr. Wilson," 234.

20. For the *Waterwitch*, see ibid.; JLW to JBW, 8 July 1842, CTS; WWD, 23 March 1843, WHS. Cf. also a detailed description of sailing in a Mpongwe boat, JLW to JBW, 7 August 1842, CTS. For JLW's adventure on the *Waterwitch*, see JLW to JBW, 23 June 1842, CTS; Wilson, "Extracts from the Journal of Mr. Wilson," 234.

21. Wilson, "Extracts from the Journal of Mr. Wilson," 234; JLW to JBW, 7 August 1842, CTS; Gardinier, *Historical Dictionary of Gabon*, 108–109; Patterson, *The Northern Gabon Coast*, 50–51.

22. Quotation: Wilson, "Extracts from the Journal of Mr. Wilson," 235.

23. Ibid., 234–236. It was not uncommon for Africans to be sold into slavery by other Africans because of debts. See, for example, Toyin Falola and Paul E. Lovejoy, eds., *Pawnship in Africa: Debt Bondage in Historical Perspective* (Boulder, 1994); Paul E. Lovejoy, *Transformations in Slavery: A History of Slavery in Africa*, 2nd ed. (Cambridge, UK, 2000), esp. 188–189; Rich, *A Workman Is Worthy of His Meat*, 7, 27–28; Patterson, *The Northern Gabon Coast*, 56–58; Vansina, *Paths in the Rainforests*, 155. For an overview of the developing historiography of slavery and Africa, see the dated but still helpful review article by William Gervase Clarence-Smith, "The Dynamics of the African Slave Trade," *Africa* 64, no. 2 (1994): 275–286.

24. Quotations: Wilson, "Extracts from the Journal of Mr. Wilson," 237.

25. Ibid., 237–238. For musical instruments from the interior of Gabon, see, from the Metropolitan Museum of Art exhibit in New York, Alisa Lagamma, ed., *Eternal Ancestors: The Art of the Central African Reliquary* (New Haven, CT, 2007), 52–53.

26. Quotations: Wilson, "Extracts from the Journal of Mr. Wilson," 237. Cf. Lagamma, *Eternal Ancestors*, fig. 60, 103. For European and European American images of healthy, vigorous interior peoples in contrast to the supposedly weak and degenerate maritime peoples of the African coast, see K David Patterson, "The Vanishing Mpongwe: European Contact and Demographic Change in the Gabon River," *Journal of African History* 16, no. 2 (1975): 217–238, esp. 221. For the movement of the Fang, see ibid.; Christopher Chamberlin, "The Migration of the Fang into Central Gabon During the Nineteenth Century: A New Interpretation," *International Journal of African Historical Studies* 11 (1978): 429–456; James Fernandez, *Bwiti: An Ethnography of the Religious Imagination in Africa* (Princeton, NJ, 1982), 29–41; John Manning Cinnamon, "The Long

March of the Fang: Anthropology and History in Equatorial Africa" (PhD diss., Yale University, 1998); Kairn Klieman, "Of Ancestors and Earth Spirits: New Approaches for Interpreting Central African Politics, Religion, and Art," in Lagamma, *Eternal Ancestors*, 40–42, 57–58.

27. Quotation: Wilson, "Extracts from the Journal of Mr. Wilson,"239–240. For early smelting sites for iron in Gabon, see Vansina, *Paths in the Rainforests*, 58–60.

28. Quotation: Wilson, "Extracts from the Journal of Mr. Wilson," 239–240.

29. Quotation: ibid. For the issues surrounding JLW's use of the English word "devil," see Lamin Sanneh, *Translating the Message: The Missionary Impact on Culture*, 2nd ed. (New York, 2009), esp. 191–228; V. Y. Mudimbe, "The Power of Speech," in *The Invention of Africa: Gnosis, Philosophy, and the Order of Knowledge* (Bloomington, IN, 1988), 44–97; Birgit Meyer, "Confessions of Satanic Riches in Christian Ghana," *Africa* 65 (1995): 236–255; Rosalind I. J. Hackett, "African Religions: Images and I-Glasses," *Religion* 20 (1990): 303–309; Dmitri van den Bersselaar, "Creating 'Union Ibo': Missionaries and the Igbo Language," *Africa* 67, no. 2 (1997): 273–295.

30. Quotations: Wilson, *Western Africa*, 391. For the "African devil" on stilts, cf. images from Musée D'Ethnographie Genève, *Le Gabon de Fernand Grébert, 1913–1932* (Geneva, Switzerland, 2003), 169, 214. See also André Raponda-Walker and Roger Sillans, *Rites et Croyances des Peuples du Gabon* (Libreville, Gabon, 2005), 16–28.

31. Cf. Walter H. Sangree, *Age, Prayer and Politics in Tiriki, Kenya* (London, 1966), esp. 164; Richard Gray, "Christianity and Concepts of Evil in Sub-Saharan Africa," in *Black Christians and White Missionaries* (New Haven, CT, 1990), 99–117; J. D. Y. Peel, *Religious Encounter and the Making of the Yoruba* (Bloomington, IN, 2000), 259–265; Philip Jenkins, "Good and Evil," in *The New Faces of Christianity: Believing the Bible in the Global South* (Oxford, 2006), 98–127.

32. For the sale of the *Waterwitch* to the Spanish slave trader, see WWD, 23 March 1843, WHS. William Walker estimated that Toko received the equivalent of $700 for the boat.

33. See Wilson, "Extracts from the Journal of Mr. Wilson," *Missionary Herald*, June 1843.

34. For JLW's reports being read regularly to slaves, see *Eleventh Annual Report of the Association for the Religious Instruction of the Negroes, in Liberty County, Georgia* (Savannah, GA, 1846), 9.

Chapter Fifteen: A Sophisticated, Hospitable, and Heathen People

1. JLW to JBW, 15 March 1843, CTS.

2. "Report of the Gaboon Mission to Prudential Committee," 28 December 1843, ABCFM; JLW to RA, 15 July 1843, ABCFM.

3. JLW to RA, 15 July 1843, ABCFM.

4. For Jane Cooper, see WWD, July–November 1842, WHS; JLW to RA, 17 September 1850, ABCFM; David E. Gardinier, "The Schools of the American Protestant Mission in Gabon (1842–1870)," *Revue Française d'Histoire d'Outre-Mer* 75, no. 2 (1988): 168–184. For Francis Allison, see Francis Allison to RA, 26 March 1843, ABCFM; JLW to RA, 15 July 1843, ABCFM; "Report of the Gaboon Mission to Prudential Committee," 28 December 1843, ABCFM.

5. WWD, July–November 1843, WHS.

6. Quotation: JBR to JHBL, 26 June 1843, MSCS.

7. For a vivid description of the requirements for safely sailing into the estuary and of the appearance of the surrounding landscape, see T. Edward Bowdich, *Mission from Cape Coast Castle to Ashante*, 3rd ed. (Oxford, UK, 1966 [1819]), 423–424. See also JLW to "Dear Father," 30 June 1843, SCL; WWD, 11 July 1843, WHS; JLW to RA, 15 July 1843, ABCFM.

8. JLW to "Dear Father," 30 June 1843, SCL; WWD, 11 July 1843, WHS; JLW to RA, 15 July 1843, ABCFM. Cf. Mrs. J. S. Preston, *Gaboon Stories* (New York, 1872), 11. For descriptions of Mpongwe dress, see JLW to JBW, 25 June 1842, CTS. Cf. also Jeremy Rich, "Civilized Attire: Refashioning Tastes and Social Status in the Gabon Estuary, c. 1870–1914," *Cultural and Social History* 2 (2005): 189–213.

9. For descriptions of Glass's Town, see Bowdich, *Mission from Cape Coast Castle to Ashante*, 422–425; JLW to JBW, 23 June 1842, CTS; WWD, December 1842, WHS; Preston, *Gaboon Stories*, 16–17; Henry H. Bucher, Jr., "The Village of Glass and Western Intrusion: An Mpongwe Response to the American and French Presence in the Gabon Estuary, 1842–1845," *International Journal of African Historical Studies* 6, no. 3 (1973): 363–400.

10. Quotation: WWD, 13 February 1843, WHS. For JLW's estimate of the number of slaves owned by Glass, see Jeremy Rich, *A Workman Is Worthy of His Meat: Food and Colonialism in the Gabon Estuary* (Lincoln, NE, 2007), 7–8.

11. David E. Gardinier, *Historical Dictionary of Gabon* (Metuchen, NJ, 1981), 109; K. David Pat-

terson, *The Northern Gabon Coast to 1875* (Oxford, 1975), 31.

12. Quotation: Patterson, *The Northern Gabon Coast*, 14. For Mpongwe as middlemen in the slave trade, see JLW to JBW, 7 August 1842, CTS; Patterson, *The Northern Gabon Coast*, 1–67; Rich, *A Workman Is Worthy of His Meat*, 6–8, 27–28; Jan Vansina, *Paths in the Rainforests: Toward a History of Political Tradition in Equatorial Africa* (Madison, WI, 1990), 204–207. For the character of Mpongwe slavery, see Bucher, "The Village of Glass," 374; K. David Patterson, "The Vanishing Mpongwe: European Contact and Demographic Change in the Gabon River," *Journal of African History* 16, no. 2 (1975): 217–238.

13. JLW to JBW, 18 July 1842, CTS; JLW to JBW, 29 July 1842, CTS. Cf. David E. Gardinier, "The American Board (1842–1870) and Presbyterian Board (1870–1892) Missions in Northern Gabon and African Responses," *Africana Journal* 17 (1998): 215.

14. Preston, *Gaboon Stories*, 18–19; WWD, 21 March 1844, WHS.

15. JLW to JBW, 7 August 1842, CTS; WWD, 10 April 1842, WHS; Rich, *A Workman Is Worthy of His Meat*, 6–9. Cf. Patterson, *The Northern Gabon Coast*, 68–89. For US ships and the slave trade, see David Eltis, "The U.S. Transatlantic Slave Trade, 1644–1867: An Assessment," *Civil War History* 54, no. 4 (December 2008), 347–380.

16. WWD, 19 December 1842, WHS; WWD, 26 December 1842, WHS; JLW to "Dear Father, Mother, Brothers and Sisters," 23 September 1846, SCL. See also Preston, *Gaboon Stories*, 14; Paul B. DuChaillu, *Explorations and Adventures in Equatorial Africa* (London, 1861), 4.

17. Quotation: WWD, 11 July 1843, WHS. For other comments by Walker, see WWD, 21 July 1843, WHS.

18. Quotations: JLW to JBW, 15 January 1843, CTS; WWD, 27 July 1843, WHS.

19. WWD, 18 January 1843, WHS; WWD, 27 July 1843, WHS.

20. For JLW's trips up and down the West African coast, see J. Leighton Wilson, "Journal of J. Leighton Wilson on a Missionary Tour to Western Africa," January–March 1843, ABCFM; JLW to JBW, 11 March 1843, CTS; JLW to RA, 14 April 1843, ABCFM; JLW to RA, 25 November 1843, ABCFM; JLW to RA, 25 April 1839, ABCFM; JBW to "Family," 22 September 1841, SCL; JLW to RA, 7 April 1842, ABCFM. For the origin of the Mpongwe and of their name, see Henry H. Bucher, Jr., "Mpongwe Origins: Histo-

riographical Perspectives," *History in Africa* 2 (1975): 59–89.

21. Quotation: JLW to JBW, 18 July 1842, CTS.

22. Quotation: J. Leighton Wilson, *Western Africa: Its History, Condition, and Prospects* (New York, 1856), 252. See also ibid., 292–293.

23. WW to the Prudential Committee, 28 December 1843, ABCFM; Benjamin Griswold, "Journal of Benjamin Griswold," 26 June 1842, ABCFM. For European reports on the sophistication of the Mpongwe, see Bucher, "The Village of Glass," 371; Patterson, "The Vanishing Mpongwe," 221–222.

24. Quotation: WW to the Prudential Committee, 28 December 1843, ABCFM.

25. Quotation: ibid. For Râgombe as the leader of the Ndiwa clan of the Mpongwe near the end of the seventeenth century, see Patterson, *The Northern Gabon Coast*, 7; David E. Gardinier, "The American Board (1842–1870) and Presbyterian Board (1870–1892), 220.

26. Quotations: JLW to JBW, 18 July 1842, CTS; WW to the Prudential Committee, 28 December 1843, ABCFM. See also Wilson, "Extracts from the Journal of Mr. Wilson," *Missionary Herald*, June 1843, 233. Cf. Patterson, "The Vanishing Mpongwe," 221–223; Patterson, *The Northern Gabon Coast*, 12–13.

27. Quotation: Wilson, *Western Africa*, 341. For mission strategy, see "Annual Report," *Missionary Herald*, January 1835, 14; "Annual Report," *Missionary Herald*, January 1837, 30. Rufus Anderson of the ABCFM and Henry Venn, executive of the Anglican Church Missionary Society, are most often associated with the "three-self" mission strategy— self-supporting, self-propagating, and self-governing. Missionaries were to lay the foundation for such an indigenous church through preaching and teaching and were to have authority only until an indigenous leadership was in place. See C. P. Williams, *The Ideal of the Self-Governing Church: A Study in Victorian Missionary Strategy* (Leiden, 1990).

28. In order to help meet the demands of missionary work, the American Board developed what it called "The Social Principle." In this approach, isolated missionaries were brought together to a central mission station for mutual encouragement and for opportunities to address any simmering disputes. See *Missionary Herald*, January 1825, 12. For salaries of Walker and James, see J. Leighton Wilson, "Schedule of Funds for the West African Mission," 2 December 1843, ABCFM. For confidence

in providence and hope for the future conversion of Africa, see, for example, WWD, 6 June 1849, WHS. Cf. the missionary hymn "God Is Working His Purpose Out," by Arthur C. Ainger, written for his students at Eton, UK, in 1894.

29. "Report of the Gaboon Mission to Prudential Committee," 28 December 1843, ABCFM; JLW to RA, 15 July 1843, ABCFM; BVRJ to RA, 9 January 1844, ABCFM; Gardinier, "The Schools of the American Protestant Mission in Gabon," 172.

30. Missionaries of the ABCFM Gaboon Mission, *A Grammar of the Mpongwe Language, with Vocabularies* (New York, 1847), vi–vii.

31. For the schedule and curriculum of the school, see JLW to JBW, 15 January 1843, CTS; WWD, 24 September 1847, WHS; Paul B. DuChaillu, *Explorations and Adventures in Equatorial Africa* (London, 1861), 28–29; Gardinier, "The Schools of the American Protestant Mission in Gabon." For developments in the school later in the nineteenth century, see Robert Hamill Nassau, *Tales Out of School* (Philadelphia, 1911).

32. WWD, 14 December 1846, WHS; JLW to JBW, 23 June 1842, CTS. Cf. Rich, *A Workman Is Worthy of His Meat,* 86–90.

33. Wilson, *Western Africa,* 243–244.

34. Quotation: JLW to JBW, 23 June 1842, CTS. This lack of enthusiasm is said to be the reaction to "bâton de manioc" by many Europeans in Libreville today. E-mail correspondence with Mary Coultier, 12 August 2011. Cf. Rich, *A Workman Is Worthy of His Meat,* 24.

35. For the hiring of a young boy to secure fish, see JLW to JBW, 23 June 1842, CTS. For preparation of fish, see Rich, *A Workman Is Worthy of His Meat,* 26. Cf. Nassau, *Tales Out of School,* 33, 37, 65. For a leopard taking a goat at Baraka, see, for example, WWD, 7 June 1861, WHS. For goat being barbecued and served, see JLW to JBW, 18 July 1842, CTS; "Western Africa," *Missionary Herald,* June 1843, 231. For a sample of the variety and beauty of "légumes et fruits indigènes," and for "importés," see the sketches in Musée D'Ethnographie Genève, *Le Gabon de Fernand Grébert, 1913–1932* (Geneva, 2003), 109–110.

36. JLW to JBW, 10 June 1842, CTS; JLW to JBW, 18 July 1842, CTS; JLW to JBW, 15 January 1843, CTS; WWD, 28 December 1842, WHS. Cf. Judith A. Carney and Richard Nicholas Rosomoff, *In the Shadow of Slavery: Africa's Botanical Legacy in the Atlantic World* (Berkeley, CA, 2009), 54, 108–111.

37. Quotations: JLW to JBW, 18 July 1842, CTS; Wilson, *Western Africa,* 262. For use of knives and forks by Mpongwe away from the estuary, see WWD, 23 February 1842, WHS. For a "knife and fork doctrine" on a Baptist mission in the Congo and the ways in which it promoted European domesticity and hygiene in the twentieth century, see Nancy Rose Hunt, *A Colonial Lexicon of Birth Ritual, Medicalization, and Mobility in the Congo* (Durham, NC, 1999), 118–123.

38. JLW to JBW, 7 August 1842, CTS. For slave production of food, see Rich, *A Workman Is Worthy of His Meat,* 27–35. Cf. Preston, *Gaboon Stories,* 69–70.

39. Quotation: JLW to JBW, 7 August 1842, CTS. For details of the international slave trade, see "Voyages: The Trans-Atlantic Slave Trade Database" at www.slavevoyages.org, especially the "Voyages Database" section of the site, which provides a database of 34,941 slave voyages. For a summary drawing from the "Voyages Database," see Eltis, "The U.S. Transatlantic Slave Trade." For a contemporary summary account of the British navy's efforts to suppress the international slave trade, see "The Slave Trade: From the Parliamentary Papers, Commissioners at Sierra Leone, to Viscount Palmerston, Sierra Leone, December 31, 1840," in *The British and Foreign Anti-Slavery Reporter: Under the Sanction of the British and Foreign Anti-Slavery Society* (London), 5 October 1842, 162. Rich, *A Workman Is Worthy of His Meat,* 6–8, provides a succinct summary of slave trading in the Gabon estuary. For slave ships built in New England and Baltimore, see Griswold, "Journal," 26 June 1842, ABCFM. Cf. JLW to JBW, 25 February 1843, CTS; "United States Slave-Trade," *The British and Foreign Anti-Slavery Reporter: Under the Sanction of the British and Foreign Anti-Slavery Society* (London), 20 April 1842, 62.

40. For King Glass's slave trading and trading at Glass's Town, see WWD, 10 February 1843, WHS; WWD, 3 June 1843, WHS. See also Tom Standage, *A History of the World in 6 Glasses* (New York, 2005), Chapters 5 and 6, for an accessible account of the role of distilled spirits in the slave trade. The chapters are entitled "High Spirits, High Seas" and "The Drinks That Built America."

41. Quotation: WWD, 10 February 1843, WHS. See Griswold, "Journal," 26 June 1842, ABCFM. For JLW's attack on Southerners who were seeking to reopen the international slave trade to the United States, see Wilson, "The Foreign Slave-Trade: Can It Be Revived Without Violating the Most Sacred Principles of Honor, Humanity,

and Religion?" *Southern Presbyterian Review* 12 (1859): 491–512. Cf. WWD, 10 February 1843, WHS.

42. For JLW's evaluation of the character of Mpongwe slavery, see Wilson, *Western Africa*, 271–272.

43. Quotation: WWD, 30 December 1842, WHS.

44. Quotation: Robert Hamill Nassau, *Fetichism in West Africa* (New York, 1904), 263. For plants and poisons available, see André Raponda-Walker and Roger Sillans, *Les Plantes Utiles du Gabon* (Paris, 1961), passim; and Muse D'Ethnographie Genève, *Le Gabon de Fernand Grébert*, passim. For the knowledge of and use of poisonous plants by the indigenous people of Gabon, see Raponda-Walker and Sillans, *Rites et Croyances des Peuples du Gabon* (Libreville, Gabon, 2005 [1962]), 43–55. For eating as a dangerous act that makes a person vulnerable to malevolent spirits, see WWD, 23 February 1843, WHS; Bowdich, *Mission from Cape Coast Castle to Ashantee*, 422–425; Rich, *A Workman Is Worthy of His Meat*, 31.

45. Quotation: Wilson, *Western Africa*, 271. Cf. Wilson, "Mr. Wilson's Description of the Country Near the Mouth of the Gaboon," *Missionary Herald*, June 1843, 233. Cf. James C. Scott, *Domination and the Art of Resistance: Hidden Transcripts* (New Haven, CT, 1990), 3–4, 31–36. For slave use of poisons in the Lowcountry, see Philip Morgan, *Slave Counterpoint: Black Culture in the Eighteenth-Century Chesapeake and Lowcountry* (Chapel Hill, NC, 1998), 614–618. For "weapons of the weak," see James C. Scott, *Weapons of the Weak: Everyday Forms of Peasant Resistance* (New Haven, CT, 1985).

46. WWD, 20 November 1843, WHS. WW saw the woman being pulled into the brush on 13 November 1843.

47. Quotation: WWD, 20 November 1843, WHS. See also Benjamin Griswold to Rev. Greene, [?] 1844, ABCFM. WW saw the woman being burned on 20 November 1843, a week after having buried the first woman.

Chapter Sixteen: Rainforest Lessons

1. Benjamin Griswold to RA, 26 December 1843; WW to the Prudential Committee, 28 December 1843, ABCFM.

2. WWD, 10 December 1842, WHS; Mary Griswold to RA, 26 November 1847, ABCFM; JLW to RA, 13 December 1847, ABCFM; Jane Preston, *Gaboon Stories* (New York, 1872), 80–82.

3. WW to the Prudential Committee, 28 December 1843, ABCFM.

4. Quotations: JLW to Charles Hodge, 1 December 1844, CTS; J. Leighton Wilson, *Western Africa: Its History, Condition, and Prospects* (New York, 1856), 239–240. For JLW's work on the Bantu language family, see J. Leighton Wilson, "Comparative Vocabularies of Some of the Principal Negro Dialects of Africa," *Journal of the American Oriental Society* 1, no. 4 (1849): 337–381. Cf. JLW to Rev. Lewis Grout, South African Mission, 13 January 1851, ABCFM.

5. WWD, 1842–1860, WHS, passim.

6. Quotation: Robert Hamill Nassau, *Fetichism in West Africa* (New York, 1904), 258. For WW's relationship with JLW and JBW, see, for example, WWD, 11 July 1843, WHS. For WW's continuing grief, see, for example, WWD, 2 February 1843, WHS; WWD, 2 May 1843, WHS.

7. For the decline of the Shékiani and their role in the slave trade around the estuary, see WWD, 2 September 1848, WHS; WWD, 20 September 1848, WHS; WWD, 14 October 1848, WHS; Wilson, *Western Africa*, 300; K. David Patterson, "The Vanishing Mpongwe: European Contact and Demographic Change in the Gabon River," *Journal of African History* 16, no. 2 (1975): 217–238. For King George's account of the decline of the Shékiani, see Rollin Porter to RA, 1 October 1851, ABCFM.

8. For earlier visits to George's Town, see WWD, 20–23 March 1843, WHS; WWD, 28–29 July 1843, WHS.

9. WWD, 20 March 1843, WHS. Cf. Rollin Porter to RA, 1 October 1851, ABCFM.

10. For George's character, see WWD, 26 October 1843, WHS; WWD, 14 March 1844, WHS; WWD, 1 February 1847, WHS; "West Africa," *Missionary Herald*, June 1848, 195–196; Wilson, *Western Africa*, 254–256. For George's account of the history of the Mpongwe, see Rollin Porter to RA, 1 October 1851, ABCFM. Cf., for traditions about the origins of the Ndiwa and the Mpongwe, Abbé André Raponda-Walker, *Notes d'histoire du Gabon* (Brazzaville, 1960), 58.

11. For the two Mpongwe sent to France, see T. Edward Bowdich, *Mission from Cape Coast Castle to Ashantee*, 3rd ed. (London, 1966 [1819]), 425.

12. Quotation: WWD, 23 October 1843, WHS; WWD, 5 December 1843, WHS. For the slave trade route through King George's Town, see the map in Christopher J. Gray, *Colonial Rule and Crisis in Equatorial Africa: Southern Gabon, ca. 1850–1940* (Rochester, NY, 2002), 28. For a detailed description of the slave trade in Gabon, see ibid., 27–35.

For the role of New England rum in debauching the people, see, for example, "West Africa: Report of the Mission for 1849," *Missionary Herald*, July 1850, 226; Wilson, *Western Africa*, 124. For an evaluation of these charges by the missionaries and similar charges by other Europeans and Americans, see Patterson, "The Vanishing Mpongwe," 230; Henry Hale Bucher, Jr., "The Mpongwe of the Gabon Estuary: A History to 1860" (PhD diss., University of Wisconsin–Madison, 1977), 151–152; George E. Brooks, *Yankee Traders, Old Coaster and African Middlemen: A History of American Legitimate Trade with West Africa in the Nineteenth Century* (Boston, 1970), 19–23, 273–275.

13. WWD, 5 December 1843, WHS; WWD, 14 March 1844, WHS.

14. For WW's discussion of these matters and for the use of the name Mpongwe, see WW to the British antislavery leader Thomas Fowell Buxton, contained in WW to RA, 29 December 1843, ABCFM. For the Bantu political tradition of lineages being divided into houses, villages, and districts, see Jan Vansina, *Paths in the Rainforests: Toward a History of Political Tradition in Equatorial Africa* (Madison, WI, 1990), 74–83. For the development of clans and clan heads around the Gabon Estuary, see ibid., 232–234. For the role of missionaries in creating a distinct identity that transcended local villages, cf. J. D. Y. Peel, *Religious Encounter and the Making of the Yoruba* (Bloomington, IN, 2000), 283–288; and Dmitri van den Dersselaar, "Creating 'Union Ibo': Missionaries and the Igbo Language," *Africa* 67, no. 2 (1997): 275.

15. Quotation: "Report of the Gaboon Mission to Prudential Committee," 28 December 1843, ABCFM. For the terminology of "Big Men"—the technical term in anthropology for leaders such as Glass and George—and its history among Bantu-speaking people, see Vansina, *Paths in the Rainforests*, 73–74, 274–275.

16. Quotations: WWD, 5–6 June 1849, WHS. Note WW's efforts to "reduce" the language to "order" and cf. Van den Dersselaar, "Creating 'Union Ibo.'"

17. Quotation: WWD, 21 March 1843, WHS. Cf. WWD, 3 May 1843, WHS. The dollar amount was what the slave traders told William Walker and is not the equivalent of what it would be today.

18. Quotations: WWD, 12 February 1843, WHS; WWD, 6 March 1843, WHS. For the drums, see "Types de Tambours," in Raponda-Walker and Sillans, *Rites et Croyances des Peuples du Gabon*, 72–74; and cf. Musée D'Ethnographie

Genève, *Le Gabon de Fernand Grébert, 1913–1932* (Geneva, 2003), 47, 217, 270.

19. Quotation: WWD, 5 March 1843, WHS. See also WWD, 21 March 1843, WHS.

20. Quotations: Benjamin Griswold, "Mr. Griswold's Visit to Corisco Island," *Missionary Herald*, December 1843, 449; JLW to RA, 28 March 1851, ABCFM. See also JLW to JBW, 23 June 1843, CTS.

21. Wilson, *Western Africa*, 270–272; Patterson, "The Vanishing Mpongwe," 227; Henry H. Bucher, Jr., "The Village of Glass and Western Intrusion: An Mpongwe Response to the American and French Presence in the Gabon Estuary, 1842–1845," *International Journal of African Historical Studies* 6, no. 3 (1973): 363–400.

22. WWD, 8 June 1849, WHS.

23. Quotations: WW to Brother Alfred, 7 February 1849, ABCFM. For examples of runaway wives, see WWD, 4 April 1843, WHS; WWD, 14 April 1843, WHS; WWD, 24 December 1847, WHS. Cf. Patterson, "The Vanishing Mpongwe," 229–233.

24. For missionary experience of the rainforest, see Wilson, *Western Africa*, 364–365, 374–378; WWD, 10 November 1847, WHS; William Walker, "Western Africa," *Missionary Herald*, 31 December 1847. For white images of jungles and the contrasting reality of rainforests, see Vansina, *Paths in the Rainforests*, 39–46. On the complex place of the leopard in Mpongwe life, see Wilson, *Western Africa*, 365–366; Nassau, *Fetichism in West Africa*, 200–203; Vansina, *Paths in the Rainforest*, 74, 78, 276–277; Raponda-Walker and Sillans, *Rites et Croyances des Peuples du Gabon*, 178–182; Jeremy Rich, "'Leopard Men,' Slaves, and Social Conflict in Libreville (Gabon), c. 1860–1879," *International Journal of African Historical Studies* 34, no. 3 (2001): 619–639. For a comprehensive overview of the role of leopard men and their relationship to the secret Mwiri societies in nineteenth- and twentieth-century Gabon, see Gray, *Colonial Rule and Crisis in Equatorial Africa*, 196–203.

25. Quotations: WWD, 23 and 26 October 1843, WHS; WWD, 11 March 1844, WHS. Walker still used "tiger" for "leopard" in 1844. He later used the correct name "leopard." I have quietly used "leopard" where he used "tiger."

26. Quotations: WWD, 1 February 1847, WHS; Albert Bushnell to RA, 22 June 1854, ABCFM. Cf. Psalm 73:3–14, Job 21:1–26; and Georgia Writers Project, Savannah Unit, Works Projects Administration, [Mary Granger], *Drums*

and Shadows: Survival Studies Among the Georgia Coastal Negroes (Savannah, 1940), 142, 147, 183.

27. Quotations: William Walker, "Letters from Mr. Walker," *Missionary Herald*, December 1847, 195–196. For the steady decline of George's Town in the 1840s and 1850s, see, for example, WWD, 5 December 1843, WHS; WWD, 14 March 1844, WHS; WWD, 9 November 1847, WHS; Walker, "Letters from Mr. Walker," *Missionary Herald*, December 1847, 195–196. Patterson estimated that the population of George's Town and its villages declined from approximately 550–650 in 1843 to 170 by 1863. See Patterson, "The Vanishing Mpongwe," 217–238.

28. For descriptions of traveling narrow trails at night, see, for example, WWD, 23 February 1843, WHS; WWD, 20 March 1843, WHS; WWD, 22 March 1843, WHS; WWD, 30 March 1844, WHS; Walker, "Mr. Walker's Visits to the Interior," *Missionary Herald*, April 1849, 120–123. For the character and use of the *ojo* for travel at night, see Rollin Porter to RA, 1 October 1851, ABCFM.

29. For descriptions of sailing on the estuary at night, see, for example, JLW to JBW, 7 August 1842, CTS; WWD, 21 February 1843, WHS; WWD, 23 February 1843, WHS; WWD, 22 March 1843, WHS; Rollin Porter to RA, 1 October 1851, ABCFM. Cf. WW to S. L. Pomeroy, 17 September 1854, ABCFM.

30. WWD, 3–14 July 1844, WHS; Hampden C. DuBose, *Memoirs of Rev. John Leighton Wilson, D.D., Missionary to Africa and Secretary of Foreign Missions* (Richmond, VA, 1895), 94.

31. Quotation: Benjamin Griswold to RA, 17 July 1842, ABCFM.

32. JLW to RA, 25 July 1842, ABCFM; "West Africa," *Missionary Herald*, July 1845; WWD, 6–14 July 1844, WHS. Cf. Albert Bushnell to RA, 16 February 1850, ABCFM, and WWD, 30 January 1848, WHS.

Chapter Seventeen: The French: "The Most Dishonest and Shameless People"

1. For French interest in Gabon, see Henry H. Bucher, Jr., "The Village of Glass and Western Intrusion: An Mpongwe Response to the American and French Presence in the Gabon Estuary, 1842–1845," *International Journal of African Historical Studies* 6, no. 3 (1973): 363–400; Hubert Deschamps, *Quinze Ans de Gabon: Les débuts de l'établissement français, 1839–1853* (Paris, 1965), esp. 289. For the outlaw-ing of French vessels carrying slaves, see Hugh Thomas, *The Slave Trade* (New York, 1997), 622–628.

2. K. David Patterson, *The Northern Gabon Coast to 1875* (Oxford, 1975), 90–91.

3. Ibid.

4. Quotation: ibid., 91. See also Deschamps, *Quinze Ans*, 292; Bucher, "The Village of Glass," 389.

5. Deschamps, *Quinze Ans*, 295.

6. Bucher, "The Village of Glass," 379–384.

7. WWD, 26 April 1843, WHS; WW to the Prudential Committee, 28 December 1843, ABCFM; RA to the Gaboon Mission, 19 November 1843, ABCFM.

8. For charges of missionary meddling in political affairs, see, for example, JBR to Oliver Holmes, 27 December 1837, MSCS; JLW to JBW, 25 February 1843, CTS. The charge was echoed by some twentieth-century historians. Jane Jacks Martin, for example, in writing about JLW's charges of imperialism by the Maryland Colonization Society and its settlers, remarked that "Wilson's conduct in later years [in Gabon] indicated his penchant of meddling in political affairs." See Jane Jackson Martin, "The Dual Legacy: Government Authority and Mission Influence Among the Glebo of Eastern Liberia, 1834–1910" (PhD diss., Boston University, 1968), 155.

9. For efforts to stir public opinion in the United States and Britain against French moves in Gabon, see, for example, "West Africa," *Missionary Herald*, November 1844, 381. For the efforts of missionaries to protect "aboriginal rights" in the face of aggressive white settlers in South Africa, Australia, and New Zealand, see Alan Lester, "Humanitarians and White Settlers in the Nineteenth Century," in *Mission and Empire*, ed. Norman Etherington (Oxford, 2005), 64–85. For the role of the Southern Presbyterian Church, and especially the African American missionary William Shepherd, in exposing the atrocities in the Congo under Belgium colonization, see Adam Hochschild, *King Leopold's Ghost: A Story of Greed, Terror, and Heroism in Colonial Africa* (New York, 1999).

10. For Buxton and the Aborigines' Protection Society and for the ridicule they faced, see Lester, "Humanitarians and White Settlers."

11. Quotation is found in a copy of WW's letter to Buxton in WW to the Prudential Committee, 28 December 1843, ABCFM.

12. Quotations: WWD, 14 March 1844, WHS. See also WWD, 3 July 1843, WHS.

13. WWD, 1 November 1843, WHS.

14. Quotation: WWD, 30 March 1844, WHS. For the story of Glass's signing and what followed immediately, see J. Leighton Wilson, "Letter of Mr. Wilson," *Missionary Herald*, 25 November 1843, 112; William Walker, "Letter from Mr. Walker," *Missionary Herald*, July 1844, 248; J. Leighton Wilson, "Letter from Mr. Wilson," *Missionary Herald*, November 1844, 381; JLW to Charles Hodge, 1 December 1844, CTS. For a summary of the French version of what happened, see Deschamps, *Quinze Ans*, 300–302. For a sharp critique of the French account, see Patterson, *The Northern Gabon Coast to 1875*, 96–100; and Bucher, "The Village of Glass," 391–393. Both Patterson and Bucher make extensive use of WW's diary.

15. WWD, 19–23 January 1844, WHS.

16. Quotation: Bucher, "The Village of Glass," 388.

17. *Missionary Register* (London), 1 January 1846, 7.

18. WWD, 26 August 1844, WHS.

19. Quotation: WWD, 6 January 1845, WHS. See also WWD, 31 December 1844 to 30 March 1845, WHS.

20. JLW to RA, 30 January 1845, ABCFM.

21. Quotation: WWD, 22 June 1845, WHS. See also WWD, 30 March 1845 to 22 June 1845, WHS.

22. WWD, 4 July 1845 to 24 November 1845, WHS.

23. WWD, 2 December 1845, WHS.

24. Quotation: Bucher, "The Village of Glass," 395. See also J. Leighton Wilson, "Letter from Mr. Wilson, July 25, 1845," *Missionary Herald*, January 1846, 25–31. The most detailed treatments of the French move against Glass's Town are Bucher, "The Village of Glass," 363–400; Henry Hale Bucher, Jr. "The Mpongwe of the Gabon Estuary: A History to 1860" (PhD diss., University of Wisconsin–Madison, 1977), 259–296; Patterson, *The Northern Gabon Coast to 1875*, 90–107. French perceptions are provided by Deschamps, *Quinze Ans*, 305–308.

25. Quotation: J. Leighton Wilson, "Letter from Mr. Wilson, July 25, 1845," *Missionary Herald*, January 1846, 27. See also ibid., 31.

26. Quotation: ibid., 29–30.

27. Quotations: ibid.

28. For the judgment that a diplomatic incident had been narrowly avoided, see Deschamps, *Quinze Ans*, 307. See also ibid., 303. Deschamps summarizes positive French perceptions of JLW:

"Wilson a été certainement un homme remarquable. Il a frappé Bouet, Darricau, Méquet qui ont admiré son œuvre, son activité, sa modération; la largeur et la justesse de ses jugements sont frappants." Ibid., 101. Cf. as well Patterson, *The Northern Gabon Coast to 1875*, 106–107. See also J. Leighton Wilson, "West Africa," *Missionary Herald*, June 1846, 210–211.

29. Quotation: Bucher, "The Village of Glass," 398–399.

30. For the continuing defiance of Glass and Toko, see WWD, 25 January 1848, WHS; "West Africa," *Missionary Herald*, December 1848, 196.

Chapter Eighteen: Home Visit

1. Quotation: JLW to RA, 28 March 1851, ABCFM. In many places WW's diary describes Catholic/Protestant relationships at the estuary. See, for example, WWD, 15 February 1847, 12 May 1848, 29 April 1849, WHS.

2. "Western Africa," *Missionary Herald*, January 1846, 3.

3. Quotation: JLW to RA, 13 December 1847, ABCFM. See also JLW to RA, 17 January 1848, ABCFM; JLW to RA, 30 January 1849, ABCFM.

4. David E. Gardinier, "The Schools of the American Protestant Mission in Gabon (1842–1870)," *Revue Française d'Histoire d'Outre-Mer* 74, no. 2 (1988): 172. For recent converts as key players in mission work, see Peggy Brock, "New Christians as Evangelists," in *Mission and Empire*, ed. Norman Etherington (Oxford, 2005), 132–152.

5. JLW to RA, 18 March 1838, ABCFM; JLW to RA, 15 July 1843, ABCFM; Jane Preston, *Gaboon Stories* (New York, 1872), 69–70; Gardinier, "The Schools of the American Protestant Mission in Gabon," 172.

6. For Dorsey, see Richard L. Hall, *On Afric's Shore: A History of Maryland in Liberia, 1834–1857* (Baltimore, 2003), 456. JLW to JHBL, 6 July 1837, MSCS; Gardinier, "The Schools of the American Protestant Mission in Gabon," 172. For Mary Clealand, see Preston, *Gaboon Stories*, 70. For their marriage, see Gardinier, "The Schools of the American Protestant Mission in Gabon," 172. For the birth of William Leighton Dorsey, see WWD, 2 July 1848, WHS; David E. Gardinier, *Historical Dictionary of Gabon* (Metuchen, NJ, 1981), 109. For their daughter Sara Dorsey, see "Ma Sara," teacher and wife of pastor Owondo Lewis, in Jean Kenyon MacKenzie, *Black Sheep: Adventures in Africa* (Boston, 1916), 163–165, 198–200. For their daughter

Celia, see Robert Hamill Nassau, *My Ogowe: Being a Narrative of Daily Incidents During Sixteen Years in Equatorial West Africa* (New York, 1914), 314–315.

7. WWD, 16 September 1846, 6 November 1846, WHS. See also JBR to Dr. James Hall, 11 July 1846, MSCS.

8. For the continuing relations between the James and Wilson families, see, for example, JLW to BVRJ, 6 May 1857, CTS; BVRJ to JLW, 8 July 1859, CTS.

9. WWD, 27 November 1846, WHS. For the conflict between settlers and Grebo in 1844, see Hall, *On Afric's Shore*, 225–246; Jane Jackson Martin, "The Dual Legacy: Government Authority and Mission Influence Among the Glebo of Eastern Liberia, 1834–1910" (PhD diss., Boston University, 1968), 164–178; and cf. King Freeman to JHBL, 1 April 1844, MSCS. For the role of Matthew Perry and the Africa Squadron, see Donald L. Canney, *Africa Squadron: The U.S. Navy and the Slave Trade, 1842–1861* (Washington, DC, 2006), 45–68. For a report on the Episcopal mission at Cape Palmas in 1846, see *Missionary Register* (London), 1 January 1848, 3.

10. Quotation: WWD, 28 November 1846, WHS.

11. "Appointments by Agent Maryland State Colonization Society," March 1845, MSCS; JBR to Dr. James Hall, 1 January 1844, MSCS; JHBL to Dr. James Hall, 1 March 1847, MSCS.

12. "Appointments by Agent Maryland State Colonization Society," March 1845, MSCS; JBR to Dr. James Hall, 1 January 1844, MSCS; JBR to JHBL, 30 December 1845, MSCS.

13. Quotation: WWD, 26 December 1846, WHS.

14. JLW to RA, 11 April 1847, ABCFM.

15. Quotation: J. Leighton Wilson, *Western Africa: Its History, Condition, and Prospects* (New York, 1856), 366.

16. Quotation: JLW to RA, 6 April 1848, ABCFM. For JLW's securing of another gorilla in 1848 and for its measurements made by Dr. Gautier, a French physician then in Gabon, see WWD, 21–23 September 1848, WHS. For JLW's securing of still another in 1851, which he again sent to Boston, see JLW to RA, 7 October 1851, ABCFM.

17. Quotation: Thomas S. Savage and Jeffries Wyman, "Notice of the External Characters and Habits of Troglodytes Gorilla, a New Species of Orang from The Gaboon River," *Boston Journal of Natural History* 5 (1847): 441. For JLW's role in the "discovery of the gorilla," see Paul Belloni Du Chaillu, *Explorations and Adventures in Equatorial Africa*

(New York, 1861), 347. JLW's role in the "discovery" has long been downplayed, as if he did not realize the scientific importance of the *njina*. For the controversy that followed after JLW turned over the skulls and bones to Savage in New York, see Richard Conniff, *The Species Seekers: Heroes, Fools, and the Mad Pursuit of Life on Earth* (New York, 2011), 227–239. For an analysis of degrading portrayals of Africans as apes and, in particular, as gorillas, see Jan Nederveen Pieterse, *White on Black: Images of Africa and Blacks in Western Popular Culture* (New Haven, CT, 1995), 39–44, 180.

18. JLW to RA, 21 June 1847, ABCFM.

19. Quotations: JLW to SSW, 28 February 1844, SCL.

20. Quotations: ibid. Cf. the Apostle Paul's position in 1 Corinthian 8 about refraining from eating meat offered to idols.

21. Quotation: ibid. For JLW's continuing conversations about slavery with family members and other Southern whites, see JLW to RA, 9 December 1852, ABCFM. For the growth of wealth in the Wilson family, see, for example, Last Will and Testament of William Wilson, Will Records 1 A, 13 May 1850, PCSC. For Sumter County developments, see J. D. B. DeBow, *Statistical View of the United States . . . Being a Compendium of the Seventh Census* (Washington, DC, 1854), 302; Walter Edgar, *South Carolina: A History* (Columbia, SC, 1998), 286.

22. For a report of JLW's visits and the content of his addresses, especially his accounts of French aggression and his denunciation of the export of New England rum to Gabon, see *Boston Daily Atlas*, 8 July 1847, 1. For his article on languages, see J. Leighton Wilson, "Comparative Vocabularies of Some of the Principal Negro Dialects of Africa," *Journal of the American Oriental Society* 1, no. 4 (1849): 337–381. For JLW's role as an early student of Bantu, see Robert Needham Cust, *A Sketch of the Modern Languages of Africa*, vol. 2 (London, 1883), passim.

23. JLW to RA, 13 December 1847, ABCFM. For reports on JLW's sermons and talks in Charleston and Savannah, see Laura Maxwell to Mary Jones, 4 December 1847, Charles Colcock Jones Papers, Howard-Tilton Memorial Library, Tulane University; see also letter of 17 December 1847. For the sale of Fair Hope plantation, see Buddy Sullivan, *Early Days on the Georgia Tidewater: The Story of McIntosh County and Sapelo* (Darien, GA, 2001), 258, 284n145. For the settlement of Roswell by wealthy Lowcountry families and the development of its mills, see Erskine Clarke, *Dwelling Place: A Plantation Epic* (New Haven, CT, 2005), 190–201.

24. For JLW's experience of his old home, see JLW to RA, 7 January 1848, ABCFM; Mrs. Shaw, "Mt. Zion Presbyterian Church: 1809–1976" (n.p., 1976), 15; S. E. Wilson to JLW, 19 July 1847, copy, ABCFM. In 1850, JLW wrote of Pine Grove as "identified almost with our existence." See JLW to "Dear Sister," 15 October 1850, SCL.

25. Quotation: "Anniversary Week in New York," *New York Herald*, 15 May 1848.

26. Quotations: ibid. For continuing anger over the French attack of the American mission at Baraka, see "Louis Philippe," *New York Herald*, 30 August 1848. Cf., for similar observations about the intelligence of Africans and the spirituality that marked many African cultures, JLW to Elipha White, 8 July 1837, in "Fair Hope, Cape Palmas," *Charleston Observer*, 21 October 1837; JLW to Elipha White, 10 March 1838, in "Fair Hope, Cape Palmas," *Charleston Observer*, 15 December 1838. See, esp., Wilson, *Western Africa*, 379–381.

Chapter Nineteen: "He Worships with Sincere Devotion the Customs of His Ancestors"

1. Leighton Wilson, "Mr. Wilson's Journal, November 1842," ABCFM. See also J. Leighton Wilson, "Extracts from the Journal of Mr. Wilson," *Missionary Herald*, June 1843. For demographic figures and reasons for the decline in the Mpongwe population, see K. David Patterson, "The Vanishing Mpongwe: European Contact and Demographic Change in the Gabon River," *Journal of African History* 16, no. 2 (1975): 217–238.

2. Quotation: WWD, 3 March 1843, WHS.

3. Quotations: WWD, 5 January 1848, WHS. See also K. David Patterson, *The Northern Gabon Coast to 1875* (Oxford, 1975), 105, 128.

4. Quotation: "Western Africa," *Missionary Herald*, 12 January 1848.

5. Quotations: WWD, 29–30 January 1848, WHS. Cf. JLW's description of Indâ, or Ndâ, in J. Leighton Wilson, *Western Africa: Its History, Condition, and Prospects* (New York, 1856), 395–396.

6. Quotations: WWD, 29–30 January 1848, WHS. For burial ceremonies, cf. Robert Hamill Nassau, *Fetichism in West Africa* (New York, 1904), 215–222.

7. WWD, 15 May 1848, WHS.

8. Quotation: WWD, 17 October 1847, WHS. For Mpongwe girls educated at Baraka entering liaisons with white traders, see David E. Gardinier, "The American Board (1842–1870) and Presbyterian Board (1870–1892) Missions in Northern Gabon and African Responses," *Africana Journal* 17 (1998): 221.

9. Quotation: WWD, 8 April 1848, WHS.

10. For a report of their departure from Providence, Rhode Island, see "Sailing of Missionaries," *Daily National Intelligencer* (Washington, DC), 17 June 1848, 1.

11. Quotations: WWD, 7–8 May 1848, WHS. For Zeniah Walker's illness and death, see WWD, 26 February 1848, WHS; WWD, 22 April 1848, WHS.

12. WWD, 14 July 1848, WHS; WWD, 26 October 1848, WHS.

13. Quotation: WWD, 31 March 1849, WHS. See also Albert Bushnell, "Report of the West African Mission for 1848," ABCFM; J. Leighton Wilson, "Letter from Mr. Wilson," *Missionary Herald*, February 1850, 37.

14. Quotation: WWD, 20 May 1849, WHS.

15. Wilson, *Western Africa*, 391–396.

16. Quotation: ibid., 394. For the use of the decomposing brain, see ibid. For the complex relationship of Mbwiri to other male secret societies, such as the Bwiti among the Fang and the Mwetyi among the Shékiani, see Kairn Klieman, "Of Ancestors and Earth Spirits: New Approaches for Interpreting Central African Politics, Religion, and Art," in *Eternal Ancestors: The Art of the Central African Reliquary*, ed. Alisa Lagamma (New Haven, CT, 2007), esp. 54–59. See also André Raponda-Walker and Roger Sillans, *Rites et Croyances des Peuples du Gabon* (Libreville, Gabon, 2005), 189–237.

17. Quotation: WWD, 15 July 1849, WHS. See also Wilson, *Western Africa*, 391.

18. Quotation: Wilson, *Western Africa*, 394.

19. Nassau, *Fetichism in West Africa*, 255; Walker and Sillans, *Rites et Croyances*, 241–243.

20. Quotations: WWD, 21–23 March 1848, WHS; Nassau, *Fetichism in West Africa*, 260–261.

21. Quotation: JLW to RA, 28 March 1851, ABCFM. See also Wilson, *Western Africa*, iii, 390–391.

22. Quotation: WWD, 1 July 1849, WHS.

23. For boils, see WWD, 31 March 1849, WHS. For a student's death from an ulcerated foot, see WWD, 23 October 1848, WHS. For liver problems, see Albert Bushnell to RA, 16 February 1850, ABCFM; JLW to RA, 2 August 1850, ABCFM. For the West African pathogens that most afflicted Europeans, see Robert A. McGuire and Philip R. P. Coelho, *Parasites, Pathogens, and Progress: Diseases and Economic Development* (Cambridge, MA,

2011), 88–97. The author discussed health issues in tropical Gabon with Drs. Fuka Bamanga Jomain and Wayne Fricke of Bongolo Evangelical Hospital, Gabon, 19 August 2007, Libreville, Gabon.

24. Quotation: JLW to RA, 6 February 1849, ABCFM. See also WWD, 1 February 1849, WHS; Jane Preston, *Gaboon Stories* (New York, 1872), 82–84.

25. Quotations: JLW to RA, 6 February 1849, ABCFM; WW to Prudential Committee, 7 February 1849, ABCFM; *Missionary Herald*, June 1849, 210.

26. Quotations: WW to L. B. Treat, 19 February 1849, ABCFM; JLW to RA, 6 February 1849, ABCFM.

27. Quotation: JLW to Charles Hodge, 2 October 1849, CTS. See also David E. Gardinier, *Historical Dictionary of Gabon* (Metuchen, NJ, 1981), 165–166; Gardinier, "The American Board (1842–1870) and Presbyterian Board (1870–1892)," 223–224.

28. Quotations: John 1; JLW to RA, 7 October 1851, ABCFM. Conversations with Professor John Ellington, who had translated the Gospel of John into several Bantu languages, November 2011, Montreat, North Carolina.

29. Quotation: Preston, *Gaboon Stories*, 69–70.

30. For improving relationships between the French and the missionaries, see, for example, JLW to William Wilson, 12 September 1850, SCL. For Du Chaillu's relationship with the mission and especially the Wilsons, see Paul Belloni Du Chaillu, *Explorations and Adventures in Equatorial Africa* (New York, 1861), 27; Hampden C. DuBose, *Memoirs of Rev. John Leighton Wilson, D.D., Missionary to Africa and Secretary of Foreign Missions* (Richmond, VA, 1895), 147; K. David Patterson, "Paul B. Du Chaillu and the Exploration of Gabon, 1855–1865," *International Journal of African Historical Studies* 7, no. 4 (1973): 649. For Du Chaillu and the gorilla, see Richard Conniff, *The Species Seekers: Heroes, Fools, and the Mad Pursuit of Life on Earth* (New York, 2011), 285–303.

31. Henry Hale Bucher, Jr., "The Mpongwe of the Gabon Estuary: A History to 1860" (PhD diss., University of Wisconsin–Madison, 1977), 300; K. David Patterson, *The Northern Gabon Coast to 1875* (Oxford, 1975), 128.

32. Jeremy Rich, *A Workman Is Worthy of His Meat: Food and Colonialism in the Gabon Estuary* (Lincoln, NE, 2007), 11, 27–35.

33. Quotation: WWD, 6 February 1849, WHS. For missionary observations of the slave trade in the estuary, see WWD, 10 August 1848,

WHS; WWD, 6 February 1849, WHS; WWD, 11 August 1858, WHS; WWD, 14 August 1866, WHS. For the continuing slave trade in the estuary and the continuing role of domestic slavery, see K. David Patterson, "Early Knowledge of the Ogowe River and the American Exploration of 1854," *International Journal of African Historical Studies* 5, no. 1 (1972): 75–87.

34. Quotations: JLW to RA, 27 December 1850, ABCFM; J. Leighton Wilson, "Suppression of the Foreign Slave Trade," to RA, 12 October 1852, ABCFM. See also JLW to Samuel Wilson, 1 January 1851, SCL. The pamphlet, with an introduction, was reproduced in Wilson, *Western Africa*, 430–451. For a succinct review of the debates about the "noble achievement" of the British, see David Brion Davis, "Honor Thy Honor," *New York Review of Books*, October 27, 2011, 46–48.

35. Albert Bushnell to RA, 16 February 1850, ABCFM; JLW to RA, 17 September 1850, ABCFM; JLW to William Wilson, 12 September 1850, SCL; WWD, 6–14 July 1852, WHS.

36. For Jane Cooper staying with the Eckards, see JLW to RA, 17 September 1850, ABCFM. For WW and Kate Hardcastle, see WWD, 29 September 1851, WHS.

37. For an evaluation of the Wilsons' health, see C. A. Ford to RA, 25 February 1852, ABCFM. Cf. also WWD, 1 March 1852, WHS.

Chapter Twenty: An Unsought and Unexpected Appointment

1. JLW to RA, 2 June 1852, ABCFM. Cf. George Brooks, *Yankee Traders, Old Coasters and African Middlemen: A History of American Legitimate Trade with West Africa in the Nineteenth Century* (Boston, 1970), esp. 73–131.

2. Ibid. For a detailed description of Harper in 1852 and the area where Fair Hope had once been located, see Richard L. Hall, *On Afric's Shore: A History of Maryland in Liberia, 1834–1857* (Baltimore, 2003), 328–331. For Freeman's death, see ibid., 368–369.

3. Winston James, *The Struggles of John Brown Russwurm: The Life and Writings of a Pan-Africanist Pioneer, 1799–1851* (New York, 2010), 105–107. For the feeling of insecurity in the colony following Russwurm's death, see WWD, 26 December 1851, WHS. Maryland in Liberia gained its independence from the Baltimore board in 1854. It became a state of the Liberian nation shortly after the war of 1857.

4. Quotation: Amos J. Beyan, *African American Settlements in West Africa: John Brown Russwurm and the American Civilizing Efforts* (New York, 2005), 92.

5. WWD, 12 December 1851, WHS. For James's letter, see Carl Patrick Burrowes, *Power and Press Freedom in Liberia, 1830–1970: The Impact of Globalization and Civil Society on Media-Government Relations* (Trenton, NJ, 2004), 174.

6. JLW to "Dear Sister," 18 July 1852, SCL.

7. JLW to RA, 15 August 1852, ABCFM; JLW to "Dear Sister," 15 October 1850, SCL; JLW to RA, 9 December 1852, ABCFM.

8. John Adger, *My Life and Times* (Richmond, VA, 1899), 164–200; Erskine Clarke, *Our Southern Zion: Calvinism in the South Carolina Low Country, 1690–1990* (Tuscaloosa, AL, 1996), 189–199.

9. Quotations: William Sumner Jenkins, *Pro-Slavery Thought in the Old South* (Chapel Hill, NC, 1935), 250. See also Michael O'Brien, *Conjectures of Order: Intellectual Life and the American South, 1810–1860* (Chapel Hill, NC, 2004), 215–252; Thomas Smyth, *Unity of the Human Races* (New York, 1850), 74. For Smyth's library, see O'Brien, *Conjectures of Order*, 488–489.

10. JLW to RA, 9 December 1852, ABCFM. For the hurricane, see Jacqueline Jones, *Saving Savannah: The City and the Civil War* (New York, 2008), 30.

11. For the rapid development of railroads in Georgia, see George White, *Statistics of the State of Georgia: Including an Account of Its Natural, Civil, and Ecclesiastical History; Together with a Particular Description of Each County, Notices of the Manners and Customs of Its Aboriginal Tribes, and a Correct Map of the State* (Savannah, GA, 1849), 87–93.

12. JLW to "Dear Sister," 15 October 1850, SCL.

13. JLW to RA, 9 December 1852, ABCFM.

14. JLW to RA, 11 January 1853, ABCFM; JLW to RA, 16 June 1853, ABCFM.

15. Quotation: Hampden C. Dubose, *Memoirs of Rev. John Leighton Wilson, D.D., Missionary to Africa and Secretary of Foreign Missions* (Richmond, VA, 1895), 230.

16. Ibid., 235.

17. For the rapid expansion of Protestant missions in the nineteenth century, see Diarmaid MacCulloch, *Christianity: The First Three Thousand Years* (New York, 2010), 879–891. For the expansion of Presbyterian missions, see John C. Lowrie, *A Manual of Missions: Or, Sketches of the Foreign Missions of the Presbyterian Church: With Maps, Showing the Stations, and Statistics of Protestant Missions Among Unevangelized Nations* (New York, 1854). See also "Annual Report: Board

of Foreign Missions, 1857," Presbyterian Church, USA (Old School), PHS.

18. For JLW's administrative work, see, for example, JLW to BVRJ, 23 December 1856, PHS; JLW to BVRJ, 31 December 1859, PHS; "Report of J. Leighton Wilson," *Minutes of the General Assembly of the Presbyterian Church in the United States of America* [Old School], 1856, 851. For JLW's travels, especially to visit the Indian Nations of the old Southwest, see DuBose, *Memoirs*, 241; and see, for example, "Indian Tribes," *Home and Foreign Record*, October 1854, 303.

19. Quotation: J. Leighton Wilson, *Western Africa: Its History, Condition, and Prospects* (New York, 1856), iii.

20. Quotation: ibid., 208.

21. Quotation: ibid., iii.

22. Ibid., 505–507.

23. Quotations: ibid., 379–380.

24. For examples of expressed mutual affection between BVRJ and JLW, see BVRJ to JLW, 15 March 1856, PHS; BVRJ to JLW, 8 July 1859, PHS; BVRJ to JLW, 20 December 1859, PHS; JLW to BVRJ, 31 December 1859, PHS. For an example of a member of the James family staying, while on furlough, with the Wilsons, see JLW to BVRJ, 6 May 1857, PHS.

25. Quotation: BVRJ to JLW, 22 August 1859, PHS. For JLW assigning financial responsibility and administrative leadership to BVRJ, see JLW to BVRJ, 6 May 1857, PHS; "Liberia," in "Twenty-Seventh Annual Report of the Board of Foreign Missions of the Presbyterian Church in America, New York, 1864," CTS. See, as well, BVRJ to JLW, 20 December 1859, PHS. For the tensions surrounding the question of white missionaries in Liberia, see Susan Wilds McArver, "'The Salvation of Souls' and the 'Salvation of the Republic of Liberia': Denominational Conflict and Racial Diversity in Antebellum Presbyterian Foreign Missions," in *North American Foreign Missions, 1810–1914: Theology, Theory, and Policy*, ed. Wilbert R. Shenk (Grand Rapids, MI, 2004), 133–160, esp. 144n24.

26. For Drayton's background in Charleston, see Raymond Morris Bost, "The Reverend John Bachman and the Development of Southern Lutheranism" (PhD diss., Yale University, 1963), 290–403. For the 1857 war between Grebo and settlers and the destruction of Big Town, see Richard L. Hall, *On Afric's Shore: A History of Maryland in Liberia, 1834–1857* (Baltimore, 2003), 398–431; Jane Jackson Martin, "The Dual Legacy:

Government Authority and Mission Influence Among the Glebo of Eastern Liberia, 1834–1910" (PhD diss., Boston University, 1968), 186–205.

27. Quotation: Martin, "The Dual Legacy," 203–204.

28. BVRJ to JLW, 8 July 1859, PHS.

29. For list of letters written by WW to JLW, see "Appendix: Wrote," following WWD, 18 January 1858, WHS.

30. For the close relationships between the missionaries on Corisco and at Baraka, see, for example, Cornelius DeHeer to JLW, 1 October 1856, PHS; JLW to Corisco Mission, 4 May 1860, PHS. For Cornelia DeHeer, see Cornelius DeHeer to JLW, 23 October 1857, PHS.

31. Quotation: "Journal of Mr. Bushnell," *Missionary Herald*, January 1855, 38. For sickness and death among the missionaries, see G. W. Simpson to Walter Lowrie, 1 February 1851, PHS; "Gaboon," *Missionary Herald*, January 1859, 3; "Annual Report," *Missionary Herald*, May 1854, 129–130; "Gabon Mission," *Missionary Herald*, January 1856, 2.

32. David E. Gardinier, "The Schools of the American Protestant Mission in Gabon (1842–1870)," *Revue Française d'Histoire d'Outre-Mer* 75, no. 2 (1988): 182; K. David Patterson, "The Vanishing Mpongwe: European Contact and Demographic Change in the Gabon River," *Journal of African History* 16, no. 2 (1975): 232.

33. Quotation: WWD, 1 July 1849, WHS. See also WWD, 1 August 1858, WHS.

34. Quotation: WWD, 21 February 1857, WHS.

35. WWD, 3–6 December 1858, WHS. Cf. WWD, 22 December 1848, WHS.

Chapter Twenty-One: A Patriot's Choice

1. Quotation: JLW to "Dear Sister," 15 October 1850, SCL. Cf. JLW to JBW, 25 February 1843, CTS.

2. For examples of JLW's travels to different parts of the country, see *Minutes of the General Assembly of the Presbyterian Church in the United States of America (MGAPCUS)*, 1854, 191, CTS; *Home and Foreign Mission*, January 1857, 13–19; JLW to BVRJ, 31 December 1859, PHS; Hampden C. DuBose, *Memoirs of Rev. John Leighton Wilson, D.D., Missionary to Africa and Secretary of Foreign Missions* (Richmond, VA, 1895), 248.

3. For the development of the concept of a "Second Middle Passage" and for its bitter details,

see Ira Berlin, *Generations of Captivity: A History of African-American Slaves* (Cambridge, MA, 2003), 161–244.

4. For the development of the proslavery argument, see Larry E. Tise, *Proslavery: A History of the Defense of Slavery in America, 1701–1840* (Athens, GA, 1987); Elizabeth Fox-Genovese and Eugene D. Genovese, *The Mind of the Master Class: History and Faith in the Southern Slaveholders' Worldview* (New York, 2005); Lacy K. Ford, *Deliver Us from Evil: The Slavery Question in the Old South* (Oxford, 2009), 481–563.

5. Quotation: JLW to JB, 1 September 1833, CTS. For examples of JLW's letters, see "Mission to Western Africa," *Charleston Observer*, 8 November 1834; "Cape Palmas," *Charleston Observer*, 7 May 1836; "Letter of J. L. Wilson," *Charleston Observer*, 5 August 1837; JLW to Elipha White, 8 July 1837, in "Fair Hope, Cape Palmas," *Charleston Observer*, 21 October 1837; "Extracts from letters of Mr. Wilson, at Cape Palmas," *Charleston Observer*, 8 September 1838. For the broader context for the attempted revival of the slave trade, see Hugh Thomas, *The Slave Trade* (New York, 1997), 765–768.

6. Quotations: JLW, "The Foreign Slave Trade: Can It Be Revived Without Violating the Most Sacred Principles of Honor, Humanity, and Religion?" *Southern Presbyterian Review* 12 (1859): 491–512. Cf. John Adger, "Review of the Report to the Legislature of South Carolina on the Revival of the Slave Trade," *Southern Presbyterian Review* 11 (1858): 100–154. See also Michael Robert Mounter, "Wanderer," in *The South Carolina Encyclopedia*, ed. Walter Edgar (Columbia, SC, 2006), 1006.

7. JLW to RA, 9 December 1852, ABCFM. For a revealing analysis of the extent of white fears of freed black slaves living in the midst of a "white America," see Phillip W. Magness and Sebastian N. Page, *Colonization After Emancipation: Lincoln and the Movement for Black Resettlement* (Columbia, MO, 2011). Cf. JLW to BVRJ, 31 December 1859, PHS.

8. Quotation: BVRJ to J. Amos, 7 November 1860, PHS. See also JLW to BVRJ, 31 December 1859, PHS.

9. Quotation: Eric Foner, *The Fiery Trial: Abraham Lincoln and American Slavery* (New York, 2010), 144. See also Ernest Trice Thompson, *Presbyterians in the South*, vol. 1, *1607–1861* (Richmond, VA, 1963), 554.

10. Gertrude McLaurin Shaw, "Mt. Zion Presbyterian Church: 1809–1977" (n. d., n. p.), 19.

11. JLW to Charles Hodge, 19 December 1860, CTS.

12. Ibid.

13. Quotation: James M. McPherson, *Abraham Lincoln and the Second American Revolution* (New York, 1990), 43–44.

14. Quotation: Benjamin Morgan Palmer, *The Life and Letters of James Henley Thornwell* (Richmond, VA, 1875), 607. Cf. Erskine Clarke, *Our Southern Zion: Calvinism in the South Carolina Low Country* (Tuscaloosa, AL, 1996), 200–207.

15. For Hodge's place in US religious history, see Paul C. Gutjahr, *Charles Hodge: Guardian of American Orthodoxy* (New York, 2011).

16. Quotation: Charles Hodge, "The State of the Country," *Biblical Repertory and Princeton Review* 33, no. 1 (1861): 1–36.

17. Quotation: JLW to Charles Hodge, 19 December 1860, CTS.

18. Quotations: Charles Hodge to JLW, 20 December 1860, SCL.

19. Quotations: JLW to Charles Hodge, 22 December 1860, CTS.

20. Quotation: BVRJ to JLW, 9 April 1861, PHS. See also JLW to Corisco Mission, 31 December 1860, PHS; JLW to BVRJ, 1 February 1861, PHS; JLW to Corisco Mission, 1 March 1861, PHS. For the efforts to find some compromise between North and South, see Foner, *The Fiery Trial*, 144–165.

21. DuBose, *Memoirs*, 232–233. For the sale of their New York home, see "Indenture Between Harriet Hunter and J. Leighton Wilson," recorded in Savannah, 18 July 1861, record 3 U, SCCC. The transaction in New York was witnessed by JLW's colleague John Lowrie.

22. For Alexander Henry, see J. Mathew Gallman, *Mastering Wartime: A Social History of Philadelphia During the Civil War* (Philadelphia, 2000).

23. Thompson, *Presbyterians in the South*, 1:563–564.

24. Quotation: Ibid., 564–566. The doctrine of the spirituality of the church was spelled out forcefully by the General Assembly in 1845. See *MGAPCUS* [Old School] (Philadelphia, 1845), 11–17.

25. For Hodge's extended review and discussion of the assembly's action, see Charles Hodge, "The General Assembly," *Biblical Repertory and Princeton Review* 33, no. 2 (1861): 542–568.

26. Quotation: *MGAPCUS*, 1861, 329–343.

27. Quotations: Walter Lowrie to BVRJ, 19 June 1861, PHS; BVRJ to Walter Lowrie, 27 August 1861, PHS.

28. Quotation: DuBose, *Memoirs*, 247.

29. Thompson, *Presbyterians in the South*, 1:566–567.

30. George Howe to Thomas Smyth, in Thomas Smyth, *Autobiographical Notes, Letters and Reflections*, ed. Louisa Cheves Stoney (Charleston, SC, 1914), 621; DuBose, *Memoirs*, 249–250.

31. For Southern interest in the annexation of Cuba, see Jonathan M. Hansen, *Guantánamo: An American History* (New York, 2011), 58–74. Cf. Michael O'Brien, *Conjectures of Order: Intellectual Life and the American South, 1810–1860* (Chapel Hill, NC, 2004), 2–7.

32. Instead of arguing for any determinism at work on white Southerners, Michael O'Brien has argued vigorously that the "Old South had chosen its own way with clarity of mind" and had "even understood things about the intractability of the human condition." See O'Brien, *Conjectures of Order*, 1199–1202.

33. Cf. Robert E. Lee's decision when Virginia seceded: "I cannot raise my hand against my birthplace, my home, my children." But note that some Southerners cast their lot with the Union. See James M. McPherson, *The Battle Cry of Freedom: The Civil War Era* (New York, 1988), 281–282.

Chapter Twenty-Two: Civil War

1. Ernest Trice Thompson, *Presbyterians in the South*, vol. 2, *1861–1890* (Richmond, VA, 1973), 20–22.

2. Ibid.

3. *Minutes of the General Assembly of the Presbyterian Church in the Confederate States of America*, 1861, 47–48.

4. Thompson, *Presbyterians in the South*, 2:13–35.

5. Quotation: *Minutes of the General Assembly of the Presbyterian Church in the Confederate States of America*, 1861, 53.

6. Quotations: ibid., 55–60. The debate over slavery and the Bible has drawn considerable scholarly attention in recent years. For an important summary of the issues and scholarship, see Mark A. Noll, *The Civil War as a Theological Crisis* (Chapel Hill, NC, 2006), 31–50. For the debate itself, see David Brion Davis, *The Problem of Slavery in the Age of Revolution, 1770–1823* (New York, 1975), 523–556; Stephen R. Haynes, *Noah's Curse: The Biblical Justification of American Slavery* (New York, 2002); Elizabeth Fox-Genovese and Eugene D. Genovese, *The Mind of the Master Class: History and Faith in the Southern Slaveholders' Worldview* (Cambridge, UK, 2005), esp. 473–504.

7. Thompson, *Presbyterians in the South*, 2:20–23.

8. *Minutes of the General Assembly of the Presbyterian Church in the Confederate States of America*, 1861, 15–17, 47–48; Thompson, *Presbyterians in the South*, 2:294–307.

9. For the history of the various battles, see McPherson, *The Battle Cry of Freedom: The Civil War Era* (New York, 1988), passim. For Antietam and its consequences, see James M. McPherson, *Cross Roads of Freedom: Antietam* (New York, 2002), 138–156; Eric Foner, *The Fiery Trial: Abraham Lincoln and American Slavery* (New York, 2010), 206–247.

10. J. E. Cousar, "Mt. Zion During the War Between the States," in Mrs. Shaw, "Mt. Zion Presbyterian Church: 1809–1976" (n.p., 1976), 72–85. For an analysis of the ways in which Americans, North and South, confronted death during the Civil War and went about the horrendous task of burying the hundreds of thousands of soldiers who died in battles and hospitals, see Drew Gilpin Faust, *This Republic of Suffering: Death and the American Civil War* (New York, 2008). For the issues of "Believing and Doubting" created by the death and suffering of the war, see ibid., 171–210.

11. Quotation: Hampden C. DuBose, *Memoirs of Rev. John Leighton Wilson, D.D., Missionary to Africa and Secretary of Foreign Missions* (Richmond, VA, 1895), 253–254. For JLW's organization of chaplains, see Thompson, *Presbyterians in the South*, 2:40–51. For diseases faced by troops North and South, see McPherson, *Cross Roads of Freedom*, 487–488; Horace H. Cunningham, *Doctors in Gray: The Confederate Medical Service* (Baton Rouge, LA, 1958).

12. Cousar, "Mt. Zion," 79.

13. Ibid.

14. Dubose, *Memoirs*, 104–105.

15. Stanley P. Hirshson, *The White Tecumseh: A Biography of General William T. Sherman* (New York, 1997), 213; "An Act to Incorporate the Calhoun and Rome Railroad Company," 1859, GLD; "An Act to Incorporate the Alabama Planters Steamboat Company," 1860, GLD; "Nicholas James Bayard," in Robert Manson Myers, ed., *The Children of Pride: A True Story of Georgia and the Civil War* (New Haven, CT, 1972), 1462–1463.

16. Hirshson, *The White Tecumseh*, 241–264.

17. For the burning of Richmond-on-Ogeechee, see Carolyn Clay Swiggart, *Shades of Gray: The Clay and McAllister Families of Bryan County, Georgia During the Plantation Years (ca. 1760–1888)* (Darien, CT, 1999), 32. For the destruction in and around Darien, including at Fair Hope Plantation, see Buddy Sullivan, *Early Days on the Georgia Tidewater: The Story of McIntosh County and Sapelo* (Darien, GA, 2001), 289–293.

18. Quotations: Jacqueline Jones, *Saving Savannah: The City and the Civil War* (New York, 2008), 207; Leon Litwack, *Been in the Storm So Long: The Aftermath of Slavery* (New York, 1979), 144; James M. Simms, *The First Colored Baptist Church in North America* (Philadelphia, 1888), 137. For the ways in which the coming of the Yankees was filled with religious meaning for many slaves, see Litwack, *Been in the Storm So Long*, 104–166.

19. Quotations: Hirshson, *The White Tecumseh*, 275, 277. For the controversy surrounding the burning of Columbia, see ibid., 280–286; Marion Brunson Lucas, *Sherman and the Burning of Columbia* (College Station, TX, 1976); John Hammond Moore, *Columbia and Richland County: A South Carolina Community, 1740–1990* (Columbia, SC, 1993), 181–208.

20. Cousar, "Mt. Zion," 82–85.

21. Quotations: BVRJ to Walter Lowrie, 30 September 1864, PHS.

Chapter Twenty-Three: Home Ground

1. For the massive movement of Freedpeople after the war, see Leon F. Litwack, *Been in the Storm So Long: The Aftermath of Slavery* (New York, 1979), 229–335.

2. Hampden C. DuBose, *Memoirs of Rev. John Leighton Wilson, D.D., Missionary to Africa and Secretary of Foreign Missions* (Richmond, VA, 1895), 256.

3. For the sale of the New York house, see "Indenture" between Harriet Hunter and J. Leighton Wilson, recorded in Savannah 18 July 1861, record 3 U, SCCC; "Indenture" between J. Leighton Wilson and Thomas Dowell, recorded in Savannah 23 September 1862, record 3 V, SCCC. For the purchase of Pine Grove house and adjacent land, see DuBose, *Memoirs*, 286; N. H. Anderson to Rev. J. L. Wilson, "Deed of Land," 7 March 1867, SCSC.

4. For the immediate issues facing Freedpeople, see Litwack, *Been in the Storm So Long*, 222–229; David Blight, *Race and Union: The Civil War in American Memory* (Cambridge, MA, 2001), 44–63. For African Americans' desire for, and sense of entitlement to, land, see Steven Hahn, *A Nation Under Our Feet: Black Political Struggles in the Rural South from Slavery to the Great Migration* (Cambridge, MA, 2003), 127–154.

5. Jessie Wilson, US Census, 1870, Sumter, SC, ID M593 roll 1509, number 347; DuBose, *Memoirs*, 104–105.

6. Cf. Hahn, *A Nation Under Our Feet*, 154–156. For these economic arrangements, especially in South Carolina, see Joel Williamson, *After Slavery: The Negro in South Carolina During Reconstruction, 1861–1877* (Chapel Hill, NC, 1965), 126–163. For a dispute between JLW and Julia English, a domestic servant under contract, over the charge of stealing, see DuBose, *Memoirs*, 290.

7. Quotation: JLW to RA, 23 January 1843, ABCFM and CTS. See also DuBose, *Memoirs*, 104.

8. For the use of "Old Homestead," see, for example, JLW to the "Venerable General Assembly," 22 May 1886, in DuBose, *Memoirs*, 313.

9. Quotation: Drew Gilpin Faust, *This Republic of Suffering: Death and the American Civil War* (New York, 2008), 192. For Southern whites' sense of invincibility, see Jason Phillips, *Diehard Rebels: The Confederate Culture of Invincibility* (Athens, GA, 2007). For issues raised by the suffering and death of the war and by the Southern defeat, see Faust, *This Republic of Suffering*; cf. Walter Brueggemann, "Some Aspects of Theodicy in Old Testament Faith," *Perspectives in Religious Studies* 26, no. 3 (1999): 253–268. For widely influential reflections on these questions, see two books by James McBride Dabbs: *Who Speaks for the South?* (New York, 1964), and *Haunted by God* (Atlanta, 1972). Dabbs lived on a plantation not far from Pine Grove and was an elder at the Salem Black River Presbyterian Church.

10. See "The Crisis over Providence," in Mark A. Noll, *The Civil War as a Theological Crisis* (Chapel Hill, NC, 2006), 75–94; cf. Phillips, *Diehard Rebels*, esp. 187–189.

11. Quotations: John Adger, "Northern and Southern Views of the Province of the Church," *Southern Presbyterian Review* 16 (March 1866), 384–411.

12. Cf. C. Vann Woodward, *The Burden of Southern History* (New York, 1961), esp. 3–25; James C. Cobb, *A Way Down South: A History of Southern Identity* (New York, 2005), 34–66.

13. DuBose, *Memoirs*, 288–290.

14. Ibid.

15. Quotation: ibid., 289.

16. Quotation: JLW to Col. Franklin Moses, 7 September 1865, CTS. For JLW's evening classes for blacks, see DuBose, *Memoirs*, 291. For the disenfranchisement of African American Southerners, see Douglas A. Blackmon, *Slavery by Another Name: The Re-Enslavement of Black Americans from the Civil War to World War II* (New York, 2008), esp. 102–104, 121–122, 139–140. For disenfranchisement in South Carolina, see Rod Andrew, Jr., *Wade Hampton:*

Confederate Warrior to Southern Redeemer (Columbia, SC, 2008), esp. 430–431, 455–456.

17. For the destitute conditions of the churches, see Ernest Trice Thompson, *Presbyterians in the South*, vol. 2, *1861–1890* (Richmond, VA, 1973), 89–92. For the establishment of a sustentation fund, see "Memorial to the General Assembly of the Presbyterian Church in the United States, on the Work of Domestic Missions and Sustentation," *Minutes of the General Assembly of the Presbyterian Church of the United States* (*MGAPCUS*), 1866, 49–51. After the war, the Presbyterian Church in the Confederate States of America adopted the name "Presbyterian Church in the United States." The church was generally referred to as the "Southern Presbyterian Church." The "Northern Presbyterian Church" was the Presbyterian Church in the United States of America.

18. Quotation: *MGAPCUS*, 1865, 369–370.

19. For black membership at Mt. Zion and Salem Black River, see *MGAPCUS*, 1867, 227. For blacks leaving their white-dominated churches, see Thompson, *Presbyterians in the South*, 2:307–331; Erskine Clarke, *Our Southern Zion: A History of Calvinism in the South Carolina Low Country, 1690–1990* (Tuscaloosa, AL, 1995), 229–242.

20. Inez Moore Parker, *The Rise and Decline for the Program of Education for Black Presbyterians of the United Presbyterian Church U.S.A., 1865–1970* (San Antonio, TX, 1977), 139–186.

21. The correspondence between Logan and JLW can be found in "Fourth Annual Report: The General Assembly's Committee on Freedmen, of the Presbyterian Church in the United States of America," PHS, 22–51.

22. Quotations: ibid., 29–31.

23. Quotations: ibid., 41, 48, 49.

24. For the work of Girardeau at Zion before the Civil War, see Clarke, *Our Southern Zion*, 189–199.

25. Quotations: John L. Girardeau, *Confederate Memorial Day at Charleston, S.C.: Re-interment of the Carolina Dead from Gettysburg* (Charleston, SC, 1871).

26. For an ideology and its language as a guardian of identity, see Clifford Geertz, "Ideology as a Cultural System," in *The Interpretation of Cultures: Selected Essays* (New York, 1973), esp. 218–219; Paul Ricoeur, *Lectures on Ideology and Utopia*, ed. George H. Taylor (New York, 1986), 258–261.

27. For the Ku Klux Klan and other vigilante groups, see Hahn, *A Nation Under Our Feet*, 265–313.

Chapter Twenty-Four: Distant Voices

1. Quotation: Matthew 28:19. Ernest Trice Thompson, *Presbyterians in the South*, vol. 2, *1861–1890* (Richmond, VA, 1973), 306.

2. For the expansion of Southern Presbyterian missions, see Thompson, *Presbyterians in the South*, 2:294–307.

3. Quotation: JLW to JBW, 18 July 1842, CTS. For JLW's awareness of the massive number of slaves carried to Brazil, see J. Leighton Wilson, *Western Africa: Its History, Condition, and Prospects* (New York, 1856), 430–451. For the number of slaves carried to the North American mainland between 1619 and 1860, see David Eltis and David Richardson, *Atlas of the Transatlantic Slave Trade* (New Haven, CT, 2010), 205. For the number carried to Brazil between 1791 and 1856, see ibid., 261. See also ibid., 4–5, 17, 261–269. For slavery in Brazil, see Katia M. De Queirós Mattoso, *To Be a Slave in Brazil, 1550–1888*, trans. Arthur Goldhammer (New Brunswick, NJ, 1989), esp. 125–128. For the final abolition of slavery in Brazil, see Seymour Drescher, "Brazilian Abolition in Comparative Perspective," in Rebecca J. Scott et al., *The Abolition of Slavery and the Aftermath of Emancipation in Brazil* (Durham, NC, 1988), 23–54.

4. Quotation: J. J. Bullock to Hamden DuBose, letter reprinted in Hampden C. DuBose, *Memoirs of Rev. John Leighton Wilson, D.D., Missionary to Africa and Secretary of Foreign Missions* (Richmond, VA, 1895), 247–248.

5. Quotation: J. Leighton Wilson, "Notes of Travel: Trip to Brazil," CTS. The notes begin on 23 November 1874 and have no page numbers. The dates are often unclear.

6. Quotation: ibid.

7. Ibid. See also Frank L. Arnold, *Long Road to Obsolescence: A North American Mission to Brazil* (n.p., 2009).

8. For the reasons for the move to Baltimore, see J. Leighton Wilson, "Our Removal," *The Missionary*, September 1875, 197.

9. Quotation: "Mr. B. V. R. James," in "Annual Report, Board of Foreign Missions," 1869, PHS.

10. For the "Back to Africa Movement" of this period, see Steven Hahn, *A Nation Under Our Feet: Black Political Struggles in the Rural South from Slavery to the Great Migration* (Cambridge, MA, 2003), 320–363.

11. For Blyden's correspondence with JLW, see, for example, Edward W. Blyden to JLW, 10 March 1859, PHS; Edward W. Blyden to JLW, 9 June 1860, PHS. For important overviews of Blyden's work and influence, see Lamin Sanneh, *Abolitionist Abroad: American Blacks and the Making of Modern West Africa* (Cambridge, MA, 1999), 230–235; V. Y. Mudimbe, *The Invention of Africa: Gnosis, Philosophy, and the Order of Knowledge* (Bloomington, IN, 1988), 98–134.

12. Quotations: "Letter from President Latrobe," *African Repository*, April 1877, 59–61. For the holocaust Leopold unleashed on the Congo, see Adam Hochschild, *King Leopold's Ghost: A Story of Greed, Terror, and Heroism in Colonial Africa* (New York, 1998).

13. Phillip W. Magness and Sebastian N. Page, *Colonization After Emancipation: Lincoln and the Movement for Black Resettlement* (Columbia, MO, 2011).

14. Jane Jackson Martin, "The Dual Legacy: Government Authority and Mission Influence Among the Glebo of Eastern Liberia, 1834–1910" (PhD diss., Boston University, 1968), 258–289. For the American Colonization Society's report on the war, see "War with Greboes," *African Repository*, April 1876, 40–42.

15. Martin, "Dual Legacy," 284–287.

16. See, for example, Bella A. Nassau, "Woman in Africa," *The Missionary*, June 1873, 163–165; "A Call from Gaboon," *The Missionary*, April 1877, 92; "Africa—Gaboon Mission," *The Missionary*, September 1878, 210–212; "Africa and the African Mission," *The Missionary*, December 1882, 268–271.

17. For WW's explorations of the Ogowe River, see K. David Patterson, "Early Knowledge of the Ogowe River and the American Exploration of 1854," *International Journal of African Historical Studies* 5, no. 1 (1971): 75–87. The Walkers retired to the United States in 1870. At the death of Albert Bushnell in 1879, Walker returned at the urgent request of the Mission Board and remained until 1883. For Bushnell, see, for example, "Gaboon and Corisco Mission, West Africa, by Rev. A. Bushnell," *The Missionary*, January 1872, 13–14; "Letter of Rev. A. Bushnell," *The Missionary*, December 1873, 278–279.

18. Quotations: WWD, 27 June 1867, WHS; WWD, 25 August 1865, WHS. For King William's burial of the two women, see WWD, 14 March 1865, WHS.

19. For details of the decline of domestic slavery among the Mpongwe and the role of the leopard men, see Jeremy Rich, "Leopard Men, Slaves, and Social Conflict in Colonial Libreville, c. 1860–1880," *International Journal of African Historical Studies* 34 (2001): 619–638. See also, for the "leopard men," Abbé André Raponda-Walker, *Notes d'histoire*

du Gabon (Brazzaville, 1960), 178–182. For Toko's son Ntâkâ Truman's description of the leopard men, see Ntâkâ Truman to John Lowrie, 1 November 1878, PHS. For a comprehensive overview of the role of leopard men and their relationship to the secret Mwiri societies in nineteenth- and twentieth-century Gabon, see Christopher J. Gray, *Colonial Rule and Crisis in Equatorial Africa: Southern Gabon, ca. 1850–1940* (Rochester, NY, 2002), 196–203.

20. Quotation: WWD, 29 March 1867, WHS. For the Mpongwe loss of their political and economic independence, see K. David Patterson, *The Northern Gabon Coast to 1875* (Oxford, 1975), 107–130.

21. Quotation: Ntâkâ Truman to John Lowrie, 3 August 1875, PHS. For Ntâkâ Truman's conversion as a "passage," see Diane Austin-Broos, "The Anthropology of Conversion: An Introduction," in *The Anthropology of Religious Conversion*, eds. Andrew Buckser and Stephen D. Glazier (Lanham, MD, 2003), 1–12; cf. Terence Ranger, "The Local and the Global in Southern African Religious History," in *Conversion to Christianity: Historical and Anthropological Perspectives on a Great Transformation*, ed. Robert W. Hefner (Berkeley, CA, 1993), 65–98. For Ntâkâ Truman, his relationship with the American missionaries, and the story of the mission during these years, see David E. Gardinier, "The American Presbyterian Mission in Gabon: Male Mpongwe Converts and Agents, 1870–1883," *American Presbyterians*, Spring 1991, 61–70; David E. Gardinier, "The American Board (1842–1870) and Presbyterian Board (1870–1892) Missions in Northern Gabon and African Responses," *Africana Journal* 17 (1998): 215–234; David E. Gardinier, "The Schools of the American Protestant Mission in Gabon (1842–1870)," in *Revue Française d'Histoire d'Outre-Mer* 75 (1988): 164–184. For an example of the shift in mission strategy and for mission boards' support of imperialism in the last part of the nineteenth century, see, for example, Susan K. Harris, *God's Arbiters: Americans and the Philippines, 1898–1902* (Oxford, 2011), 29–30, 104–125. Cf. also Wendy J. Deichmann Edwards, "Forging an Ideology for American Missions: Josiah Strong and Manifest Destiny," in Wilbert R. Shenk, ed., *North American Foreign Missions, 1810–1914: Theology, Theory, and Policy* (Grand Rapids, MI, 2004), 163–191.

22. For the insistence that indigenous peoples were not passive in the face of any missionary imperialism and for the complexity of the mission movement's relationship to cultural imperialism, see Andrew Porter, "'Cultural Imperialism' and Protes-

tant Missionary Enterprise, 1780–1914," *Journal of Imperial and Commonwealth History* 25, no. 3 (1997): 367–391. For the continuing power of the old ideal of a self-governing church emerging from missionary efforts, see C. P. Williams, *The Ideal of the Self-Governing Church: A Study in Victorian Missionary Strategy* (Leiden, 1990).

23. For William Leighton Dorsey, see Gardinier, "The Schools of the American Protestant Mission in Gabon," 172. For "Ma Sara," see Jean Kenyon MacKenzie, *Black Sheep: Adventures in West Africa* (Cambridge, MA, 1916), 163–165, 198–202. For Celia, see Jane Preston, *Gaboon Stories* (New York, 1872), passim.

24. For Mary Clealand Dorsey's marriage to a Scotsman, see Preston, *Gaboon Stories*, 69–70.

25. For the impact of translations, see "Missionary Translation in African Perspective," in Lamin Sanneh, *Translating the Message: The Missionary Impact on Culture*, rev. ed. (New York, 2009), 191–228. The ABCFM had transferred the Gabon mission to the Northern Presbyterian Board of Foreign Mission in the 1870s. With French pressure on the American missionaries, the Presbyterian board transferred the mission to the Société des Missions Évangéliques of Paris in 1892. The last Americans left Baraka in 1913. See Gardinier, "The American Board (1842–1870) and Presbyterian Board (1870–1892)," 182–183.

26. For JLW's work in Baltimore, see Thompson, *Presbyterians in the South*, 2:294–307. For Margaret Eckard's death, see DuBose, *Memoirs*, 297–308.

27. Quotation: JLW to A. A. Hodge, 24 February 1881, CTS. See also JLW to "My Dear Sister," 12 August 1880, SCL; JLW to "My Dear Sister," 3 June 1881, SCL; JLW to "My Dear Sister," 7 April 1884, SCL.

28. See "Bayard, Nicholas James," in *The Children of Pride: A True Story of Georgia and the Civil War*, ed. Robert Manson Myers (New Haven, CT, 1972), 1462–1463.

29. For JLW preaching regularly at Mt. Sinai, see DuBose, *Memoirs*, 309–317. For the Good Will school, see "Teacher's Monthly School Report," 1867–1869, Good Will School, Sumter, South Carolina, in Freedmen's Bureau Records, National Archives, Washington, DC; Annual Reports, "The General Assembly's Committee on Freedmen, of the Presbyterian Church in the United States of America," 1867–1876, PHS; Inez Moore Parker, *The Rise and Decline for the Program of Education for Black Presbyterians of the United Presbyterian Church U.S.A.*,

1865–1970 (San Antonio, TX, 1977), 139–186. For Freedpeople being taught a "Yankee ethic," see Leon F. Litwack, *Been in the Storm So Long: The Aftermath of Slavery* (New York, 1979), 450–556; and, especially, Edmund L. Drago, *Initiative, Paternalism, and Race Relations: Charleston's Avery Normal Institute* (Athens, GA, 1990). For the ethos of the school during the early decades of the twentieth century, author's interview with former students of the Good Will school, 13 May 2011, Good Will Presbyterian Church, Sumter County, South Carolina. For the ways in which memory can shatter the ideological claims of a dominant class, see Michael Walzer, *Interpretation and Social Criticism* (Cambridge, MA, 1987); Hans-Georg Gadamer, *Truth and Method* (New York, 1984), esp. "Hermeneutics and Historicism," 460–491; Paul Ricoeur, *Conflict of Interpretation* (Evanston, IL, 1977).

30. DuBose, *Memoirs*, 309–317.

31. Quotation: JLW to "My Dear Sister," 3 June 1881, SCL. See also JLW to "My Dear Sister," 12 August 1881, SCL; JLW to "My Dear Sister Martha," 22 January 1884, SCL; JLW to "My Dear Sister," 7 April 1884, SCL; JLW to "My Dear Bro William," 10 June 1884, SCL.

32. Quotation: DuBose, *Memoirs*, 263.

33. Ibid., 310–312.

34. Ibid., 318–319.

35. Ibid., 319–320.

Epilogue

1. Dahleen Glanton and Stacy St. Clair, "Michelle Obama's Family Tree Has Roots in a Carolina Slave Plantation," *Chicago Tribune*, 1 December 2008; Rachel L. Swarns, *American Tapestry: The Story of the Black, White, and Multiracial Ancestors of Michelle Obama* (New York, 2012), 234–239.

2. For the Anglican Mission in the Americas, see www.theamia.org/. According to the website, "The Americas" includes only the United States and Canada. For All Saints Anglican Church, Pawley Island, South Carolina, see www.allsaintspawleys.org/. A major dispute erupted in 2011 when the Rwan-

dan bishops asked US leaders of the mission for more transparency and accountability in regard to finances. See Bob Smietana, "Anglican Mission in the Americas Confronts a New Power Struggle with Rwandan Patrons," *Huffington Post*, February 10, 2012, www.huffingtonpost.com/2012/02/10/anglican-mission-in-the-americas-rwanada_n_126 6831.html. For the relation of US Christianity to globalization, see Robert Wuthnow, *Boundless Faith: The Global Outreach of American Churches* (Berkley, CA, 2009).

3. Quotation: Philip Jenkins, *The New Faces of Christianity: Believing the Bible in the Global South* (Oxford, 2006), 9. For details of the Pew report, see "Global Christianity: A Report on the Size and Distribution of the World's Christian Population," December 19, 2011, www.pewforum.org/Christian/Global-Christianity-exec.aspx. For important studies of the changes taking place in global Christianity, see Philip Jenkins, *The Next Christendom: The Coming of Global Christianity* (Oxford, 2002); Mark A. Noll, *The New Shape of World Christianity: How American Experience Reflects Global Faith* (Westmont, IL, 2009); Todd M. Johnson and Kenneth R. Ross, eds., *Atlas of Global Christianity* (Edinburgh, 2010).

4. David A. Shank, *Prophet Harris, the 'Black Elijah' of West Africa* (Leiden, 1994). See also Norbert C. Brockman, "William Wadé Harris," in *Dictionary of African Biography*, www.dacb.org/stories/liberia/harris1_william.html.

5. Quotation: J. Leighton Wilson, *Western Africa: Its History, Condition, and Prospects* (New York, 1856), 21. For RA's emphasis on an indigenous leadership for new churches, see "The Rev. John Leighton Wilson Received the Instructions of the Prudential Committee in the Central Presbyterian Church, Philadelphia," *Missionary Herald*, 19 October 1834; cf. Paul Harris, "Denominationalism and Democracy: Ecclesiastical Issues Underlying Rufus Anderson's Three Self Program," in *North American Foreign Mission, 1810–1914: Theology, Theory, and Policy*, Wilbert R. Shenk, ed. (Grand Rapids, MI, 2004), 61–85.

INDEX

INDEX OF NAMES